Featured Collections:

The Greg Southward Collection, The Jacob and Heather Dedman Collection,
The William A. "Bill" Bond Collection of Confederate and Southern States Bonds,
The Lincoln Collection of Illinois Nationals, and The Rolling Plains Collection of Oklahoma and Texas Nationals.

EXHIBITION OF LOTS

America's Center | Room 132 | 701 Convention Plaza

Tuesday, May 8	11am-7pm CDT
Wednesday, May 9	8am-7pm CDT
Thursday, May 10	8am-7pm CDT
Friday, May 11	8am-7pm CDT
Saturday, May 12	8am-12pm CDT

During the Hours of Lot Exhibition,
Our DIRECT Phone Number is (407) 685-6223
Our DIRECT FAX Number (24 Hours) is (407) 685-6224

LIVE, INTERNET AND MAIL BID SIGNATURE AUCTION #436

America's Center | Room 130 | 701 Convention Plaza

Session 1	Wed., May 9	6 PM CDT	Lots 12001-12886
Session 2	Thurs., May 10	6 PM CDT	Lots 12887-13662
Session 3	Fri., May 11	1 PM CDT	Lots 13663-14262
Session 4	Fri., May 11	6 PM CDT	Lots 14263-15474

Lots are sold at an approximate
rate of 225 lots per hour.
This auction is subject to a
15% Buyer's Premium.

3500 Maple Avenue | 17th Floor | Dallas, Texas 75219-3941
214-528-3500 | 1-800-872-6467
Direct Client Service Line: Toll Free 1-866-835-3243

FAX BIDS TO:
214-443-8425

FAX DEADLINE:
Tues., May 8, Noon CT

INTERNET BIDDING:
Closes at 10 pm CT
the day before
the session on sale

You can now view full-color images and bid via the Internet,
at the Heritage website: HA.com/Currency

Catalogued by: Frank Clark, Jim Fitzgerald, Len Glazer, Dustin Johnston,
Allen Mincho, and Michael Moczalla

Photography and Imaging by: Leticia Crawford, Lucas Garritson,
Lori McKay, Bea Faustino, Patric Glenn, Haley Hagen,
Lindsey Johnson, Brittney Lovelace.

Design and Production by: Cindy Brenner, Lisa Fox,
Kelley Norwine, Michael Puttonen

Auctioneer: Samuel Foose - Licensed by the City of St. Louis
Heritage Numismatic Auctions, INC - AB0000665

LOT PICK UP:
Room 132
Thurs., May 10, 10am-1pm
Fri., May 11, 10am-1pm
Sat., May 12, 9am-12pm

Auction Results
Available Immediately
at our website:
HA.com/Currency

Auction #436

Steve Ivy
CEO
Co-Chairman
of the Board

Jim Halperin
Co-Chairman
of the Board

Greg Rohan
President

Paul Minshull
Chief Operating
Officer

Allen Mincho
Director of Auctions

Jim Fitzgerald
Director of Auctions

Len Glazer
Director of Auctions

David Lisot
Consignment Director

Dustin Johnston
Director of Auctions

Michael Moczalla
Consignment Director

3500 Maple Avenue • 17th Floor • Dallas, Texas 75219-3941
1-800-872-6467 • 214-528-3500 • FAX: 214-443-8425
e-mail: Bid@HA.com
HA.com/Currency

TERMS AND CONDITIONS OF AUCTION

Auctioneer and Auction:
1. This Auction is presented by Heritage Auction Galleries, a d/b/a/ of Heritage Auctions, Inc., or their affiliates Heritage Numismatic Auctions, Inc. or Currency Auctions of America, Inc., d/b/a as identified with the applicable licensing information on the title page of the catalog or on the HA.com Internet site (the "Auctioneer"). The Auction is conducted under these Terms and Conditions of Auction and applicable state and local law. Announcements and corrections from the podium and those made through the Terms and Conditions of Auctions appearing on the Internet at HA.com supersede those in the printed catalog.

Buyer's Premium:
2. On bids placed through Heritage, a Buyer's Premium of fifteen percent (15%) will be added to the successful hammer price bid on lots in Coin and Currency auctions, or nineteen and one-half percent (19.5%) on lots in all other auctions. If your bid is placed through eBay Live, a Buyer's Premium equal to the normal Buyer's Premium plus an additional five percent (5%) of the hammer price will be added to the successful bid up to a maximum Buyer's Premium of Twenty Two and one-half percent (22.5%). There is a minimum Buyer's Premium of $9.00 per lot. In Gallery Auctions only, a ten percent (10%) handling fee is applied to all lots based upon the total of the hammer price plus the 15% Buyer's Premium.

Auction Venues:
3. The following Auctions are conducted solely on the Internet: Heritage Weekly Internet Coin, Currency, Comics, and Vintage Movie Poster Auctions; Heritage Monthly Internet Sports and Marketplace Auctions; OnLine Sessions. Signature Auctions and Grand Format Auctions accept bids on the Internet first, followed by a floor bidding session; bids may be placed prior to the floor bidding session by Internet, telephone, fax, or mail.

Bidders:
4. Any person participating or registering for the Auction agrees to be bound by and accepts these Terms and Conditions of Auction ("Bidder(s)").
5. All Bidders must meet Auctioneer's qualifications to bid. Any Bidder who is not a customer in good standing of the Auctioneer may be disqualified at Auctioneer's sole option and will not be awarded lots. Such determination may be made by Auctioneer in its sole and unlimited discretion, at any time prior to, during, or even after the close of the Auction. Auctioneer reserves the right to exclude any person it deems in its sole opinion is disruptive to the Auction or is otherwise commercially unsuitable.
6. If an entity places a bid, then the person executing the bid on behalf of the entity agrees to personally guarantee payment for any successful bid.

Credit References:
7. Bidders who have not established credit with the Auctioneer must either furnish satisfactory credit information (including two collectibles-related business references) well in advance of the Auction or supply valid credit card information. Bids placed through our Interactive Internet program will only be accepted from pre-registered Bidders; Bidders who are not members of HA.com or affiliates should pre-register at least two business days before the first session to allow adequate time to contact references.

Bidding Options:
8. Bids in Signature Auctions or Grand Format Auctions may be placed as set forth in the printed catalog section entitled "Choose your bidding method." For auctions held solely on the Internet, see the alternatives on HA.com. Review at HA.com/common/howtobid.php.
9. Presentment of Bids: Non-Internet bids (including but not limited to podium, fax, phone and mail bids) are treated similar to floor bids in that they must be on-increment or at a half increment (called a cut bid). Any podium, fax, phone, or mail bids that do not conform to a full or half increment will be rounded up or down to the nearest full or half increment and this revised amount will be considered your high bid.
10. Auctioneer's Execution of Certain Bids. Auctioneer cannot be responsible for your errors in bidding, so carefully check that every bid is entered correctly. When identical mail or FAX bids are submitted, preference is given to the first received. To ensure the greatest accuracy, your written bids should be entered on the standard printed bid sheet and be received at Auctioneer's place of business at least two business days before the Auction start. Auctioneer is not responsible for executing mail bids or FAX bids received on or after the day the first lot is sold, nor Internet bids submitted after the published closing time; nor is Auctioneer responsible for proper execution of bids submitted by telephone, mail, FAX, e-mail, Internet, or in person once the Auction begins. Internet bids may not be withdrawn until your written request is received and acknowledged by Auctioneer (FAX: 214-443-8425); such requests must state the reason, and may constitute grounds for withdrawal of bidding privileges. Lots won by mail Bidders will not be delivered at the Auction unless prearranged.
11. Caveat as to Bid Increments. Bid increments (over the current bid level) determine the lowest amount you may bid on a particular lot. Bids greater than one increment over the current bid can be any whole dollar amount. It is possible under several circumstances for winning bids to be between increments, sometimes only $1 above the previous increment. Please see: "How can I lose by less than an increment?" on our website.

The following chart governs current bidding increments.

Current Bid	Bid Increment	Current Bid	Bid Increment
< $10	$1	$3,000 - $4,999	$250
$10 - $29	$2	$5,000 - $9,999	$500
$30 - $59	$3	$10,000 - $19,999	$1,000
$60 - $99	$5	$20,000 - $29,999	$2,000
$100 - $199	$10	$30,000 - $49,999	$2,500
$200 - $299	$20	$50,000 - $99,999	$5,000
$300 - $499	$25	$100,000 - $249,999	$10,000
$500 - $999	$50	$250,000 - $499,999	$25,000
$1,000 - $1,999	$100	$500,000 - $1,499,999	$50,000
$2,000 - $2,999	$200	> $1,500,000	$100,000

12. If Auctioneer calls for a full increment, a floor/phone bidder may request Auctioneer to accept a bid at half of the increment ("Cut Bid") which will be that bidders final bid; if the Auctioneer solicits bids other the expected increment, they will not be considered Cut Bids, and bidders accepting such increments may continue to participate.

Conducting the Auction:
13. Notice of the consignor's liberty to place reserve bids on his lots in the Auction is hereby made in accordance with Article 2 of the Texas Uniform Commercial Code. A reserve is an amount below which the lot will not sell. THE CONSIGNOR OF PROPERTY MAY PLACE WRITTEN RESERVE BIDS ON HIS LOTS IN ADVANCE OF THE AUCTION; ON SUCH LOTS, IF THE HAMMER PRICE DOES NOT MEET THE RESERVE, THE CONSIGNOR MAY PAY A REDUCED COMMISSION ON THOSE LOTS. Reserves are generally posted online several days prior to the Auction closing. Any successful bid placed by a consignor on his Property on the Auction floor or by telephone during the live session, or after the reserves for an Auction have been posted, will be considered an Unqualified Bid, and in such instances the consignor agrees to pay full Buyer's Premium and Seller's Commissions on any lot so repurchased.
14. The highest qualified Bidder shall be the buyer. In the event of any dispute between floor Bidders at a Signature Auction, Auctioneer may at his sole discretion reoffer the lot. Auctioneer's decision and declaration of the winning Bidder shall be final and binding upon all Bidders.
15. Auctioneer reserves the right to refuse to honor any bid or to limit the amount of any bid which, in his sole discretion, is not submitted in "Good Faith," or is not supported by satisfactory credit, numismatic references, or otherwise. A bid is considered not made in "Good Faith" when an insolvent or irresponsible person, or a person under the age of eighteen makes it. Regardless of the disclosure of his identity, any bid by a consignor or his agent on a lot consigned by him is deemed to be made in "Good Faith".
16. Nominal Bids. The Auctioneer in its sole discretion may reject nominal bids, small opening bids, or very nominal advances. If a lot bearing estimates fails to open for 40–60% of the low estimate, the Auctioneer may pass the item or may place a protective bid on behalf of the consignor.
17. Lots bearing bidding estimates shall open at Auctioneer's discretion (approximately 50% of the low estimate). In the event that no bid meets or exceeds that opening amount, the lot shall pass as unsold.
18. All items are to be purchased per lot as numerically indicated and no lots will be broken. Bids will be accepted in whole dollar amounts only. No "buy" or "unlimited" bids will be accepted. Off-increment bids may be accepted by the Auctioneer at Signature Auctions and Grand Format Auctions. Auctioneer reserves the right to withdraw, prior to the close, any lots from the Auction.
19. Auctioneer reserves the right to rescind the sale in the event of nonpayment, breach of a warranty, disputed ownership, auctioneer's clerical error or omission in exercising bids and reserves, or otherwise.
20. Auctioneer occasionally experiences Internet and/or Server service outages during which Bidders cannot participate or place bids. If such outage occurs, we may at our discretion extend bidding for the auction. This policy applies only to widespread outages and not to isolated problems that occur in various parts of the country from time to time. Auctioneer periodically schedules system downtime for maintenance and other purposes, which may be covered by the Outage Policy. Bidders unable to place their Bids through the Internet are directed to bid through Client Services at 1-800-872-6467.
21. The Auctioneer or its affiliates may consign items to be sold in the Auction, and may bid on those lots or any other lots. Auctioneer or affiliates expressly reserve the right to modify any such bids at any time prior to the hammer based upon data made known to the Auctioneer or its affiliates. The Auctioneer may extend advances, guarantees, or loans to certain consignors, and may extend financing or other credits at varying rates to certain Bidders in the auction.
22. The Auctioneer has the right to sell certain unsold items after the close of the Auction; Such lots shall be considered sold during the Auction and all these Terms and Conditions shall apply to such sales including but not limited to the Buyer's Premium, return rights, and disclaimers.

Payment:
23. All sales are strictly for cash in United States dollars. Cash includes: U.S. currency, bank wire, cashier checks, travelers checks, and bank money orders, all subject to reporting requirements. Checks may be subject to clearing before delivery of the purchases. Credit Card (Visa or Master Card only) and PayPal payments may be accepted up to $10,000 from non-dealers at the sole discretion of the auctioneer, subject to the following limitations: a) sales are only to the cardholder, b) purchases are shipped to the cardholder's registered and verified address, c) Auctioneer may pre-approve the cardholder's credit line, d) a credit card transaction may not be used in conjunction with any other financing or extended terms offered by the Auctioneer, and must transact immediately upon invoice presentation, e) rights of return are governed by these Terms and Conditions, which supersede those conditions promulgated by the card issuer, f) floor Bidders must present their card.

24. Payment is due upon closing of the Auction session, or upon presentment of an invoice. Auctioneer reserves the right to void an invoice if payment in full is not received within 7 days after the close of the Auction.
25. Lots delivered in the States of Texas, California, or other states where the Auction may be held, are subject to all applicable state and local taxes, unless appropriate permits are on file with us. Bidder agrees to pay Auctioneer the actual amount of tax due in the event that sales tax is not properly collected due to: 1) an expired, inaccurate, inappropriate tax certificate or declaration, 2) an incorrect interpretation of the applicable statute, 3) or any other reason. Lots from different Auctions may not be aggregated for sales tax purposes.
26. In the event that a Bidder's payment is dishonored upon presentment(s), Bidder shall pay the maximum statutory processing fee set by applicable state law.
27. If any Auction invoice submitted by Auctioneer is not paid in full when due, the unpaid balance will bear interest at the highest rate permitted by law from the date of invoice until paid. If the Auctioneer refers any invoice to an attorney for collection, the buyer agrees to pay attorney's fees, court costs, and other collection costs incurred by Auctioneer. If Auctioneer assigns collection to its in-house legal staff, such attorney's time expended on the matter shall be compensated at a rate comparable to the hourly rate of independent attorneys.
28. In the event a successful Bidder fails to pay all amounts due, Auctioneer reserves the right to resell the merchandise, and such Bidder agrees to pay for the reasonable costs of resale, including a 10% seller's commission, and also to pay any difference between the resale price and the price of the previously successful bid.
29. Auctioneer reserves the right to require payment in full in good funds before delivery of the merchandise.
30. Auctioneer shall have a lien against the merchandise purchased by the buyer to secure payment of the Auction invoice. Auctioneer is further granted a lien and the right to retain possession of any other property of the buyer then held by the Auctioneer or its affiliates to secure payment of any Auction invoice or any other amounts due the Auctioneer or affiliates from the buyer. With respect to these lien rights, Auctioneer shall have all the rights of a secured creditor under Article 9 of the Texas Uniform Commercial Code, including but not limited to the right of sale. In addition, with respect to payment of the Auction invoice(s), the buyer waives any and all rights of offset he might otherwise have against the Auctioneer and the consignor of the merchandise included on the invoice. If a Bidder owes Auctioneer or its affiliates on any account, Auctioneer and its affiliates shall have the right to offset such unpaid account by any credit balance due Bidder, and it may secure by possessory lien any unpaid amount by any of the Bidder's property in their possession.
31. Title shall not pass to the successful Bidder until all invoices are paid in full. It is the responsibility of the buyer to provide adequate insurance coverage for the items once they have been delivered.

Delivery; Shipping and Handling Charges:
32. Shipping and handling charges will be added to invoices. Please refer to Auctioneer's website www.HA.com/common/shipping.php for the latest charges or call Auctioneer. Auctioneer is unable to combine purchases from other auctions or affiliates into one package for shipping purposes.
33. Successful overseas Bidders shall provide written shipping instructions, including specified customs declarations, to the Auctioneer for any lots to be delivered outside of the United States. NOTE: Declaration value shall be the item(s) hammer price together with its buyer's premium.
34. All shipping charges will be borne by the successful Bidder. Any risk of loss during shipment will be borne by the buyer following Auctioneer's delivery to the designated common carrier or third-party shipper, regardless of domestic or foreign shipment.
35. Due to the nature of some items sold, it shall be the responsibility for the successful bidder to arrange pick-up and shipping through third-parties; as to such items Auctioneer shall have no liability.
36. Any request for shipping verification for undelivered packages must be made within 30 days of shipment by Auctioneer.

Cataloging, Warranties and Disclaimers:
37. NO WARRANTY, WHETHER EXPRESSED OR IMPLIED, IS MADE WITH RESPECT TO ANY DESCRIPTION OR CONDITION REPORT CONTAINED IN THIS AUCTION OR ANY SECOND OPINE. Any description of the items or second opine contained in this Auction is for the sole purpose of identifying the items for those Bidders who do not have the opportunity to view the lots prior to bidding, and no description of items has been made part of the basis of the bargain or has created any express warranty that the goods would conform to any description made by Auctioneer.
38. Auctioneer is selling only such right or title to the items being sold as Auctioneer may have by virtue of consignment agreements on the date of auction and disclaims any warranty of title to the Property. Auctioneer disclaims any warranty of merchantability or fitness for any particular purposes.
39. Translations of foreign language documents may be provided as a convenience to interested parties. Heritage makes no representation as to the accuracy of those translations and will not be held responsible for errors in bidding arising from inaccuracies in translation.
40. Auctioneer disclaims all liability for damages, consequential or otherwise, arising out of or in connection with the sale of any Property by Auctioneer to Bidder. No third party may rely on any benefit of these Terms and Conditions and any rights, if any, established hereunder are personal to the Bidder and may not be assigned. Any statement made by the Auctioneer is an opinion and does not constitute a warranty or representation. No employee of Auctioneer may alter these Terms and Conditions, and, unless signed by a principal of Auctioneer, any such alteration is null and void.
41. Auctioneer shall not be liable for breakage of glass or damage to frames (patent or latent); such defects, in any event, shall not be a basis for any claim for return or reduction in purchase price.

Release:
42. In consideration of participation in the Auction and the placing of a bid, Bidder expressly releases Auctioneer, its officers, directors and employees, its affiliates, and its outside experts that provide second opines, from any and all claims, cause of action, chose of action, whether at law or equity or any arbitration or mediation rights existing under the rules of any professional society or affiliation based upon the assigned description, or a derivative theory, breach of warranty express or implied, representation or other matter set forth within these Terms and Conditions of Auction or otherwise. In the event of a claim, Bidder agrees that such rights and privileges conferred therein are strictly construed as specifically declared herein; e.g., authenticity, typographical error, etc. and are the exclusive remedy. Bidder, by non-compliance to these express terms of a granted remedy, shall waive any claim against Auctioneer.

Dispute Resolution and Arbitration Provision:
43. By placing a bid or otherwise participating in the auction, Bidder accepts these Terms and Conditions of Auction, and specifically agrees to the alternative dispute resolution provided herein. Arbitration replaces the right to go to court, including the right to a jury trial.
44. Auctioneer in no event shall be responsible for consequential damages, incidental damages, compensatory damages, or other damages arising from the auction of any lot. In the event that Auctioneer cannot deliver the lot or subsequently it is established that the lot lacks title, provenance, authenticity, or other transfer or condition issue is claimed, Auctioneer's liability shall be limited to rescission of sale and refund of purchase price; in no case shall Auctioneer's maximum liability exceed the high bid on that lot, which bid shall be deemed for all purposes the value of the lot. After one year has elapsed, Auctioneer's maximum liability shall be limited to any commissions and fees Auctioneer earned on that lot.
45. In the event of an attribution error, Auctioneer may at its sole discretion, correct the error on the Internet, or, if discovered at a later date, to refund the buyer's purchase price without further obligation.
46. If any dispute arises regarding payment, authenticity, grading, description, provenance, or any other matter pertaining to the Auction, the Bidder or a participant in the Auction and/or the Auctioneer agree that the dispute shall be submitted, if otherwise mutually unresolved, to binding arbitration in accordance with the commercial rules of the American Arbitration Association (A.A.A.). A.A.A. arbitration shall be conducted under the provisions of the Federal Arbitration Act with locale in Dallas, Texas. Any claim made by a Bidder has to be presented within one (1) year or it is barred. The prevailing party may be awarded his reasonable attorney's fees and costs. An award granted in arbitration is enforceable in any court of competent jurisdiction. No claims of any kind (except for reasons of authenticity) can be considered after the settlements have been made with the consignors. Any dispute after the settlement date is strictly between the Bidder and consignor without involvement or responsibility of the Auctioneer.
47. In consideration of their participation in or application for the Auction, a person or entity (whether the successful Bidder, a Bidder, a purchaser and/or other Auction participant or registrant) agrees that all disputes in any way relating to, arising under, connected with, or incidental to these Terms and Conditions and purchases, or default in payment thereof, shall be arbitrated pursuant to the arbitration provision. In the event that any matter including actions to compel arbitration, construe the agreement, actions in aid or arbitration or otherwise needs to be litigated, such litigation shall be exclusively in the Courts of the State of Texas, in Dallas County, Texas, and if necessary the corresponding appellate courts. The successful Bidder, purchaser, or Auction participant also expressly submits himself to the personal jurisdiction of the State of Texas.
48. These Terms & Conditions provide specific remedies for occurrences in the auction and delivery process. Where such remedies are afforded, they shall be interpreted strictly. Bidder agrees that any claim shall utilize such remedies; Bidder making a claim in excess of those remedies provided in these Terms and Conditions agrees that in no case whatsoever shall Auctioneer's maximum liability exceed the high bid on that lot, which bid shall be deemed for all purposes the value of the lot..

Miscellaneous:
49. Agreements between Bidders and consignors to effectuate a non-sale of an item at Auction, inhibit bidding on a consigned item to enter into a private sale agreement for said item, or to utilize the Auctioneer's Auction to obtain sales for non-selling consigned items subsequent to the Auction, are strictly prohibited. If a subsequent sale of a previously consigned item occurs in violation of this provision, Auctioneer reserves the right to charge Bidder the applicable Buyer's Premium and consignor a Seller's Commission as determined for each auction venue and by the terms of the seller's agreement.
50. Acceptance of these Terms and Conditions qualifies Bidder as a Heritage customer who has consented to be contacted by Heritage in the future. In conformity with "do-not-call" regulations promulgated by the Federal or State regulatory agencies, participation by the Bidder is affirmative consent to being contacted at the phone number shown in his application and this consent shall remain in effect until it is revoked in writing. Heritage may from time to time contact Bidder concerning sale, purchase, and auction opportunities available through Heritage and its affiliates and subsidiaries.

State Notices:
Notice as to an Auction in California. Auctioneer has in compliance with Title 2.95 of the California Civil Code as amended October 11, 1993 Sec. 1812.600, posted with the California Secretary of State its bonds for it and its employees, and the auction is being conducted in compliance with Sec. 2338 of the Commercial Code and Sec. 535 of the Penal Code.

Notice as to an Auction in New York City. These Terms and Conditions are designed to conform to the applicable sections of the New York City Department of Consumer Affairs Rules and Regulations as Amended. This is a Public Auction Sale conducted by Auctioneer. The New York City licensed Auctioneers are Kathleen Guzman, No.0762165-Day, and Samuel W. Foose, No.0952360-Day, No.0952361-Night, who will conduct the Auction on behalf of Heritage Auctions, Inc. ("Auctioneer"). All lots are subject to: the consignor's right to bid thereon in accord with these Terms and Conditions of Auction, consignor's option to receive advances on their consignments, and Auctioneer, in its sole discretion, may offer limited extended financing to registered bidders, in accord with Auctioneer's internal credit standards. A registered bidder may inquire whether a lot is subject to an advance or reserve. Auctioneer has made advances to various consignors in this sale.

Rev. 10_6_06

ADDITIONAL TERMS AND CONDITIONS OF AUCTION

COINS and CURRENCY TERM A: Signature Auctions are not on approval. No certified material may be returned because of possible differences of opinion with respect to the grade offered by any third-party organization, dealer, or service. No guarantee of grade is offered for uncertified Property sold and subsequently submitted to a third-party grading service. There are absolutely no exceptions to this policy. Under extremely limited circumstances, (e.g. gross cataloging error) a purchaser, who did not bid from the floor, may request Auctioneer to evaluate voiding a sale: such request must be made in writing detailing the alleged gross error; submission of the lot to the Auctioneer must be pre-approved by the Auctioneer; and bidder must notify Ron Brackemyre (1-800-872-6467 ext. 312) in writing of such request within three (3) days of the non-floor bidder's receipt of the lot. Any lot that is to be evaluated must be in our offices within 30 days after Auction. Grading or method of manufacture do not qualify for this evaluation process nor do such complaints constitute a basis to challenge the authenticity of a lot. AFTER THAT 30-DAY PERIOD, NO LOTS MAY BE RETURNED FOR REASONS OTHER THAN AUTHENTICITY. Lots returned must be housed intact in their original holder. No lots purchased by floor Bidders may be returned (including those Bidders acting as agents for others) except for authenticity. Late remittance for purchases may be considered just cause to revoke all return privileges.

COINS and CURRENCY TERM B: Auctions conducted solely on the Internet THREE (3) DAY RETURN POLICY: Certified Coin and Uncertified Currency lots paid for within seven days of the Auction closing are sold with a three (3) day return privilege. Third party graded notes are not returnable for any reason whatsoever. You may return lots under the following conditions: Within three days of receipt of the lot, you must first notify Auctioneer by contacting Client Service by phone (1-800-872-6467) or e-mail (Bid@HA.com), and immediately ship the lot(s) fully insured to the attention of Returns, Heritage, 3500 Maple Avenue, 17th Floor, Dallas TX 75219-3941. Lots must be housed intact in their original holder and condition. You are responsible for the insured, safe delivery of any lots. A non-negotiable return fee of 5% of the purchase price ($10 per lot minimum) will be deducted from the refund for each returned lot or billed directly. Postage and handling fees are not refunded. After the three-day period (from receipt), no items may be returned for any reason. Late remittance for purchases revokes these Return privileges.

COINS and CURRENCY TERM C: Bidders who have inspected the lots prior to any Auction will not be granted any return privileges, except for reasons of authenticity.

COINS and CURRENCY TERM D: Coins sold referencing a third-party grading service are sold "as is" without any express or implied warranty, except for a guarantee by Auctioneer that they are genuine. Certain warranties may be available from the grading services and the Bidder is referred to them for further details: ANACS, P.O. Box 182141, Columbus, Ohio 43218-2141; Numismatic Guaranty Corporation (NGC), P.O. Box 4776, Sarasota, FL 34230; Professional Coin Grading Service (PCGS), PO Box 9458, Newport Beach, CA 92658; and Independent Coin Grading Co. (ICG), 7901 East Belleview Ave., Suite 50, Englewood, CO 80111.

COINS and CURRENCY TERM E: Notes sold referencing a third-party grading service are sold "as is" without any express or implied warranty, except for guarantee by Auctioneer that they are genuine. Grading, condition or other attributes of any lot may have a material effect on its value, and the opinion of others, including third-party grading services such as PCGS Currency, PMG, and CGA may differ with that of Auctioneer. Auctioneer shall not be bound by any prior or subsequent opinion, determination, or certification by any grading service. Bidder specifically waives any claim to right of return of any item because of the opinion, determination, or certification, or lack thereof, by any grading service. Certain warranties may be available from the grading services and the Bidder is referred to them for further details: Paper Money Guaranty (PMG), PO Box 4711, Sarasota FL 34230; PCGS Currency, PO Box 9458, Newport Beach, CA 92658; Currency Grading & Authentication (CGA), PO Box 418, Three Bridges, NJ 08887. Third party graded notes are not returnable for any reason whatsoever.

COINS and CURRENCY TERM F: Since we cannot examine encapsulated coins or notes, they are sold "as is" without our grading opinion, and may not be returned for any reason. Auctioneer shall not be liable for any patent or latent defect or controversy pertaining to or arising from any encapsulated collectible. In any such instance, purchaser's remedy, if any, shall be solely against the service certifying the collectible.

COINS and CURRENCY TERM G: Due to changing grading standards over time, differing interpretations, and to possible mishandling of items by subsequent owners, Auctioneer reserves the right to grade items differently than shown on certificates from any grading service that accompany the items. Auctioneer also reserves the right to grade items differently than the grades shown in the prior catalog should such items be reconsigned to any future auction.

COINS and CURRENCY TERM H: Although consensus grading is employed by most grading services, it should be noted as aforesaid that grading is not an exact science. In fact, it is entirely possible that if a lot is broken out of a plastic holder and resubmitted to another grading service or even to the same service, the lot could come back with a different grade assigned.

COINS and CURRENCY TERM I: Certification does not guarantee protection against the normal risks associated with potentially volatile markets. The degree of liquidity for certified coins and collectibles will vary according to general market conditions and the particular lot involved. For some lots there may be no active market at all at certain points in time.

COINS and CURRENCY TERM J: All non-certified coins and currency are guaranteed genuine, but are not guaranteed as to grade, since grading is a matter of opinion, an art and not a science, and therefore the opinion rendered by the Auctioneer or any third party grading service may not agree with the opinion of others (including trained experts), and the same expert may not grade the same item with the same grade at two different times. Auctioneer has graded the non-certified numismatic items, in the Auctioneer's opinion, to their current interpretation of the American Numismatic Association's standards as of the date the catalog was prepared. There is no guarantee or warranty implied or expressed that the grading standards utilized by the Auctioneer will meet the standards of any grading service at any time in the future.

COINS and CURRENCY TERM K: Storage of purchased coins and currency: Purchasers are advised that certain types of plastic may react with a coin's metal or transfer plasticizer to notes and may cause damage. Caution should be used to avoid storage in materials that are not inert.

COINS and CURRENCY TERM L: NOTE: Purchasers of rare coins or currency through Heritage have available the option of arbitration by the Professional Numismatists Guild (PNG); if an election is not made within ten (10) days of an unresolved dispute, Auctioneer may elect either PNG or A.A.A. Arbitration.

WIRING INSTRUCTIONS:
Bank Information: JP Morgan Chase Bank, N.A., 270 Park Avenue, New York, NY 10017
Account Name: HERITAGE NUMISMATIC AUCTIONS MASTER ACCOUNT
ABA Number: 021000021
Account Number: 1884827674
Swift Code: CHASUS33

Rev. 02_15_07

CHOOSE YOUR BIDDING METHOD

Mail Bidding at Auction

Mail bidding at auction is fun and easy and only requires a few simple steps.

1. Look through the catalog, and determine the lots of interest.
2. Research their market value by checking price lists and other price guidelines.
3. Fill out your bid sheet, entering your maximum bid on each lot using your price research and your desire to own the lot.
4. Verify your bids!
5. Mail Early. Preference is given to the first bids received in case of a tie. When bidding by mail, you frequently purchase items at less than your maximum bid.

Bidding is opened at the published increment above the second highest mail or Internet bid; we act on your behalf as the highest mail bidder. If bidding proceeds, we act as your agent, bidding in increments over the previous bid. This process is continued until you are awarded the lot or you are outbid.

An example of this procedure: You submit a bid of $100, and the second highest mail bid is at $50. Bidding starts at $51 on your behalf. If no other bids are placed, you purchase the lot for $51. If other bids are placed, we bid for you in the posted increments until we reach your maximum bid of $100. If bidding passes your maximum: if you are bidding through the Internet, we will contact you by e-mail; if you bid by mail, we take no other action. Bidding continues until the final bidder wins.

Mail Bidding Instructions

1. **Name, Address, City, State, Zip**
   Your address is needed to mail your purchases. We need your telephone number to communicate any problems or changes that may affect your bids.

2. **References**
   If you have not established credit with us from previous auctions, you must send a 25% deposit, or list dealers with whom you have credit established.

3. **Lot Numbers and Bids**
   List all lots you desire to purchase. On the reverse are additional columns; you may also use another sheet. Under "Amount" enter the maximum you would pay for that lot (whole dollar amounts only). We will purchase the lot(s) for you as much below your bids as possible.

4. **Total Bid Sheet**
   Add up all bids and list that total in the appropriate box.

5. **Sign Your Bid Sheet**
   By signing the bid sheet, you have agreed to abide by the Terms of Auction listed in the auction catalog.

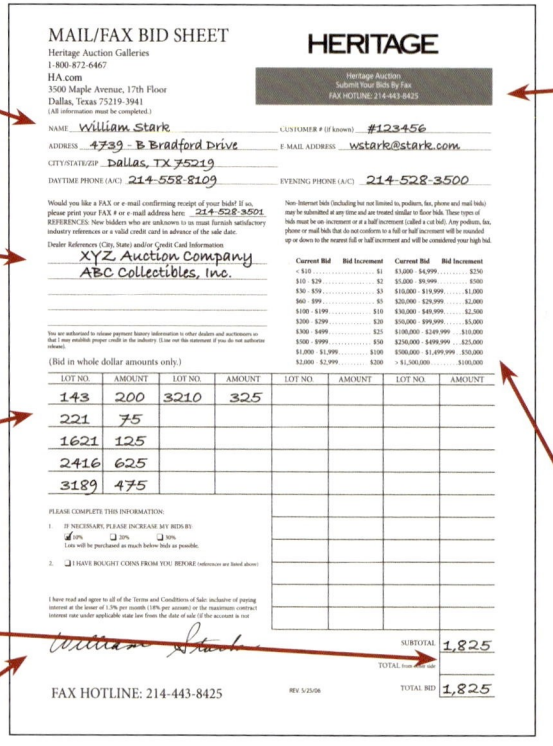

The official prices realized list that accompanies our auction catalogs is reserved for bidders and consignors only. We are happy to mail one to others upon receipt of $1.00. Written requests should be directed to Customer Service.

6. **Fax Your Bid Sheet**
   When time is short submit a Mail Bid Sheet on our exclusive Fax Hotline. There's no faster method to get your bids to us *instantly*. Simply use the **Heritage Fax Hotline number: 214-443-8425**.

   When you send us your original after faxing, mark it "Confirmation of Fax" (preferably in red!)

7. **Bidding Increments**
   To facilitate bidding, please consult the following chart. Bids will be accepted on the increments or on the half increments.

10_5_06

CHOOSE YOUR BIDDING METHOD (CONT'D.)

Interactive Internet Bidding

You can now bid with Heritage's exclusive *Interactive Internet* program, available only at our web site: HA.com. It's fun, and it's easy!

1. Register online at: **HA.com**
2. View the full-color photography of every single lot in the online catalog!
3. Construct your own personal catalog for preview.
4. View the current opening bids on lots you want; review the prices realized archive.
5. Bid and receive immediate notification if you are the top bidder; later, if someone else bids higher, you will be notified automatically by e-mail.
6. The *Interactive Internet* program opens the lot on the floor at one increment over the second highest bid. As the high bidder, your secret maximum bid will compete for you during the floor auction, and it is possible that you may be outbid on the floor after Internet bidding closes. Bid early, as the earliest bird wins in the event of a tie bid.
7. After the sale, you will be notified of your success. It's that easy!

Interactive Internet Bidding Instructions

1. **Log Onto Website**
   Log onto **HA.com** and choose the portal you're interested in (i.e., coins, comics, movie posters, fine arts, etc.).

2. **Search for Lots**
   Search or browse for the lot you are interested in. You can do this from the home page, from the Auctions home page, or from the home page for the particular auction in which you wish to participate.

3. **Select Lots**
   Click on the link or the photo icon for the lot you want to bid on.

4. **Enter Bid**
   At the top of the page, next to a small picture of the item, is a box outlining the current bid. Enter the amount of your secret maximum bid in the textbox next to "Secret Maximum Bid." The secret maximum bid is the maximum amount you are willing to pay for the item you are bidding on (for more information about bidding and bid increments, please see the section labeled "Bidding Increments" elsewhere in this catalog). Click on the button marked "Place Absentee Bid." A new area on the same page will open up for you to enter your username (or e-mail address) and password. Enter these, then click "Place Absentee Bid" again.

5. **Confirm Absentee Bid**
   You are taken to a page labeled, "Please Confirm Your Bid." This page shows you the name of the item you're bidding on, the current bid, and the maximum bid. When you are satisfied that all the information shown is correct, click on the button labeled, "Confirm Bid."

6. **Bidding Status Notification**
   One of two pages is now displayed.

   a. If your bid is the current high bid, you will be notified and given additional information as to what might happen to affect your high bidder status over the course of the remainder of the auction. You will also receive a Bid Confirmation notice via email.

   b. If your bid is not the current high bid, you will be notified of that fact and given the opportunity to increase your bid.

ORDER OF SALE #436

SESSION ONE — LOTS 12001-12886
WEDNESDAY, MAY 9
PROMPTLY AT 6 PM

CONTINENTAL	12001-12022
COLONIAL	12023-12234
POSTAGE ENVELOPES	12235-12236
ENCASED POSTAGE	12237-12288
FRACTIONAL CURRENCY	12289-12495
CONFEDERATE CURRENCY	12496-12583
CONFEDERATE BONDS	12584-12616
SOUTHERN STATES BONDS	12617-12663

OBSOLETE CURRENCY

ALABAMA	12664-12666
ARKANSAS	12667-12694
DISTRICT OF COLUMBIA	12695
FLORIDA	12696-12699
GEORGIA	12700
ILLINOIS	12701-12705
INDIANA	12706
IOWA	12707-12713
KENTUCKY	12714
LOUISIANA	12715-12718
MARYLAND	12719-12720
MICHIGAN	12721
MINNESOTA	12722
MISSISSIPPI	12723-12724
MISSOURI	12725
NEBRASKA	12726-12729
NEW HAMPSHIRE	12730-12733
NEW JERSEY	12734-12735
NEW MEXICO	12736
NEW YORK	12737-12771
NORTH CAROLINA	12772
OHIO	12773-12774
PENNSYLVANIA	12775-12777
RHODE ISLAND	12778-12780
SOUTH CAROLINA	12781-12784
TENNESSEE	12785-12786
TEXAS	12787-12811
VIRGINIA	12812-12815
WISCONSIN	12816-12818

MISCELLANEOUS	12819-12832
MILITARY PAYMENT CERTIFICATES	12833-12862
FOREIGN CURRENCY	12863-12882
CANADIAN CURRENCY	12883-12886

SESSION TWO — LOTS 12887-13662
THURSDAY, MAY 10
PROMPTLY AT 6 PM

EARLY US BONDS	12887-12888

LARGE SIZE TYPE NOTES

DEMAND NOTE	12889
LEGAL TENDER NOTES	12890-13098
REFUNDING CERTIFICATE	13099
SILVER CERTIFICATES	13100-13385
TREASURY NOTES	13386-13413
FEDERAL RESERVE BANK NOTES	13414-13516
FEDERAL RESERVE NOTES	13517-13605
GOLD CERTIFICATES	13606-13662

SESSION THREE — LOTS 13663-14262
FRIDAY, MAY 11
PROMPTLY AT 1 PM

SMALL SIZE TYPE NOTES	13663-14209
ERROR NOTES	14210-14262

ORDER OF SALE #436

SESSION FOUR — LOTS 14263-15474
FRIDAY, MAY 11
PROMPTLY AT 6 PM

NATIONAL BANK NOTES

ALABAMA 14263-14266
ARKANSAS 14267-14323
CALIFORNIA 14324-14340
COLORADO 14341-14357
CONNECTICUT 14358-14360
DELAWARE 14361-14362
FLORIDA 14363-14366
GEORGIA 14367-14369
HAWAII 14370-14376
IDAHO 14377-14378
ILLINOIS 14379-14718
INDIANA 14719-14747
IOWA 14748-14764
KANSAS 14765-14774
KENTUCKY 14775-14803
LOUISIANA 14804-14810
MAINE 14811-14816
MARYLAND 14817-14824
MASSACHUSETTS 14825-14839
MICHIGAN 14840-14850
MINNESOTA 14851-14861
MISSISSIPPI 14862-14867
MISSOURI 14868-14880
MONTANA 14881-14882
NEBRASKA 14883-14889
NEVADA 14890
NEW HAMPSHIRE 14891-14893
NEW JERSEY 14894-14913
NEW MEXICO 14914-14917
NEW YORK 14918-14970
NORTH CAROLINA 14971-14986
NORTH DAKOTA 14987-14993
OHIO 14994-15038
OKLAHOMA 15039-15180
PENNSYLVANIA 15181-15236
RHODE ISLAND 15237-15238
SOUTH CAROLINA 15239-15242
SOUTH DAKOTA 15243-15248
TENNESSEE 15249-15256
TEXAS 15257-15441
UTAH 15442-15443
VERMONT 15444-15447
VIRGINIA 15448-15455
WASHINGTON 15456
WEST VIRGINIA 15457-15461
WISCONSIN 15462-15471
WYOMING 15472-15474

END OF SALE
THANK YOU FOR PARTICIPATING

Heritage Auction Galleries Staff

Steve Ivy - Co-Chairman and CEO

Steve Ivy began collecting and studying rare coins in his youth, and as a teenager in 1963 began advertising coins for sale in national publications. Seven years later, at the age of twenty, he opened Steve Ivy Rare Coins in downtown Dallas, and in 1976, Steve Ivy Numismatic Auctions was incorporated. Steve managed the business as well as serving as chief numismatist, buying and selling hundreds of millions of dollars of coins during the 1970s and early 1980s. In early 1983, James Halperin became a full partner, and the name of the corporation was changed to Heritage Rare Coin Galleries. Steve's primary responsibilities now include management of the marketing and selling efforts of the company, the formation of corporate policy for long-term growth, and corporate relations with financial institutions. He remains intimately involved in numismatics, attending all major national shows. Steve engages in daily discourse with industry leaders on all aspects of the rare coin/currency business, and his views on grading, market trends and hobby developments are respected throughout the industry. He serves on the Board of Directors of the Professional Numismatists Guild (and was immediate past president), is the current Chairman of The Industry Council for Tangible Assets, and is a member of most leading numismatic organizations. Steve's keen appreciation of history is reflected in his active participation in other organizations, including past or present board positions on the Texas Historical Foundation and the Dallas Historical Society (where he also served as Exhibits Chairman). Steve is an avid collector of Texas books, manuscripts, and national currency, and he owns one of the largest and finest collections in private hands. He is also a past Board Chair of Dallas Challenge, and is currently the Finance Chair of the Phoenix House of Texas.

James Halperin - Co-Chairman

Jim Halperin and the traders under his supervision have transacted billions of dollars in rare coin business, and have outsold all other numismatic firms every year for over two decades. Born in Boston in 1952, Jim attended Middlesex School in Concord from 1966 to 1970. At the age of 15, he formed a part-time rare coin business after discovering that he had a knack (along with a nearly photographic memory) for coins. Jim scored a perfect 800 on his math SATs and received early acceptance to Harvard College, but after attending three semesters, he took a permanent leave of absence to pursue his full-time numismatic career. In 1975, Jim personally supervised the protocols for the first mainframe computer system in the numismatic business, which would catapult New England Rare Coin Galleries to the top of the industry in less than four years. In 1983, Jim merged with his friend and former archrival Steve Ivy, whom Jim had long admired. Their partnership has become the world's largest and most successful numismatic company, as well as the third-largest auctioneer in America. Jim remains arguably the best "eye" in the coin business today (he won the professional division of the PCGS World Series of Grading). In the mid-1980s, he authored "How to Grade U.S. Coins" (now posted on the web at www.CoinGrading.com), a highly-acclaimed text upon which the NGC and PCGS grading standards would ultimately be based. Jim is a bit of a Renaissance man, as a well-known futurist, an active collector of EC comics and early 20th-century American art (visit www.jhalpe.com), venture capital investor, philanthropist (he endows a multimillion-dollar health education foundation), and part-time novelist. His first fictional novel, "The Truth Machine," was published in 1996 and became an international science fiction bestseller, and was optioned for movie development by Warner Brothers. Jim's second novel, "The First Immortal," was published in early 1998 and immediately optioned as a Hallmark Hall of Fame television miniseries. Jim is married to Gayle Ziaks, and they have two sons, David and Michael. In 1996, with funding from Jim and Gayle's foundation, Gayle founded Dallas' Dance for the Planet, which has grown to become the largest free dance festival in the world.

Greg Rohan - President

At the age of eight, Greg Rohan started collecting coins as well as buying them for resale to his schoolmates. By 1971, at the age of ten, he was already buying and selling coins from a dealer's table at trade shows in his hometown of Seattle. His business grew rapidly, and by 1985 he had offices in both Seattle and Minneapolis. He joined Heritage in 1987 as Executive Vice-President and Manager of the firm's rare coin business. Today, as an owner and as President of Heritage, his responsibilities include overseeing the firm's private client group and working with top collectors in every field in which Heritage is active. Greg has been involved with many of the rarest items and most important collections handled by the firm, including the purchase and/or sale of the Ed Trompeter Collection (the world's largest numismatic purchase according to the Guinness Book of World Records), the legendary 1894 San Francisco Dime, the 1838 New Orleans Half Dollar, and the 1804 Silver Dollar. During his career, Greg has handled more than $1 billion of rare coins, collectibles and art, and provided expert consultation concerning the authenticity and grade condition of coins for the Professional Coin Grading Service (PCGS). He has provided expert testimony for the United States Attorneys in San Francisco, Dallas, and Philadelphia, and for the Federal Trade Commission (FTC). He has worked with collectors, consignors, and their advisors regarding significant collections of books, manuscripts, comics, currency, jewelry, vintage movie posters, sports and entertainment memorabilia, decorative arts, and fine art. Additionally, Greg is a Sage Society member of the American Numismatic Society, and a member/life member of the PNG, ANA, and most other leading numismatic organizations. Greg is also Chapter Chairman for North Texas of the Young Presidents' Organization (YPO), and is an active supporter of the arts. Greg co-authored "The Collectors Estate Handbook," winner of the NLG's Robert Friedberg Award for numismatic book of the year. Mr. Rohan currently serves on the seven-person Advisory Board to the Federal Reserve Bank of Dallas, in his second appointed term. He and his wife, Lysa, are avid collectors of rare wine, Native American artifacts, and American art.

Paul Minshull - Chief Operating Officer

As Chief Operating Officer, Paul Minshull's managerial responsibilities include integrating sales, personnel, inventory, security and MIS for Heritage. His major accomplishments include overseeing the hardware migration from mainframe to PC, the software migration of all inventory and sales systems, and implementation of a major Internet presence. Heritage's successful employee-suggestion program has generated 200 or more ideas each month since 1995, and has helped increase employee productivity, expand business, and improve employee retention. Paul oversees the company's highly-regarded IT department, and has been the driving force behind Heritage's web development, now a significant portion of Heritage's future plans. As the only numismatic auction house that combines traditional floor bidding with active Internet bidding, the totally interactive system has catapulted Heritage to the top rare coin website (according to Forbes Magazine's "Best of the Web"). Paul was born in Michigan and came to Heritage in 1984 after 12 years as the General Manager of a plastics manufacturing company in Ann Arbor. Since 1987, he has been a general partner in Heritage Capital Properties, Sales Manager, Vice President of Operations, and Chief Operating Officer for all Heritage companies and affiliates since 1996. Paul maintains an active interest in sports and physical fitness, and he and his wife have three children.

Steven R. Roach, J.D. - Director, Trusts and Estates
As both a licensed attorney and a seasoned numismatist, Steve is in a unique position to help heirs, nonprofit institutions, attorneys, and advisors with their collectible assets. In his more than 15 years in the coin industry, he has worked with many of the best, including positions at Heritage as a senior grader and numismatist, ANACS as a grader, and stints with Christie's and Spink-America in New York, and PCGS in Los Angeles. Steve writes the popular "Inside Collecting" column in Coin World, and has received two Numismatic Literary Guild (NLG) awards. He received his JD from The Ohio State University Moritz College of Law. He was a judicial extern to United States District Court Judge Gregory Frost, and a summer research fellow for the American Bar Association Section on Dispute Resolution in Washington, D.C. Steve received his BA with high honors from the University of Michigan with a dual degree in the History of Art and Organizational Studies, receiving the Tappan award for outstanding performance in the History of Art program, and studied in Florence, Italy. He is a life member of the American Numismatic Association, and a member of the American Bar Association, the Dallas Bar Association, the Dallas Association of Young Lawyers, and the Dallas Estate Planning Council.

Norma L. Gonzalez - VP of Operations - Numismatic Auctions
Born in Dallas, Texas, Norma joined the U.S. Navy in August of 1993. During her five-year enlistment, she received her Bachelor's Degree in Resource Management and traveled to Japan, Singapore, Thailand and lived in Cuba for three years. After her enlistment, she moved back to Dallas where her family resides. Norma joined Heritage in 1998; always ready for a challenge, she spent her days at Heritage and her nights pursuing an M. B. A. She was promoted to Vice President in 2003. She currently manages the operations departments, including Coins, Currency, World & Ancient Coins, Sportscards & Memorabilia, Comics, Movie Posters, Pop Culture and Political Memorabilia. Norma enjoys running, biking and spending time with her family. In February 2004 she ran a 26.2-mile marathon in Austin, Texas and later, in March she accomplished a 100-mile bike ride in California.

Kelley Norwine - VP - Marketing
Born and raised in South Carolina, Kelley pursued a double major at Southern Wesleyan University, earning a BA in Music Education and a BS in Business Management. A contestant in the Miss South Carolina pageant, Kelley was later Regional Manager & Director of Training at Bank of Travelers Rest in South Carolina. Relocating to Los Angeles, Kelley became the Regional Manager and Client Services Director for NAS-McCann World Group, an international Advertising & Communications Agency where she was responsible for running one of the largest offices in the country. During her years with NAS Kelley was the recipient of numerous awards including Regional Manager of the Quarter and the NAS Courage and Dedication award. After relocating to Dallas, Kelley took a job as Director of Client Services for TMP/Monster Worldwide and joined Heritage in 2005 as Director of Client Development. She was named VP of Marketing for Heritage in 2007. A cancer survivor, Kelley is an often-requested motivational speaker for the American Cancer Society. In her spare time, she writes music, sings, and plays the piano.

John Petty - Director - Media Relations
John Petty joined Heritage in 2001 as the first employee of the newly-formed Heritage Comics division, anxious to join the exciting auction industry. A passionate collector, comics historian, and Overstreet advisor, John had a life-long interest in comics. In 2004, John became the Director of Media Relations, and now handles public relations, copywriting, and media affairs for Heritage Auction Galleries. He also works on special assignments such as magazine articles, book projects, and TV productions. John is also one of Heritage's popular auctioneers, and can frequently be seen calling Movie Poster, Entertainment, and Fine & Decorative Art auctions. Currently, John co-writes monthly columns for both *The Comics Buyers Guide* and *Big Reel Magazine*. Originally from the New York area, John now lives in Texas with Judy, his significant other, two dogs, and three cats. He holds a Bachelor of Music degree in Voice from Baldwin-Wallace College in Berea, Ohio. In his spare time, John enjoys leather carving, silent movies, and Celtic music.

Marti Korver - Manager - Credits/Collections
Marti has been working in numismatics for more than three decades. She was recruited out of the banking profession by Jim Ruddy, and she worked with Paul Rynearson, Karl Stephens, and Judy Cahn on ancients and world coins at Bowers & Ruddy Galleries, in Hollywood, CA. She migrated into the coin auction business, running the bid books for such memorable sales as the Garrett Collection and representing bidders as agent at B&R auctions for 10 years. She also worked as a research assistant for Q. David Bowers for several years. Memorable events included such clients (and friends) as Richard Lobel, John Ford, Harry Bass, and John J. Pittman. She is married to noted professional numismatist and writer, Robert Korver, (who is sometimes seen auctioneering at coin shows) and they migrated to Heritage in Dallas in 1996. She has an RN daughter (who worked her way through college showing lots for Heritage) and a son (who is currently a college student and sometimes a Heritage employee) and a type set of dogs (one black and one white). She currently collects kitschy English teapots and compliments.

Todd Imhof - Vice President

Unlike most professional numismatists, Todd Imhof did not start as a coin collector. Shortly after graduating college in 1987, Todd declined an offer from a prestigious Wall Street bank to join a former high school classmate who was operating a small rare coin company in the Seattle area. The rare coin industry was then undergoing huge changes after the advent of certified grading and growing computer technologies. Being new to the industry, Todd had an easier time than most embracing the new dynamics. He soon discovered a personal passion for rare coins, and for working with high-level collectors. Through his accomplishments, Todd enjoys a reputation envied by the entire numismatic community. During his earlier tenure with Hertzberg Rare Coins, it was named by Inc. magazine as one of the nation's fastest growing private companies 1989-1991. In 1991, Todd co-founded Pinnacle Rarities, Inc., a boutique-styled firm that specialized in servicing the rare coin industry's savviest and most prominent collectors. At 25, he was among the youngest people ever accepted into the Professional Numismatists Guild, and currently serves on its Consumer Protection Committee. In 1992, he was invited to join the Board of Directors for the Industry Council for Tangible Assets, serving as its Chairman 2002-2005. Todd served as Pinnacle's President until his decision to join Heritage in 2006. In the Morse Auction, he became the only person in history to purchase two $1mm+ coins during a single auction session! Todd serves Heritage's Legacy clients, many of whom had previously sought his counsel and found his expertise and integrity to be of great value. Todd really understands what collectors are trying to accomplish, and he has an uncanny ability to identify the perfect coins at the right prices while navigating complex and difficult deals with unsurpassed professionalism.

Allen Mincho - Director of Auctions

Starting as a collector of paper money in 1968, Allen Mincho has become one of the foremost experts in the field of United States currency during the past three decades. After graduating from New York University Law School in 1971, Allen formed what is still the definitive collection of National Bank Notes from the City of New York, eventually comprising notes from over 130 of the 162 issuing banks within the city's five boroughs. Although serving for eight years as an Assistant District Attorney in the Rackets Bureau of the Kings County DA's office and as a Special Assistant Attorney General for the State of New York, the allure of a career dealing in paper money proved too attractive, and in 1980 he became a full time dealer. Specializing in National Bank Notes and large size type material, he has had the opportunity to handle nearly every significant rarity which has been offered since that time. After authoring a fixed price list since 1971, Allen became one of the three founders of Currency Auctions of America in 1990. This firm, which has now joined the Heritage family, quickly became the largest and most successful currency auction house ever, selling over 65,000 lots in its 27 sales. Allen was one of the founding members of the Professional Currency Dealers Association, serving as its first Vice President and then as the group's legal counsel. He is a contributor to many publications, including the standard reference in the field, Friedberg's Paper Money of the United States, and his articles have appeared in the Green Sheet and Paper Money Magazine. He has been a member of the Society of Paper Money Collectors since 1969. He currently contributes a column called Notes on the Market, which has run every month in Bank Note Reporter since January of 1998. Allen and his wife Penny were married in 1969. They are avid travelers and enjoy and collect fine wines. Both have served as officers in the Austin Branch of the International Wine and Food Society, and Allen is also actively involved with the Salvation Army in Austin.

Len Glazer - Director of Auctions

Len Glazer, co-founder and president of Currency Auctions of America, is widely recognized as one of the country's foremost authorities on paper money. Born and raised in Kew Gardens, NY, Len started collecting coins when he was in the seventh grade. Both his collection and his fondness for the hobby grew steadily over the years, and while he was still attending high school, he entered the market as a coin dealer at local trade shows. He continued to buy and sell coins throughout his years at St. John's University. Though he held a double major in Marketing and Management, he still managed to establish a reputation for himself in the coin-dealing community at nights and on weekends. But over time, he developed a greater interest in the intricacies of paper money, specifically Fractional Currency, a form of paper money produced in denominations of less than a dollar in response to the coin shortage created by the Civil War. Before graduating from college, Len had become a recognized dealer of - and authority on - Fractional Currency. In 1975, Len founded Fractional Currency Incorporated. On the merits of his accomplishments with this company over the following years, he was appointed Founding President of the Professional Currency Dealer's Association (PCDA), an organization he helped establish in 1985. He served two terms, from 1985-1987. In 1990, Len, along with friend and dealer Allen Mincho, started Currency Auctions of America, Inc. They held their first auction as CAA in November of that year. That auction sold $700,000 worth of currency. Now, over 30 auctions later, CAA sales average over $3 million. In September of 1997, CAA set the world record for the most expensive single piece of currency ever sold. They then broke their own record twice, before losing it briefly in December of 1998. They have recently reclaimed the record, having sold a note in January 2000 for the once-inconceivable price of $935,000. Len and Jean have been married for 30 years and have two adult children: Karen, a Wall-Street yuppie, and Daniel, who works with Len in the currency business. Today, Len Glazer is recognized as the country's foremost authority on Fractional Currency, as well as one of the most respected figures in the entire paper money community. In addition, Currency Auctions of America, the largest firm of its kind has become synonymous with quality consignments, honest dealing, and edge-of-your-seat auctions. Entering its second decade - and Len's fourth in the business - CAA is the strongest it has ever been.

Jim Fitzgerald - Director of Auctions

Jim joined the Heritage team in 2005, after working the past 16 years within the Travel and Hotel industry. Jim began collecting coins as a child, filling up Whitman folders with the assistance of his grandfather, who would pay for Jim's "extra" silver coins and wheat pennies found during the late 1960's - early 1970's. Upon his grandfather's death in 1983, Jim as entrusted by the estate to divide up those "extra" coins found as a child. While still collecting coins, Jim's primary focus has been on collecting paper money - small-size US notes, Texas Obsoletes, and most specifically, National Bank Notes. Ten years ago, he was introduced to a $100 National Bank Note from the Fort Worth National Bank, and ever since then, Jim has sharpened that collecting focus to all banks from Fort Worth, his hometown to this day, along with all ephemera from that era. He has given educational lectures on his collection and research at the Texas Numismatic Association shows, Tarrant County Historical Society, as well as all of the local coin clubs within the DFW area. Jim is a member of the Society of Paper Money Collectors, Texas Numismatic Association, Central States Numismatic Society, Dallas Coin Club, Northeast Tarrant Coin Club, as well as a founding member and past president of the Mid-Cities Coin Club. He also serves as the Show Chairman for the annual Texas Numismatic Association Show held presently in Fort Worth. Jim and his wife Sheli will celebrate their 10th year of marriage in September, 2007. While in his spare time, Jim enjoys travel, outdoor photography, hunting and fishing.

Dustin Johnston - Director of Auctions

Dustin Johnston joined the Heritage team in 1998 and has been active in nearly every aspect of the business. Prior to starting his full-time numismatic career with Heritage, he lived in Tucson, where he studied Accounting and Finance at the University of Arizona. Dustin's numismatic interests started at the age of 10 when he received a number of U.S. and foreign coins from his grandfather. At the age of 15 he was already attending national conventions including the annual ANA Convention. Though he was buying and selling coins and currency, his interests were mostly academic prior to joining Heritage and his accomplishments include a number of literary and exhibiting awards from the ANA. Dustin also served as an Exhibit Judge and Numismatic Theater Speaker for the ANA. As the Director of Auctions for Heritage-Currency Auctions of America, Dustin is responsible for consignment acquisitions, purchasing, cataloging, catalog production as well as managing the currency inventory. His broad numismatic knowledge has allowed him to assist thousands of consignors with the disposition of tens of millions of dollars worth of U.S. and foreign coins and currency. Dustin is a member of the ANA, CSNS, and PCDA.

Michael Moczalla - Consignment Director

Born and raised in and around Chicago, Michael's interest in coins and currency began at the age of 8. His paternal grandmother fueled his collecting ambitions by visiting local shops and giving him coins. This was when he decided that he would one day own a coin shop. His dream became a reality, when he opened MGM Currency & Coins in Vernon Hills, IL. After a successful tenure with various paper money discoveries, the opportunity to work for Heritage Galleries and share his talents presented itself. He is a member of ANA, CSNS, ILNA, and SPMC. He served as Vice-President of the Mundelein, IL Coin Club for three years and was a member of Lake County Coin Club. For two years he shared the joys of collecting with ten youngsters at a local school by forming a club there. His civic contributions include serving on the Lake County, IL Crimestoppers board and serving as Exalted Ruler at Waukegan, IL Lodge #702 of the Benevolent and Protective Order of Elks of the United States of America. He also aided in corralling a coin theft ring in Northern Illinois that involved numerous burglaries. Michael has been married to his wife, Debra, for almost 20 years and they have a son, Christopher and a daughter, Nathalie. During his leisure time, he enjoys his family, golf, travel, and tournament fishing for bass or walleye. He also speaks fluent French.

Frank Clark - Cataloger

Frank has been with Heritage/Currency Auctions of America since June 2003. He has been able to take a thirty year paper money avocation and make it his vocation. Along the way, he has enjoyed an active involvement with many numismatic societies. These include president of the Society of Paper Money Collectors, president Dallas Coin Club, president Garland Coin Club, district governor Texas Numismatic Association, and out-of-state board member of the Paper Money Collectors of Michigan. Frank has written over a hundred numismatic articles and displayed over fifty exhibits at the local, state, and national levels. He also has given more than sixty programs before numismatic societies across the nation. In October 2002, he participated as an invited member of the Bureau of Engraving Western Currency Facility focus group. Finally, Frank says that the best part of numismatics is sharing the knowledge that you gain along the way. That is why he enjoys cataloging so much, it helps him in distributing information to paper money collectors.

Paquet Liberty Double Eagle
Realized: $1,610,000
August 14, 2006

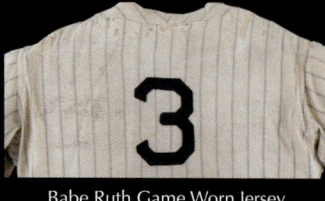

Babe Ruth Game Worn Jersey
Realized: $657,250
October 27, 2006

A WORLD OF COLLECTIBLES

HERITAGE IS THE WORLD'S LARGEST Collectibles Auctioneer, with on-staff experts in a variety of fields, including:

- Coins
- Currency
- Fine Art
- Decorative Arts
- Comic Books
- Original Comic Art
- Sports Memorabilia
- Political Memorabilia & Americana
- Entertainment & Music Memorabilia
- Jewelry & Timepieces
- Vintage Movie Posters
- Character Memorabilia & Vintage Toys
- Autographs & Rare Manuscripts
- And Much More!

Thomas Moran Oil Painting
Realized: $567,625
November 8, 2006

Pre-Columbian Gold Figure
Realized: $155,350
September 28, 2006

- **CASH FOR YOUR ITEMS**
- Always Accepting Consignments
- Free Appraisals by Appointments

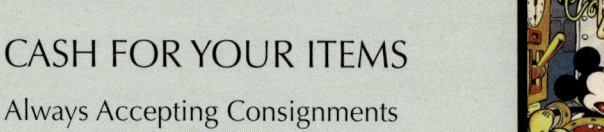

Kurt Cobain Guitar
Realized: $131,450
April 15, 2006

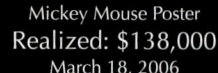

Mickey Mouse Poster
Realized: $138,000
March 18, 2006

Whatever your area of interest, Heritage can help! Interested in selling the collection you've spent years putting together? Call one of our expert Consignment Directors today at 1-800-872-6467 and find out how easy it is to turn your treasures into cash.

And be sure to visit HA.com, where you can explore all of our exciting categories and join our on-line community of 275,000 members, all of whom enjoy a host of benefits that only Heritage can offer!

To receive a complimentary catalog of your choice, register online at HA.com/CAT6709, or call 866-835-3243 and mention reference #CAT6709.

Annual Sales Exceeding $500 Million • Over 275,000 Registered Online Bidder-Members

3500 Maple Ave, 17th Floor • Dallas, Texas 75219 • 214-528-3500 • 800-872-6467 • HA.com

Auctioneer: John Petty, TX license #00013740

HERITAGE HA.com
Auction Galleries

6709

SESSION ONE

Live, Internet, and Mail Bid Auction 436 • St. Louis, Missouri
Wednesday, May 9, 2007, 6:00 PM CT • Lots 12001-12886

A 15% Buyer's Premium ($9 minimum) Will Be Added To All Lots
You can now view full-color images and bid via the Internet at the Heritage website: HA.com

CONTINENTAL CURRENCY

12001 **Continental Currency May 10, 1775 $4 About New.** A single center fold and a minor repaired split hold this First Issue Continental from a far higher grade. The note has the eye appeal of a choice new example. (200-up)

12002 **Continental Currency May 10, 1775 $8 Gem New.** Pristine original paper surfaces, bold signatures and excellent margins on both sides all combine on this extremely pretty, essentially flawless First Issue Continental. Continentals this nice from this issue were never common, but they used to be seen on occasion. The supply dried up long ago, and in today's market, May '75 Continentals in Gem condition are decidedly rare. (750-up)

12003 **Continental Currency November 29, 1775 $1 Very Choice New.** A near-Gem example of this desirable One Dollar Denomination Continental. The signatures are bold, and the note is well margined all the way around on both sides. One Dollar Continentals were issued for only five of the eleven issues. (550-up)

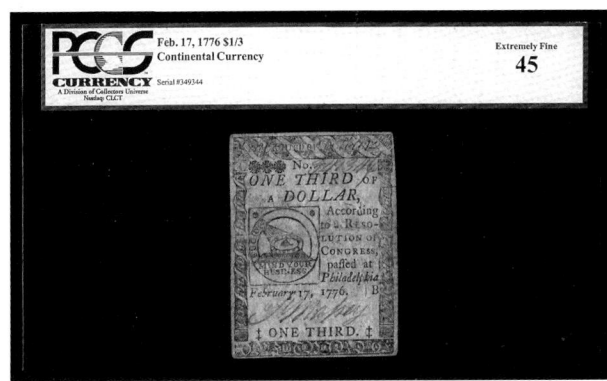

12004 **Continental Currency February 17, 1776 $1/3 PCGS Extremely Fine 45.** This Fugio fractional note has light folds, as well as bright signatures and serial number. (350-up)

12005 **Continental Currency February 17, 1776 $1/2 Choice About New.** This most pleasing and original piece is the nicest of this denomination to appear in our auctions in nearly a year. A lone horizontal center fold precludes the Gem grade. (650-up)

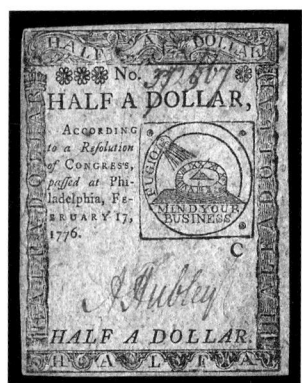

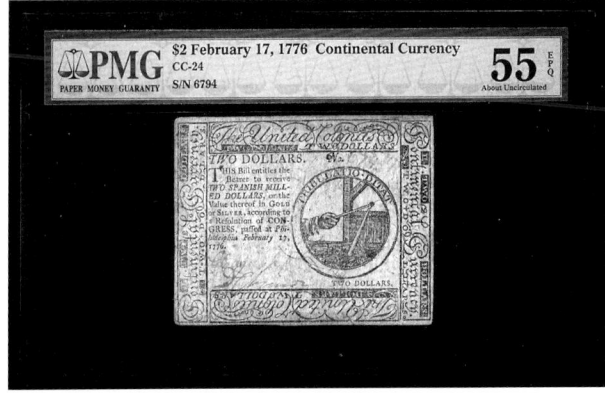

12006 **Continental Currency February 17, 1776 $2 PMG About Uncirculated 55 EPQ.** This pretty Continental is one extremely light center fold away from the Choice New grade. It's well-signed, well-margined, and has a razor-sharp vignette. (350-up)

12007 **Continental Currency February 17, 1776 $3 PCGS Choice About New 58PPQ.** The margins are complete on this pleasing example. **(375-up)**

12008 **Continental Currency February 17, 1776 $5 About New.** This note with dark signatures is a single center fold away from the Choice New grade. **(350-up)**

12009 **Continental Currency February 17, 1776 $8 New.** This fully uncirculated Eight Dollar note is held from the Choice grade, as all four corners have been clipped. Only the very outer frame line is touched by the clipping, with none of the design affected. **(500-up)**

12010 **Continental Currency February 17, 1776 $8 New.** This is a very pleasing example from this popular issue which is nicely margined, crisp, and well printed. A moisture spot affects the second signature. **(500-up)**

12011 **Continental Currency February 26, 1777 $7 PCGS Extremely Fine 40.** This is a lightly circulated example of this scarcer Baltimore issue which has a couple of light folds. **(250-up)**

12012 **Continental Currency February 26, 1777 $8 Very Choice New.** High-grade notes from this February 1777 Baltimore issue are deceptively scarce, and this one is a real beauty. The note has bold signatures, good print quality, strictly original paper surfaces, and perfect colors. It is very close to the full Gem grade. **(750-up)**

12013 **Continental Currency Blue Counterfeit Detector September 26, 1778 $5 Extremely Fine-About New.** This note is sharply printed and problem free save for two light folds. **(750-up)**

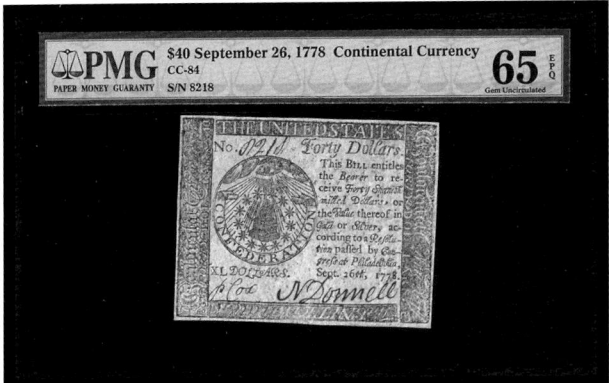

12014 **Continental Currency September 26, 1778 $40 PMG Gem Uncirculated 65 EPQ.** Boldly signed with clearly original paper surfaces and excellent margins. It's still rather early in the grading game, but it is safe to say that 65 EPQ Continentals are never going to be common. **(750-up)**

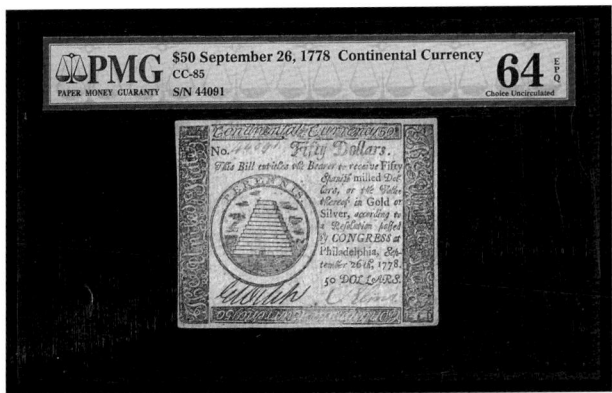

12015 **Continental Currency September 26, 1778 $50 PMG Choice Uncirculated 64 EPQ.** A handsome Continental with the important "Exceptional Paper Quality" comment. **(600-up)**

12016 **Continental Currency September 26, 1778 $50 PCGS Choice About New 58PPQ.** This is a pleasing lightly circulated example that has good signatures and bright serial number. **(300-up)**

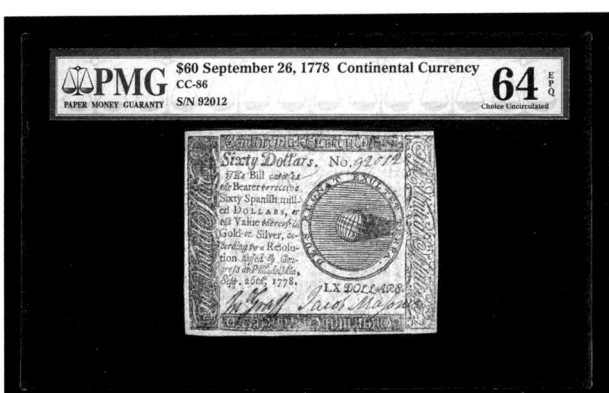

12017 **Continental Currency September 26, 1778 $60 PMG Choice Uncirculated 64 EPQ.** The margins are a bit tight on the right but present all around. The signatures are strong, and the original embossing, which has earned this note its EPQ designation, can be easily seen through the third-party holder. **(600-up)**

12018 **Continental Currency September 26, 1778 $60 PCGS Choice About New 58PPQ.** It is unlikely this piece spent more than a day or two in circulation, if any time at all. The signatures and serial number remain bold and the paper is most pleasing. **(300-up)**

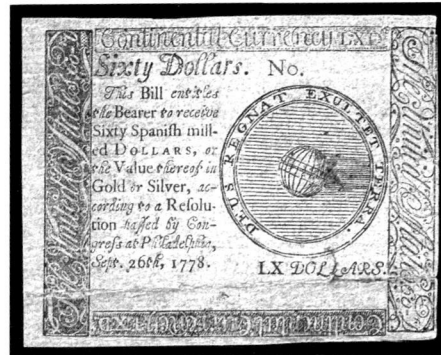

12019 **Continental Currency September 26, 1778 $60 Counterfeit Detector Extremely Fine.** This is a blue-paper detector note that has picked up a few folds over the years. It has excellent eye appeal and it is an inexpensive way to represent a rare type. Most collectors try to obtain at least one counterfeit detector. It is an ideal association item for a Continental set. **(400-up)**

12020 **Continental Currency January 14, 1779 $1 PMG Choice Extremely Fine 45.** This is a wonderfully margined and boldly signed example of this infrequently seen denomination that exhibits no folds through the holder. **(250-up)**

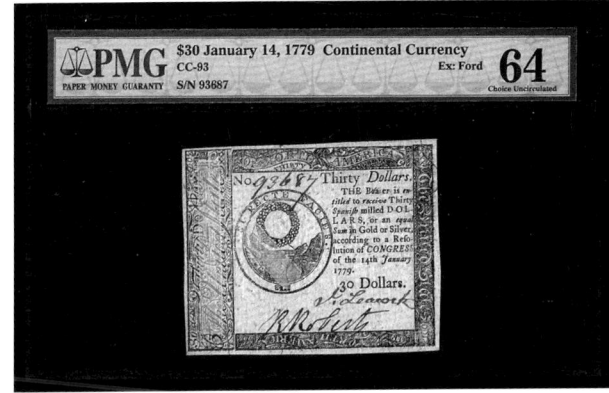

12021 **Continental Currency January 14, 1779 $30 PMG Choice Uncirculated 64.** Not many Continentals wind up in premium TPG holders and this one seems to have earned its 64 grade. Its well margined, bright, boldly signed and with clearly original paper surfaces. From the final issue of Continentals. **(750-up)**

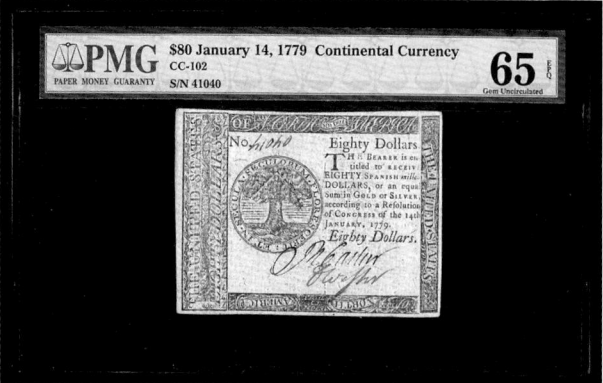

12022 **Continental Currency January 14, 1779 $80 PMG Gem Uncirculated 65 EPQ.** As the largest Continental denomination, this issue is well sought after. This piece which boasts solid margins also has two strong remaining signatures. **(750-up)**

COLONIAL NOTES

CONNECTICUT

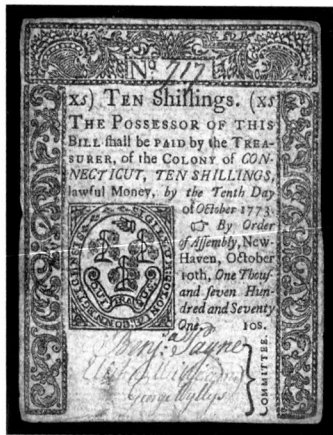

12023 **Connecticut October 10, 1771 10s Very Fine+.** This is a seldom seen note. The signatures are clear and the serial number is bold on this sharp-looking example. A bit of a small split is at right under the fold line. **(850-up)**

12024 **Connecticut October 11, 1777 7d Uncancelled Choice About New.** A very light fold is found on this well margined small pence note that has a bold signature, excellent printing, and most importantly no cancellation. **(200-up)**

DELAWARE

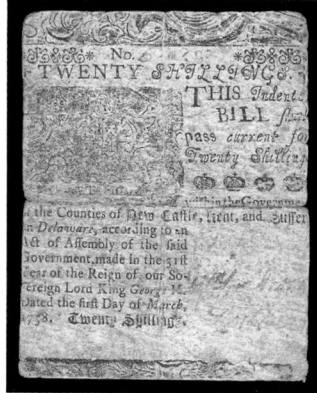

12025 **Delaware March 1, 1758 20s Fine.** This is an ideal example for the grade with a slightly stronger face than back. It appears to be restoration free, and the corners are nowhere near as rounded as most known examples. The all-important "Printed by B. Franklin" is easily seen. **(400-up)**

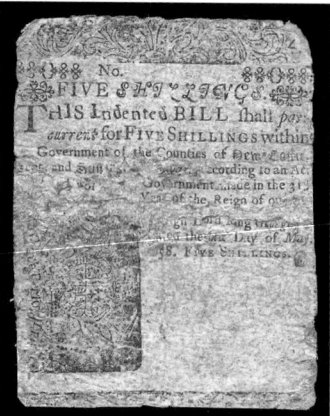

12026 **Delaware May 1, 1758 5s Fine.** The signatures and serial number have faded, and some minor old repairs have affected parts of the text. The "Printed by B. Franklin" on the back is clear, as is the majority of the text on both sides of the note. This is a fairly typical example of the issue. **(400-up)**

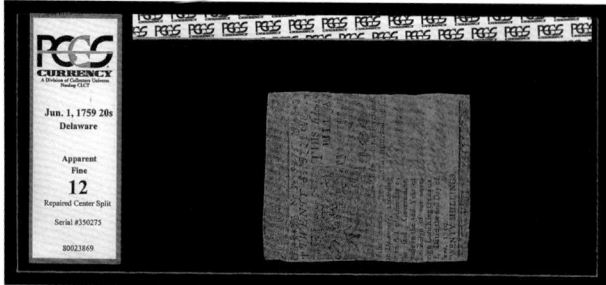

12027 **Delaware June 1, 1759 20s PCGS Apparent Fine 12, Repaired Center Split.** The repair on this note was very well executed, as only a professional would notice it. **(150-up)**

12028 Delaware January 1, 1776 5s PMG Gem Uncirculated 66 EPQ. While large margins on Colonials are seen with some regularity, this issue is not as often seen with behemoth margins such as these. The dark signatures and pleasing paper quality are quite complementary. **(750-up)**

12029 Delaware January 1, 1776 6s PCGS Very Choice New 64. The back is well centered on this example that has a slight stain on the front. **(350-up)**

12030 Delaware January 1, 1776 10s Choice New. This is a lovely example of this issue that has bold penmanship as well as exceptional print quality. Only at the back lower left corner does the edge drift inside the ornamentation line. **(400-up)**

12031 Delaware January 1, 1776 20s PCGS Very Choice New 64PPQ. The only grade limiting factor on this note is lightly toned paper. The signatures are strong, the margins are solid and the note is wholly original. **(400-up)**

12032 Delaware January 1, 1776 20s PCGS Choice New 63PPQ. Full margins around the face design and perfect signatures add allure to this piece of Colonial history. **(325-up)**

12033 Delaware January 1, 1776 20s PCGS Choice New 63PPQ. Another nice third-party graded example of this popular Delaware type. **(325-up)**

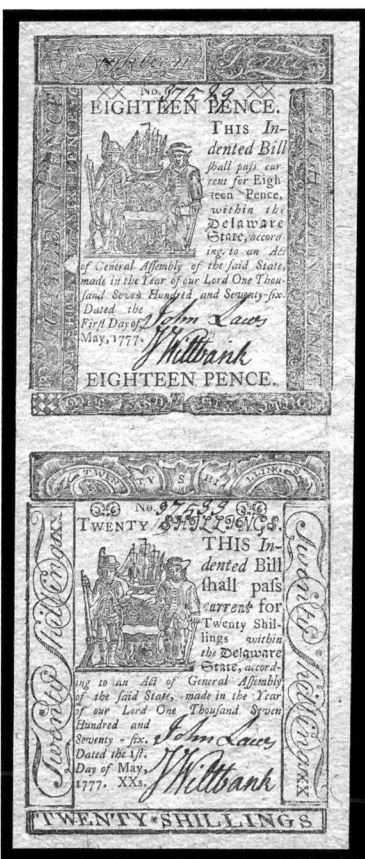

12034 Delaware May 1, 1777 18d and 20s Vertical Pair Choice About New. This is an unsevered pair from a difficult issue. There is an old sheet fold near the right edge of both notes, but they are otherwise Superb, with perfect color, strong signatures, broad margins, and no problems of any kind. **(1,500-up)**

GEORGIA

12035 Georgia 1776 1s/6d About New. This is an incredibly margined, high grade example of an issue that is almost never seen anywhere near this nice. All three signatures are bold including that of William Few, who signed two Georgia issues of Colonial currency and eleven years later, was one of the signers of the United States Constitution. The note has one or two extremely light folds, but appears to have never actually circulated. This is by far the highest grade example of this note that we have had the opportunity to handle and a piece of the highest interest to serious collectors of Georgia's early paper money. A small split at right center has been nicely repaired. (2,200-up)

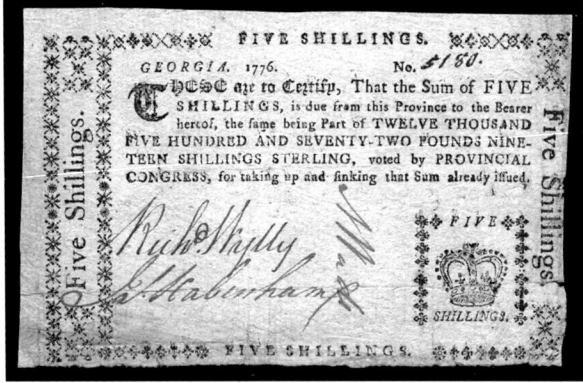

12036 Georgia 1776 - Crown Variety 5s Choice Very Fine. This is by far the finest example of this elusive Georgia note that HCAA has had the opportunity to offer. The note is totally free of repairs and restorations that are near ubiquitous on issues of this colony. The note's only problem (which scarcely rises to the level of problem) is a tiny split to the right of the *Crown* vignette and a couple of nearby tiny holes. Although notes of this colony have increased dramatically in price over the past four years, the price-versus-rarity relationship is still bizarrely low compared to all other areas of American Numismatics. A note that would make any Georgia collector proud to own. (2,200-up)

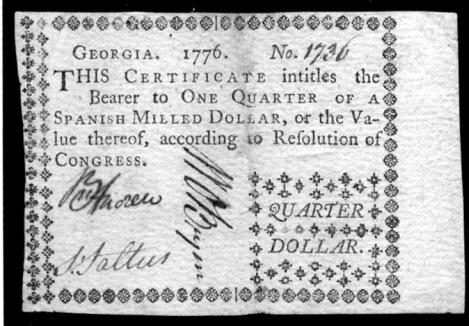

12037 Georgia 1776 $1/4 Extremely Fine-About New. This is a gorgeous Georgia note from a scarce two-note issue. The note has virtually no circulation, just a few corner folds. At one time it had a split along its center fold which has been beautifully repaired to the point of being virtually undetectable. No paper or ink has been added. All three signatures and the serial number are strong and the margins are extraordinary. (1,700-up)

12038 Georgia 1776 $1/4 Very Fine. The center split has been reinforced on the blank back by a paper strip, but the note "faces up" like a XF piece. All three signatures are strong. This is the lower of the only two denominations from this issue. (900-up)

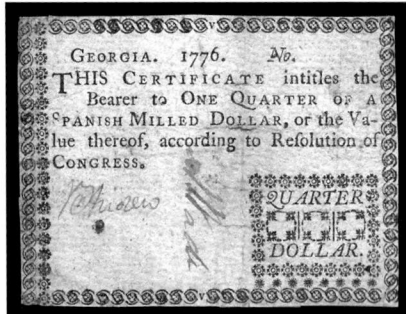

12039 Georgia 1776 $1/4 Very Fine. This note is attractive from the face, but somewhat soiled on the back. A scarce and underrated issue particularly damage-free and unrestored as this piece is. (900-up)

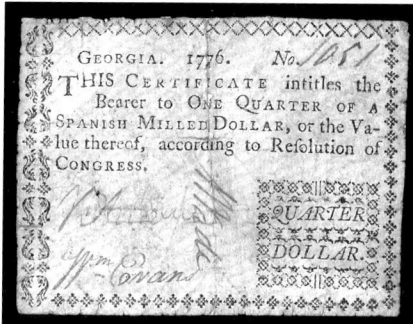

12040 **Georgia 1776 $1/4 Fine.** This note is from a scarce two note fractional issue. This example has nice signatures and edges for the grade. The center fold has been strengthened and a couple of pinholes are noticed. **(600-up)**

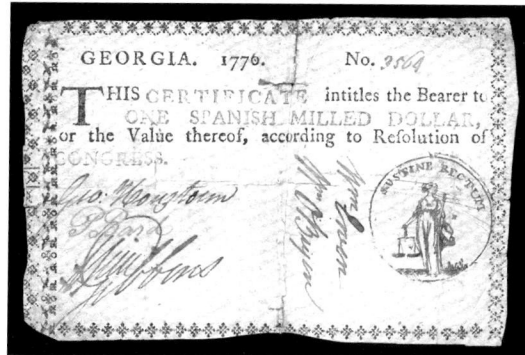

12041 **Georgia 1776 $1 Choice Very Fine.** The only repair on this lovely note is a tear in the top margin. There has been no paper replacement, save for that minor flaw, as the note is otherwise totally natural. The blue seal is wonderfully dark and embossed through to the back, and all five signatures are strong and sharp. Colored Seal Georgia notes have been bringing very strong prices of late. **(1,500-up)**

12042 **Georgia 1776 $1 Very Fine.** This note has a bold blue seal and five very strong signatures. There are a few minor internal splits, and several short edge splits, but there is no paper loss and the note is free of repairs and restorations. This is a well-above average example of this scarce note. In spite of its moderate circulation, the original embossing of the text and the seal remain visible. **(1,400-up)**

12043 **Georgia 1776 $2 Very Fine.** This note is well-signed with a bold blue seal. There are a few minor internal splits, and several short-edge splits, but there is no paper loss and the note is free of repairs and restorations. A well-above average example of this scarce note. In spite of its moderate circulation, the original embossing of the text and the seal remain visible. **(1,500-up)**

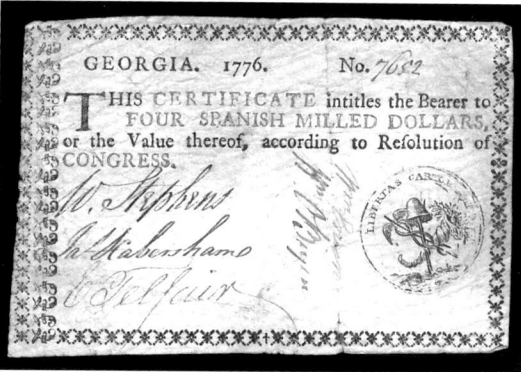

12044 **Georgia 1776 $4 Very Fine-Extremely Fine.** This is a problem-free example, with excellent margins, strong signatures, and a deeply colored blue seal that is impressed through to the back. The note exhibits some light circulation, but it is wholly free of the repairs and restorations generally seen on this colony's notes. **(1,700-up)**

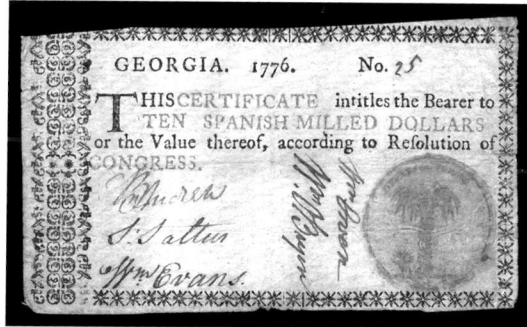

12045 **Georgia 1776 $10 Very Fine.** Perfect for the grade, without a hint of a repair, restoration, or problem of any kind. The margins are generous all around and touch the border designs only at the top left end. The signatures are strong, as is the very low serial number of 25. An utterly unmolested example for the Georgia purist. **(1,700-up)**

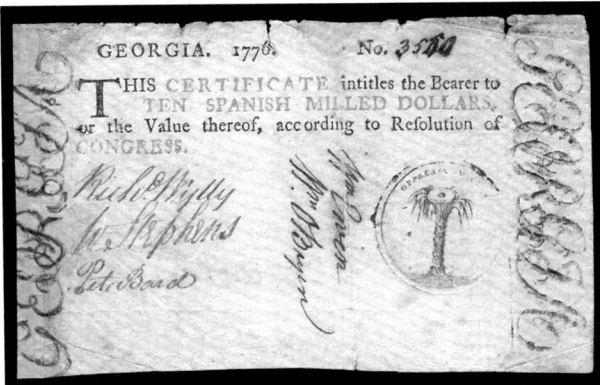

12046 Georgia 1776 $10 Very Fine. A handsome enough note, but with a considerable amount of deft restoration at the left edge and a smaller repaired area at the top center to the left of the serial number. All five signatures remain strong as does the maroon seal. **(1,400-up)**

12047 Georgia 1776 $2 Very Fine. We've net graded this scarce note, as it is extensively repaired along the right edge and the upper part of the left edge. The central portions of the note including the vignette, signatures and all the text, are untouched by these restorations, and the note grades substantially XF in these areas. The note has the appearance of a four-figure example, but will likely sell for about half that. **(500-up)**

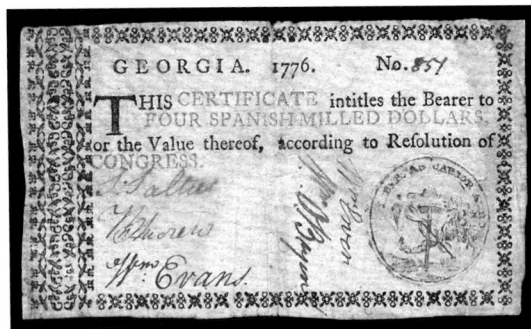

12048 Georgia 1776 $4 Very Good-Fine. The signatures are sharp on this bi-color example that has a nice repair in the upper right corner. This type does not appear with regularity, in the last seven years we have been able to offer only two different examples. **(600-up)**

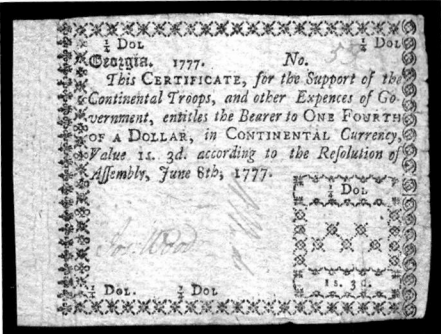

12049 Georgia June 8, 1777 $1/4 Very Fine-Extremely Fine. We have been able to offer only three different examples of this scarce note during this millennium. This nice example is free of problems, repairs, and restorations of any kind with the margins being clear of the outer-edge of the boarder elements. The fractional denominated notes of this issue are considerably scarcer than the dollar denominated pieces. **(1,700-up)**

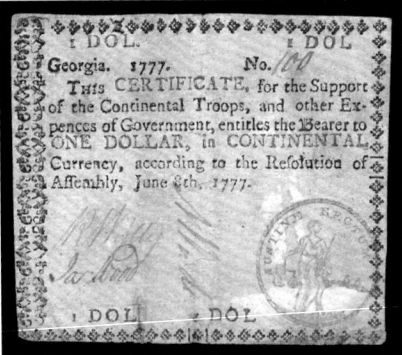

12050 Georgia June 8, 1777 $1 Fine. Serial number 100 graces this note. It is evenly toned over most of its surface. What looks to be a repair on the back is actually a strip of soiling and all of the details remain strong. This is the variety with identical ornaments in the top border. **(600-up)**

12051 Georgia June 8, 1777 $3 Very Fine. There is an approximate half inch internal split that is easily repairable on this otherwise problem-free note. It is the far scarcer variety with the word "in" in the fourth line printed in black. As with most examples of this black "in" type, it is a very low serial numbered piece. In this instance—17. The orange vignette is also better printed than most and the signatures remain strong. This is an under appreciated variety that is seldom seen. **(1,800-up)**

12052 **Georgia June 8, 1777 $4 Very Fine-Extremely Fine.** Several long splits have been beautifully restored, leaving virtually no trace of the work on this handsome, well margined Orange Vignette Georgia. It bears the low serial number 6 and all five of its signatures remain dark and clear. A lovely piece, with considerable value in spite of its restorations. (1,500-up)

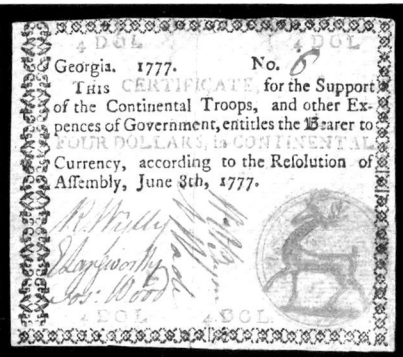

Historic Georgia Vertical Strip

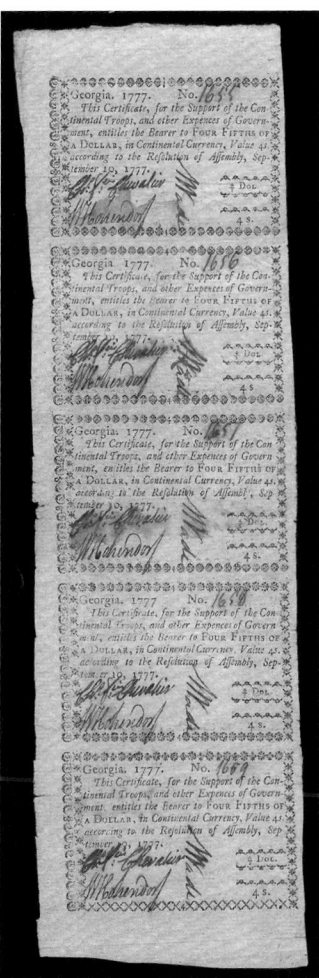

12053 **Georgia September 10, 1777 Uncut Vertical Strip of Five $4/5 Extremely Fine.** This is a fully signed strip from the left side of a ten-subject sheet. These are extremely rare in multiples and practically unheard of as a quintet. There is ink haze as-made and the notes grade XF or better individually. Certainly a great multiple for a top drawer collection. (7,500-up)

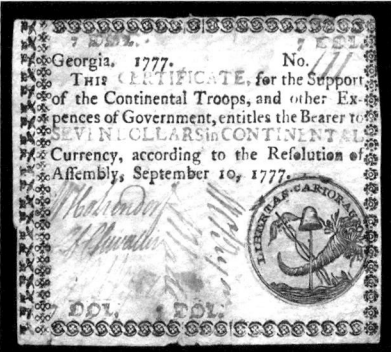

12054 **Georgia September 10, 1777 $7 Very Fine.** The colored seal is razor sharp, showing every detail of the caduceus, liberty pole and cap, and horn of plenty. The note also bears not the slightest hint of repair or restoration. This handsome note appears XF or better when viewed from the face, but the VF grade has been assigned as the blank back has picked up a considerable amount of soil over approximately two-thirds of the paper. Georgia is at the same time one of the rarest issuers of Colonial Currency and one of the most actively collected. Notes of this quality almost never reach the auction block and are sure to be hotly contested when the opportunity to purchase one arises. (1,600-up)

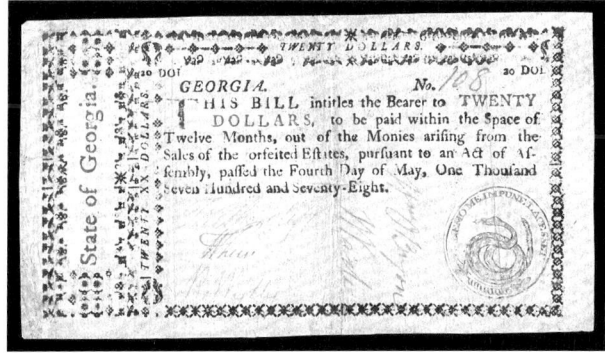

12055 **Georgia May 4, 1778 $20 Very Fine-Extremely Fine.** The blue seal rattlesnake vignette is sharp and bold, and the signature of William Few, who was a signer of the United States Constitution, can be clearly seen. There are a few rough places on the paper surface, and the five signatures, although totally legible, are a bit light overall. (1,500-up)

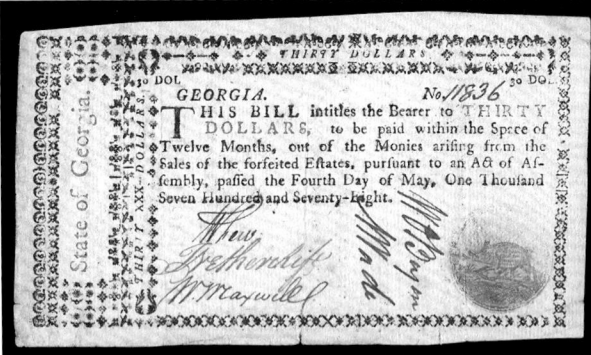

12056 **Georgia May 4, 1778 $30 Extremely Fine-About New.** This is a bright, nicely margined note with strong signatures, including that of William Few who later became a signer of the United States Constitution in 1787. The boar vignette is strong from the boar on down, but weak at the upper right. The note is problem-free save for a few very minor edge splits that, due to the wide margins, do not reach the design. The overall quality of the note is high. **(1,700-up)**

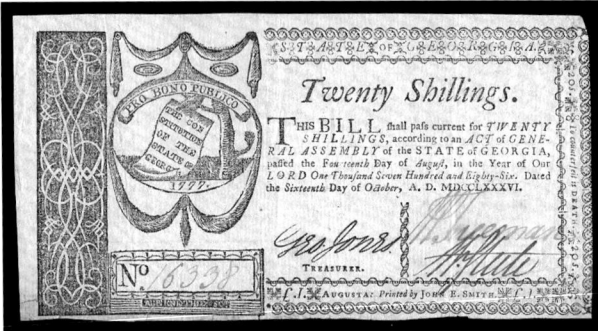

12057 **Georgia October 16, 1786 20s Very Fine.** Save for extremely minor restorations at the lower left and right corner tips, this handsome, scarce note from the final Georgia issue is nice for the grade. It has picked up a few light folds, but it is free from any circulation soil. All three signatures are beautifully bright. **(1,700-up)**

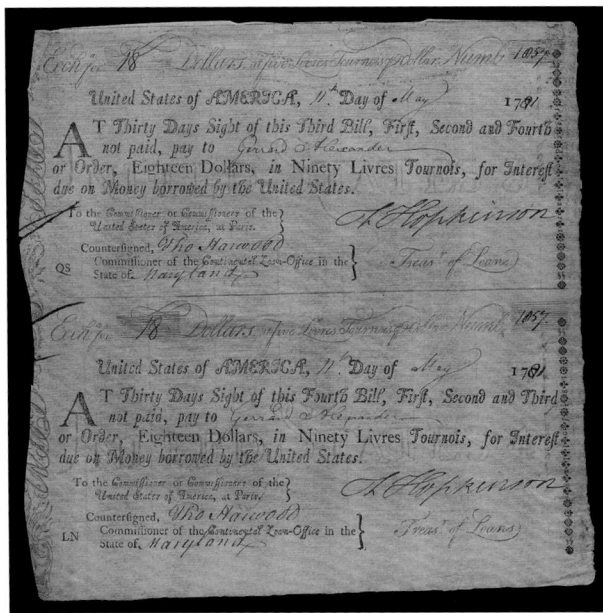

MARYLAND

12058 **Maryland 17__ 15s Uncut Pair New.** This remainder is from Maryland's first issue. This example does not have any folds, but the right-hand edge shows a few small tears that have repaired with archival tape along its entire length. This note is printed on "MARYLAND" watermarked paper and it also has a complete indent. This is also the first time we have handled a multiple on this denomination from this issue. **(800-up)**

12059 **Maryland April 10, 1774 $2/3 PMG Choice Uncirculated 64EPQ.** Anyone who has spent any time collecting or dealing in Colonial currency is well aware that this issue is one of the most common in Fine to Extremely Fine grades, but is a major rarity at 60 and above. This piece is to date the highest note graded by PMG for the eleven different denominations of this issue. Only three other pieces have been graded 60 and above. **(750-up)**

12060 **Maryland Continental Loan Office Bill of Exchange May 11, 1781 Choice About New.** Listed as US 95 in Anderson, it's an uncut pair consisting of a Third and Fourth of Exchange made out for $18. Both notes from this vertical pair are signed by Francis Hopkinson (a signer of the Declaration of Independence) as Treasurer of Loans, and by Thomas Harwood for the state of Maryland. Maryland is the second most difficult colony from which to obtain these certificates. They're rated as a high R7, which William G. Anderson considers to be four to six known, in his excellent book, *The Price of Liberty*. Only Virginia, with one to three known, is considered rarer. This unsevered pair is in essentially as-issued condition, but for a slight bend between the notes and a minor corner fold. This lovely and valuable pair should create considerable bidder interest. **(2,000-up)**

MASSACHUSETTS

Historic Note Printed by Paul Revere

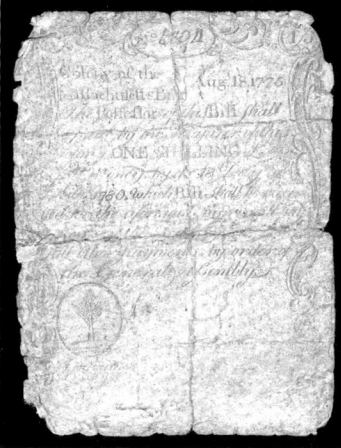

12061 Massachusetts August 18, 1775 1s Good. This is the first Sword in Hand issue. It was engraved and printed by the famous Colonial patriot Paul Revere. Sixteen different denominations were printed and fifteen of the sixteen had a small ship vignette on the face. Only this 1s denomination bears a pine tree vignette on the face where the ship is normally found. This note is very well worn with somewhat tattered edges, and although free of noteworthy problems, much of the text both face and back is quite light. In spite of its heavy use, it retains considerable collector value due to its historic importance and lack of availability in higher grades. **(900-up)**

12062 Massachusetts August 18, 1775 2s Fine. The details of this note match those of Newman's plate note exactly, allowing us to conclude this was printed from the same plate (minor variances of the hand engraved designs exist from plate to plate). The historical significance adds to the appeal of this popular design. This issue was both engraved by Paul Revere and printed in his shop just a few months after his famous ride. This piece was once sewn together along the center fold, but has since been professionally repaired. **(2,000-up)**

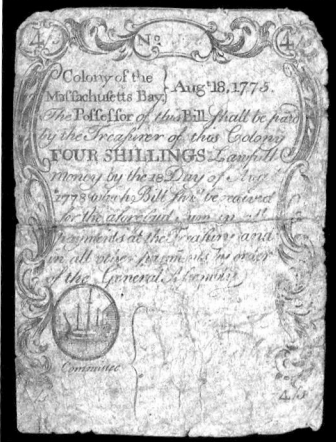

12063 Massachusetts August 18, 1775 4s Fine. This is the only example of this denomination that we have handled. On the back, in bold detail, is the all-important vignette of a Continental Soldier who holds his sword upright "In defence of American Liberty." Some minor repairs are noted, most notable of which is the reinforced center fold. **(2,000-up)**

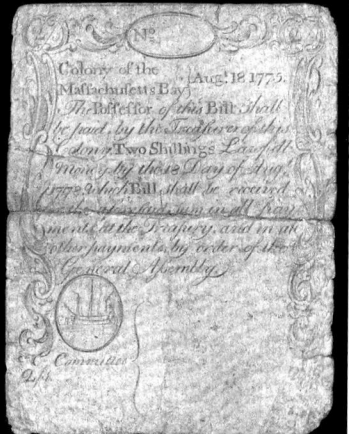

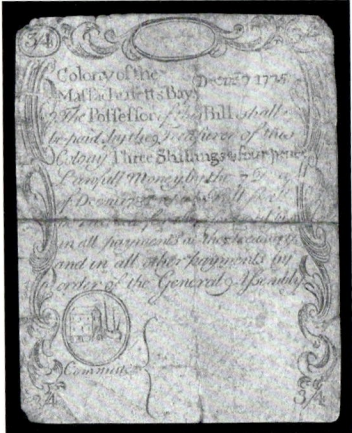

12064 Massachusetts December 7, 1775 3s/4d Very Good. This has always been a tough series that is very much in demand. The center fold has several breaks in the paper, but the all important *Sword in Hand* vignette is sharp for the grade. **(2,000-up)**

Genuine Sword in Hand

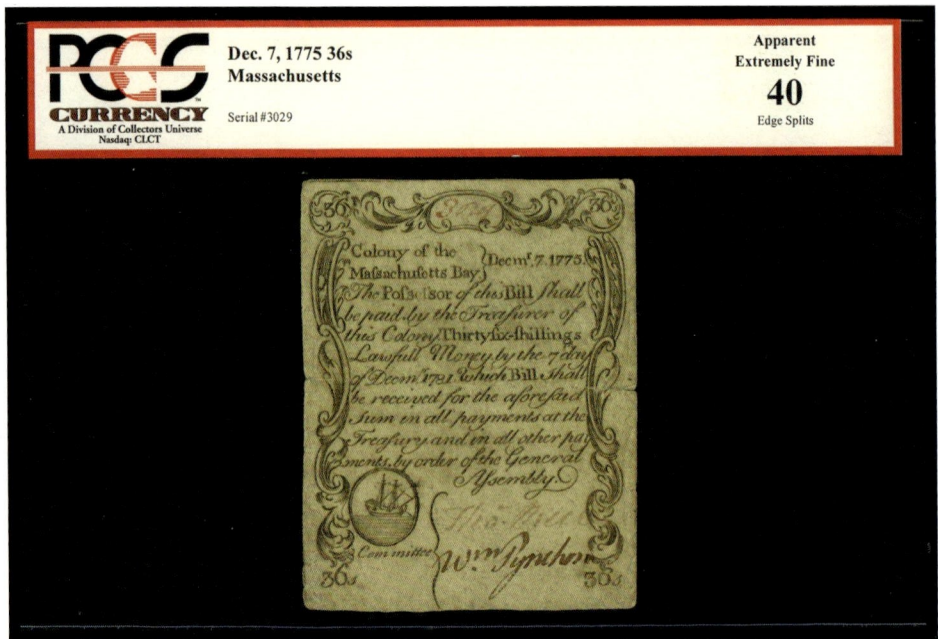

12065 Massachusetts December 7, 1775 36s PCGS Apparent Extremely Fine 40. This is the first genuine example for this denomination "Sword in Hand" engraved and printed by Paul Revere that we have seen in quite some time. The edge splits mentioned are minor when the scarcity of the issue is considered. Our estimate may prove conservative as this issue is not priced above Very Fine in Friedberg. A must to complete a type set for this important Revolutionary issue. **(6,000-up)**

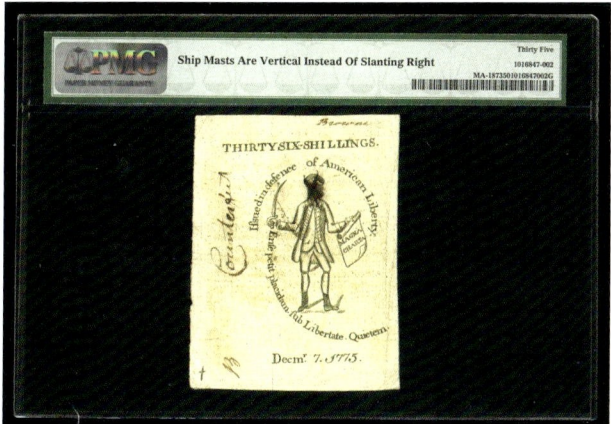

12066 Massachusetts December 7, 1775 36s PMG Choice Very Fine 35. This is one of the more deceptive contemporary counterfeits and the highest grade example that we have handled. The note is well printed, well signed, and clearly circulated, at least briefly, alongside the genuine notes. The note has the look of a genuine example and is distinguished from the genuine only by minute differences in engraving. The easiest ones to spot are the straight vertical main masts on the ship vignette. On the genuine examples, the masts slant to the right. An unusually bright, clean and very attractive note that will not realize anywhere near the $7,000 or so that a genuine in this grade would realize. Pen cancelled on front, with counterfeit written on back and penned "X" on soldier's face. **(2,500-up)**

12067 Massachusetts June 18, 1776 10d Very Fine-Extremely Fine. This is a very rare note in high grade and this piece is a beauty. It's signed and numbered in red and it is totally free of repairs or restorations. The note has four meaningless pinholes that can only be seen when held to light, and even *with* them it's as perfect an example of this issue as we have handled, which is very, very few over the years. **(1,200-up)**

12068 Massachusetts June 18, 1776 10d PMG Very Good 08. This piece is perfect for the budget minded collector looking to fill their collection with this scarce issue. **(350-up)**

12069 Massachusetts June 18, 1776 1s/8d Fine-Very Fine. The center fold is a touch weak, though the note faces up well. The signature of D. Hopkins remains. On back, the denomination is scribbled on all four edges of the note, expressed simply as 1/8. We do not recall having seen this on any note before now. **(500-up)**

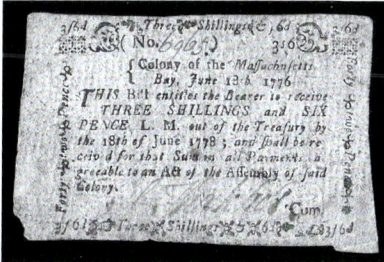

12070 Massachusetts June 18, 1776 3s/6d Very Fine-Extremely Fine. This appealing and original example boasts all of its original detail save for a light signature. **(500-up)**

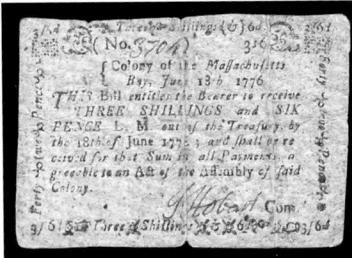

12071 **Massachusetts June 18, 1776 3s/6d Fine.** This is a nice example of the seldom seen smaller size low denomination notes from this very scarce June 18, 1776 issue. The margins are pleasing and the signature and serial number are clear. A solid note, free of restorations, with all of its text quite legible. **(600-up)**

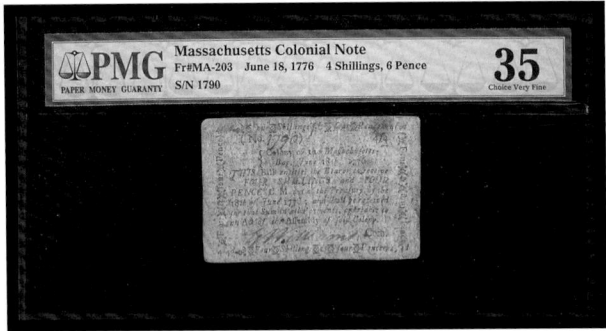

12072 **Massachusetts June 18, 1776 4s/6d PMG Choice Very Fine 35.** This is the first time a note of this type has appeared at auction with us in over five years. The signature and serial number remain legible. **(650-up)**

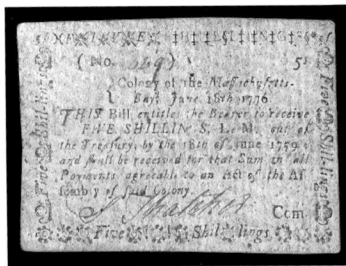

12073 **Massachusetts June 18, 1776 5s Extremely Fine.** A scarce and highly underrated issue, particularly as a well-margined, boldly signed high-grade piece. There is a very light stain that affects only the back, and the note has one or two extremely light folds. It is one of the better examples we've seen of this underrated and undervalued issue. It should attract considerable interest, and should realize at least... **(750-up)**

12074 **Massachusetts October 16, 1778 4d Very Fine.** We have had only two examples from this date and denomination over the last seven years. This scarce note has had some restorations at both the upper right and lower left corner tips. The eye appeal is still excellent and what would otherwise have been a $750 note or more will likely sell for about... **(450-up)**

12075 **Massachusetts October 16, 1778 4d Very Fine.** This is a desirable and popular issue where the important Codfish and Pine Tree designs are well printed, and one of only a couple that we have handled in this denomination. The technical grade for this note is Very Fine or better as there really are not many folds in the paper but the face is uniformly toned and there are some clear tape remnants which subtly mask a couple of edge tears. **(350-up)**

12076 **Massachusetts October 16, 1778 1s/6d PMG Choice Extremely Fine 45.** This is a very high grade example of this always popular Codfish note that has a light fold or two on crisp, well margined paper. The print detail is much better than that seen on most notes from this issue. When we have had notes in this grade range in the past they teeter upon the four figure price range. In today's post-Ford colonial marketplace we would expect a prize such as this to be greatly treasured by its new owner. **(1,000-up)**

Paul Revere Engraved Note

12077 Massachusetts 1779 2s/6d Extremely Fine. This is a beautifully margined Rising Sun note that is quite well printed on both sides. There is a scattering of light stains that affect nothing, and the right-hand margin extends all the way out to the sheet edge. A handsome note, partially engraved by Paul Revere. (800-up)

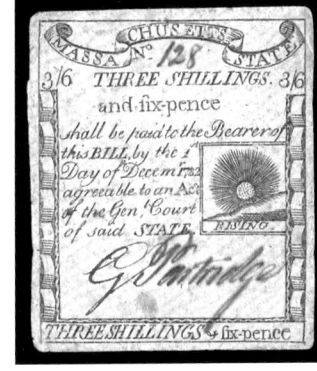

12078 Massachusetts 1779 3s/6d Very Fine. This is a lightly circulated, ideally centered Rising Sun note without a hint of a problem. This Rising Sun issue was printed from face plates that had been engraved by Colonial printer, silversmith, and legendary forefather Paul Revere, who also printed the faces of the notes themselves. The backs employed set-type and cast cuts from the previous Codfish issue and were printed by Thomas Fleet. (900-up)

12079 Massachusetts 1779 3s/6d Fine. This note is off-center a little bit on both sides, but otherwise problem free for the grade. An inexpensive example of this popular Paul Revere engraved type. (200-up)

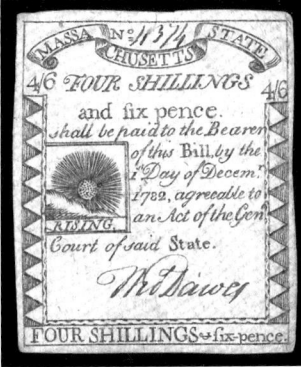

12080 Massachusetts 1779 4s/6d Extremely Fine-About New. A really lovely, lightly circulated Rising Sun note. The overall eye appeal is excellent, and it's augmented considerably by four nice, even margins. The back plate uses the same type and cast cuts as the Codfish issues, but the face plate is newly engraved by Paul Revere. Revere also printed the faces, and as with the previous Codfish issue, Thomas Fleet printed the backs. An exceptional note, far superior to most technical Uncs due to its exceptional centering and beautifully sharp printing on both sides. (1,250-up)

12081 Massachusetts 1779 4s/6d Extremely Fine. Another really lovely, lightly circulated Rising Sun note. The paper has some light scattered aging, but the eye appeal is quite good, and it's boxed in nicely by four even margins. The back plate uses the same type and cast cuts as the Codfish issues, but the face plate is newly engraved, again by Paul Revere. Revere also printed the faces, and as with the previous Codfish issue, Thomas Fleet printed the backs. (1,000-up)

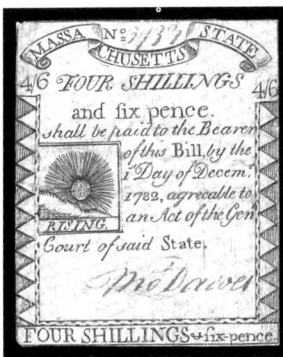

12082 Massachusetts 1779 4s/6d Very Fine-Extremely Fine. This note is closely margined, but beautifully well-printed. These historic Massachusetts notes, with their close association to Paul Revere, have always been highly sought after. (750-up)

12083 Massachusetts 1779 4s/6d PCGS Very Fine 20. A nice, evenly circulated Rising Sun note. The face plates for these notes were engraved by Colonial patriot, silversmith, and printer Paul Revere, and the faces were printed in his shop. The backs were typeset and printed by Thomas Fleet. (700-up)

12084 **Massachusetts 1779 4s/6d Fine-Very Fine.** This lovely Rising Sun note is well printed on both sides with period arithmetic ciphering on the back. (600-up)

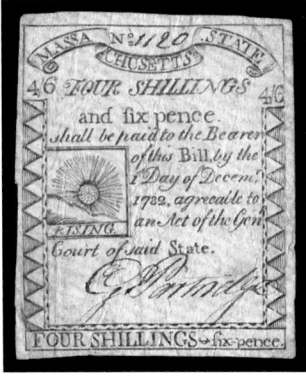

12085 **Massachusetts 1779 5s Fine-Very Fine.** The upper right corner has been professionally replaced, adding to the eye appeal of this lightly circulated, scarce issue. (250-up)

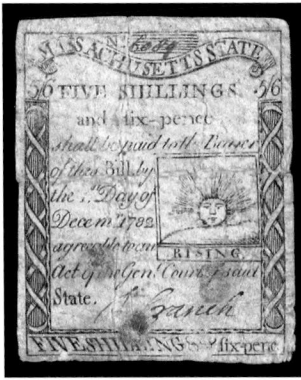

12086 **Massachusetts 1779 5s/6d Fine.** This is a nice circulated example of this extremely popular issue. The face plates for this issue were engraved by Paul Revere and in fact the faces of the notes were printed in his shop. The back uses the same type and cast cuts that were previously employed on the Codfish issue and they were printed in the shop of Thomas Fleet. (500-up)

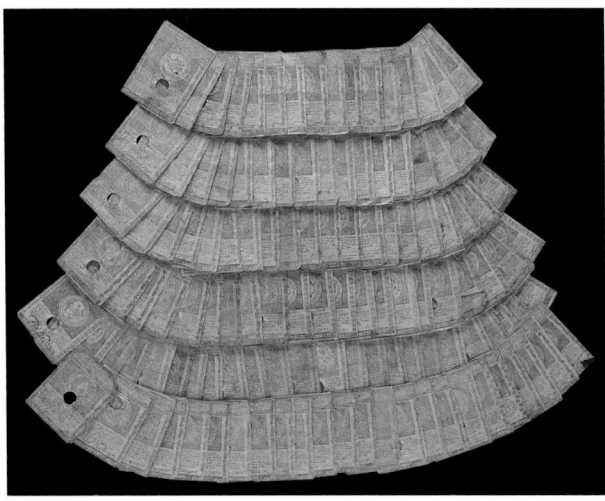

12087 **Massachusetts May 5, 1780 $2 (19); $3 (15); $4 (15); $5 (5); $7 (42); $8 (16); $20 (2) Very Good to Very Fine, HOC.** Most notes fall in the middle of the grade range.. A couple of notes have large tears. (Total: 114 notes) (5,000-up)

12088 **Massachusetts May 5, 1780 $7 PMG Choice Uncirculated 64.** PMG comments "Hole Cancelled," which on this note is a somewhat smaller hole than the normal nickel-sized hole. The note is bright, well-margined, and boldly signed. (200-up)

12089 **Massachusetts May 5, 1780 $7 PMG Choice Uncirculated 63.** PMG comments "Hole Cancel" on this bright, well-signed Massachusetts guarantee note. (200-up)

12090 **Massachusetts May 5, 1780 $7 PMG Choice Uncirculated 63.** "Hole Cancelled" is the only comment on the PMG Choice Uncirculated holder. (175-up)

12091 **Massachusetts May 5, 1780 $8 PMG Choice Uncirculated 64 EPQ.** An adequately margined, crisp, and well embossed example of this more available Massachusetts issue that does not have the usual hole cancellation. (300-up)

12092 **Massachusetts May 5, 1780 $8 PMG Choice Uncirculated 63.** The "Hole Cancel" is mentioned on the PMG holder of this bright, and attractive Massachusetts note. (175-up)

One of Only Five Reported Examples

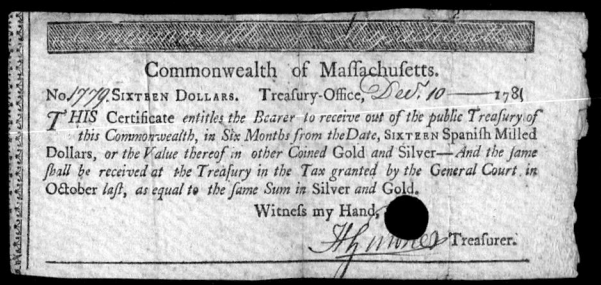

12093 **Massachusetts 1781 $16 Extremely Fine.** This denomination had been unknown until about two years ago when five pieces surfaced. It's listed both in Newman as a note, and in Anderson as fiscal paper. No new pieces have surfaced since this first small group came out, and this may well be the final opportunity to acquire this extremely rare type for some time to come. (6,000-up)

12094 **Massachusetts Commodity Bond January 1, 1780 Very Fine, repairs.** This bond is listed in Anderson as MA-21 and considered by him to be an R5 (31 to 75 known). These Commodity Bonds are perhaps the most interesting of all the Massachusetts fiscal paper, because both their principal and interest were tied to the current price of various commodities (corn, beef, sheep's wool, sole leather) at the date the bond was due. The bonds were authorized to cover the depreciation of pay received by Continental soldiers and sailors. This specimen was payable to Benjamin Barron, a lieutenant in the Continental Navy. This is also the scarcer variety, with the engraver's name, J.M. Furnass, incorporated in small letters within the loop of the final "r" in Treasurer in the lower right corner. However, only remnants of that imprint remain. The wear on this note consists of three vertical folds, three archival tape repairs, soiling near the right edge, small internal apertures, edge nicks, and a clipped corner tip. Still a rare item that is much better in appearance than it is in description, and it is also a direct link to America's fight for independence. (1,200-up)

NEW HAMPSHIRE

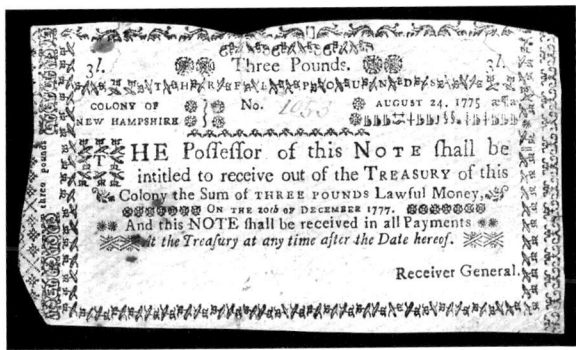

12095 **New Hampshire August 24, 1775 £3 Very Fine.** Very few pieces in total were printed for this issue, which was authorized for just £8,000 of notes. This example has uneven margins, but they are generous in most all places. The signatures are a bit faded and the restoration of three splits can be seen on the blank back. Unlike the November 3, 1775 notes, there are no counterfeits known for any of the five denominations of this issue. (2,000-up)

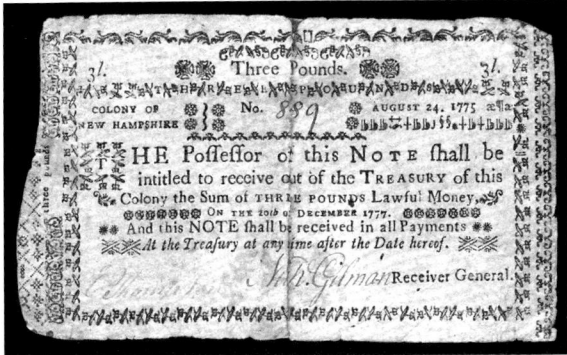

12096 **New Hampshire August 24, 1775 £3 Fine.** Only 1,333 pieces in total were printed for the £3 denomination of this issue, which was authorized for just $8,000. This example has uneven margins, but they are generous in most places. The signatures are a bit faded and restorations and reinforcements of splits and roughness can be seen on the blank back. (1,600-up)

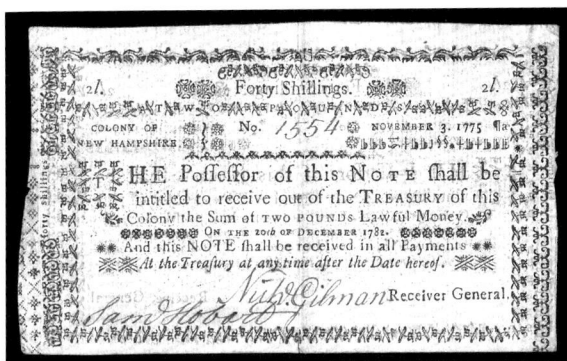

12097 **New Hampshire November 3, 1775 40s Contemporary Counterfeit About New.** Listed as a Contemporary Counterfeit in Newman, but properly signed and printed in the shop of the man who printed the genuine. These notes have always been collected as avidly as the genuinely issued pieces, and this one is an extremely nice example. The note is extraordinarily well margined and boldly signed. It shows no circulation save for a single center fold. An attractive and important piece. (1,750-up)

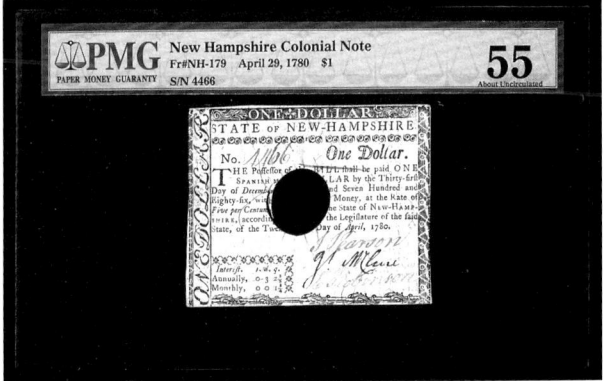

12098 **New Hampshire April 29, 1780 $1 PMG About Uncirculated 55 HOC.** This hole cancelled issue appears fully uncirculated as the corner tip fold that accounts for the grade is mostly visible from the back. (750-up)

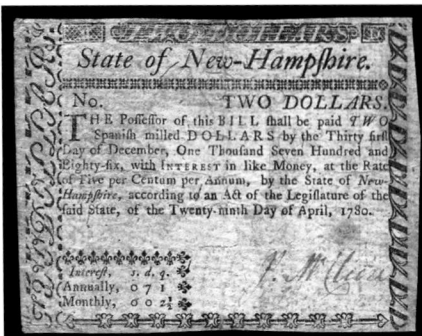

12099 **New Hampshire April 29, 1780 $2 Very Fine.** Cancelled New Hampshire Guaranteed Notes probably outnumber uncancelled issues by a factor of 10 to 1. This example circulated for a very short time and was never cancelled. The paper is excellent and is absolutely problem free. **(1,000-up)**

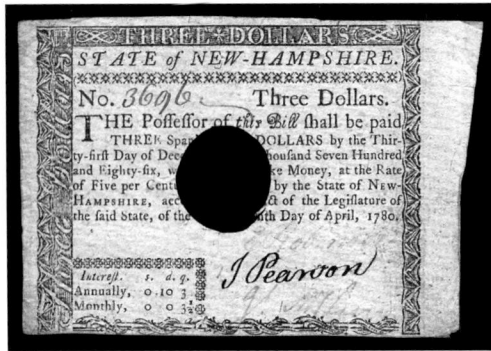

12100 **New Hampshire April 29, 1780 $3 About New.** A light fold and a corner tip nick are seen on this hole cancelled example that has a strong black signature, while the signatures in red ink show the usual fading. **(750-up)**

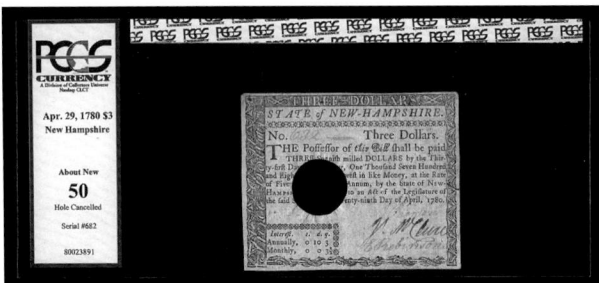

12101 **New Hampshire April 29, 1780 $3 PCGS About New 50.** Unusually well margined and with a very nice overall appearance. **(750-up)**

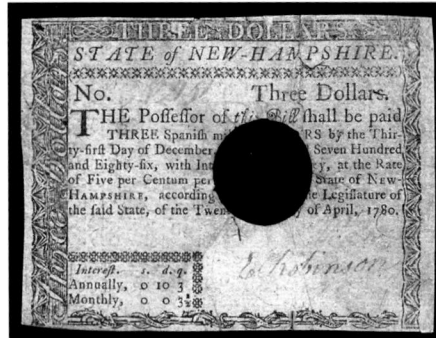

12102 **New Hampshire April 29, 1780 $3 Fine.** A split has been nicely resealed on this evenly circulated, hole canceled note from a scarcer colony. The serial number has almost faded away. **(450-up)**

12103 **New Hampshire April 29, 1780 $4 Extremely Fine.** This note is hole-cancelled with the normal nickel-sized hole. It shows very light signs of circulation, but with three strong signatures, nice margins, and an excellent overall appearance. **(600-up)**

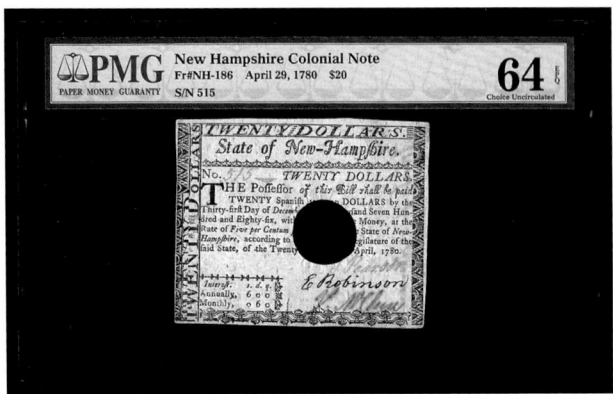

12104 **New Hampshire April 29, 1780 $20 PMG Choice Uncirculated 64 EPQ HOC.** An attractive example of this hole cancelled issue, with margins on all sides protecting the important design elements. **(750-up)**

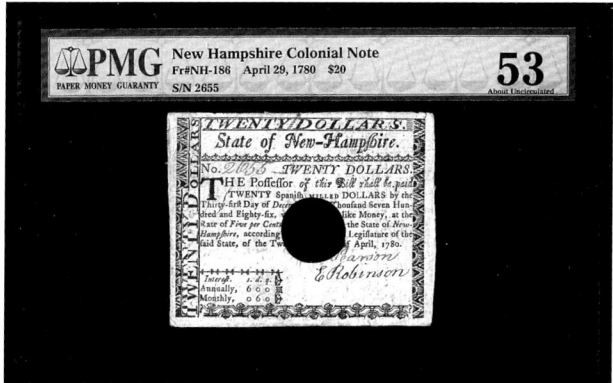

12105 **New Hampshire April 29, 1780 $20 PMG About Uncirculated 53 HOC.** A lightly circulated, problem free and well margined example of this highest denomination. **(500-up)**

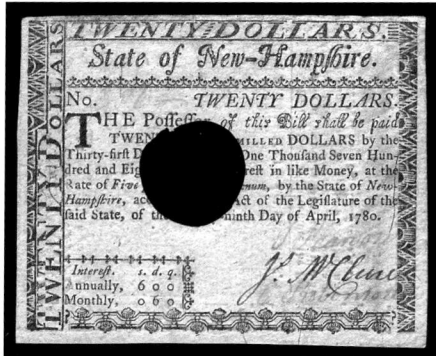

12106 **New Hampshire April 29, 1780 $20 Extremely Fine-About New HOC.** A fold is noticed on this cancelled example which possibly was wet at one time as the back countersignature has faded. **(400-up)**

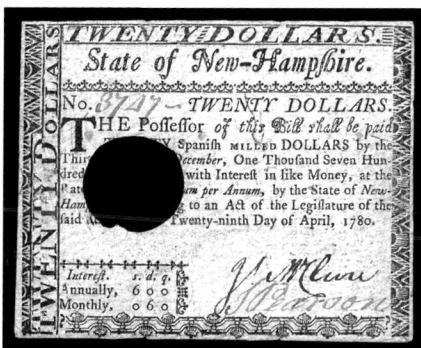

12107 **New Hampshire April 29, 1780 $20 Very Fine-Extremely Fine HOC.** An attractive, wholly original example, with great remaining details and signatures. Some penciled catalog numbers are noted on back. **(300-up)**

NEW JERSEY

12108 **New Jersey June 22, 1756 1s PCGS Choice New 63PPQ.** Tremendously high-grade for this scarce issue. Boldly signed, and problem-free save for the normal close centering. **(750-up)**

12109 **New Jersey June 22, 1756 12s PCGS Very Choice New 64PPQ.** The bottom margin touches very slightly, but the note has three full margins, which is incredible for this issue. It's also far brighter than normally encountered, with three strong signatures that are totally free of blurring. This is the earliest Jersey issue that is seen in top grade with any regularity. **(800-up)**

12110 **New Jersey June 22, 1756 15s Choice New.** This note is beautifully crisp with bold signatures, a Gem in all respects, but for the normally tight margins that are always seen on this issue. The three lowest denominations of this issue are relatively common uncirculated, but the 15s are seldom seen this nice. **(600-up)**

12111 **New Jersey June 22, 1756 15s PCGS Choice New 63.** This is the only New Jersey issue prior to 1763 that is ever seen in this grade. The margins on most known pieces are extremely poor. This piece, while it is slightly cut-in at two sides, has two nearly full margins, missing only two minor pieces of the border at the other two. Bright and original and with three strong signatures. **(750-up)**

12112 **New Jersey May 1, 1758 30s Extremely Fine.** This colorful example bears a single vertical fold and may have claims to a higher grade. Tremendous grade for an early Jersey, with only slightly rounded corners, bold text, clear signatures, and no repairs or restorations of any kind. The cut is a bit typical with some trimming in at the upper left. This lot is accompanied by a lot tag from a New Netherlands auction in December 1975 where it was lot 343. **(800-up)**

12113 **New Jersey May 1, 1758 £3 Extremely Fine.** This is a splendid example from this much scarcer early New Jersey issue from which notes are usually found in the VG grade range or lower. In fact Friedberg does not even list a value above VG, just the comments, "Rare" and "Very Rare" for the VF and Unc grades. The signatures are above average, but the border printing shows a little weakness. There is also a quarter inch split at top center. **(800-up)**

12114 **New Jersey April 10, 1759 £3 About New.** Only 2,850 examples were printed for this denomination on this issue. This 1759 issue is scarce in any grade. In fact this is the nicest example we have ever handled. There are some lighter spots on the face where the ink did not adhere well. **(1,200-up)**

12115 **New Jersey April 10, 1759 £3 PCGS Very Fine 20PPQ.** A second chance for the underbidders. This issue is unpriced above Very Good. Very well signed, and the PPQ designation attests to its problem-free originality. **(750-up)**

12116 **New Jersey April 23, 1761 £6 PCGS Extremely Fine 40.** Extraordinarily high-grade for a note that is listed as rare and unpriced in Very Fine. All the signatures and every bit of the text is bold and clear. **(1,250-up)**

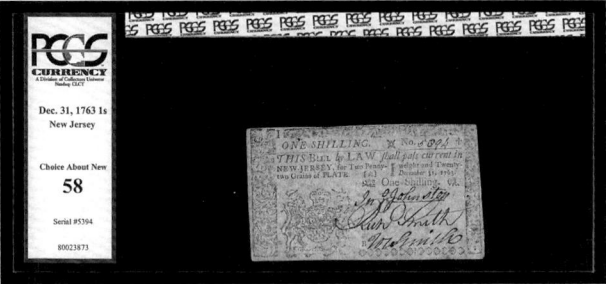

12117 **New Jersey December 31, 1763 1s PCGS Choice About New 58.** Here is a bright representative with dark signatures. **(350-up)**

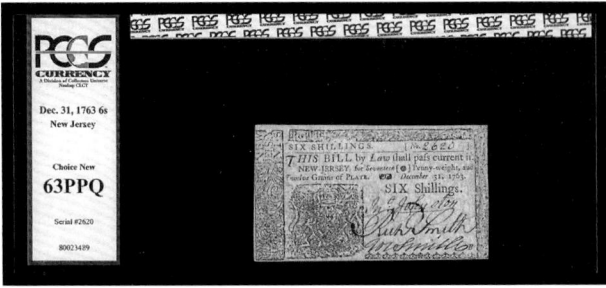

12118 **New Jersey December 31, 1763 6s PCGS Choice New 63PPQ.** Bright, beautifully signed and very well printed. The margins are close, as is typical for the issue, but the note is flawless in every other respect. This is a very good looking, highly desirable example. **(600-up)**

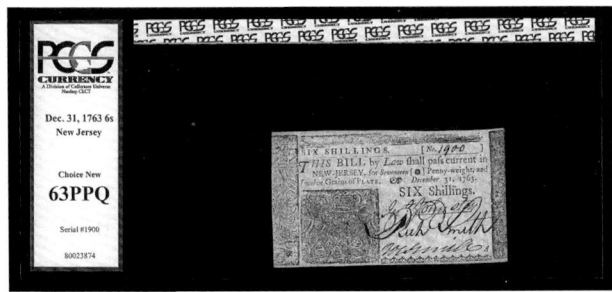

12119 **New Jersey December 31, 1763 6s PCGS Choice New 63PPQ.** Here is another deeply inked example of this popular issue. **(600-up)**

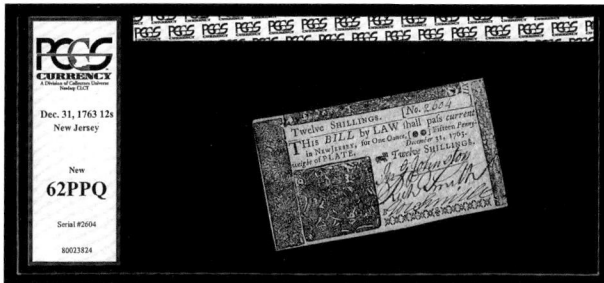

12120 **New Jersey December 31, 1763 12s PCGS New 62PPQ.** Closely margined, as is virtually always the case for this issue, but bright, crisp and problem free. The printing and signatures are quite dark. This is the earliest New Jersey issue from which high-grade pieces are relatively available. **(500-up)**

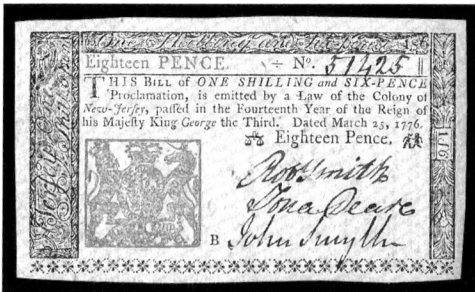

12121 **New Jersey March 25, 1776 18d Superb Gem New.** A simply gorgeous example, with broad even margins and sharp print quality. The red vignette, showing the New Jersey coat of arms, almost always prints very indistinctly. This particular example is razor-sharp, showing all the detail of the crowned lion, the unicorn and the shield between them. **(500-up)**

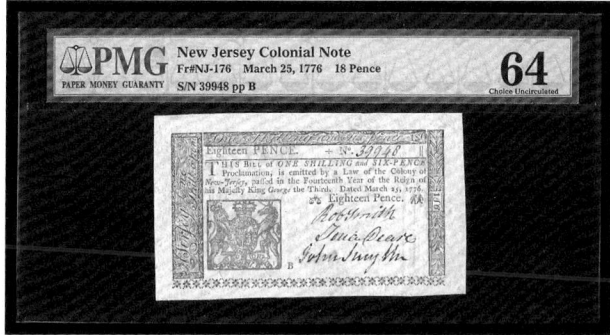

12122 **New Jersey March 25, 1776 18d PMG Choice Uncirculated 64.** A jumbo-margined, flawless example with razor sharp print quality on both sides. Even the red New Jersey coat of arms is sharply printed, allowing every letter of every word to be clearly seen. The signatures are strong. **(350-up)**

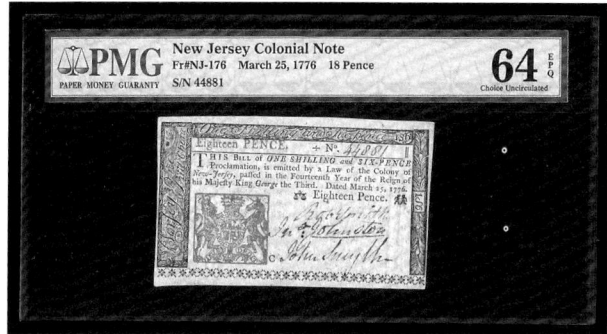

12123 **New Jersey March 25, 1776 18d PMG Choice Uncirculated 64 EPQ.** A wonderfully embossed and superbly printed New Jersey note. Very few have the exceptional detail on the face design. If the right margin did not stray too close this would easily make the gem grade. **(350-up)**

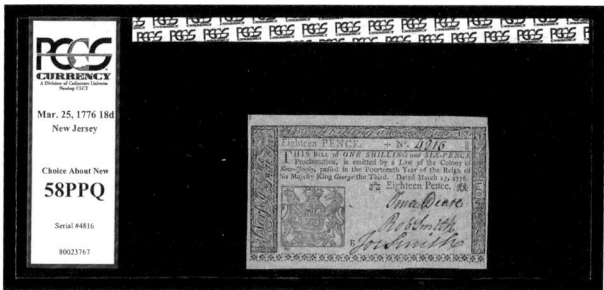

12124 **New Jersey March 25, 1776 18d PCGS Choice About New 58PPQ.** Only a corner bend is visible on this note with dark signatures. **(350-up)**

12125 **New Jersey March 25, 1776 18d PCGS Very Fine 25.** This is a strong example with the bold signature of John Hart, one of the signers of the Declaration of Independence. **(400-up)**

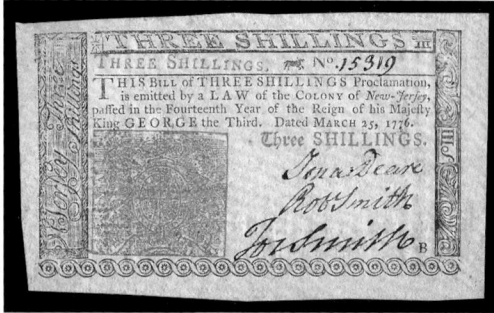

12126 **New Jersey March 25, 1776 3s Superb Gem New.** A flawless piece, with bold signatures, broad, even margins, fresh, original paper surfaces and super eye appeal. An exceptional example of this readily available issue. **(500-up)**

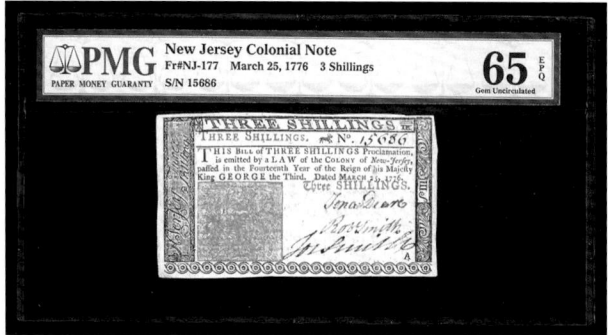

12127 **New Jersey March 25, 1776 3s PMG Gem Uncirculated 65 EPQ.** A nicely margined, well signed example. **(400-up)**

12128 **New Jersey March 25, 1776 6s PMG Superb Gem Unc 67 EPQ.** Jumbo margins all the way around, deep original embossing, bold, dark signatures and ideal centering of both sides all combine on this utterly pristine New Jersey Colonial. Simply as nice as they come. **(750-up)**

12129 **New Jersey March 25, 1776 6s PMG Gem Uncirculated 66 EPQ.** An enormously margined example of this popular New Jersey issue that is boldly signed and numbered with superb embossing and flawless paper quality. Notes in this grade are always popular as there is the belief that they could just as easily reach the superb gem grade. **(600-up)**

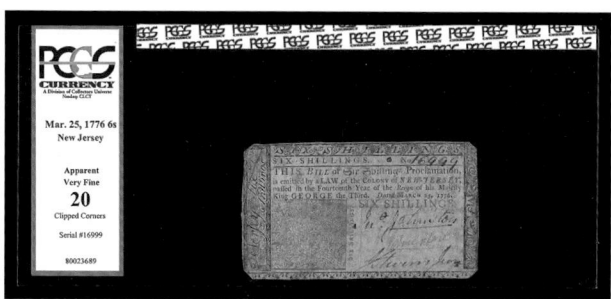

12130 **New Jersey March 25, 1776 6s PCGS Apparent Very Fine 20.** "Clipped Corners" are the reason PCGS has encased this John Hart-signed note in a red holder. **(400-up)**

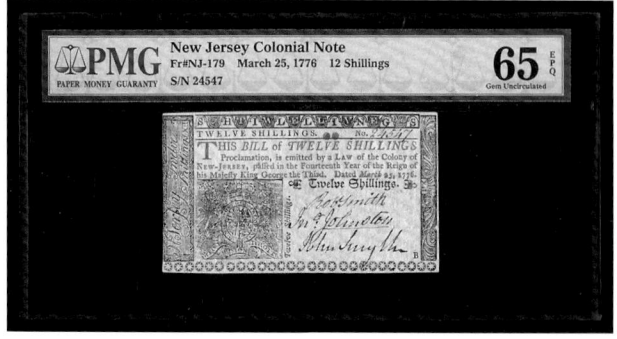

12131 **New Jersey March 25, 1776 12s PMG Gem Uncirculated 65 EPQ.** Superb printing and crackerjack embossing are found on this New Jersey note that has exceptional eye appeal and wonderful paper quality. **(400-up)**

12132 **New Jersey March 25, 1776 12s PCGS Apparent Extremely Fine 45.** According to the holder someone unfortunately has clipped the corners on this pretty note which was signed by John Hart. **(500-up)**

12133 **New Jersey March 25, 1776 15s New.** This note has a perfect face with wide margins and dark signatures. There are no folds, but the note was mounted long ago with stamp hinge tape. Removal from the mounting left a skin mark at back bottom center. **(275-up)**

12134 **New Jersey March 25, 1776 15s Choice About New.** The tiniest of corner folds precludes a full Gem grade on this colorful issue. **(250-up)**

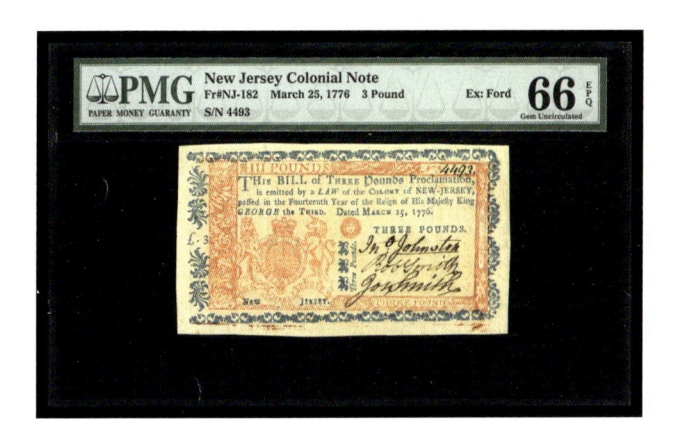

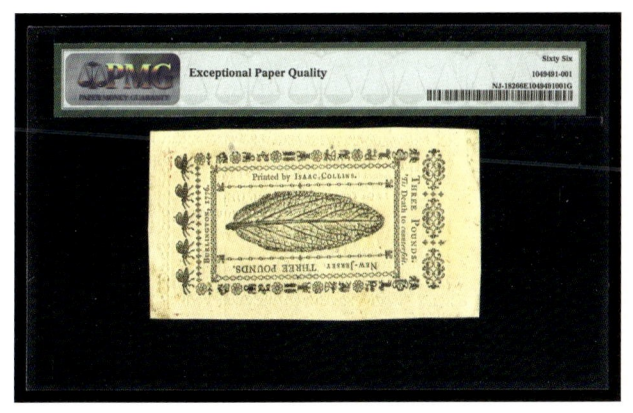

12135 **New Jersey March 25, 1776 £3 PMG Gem Uncirculated 66 EPQ.** A spectacular tricolor £3 Jersey that has broad margins, deep original embossing, and great eye appeal. When this note appeared in the Ford Sale, it realized just a hair under $2,000 raw. In its 66 EPQ holder, we would expect that number to be left behind. **(2,500-up)**

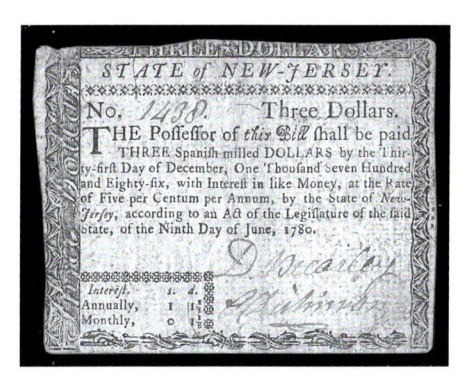

12136 **New Jersey June 9, 1780 $3 Very Fine.** A solid, problem-free example likely to evoke considerable bidder fervor. Cut close on two sides, but with good color and the signatures of Brearly and Borden. **(800-up)**

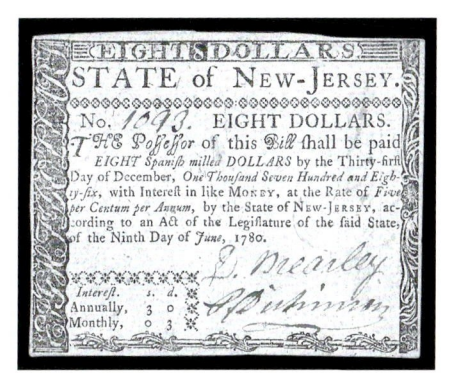

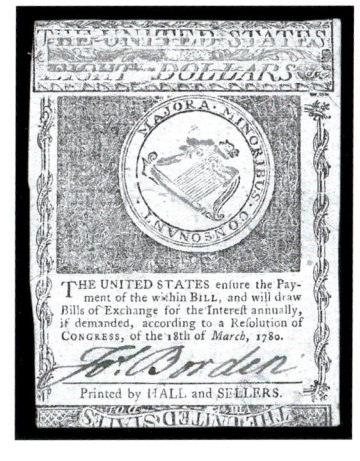

12137 **New Jersey June 9, 1780 $8 Choice About New.** Fully signed on both sides, with the signature of David Brearley on the face. Brearley was one of the signers of the United States Constiution seven years after he signed this note. The guarantee on the back is signed by Joseph Borden, who signed only this issue. He was also a delegate to the Stamp Act Congress of 1765. New Jersey is a scarce Colony for Guaranteed Issue notes. We've handled only eleven in all our sales combined, and this is only the third $8 denomination. The piece has the color and appearance of a fully uncirculated note, with only very minor handling separating it from that grade. **(1,500-up)**

NEW YORK

12138 **New York April 20, 1756 £3 Extremely Fine-About Uncirculated.** This note is in very nice condition given the scarcity of the issue. In fact, it is the only example that we have handled in many years. It has been backed by a thin dark paperboard, but it only exhibits one fold as seen from the face. (1,250-up)

12139 **New York April 20, 1756 £5 Very Fine-Extremely Fine.** This note is listed in Friedberg with a price only in the VG column and "rare" in the VF column. This is the second finest example that we've handled of this note in 40+ years of dealing in currency. A very important early date New York piece. (700-up)

12140 **New York April 15, 1758 £5 Fine.** This is only the fourth example of this note in our over 40 catalog auctions. All three signatures remain and there is a reinforced center split. Rare, underappreciated, and highly undervalued. (500-up)

12141 **New York April 15, 1758 £10 PCGS Apparent About New 50.** PCGS has red holdered this note due to "Small Repaired Splits at Top and Bottom." The splits are indeed small, and this piece is tremendous quality for this early New York issue. (800-up)

12142 **New York April 15, 1758 £10 Choice Very Fine.** This is a very scarce issue in any grade, but particularly so this nice. (600-up)

12143 **New York April 2, 1759 £5 Very Fine.** Some minor restoration work has been perfectly executed, most notably on the center fold. The design elements are still incredibly bold, as are the signatures. (250-up)

12144 **New York April 2, 1759 £10 PCGS Apparent Fine 15.** The holder notates the obvious on this not often seen issue that there are corners missing and minor edge repairs. (500-up)

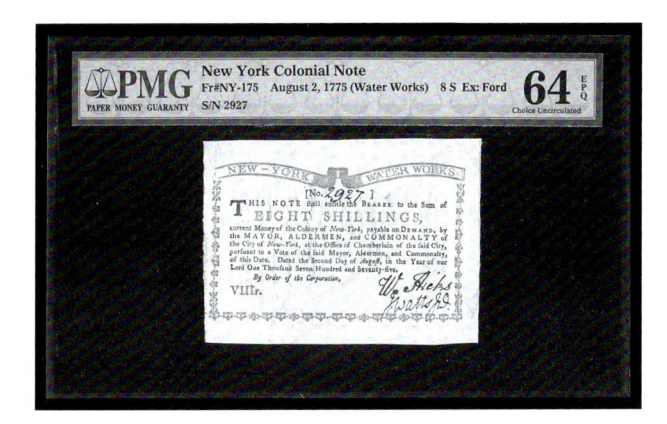

12145 **New York August 2, 1775 (Water Works) 8s PMG Choice Uncirculated 64 EPQ.** This note, which is from the Ford Collection, is one of the nicest Water Works notes that we have seen. Signatures are bold, the margins are broad all the way around on both sides, and it appears to us that a point or two more might have been in order. Nonetheless, 64 EPQ is the highest example yet graded, and the note should easily reach... **(750-up)**

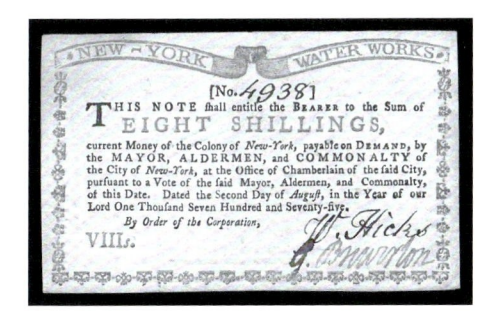

12146 **New York August 2, 1775 (Water Works) 8s Choice New.** This is a bright and nicely printed Water Works note that has very bold signatures and serial number as well. **(550-up)**

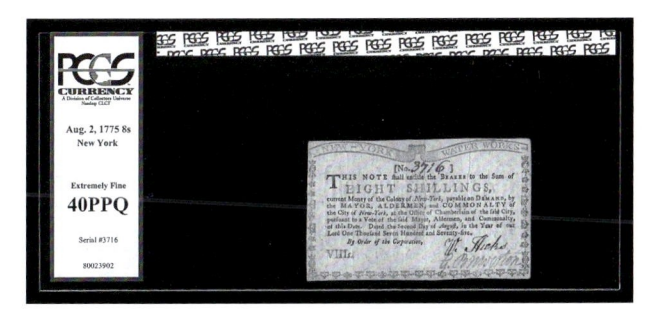

12147 **New York August 2, 1775 (Water Works) 8s PCGS Extremely Fine 40PPQ.** This red and black issue exhibits a couple of folds and a small stain on the back, but faces up nicely in the third party holder. **(200-up)**

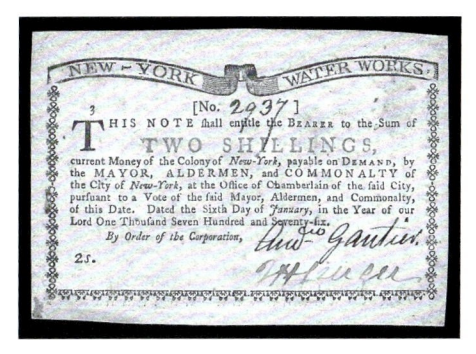

12148 **New York January 6, 1776 (Water Works) 2s Gem New.** This is an outstanding example of this scarcest of the four New York Water Works issues. All its original embossing is intact, the margins are broad all the way around, and the mounting is perfect. Mounting in this case refers to the gluing together of the face and back of the note. The faces of the notes were printed on a fine buff stock and the backs on a much coarser, darker paper. The two pieces were mounted together prior to the printing of the note, which oft-time has led to wrinkles, holes, gaps, and other problems. This note is totally problem free. **(750-up)**

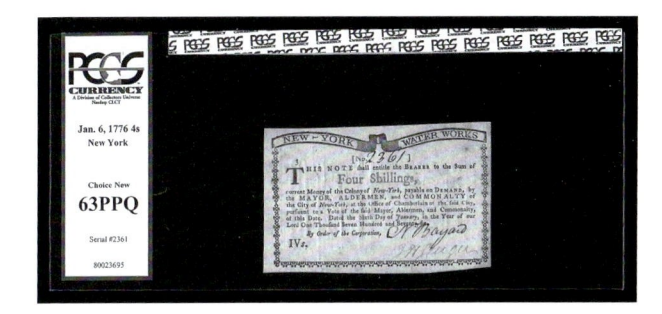

12149 **New York January 6, 1776 (Water Works) 4s PCGS Choice New 63PPQ.** A handsome example of a New York Water Works note. Although these are occasionally seen high grade, it's rather unusual to find one with no faults. This one is an excellent example. **(750-up)**

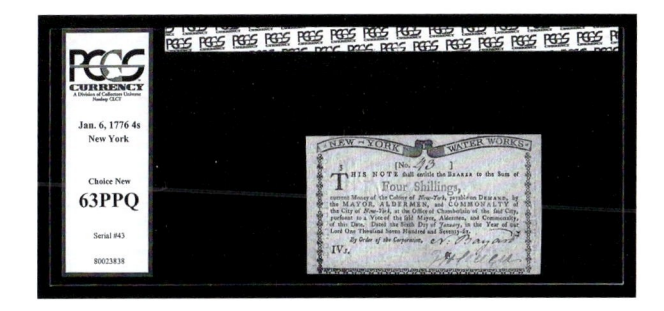

12150 **New York January 6, 1776 (Water Works) 4s PCGS Choice New 63PPQ.** A very nice example of this popular type. **(750-up)**

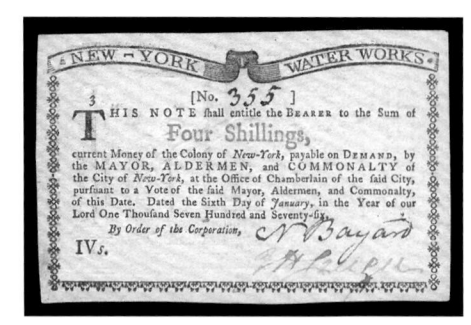

12151 **New York January 6, 1776 (Water Works) 4s Choice New.** This is a nice Water Works note. The original embossing can be seen on this evenly margined example with its low serial number of 355. The brown signature is strong, while the red signature is expectedly somewhat less so. **(650-up)**

12152 **New York March 5, 1776 $2/3 Choice About New.** A lone corner fold prohibits a full New grade for this attractive issue. The margins are solid and Andrew Stockholm's well executed signature remains dark. **(650-up)**

12153 **New York March 5, 1776 $2/3 About New.** While not quite as nice as the other About New offered here, this piece is still attractive and separated from a New grade by a mere center fold and corner bend. **(600-up)**

12154 **New York March 5, 1776 $2 Extremely Fine.** The rarity of this issue may not fully be illustrated by price guides as we last handled an example of this denomination over two years ago. The signature of Cornelius Ray is still bold. **(300-up)**

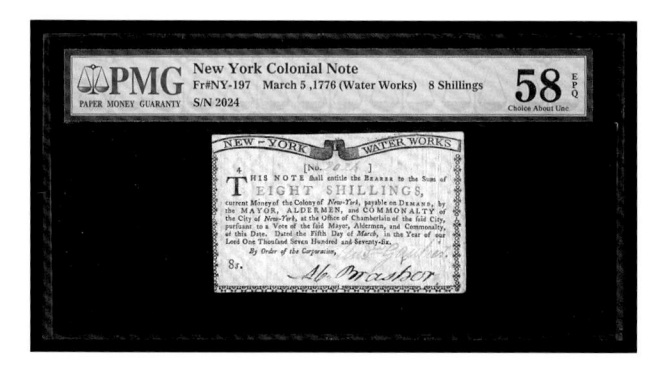

12155 **New York March 5, 1776 (Water Works) 8s PMG Choice About Unc 58 EPQ.** This is a lovely example of this more challenging Water Works issue that has great signatures, printing and paper quality. This note has all the eye appeal of a lovely Choice New note and will likely see such bidding as that which is accorded a note of that stature. **(400-up)**

12156 **New York August 13, 1776 $1/16 Very Fine-Extremely Fine.** This is a beautifully margined example, with very little actual wear, good signatures, and lots of eye appeal. **(600-up)**

NORTH CAROLINA

12157 North Carolina March 9, 1754 20s PCGS Apparent Fine 12. This note was red holdered for "Edge Splits, Repairs, and Restorations"—all of which affect blank paper areas only. The signatures, text, vignette, and indent are untouched, and both the appearance and value of the note are far in excess of the assigned grade. (250-up)

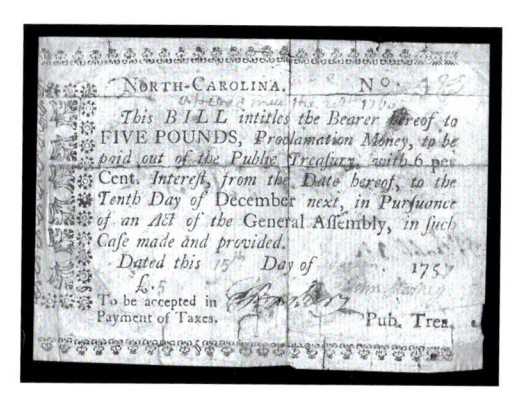

12158 North Carolina 1756 - 1757 (written dates) £5 Very Good-Fine. This example which has been professionally restored shows a handwritten date of Decem. 15, 1757. This issue is particularly scarce and few examples are known to be in unadulterated states of preservation. (700-up)

12159 North Carolina July 14, 1760 £3 Very Fine. There is a single minor repaired edge split on this well margined, solid, attractive piece. This is a scarce North Carolina issue, not often seen and particularly not this nice. The VF price in Friedberg is $600, and we would expect that to be nearly reached. (500-up)

12160 North Carolina December, 1768 20s Very Fine. This pleasingly original piece is solid, save for a few very minor margin nicks. The signatures and serial number remain strong. (300-up)

12161 North Carolina December, 1771 2s/6p, £1, 10s Uncut Sheet Very Choice New. The top note of the 2s/6d House Variety has the normal needle-hole at top center from when original bundles were sewn together. The other two notes are problem-free. (1,200-up)

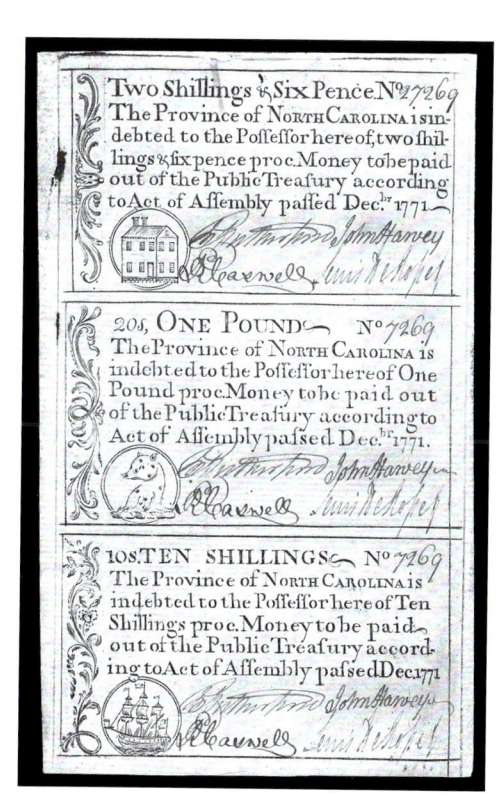

12162 North Carolina December, 1771 2s/6d, £1, 10s Uncut Sheet Very Choice New. The 2s/6d has the normal pinhole in its top margin, which is common to all three-subject sheets of this issue as they were issued in sewn packs of 50. The £1 and 10s notes are both perfect Gems. (1,200-up)

View color images of virtually every lot and place bids at HA.com

Session One, Auction 436 • Wednesday, May 9, 2007 • 6:00 PM CT   27

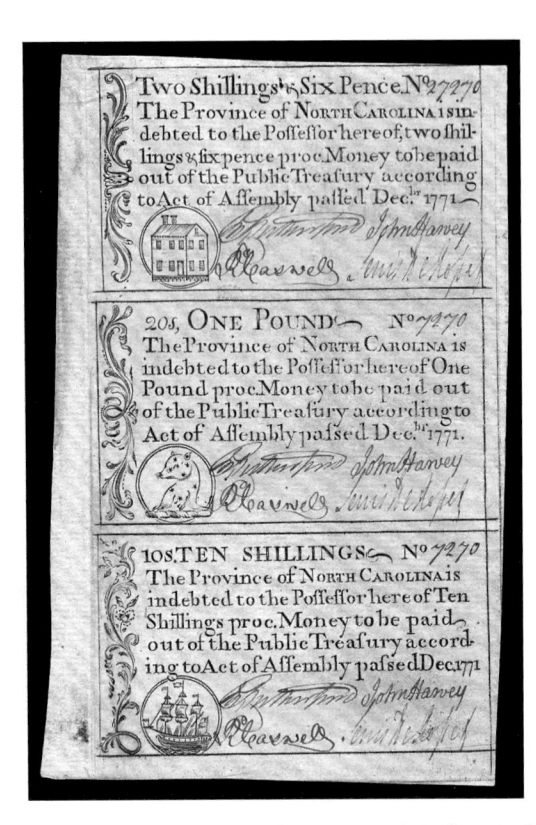

12163 **North Carolina December, 1771 2s/6d, £1, 10s Uncut Sheet Very Choice New.** The first note has the normal pinhole at top center and a pen notation on the back. The bottom two notes are pristine. **(1,200-up)**

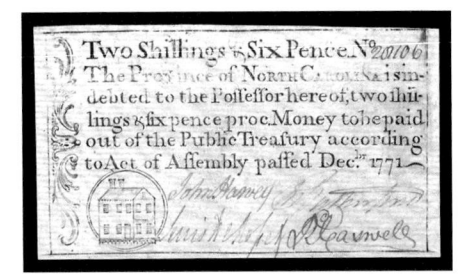

12164 **North Carolina December, 1771 2s/6d Choice New.** This note has a nice house vignette plus ample margins. **(300-up)**

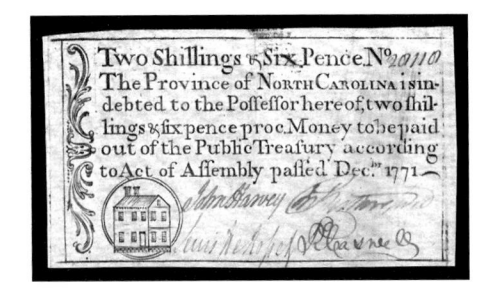

12165 **North Carolina December, 1771 2s/6d Choice New.** This is a nicely margined, well-signed example of this popular type with its charming house vignette. The house vignette was strengthened during the later printing. The pinhole at top center is from the custom of sewing sheets together. **(300-up)**

12166 **North Carolina December, 1771 Vertical Strip of Three 2s/6d, £1, 10s New.** A corner fold not into the design plus a little more edge handling is noticed on this three-subject strip. **(1,000-up)**

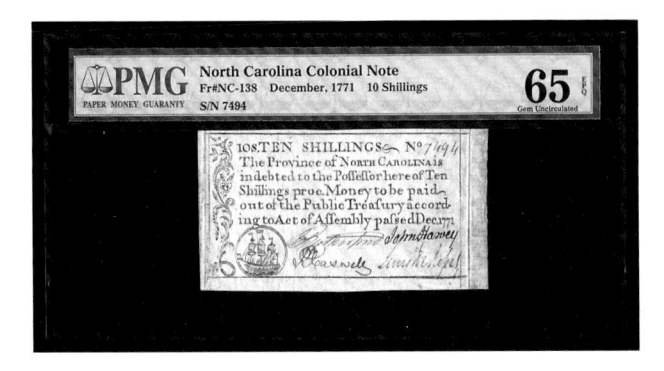

12167 **North Carolina December, 1771 10s PMG Gem Uncirculated 65 EPQ.** Beautifully margined, bright, and as attractive as the high grade would imply. **(450-up)**

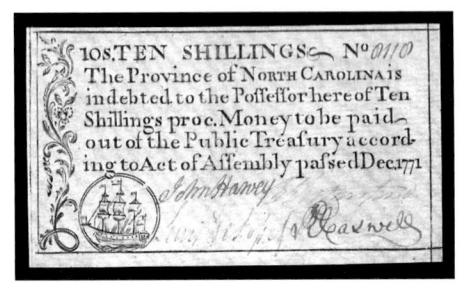

12168 **North Carolina December, 1771 10s Choice New.** Four nice margins and signatures typical of the issue are found on this note that has a minute pull mark in the vignette frame of the ship. **(400-up)**

28 Please visit HA.com to view other collectibles auctions. A 15% Buyer's Premium ($9 min.) Applies To All Lots

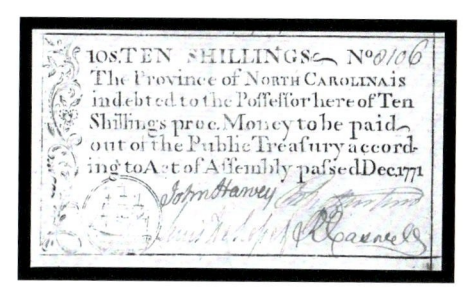

12169 North Carolina December, 1771 10s Choice New. The ship vignette is weak on this nicely preserved example. This note has serial number 2106, the same serial number as the following £1 note. (300-up)

12170 North Carolina December, 1771 10s PCGS About New 53PPQ. A handsome, broadly margined North Carolina "Ship" note with four bold signatures. (250-up)

12171 North Carolina December, 1771 10s PCGS Extremely Fine 45. Beautifully printed and signed. (225-up)

12172 North Carolina December, 1771 10s PCGS Extremely Fine 40PPQ. Another well-printed "Ship" note. (225-up)

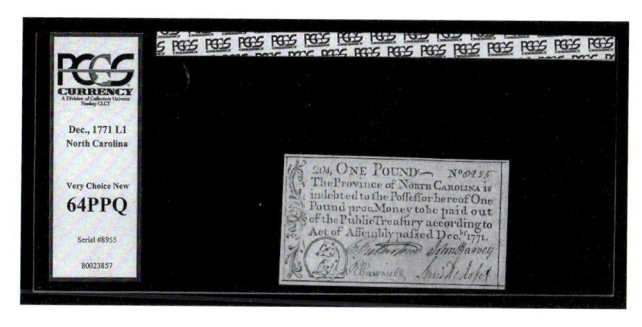

12173 North Carolina December, 1771 £1 PCGS Very Choice New 64PPQ. A lovely example, with four strong signatures and excellent margins. (400-up)

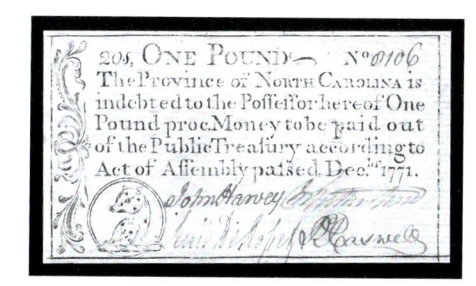

12174 North Carolina December, 1771 £1 Choice New. The vignette is of the constellation Ursa Minor. This note has serial number 2106, the same serial number as the preceeding 10s note. (300-up)

12175 North Carolina December, 1771 £2 Extremely Fine. This is a really nice example of a much scarcer denomination from this popular issue. Pieces up through the £1 are seen with some frequency in higher grade, but the four highest denominations are far scarcer. (300-up)

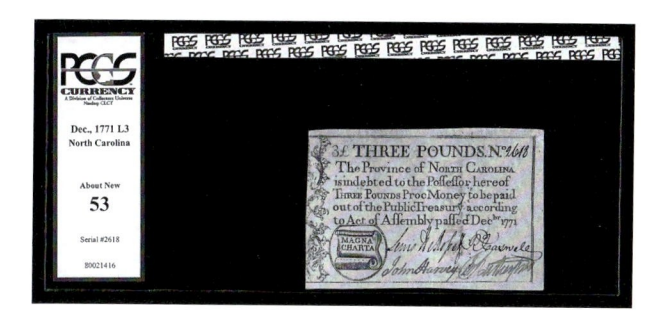

12176 North Carolina December, 1771 £3 PCGS About New 53. A beautifully signed, boldly printed example of this scarcer Three Pound denomination. (500-up)

12177 North Carolina December, 1771 £5 PCGS Extremely Fine 45. The highest denomination and the scarcest note from the issue. (900-up)

Incredibly Scarce North Carolina Issue

12178 North Carolina August 21, 1775 $4 Extremely Fine, Repaired. This note, from one of the most elusive issues of Colonial Currency, is the first example that Heritage-CAA has handled. The Friedberg catalog prices only the $1/4 from this issue, and refers to all the other denominations as very rare in all grades. This rare Colonial note was previously part of Stack's October 2006 sale, where it realized over $4900. At that time, a center split was reinforced with paper tape on the back. The note has had that tape removed, and the split properly dealt with. The note has a few minor edge splits and tiny pinholes, but it is well margined, boldly signed and faces-up beautifully. The Masonic symbol at the lower left is clean, sharp and with all its varied elements crystal clear. This is likely one of the nicest, if not the nicest example known, and it should certainly move far past its previous level. **(7,500-up)**

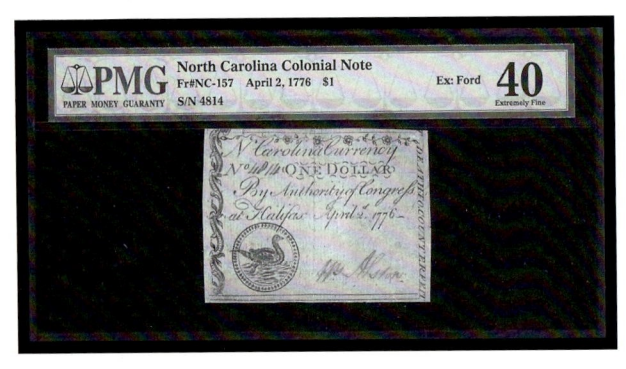

12179 North Carolina April 2, 1776 $1 PMG Extremely Fine 40. This is the first example of this design that Heritage-CAA has offered, and it's an extremely nice one. The waterfowl vignette is razor-sharp, and the note is well-margined and well-printed. The center split (noted on the PMG holder) has been carefully restored and this piece should easily surpass its previous auction realization of over $800. **(1,250-up)**

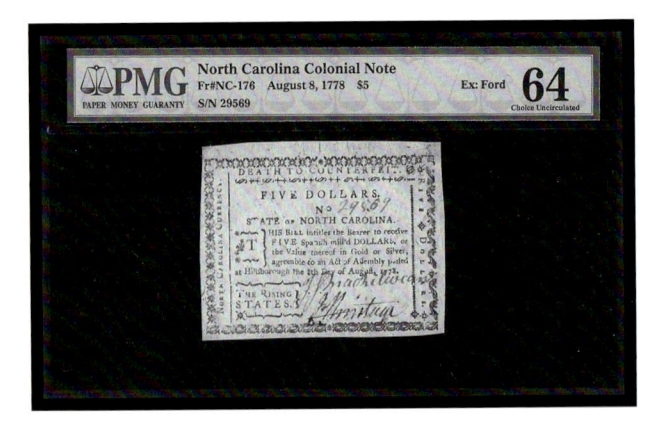

12180 North Carolina August 8, 1778 $5 PMG Choice Uncirculated 64. This is not a common note in any grade, and it is a major rarity this nice. At this early date, PMG has graded only four examples of this note, the other three all being circulated. That count will go way up over the years, but it will be a very long time, if ever, before another 64 will be graded. This is a popular issue due to the patriotic mottos on the notes, and this one, with its "THE RISING STATES" motto is one of the most popular of them all. **(1,000-up)**

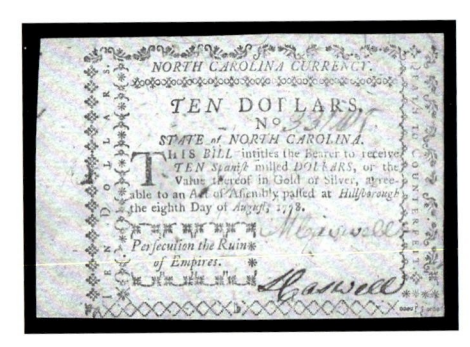

12181 North Carolina August 8, 1778 $10 Choice About New. This note is beautifully margined and a great-looking example of this issue, with a light centerfold that could easily be overlooked. The note bears the motto "Persecution the Ruin of Empires." **(450-up)**

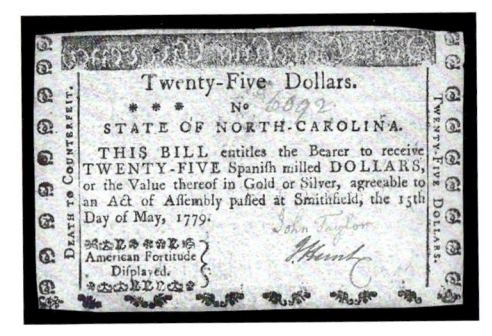

12182 North Carolina May 15, 1779 $25 Extremely Fine. Many examples of this issue are seen with serious defects. This piece is wholly original and absolutely free of any paper problems. **(400-up)**

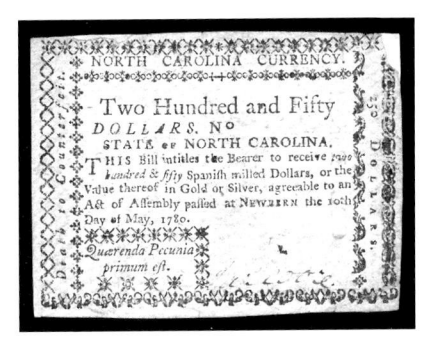

12183 **North Carolina May 10, 1780 $250 Extremely Fine.** The signatures are faded, and the upper right corner tip has been replaced. Still, a high-grade piece for the issue. **(400-up)**

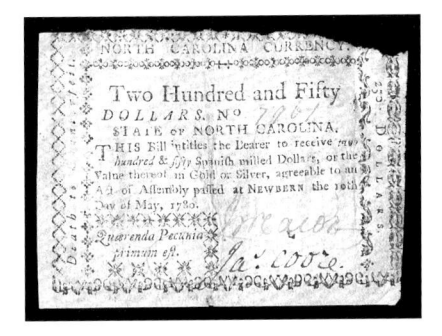

12184 **North Carolina May 10, 1780 $250 Fine-Very Fine.** Held back just a bit by an irregular cut across the top **(200-up)**

PENNSYLVANIA

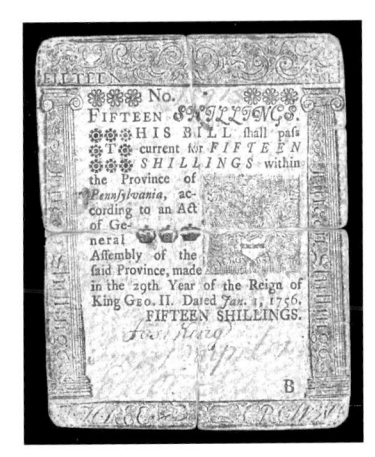

12185 **Pennsylvania January 1, 1756 15s Very Good-Fine.** The back has a slight reinforcement with a brown paper strip across the horizontal fold. At top center is an approximate quarter inch tear and at bottom center is an approximate three-fourths inch tear. The corners are also slightly rounded on this elusive Franklin/Hall collaboration. This is how notes of this issue are usually found as the entire issue is not priced above VG in Friedberg. In fact, we have handled very few January 1, 1756 notes over the years. **(400-up)**

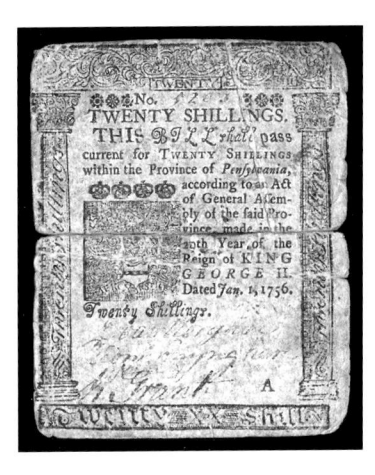

12186 **Pennsylvania January 1, 1756 20s Very Good.** This Franklin note has a split on the horizontal crease which is strip repaired with a silk cloth backing. There is some minor edge roughness, but it is well printed and still attractive. **(500-up)**

12187 **Pennsylvania May 20, 1758 20s Fine.** Benjamin Franklin and David Hall printed this scarce issue. This example carries a hard horizontal fold that is showing some signs of an impending split. The note has been trimmed in a bit, and the back print is quite subdued. A couple of small spots are noticed on the face and back. **(600-up)**

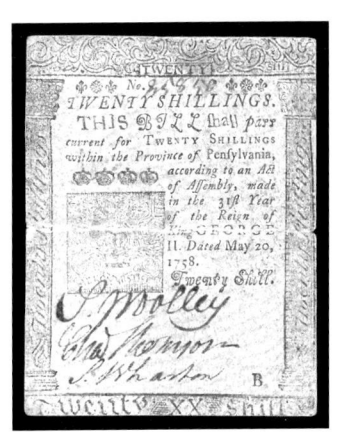

12188 **Pennsylvania March 10, 1769 10s PMG Choice Extremely Fine 45 EPQ.** Not a very rare note in lower grade even though only 2000 pieces of this denomination were originally printed. In Very Fine and above it is a major rarity, and this XF45 EPQ is the finest example we have ever seen. This issue was printed "for the relief and employment of the poor in the city of Philadelphia" and is often referred to as Bettering House money. This piece from the Ford Collection realized $1,060 when last auctioned. Now, in its 45 EPQ holder, it is likely to do a fair bit better. **(1,500-up)**

12189 **Pennsylvania April 3, 1772 9d PMG Choice Uncirculated 64.** A Gem appearing note that has the PMG comment "hinged" on the back. Well signed and beautifully margined. **(300-up)**

12190 **Pennsylvania April 3, 1772 1s Choice New.** A Gem but for a somewhat tight margin at the bottom. Well signed, with perfect original paper surfaces. **(300-up)**

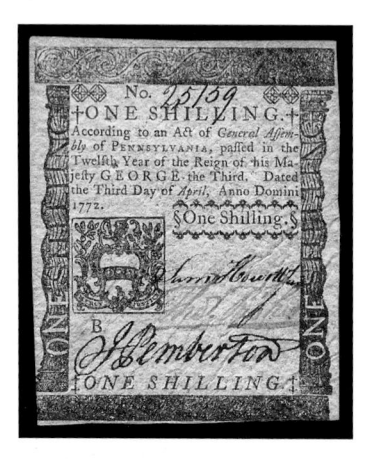

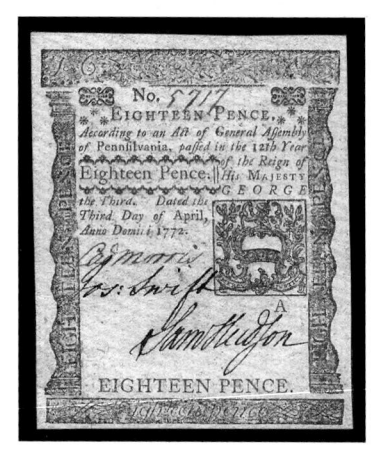

12191 **Pennsylvania April 3, 1772 18d Superb Gem New.** A gorgeous note, with three bold signatures, broad, even margins all the way around on both sides and super eye appeal. This is a rather common issue, but it is just about never seen anywhere near this nice. **(700-up)**

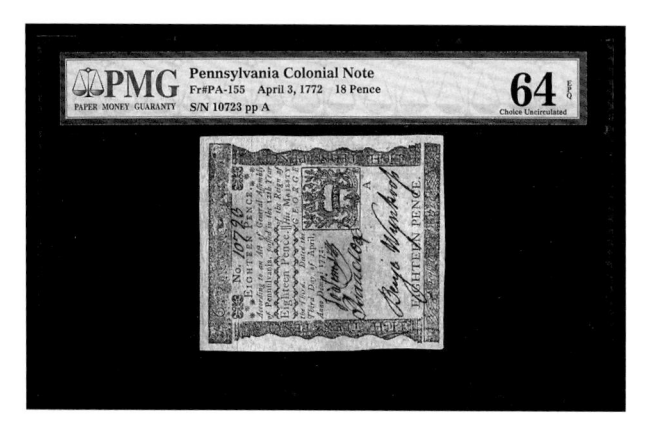

12192 **Pennsylvania April 3, 1772 18d PMG Choice Uncirculated 64 EPQ.** Solid margins surround this boldly signed, original issue. Though this is not a particularly scarce issue, it is not often seen in grades approaching Gem. **(500-up)**

12193 **Pennsylvania April 3, 1772 2s Choice New.** Three good signatures and fresh paper surfaces highlight this nice note. **(300-up)**

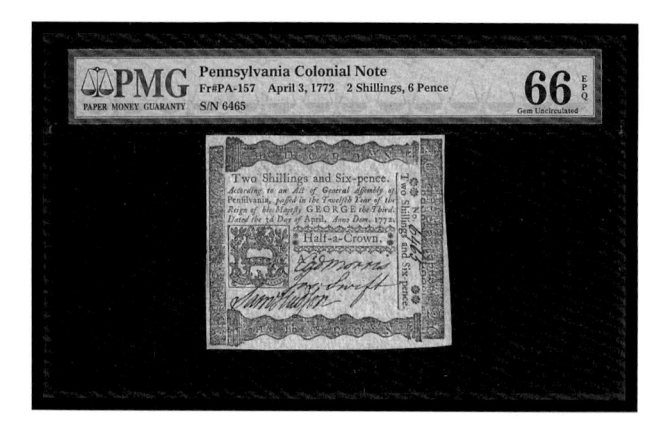

12194 **Pennsylvania April 3, 1772 2s/6d PMG Gem Uncirculated 66 EPQ.** An exceptional example of the issue and by far, the highest grade yet assigned to a PA-157 by PMG. Only one piece from this issue—a different denomination—has been graded 65, and this is the lone 66 from any of the April 3, 1772 denominations. **(750-up)**

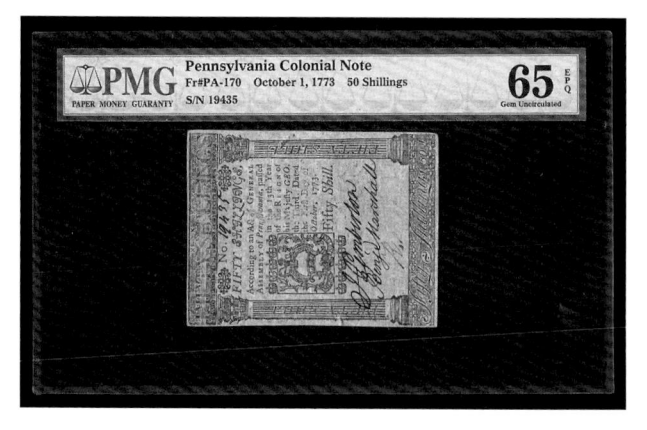

12195 **Pennsylvania October 1, 1773 50s PMG Gem Uncirculated 65 EPQ.** This piece is likely as fresh as it was the day it was printed. The signatures of Pemberton and Marshall are still bold. **(450-up)**

12196 **Pennsylvania October 1, 1773 50s PMG Choice Uncirculated 63 EPQ.** A crisp example of this columned issue that has three superb signatures as well as crackling fresh paper. **(275-up)**

12197 **Pennsylvania October 25, 1775 9d PMG Choice Uncirculated 64 EPQ.** Bold embossing and superb paper quality are both clearly evident on this small change note. With a touch more left margin this well signed and numbered note would easily reach the Gem grade. **(400-up)**

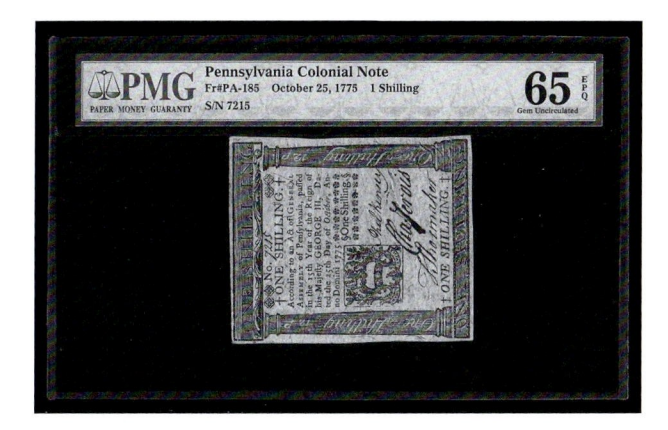

12198 Pennsylvania October 25, 1775 1s PMG Gem Uncirculated 65 EPQ. An enormously margined example of this available issue that has very sizeable margins for this type. The penned signatures and number are as bold as the day they were printed and the print quality is razor sharp. (500-up)

12199 Pennsylvania December 8, 1775 40s PMG Choice Uncirculated 64 EPQ. This attractive near-Gem is fully margined on all sides and boasts exceptional paper quality. The signatures and serial number are perfectly penned while the design shows great detail and excellent centering. (400-up)

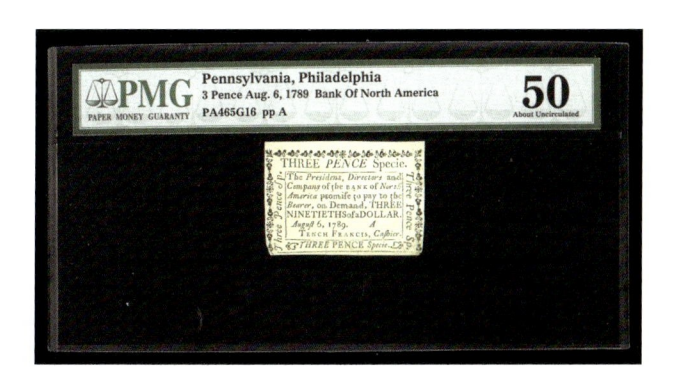

12200 Pennsylvania Bank of North America August 6, 1789 3d PMG About Uncirculated 50. Bold swaths of color are noted on back, and a mere corner tip fold accounts for the grade on this otherwise uncirculated issue. According to Newman, "Bank of North America Small Change Bills Payable in Specie were issued because of the 'Copper Panic' of July 1789, when circulating copper coin was refused." He goes on to say they were "printed by Benjamin F. Bache on paper furnished by Benjamin Franklin which had a polychrome or marbled edge on both sides." (2,000-up)

RHODE ISLAND

12201 Rhode Island May 22, 1777 $1/6 Fine. This Fractional-only issue consisted of nine different denominations from $1/36 to $1/3. This is the first example of this "higher" denomination. The note faces up nicely as a Very Fine with clear text and signature. Some clear tape repairs have reinforced the center of the note but do not greatly interfere with the integrity or aesthetic appeal of the note. (300-up)

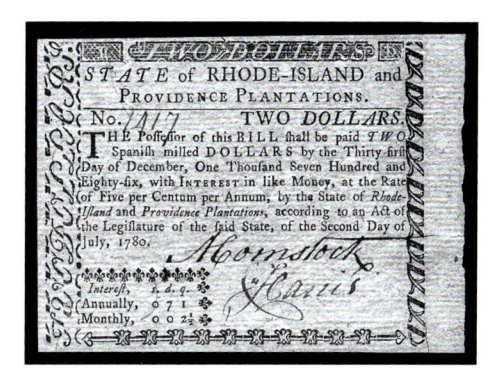

12202 Rhode Island July 2, 1780 $2 Gem New. This is a perfect remainder, fully signed on the face, but with an unsigned guarantee on the back. (300-up)

12203 Rhode Island July 2, 1780 $2 Choice About New. Signatures are bold and the paper is bright on this Rhode Island $2 that has a weak center fold. (250-up)

12204 Rhode Island July 2, 1780 $3 Extremely Fine-About New. This note should grade New, however, an expertly repaired upper left corner must be noted. (200-up)

12205 Rhode Island July 2, 1780 $5 Gem New. The face of this well preserved remainder with serial number 656 has wide margins at the left and right. (250-up)

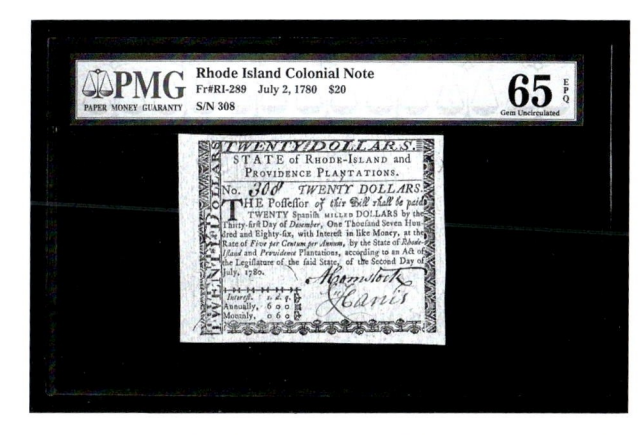

12206 Rhode Island July 2, 1780 $20 PMG Gem Uncirculated 65 EPQ. A touch close along the top margin, but absolute perfection in every other respect. The colors are spectacular, the signatures are strong, the paper is beautifully bright and the note is perfectly crisp. (450-up)

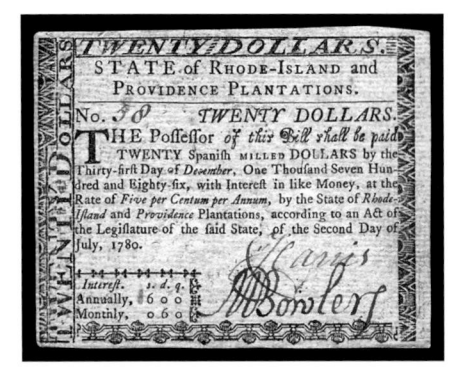

12207 **Rhode Island July 2, 1780 $20 Choice New.** Serial number 58 adorns this attractive colorful note that is without any folds, but intense scrutiny did notice a couple of pinholes. (300-up)

12208 **Rhode Island July 2, 1780 $20 New.** This is an attractive note with nice print quality. A corner bump and an approximate 3mm split at top center is noticed. (250-up)

12209 **Rhode Island July 2, 1780 $20 Choice About New.** A brief sojourn into circulation resulted in a center fold. (225-up)

12210 **Rhode Island May 1786 1s PMG Choice Uncirculated 64.** A tiny tear in the right margin, which is extremely difficult to see, has kept the EPQ away from this broadly margined, bright note. (200-up)

12211 **Rhode Island May 1786 5s PMG Gem Uncirculated 66 EPQ.** It has been more than a couple of years since we sold an example of this denomination this nice. The margins are exceptionally big, the signatures remain bold, and the printing quality is most pleasing. (300-up)

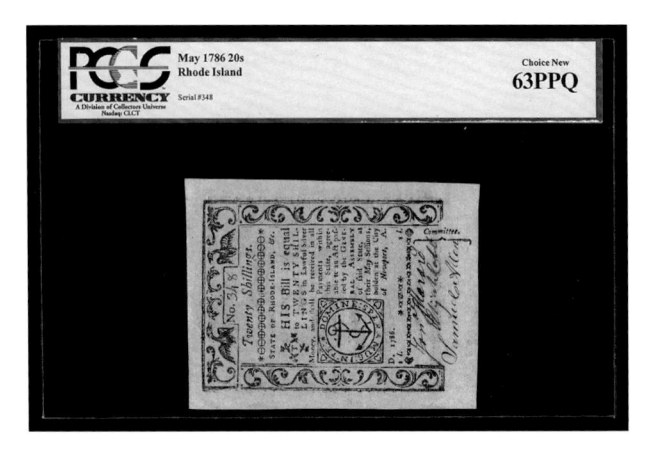

12212 **Rhode Island May 1786 20s PCGS Choice New 63PPQ.** The margins are quite large on this bright example. (300-up)

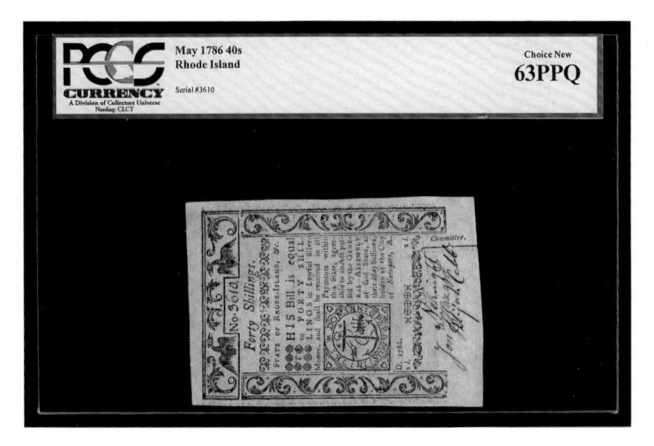

12213 **Rhode Island May 1786 40s PCGS Choice New 63PPQ.** A lovely Rhode Island note with excellent paper quality and tremendous eye appeal for the grade. (300-up)

SOUTH CAROLINA

12214 **South Carolina December 23, 1776 $1 PCGS Choice New 63PPQ.** A Remainder Note with no serial number and signed by Dart and Wakefield only. This note uses four Hebrew characters on the back as an anticounterfeiting device. (500-up)

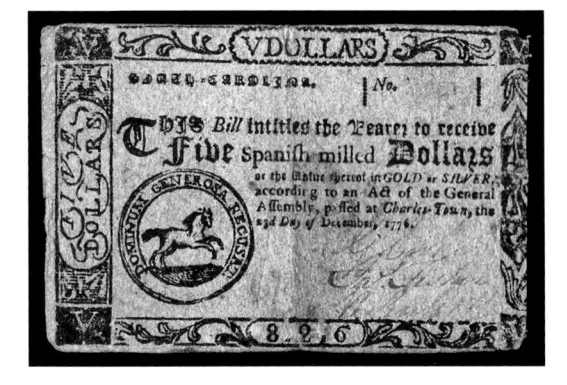

12215 **South Carolina December 23, 1776 $5 Extremely Fine.** The horse vignette is razor sharp, as is the Latin motto surrounding it, "DOMINUM GENEROSA RECUSAT," which Newman translates as, "The well born refuses a master." This note was once mounted with a stamp hinge. The center fold is flanked by two weaker folds. A couple of tiny edge nicks are noticed, too. (350-up)

12216 South Carolina April 10, 1778 Block of Four. A Very Fine sheet of four made up of a 2s6d; 3s9d; 5s; and 10s note. Each is signed by Beale only and unnumbered. All four vignettes are well printed. Scarce and desirable. (1,200-up)

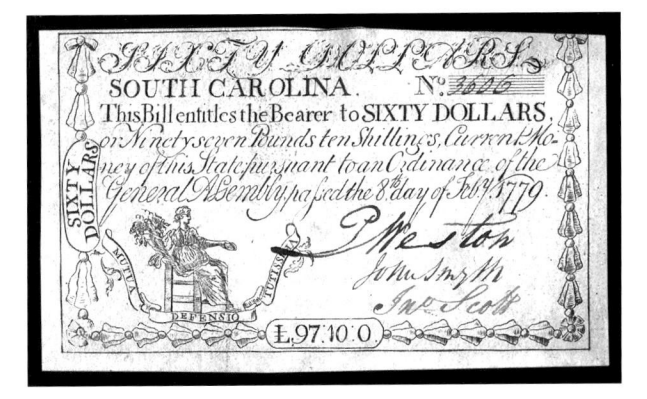

12217 South Carolina February 8, 1779 $60 Choice About New. This piece has three broad margins, but the top margin is quite tight. It's a very well signed, bright and attractive example of this extremely popular issue. Both the faces and backs of these notes were elaborately engraved by Thomas Coram of Charleston, South Carolina. The face vignette is of a seated Liberty figure holding a cornucopia, surrounded by a ribbon with the Latin motto "MUTUA DEFENSIO TUTISSIMA," which Newman translates as "Mutual defense is safest." The back features a lyre surrounded by horns, flags, and vines. (2,000-up)

VIRGINIA

12218 Virginia April 1, 1773 £8 Very Fine. This is the earlier and much rarer James River Bank form issue, and, in spite of numerous edge splits and problems, it's one of the nicest examples we've seen from this issue. None of the problems have caused meaningful paper loss, and the only repair is an archival tape reinforcement of the lengthy center-slit. (1,200-up)

Spectacular Grade March 4, 1773

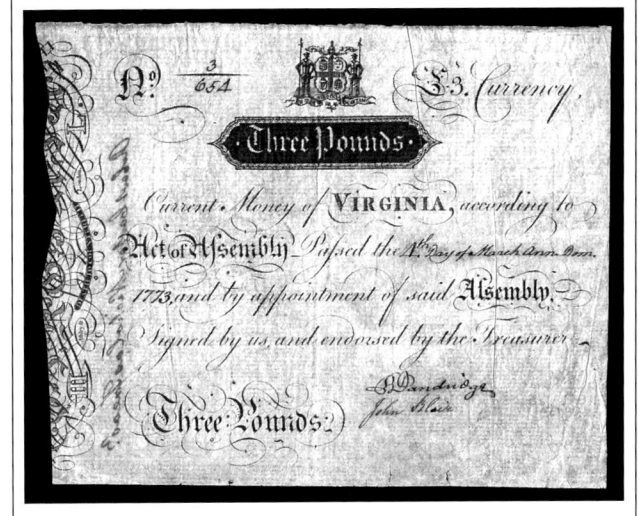

12219 Virginia March 4, 1773 £3 Extremely Fine-About New. We have handled a tremendous amount of Colonial currency in our 40+ sales, including over a dozen examples from this very rare issue—none have even vaguely approached the quality of this incredible piece. But for a minute hole in the Blair signature, a few pinholes, and some extremely minor touches of circulation, this piece is as issued and impeccable. It's from a very large issue, printed on thin, weak paper that practically disintegrated at first touch. These notes were printed in London from plates engraved by Harry Ashby. They did not reach Virginia until September 1773, when they were completed, signed, indented, and released. The issue is rare in all grades, and prohibitively rare in high grade. This note is totally intact, beautifully margined, well signed, and problem-free. This is very likely one of the finest existing examples of this rare Virginia issue. We would not be surprised if this piece were the finest known example of its issue and denomination. (4,500-up)

12220 **Virginia July 17, 1775 £2 Very Fine.** There are some juncture holes and edge splits, but this note is vastly superior to what is usually seen for this issue. We have offered scant few of these in 46 major auctions spread over 18 years. **(1,200-up)**

12221 **Virginia July 17, 1775 £3 Very Fine.** This note is clearly well-circulated, but amazingly problem-free with perfect print quality and ideal signatures. There are a few very minor edge problems, but the note is vastly superior to the usual tattered examples seen from this issue. **(1,200-up)**

12222 **Virginia September 1, 1775 20s Extremely Fine.** Strong signatures, a gorgeous ship vignette, along with perfectly clear text and handwriting are highlights of this example. Some very well done repair work is noted, obviously to strengthen some edge tears encountered in these past 231 years. **(1,000-up)**

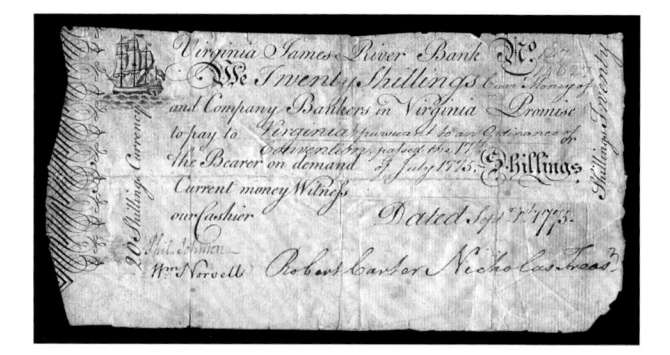

12223 **Virginia September 1, 1775 20s Very Fine.** A number of splits have been repaired with paper patches on the blank back. The repairs appear to be contemporary to the circulation period. There are no pieces missing nor paper restorations on this scarce and popular type. All the signatures are perfect, as is the all-important ship vignette. **(800-up)**

12224 **Virginia October 7, 1776 $6 Choice Very Fine.** Closely margined all the way around, but a really nice unsplit problem-free Virginia example. **(250-up)**

12225 **Virginia Partial Proof $10 Extremely Fine-About New.** This lot appears to be similar to lot # 4429 of the Stack's Ford XVII sale, and was described as, "A partial proofing with incomplete cast border cuts. These were struck privately from seized and partially broken plates at Richmond during the Civil War. Rare and the first we have catalogued for the sale. The only example for which we have a pedigree was in Pine Tree's 1975 Elizabeth Morton Sale." This piece is on different paper than the actual issue, thus leading us to believe this is also a Civil War restrike. **(400-up)**

12226 **Virginia October 20, 1777 $1 Very Fine-Extremely Fine.** The paper quality on this hand dated issue is exceptional. Only a few folds account for the grade and the design remains bold. **(250-up)**

12227 **Virginia May 4, 1778 (Dates Printed) $3 Very Fine-Extremely Fine.** This piece was only briefly circulated before ultimately ending up in the collection of a numismatist. There are four paper pulls at each of the corners indicating that it may have been mounted at one time. (300-up)

12228 **Virginia May 4, 1778 (Dates Printed) $10 Very Fine-Extremely Fine.** This unadulterated Virginia issue has the printed dates and is on thick paper. A tiny "tc" is branded on the front, clear of the design. (250-up)

12229 **Virginia July 14, 1780 $80 Extremely Fine.** The thin paper on this issue has held up extraordinarily well. Add four solid margins all around and great remaining signatures and this is an eye appealing example of this type. (400-up)

12230 **Virginia October 16, 1780 $400 Very Fine-Extremely Fine.** Solid margins are noted on this lightly circulated, thin paper issue. The signatures are ideal as is the paper, save for a tiny repair in the center of the note. (250-up)

12231 **Virginia March 1, 1781 $500 Extremely Fine.** This thick paper variety sustained only a few light folds, only one of which is readily visible on the face. The signatures are strong, though there is a corner nick and some weakness in the center fold that must be noted. (500-up)

12232 **Virginia March 1, 1781 $500 Very Fine-Extremely Fine.** The signatures and serial number are bold, while a few edge nicks and tears are noticed on this thin paper variety. (350-up)

12233 **Virginia May 7, 1781 $50 About New.** The design details are all fully legible. Though there are some repairs noted, they are mostly confined to the top of the note and were well executed. (300-up)

12234 **Virginia May 7, 1781 $1500 Very Fine-Extremely Fine.** The design details are solid and the paper is bright. The bottom portion of the note shows signs of professional restoration. (250-up)

POSTAGE ENVELOPES

12235 **Postage Stamp Envelope 25¢ Snow & Hapgood Boston Extremely Fine.** Listed in the Krause and Lemke book as KL130-25. This is an extremely rare Boston issuer. Almost all known postage stamp envelopes are from New York City. As a category, these envelopes are among the rarest of all Civil War era emergency money collectibles. The envelope is a bit soiled, but wholly intact with no tears or problems. Apparently, either a silver quarter or piece of encased postage was stored in this envelope for years as its imprint remains. (600-up)

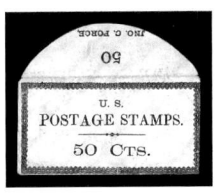

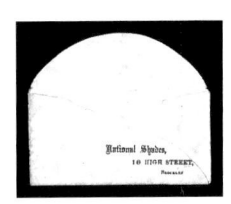

12236 **Postage Stamp Envelope 50¢ JNO. Force Brooklyn, NY About New.** Listed in Krause and Lemke as number KL34-50, this very rare issuer was located in Brooklyn, NY. Now part of New York City, Brooklyn, at the time when these pieces were issued in 1862, was an independent city. The piece is in perfect condition printed in blue on the face and black on the back. Force's full business address "JNO. C. Force, National Shades, 16 High Street, Brooklyn" is listed on four lines on the flap and back of the envelope. A great piece. (750-up)

ENCASED POSTAGE

United States Encased Postage Stamps came into being as a "Money of Necessity" at the same time and for the same reasons as Fractional Currency. For several years there had been a shortage of small change. This condition was at its worst in the Spring and Summer of 1862. It had become nearly impossible for merchants (and the public) to get along without being able to make change. Private scrip, bank and merchant scrip, small private copper tokens, and postage stamps (both loose and in pre-printed envelopes) were all being pressed into service.

The inventor of Encased Postage, John Gault of Boston (later with Kirkpatrick of New York City) cleverly solved the problem of quick disintegration of stamps in circulation by encasing them in a metal case with a mica "window" so the stamp was visible. His profit was made by selling advertising on the back of the case to various merchants.

John Gault obtained a patent on Encased Postage Stamps on August12, 1862. Most, if not all of the Encased Postage was produced from this patent date; until early 1863 when Postage Currency (First Issue Fractional Currency) was beginning to fill the small change gap (Postage Currency was first printed on August of 1862 and most likely was placed into circulation at once, or for sure by early September, but it was several months before it began to circulate freely). Mr. Gault was also hard pressed to obtain stamps, because after the July and August rush on post offices (to obtain stamps to replace the hoarded coins) the post office department cut off supplies of stamps for all but postage use.

Most major collections of Fractional Currency have had several pieces of Encased Postage in them as association items; and, needless to say, a collection of Encased Postage stands well in its own right.

The average collectable condition for Encased Postage is Very Fine with an exceptional piece being Extra Fine to About New. A fully New piece of Encased Postage is a major rarity even for the most common issues, and most varieties are unknown in even About New condition.

Possibly Finest Known "Aerated Bread"

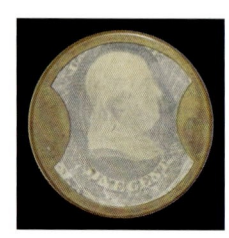

12237 HB-1 EP-1 1¢ Aerated Bread Choice About New. The finest Aerated Bread encasement by far that we have seen. Aerated Bread is a very rare merchant, represented by only the One Cent denomination and a unique Five Cent example. Only about fifteen Aerated Bread pieces are known, and they very seldom reach the market. This one is simply incredible, with the back of the case very nearly fully silvered. The mica is perfect, and the stamp has its full bright blue color with the white portions only lightly toned. If you are trying to assemble a high-quality merchant set, this Aerated Bread piece is a must-have. **(7,500-up)**

12238 HB-6 EP-32a 3¢ Ayer's Cathartic Pills Long Arrows Choice About New. The case is a glossy medium mahogany color, without any distractions whatsoever. The stamp is 90+% fully bright, and the mica is as close to flawless as will ever be found. This is a rather common variety, but it is rarely found anywhere near this nice. **(600-up)**

12239 HB-6 EP-32a 3¢ Ayer's Cathartic Pills Long Arrows Choice About New. A little silvering remains on the back between the letters. The stamp and mica are both as perfect as they come. The only flaw at all on this near-perfect piece is the presence of two unobtrusive dark spots on the back. **(600-up)**

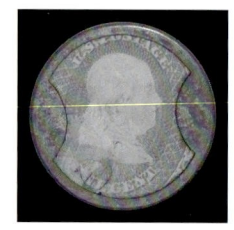

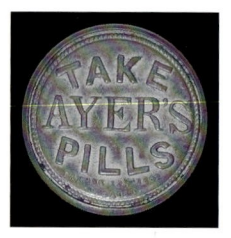

12240 HB-17 EP-3 1¢ Take Ayer's Pills About New. The case is an even, medium brass color, with a considerable amount of silvering remaining between the letters. The stamp is well centered and fully bright, with all its original blue color. The mica has a separation at the bottom where the top layer has broken off, but the lower layers still cover the stamp completely. It's rather unobtrusive, and the overall appearance of this piece is quite nice. **(500-up)**

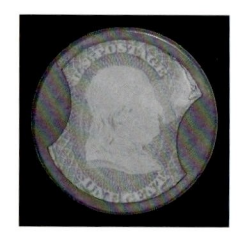

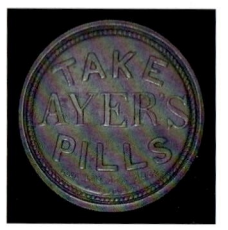

12241 HB-17 EP-3 1¢ Take Ayer's Pills About New. The case is a lovely glossy medium-mahogany color, and it is without a hint of a flaw, the stamp is very nearly fully bright and the mica perfect save for a very minor craze mark just above the right tab. The piece is virtually identical to Lot 12423 from our January sale which realized $632.50. **(650-up)**

12242 **HB-17 EP-3 1¢ Take Ayer's Pills Extremely Fine.** The problem-free case is a nice, even dark-mahogany color, the stamp is bright and the mica above average with some very minor flaws at its edge. **(450-up)**

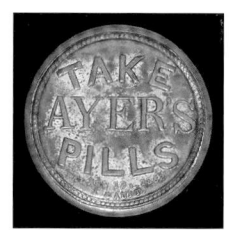

12243 **HB-18 EP-33 3¢ Take Ayer's Pills Choice About New.** The back of this high-quality piece has nearly half its original silvering. The case is essentially perfect, without a hint of a flaw. The mica is completely clean and flawless, and the stamp remains bright and attractive. A common piece becomes elusive in this grade. **(550-up)**

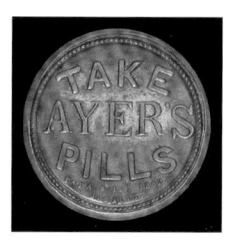

12244 **HB-23 EP-136 12¢ Take Ayer's Pills About New.** Some silvering remains behind the lettering on the back of this very scarce Twelve Cent Encasement. The case is essentially flawless, as is the mica, and the stamp is bright and attractive. While not highly rated in the various catalogs, we have always found this to be an extremely elusive piece, and we can trace only five examples in our records. This piece is considerably nicer than either of the two examples in Stack's June 2004 sale. **(3,000-up)**

12245 **HB-28 EP-4A 1¢ Ayer's Sarsaparilla Medium "Ayer's" Choice About New.** This beautiful piece has over 95% of its original silvering remaining, including the front of the case, which is almost never seen. "A very good case" could be made to call this piece fully uncirculated. What will appear in the photograph as a spot by the second "s" of "sarsaparilla" is a minor area where the original silvering did not take. While this is a common piece, any encasement with this much silvering should be considered very rare. The mica is as flawless as they ever come, and the stamp is beautifully bright. **(1,250-up)**

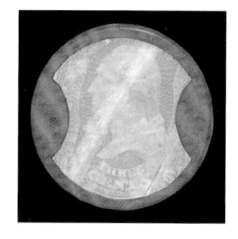

12246 **HB-30 EP-34a 3¢ Ayer's Sarsaparilla About New.** Last appearing in our 2006 FUN Sale, "A beautiful case, with traces of silver remaining and a fully bright stamp. The mica has two as-made imperfections, one crossing fully across the face of the stamp. At a glance, these appear to be cracks, but they are not." **(450-up)**

12247 **HB-30 EP-34A 3¢ Ayer's Sarsaparilla Medium "Ayer's" About New.** The perfect case is a glossy problem-free medium-mahogany color, the stamp is 100% fully bright and the mica is perfect save for the most minor of surface marks. A common number and an ideal piece for type. **(450-up)**

12248 **HB-30 EP-34A 3¢ Ayer's Sarsaparilla Medium "Ayer's" Extremely Fine.** The case had been cleaned at one time, but a bit of silver remains in spite of the old cleaning. The stamp is beautifully bright and very nearly perfectly centered, and the mica is essentially perfect. **(400-up)**

12249 **HB-32 EP-34b 3¢ Ayer's Sarsaparilla Large "Ayer's" Choice About New.** The case is a beautiful chocolate brown with not a hint of a mark or defect. The stamp is fully bright, and the mica is flawless save for a single craze mark at the very bottom. A beautiful example of this scarcer Large "Ayer's" type. **(800-up)**

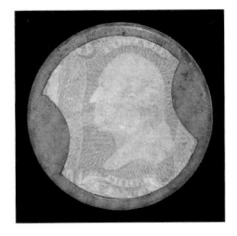

12250 **HB-32 EP-34b 3¢ Ayer's Sarsaparilla About New.** Last appearing in our 2006 FUN Sale, where we described, "This is the variety with the large "Ayer's." The case is a perfect medium brown, the stamp is fully bright and the mica is close to perfect. A much harder variety to find this nice." (800-up)

12251 **HB-32 EP-34B 3¢ Ayer's Sarsaparilla Large "Ayer's" Extremely Fine.** The case is a most attractive brass-to-medium-brown color, with no marks or problems. The stamp is perfectly centered under flawless mica, and it has retained every bit of its original bright color. An extraordinary piece, likely one of the very finest known for this number. (700-up)

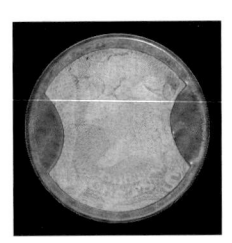

12252 **HB-32 EP-34B 3¢ Ayer's Sarsaparilla Large "Ayer's" Very Fine.** A nice evenly circulated example of this much scarcer variety. The case is problem-free, the stamp somewhat toned and the mica with a number of small chips, cracks and crazes. (350-up)

12253 **HB-34 EP-106 10¢ Burnett's Standard Cooking Extracts Very Fine.** A nice evenly circulated piece, with a reasonably bright stamp, a case with no problems save for a few stains and an essentially perfect mica. (350-up)

12254 **HB-45 EP-36 3¢ Bailey & Co. Extremely Fine.** The stamp is about 80% fully bright, the mica is excellent, with just a few minor surface marks and the case is lightly circulated and mark free. Unfortunately, the case has been cleaned to an unnatural, bright brassy color. Save for that, this would be a four-figure encasement, as Bailey is a rather scarce merchant. (600-up)

12255 **HB-74 EP-39 3¢ Burnett's Cocoaine Kalliston Choice About New.** The case is a glossy, attractive medium-olive brown, the stamp is beautifully bright and the mica crystal clear save for a small craze behind Washington's head. We sold a comparable piece of this number in our January sale for just under $800 and would expect about the same for this beauty. (750-up)

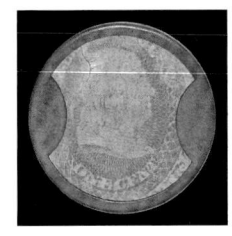

12256 **HB-96 EP-12 1¢ Dougan Choice About New.** A fair amount of original color remains behind the hat and among the letters. This piece is a very beautiful example of the only merchant that bears an illustration on the case. Roughly thirty examples are known for all denominations combined, with about ten of them of this One Cent denomination. The mica on this piece is clear and problem-free, with just a minor natural mark behind Franklin's head. The stamp, while not fully bright, remains attractive, and this piece has excellent eye appeal. A terrific example of a very scarce and highly popular merchant. (3,500-up)

12257 **HB-96 EP-12 1¢ Dougan Very Fine.** Dougan is a rare merchant, with only about 30 examples known for all denominations combined. About ten examples of this One Cent denomination have been traced, and this piece is safely in the top half for condition. Dougan is the only merchant in the Encased Postage series that has an illustration on the case. The mica on this piece is very nearly perfect, with only a few surface marks. The stamp, while not fully bright, has retained strong color. The case itself is a nice natural brass color, flawed only by two small dents at the top: one above the "U" in "DOUGAN," and the other right on the rim. (2,500-up)

Finest Known Dougan

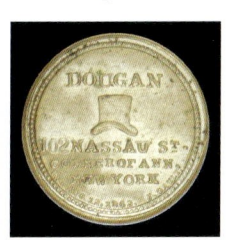

12258 **HB-97 EP-41 3¢ Dougan Choice About New.** About 70% of the original silvering remains on this piece, including some traces on the front of the case. The mica is perfect, and the stamp only slightly toned. This is easily the finest-condition Dougan that we have handled, and it's certainly one of the very finest known. All Dougan encasements are quite rare, with only a total of about 30 examples known for all denominations combined. The 1¢ and 3¢ pieces are represented by about ten examples each. (5,000-up)

12259 **HB-100 EP-13 1¢ Drake's Plantation Bitters About New.** The case is a gorgeous, natural glossy brass color, with virtually no traces of circulation. The stamp is a fully brilliant blue and it is very nicely centered. The mica is essentially perfect, too. Not a rare piece, but in extraordinary condition. (500-up)

12260 **HB-100 EP13 1¢ Drake's Plantation Bitters About New.** A considerable amount of silvering remains between the letters on the back. The case is a medium-brass color, the stamp is very nearly 100% bright, and the mica is clear save for some very minor surface disturbances. A solid problem-fee example. (500-up)

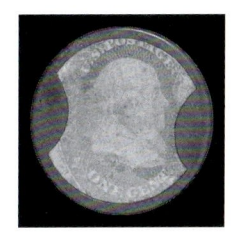

12261 **HB-100 EP-13 1¢ Drake's Plantation Bitters Very Fine.** Clearly circulated but still attractive, with a rather bright stamp and a surprisingly problem-free mica. (350-up)

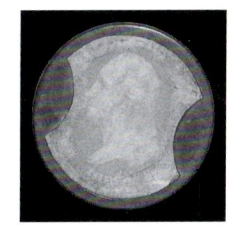

12262 **HB-101 EP-42 3¢ Drake's Plantation Bitters Fine.** Well worn but problem free. This piece has clearly circulated for an extended period of time. It has as much actual wear as we've ever seen on a piece of Encased Postage. It's held up amazingly well, with a problem-free case, a mica that has surface marks only, without cracks or breaks and a slightly wrinkly, toned-down stamp. (300-up)

12263 **HB-122 EP-77 5¢ Tremont House Extremely Fine.** The case is a lovely natural multicolor with no flaws. The stamp is nearly fully bright, and the mica is clear and problem free over most of its surface but with a medium-size hole through to the stamp at the upper right of Jefferson's head. Still a presentable piece that faces-up quite well. (450-up)

12264 **HB-131 EP-78 5¢ J. Gault Choice About New.** A very nearly perfect example with a tightly closed case, a beautifully bright stamp and a mica that comes very close to perfect. A little silvering remains on the back, which is almost never the case on these plain-back Gault pieces, as the lack of relief allowed the silvering to disappear quite rapidly. This is an exceptional little piece! **(550-up)**

12265 **HB-132 EP-79 5¢ J. Gault Ribbed Frame Extremely Fine.** A handsome example with a high-grade problem-free case, a nicely centered, bright stamp and a crystal clear, problem-free mica. This 5¢ Gault is the most available of the ribbed-frame encasements, and is an excellent piece for type. **(800-up)**

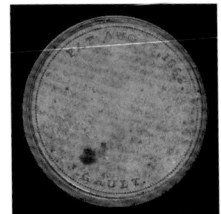

12266 **HB-132 EP79 5¢ J. Gault Ribbed Frame Extremely Fine.** This is the much scarcer ribbed frame variety—it's a nice piece at that—with an evenly colored brass frame, a decently bright stamp, and a mica with only some very minor crazing at its outer edges. There is one small spot of discoloration on the back of the case toward the bottom. **(650-up)**

12267 **HB-133 EP-116 10¢ J. Gault Extremely Fine.** The case is just about perfect, the stamp is only slightly toned and the mica is problem free save for some very minor surface marks. **(750-up)**

12268 **HB-133 EP-116 10¢ J. Gault Extremely Fine.** A decent example with a bright stamp, excellent mica and a damage-free case. A good piece to represent the denomination. **(750-up)**

12269 **HB-133 EP-116 10¢ J. Gault Extremely Fine.** The stamp and mica are perfect. The case is a lovely red mahogany on the front; the back is tricolor with some red mahogany, some medium brass and a stripe of lighter brass. **(750-up)**

12270 **HB-133 EP-116 10¢ J.Gault Very Fine.** The mica is clear and the case is a lovely brass color on this example. The stamp is clean with a little loss of paper at bottom center. **(600-up)**

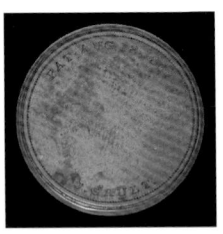

12271 **HB-134 EP-117 10¢ J. Gault Ribbed Frame Extremely Fine.** A very nice example of the much scarcer ribbed-frame variety. The case, mica and stamp are all far above average, and the piece has an excellent overall appearance. This is by far the most available of the 10¢ Ribbed Frame encasements, and it's an ideal piece for type. **(850-up)**

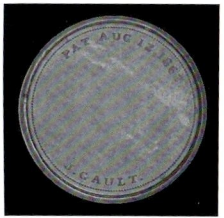

12272 **HB-135 EP-148 12¢ J. Gault About New.** A flawless, clearly original example of the most available of the 12¢ Denomination pieces. The case is a most attractive two-tone brass and reddish brown, with virtually no sign of wear. The mica is clear, with only the most minor of surface blemishes, and the stamp has retained strong color and good eye appeal. The case is tightly, evenly and perfectly closed all the way around. **(2,000-up)**

12273 **HB-137 EP-167 24¢ J. Gault Choice About New.** The case is a glossy, medium mahogany without a trace of a flaw. The mica is clear and problem free, and the stamp, although not 100% bright, is quite close to it. The case is tightly and evenly closed all around, guaranteeing that the genuineness of this piece is beyond suspicion. **(3,500-up)**

12274 **HB-137 EP-167 24¢ J. Gault Choice About New.** A super-quality 24¢ encasement with a perfectly formed, tightly closed case, an ideal mica and an attractive, beautifully centered problem-free stamp, this Gault 24¢ is the most common piece of this denomination, making it an ideal representation of the type. It's possible that as many as twenty examples of this number are known, but it is unlikely that more than one or two others are as nice as this piece. **(3,500-up)**

12275 **HB-152 EP-82 5¢ Irving House Ribbed Frame Choice About New.** This pretty piece is a real contender for the fully uncirculated grade. The case is a beautiful medium-brass color, the mica is essentially perfect and the stamp is beautifully centered and very bright. An unusually nice example of this far-from-common piece. **(1,500-up)**

12276 **HB-152 EP-82 5¢ Irving House Ribbed Frame About New.** The case is a lovely natural light-brass color, the stamp is well centered and fully bright and the mica is clear save for two crazed areas to the right of Jefferson's head. **(1,000-up)**

24¢ Kirkpatrick & Gault

12277 **HB-165 EP-171 24¢ Kirkpatrick & Gault About New.** About 50% of the original silvering remains on the back of this most attractive 24¢ encasement. The mica is clear and undamaged, and the stamp has retained a fair amount of its original lilac color, unlike most 24¢ examples, which have faded to gray. The stamp is also beautifully centered, allowing the entire denomination to be read. If you have been looking for an extremely nice example of this denomination for your set, this is a piece that should be pursued. **(3,000-up)**

12278 **HB-176 EP-21 1¢ Mendum's Family Wine Emporium About New.** The case is a beautifully natural two-tone red and brass, and the mica and stamp are simply as perfect as anyone could hope to find. Mendum's, while not rare, is a much scarcer merchant, and this is a beautiful example that must number among the finest known. **(1,000-up)**

12279 HB-177 EP-52 3¢ Mendum's Family Wine Emporium Extremely Fine. From our FUN 2006 catalog description, "The case shows almost no wear, but the stamp is badly stained and the mica quite cracked. This piece is ex-Stack's Arnold Perl Collection from December 1969. It is either unique or one of two known, depending on the source consulted. No three cent Mendum's was in the massive collection sold by Stacks in June of 2004. This piece has always been considered genuine, and in fact, it may well be. But it certainly has elements that this cataloger considers suspicious." **(3,000-up)**

12280 HB-189 EP-24a 1¢ North America Life Insurance Company "Insurance" Curved Choice About New. A super piece, with 95+% of its original silvering on both sides. The mica is primarily perfect, with a small crazed area at the very bottom, and the stamp is nearly fully bright with one slightly darker area in Franklin's hair. A top-condition encasement that is very likely one of the finest examples of its number. **(1,500-up)**

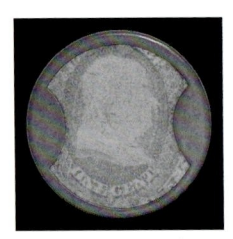

12281 HB-189 EP-24a 1¢ North America Life Insurance Company "Insurance" Curved Choice About New. A second example of this scarcer issue. The case is very nearly uncirculated, with an attractive even-mahogany color and undisturbed glossy surfaces. The mica is perfect, and this piece would be incredible all the way around were it not for a lightly faded stamp. Our January sale had three examples of the "insurance"-straight 1¢, and none of this scarcer, curved variety. Scarce and most attractive. **(1,500-up)**

12282 HB-189 EP-24a 1¢ North America Life Insurance Company About New. A gorgeous piece, with about 50% of its original silvering remaining. The stamp is lightly toned, but its blue remains quite bright. The mica is very nice, with only the most minor of marks. Quite a scarce piece, especially so with this much silver and strong eye appeal. **(1,250-up)**

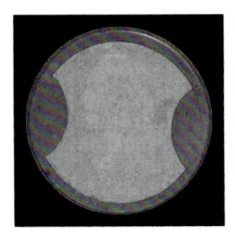

12283 HB-212 EP-55 3¢ Schapker and Bussing Extremely Fine. A scarcer encasement, Schapker & Bussing ordered only the 1¢ through 12¢ denominations from Gault. The 3¢ and 5¢ are the only ones usually seen. This piece has a beautiful dark-mahogany case that comes very close to the full About New grade. The mica is essentially perfect, but unfortunately, the red 3¢ stamp is considerably faded. This should prove to be a relatively inexpensive piece for a merchant set. **(750-up)**

12284 HB-221 EP-27 1¢ S. Steinfeld Extremely Fine. A very attractive example of one of the rarest merchants. The case is a problem-free medium brown color, the mica is essentially perfect and the stamp remains bright and attractive. This 1¢ is the only collectable denomination for Steinfeld; no 3¢ is known, and the 5¢, 10¢ and 12¢ are all considered to be unique. Only about 20 examples of this merchant are known in all grades combined, and this solid problem-free piece is certainly more than halfway up the census for condition. **(5,000-up)**

N&G Taylor & Co.

12285 **HB-225 EP-28 1¢ N & G Taylor & Co. Choice About New.** One of the very rarest of the Encased Postage merchants, with less than 20 examples known for all denominations combined. The 1¢ and 3¢ account for more than half of that total, with the other three known denominations represented by one or two pieces each. This gorgeous One Cent has a beautifully bright stamp, a clear mica and a glossy, light brown, flawless case. The mica has a few minor natural flaws at its bottom, but it is unaffected by circulation-caused defects. This piece is certainly among the top two or three examples of this merchant, and it's the nicest One Cent we have ever seen. **(5,500-up)**

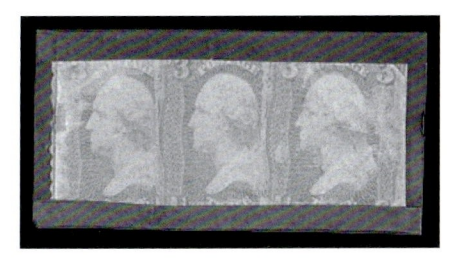

12286 **HB-unl EP-95a 9¢ Strip Extremely Fine.** Often called a Feuchtwanger strip, as the back bears an eagle reminiscent of the Hard Times Tokens from 1837 designed by Dr. Feuchtwanger. This cataloger (among others) has long believed these 9¢ (as well as the identical 27¢) strips were produced in New York City in the 1890's. By the late 1890's, they were appearing on dealer price lists. Nonetheless, they have a long history of collectability, and this is a particularly nice one, with brightly colored stamps, a mica with only a few minor flaws and an attractive high-grade case. **(500-up)**

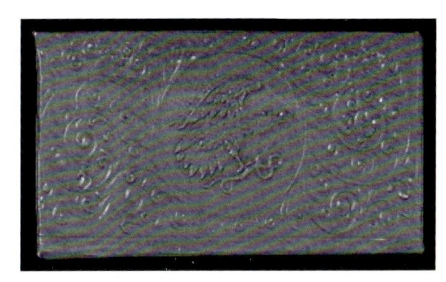

12287 **HB-unl EP-95a 9¢ Feuchtwanger Strip Extremely Fine.** Another example, whose history appears in the previous lot. The stamps are bright, and the case a nice high grade. **(500-up)**

12288 **HB-unl EP-95? 21¢ Feuchtwanger Strip Extremely Fine.** This strip is identical in size to the more-commonly-seen Nine Cent strips, two of which are featured above. This one contains seven Three Cent stamps arranged vertically. The mica is missing, and some light soil at the top of each stamp seems to indicate that this piece circulated in this form at least briefly. **(500-up)**

FRACTIONAL CURRENCY
FIRST ISSUE

12289 **Fr. 1228 5¢ First Issue PMG Gem Uncirculated 65 EPQ.** The colors are completely fresh, and the note would be absolutely superb if the bottom margin were just a touch better. An exceptional example destined for a premium collection. **(500-up)**

12290 **Fr. 1228 5¢ First Issue About New.** Nicely perforated and a single light fold from the Choice New grade. **(150-up)**

12291 **Fr. 1229 5¢ First Issue Very Choice New.** Fully perforated, with only a few short perfs at the right. The colors are excellent, and this much rarer no-monogram piece comes extremely close to the full Gem grade. High grade, no-monogram perforated notes are very underrated in this cataloger's opinion, and this nice piece should garner considerable bidder activity.
From The Jacob and Heather Dedman Collection **(500-up)**

12292 **Fr. 1230 5¢ First Issue Superb Gem New.** Just about as nice as these come, with fresh, original paper surfaces, broad margins all around, bright colors and tons of eye appeal. A note that would likely find its way into a 66 or 67 holder.
From The Jacob and Heather Dedman Collection **(300-up)**

12293 **Fr. 1230 5¢ First Issue Choice New.** Bold ink colors are found on this nicely centered first issue type note. **(100-up)**

12294 **Fr. 1231SP 5¢ First Issue Wide Margin Pair PMG Superb Gem Unc 68 EPQ/65 EPQ.** The face of this lovely pair has earned the 65 EPQ grade, and the back the Superb grade of 68 EPQ. 68 EPQ Specimens will always remain very rare, and this 65 face is quite a nice note in its own right. Expect some strong bids on this pair that could easily reach of four-figure mark. (Total: 2 notes) **(1,000-up)**

12295 **Fr. 1231SP 5¢ First Issue Narrow Margin Pair Superb Gem New.** This strictly original, beautifully bright pair have been cut down from Wide Margin notes. They have broad, even, eighth-inch margins all the way around. (Total: 2 notes) **(300-up)**

12296 **Fr. 1231SP 5¢ First Issue Wide Margin Face Superb Gem New.** An absolutely perfect example, with huge margins, fresh paper surfaces, ideal originality and not so much as a handling mark. Very rarely seen this nice.
From The Jacob and Heather Dedman Collection **(400-up)**

12297 **Fr. 1240 10¢ First Issue PMG Choice Uncirculated 64.** Full perforations all around are noticed with a touch of weakness in them at lower left. **(400-up)**

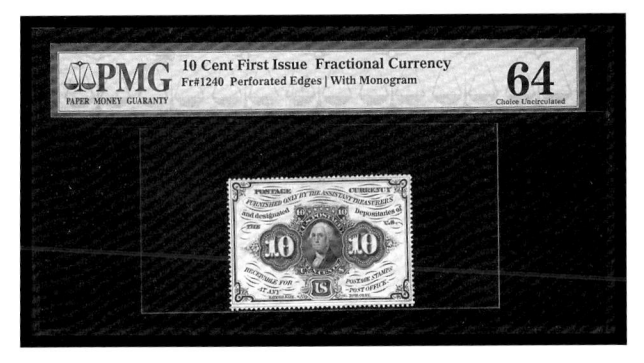

12298 **Fr. 1240 10¢ First Issue PMG Choice Uncirculated 64.** This is a pleasing piece with full perforations all the way around. A little better back centering and this piece is Gem. **(400-up)**

12299 **Fr. 1241 10¢ First Issue Very Choice New.** Fully and deeply perforated all the way around, and with terrific paper color and ideal back centering. The face centering is just a bit short of perfect; otherwise, this note would grade Superb. This perforated, no-monogram note is about three times rarer than the already scarce Fr. 1240, and this is one of the nicer examples we've seen. **(500-up)**

12300 **Fr. 1241 10¢ First Issue About New.** This is a bright and well perforated example of this scarcer no monogram number that displays vibrant ink colors and a light fold. **(300-up)**

12301 **Fr. 1242 10¢ First Issue Gem New.** The top and left margin are the wide sheet selvage, both measuring more than 1/4". The colors are terrific, the surfaces strictly original and the note is a Gem in every sense of the word.
From The Jacob and Heather Dedman Collection **(250-up)**

12302 **Fr. 1243 10¢ First Issue Very Choice New.** The margins are just a bit too tight for the Gem grade, but this scarce, straight-edge, no-monogram example has perfect back centering, excellent color, good paper surfaces and all the other attributes of a Gem piece.
From The Jacob and Heather Dedman Collection **(400-up)**

12303 **Fr. 1243SP 10¢ First Issue Wide Margin Pair PMG Superb Gem Unc 67 EPQ/64.** The Superb back of this First Issue pair has been graded 67 EPQ, and the face, which is its visual match, has been graded 64 by PMG. (Total: 2 notes) **(750-up)**

12304 **Fr. 1279 25¢ First Issue Gem New.** A gorgeous, fully perforated First Issue 25¢ with ideal back centering and face centering that is just a hair off. Likely a 64 at either third-party service, but this quality of perforated note has changed hands as a Gem for decades. 64 or 65 notwithstanding, this is a beautiful piece, with fresh, original surfaces and tons of eye appeal.
From The Jacob and Heather Dedman Collection **(500-up)**

12305 **Fr. 1279 25¢ First Issue PMG Gem Uncirculated 65 EPQ.** A super little note, with deep, perfect perforations all the way around, including a margin strip outside the perforations at the left. Bright, fresh, strictly original and as pretty as they get. **(500-up)**

12306 **Fr. 1280 25¢ First Issue Very Choice New.** A near Gem example of this much tougher, no-monogram perforated note. The perforations are deep and even all the way around, and the note would be Superb if the bottom and right margins were as broad as the top and left. The back is perfectly centered. **(800-up)**

12307 **Fr. 1281 25¢ First Issue PMG Gem Uncirculated 66 EPQ.** Beautifully margined, beautifully bright and a note that appears to have earned its high third-party grade. Tough to find this nice. **(350-up)**

Gutter Fold Error Fr. 1281

12308 **Fr. 1281 25¢ First Issue PMG Very Fine 20.** The PMG comment "Gutter Fold" is denoted on the back of the holder. This is a very nice example with the aforementioned prominent gutter fold error in plain view across the better part of the upper right portion of the note. Errors such as this have been realizing many hundreds of dollars and we would expect the same from this delightful prize. **(600-up)**

Fr. 1281 Inverted Back

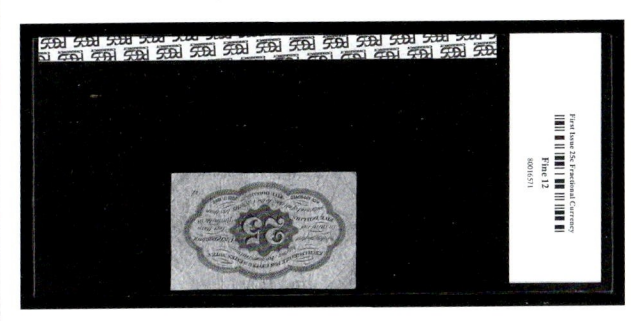

12309 Fr. 1281 25¢ First Issue Inverted Back PCGS Fine 12. While not a terribly rare invert, with about a dozen pieces known, it certainly isn't common either. **(600-up)**

12310 Fr. 1282 25¢ First Issue Very Choice New. Irregularly margined, but clear of the frame line at all points. Bright and very scarce. **(500-up)**

12311 Fr. 1282SP 25¢ First Issue Wide Margin Pair PMG Superb Gem Unc 67 EPQ/66 EPQ. A spectacular 25¢ First Issue pair with broad margins, easily seen paper originality, and razor-sharp print quality. The 67 face alone is an important piece, and the pair together might well exceed... (Total: 2 notes) **(1,500-up)**

12312 Fr. 1282SP 25¢ First Issue Wide Margin Face PMG Gem Uncirculated 66 EPQ. A great looking example on the lighter lemon-colored paper that is occasionally seen. This lighter paper provides a bolder contrast with the brown ink, and provides great eye-appeal. **(400-up)**

12313 Fr. 1310 50¢ First Issue PMG Gem Uncirculated 65 EPQ. Deep, even perforations all the way around, ideal color, fresh paper surfaces and not a hint of so much as a handling mark. The back centering is almost perfect, and the face, although shy of perfection, is nice for the type. A real beauty. **(1,250-up)**

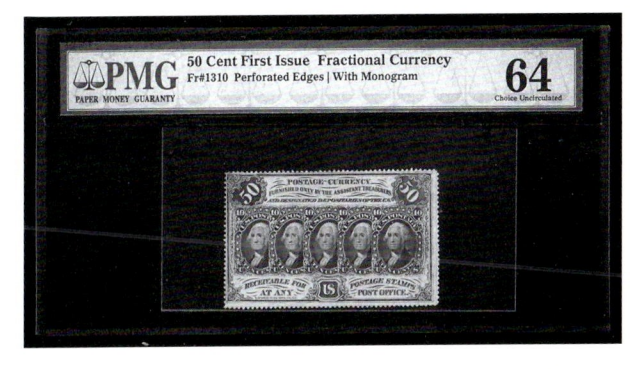

12314 Fr. 1310 50¢ First Issue PMG Choice Uncirculated 64. This is a pleasing perforated variety. **(600-up)**

12315 **Fr. 1311 50¢ First Issue PMG Gem Uncirculated 66 EPQ.** This is a Friedberg number that we have not often seen in Gem grade. It's fully perforated, bright and attractive. This is the highest third-party graded example we have yet to see of this number, and likely one of the very few we ever will see. Truly rare in this grade. **(1,500-up)**

12316 **Fr. 1311 50¢ First Issue Choice New.** Great front to back centering is noted on this original First Issue note. A tiny tip fold is noted on one of the perforated corners but misses the design.
From The Bill and Kathy Stella Currency Collection
(600-up)

12317 **Fr. 1311 50¢ First Issue Choice New.** Fully perforated all the way around, with spectacular color and more-than-acceptable centering. Fr. 1311 is many times scarcer than the with-monogram Fr. 1310, yet it typically sells for only a slight premium.
From The Jacob and Heather Dedman Collection **(600-up)**

12318 **Fr. 1311 50¢ First Issue Very Fine.** A fully perforated no-monogram 50¢ note with an inscription on the back that dates to the week these notes were released, "September 10, 1862 This is the first of this currency taken by N.H. Gleason." A scarce number made additionally desirable by the contemporary manuscript. **(250-up)**

Unique 50¢ Trial-Color Die Proof

12319 **Milton 1DP50F.1 50¢ First Issue Trial-Color Die Proof About New.** Printed on soft, white India paper in black ink, this off-color trial printing is clearly from a brand new plate, as every line of the engraving is razor sharp. There are a few light handling marks and a very tiny paper pull at the lower right, at the "C" in "OFFICE," but the overall appearance far outweighs these minor faults. This magnificent rarity is unique. Not even a rumor of another exists. Although this is a Narrow Margin Proof, the margins are free of the frame line all around the note. This Proof realized $1650 in our January 1997 auction of the Milton Friedberg Collection. Prior to that, it was lot 568 from the Chapman's October 20, 1904 auction. **(2,500-up)**

12320 **Fr. 1312 50¢ First Issue Gem New.** This is an incredible piece, with gorgeous color, broad, even margins, excellent back centering, and tons of eye appeal. An overall exceptional example of a note that is very difficult to find in this grade. **(300-up)**

12321 **Fr. 1312 50¢ First Issue Very Choice New.** Nicely margined, with excellent color, fresh, original paper surfaces and just a touch of handling.
From The Jacob and Heather Dedman Collection **(225-up)**

12322 **Fr. 1312 50¢ First Issue Choice About New.** There is an extremely light center fold on this otherwise Gem example. The margins are broad, the colors perfect, and the center fold is invisible under all but the closest of scrutiny.
From The Jacob and Heather Dedman Collection **(150-up)**

12323 **Fr. 1312 50¢ First Issue About New.** This note was once mounted with a stamp hinge. **(100-up)**

12324 **Fr. 1313 50¢ First Issue PMG Choice Uncirculated 64 EPQ.** The margins are bit tight at the top and lower right. This colorful, straight-edge no-monogram 50¢ note is very scarce in all grades. **(800-up)**

12325 **Fr. 1313 50¢ First Issue Choice New.** A nicely centered example of this very scarce note. The back is perfectly centered, and the paper surfaces are strictly original. This is one of the nicer examples we've seen of this tough number, and with just a tiny bit more margin it would be a full Gem.
From The Jacob and Heather Dedman Collection **(800-up)**

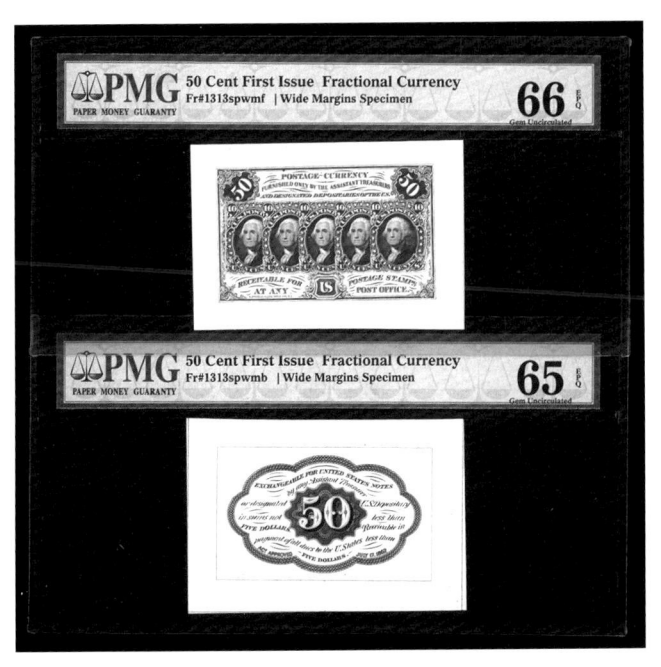

12326 **Fr. 1313SP 50¢ First Issue Wide Margin Pair PMG Gem Uncirculated 66 EPQ/65 EPQ.** Both halves of this pretty First Issue pair have earned the coveted EPQ designation. The face is graded 66, and the back 65. A lovely pair. (Total: 2 notes) **(850-up)**

12327 **Fr. 1313SP 50¢ First Issue Wide Margin Back Choice New.** A Gem but for two very minor stained areas that are visible only on the blank back of this uniface Specimen.
From The Jacob and Heather Dedman Collection **(250-up)**

SECOND ISSUE

12328 **Fr. 1232 5¢ Second Issue Gem New.** All margins are at least 1mm on this note that divulges a partial plate number in the lower left corner. The bronze oval is also placed neatly around Washington's portrait. **(400-up)**

12329 **Fr. 1232 5¢ Second Issue Gem New.** 1232 is a rather common number, but it is seldom found anywhere near as nice as this note. All four face margins are huge, and the note would be Superb but for the back's being centered a hair to the right.
From The Jacob and Heather Dedman Collection **(400-up)**

12330 **Fr. 1232 5¢ Second Issue Vertical Pair About New.** The bronze overprint is reflective on this attractive vertical pair. There is a weak fold between the notes and a long corner fold. **(350-up)**

12331 **Fr. 1232SP 5¢ Second Issue Wide Margin Pair PMG Gem Uncirculated 66 EPQ/64.** The face has been graded 66 EPQ. Both halves are fully wide, with strong eye-appeal. (Total: 2 notes) **(800-up)**

12332 **Fr. 1234 5¢ Second Issue Superb Gem New.** Fr. 1234 is not thought of as a scarce note, and in the real sense, it certainly isn't, although it's greatly outnumbered by the common 1232's and 1233's. In the higher grades, however, the note is legitimately rare, and essentially perfect examples such as this one can be years between appearances. The note is broadly margined, with ideal color, strong, clear bronze surcharges, and virtually perfect centering of both sides. We have sold all of the great Fractional Collections to have reached the market in the last fifteen years, and few of them had a 1234 the equal of this note. A definite prize for the specialist. **(600-up)**

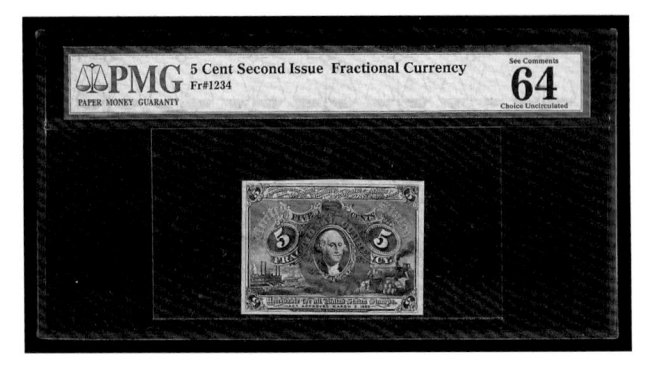

12333 **Fr. 1234 5¢ Second Issue PMG Choice Uncirculated 64 EPQ.** A reflective bronze overprint and distinct surcharges are traits of this fractional. PMG reinforces this notion by stating "Exceptional Paper Quality" on its third-party label. **(400-up)**

12334 **Fr. 1235 5¢ Second Issue Very Choice New.** A fresh, original and very nearly Gem example of this truly scarce Five Cent Second Issue Fiber Paper note. It's a bright, beautiful piece that would be a perfect Gem if it had a sliver more top margin. **(750-up)**

12335 **Fr. 1235 5¢ Second Issue Choice About New.** The bronze oval has been placed neatly over the portrait on this note that has a small corner fold. **(450-up)**

12336 **Fr. 1244SP 10¢ Second Issue Wide Margin Pair PMG Superb Gem Unc 67 EPQ/66 EPQ.** The face has earned the 66 grade and the Superb back 67. Each has the important EPQ qualifier, and both are fully wide and most attractive. (Total: 2 notes) **(1,000-up)**

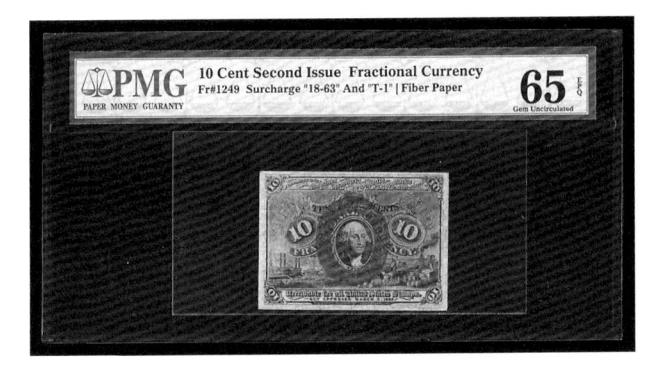

12337 **Fr. 1249 10¢ Second Issue PMG Gem Uncirculated 65 EPQ.** It is likely that fewer than a dozen examples of this Fiber Paper rarity exist in Gem states of preservation. This piece boasts bright paper, solid details, well centered bronze overprint, superb eye appeal. Though the margins are not perfectly equal, they are ample all around and the 'T-1-18-63' surcharge on the back is as sharp as one will find. **(1,600-up)**

12338 **Fr. 1249 10¢ Second Issue PMG Choice Uncirculated 63 EPQ.** This example would make Gem with just a bit more top margin. The colors and overall quality are exceptional. **(800-up)**

12339 **Fr. 1283 25¢ Second Issue PMG Choice Uncirculated 63 EPQ.** The margins vary in size, though the most important margin at top was not trimmed so far as to get rid of the partial Treasury Rectangle. There are two versions about why the stamp, "Treas Dpt." was designed and implemented. The first is the rectangle was stamped on the corner of the sheet to indicate that it had been counted. The other argument is that Congress mandated new paper to circumvent counterfeiting, but this requirement was presumably met by denoting each sheet with the stamp. **(600-up)**

12340 **Fr. 1283 25¢ Second Issue Experimental Choice New.** This uniface 25¢ piece is the most common of the Fractional Experimentals. It lacks the bronze oval, but it has the purple SPECIMEN stamp and the two half-moon cancels. The market had been flooded with these for a while, but they seem to have dried up in the past few years.
From The Jacob and Heather Dedman Collection **(300-up)**

12341 **Fr. 1283SP 25¢ Second Issue Wide Margin Face Superb Gem New.** Deep, original embossing, ideal color and very broad margins are all featured on this Wide Margin Specimen. There is a small portion of a plate number 4 in the upper right corner.
From The Jacob and Heather Dedman Collection **(350-up)**

12342 **Fr. 1283SP 25¢ Second Issue Wide Margin Pair PMG Gem Uncirculated 66 EPQ/64.** The face of this attractive pair is graded 66 EPQ. It has two full cutting guides as well as the plate number "4" in its lower right corner. The back, although it looks lovely through the holder and we can see its originality, was graded 64. (Total: 2 notes) **(750-up)**

12343 **Fr. 1286 25¢ Second Issue PMG Choice Uncirculated 64 EPQ.** Bright bronzing, excellent color and superb margins are found on this lovely example of a much scarcer number. We would not be at all surprised to see this land in a higher number holder some day. **(400-up)**

12344 **Fr. 1288 25¢ Second Issue Choice New.** Strong back to face embossing has produced lines into the portrait caused by the "2" digit in the denomination. The "18" and "63" surcharges are sharp, while the "2" surcharge is clearer than usually seen. A miniscule tear is noticed at bottom center.
From The Bill and Kathy Stella Currency Collection
(200-up)

12345 **Milton 2E50F.7 50¢ Second Issue Essay Gem New.** This note is from our January 1997 Milton Friedberg auction where it was described, "Magnificently sharp printing on stiff, thin yellow paper." The yellowish background gives this note an unfamiliar look, which at a glance makes one think there is some difference in the design. This is, however, a normal 50¢ Second Issue completed face plate, with unusually sharp print quality. The impression was made with such pressure that even elements of the design that typically do not emboss have pressed through to the back of the paper. This is a very attractive and most significant piece not known to exist when *The Encyclopedia of United States Postage & Fractional Currency* was first printed and currently is believed to be unique. A great item for the Fractional specialist. **(2,200-up)**

12346 **Fr. 1314SP 50¢ Second Issue Wide Margin Pair PMG Choice Uncirculated 64 EPQ.** Both face and back have earned the same grade. They are both fully wide and rather handsome. (Total: 2 notes) **(600-up)**

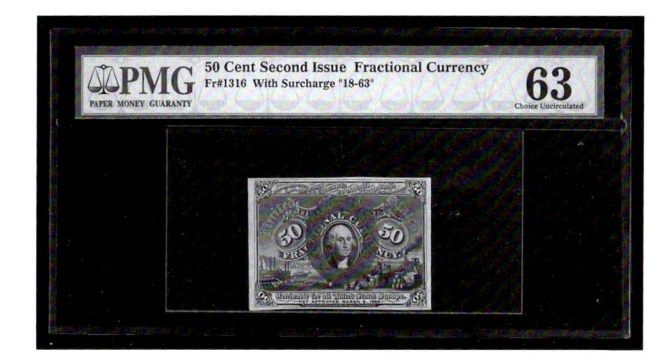

12347 **Fr. 1316 50¢ Second Issue PMG Choice Uncirculated 63.** With a touch better centering on the back at the top this "sleeper" piece would have garnered a higher grade. (500-up)

12348 **Fr. 1320 50¢ Second Issue PCGS Choice About New 58PPQ.** A scarce fiber paper note, this example has abundant margins and crystal clear surcharges which give it the allure of a much higher grade. (200-up)

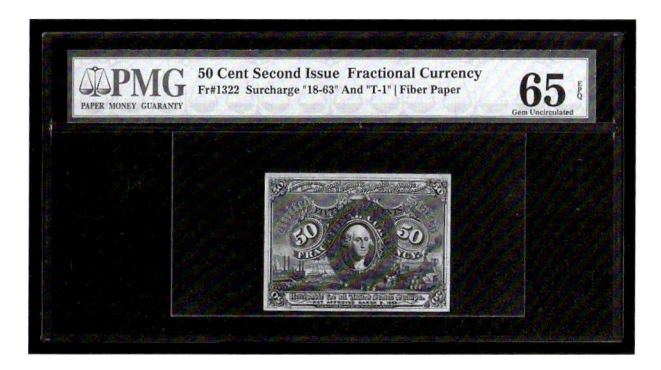

12349 **Fr. 1322 50¢ Second Issue PMG Gem Uncirculated 65 EPQ.** Though this may be the most common of the Fiber Paper issues in Gem, we rarely handle more than three or four Gem pieces in a given year. The bronze oval is nearly centered over Washington's portrait and unlike so many Fiber Paper issues that show some softness in the printed details, this piece remains bold, and perfectly detailed. (1,200-up)

THIRD ISSUE

12350 **Fr. 1226 3¢ Third Issue Gem New.** A lovely note, with broad margins, good paper surfaces, bright colors and loads of eye appeal.
From The Jacob and Heather Dedman Collection (250-up)

12351 **Fr. 1227 3¢ Third Issue Gem New.** Previously Lot 110 from CAA's January 1995 sale of the Gengerke Collection. It was described there, "an utterly amazing Dark Curtain 3¢. While Light Curtain Fr. 1226's are occasionally seen like this, we have never seen or heard of another 1227 in this class. Face-plate number 63 appears at the lower left." This piece realized $577.50 twelve years ago. Also included is the original "Certificate of Provenance" from that sale.
From The Jacob and Heather Dedman Collection (Total: 2 items) (750-up)

12352 **Fr. 1227 3¢ Third Issue PMG Choice Uncirculated 63 EPQ.** A slightly large margin at right and this piece would likely have garnered a higher grade. The details are photographic in quality. (350-up)

12353 **Fr. 1227SP 3¢ Third Issue Wide Margin Pair Superb Gem New.** Both the face and the back are pure white, with bold ink color, broad margins and a wonderful overall appearance. Each is printed on CSA paper.
From The Jacob and Heather Dedman Collection (Total: 2 notes) (750-up)

12354 **Fr. 1227SP 3¢ Third Issue Wide Margin Pair Choice New.** Both the face and back have some minor traces of handling, but the pair have strictly original paper surfaces, good color, and excellent margins. (Total: 2 notes) **(600-up)**

12355 **Fr. 1227SP 3¢ Third Issue Wide Margin Pair.** The face is a beautiful **Gem New** example, and the back has a single, light diagonal fold as well as a few small pinholes. Both pieces are fully bright and fully wide. The back is printed on CSA paper, with two full letters visible; the face appears to be on CSA paper, but the watermark has missed the note. (Total: 2 notes) **(600-up)**

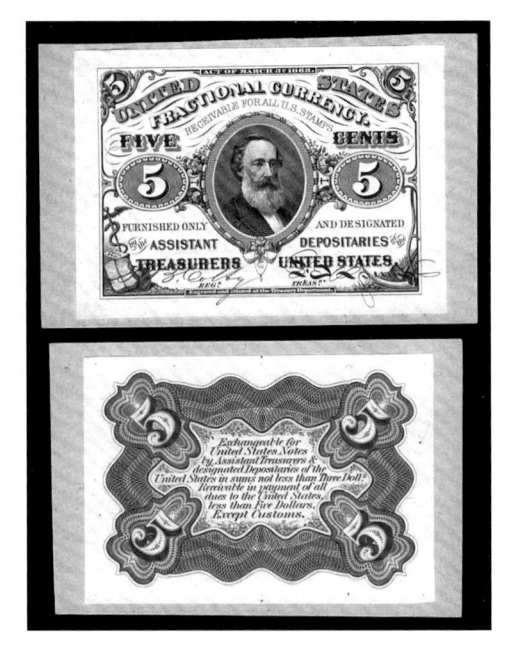

12356 **Milton 3S5F.1c & 3S5R.2b 5¢ Third Issue Proof Pair Gem New.** This pair is from our sale of the Dr. Wallace Lee Collection in January 1999, where they were described as, "Acquired by Dr. Lee from NASCA's April 12, 1981 sale of the Rockholt Collection. These are exceptionally sharp, perfect proofs done on soft white paper which is glued lightly at the tips to a gray light-cardboard backing. They are identical to the notes that appear mounted in the Treasury Presentation books." At that sale 26 years ago, the pair was estimated at $1,000-up and tripled the estimate, realizing $3080. We would expect that they will do somewhat better than that this evening. (Total: 2 notes) **(3,500-up)**

12357 **Fr. 1236 5¢ Third Issue Very Choice New.** A nice Red Back Clark, free of the normal ink smears and quite near the full Gem grade.
From The Jacob and Heather Dedman Collection **(200-up)**

12358 **Fr. 1236 5¢ Third Issue Choice New.** A very minor ink trace at the bottom right of the back holds this broadly margined Red Back Clark from the Gem grade. **(200-up)**

12359 **Fr. 1236 5¢ Third Issue PMG Choice Uncirculated 63 EPQ.** This is a nice red back Clark with four full margins. **(200-up)**

12360 **Fr. 1236/38SP 5¢ Third Issue Wide Margin Set of Three PMG Gem Uncirculated 67 EPQ/66 EPQ/64 EPQ.** All three pieces of this Clark Wide Margin trio have earned the "Exceptional Paper Quality" comment. The face is graded 64, the Green Back, which has the full plate number "19" in its upper right corner, is graded 66 and the Red Back bears the Superb 67 grade. All three have great visual appeal, and this set should prove quite popular with bidders, as high quality Specimens are getting harder and harder to find. (Total: 3 notes) **(1,500-up)**

12361 **Fr. 1236/38SP 5¢ Third Issue Wide Margin Set of Three Gem New.** The Face, as well as the Red and Green Backs, is beautifully wide and brightly colored. There has been tremendous buying pressure on Wide Margin Specimens of late, and we would not be at all surprised to see this lovely trio approach the four-figure mark.
From The Jacob and Heather Dedman Collection (Total: 3 notes) **(800-up)**

12362 **Fr. 1238 5¢ Third Issue Superb Gem New.** A glorious little note, with huge margins, perfect print quality, terrific centering of both sides and all its original embossing present. About as nice an example as you are ever likely to encounter. This one should be headed into a very high grade TPG holder.
From The Jacob and Heather Dedman Collection **(400-up)**

12363 **Fr. 1239 5¢ Third Issue Choice New.** Sizeable margins and embossing are found on this scarcer number with an "a" position indicator on its face. **(150-up)**

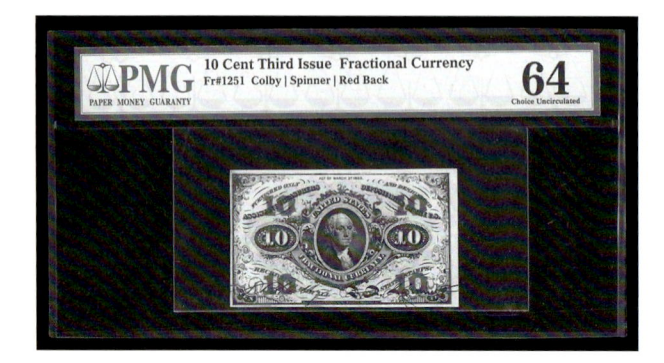

12364 **Fr. 1251 10¢ Third Issue PMG Choice Uncirculated 64.** PMG has added the comment, "As Made Flaw On Back." It's a bit hard to tell through the holder what this is, but it's large, quite noticeable, and it turns this Ten Cent Red Back into a rather interesting Error Note. **(350-up)**

12365 **Fr. 1251 10¢ Third Issue PMG Choice About Unc 58.** Nice margins surround this pretty red back. **(150-up)**

12366 **Fr. 1251/55SP 10¢ Third Issue Wide Margin Set of Three PMG Gem Uncirculated 66 EPQ/66 EPQ/65 EPQ.** All three Wide Margin Specimens have earned the coveted PMG "EPQ" designation. The Face and Red Back have been graded 66, and the Green Back is just a point lower at 65. This lovely Gem trio has terrific eye appeal to go along with the technical accolades assigned by the TPG service. Using "TPG" to mean "third-party grading" leaves this cataloger ill at ease, but as I seem to be the final civilized human still typing out "third-party grading," I have decided to throw in the towel. (Total: 3 notes) **(1,500-up)**

12367 **Fr. 1252 10¢ Third Issue PMG Gem Uncirculated 65 EPQ.** Attractive and deep bronzing is noted on the front and back. The margins are solid for the issue and nearly even all around. **(400-up)**

12368 **Fr. 1253 10¢ Third Issue PMG Gem Uncirculated 66 EPQ.** Four huge margins encircle the frame on this very well printed and boldly signed note. The back displays bright bronzing and fire engine red ink colors. The quality of this note is hard to improve on as there may be no equal. **(1,000-up)**

12369 **Fr. 1253 10¢ Third Issue Gem New.** A broadly margined, well printed, beautiful example with deep original embossing and perfect colors. Both the Colby and Spinner signatures are dark and bold, but neither has begun to erode the paper.
From The Jacob and Heather Dedman Collection **(500-up)**

12370 **Fr. 1253SP 10¢ Third Issue Wide Margin Face PMG Choice Uncirculated 64 EPQ.** A handsome Hand Signed Specimen note with the important EPQ qualifier. **(250-up)**

12371 **Fr. 1254 10¢ Third Issue Very Choice New.** There are a few random offset smears on both sides of this strictly original beauty. If the top margin were just a shade broader, the note would be a perfect Gem. As it is, it's a highly desirable piece, likely in the top ten known. This Jeffries-Spinner signature combination is a true sleeper note. **(750-up)**

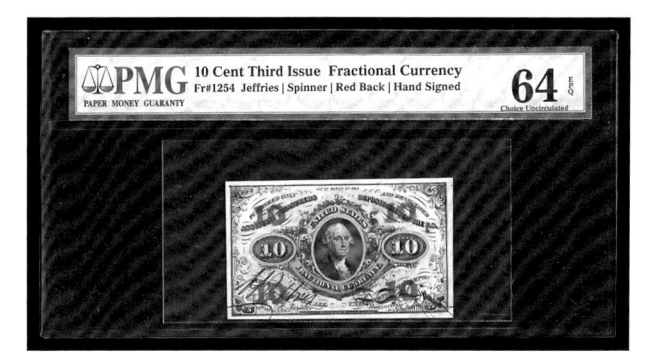

12372 **Fr. 1254 10¢ Third Issue PMG Choice Uncirculated 64 EPQ.** The margins on this Jeffries-Spinner hand-autographed Ten Cent note are a bit irregular, but they are broad enough at all points to support the Very Choice grade. The colors are perfect, the hand signatures are bold and clean, and the eye appeal is exceptional. Fr. 1254 is a very scarce note in any grade. We have always felt it to be outnumbered - about 25 to one - by Fr. 1253, the Colby-Spinner hand-signed note. **(750-up)**

12373 **Fr. 1254 10¢ Third Issue About New.** The top margin touches the design at the right. The paper color is a bit dull, and there are a half-dozen small pinholes. A much scarcer variety. **(200-up)**

12374 **Fr. 1255 10¢ Third Issue Superb Gem New.** Previously Lot 120 from CAA's January 1995 sale of the Martin Gengerke Collection. Re-examining this note over a decade later, we have the same thing to say about it. This is a very common number, but they simply do not come this nice. An exquisite piece worth multiples of a normal Gem 1255. Also included is the "Certificate of Provenance" from that sale.
From The Jacob and Heather Dedman Collection **(350-up)**

12375 **Fr. 1255 10¢ Third Issue PMG Gem Uncirculated 65 EPQ.** The back centering is a touch off, but the face margins are quite even. **(250-up)**

12376 **Milton 3S10F.2c 10¢ Third Issue Proof Choice New.** This is a beautiful proof printing on soft white paper well embossed through to the back. It grades fully Gem, but for some very minor handling marks visible only on the back. This proof appears identical to the pieces found in the very rare Fractional Currency presentation books. **(1,300-up)**

12377 **Fr. 1256 10¢ Third Issue Superb Gem New.** As perfect a Fractional note as one will ever encounter for *any* issue or denomination. The margins are utterly huge all the way around, the bronze is blazing bright, the back centering absolutely perfect and the eye appeal exquisite. Added to that, a partial face plate number appears in the lower right corner. Although this is a rather common number, this piece could easily run away, as no finer example exists to our knowledge. **(250-up)**

12378 **Fr. 1256 10¢ Third Issue PMG Gem Uncirculated 65 EPQ.** This is a lovely example of this much scarcer "1" on face variety. **(250-up)**

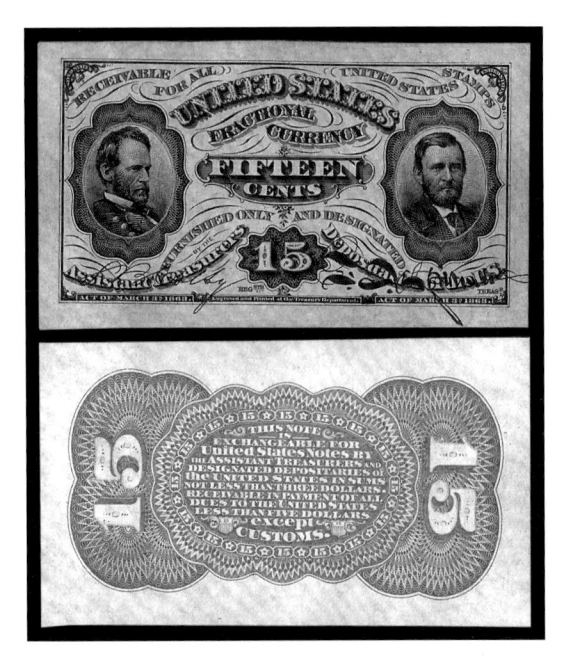

12379 **Fr. 1272/73SP 15¢ Third Issue Medium-Wide Pair Gem New.** Clearly cut down from Wide Margin Specimens with margins that are roughly 1/4" at all points. The printed signature face is paired with a Red Back. (Total: 2 notes) **(1,000-up)**

Exceptional Wide Margin Grant Sherman Pair

12380 **Fr. 1272SP 15¢ Third Issue Wide Margin Pair Gem New.** Both the face and back are fully wide, flawless beauties with ideal color and strong eye appeal. Really nice Grant-Sherman pairs have almost entirely left the market over the previous 24 months, and the prices that these notes are realizing are surprising to some of the old timers. But in reality, the current prices are simply in line with the true rarity and extreme popularity of these pieces.
From The Jacob and Heather Dedman Collection **(2,500-up)**

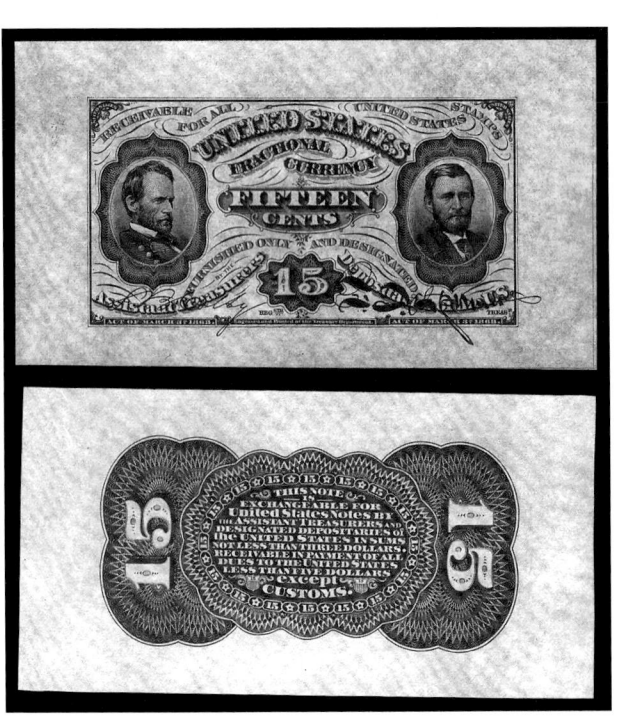

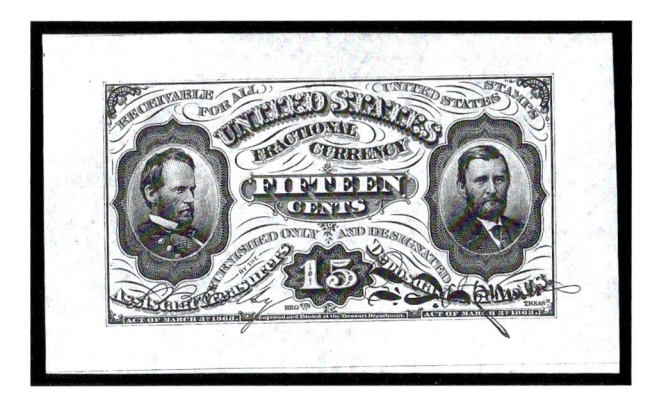

12381 **Fr. 1272SP 15¢ Third Issue Medium-Wide Face Gem New.** This specimen was cut down from a Wide Margin Specimen. The left and right margins are 1/4" deep, while the top and bottom margins are approximately 3/8". The bottom frame line is visible. **(450-up)**

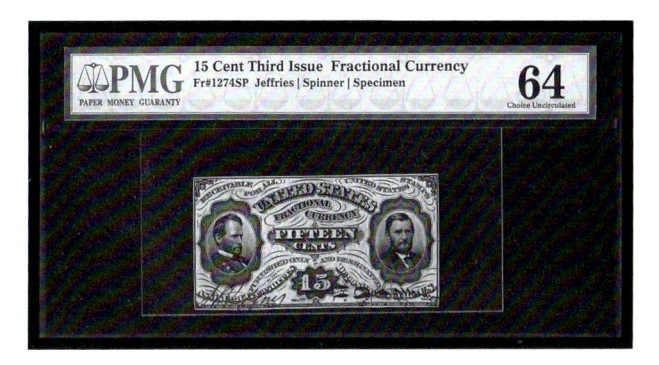

12382 **Fr. 1272SP/1274SP 15¢ Third Issue PMG Choice Uncirculated 64.** This Grant/Sherman pair has been glued together and third party graded. These certainly would have been well received had they actually circulated. **(500-up)**

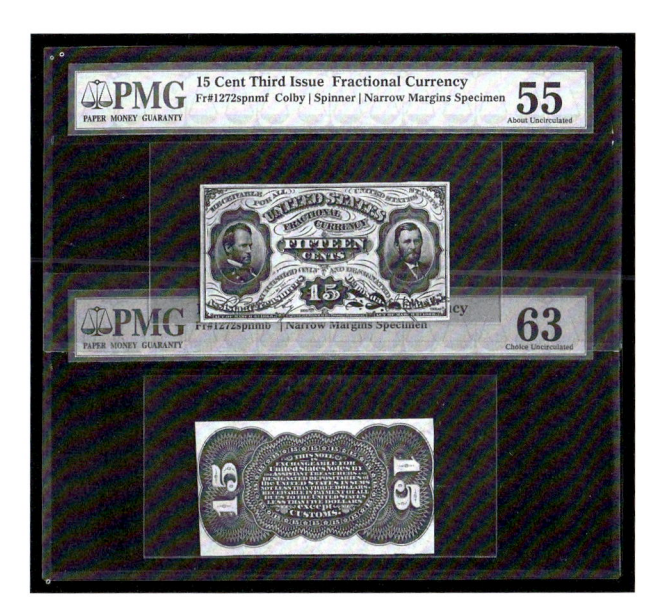

12383 **Fr. 1272SP 15¢ Third Issue Narrow Margin Pair PMG About Uncirculated 55; PMG Choice Uncirculated 63.** This narrow margin pair has both the technical merit and aesthetic appeal of a higher grade, but with some minor shield remnants on the back. (Total: 2 notes) **(900-up)**

12384 **Fr. 1272SP 15¢ Third Issue Glued Pair Extremely Fine.** The back is glued upside-down on this pair that clearly circulated as a 15¢ note—at least briefly. **(300-up)**

12385 **Fr. 1272SP 15¢ Third Issue Wide Margin Back PMG Extremely Fine 40 EPQ.** This Grant-Sherman Green Back has earned the "Exceptional Paper Quality" appellation. **(250-up)**

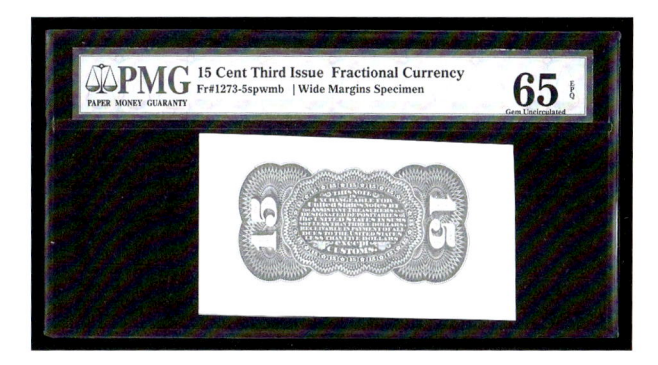

12386 **Fr. 1273SP 15¢ Third Issue Wide Margin Back PMG Gem Uncirculated 65 EPQ.** A handsome and bright Red Back with its bold embossing easily visible through the third-party holder. **(450-up)**

12387 **Fr. 1273SP 15¢ Medium-Wide Margin Back Specimen Third Issue Choice About New.** This is a lovely medium margin back specimen that is of the scarcer red back variety. This specimen was cut down from a Wide Margin specimen and it shows a fold from the bottom edge that disappears shortly after it crosses the red design. **(250-up)**

12388 **Fr. 1274SP 15¢ Third Issue Narrow Margin Pair Very Choice New.** Cut down from wide margins as the margins are broader than typically seen. The signatures are strong, the colors are excellent, and the pair has great eye appeal. (Total: 2 notes) **(750-up)**

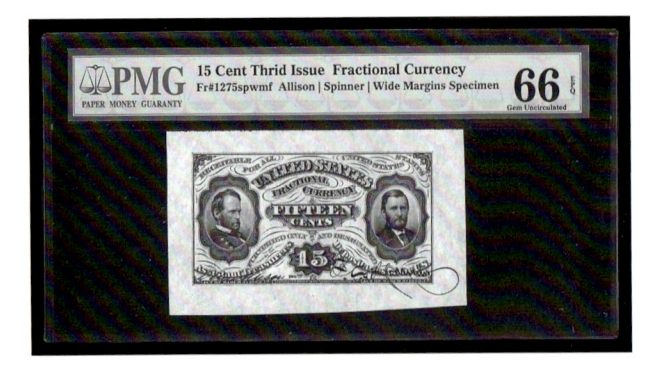

12389 Fr. 1275SP 15¢ Third Issue Wide Margin Face PMG Gem Uncirculated 66 EPQ. Clearly original with good signatures, broad margins, and strong eye appeal. These don't come much nicer than this. **(2,000-up)**

12390 Fr. 1275SP 15¢ Third Issue Narrow Margin Pair Very Choice New. There is a minor stain at the top center of the face on this otherwise Gem pair. The hand signatures are bold and the pair has broader margins than are typically seen on Narrow Margin Specimens. (Total: 2 notes) **(750-up)**

12391 Fr. 1291 25¢ Third Issue Superb Gem New. Flashy bright bronze, huge margins, ideal centering of both sides and fully fresh ink and paper color all combine on this impeccable Fessenden. The deep, original embossing can be easily seen. Simply as nice as it can possibly be.
From The Jacob and Heather Dedman Collection **(500-up)**

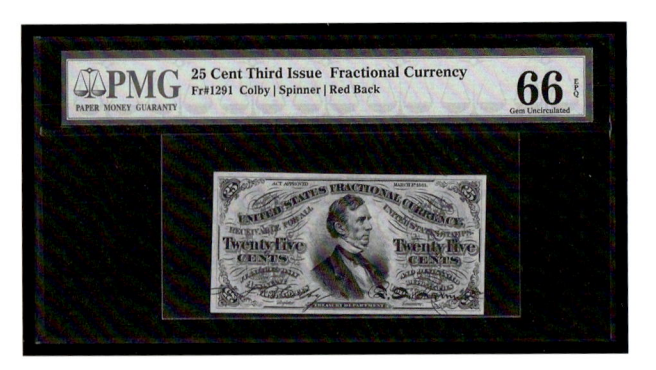

12392 Fr. 1291 25¢ Third Issue PMG Gem Uncirculated 66 EPQ. This note is very similar to one that appeared in our FUN sale earlier this year. It is a stunning Red Back Fessenden with cavernous original embossing, and perfect paper and flashy ink color. **(500-up)**

12393 Fr. 1291/94SP 25¢ Third Issue Wide Margin Set of Three PMG Gem Uncirculated 66 EPQ/66 EPQ/65 EPQ. All three pieces of this Wide Margin Fessenden Set have earned the PMG EPQ designation. The Face and Green Back are both graded 66, and the Red Back is just a hair behind them at 65. A beautiful set, well worth a very strong bid. (Total: 3 notes) **(1,500-up)**

12394 **Fr. 1292 25¢ Third Issue Gem New.** A gorgeous Red Back Fessenden with blazing bright bronze, outsize margins, perfect colors and pronounced original embossing.
From The Jacob and Heather Dedman Collection **(500-up)**

12395 **Fr. 1294 25¢ Third Issue Very Choice New.** This brightly colored Green Back Fessenden comes quite close to the full Gem grade.
From The Jacob and Heather Dedman Collection **(200-up)**

12396 **Fr. 1298 25¢ Third Issue PMG Choice Uncirculated 64 EPQ.** A beautiful example of this much more difficult "a" on face fiber paper fractional that has been blessed with excellent margins, clear surcharges and blinding bronzing. PMG has stated that this note exhibits "Exceptional Paper Quality." This is a much tougher number than the Fr. 1297 type note and will require a healthy premium bid to obtain it. **(750-up)**

12397 **Fr. 1324 50¢ Third Issue Spinner PMG Gem Uncirculated 65 EPQ.** This is a delightful example of this red back Spinner type that has a bright bronze overprint, wide margins, and nice color. **(600-up)**

12398 **Fr. 1324SP 50¢ Third Issue Wide Margin Pair PMG 66EPQ.** A lovely, perfectly matched Wide Margin Spinner pair, both of which have earned the very high 66 grade as well as the EPQ qualifier. Hard to say exactly what these will bring, but they certainly are rare this nice, and Wide Margin Specimens have been fetching strong prices even in far lower grade. (Total: 2 notes) **(1,000-up)**

12399 **Fr. 1325 50¢ Third Issue Spinner PMG Gem Uncirculated 65 EPQ.** Very nice margins, deep, original embossing and perfect color all come together on this "1" and "a" Red Back Spinner. The bottom face margin is a hair tight, which is all that holds this beauty from the Superb grade. **(1,500-up)**

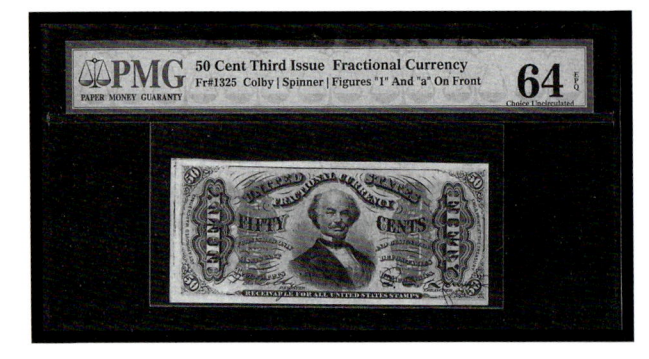

12400 **Fr. 1325 50¢ Third Issue Spinner PMG Choice Uncirculated 64 EPQ.** A near-Gem example of this "1" and "a" red back Spinner. The margins are broad and with a bit of tightness on the right side, and the note has exceptional color and all its original embossing. **(1,250-up)**

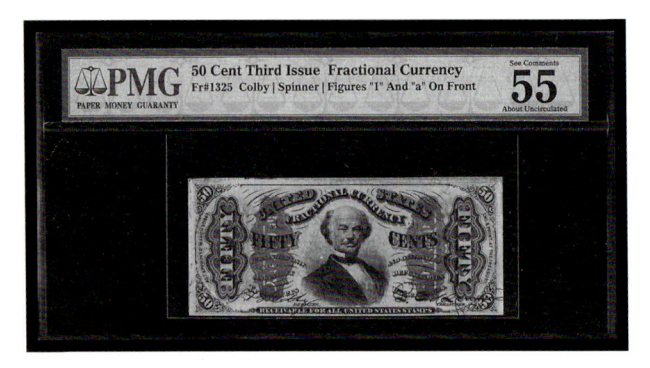

12401 **Fr. 1325 50¢ Third Issue Spinner PMG About Uncirculated 55 EPQ.** A well margined and very well embossed example of this scarce "1" and "a" red back Spinner. Although the centering is not picture perfect the margins are more than acceptable. This is a pleasing example with a couple of small corner folds that account for the grade. **(500-up)**

12402 **Fr. 1326 50¢ Third Issue Spinner Superb Gem New.** Dark inks, overly wide and even margins, plus great centering combine to deliver a note that Fractional specialists will appreciate. **(1,250-up)**

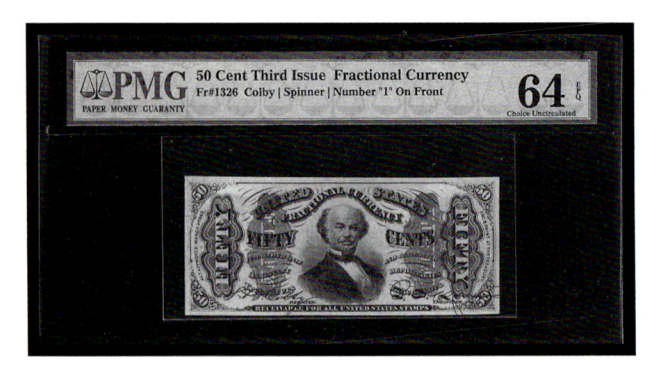

12403 **Fr. 1326 50¢ Third Issue Spinner PMG Choice Uncirculated 64 EPQ.** This Spinner is widely margined and back centering is the only issue that affects the grade. **(450-up)**

12404 **Fr. 1327 50¢ Third Issue Spinner Very Choice New.** This scarcer Red Back Spinner is a Superb Gem from the face. The back is centered a tad toward the right. Save for that trifle, this fully original, deeply embossed beauty, is Superb. **(600-up)**

12405 **Fr. 1327 50¢ Third Issue Spinner Very Choice New.** This is a broadly margined and wonderfully embossed example of this scarcer red back Spinner number that does not get the credit it deserves in terms of relative rarity. Only margin size is the grade limiting factor as the paper surface quality is impeccable. **(600-up)**

12406 **Fr. 1328 50¢ Third Issue Spinner PMG Gem Uncirculated 66 EPQ.** This Spinner variety has a Red Back with "A-2-6-5" surcharges and the large hand signed autographs of Colby and Spinner. Perfectly even margins are noted, with no grade limiting factors visible through the holder. **(750-up)**

12407 **Fr. 1328 50¢ Third Issue Spinner Gem New.** A boldly signed, handsome Spinner with strong original embossing, ideal color and excellent centering of both sides.
From The Jacob and Heather Dedman Collection **(500-up)**

12408 **Fr. 1328 50¢ Third Issue Spinner Very Choice New.** A near Gem example of this always popular hand-signed Red Back Spinner. **(400-up)**

12409 **Fr. 1328 50¢ Third Issue Spinner Very Choice New.** This hand-signed Red Back Spinner has great paper originality, deep embossing, strong signatures and a wonderful overall appearance. It comes quite close to the full Gem grade, but falls short by centering that is only slightly off. **(400-up)**

12410 **Fr. 1328 50¢ Third Issue Spinner PCGS Choice New 63.** Bold signatures and fiery red inks are found on this popular number. **(350-up)**

12411 **Fr. 1328 50¢ Third Issue Spinner PCGS New 62PPQ.** This hand-signed Colby-Spinner note has large margins, good embossing and exceptional eye appeal for the grade. There is a light corner tip fold that is completely contained within the wide left border. **(300-up)**

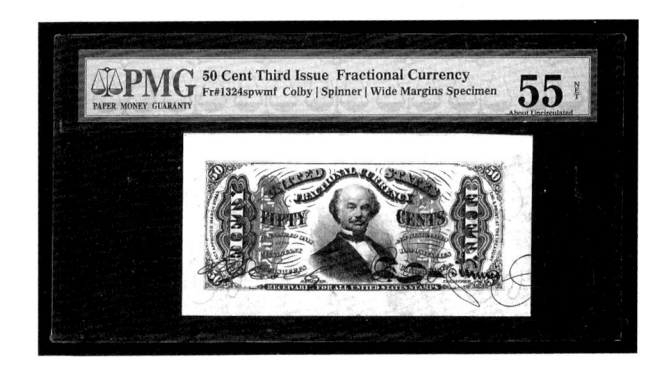

12412 **Fr. 1328SP 50¢ Third Issue Spinner Wide Margin Face PMG About Uncirculated 55.** This hand-signed Spinner is mistakenly called 1324SP on the PMG holder. They seem to have gotten the grade right; they've assigned a "Net 55" grade due to ink burn. This kind of error is re-holdered at no charge, should the buyer care to have it fixed. **(200-up)**

12413 **Fr. 1328SP 50¢ Third Issue Spinner Wide Margin Face About New.** There are a few light folds and some minor ink-erosion holes, but this hand-signed Wide Margin Specimen faces-up very nicely.
From The Jacob and Heather Dedman Collection **(200-up)**

12414 Fr. 1329 50¢ Third Issue Spinner PMG Gem Uncirculated 66 EPQ. Beautiful face margins, ideal color, bright bronze and incredibly deep, original embossing all highlight this much scarcer Allison-Spinner hand-signed note. A little miscut in the upper right margin keeps this piece from an even higher grade. As it is, it's one of the nicest of its number we've seen with back plate 44 seen at lower right. **(1,250-up)**

12415 Fr. 1329 50¢ Third Issue Spinner Gem New. This Allison-Spinner hand-signed note is scarcer than the Colby-Spinner variety by a ratio of at least ten to one. This strictly original note is well embossed and beautifully centered on both sides; well signed with bright bronze and terrific eye appeal. **(800-up)**

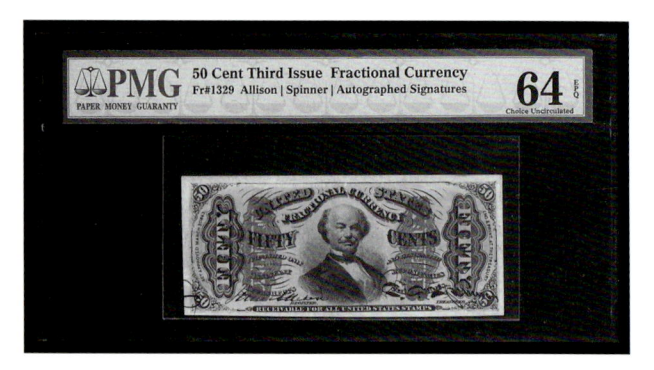

12416 Fr. 1329 50¢ Third Issue Spinner PMG Choice Uncirculated 64 EPQ. This scarcer-signature-combination note has excellent margins, terrific color and original embossing that is readily apparent through the third-party holder. **(750-up)**

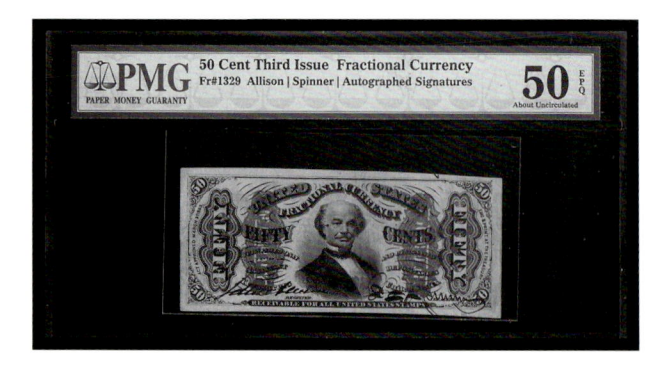

12417 Fr. 1329 50¢ Third Issue Spinner PMG About Uncirculated 50 EPQ. Despite the slight cut at the upper right margin, this is still a pleasing example of the tough Allison - Spinner signature combination. **(350-up)**

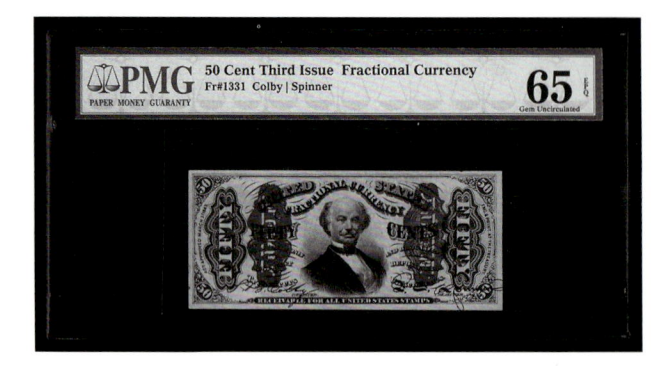

12418 Fr. 1331 50¢ Third Issue Spinner PMG Gem Uncirculated 65 EPQ. Solid margins are noted on both sides of this deeply embossed note. **(600-up)**

12419 Fr. 1331/58SP 50¢ Third Issue Wide Margin Green Back Choice New. Fully wide, with terrific paper originality and just a few light age spots holding it from the Superb grade. **(250-up)**

12420 **Fr. 1332 50¢ Third Issue Spinner Very Choice New.** The most common of the "1" and "a" Spinners, and a very nice example. (600-up)

12421 **Fr. 1332 50¢ Third Issue Spinner Extremely Fine.** A nice, natural problem-free example of this "1" and "a" Green Back Spinner. There are a few as-made press-bed smudges on the back, but the note overall is a lightly circulated, nicely margined, desirable piece. (350-up)

12422 **Fr. 1333 50¢ Third Issue Spinner Gem New.** Excellent centering of both sides as well as deep, original embossing highlight this scarcer Green Back Spinner. (500-up)

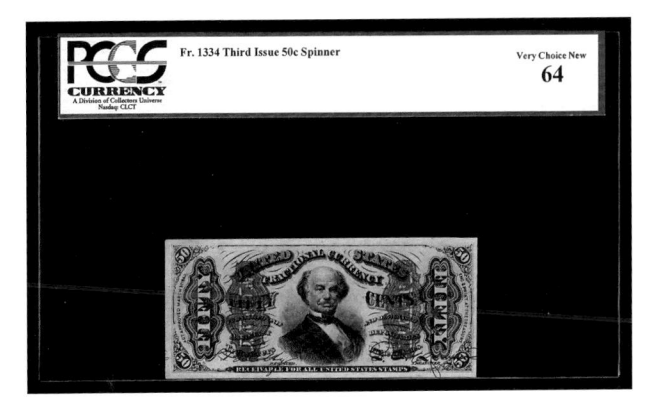

12423 **Fr. 1334 50¢ Third Issue Spinner PCGS Very Choice New 64.** A little tightness is seen in the right margin on this otherwise original example. This is the only distraction on an otherwise Gem piece. (450-up)

12424 **Fr. 1338 50¢ Third Issue Spinner Choice New.** Hugely margined, and close to the full Gem grade. A much tougher Green Back Spinner. (500-up)

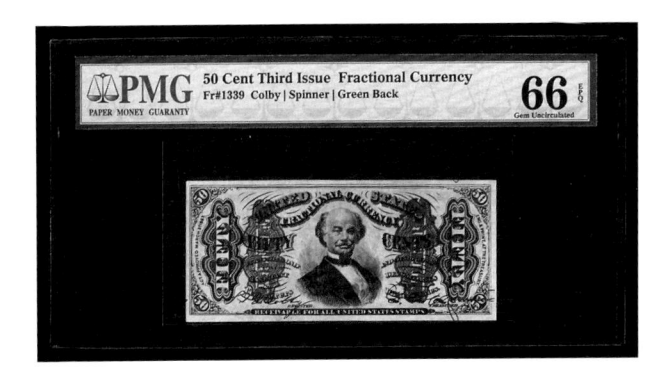

12425 **Fr. 1339 50¢ Third Issue Spinner Type II PMG Gem Uncirculated 66 EPQ.** Unlike many so-called Gems, this exceptional piece boasts broad margins and near perfect front to back centering. (800-up)

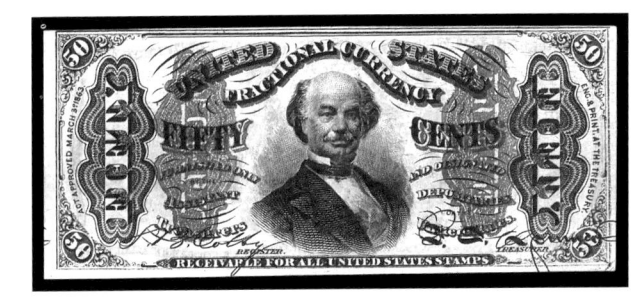

12426 **Fr. 1339 50¢ Third Issue Spinner Type II Very Choice New.** Deep, original embossing, super color and bright bronze all highlight this Type II Spinner. A slightly broader top face margin would carry this beauty to the Gem grade.
From The Jacob and Heather Dedman Collection (400-up)

12427 **Fr. 1339 50¢ Third Issue Spinner Type II Choice New.** A problem-free, evenly margined Type II Spinner example.
From The Jacob and Heather Dedman Collection (300-up)

12428 Fr. 1340 50¢ Third Issue Spinner Type II Choice New.
A bit tight across the bottom, but otherwise a full Gem, with excellent color, perfect paper originality, decent back centering and a most attractive overall appearance.
From The Jacob and Heather Dedman Collection **(650-up)**

12429 Fr. 1340 50¢ Third Issue Spinner Type II About New.
A very nicely margined "1" and "a" Type II Spinner. It has terrific color and all its deep, original embossing.
From The Jacob and Heather Dedman Collection **(500-up)**

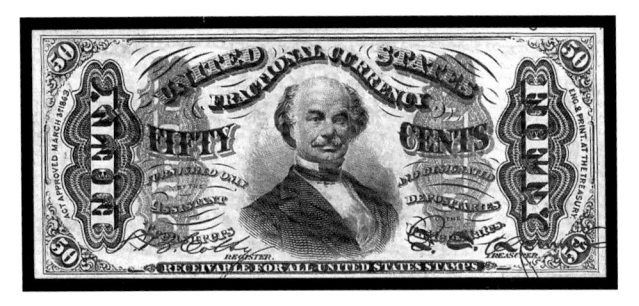

12430 Fr. 1341 50¢ Third Issue Spinner Type II Very Choice New. The margins are just a hair shy of the full Gem grade, but this lovely Type II Spinner qualifies in every other sense. The colors are perfect, and the original embossing is unusually deep and pronounced. **(450-up)**

12431 Fr. 1341 50¢ Third Issue Spinner Type II PCGS Choice About New 58. Superb margins, bright bronzing and exceptional eye appeal are all found on this tougher Type II Spinner note. There is no evidence of any folds visible through the holder. **(175-up)**

12432 Fr. 1342 50¢ Third Issue Spinner Type II PMG Gem Uncirculated 65 EPQ. We handle an average of one or two Gem Fr. 1342's in any given year. This piece, which features broad margins, bright paper, and bold overprints is among the nicest of those Gems. **(600-up)**

12433 Fr. 1343/58 SP 50¢ Third Issue Wide Margined Pair Justice PMG Choice Uncirculated 64. A handsome pair, both with good margins and excellent color. (Total: 2 notes) **(750-up)**

12434 Fr. 1343SP 50¢ Third Issue Wide Margin Face Justice PMG Choice Uncirculated 64. A broadly margined, bright Specimen with reflective bronze. **(400-up)**

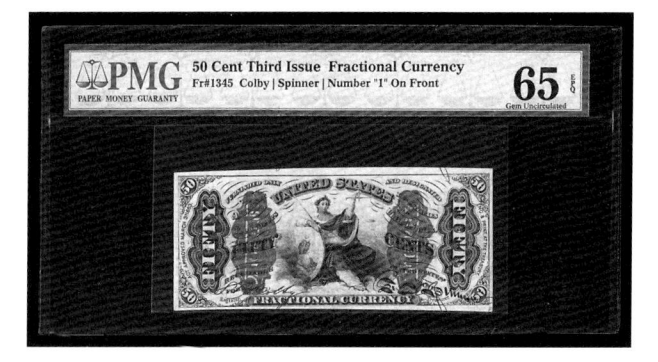

12435 **Fr. 1345 50¢ Third Issue Justice PMG Gem Uncirculated 65 EPQ.** Most examples of this issue have one or more margins that are cut into the design. This issue retains full margins all around. Deep embossing is noted in the bare areas of the red back design. **(800-up)**

12436 **Fr. 1345 50¢ Third Issue Justice PCGS Very Choice New 64PPQ.** The bronzing is very deep on this Red Backed Justice which has nice back centering. Expect the hammer to fall in the area of . . . **(750-up)**

12437 **Fr. 1345 50¢ Third Issue Justice New.** The technical grade does not do justice (no pun intended) to the sheer beauty of this Red Back note. Although the top and left margins are both tightly trimmed, the bronzing is bright, the ink colors are bold and every minute aspect of the embossing can be seen on both sides. There is a small natural spot to the right of the bronzing which should not be misconstrued as a fault. For the grade, this Justice is as nice as they come. **(450-up)**

12438 **Fr. 1347 50¢ Third Issue Justice Gem New.** This Gem has incredible margins for a Justice note, as well as blazing bright bronze, deep, original embossing and sharp printing on both sides. A beautiful, fresh note that is sure to please. **(650-up)**

12439 **Fr. 1347 50¢ Third Issue Justice PMG Choice Uncirculated 64 EPQ.** This pleasing Justice remains quite bright and is well embossed. Better margins would have raised the grade on this pretty piece. **(500-up)**

12440 **Fr. 1347 50¢ Third Issue Justice Very Choice New.** This pretty Red Back Justice comes extremely close to the full Gem grade, a grade that it can claim in every way save for the tight left-face margin. The note has terrific paper originality. **(500-up)**

12441 **Fr. 1347 50¢ Third Issue Justice Very Choice New.** A very attractive Red Back Justice which has bright colors and bold printing. The margins are solid on all sides, though they are a touch tight in a couple of places. **(500-up)**

Fr. 1348 50 Cent Third Issue
Justice PMG 62 EPQ

12442 Fr. 1348 50¢ Third Issue Justice PMG Uncirculated 62 EPQ. A near flawless example of this rare "1" and "a" Red Back variety that is very difficult to locate in any grade but certainly quite a chore to find new. The margins are broad on three sides and very adequate on the fourth. Deep and original embossing is complemented by bright bronzing and vivid ink colors. This is truly a trophy piece that should find its way into an advanced collection and which will instantly augment its status in the pantheon of fractional collections. (2,000-up)

12443 Fr. 1350 50¢ Third Issue Justice Choice About New. A strictly original example of the much scarcer Red Back Justice Number. The bronze is a hair dark and the left face margin a bit tight, but the pronounced original embossing and bright Red Back more than make up for the minor flaws. (250-up)

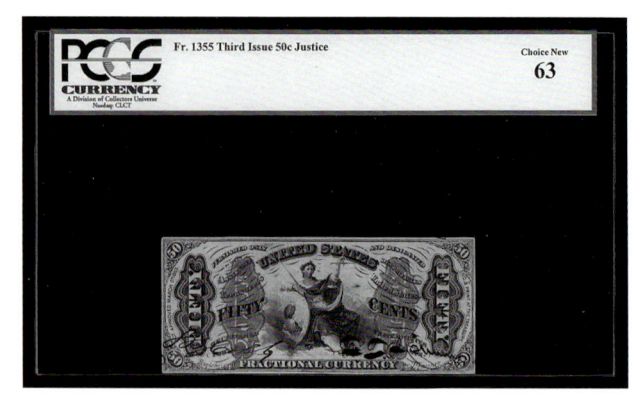

12444 Fr. 1355 50¢ Third Issue Justice PCGS Choice New 63. A nice hand-signed Red Back, with better-than-average centering, decent color and complete margins all the way around. (500-up)

12445 Fr. 1355 50¢ Third Issue Justice About New. A nice hand-signed, Red Back Justice with good paper originality. (250-up)

12446 Fr. 1355SP 50¢ Third Issue Wide Margin Face Justice PMG Gem Uncirculated 66 EPQ. Unlike the majority of hand-signed Specimens on CSA paper, the ink has not cracked. Because of this tendency, few of these will ever receive this EPQ designation. Scarce and undervalued in this grade. (750-up)

12447 Fr. 1356 50¢ Third Issue Justice PMG Choice Uncirculated 64 EPQ. Boldly signed, with good color and the coveted EPQ designation. 1356 is a slightly tougher number than the similar 1355, and it's hard to find graded this high. (600-up)

12448 **Fr. 1356 50¢ Third Issue Justice Choice About New.** A single, light, difficult-to-see fold near the edge on the back is all that holds this originally embossed, boldly signed Red Back Justice from the Choice New grade. **(250-up)**

Fr. 1357 Inverted Back Engraving

12449 **Fr. 1357 50¢ Third Issue Justice Inverted Back Engraving PMG About Uncirculated 55.** PMG comments, "Great Embossing, Vivid Details," on this high-end AU 1357 Invert. As a normal note without the inverted engraving, this would be a $1000-plus note. **(2,000-up)**

12450 **Fr. 1357 50¢ Third Issue Justice About New.** There is a short repaired split on the top center on this scarce, hand-signed, fiber-paper Justice. **(750-up)**

12451 **Fr. 1357 50¢ Third Issue Justice About New.** This hand-signed Red Back Fiber Paper Justice is a scarce and underrated note in all grades. This example, in spite of its light circulation, is one of the better pieces we've seen. It's extraordinarily well margined for a Justice note. The pen signatures are strong, the surfaces are strictly original and the bronze reflectively bright. In our opinion, high-quality circulated notes like this one should be worth more money than the higher-priced, scruffy uncirculated pieces that tend to appear. **(800-up)**

12452 **Fr. 1358 50¢ Third Issue Justice Very Choice New.** Two of the margins are huge, and two are small but more than adequate for a Justice. The back centering is excellent, as are the colors, and the original embossing is pronounced and unmistakable. A really pretty note, worth just about full Gem money.
From The Jacob and Heather Dedman Collection **(650-up)**

12453 **Fr. 1358SP 50¢ Third Issue Justice Choice About New.** Much of the appearance of a Gem, but with minor mounting marks and a bit of handling. This note exhibits the full plate number 15 which, interestingly enough, is not in one of the corners, but along the bottom margin, an inch and a half in from the edge.
From The Jacob and Heather Dedman Collection **(200-up)**

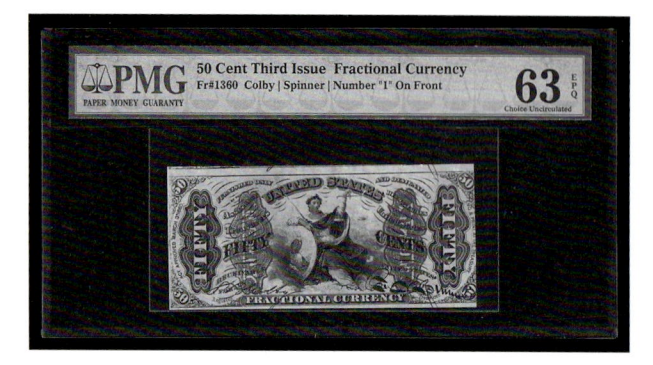

12454 **Fr. 1360 50¢ Third Issue Justice Choice Uncirculated 63 EPQ.** Natural paper ripple and embossing are traits of this tougher Justice with the unusually large "1" sheet position indicator. The right-hand edge is just inside the frame line of this EPQ note. **(700-up)**

12455 **Fr. 1360 50¢ Third Issue Justice Choice About New.** Typical Justice centering, with the right face margin cut into the design, but with terrific color and excellent paper originality. A much tougher number. **(300-up)**

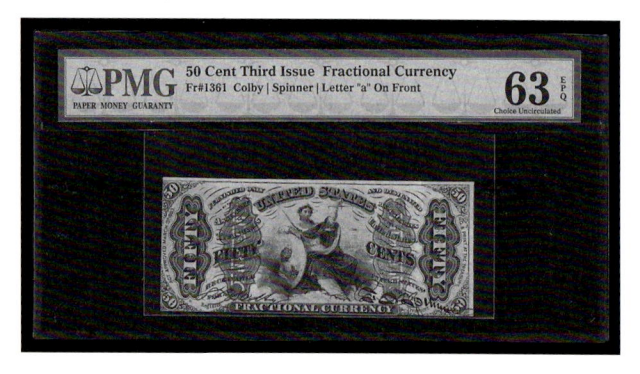

12456 **Fr. 1361 50¢ Third Issue Justice Choice Uncirculated 63 EPQ.** Wonderful inks, embossing, and a nice bronze overprint define this Justice. **(500-up)**

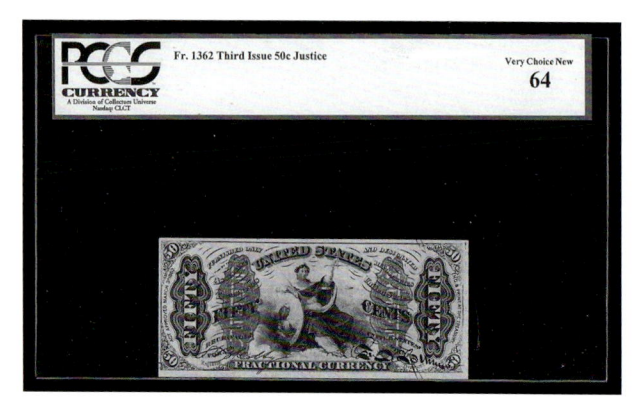

12457 **Fr. 1362 50¢ Third Issue Justice PCGS Very Choice New 64.** A near Gem example and an ideal Green Back Justice. It has bright bronze and deep inks. Three of the margins are sizeable while the fourth at left is smaller but complete. **(600-up)**

Milton 3R50.10d Inverted Back Surcharge

12458 **Fr. 1362 Milton 3R50.10d 50¢ Third Issue Justice Inverted Back Surcharge Choice Extremely Fine.** This group of Justices (Fr. 1362-1365) is very rare as Inverts, with only nine or so pieces traced, and only about three are Fr. 1362's. As a type, there are around 30 total Justice Inverts. This is a nice example for the specialist or the collector looking for a single invert example. **(2,000-up)**

12459 **Fr. 1363 50¢ Third Issue Justice About New.** A single, light center fold holds this "1" and "a" Justice from the Choice New grade. The face margins are exceptional for a Justice, and the appearance is enhanced by bright bronze and strong print quality.
From The Jacob and Heather Dedman Collection **(400-up)**

12460 **Fr. 1364 50¢ Third Issue Justice Choice New.** The bronze overprint is strong on this example that is missing its lower right corner tip starting at the frame line. The top margin is just inside the frame line. **(850-up)**

12461 **Fr. 1366 50¢ Third Issue Justice PMG Uncirculated 62 EPQ.** This is a near-Choice example of this much scarcer Justice type. **(500-up)**

12462 **Fr. 1366 50¢ Third Issue Justice About New.** The bronze overprint is bold on this lightly handled example. **(400-up)**

12463 **Fr. 1366 50¢ Third Issue Justice Choice About New.** Three of the margins are huge on this bright, strictly original example of a much tougher number. The right face margin touches the design, and there is a light center fold, but the positive attributes of this 1366 should carry it to or above... **(500-up)**

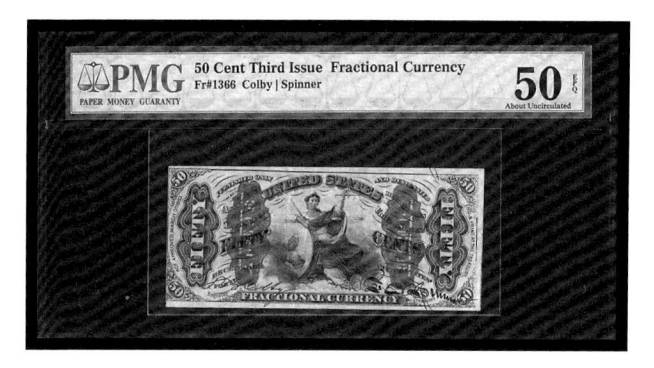

12464 **Fr. 1366 50¢ Third Issue Justice PMG About Uncirculated 50 EPQ.** A lovely note with bright colors of the paper, inks and bronze, terrific original embossing and decent margins. The side margin is close at left, and the note has a light center fold. The start of a back plate number appears partially at lower right in the form of a # 3. **(500-up)**

12465 **Fr. 1368 50¢ Third Issue Justice Choice About New.** The side margins are a bit tight on this very scarce Justice Number, but the top and bottom margins are overly generous. The colors of the ink, paper, and bronze are all terrific, and the note is a broad corner fold away from the Choice New grade. The original embossing is pronounced, and this is one of the nicer ones we've seen of this scarcer number. **(1,250-up)**

12466 **Fr. 1370 50¢ Third Issue Justice Very Choice New.** Extremely well margined, with bright bronze and unusually bright paper for a fiber-paper note. Only the somewhat low back centering holds this striking piece from the full Gem grade. Fiber Paper Justices in attractive, undamaged, uncirculated condition are extremely underrated. **(1,000-up)**

12467 **Fr. 1370 50¢ Third Issue Justice About New.** This fiber-paper Justice is a light center fold away from the Choice New grade. **(250-up)**

12468 **Fr. 1372 50¢ Third Issue Justice Choice New.** This Fiber Paper Justice has incredible print quality, fully original paper surfaces and beautifully bright bronze. With just slightly better centering, it would be one of only two or three truly Gem 1372's that we have ever seen. As it is, it clearly falls in the top ten for condition census, and even higher than that for eye appeal. An exceptional note, quite rare this nice. **(1,500-up)**

12469 **Fr. 1372 50¢ Third Issue Justice PMG Choice Extremely Fine 45 EPQ.** A wonderfully margined example of this scarce Justice fiber paper variety that certainly appears to be deserving of the grade assigned. **(400-up)**

FOURTH ISSUE

12470 **Fr. 1257 10¢ Fourth Issue Superb Gem New.** The watermark is a little hard to spot on this one, but it is definitively present. The note has broad, even margins, perfect centering of both sides, excellent color and most of seal plate #30 in the bottom face margin.
From The Jacob and Heather Dedman Collection **(450-up)**

12471 **Fr. 1257 10¢ Fouth Issue Superb Gem New.** Bright colors, beautiful margins, a bold watermark and tons of eye appeal all come together on this gorgeous little note. A large clump of bright pink fiber on Liberty's face adds an interesting touch to this beautiful piece.
From The Jacob and Heather Dedman Collection **(450-up)**

12472 **Fr. 1257 10¢ Fourth Issue PMG Gem Uncirculated 66 EPQ.** While this is certainly a common type it becomes much more challenging to locate in the upper gem grade range. This example has good centering and excellent color to lend credence to the grade. **(400-up)**

12473 **Fr. 1257 10¢ Fourth Issue PMG Gem Uncirculated 66 EPQ.** Four boardwalk margins and perfect centering combine to make this note as nice as any imaginable. This cataloger, who has seen his fair share of high grade fractionals, is left scratching his head as to how this did not garner an extra point or two from the PMG gang. As we delve more deeply into TPG (Third Party Grading) parlance this note could be a perfect candidate for a potential upgrade. **(400-up)**

12474 **Fr. 1257 10¢ Fourth Issue PMG Choice Uncirculated 64 EPQ.** Three huge margins on the front are matched with a thin one at left. The inks are deep with vibrant color throughout. **(200-up)**

12475 **Fr. 1267 15¢ Fourth Issue PMG Choice Uncirculated 64.** A little tightness at the top keeps this piece from a higher grade. **(200-up)**

12476 **Fr. 1267 15¢ Fourth Issue Choice About New.** Beautifully margined 15¢ note that has a single extremely light centerfold, and the appearance of a perfect Gem. **(125-up)**

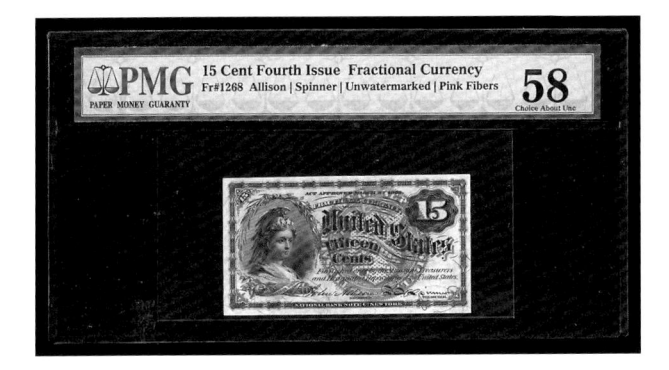

12477 **Fr. 1268 15¢ Fourth Issue PMG Choice About Unc 58.** This is the far rarer variety without the USUSUS watermark. This note has enormous margins, perfect face centering and robust ink colors. This is a real beauty which faces up as a superb gem and upon viewing the note through the holder at virtually every angle we cannot find even a hint of circulation. This is a rare number and with a bright and flawless example such as this that does not have even a trace of a watermark the attribution is rather easy. The few auction records that exist for this variety prove that even for a nice AU a four figure price is in order and with its outstanding eye appeal it could realize a runaway price. **(1,500-up)**

12478 **Fr. 1269 15¢ Fourth Issue PMG Superb Gem Unc 67 EPQ.** Spectacular Fourth Issue 15¢ pieces are more often seen among the Fr. 1267 issues. This piece is one of the nicest Fr. 1269's we've seen with deep blue color and broad, even margins. **(600-up)**

12479 **Fr. 1271 15¢ Fourth Issue Gem New.** Broadly margined with terrific color, perfect paper surfaces, and great eye appeal all adorn this note. **(350-up)**

12480 **Fr. 1271 15¢ Fourth Issue PCGS Choice New 63PPQ.** Brightly colored and with good original embossing, this 15¢ makes the Gem grade but for its bottom left margin which is slightly close. **(300-up)**

12481 **Fr. 1271 15¢ Fourth Issue Fine.** This Fifteen Cent note, though well circulated, has the most convincing brown seal we've seen for this denomination. **(250-up)**

12482 **Fr. 1307 25¢ Fourth Issue PMG Gem Uncirculated 66 EPQ.** A delightful example of this very scarce Washington variety with the smaller red seal and blue fibers. The margins are broad and the eye appeal is absolutely superb. PMG has also bestowed this note with the added "EPQ" suffix for "Exceptional Paper Quality." **(400-up)**

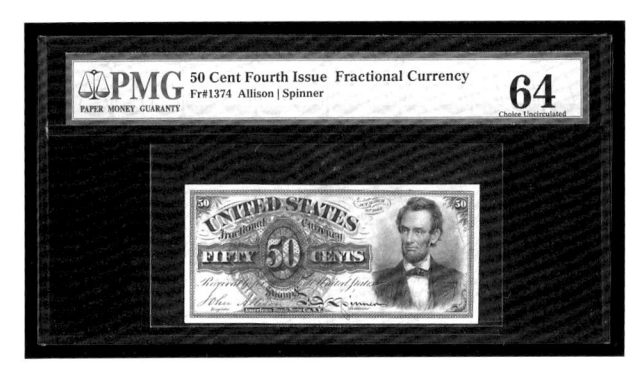

12483 **Fr. 1374 50¢ Fourth Issue Lincoln PMG Choice Uncirculated 64.** It's a bit hard to figure out what's going on here. This Lincoln has huge margins, ideal centering, spectacular eye appeal and all the visual allure of a Superb piece. We're guessing that there is a minor hidden flaw that can't be seen through the holder, as it sure looks like a 67 or better to us. **(550-up)**

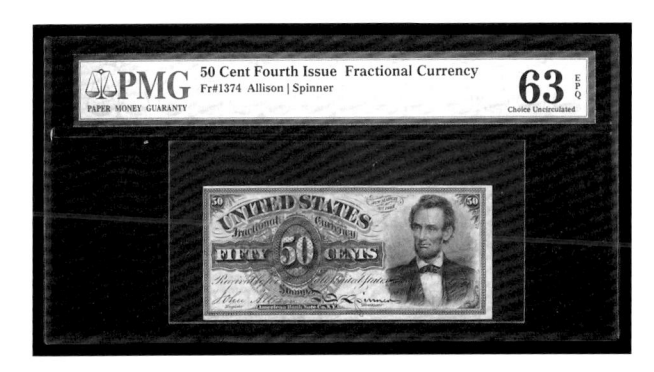

12484 **Fr. 1374 50¢ Fourth Issue Lincoln PMG Choice Uncirculated 63 EPQ.** The left side is a bit thin on this otherwise colorful Lincoln. **(500-up)**

12485 **Fr. 1376 50¢ Fourth Issue Stanton Choice New.** This solid piece is a little tight at the lower margin, though the paper quality is excellent. A touch of handling is noted. **(300-up)**

12486 Fr. 1379 50¢ Fourth Issue Dexter PMG Gem Uncirculated 66 EPQ. This is another abundantly margined and perfectly centered Dexter which appears to be graded somewhat conservatively. The ink colors are bright and the eye appeal exceptional for this lovely type note. While Dexters certainly are common up until the "64" grade they become decidedly scarcer in the gem grades. (500-up)

12487 Fr. 1379 50¢ Fourth Issue Dexter PMG Gem Uncirculated 66 EPQ. Behemoth margins and flawless paper surfaces are found on this high grade Dexter which has perfect centering seen on both sides. The few examples that we have had in this grade have realized between $500-$600 and we see no reason for anything less in today's rapidly expanding marketplace. (500-up)

12488 Fr. 1379 50¢ Fourth Issue Dexter PMG Gem Uncirculated 65 EPQ. The "Exceptional Paper Quality" designation is clearly earned on this high grade Dexter that has been blessed with sizeable margins and bold printing. (350-up)

12489 Fr. 1379 50¢ Fourth Issue Dexter PMG Gem Uncirculated 65 EPQ. Gem condition Dexters are a statistical anomaly since they infrequently are found with both the margin size and centering required for the grade. This example has both bountiful margins and exceptional centering as well as vibrant ink colors. (350-up)

12490 Fr. 1379 50¢ Fourth Issue Dexter Gem New. A really nice Dexter, with good paper color, broad margins and terrific eye appeal. (300-up)

FIFTH ISSUE

12491 Fr. 1308 25¢ Fifth Issue PMG Gem Uncirculated 65 EPQ. This long key variety is a touch scarcer than the thick key. Bright colors dominate the surface of this piece. (200-up)

FRACTIONAL SHIELDS

12492 Fractional Currency Shield, With Gray Background. This Shield gives an overall impressive appearance. It does not suffer from the water staining so typical of these majestic numismatic items. The white backing is bright for a 140 year old item that has proudly been displayed during its lifetime. The Shield also looks like it is housed in a near-period frame. The brown paper back enclosure and hanging wire are probably of a more recent vintage. About half the notes show ink fading of different degrees and the penmanship on the hand-signed notes shows some fading, too. Nonetheless an attractive, pleasing Shield that is far better than most and ready to settle down in your den or study. (4,000-up)

12493 **Fractional Currency Shield, With Pink Background.** Far and away the worst Pink Shield this cataloger has ever seen, and it is likely the worst that exists. Were it not for the fact that we are playing favorites due to the consignor being a close friend, we would say bad things about this shield. Most of the notes are damaged, but some of the damage is difficult to see because of the stains. The shield has been cut out into the design all the way around, and the notes are aged, torn, stained, and generally repulsive. Nonetheless, this is a very rare Pink Shield. Only about 20 of these exist, and for condition, this piece is clearly in the top 25. The gold-leafed elaborate frame, although not perfect, is definitely the high point of this offering. Nice Pink Shields are worth about $20,000 on the current market. Assigning a value to this presently offered piece is a challenge that we will avoid. Offered without estimate.

MIXED FRACTIONAL

12494 Three 5¢ Second Issues including Fr. 1232 **XF-About New;** Fr. 1233 **VF;** and Fr. 1234 **XF.** The bronze on the Fr. 1233 has oxidized. (Total: 3 notes) **(100-up)**

12495 A trio of Clarks including Fr. 1236 **Choice About New;** Fr. 1238 **Choice New;** and Fr. 1239 **About New,** with left edge press bed smearing. (Total: 3 notes) **(300-400)**

CONFEDERATE NOTES

12496 **T5 $100 1861.** This $100 was printed by the Southern Bank Note Company. It has been cut cancelled and nicely repaired. It has also been punch cancelled ten times. The punch cancels were repaired at one time in the distant past, but nine of the PC repairs have since failed. This was a common way to cancel this issue. A small edge tear has also been repaired. The note remains attractive and it also becomes a more affordable representative of a very difficult type as only 5798 were printed. The back reveals an endorsement, a small red "H", and an April 21, 1863 stamping for 425 days of interest. These notes were not the first notes to be issued from the new Confederate capital at Richmond, but the "First Richmond" moniker has stuck since the earliest days of collecting Confederate notes. **Fine-Very Fine,** CC and POC. (750-1,000)

PMG Choice Uncirculated 63 EPQ $50 T-6

12497 **T6 $50 1861.** This nicely embossed example has dark green ink and bright paper seen through the holder. The penmanship is dark, while the sound edges are clear of the frame line. A superior note for the grade of a type that had only 5,798 issued, this one by Major Anderson of Memphis. Graded **Choice Uncirculated 63 EPQ** by PMG. (6,000-8,000)

12498 T6 $50 1861. This scarce note has the folds of a **Very Fine,** yet the right edge has three missing notches and several other small edge tears are noticed. The far right quarter panel also shows aging while the green overprint remains dark. These were printed by the Southern Bank Note Company. These engraved notes (and T5s) were ordered in May 1861 through the ABNCo branch in New Orleans. The parent company had issued orders not to aid the South, therefore managing partner Samuel Schmidt came up with the Southern Bank Note Company name. Needless to say not very many people were fooled. (300-500)

12499 T7 $100 1861. This scarce type rarely comes with this amount of eye appeal in a moderately circulated specimen. More interesting is the missing REAS in For Treas in the lower right hand corner. A foldover error resulted in the omission and it is the first we've seen. **Very Fine.** (2,500-3,000)

12500 T8 $50 1861 Cr. 19 PF-7. This George Washington note is an attractive **Choice Crisp Uncirculated** issue with solid margins all around. Signed by C. C. Thayer and Jno. Ott. (600-800)

12501 T8 $50 1861 Cr-15/17, PF-2. Some faint handling is noted on this wholly original and bright Confederate issue, graded **Choice About Uncirculated 58** by PMG. (400-500)

12502 T8 $50 1861. Light handling is noticed on this note that may have been mounted at one time. **PMG About Uncirculated 55.** (300-400)

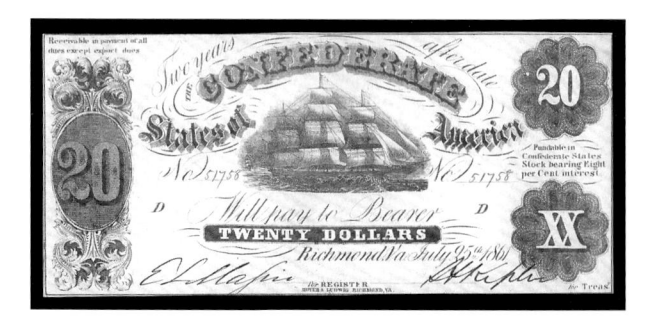

12503 T9 $20 1861. This thick paper variety grades **Crisp Uncirculated.** Just a little better cut and this note would be Choice. Overall a handsome note. (500-750)

12504 T10 $10 1861. This moderately circulated piece displays good paper quality and most importantly has not been cancelled. Overall, the design is solid and well detailed. **PMG Fine 12.** (400-500)

12505 T10 $10 1861. This is a thin paper example that also has "for" added by the signer for the Treasurer. The back reveals a right edge repair. **Very Good.** (200-300)

12506 T11 $5 1861. This is a scarce CSA note with this being a choice note for the grade. The edges and paper are nice and the circulation is evenly dispersed across the note. A lightly pencilled "15" is found on the back along with a stamped "S.H.L. October 1861." COC/HOC notes are not priced in Fricke above G-VG. **Fine,** COC. (1,000-1,500)

Scarce T-12 Manouvrier Note

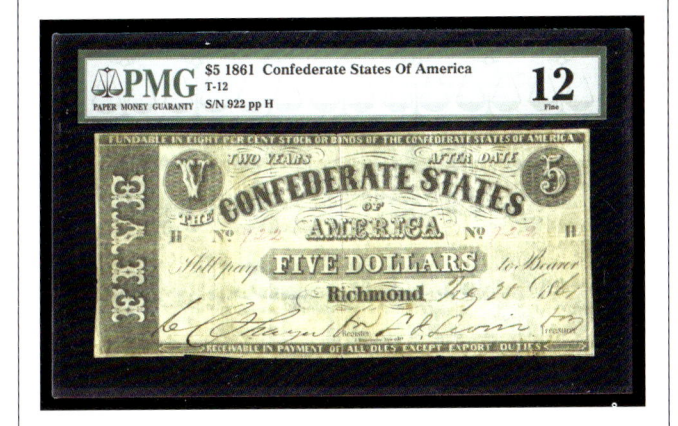

12507 T12 $5 1861 Cr-48, PF-1. This famous note was printed by Jules Manouvrier, a prominent New Orleans lithographer and printer. Because of its light blue color, the back design quickly faded on most notes, and the simplistic design caused the Confederate government to not renew its contract with the printer. Scarce in all grades, this type is especially difficult to locate in nicer circulated grades such as the note here offered. **PMG Fine 12.** (4,000-6,000)

12508 T13 $100 1861. The September 2, 1861 date for this issue was chosen arbitrarily because this was the date on which Hoyer & Ludwig started work on the notes. This example has avoided circulation while toning a shade. **Crisp Uncirculated.** (200-300)

12509 T13 $100 1861. Cr-56, PF-4. Some light handling is noted on this lightly toned issue. **Choice About Uncirculated.** (300-400)

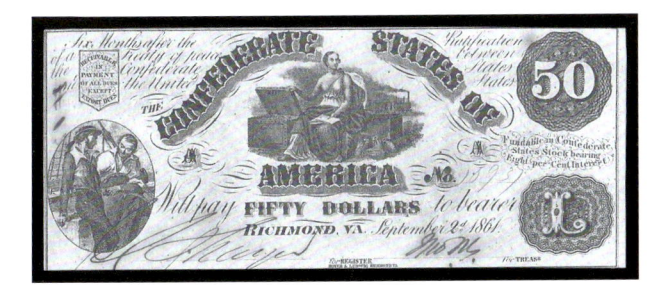

12510 T14 $50 1861 Cr. 59 PF-1. This note is quite crisp with no folds, but there is some light handling. The paper is toned, making the inks quite dark. **Crisp Uncirculated** (350-450)

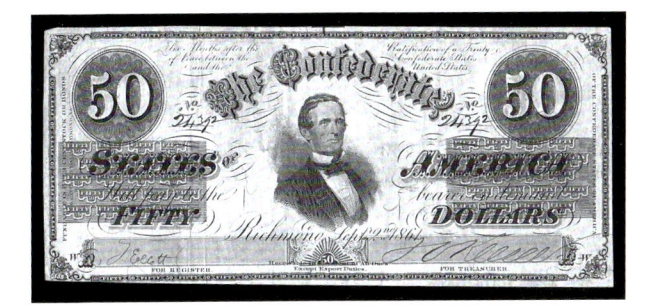

12511 T16 $50 1861. Healthy edges and original paper surfaces define this $50 that is almost fully framed. A paper guide line marker is noticed at top center. **Very Fine.** (300-500)

12512 T17 $20 1861. The folds for the most part are spread evenly across this $20 that also has a tiny amount of ink erosion. The top cut dips inside the frame line. T17s are almost always found with a poor cut. **Very Fine.** (900-1,200)

12513 T18 $20 1861. This nicely preserved $20 is completely encircled by a frame line. **Crisp Uncirculated.** (100-150)

Sheet of T-18s

12514 T18 $20 1861. This is the first time we have come across a sheet of T-18s. This sheet has been folded vertically through the center and ink erosion is seen in most of the examples of Tho. J. Miller's signature.
From The Jacob and Heather Dedman Collection
(4,000-6,000)

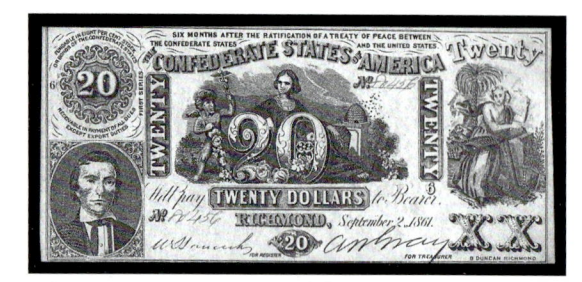

12515 **CT20 $20 1861** Cr. 141 PF-5. This Navigation & Beehive counterfeit-example is just a hair from Choice, if only for an incomplete frameline at top left. Still one of the nicest examples you will find. **Crisp Uncirculated.**
From The Jacob and Heather Dedman Collection (150-350)

12516 **T20 $20 1861.** This $20 acquired very light handling. **About Uncirculated.** (150-200)

12517 **T21 $20 1861.** This pleasing blue-green issue escaped being cancelled. The back has a hand written note, "Sale E.F. April 19 — 43." **PMG Choice Extremely Fine 45.** (1,000-1,300)

12518 **T21 $20 1861.** This blue-green $20 has original surfaces that display embossing and problem-free edges. The cut is typical for the issue. **Extremely Fine.** (900-1,200)

12519 **T22 $10 1861.** The Indian Family $10 is one of the more popular Confederate notes. It was printed by the Southern Bank Note Company. This mid-grade example is blessed with solid edges while the undertint has taken on an orange hue. The paper is snappy with ample margins on three sides. **Fine.** (700-1,000)

12520 **T23 $5 1861.** This is a scarce note in any condition and our archives over the years bear that out. This example has a colorful overprint for the grade and the edges are solid except where the COCs are. The cut is also nice as it comes into contact with the frame line only briefly. **Fine, COC.** (400-700)

12521 **T24 $10 1861.** This is a gorgeous example of this type, with great color to go along with a complete frameline. Our consignor reportedly paid $250 for his beauty, and should easily see a nice return. Referenced as a PF-11, Cr. 164. **Choice About Uncirculated.** (1,250-1,750)

12522 **T24 $10 1861** Cr-156, PF-1. This note exhibits great colors for the grade, which is encased in a **PMG Choice Fine 15** holder. (300-400)

12523 **T24 $10 1861** Cr-156, PF-1. A nice, evenly-circulated example for the type, with nice colors for the grade. Two mounting remnants are attached at each top corner on the back. **Fine.** (300-400)

12524 **T25 $10 1861** Cr-169, PF-2. No problems to report on this uncancelled **Fine** example. (300-400)

12525 **T26 $10 1861.** Cr-177 PF-8. PMG has granted the grade of **Very Fine 25** to this example of the solid "X" variety. (250-350)

12526 **T26 $10 1861.** This **Fine-Very Fine** $10 is an example of the Fine Lace subtype. The note displays heavy embossing behind "Confederate States." It is fully framed on three sides by margins while the top edge dips below the frame line as it nears the upper left corner. A little bit of soiling is noticed. (150-250)

12527 **CT29/237A Counterfeit $10 1861.** The tell-tale sign on these counterfeit examples can be found in the lower left corner as "R. Duncan" is not the actual printer's name. B. Duncan is the correct name found on genuine notes. **Very Fine.** (250-350)

12528 **T29 $10 1861.** Cr-237, PF-1. Several names in pencil appear on the back of this "Slave Picking Cotton" issue which may have been a souvenir from the time. **PMG Very Fine 20.** (350-450)

12529 **T29 $10 1861.** This $10 carries a lot of eye appeal as it is much nearer to the high-end of the split grade. A few pinholes are noticed along with an approximate quarter inch edge tear. **Fine-Very Fine.** (500-700)

12530 **T30 $10 1861** Cr. 239 PF-3. An excellent representation of the *Sweet Potato Dinner* note, possibly the nicest T-30 we have had the pleasure of offering at auction. This Second Series note is fully framed, with signatures of J.M. McKinney and Hampton C. Williams. **Choice Crisp Uncirculated.** (1,000-1,500)

View color images of virtually every lot and place bids at HA.com

12531 **T30 $10 1861.** This Second Series note has the famed *Sweet Potato Dinner* vignette. Whether this encounter between General Marion, the Swamp Fox, and an unknown British officer took place is open to debate, but it is known that General Marion ran circles around the British. This example is bright with healthy edges and paper that is hindered only by a broad corner fold. **Choice About Uncirculated.** (250-350)

12532 **T31 $5 1861.** This is a **Very Fine** example of this colorful Southern Bank Note Company $5. T31s are highly underrated in grades VF and above and this example shows even wear, sound edges, and a nice cut for the issue. A partial paper clip rust outline is found on the back. (1,300-1,800)

12533 **T31 $5 1861.** This is a snappy **Fine** $5 with uniform wear and especially nice edges for the grade.
From The William A. "Bill" Bond Collection (700-1,000)

12534 **T31 $5 1861.** This scarce mid-grade note was hand-picked with care by our consignor as he looked for choice notes for the grade. This example exhibits nice paper and edges save for one small edge tear. **Fine.** (700-1,000)

12535 **T32 $5 1861.** This is an elusive issue with this example having even wear and wholesome edges save for one tiny nick. It is a common phenomenon for the overprint of this design to fade due to circulation and/or the elements. **Fine.** (1,700-2,200)

12536 **CT33 $5 1861.** This "Plate J" counterfeit is gorgeous and boasts perfect paper quality. The signatures are printed, and the serial numbers were hand written. **Choice Crisp Uncirculated.** (250-350)

12537 **T33 $5 1861.** This is a superior note for the grade with its wholesome edges and nice color. **Fine.** (600-800)

12538 **T36 $5 1861.** Some light handling is noted on this pleasing, **PMG Choice Uncirculated 63** note. The signatures are still good and the print quality is sharp and perfectly detailed. (300-400)

12539 **T36 $5 1861** Cr. 274 PF-2. This is a lovely **Crisp Uncirculated** Ceres on Cotton note. (350-450)

12540 **T38 $2 1861.** An engraving error gave this issue an 1861 instead of an 1862 date. This note is scarce in all grades and when found is usually at the lower end of the grading spectrum due to the fact that this was the first issue of this denomination and inflation was not rampant at this time. This **Very Good** example displays the typical pinholes and edge tears for the grade. This example was once mounted leaving tell-tale evidence behind on the back. (400-600)

12541 **T39 $100 1862.** 1863 and 1864 interest paid stamps are on the back of this **Crisp Uncirculated** $100 that is adorned with serial number 840. (100-150)

12542 **T40 $100 1862.** Cr. 306. This bright representative exhibits very dark inks on crisp surfaces. The top frame line is missing as the cut was a bit off. A pair of interest stamps from Raleigh, NC are seen on the back. **Crisp Uncirculated.** (300-400)

12543 **T41 $100 1862.** The stamps on back are perfectly applied, including the issuance stamp from Jackson, MS with a date of January 7, 1863. The CSA block lettered watermark is present. **PCGS Choice New 63PPQ.** (300-350)

12544 **CT41 $100 1862.** Perfect paper quality is noted on this spectacular counterfeit. To date, this is one of the finest examples of this type that we have handled. **Choice Crisp Uncirculated.** (300-400)

12545 **T41 $100 1862.** The even margins for this handsome note are free of the frame line. This enhances the aesthetics of this eye appealing $100 that has three Augusta interest paid stamps on the back. **PCGS New 62PPQ.** (200-300)

12546 **T41 $100 1862.** This is a bright, well embossed Scroll 2 $100 with wholesome edges and no pinholes. **Very Fine.** (70-90)

12547 **CT41/316A Counterfeit $100 1862.** An interesting counterfeit with the seldom-seen "Counterfeit" stamps across the face of the note. (250-350)

12548 **T42 $2 1862.** This Third Series $2 has a pre-printing crinkle, a little bit of ink erosion at top center, and light circulation. **About Uncirculated.** (150-200)

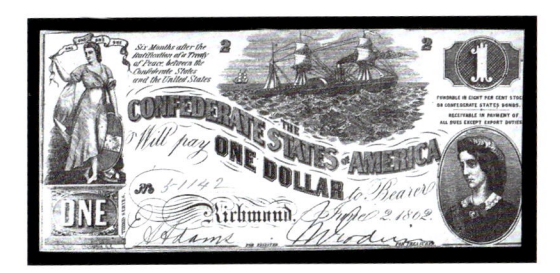

12549 **T44 $1 1862.** This is a bright $1 with a better than average cut for the type. **Crisp Uncirculated.** (200-250)

12550 **T44 $1 1862.** A couple of corner bumps are noted and account for the grade. The note is otherwise fully New with bright white paper, perfect signatures and excellent eye appeal. **Choice About Uncirculated.** (200-300)

PMG Choice Uncirculated 64 EPQ

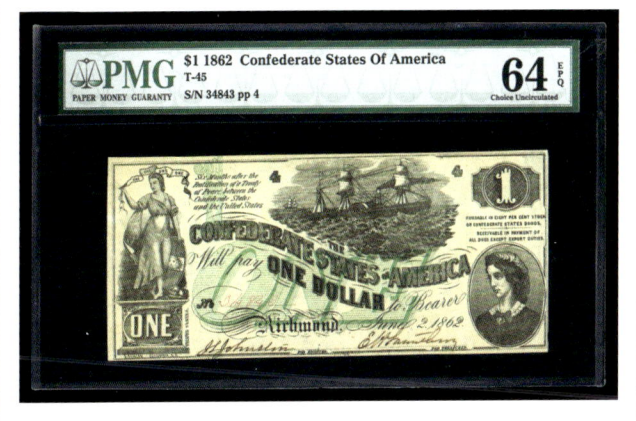

12551 **T45 $1 1862.** This is the nicest one of these we have handled in quite some time. It is nicely margined on all four sides for this design as the notes on an uncut sheet of this type leave barely any room between the notes. It may be quite awhile before another T45 this nice is available. **PMG Choice Uncirculated 64 EPQ.** (3,000-5,000)

12552 **T45 $1 1862.** This is a type that is seldom seen in high grade, yet this example has survived nearly fully new with only edge handling keeping it from being uncirculated. This $1 is tight at the top, but otherwise nicely margined, with great color and eye appeal. **PMG Choice About Unc 58 EPQ.** (1,300-1,800)

12553 **T46 $10 1862.** Although printed in 1861, this type was dated 1862 in error. This **Extremely Fine,** CC example is nicely centered and two of the folds show soiling. This note is the variety with the letter "s" after "Month" in the redemption clause. (150-200)

12554 **T49 $100 1862.** Cr-348, PF-2. While having the appearance of a Choice Unc note, closer scrutiny reveals multiple light folds, thus, the **Very Fine-Extremely Fine** grade. (350-450)

12555 **T49 $100 1862.** This $100 is a problem-free **Very Fine** with bright and healthy paper. (300-500)

12556 **T50 $50 1862.** A lone center fold is noted through the holder, though we would not disagree with a grade of About New. The color is bright and the paper is ideal, with a fairly well centered CSA watermark worthy of mention. **Choice Extremely Fine 45.** (600-800)

12557 **T50 $50 1862.** This $50 has sound edges that almost entirely escape the frame line. The color is nice and the handling is even. Two small possible rust circles are found along the right edge. **Fine-Very Fine.** (300-500)

12558 **T54 $2 1862.** This Deuce has been lightly handled. **Extremely Fine-About Uncirculated.** (125-175)

12559 **T55 $1 1862.** This $1 shows traces of foxing. **Crisp Uncirculated.** (150-200)

12560 **T56 $100 1863.** Cr-403, PF-1. A partial CSA treasury stamp is noted in the upper left corner adding to the appeal of this wholly original issue. **Choice Crisp Uncirculated.** (500-600)

12561 **T56 $100 1863.** Serial number embossing is retained by this 1st Series C-note that is only limited by its bottom edge drifting inside the frame line. **Crisp Uncirculated.** (250-350)

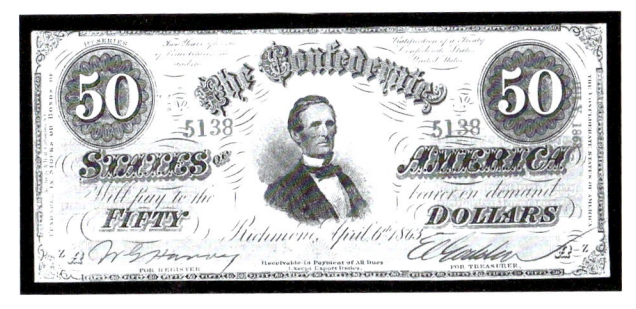

12562 **T57 $50 1863.** Cr-414, PF-8. Deep embossing of the serial numbers and series date is noted. Shull indicates there are only about a dozen examples known of this variety which features, "Keatinge & Ball, Columbia, S.C." at left end. **Choice Crisp Uncirculated.** (1,500-2,000)

12563 **T57 $50 1863.** Cr-406, PF-1. A lone corner bump keeps this note from a full Choice grade, so it is unlikely this issued note ever circulated. The penned signatures are full, the serial numbers and date are bright and the paper is perfect. **Choice About Uncirculated.** (250-350)

12564 **T57 $50 1863.** A corner fold is found on this Jeff Davis $50 that has edges clear of the frame line and serial number embossing. This example was once mounted with two stamp hinges. **About Uncirculated.** (150-200)

12565 **T58 $20 1863.** Cr-426 PF-17. This 2nd Series note would have benefited from a touch wider margin at upper left. Original surfaces have been awarded the grade of **Uncirculated 62 EPQ** by PMG. (200-300)

12566 **T58 $20 1863.** This 3rd Series $20 has bright paper that reveals a pinhole after intense scrutiny. The bottom edge drifts inside the frame line. **Crisp Uncirculated.** (150-200)

Unique Inverted Back - Fricke Example

12567 **T59 Inverted $10 1863.** Rarely, if ever, do we have the opportunity to offer a note of any kind that we feel comfortable calling "unique". However, we feel quite satisfied with that terminology, as this variety was unknown to the late Grover Criswell, Dr. Douglas Ball, Philip Chase, and all other renowned researchers of Confederate paper money. Even the vast holdings of the National Archives and the Museum of the Confederacy do not possess an example of this note. Listed as "Non-Collectible" in the Fricke tome, this is the note stated in the Condition Census, listed as a PF-26IB. This note displays great clarity on both sides, with no problems whatsoever. Expect to see spirited bidding on this note, as this is a must have for those wanting to complete a set of T-59 inverted backs. (10,000-15,000)

12568 **T60 $5 1863.** Cr.459 PF-21. An excellent example for type, with the typical closely cut margins. **Crisp Uncirculated.** (200-250)

12569 **T61 $2 1863.** Faint handling and a moisture spot are found on this $2. **Extremely Fine-About Uncirculated.** (200-300)

12570 **T63 50 Cents 1863** Cr. Unlisted PF-7. This 2nd Series note has an interesting error, in that the serial number was stamped twice on the face. This **Fine** note does have multiple pinholes, as well as a partial CSA stamp on the back. (200-300)

12571 **T64 $500 1864.** Plenty of embossing can be seen on this note that has some waviness present graded **PMG Choice Uncirculated 63.** (900-1,200)

12572 **T64 $500 1864** Cr-489, PF-1. This is one of the nicest Confederate $500 notes we've ever had to offer. Lovely **Choice Crisp Uncirculated,** just the slightest of handling removing it from the gem designation.
From The Jacob and Heather Dedman Collection
(900-1,200)

12573 **T64 $500 1864.** Cr. 489 PF-1. Signatures are of (Mrs.)V. M. Penrifoy and (Miss) A.S. Stuart. Embossing is quite strong on this **Choice Crisp Uncirculated** note. (900-1,200)

12574 **T64 $500 1864.** Strong embossing is found on this well preserved D-note that lacks only a little better cut from claiming a higher grade. This note was signed by (Mrs.) V. (M.) Penrifoy and (Miss) A. (S.) Stuart. **Crisp Uncirculated.** (800-1,000)

12575 **T64 $500 1864** Cr-489, PF-1. This light pink tinted example is **Crisp Uncirculated,** with its only flaws a couple of small edge tears at top center. (800-1,000)

12576 **T64 $500 1864.** Here is another note signed by (Mrs.) V. (M.) Penrifoy and (Miss) A. (S.) Stuart that exhibit a couple handling wrinkles. **Crisp uncirculated.** (800-1,000)

12577 **T64 $500 1864.** Cr-489, PF-1. This $500 faces up like a fully uncirculated note, though a lone center fold is noted. The color is still excellent for the issue. **PMG About Uncirculated 53.** (600-800)

12578 **T64 $500 1864** Cr-489, PF-1. This is a very pleasing example of the "Stars and Bars" $500. The paper is perfectly original and the signatures remain strong. A small repaired tear is noted at left. **About Uncirculated.**
From The Rolling Plains Collection (600-800)

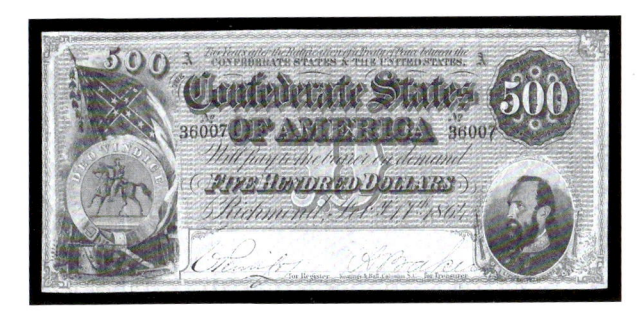

12579 **T64 $500 1864.** This colorful $500 note is of the dark red background variety with a high serial number for the issue. The upper right corner reveals a partial Confederate Treasury stamp. Serial number embossing is noticed on this delightful mid-grade note. **Very Fine.** (400-600)

12580 **T65 $100 1864** Cr. 490 PF-1. Only a light center fold keeps this gorgeous Dark Red Ink variety from Gem. Also of note on back is "Levy", and what appears to be a partial "7". **Choice Crisp Uncirculated.**
From The Jacob and Heather Dedman Collection (175-200)

12581 **T67 $20 1864. Four Examples.** These four **Crisp Uncirculated** examples are of the dark red ink variety, listed as Cr. 504, PF-1. These are not consecutive, but the serial numbers are all within a 90 number range.
From The Jacob and Heather Dedman Collection (400-600)

Beautiful Uncut $10 Confederate Sheet

12582 **T68 $10 1864 Uncut Sheet of Eight.** We have handled quite a few of these sheets over the years and this example that we originally sold back in September 1996 is still superior to any we have ever seen. It is 100% fully bright and lacks even minimal signs of handling. This sheet is unsigned and unnumbered and it also has three engraver's names in the face and back selvage. **Gem Crisp Uncirculated.**
From The Jacob and Heather Dedman Collection
(1,000-1,500)

12583 **T71 $1 1864** Cr. 574 PF-12. Nice orange tints accent this **Choice Crisp Uncirculated** Clay note. (250-300)

CONFEDERATE BONDS

12584 **Ball 1; 2; 3; 4; 6; 7; 9 Cr. 5; 5A; 6; 6A; 7; 7A; 8 $50; $50; $100; $100; $500; $500; $1000 1861 Bonds Very Good or Better.** This is a complete subset of early Montgomery bonds except for two Ball numbers that are each represented by only one known bond in a preliminary printing stage. The $50 and $100 bonds were printed by the small New Orleans printer John Douglas, while the $500 and $1000 bonds were printed by the Southern Bank Note Company (nom de guerre of the ABNCo New Orleans) without their imprint. These were once mounted with stamp hinges. The $1000 bond has a small hole.
From The William A. "Bill" Bond Collection (Total: 7 items)
(350-500)

Rare Ball 10 Criswell 1 CSA Bond

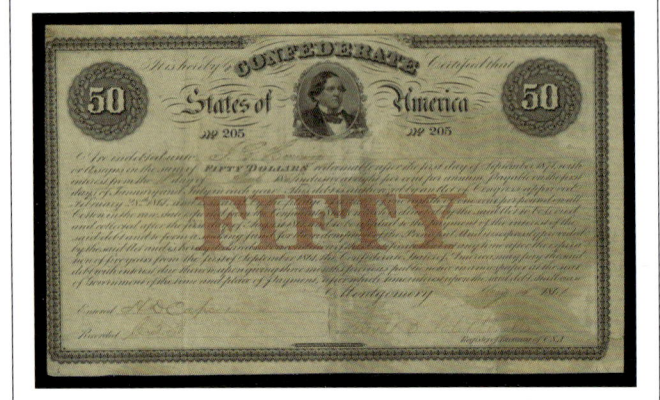

12585 Ball 10 Cr. 1 $50 1861 Bond Very Good. This is one of only 250 bonds issued for this Montgomery type. Very few of those remain for the collectors of today. June 2005 saw a Ball 10 go for $8050. The bonds of this 1861 issue have the American Bank Note Co. New Orleans imprint, though they were actually printed at the company's New York office. A large moisture stain is noticed, the top edge has been reinforced, and it was once mounted. The portrait is of Howell Cobb, president of the Confederate Provisional Congress. This bond is signed by Register of the Treasury Alex(ander) B. Clitherall. When the Confederate capital moved to Richmond in July 1861, Clitherall decided to resign and stay in his home state. Therefore Clitherall's signature is only found on the Montgomery issues of the February 28, 1861 bonds.
From The William A. "Bill" Bond Collection
(3,000-5,000)

Rare Ball 13 Criswell 2A Richmond Issue

12586 Ball 13 Cr. 2A $100 1861 Bond Very Fine. This bond was issued to Mrs. Joel Butler at Richmond as Montgomery has been crossed-out. 500 examples of this bond were issued at Richmond. It has the signature of Ro(bert) Tyler as Register of the Treasury. A couple of pinholes are mentioned for cataloging accuracy. A Ball 13 in VF sold for $15,525 in March 2006.
From The William A. "Bill" Bond Collection
(9,000-12,000)

Rare Richmond $500 1861 Issue

12587 Ball 15 Cr. 3A $500 1861 Bond Fine. This $500 bond with serial number 171 was issued at Richmond, but according to Ball, serial numbers 1-177 were issued at Montgomery. Ball credits Richmond with 314 examples of this bond. This bond has the uncommon signature of C(harles) T. Jones as Register of the Treasury. As Acting Register he would have signed this bond only if Register of the Treasury Robert Tyler was unavailable. This example was once lightly mounted with two stamp hinges. March 2006 saw a VF example of Ball 15 cross the podium at $12,650.
From The William A. "Bill" Bond Collection
(6,000-9,000)

Elusive Ball 16 Criswell 4 $1000 Bond

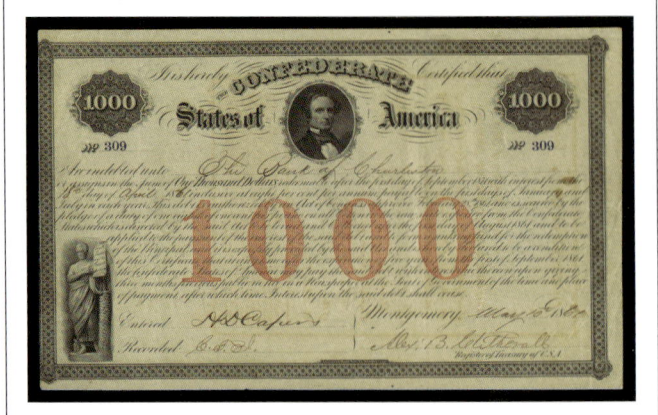

12588 Ball 16 Cr. 4 $1000 1861 Bond Very Fine. The first 810 bonds of this denomination were issued at Montgomery. The portrait is of Jefferson Davis. The Bank of Charleston stepped up to the plate to purchase this bond less than a month after Fort Sumter. This bond has lightly toned over the years. This is a trait often seen for this design. This bond was once mounted with two stamp hinges and a couple of small stains are also noticed. A couple of pinholes are mentioned for cataloging accuracy. These early Confederate bonds appear only when great collections are sold and William Bond had such a collection. He was a major contributor to the Criswell reference series.
From The William A. "Bill" Bond Collection
(5,000-8,000)

Rare Richmond Issue with C.T. Jones Signature

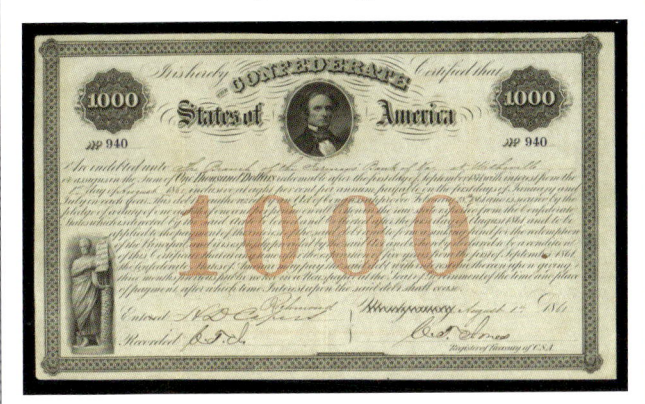

12589 Ball 17 Cr. 4A $1000 1861 Bond Extremely Fine. This Richmond bond is one of only 190 issued. Also, we see the uncommon signature of Acting Register C(harles) T. Jones. This is a bright bond that has a couple of pinholes and a small red ink spot. Two stamp hinges were once used to mount this rare bond in an artist's portfolio. It has been many years since collectors have had an opportunity to acquire this Ball number.
From The William A. "Bill" Bond Collection
(9,000-12,000)

Scarce and Popular Ben Franklin CSA Bond

12590 Ball 18D Cr. 9 $2000 1861 Bond Very Fine. The denomination is hand-written for this popular, but scarce issue that has a Benjamin Franklin portrait. This serial number 4 example is signed by Acting Register C.T. Jones. It was lightly mounted with stamp hinges.
From The William A. "Bill" Bond Collection
(2,500-4,500)

Rare Hand-written Denomination Bond

12591 Ball 19K Cr. 10 $20,000 1863 Bond Extremely Fine. This is the second highest denomination for this hand-written denomination issue. Only 23 were issued at the $20,000 level. Ball gives it a Rarity 8 listing - 1 to 3 known. Two stamp hinges held it in a portfolio where this bond had not seen the light of day for 40 years. A couple of pinholes are noticed along with a tiny internal tear.
From The William A. "Bill" Bond Collection
(3,000-5,000)

12592 Ball 22; 23; 24 Cr. 12; 12A; 13 $500; $500; $500 1861 Bonds. The Ball 22 and 23 bonds are known as *Indian Princess* bonds because they share the Indian Princess vignette with the famous and rare T35 note. The T23 has three extra hand-written coupons right below the bond. These coupons were signed by Tyler. The Ball 22 and 23 grade **VG** or better. The Ball 24 grades **AU**. All three were once mounted with stamp hinges.
From The William A. "Bill" Bond Collection (Total: 3 items)
(200-400)

12593 Ball 28 Cr. 16 $200 1861 Bond Extremely Fine. Only 503 examples of this hand-written denominated bond were issued. Further only 31 of the $200 denomination were issued. Ball also gives this number an R8 rating, 1 - 3 known. There is an internal one inch tear that has been repaired along with two stamp hinges that once held this bond in place.
From The William A. "Bill" Bond Collection **(2,000-4,000)**

Rare $11,000 Confederate Bond

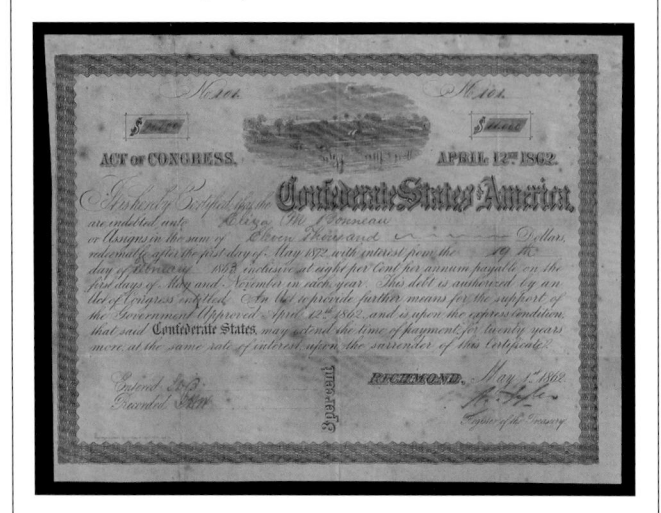

12594 Ball 150 Cr. 113 $11,000 1862 Bond Fine. This hand-written denominated bond only had 181 examples issued. They were issued in amounts from $100 to $14,550. Only three $11,000 bonds were issued. This bond with serial number 101 was issued to Eliza M. Bonneau. Ball gives this number an R7 rating, 11 - 20 known for all issued denominations. This bond was engraved and printed by George Dunn. He came to the CSA in 1862 with other Scottish printers. Dunn has been described as one of the best engraving resources of the Confederacy. The vignette on this bond is of the *Confederate Defenses at Drury's Bluff*. The vignette shows detail of stakes, a sunken ship, plus floating ships. This is a great Confederate bond that is seldom encountered. This example shows extensive foxing and some pencilled collector notations on the back. A little bit of ink erosion is noticed along with two places where stamp hinges once held this bond.
From The William A. "Bill" Bond Collection
(4,000-8,000)

12595 Ball 156 Cr. 116 £100 1863 Bond Fine. We are fortunate to have all four Erlanger bond denominations in this auction. All denominations for this issue carry a wonderful vignette of the *Confederacy*. This £100 bond has 36 coupons as is the common case. All Erlanger bonds have an embossed British tax stamp as they were printed in London. The bonds are printed in English and French and denominated in pounds sterling and francs. A little paper separation along the folds is noticed on this example. It also shows aging in the middle third section. The Erlanger bonds are signed by Confederate diplomat John Slidell. Much history surrounds these popular bonds.
From The William A. "Bill" Bond Collection **(400-800)**

12596 Ball 157 Cr. 117 £200 1863 Bond Fine. This is the second denomination for Erlanger bonds. Pinholes are noticed along with a little paper separation along the folds. Some aging also shows in the middle third section.
From The William A. "Bill" Bond Collection **(500-1,000)**

12597 Ball 158 Cr. 118 £500 1863 Bond Fine. This is the third denomination for the Erlanger bonds. These bonds steadily declined in value until March 1, 1865 when payments ceased. Some paper separation along the folds is noticed on this bond. A small hole is also noticed. The aging in the middle third section is light.
From The William A. "Bill" Bond Collection **(500-1,000)**

12598 Ball 160 Cr. 119 £1000 1863 Bond Fine-Very Fine. This is one of the fabled bond issues of the Confederacy as it was floated overseas in London and the Continent with the backing of the Erlanger financial empire. These cotton bonds are very popular with collectors and this is an example of the highest denomination issued. The printer started with the £1000 bond denomination, thus the Series A designation. In the 1960s a relative of the Erlanger family burned the remaining bonds in the family's possession thinking they were worthless paper, thus enhancing greatly their scarcity. All of these bonds were signed by Baron Emile Erlanger. This example shows some aging in the middle third section and along the top border. Small amounts of paper separation are noticed along the folds and coupon 11 has an approximate one and a half inch tear. There are also many pinholes. This is still a highly collectible bond that is very elusive.
From The William A. "Bill" Bond Collection **(1,000-1,500)**

12599 Ball 258 Cr. 127 $500 1863 Fine. This is a bright example of a popular design that was once mounted. The upper left corner is missing.
From The William A. "Bill" Bond Collection **(200-400)**

12600 Ball 268 Cr. 134 $1000 1863 Six Per Cent Stock Certificate Very Fine. This is another highly popular bond. The vignette is of *A Cotton Gin and Press* and it too was engraved by George Dunn. This bright example has been tri-folded and a repair has been made to the back of the Confederate Treasury embossed blind stamp. The top edge reveals an approximate quarter inch tear and two places where stamp hinges were once affixed.
From The William A. "Bill" Bond Collection **(800-1,200)**

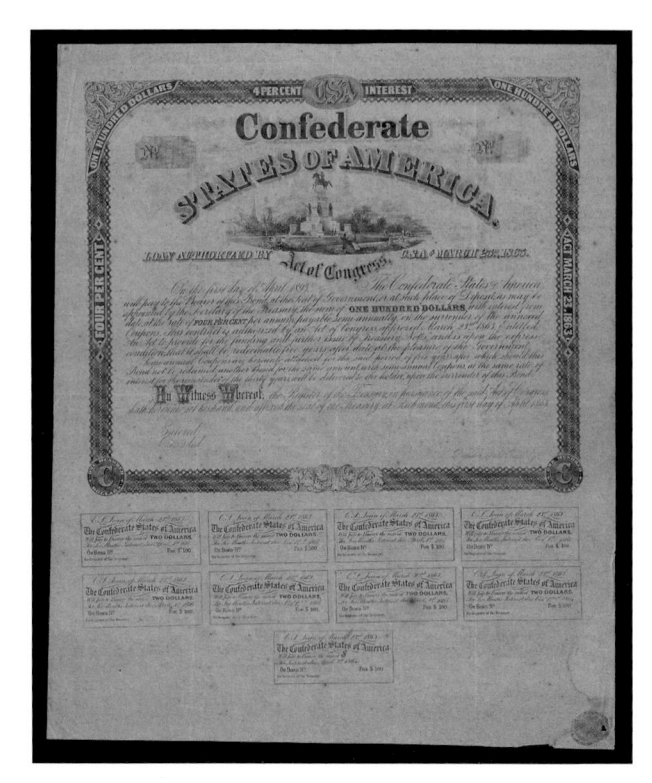

12601 **Ball 270 Cr. UNL $100 1863 Fine.** This once stamp hinge mounted remainder shows foxing and a moisture spot in the lower right corner. Only thirteen of this design were issued.
From The William A. "Bill" Bond Collection **(700-1,000)**

12602 **Ball 272 Cr. UNL $500 1863 Fine.** This is a remainder on this design, but only six were ever issued. Some foxing is noticed along with pencilled collector notations on the back. It also was once hinged in a portfolio.
From The William A. "Bill" Bond Collection **(500-800)**

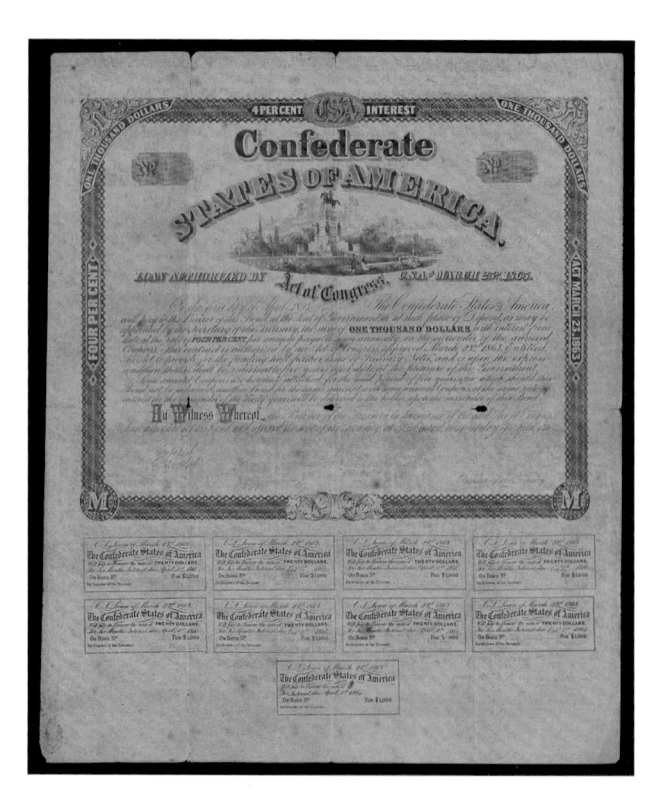

12603 **Ball 274 Cr. UNL $1000 1863 Good-Very Good.** Only 18 of this design were issued. This remainder has four edge splits with the longest being approximately four inches.
From The William A. "Bill" Bond Collection **(200-400)**

12604 **Ball 275 Cr. 135 $50,000 1863 Five Per Cent Call Certificate Fine.** This once lightly hinged example has toned a shade while acquiring a couple of small holes. It has also been cut and punch cancelled. The back has an extensive penned endorsement and a pencilled arithmetic problem.
From The William A. "Bill" Bond Collection **(200-400)**

Rare Four Per Cent Call Certificate

12605 **Ball 276 Cr. 136 $1000 1863 Four Per Cent Call Certificate Fine.** Ball 276 is known only in unissued form as all issued pieces were redeemed and destroyed. Ball estimates a population of only 11-20 extant. Two spots of stamp hinge adhesive are noticed. The vignette is *Ruins of Jamestown, Virginia*.
From The William A. "Bill" Bond Collection
(1,500-2,500)

Rare Ball 277

12606 **Ball 277 Cr. 137 $5000 1863 Four Per Cent Call Certificate Fine.** Ball 277 is known only as a remainder as all issued pieces were redeemed and destroyed. Ball estimates a population of only 4-10 extant. In his footnotes he mentions that two of those are proofs and three are remainders. This was an exciting find as it was unmounted.
From The William A. "Bill" Bond Collection
(4,000-8,000)

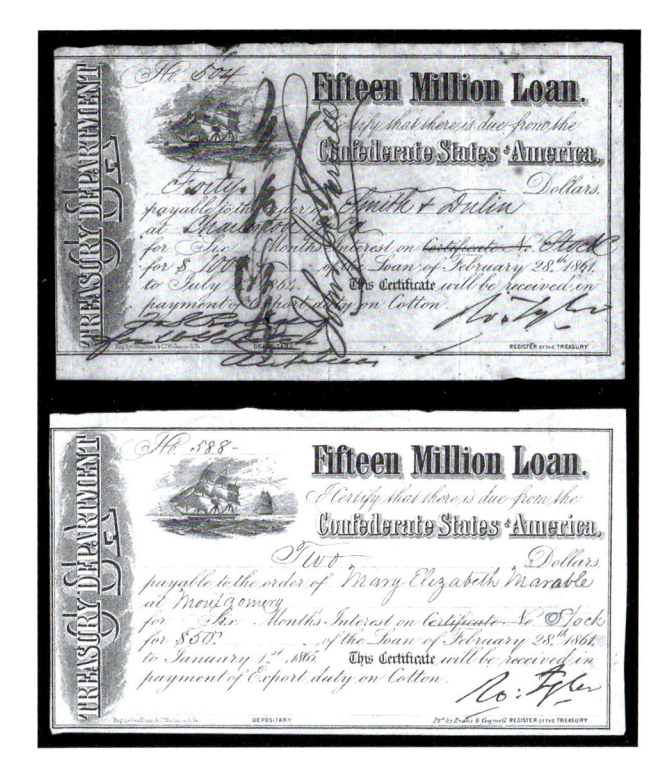

12607 **Ball 284; 285 Cr. 139; 140 $40; $2 1864 Stock Certificate Interest Forms.** These were engraved by George Dunn and printed by Evans and Cogswell. The Ball 284 has toned a shade and there is a small amount of ink erosion. The top edge also displays a small notch and it grades **Fine**. The Ball 285 is a delightful **CU**. Both of these were mounted with stamp hinges.
From The William A. "Bill" Bond Collection (Total: 2 items)
(600-900)

12608 **Ball 286; 287; 288; 294 Cr. 141; 141E; 141A; 141D $100; $100; $500; $5000 1864 Four Per Cent Registered Bonds Very Fine.** All four of these show some paper aging and they once were held captive by two stamp hinges each. The $500 has a small repair and the $5000 has some ink erosion.
From The William A. "Bill" Bond Collection (Total: 4 items)
(400-700)

12609 **Ball 323 $1000 Confederate Bond.** The vignette is of the Confederate seal, with 59 of 60 coupons remained attached to the bond. The upper right corner has a Confederate Treasury Seal stamp. The bond is not graded due to its being framed under glass. Total dimensions are approximately 31 by 40 inches. (300-400)

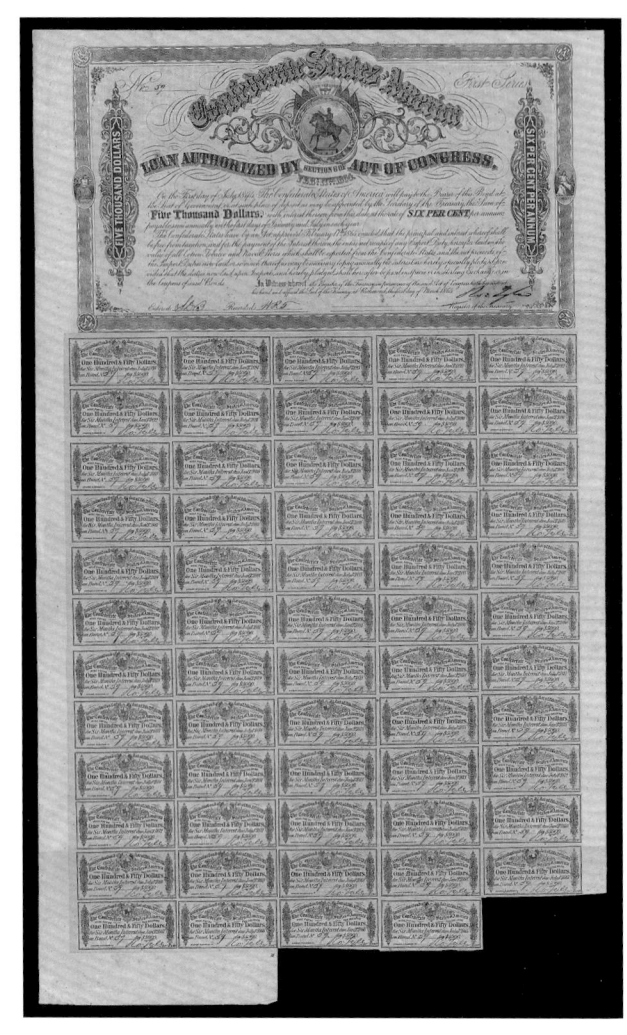

12610 **Ball 337 Cr. 145 $5000 1864 Bond Fine.** This is number 59 of only 200 issued for this Ball number. This example was once mounted with stamp hinges. Some ink erosion and pinholes were also noticed on this rarely encountered high denomination bond.
From The William A. "Bill" Bond Collection **(900-1,200)**

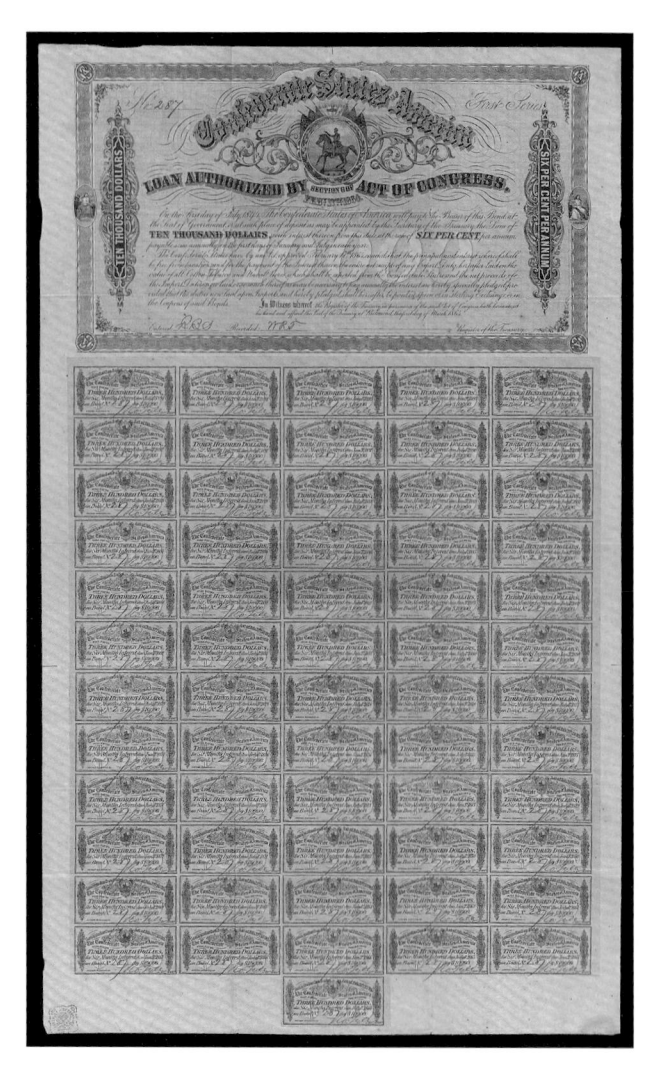

12611 **Ball 339 Cr. 146 $10,000 1864 Bond Fine.** This is a numbered remainder for this design. Only 100 bonds were issued of the 500 printed for this Ball number. This is a rarely seen high denomination bond in issued or remainder form. The back middle third section shows some aging and there is also a little paper separation in the folds. Two stamp hinges held this bond in place for nearly 50 years.
From The William A. "Bill" Bond Collection **(1,000-1,500)**

12612 **Ball 357a Cr. 147 $100 1864 Bond Fine.** This numbered remainder bond is bright for the grade and it has a few small fold splits in the center vertical fold. This popular bond has the vignette of a Confederate sergeant in front of his tent. Two stamp hinges once held this bond in place.
From The William A. "Bill" Bond Collection **(300-500)**

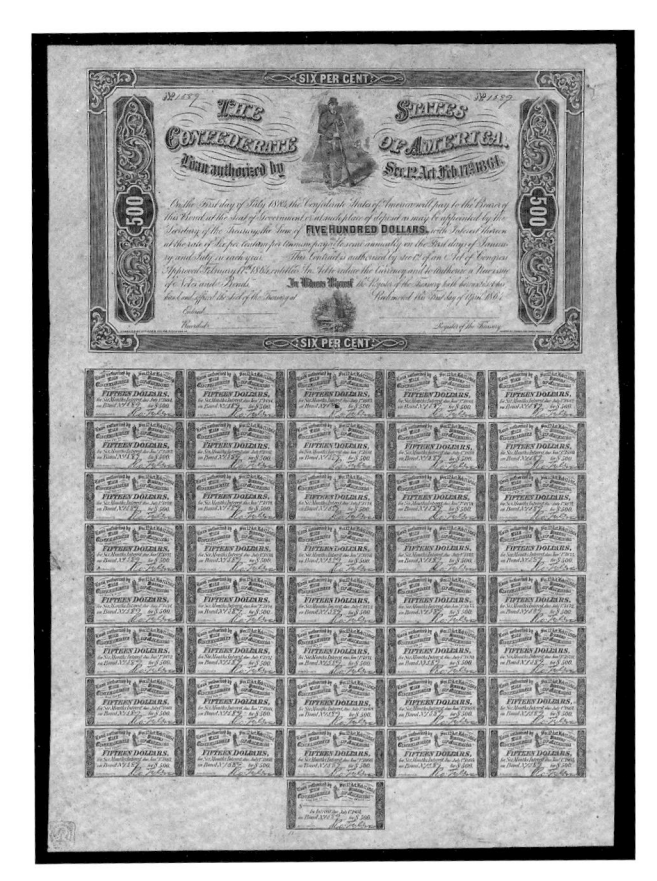

12613 **Ball 359a Cr. 148 $500 1864 Bond Fine.** This example shows some paper separation along the folds. There are also five repairs on the back and pinholes are noticed. This numbered remainder bond was once mounted with two stamp hinges.
From The William A. "Bill" Bond Collection **(400-600)**

12614 **Ball 371 Cr. UNL $10,000 1864 Six Per Cent Non Taxable Certificate Fine.** Only 60 of these were issued with serial numbers 131 - 190. This is serial number 152 and it was issued to Richard Henny. This example has been glued in two places to construction paper. Several edge splits are noticed with the longest being approximately half an inch.
From The William A. "Bill" Bond Collection **(500-800)**

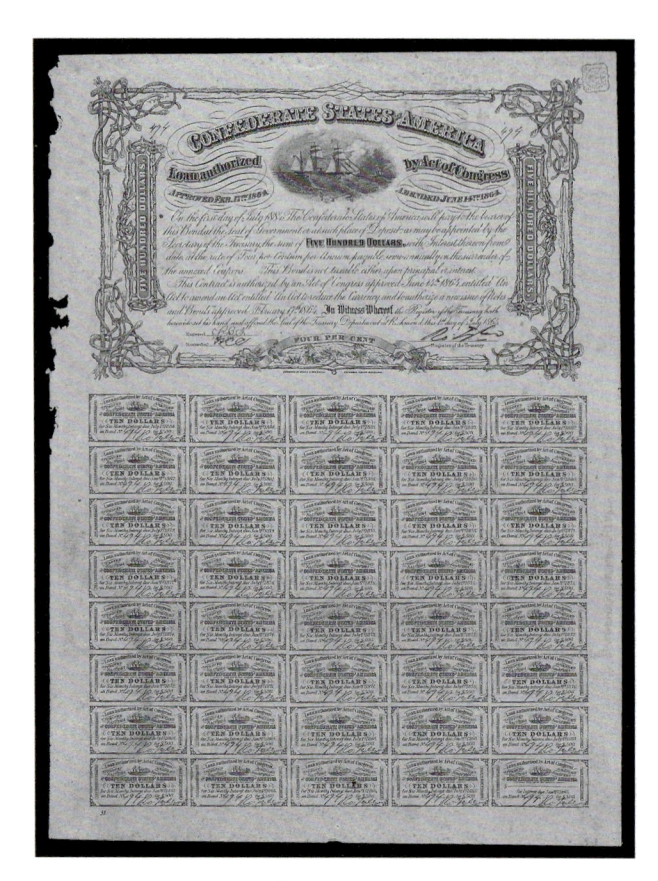

12615 **Ball 385 Cr. 167 $500 1864 Fine.** This remainder has a vignette of the *CSS Alabama*. Left edge damage is noticed along with foxing and pinholes. This bond, as with almost all of the bonds in this collection, was once mounted.
From The William A. "Bill" Bond Collection **(300-500)**

Rare Ball 386 Criswell 167

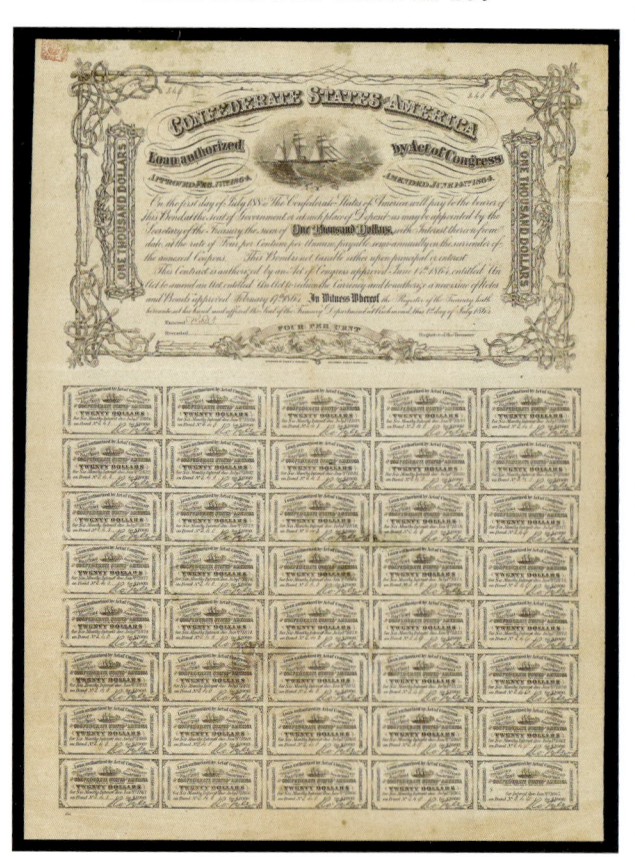

12616 **Ball 386 Cr. 167 $1000 1864 Fine.** This is a rare bond. Ball gave it a rarity of 7+, 4 - 10 known. However in his footnotes, he mentions that he has seen only two. Foxing is noticed on this example along with a stain at center. There are some pinholes and a little bit of paper separation along the folds. This remainder was once mounted. It is listed at $7500 in Fine in the Ball reference and in Fricke's *Confederate Currency and Bonds Quotes* it is unpriced. A great Confederate item.
From The William A. "Bill" Bond Collection
(5,000-10,000)

SOUTHERN STATES BONDS

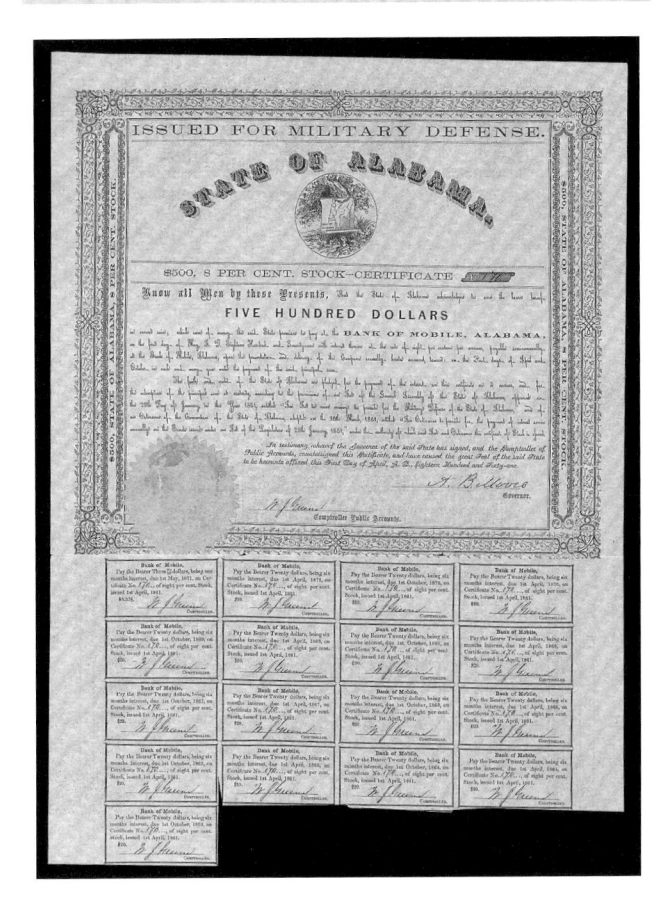

12617 **(Montgomery, AL)- State of Alabama** $500 Bond 1861 Cr. 61A
This bright **Very Fine** Military Defense bond has a pink seal. A little bit of paper separation is noticed along the folds of this once mounted bond.
From The William A. "Bill" Bond Collection **(600-900)**

12618 **(Montgomery, AL)- State of Alabama** $1000 Bond 1861 Cr. 61C
This Military Defense bond with a yellow seal shows some foxing and three top edge tears with the longest being approximately 1.5 inches. There are a few small holes in the body of this once hinged bond. **Fine.**
From The William A. "Bill" Bond Collection **(400-700)**

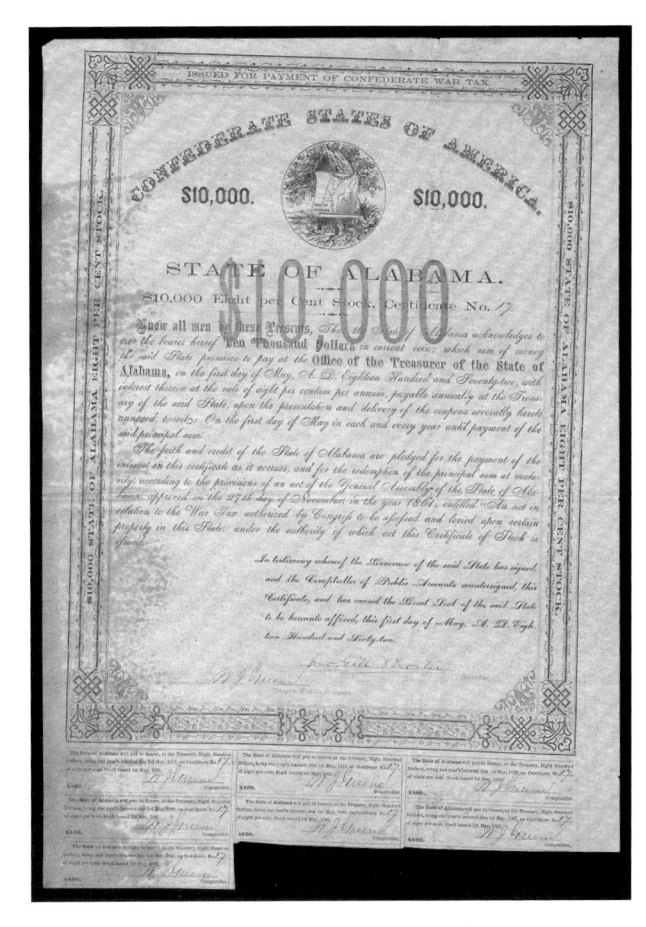

12619 **(Montgomery, AL)- State of Alabama** $10,000 Bond 1862 Cr. 61H
This rare bond with serial number 17 was issued by the state to help pay for the Confederate war tax. Criswell gives it his highest rarity rating of R11. This once lightly mounted bond grades a bright **Fine** with a half dozen repairs and it also has an approximate 1.5 inch bottom edge split.
From The William A. "Bill" Bond Collection **(1,000-1,500)**

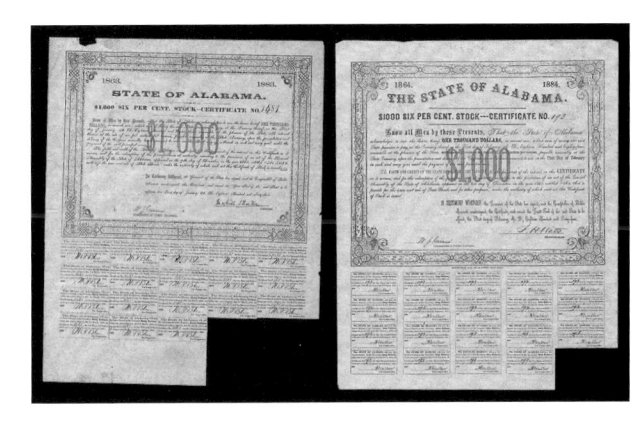

12620 **(Montgomery, AL)- State of Alabama** $1000 Bonds 1863-4 Cr. 62A; UNL
The 62A grades **Good-VG** with edge splits and some paper separation along the folds. The unlisted **Fine-VF** bond of 1864 is bright and it was printed by the Montgomery Steam Power Press Print. Both were once hinged.
From The William A. "Bill" Bond Collection (Total: 2 items) **(700-1,000)**

Bond Signed by Nathan Bedford Forrest

12621 Selma, AL- Selma, Marion and Memphis Railroad Company $1000 Bond 1868
This colorful bond has the signature of N(athan) B(edford) Forrest, former Confederate Lt. General of cavalry, on both the face and back. Forrest had much success during the war with his daring raids and tactics. However, this railroad went bankrupt under his leadership. This bond was not mounted. **Very Fine.**
From The William A. "Bill" Bond Collection
(2,000-4,000)

12622 (Little Rock), AR- State of Arkansas $5; $10; $10; $20 Bonds 1861 Cr. 61B; 61D; 61E; 61F
The 61B grades **VF,** the 61D grades **XF-AU,** the 61E grades **Fine** with an approximate 1.5 inch edge split; and the 61F grades **AU.** All have been mounted with stamp hinges except for the scarce 61E which was mounted with tape on black construction paper. The 61E also has all of its coupons.
From The William A. "Bill" Bond Collection (Total: 4 items)
(350-500)

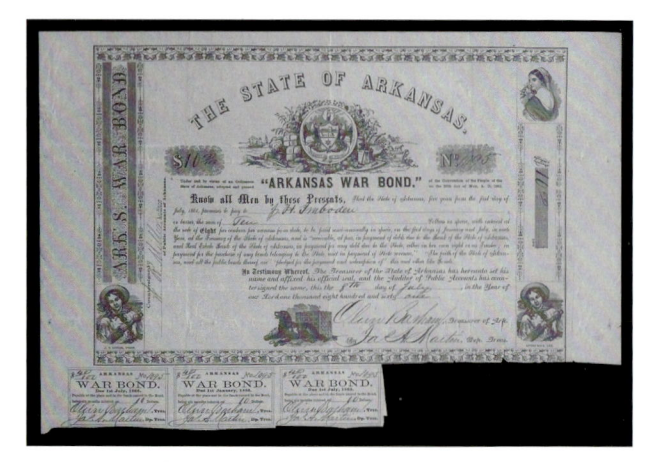

12623 (Little Rock), AR- State of Arkansas $10 Bond 1861 Cr. 61A
This Arkansas War Bond shows a little paper separation along the folds. Three coupons are present. **Fine,** hinged.
From The William A. "Bill" Bond Collection **(300-500)**

12624 (Little Rock), AR- State of Arkansas $5; $10; $20; $50; $100 Bonds 1861 Cr. 61J2; 61K2; 61L2; 61M; 61P
These bonds will grade **Very Fine** or better. Almost all will have an edge tear or two. They were all once mounted with stamp hinges.
From The William A. "Bill" Bond Collection (Total: 5 items)
(1,000-1,500)

Rare 1862 Florida Bond

12625 (Tallahassee), FL- State of Florida $500 Bond 1862 Cr. 61B
This bond weighs in as a R11, 2 - 4 known. It has a couple of "white out" repairs that are 1.5. inches or so in length. The endorsement states that this bond was paid and cancelled on November 7, 1919 by the state comptroller. An interesting story lies here. **Fine,** hinged.
From The William A. "Bill" Bond Collection
(1,000-1,500)

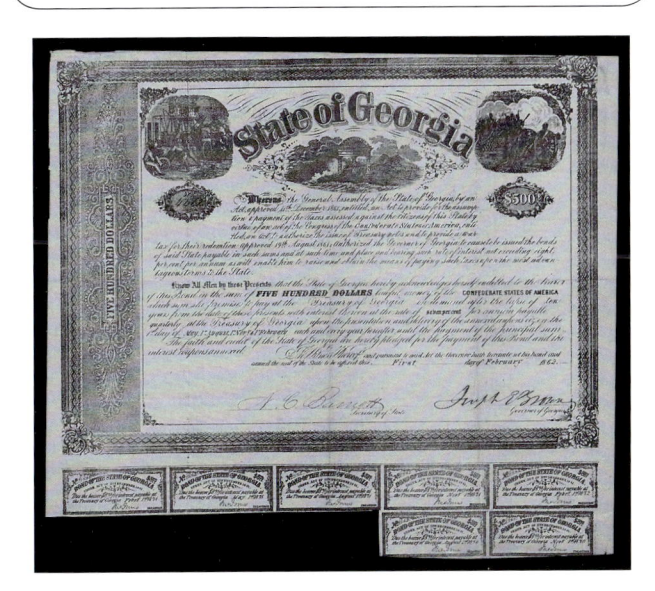

12626 (Milledgeville), GA- State of Georgia $500 Bond 1862 Cr. 61B
Governor Joseph E. Brown signed this bond. It has pinholes and stamp hinge repairs. A small amount of ink erosion is also noticed. **Fine.**
From The William A. "Bill" Bond Collection (400-700)

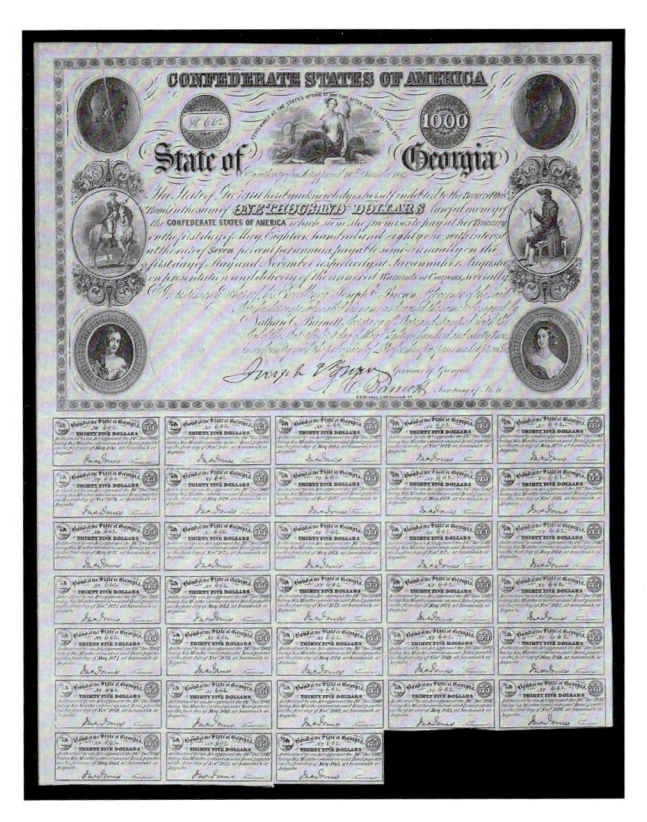

12627 (Milledgeville), GA- State of Georgia $1000 Bond 1862 Cr. 61B
This bond also carries Governor Joseph E Brown's signature. A thin gutter is found in the upper left portrait while this bond also has vignettes of George Washington and James Oglethorpe, founder of Georgia. Pinholes are spotted at center and there are a couple of places of stamp hinge residue along the top edge. **Very Fine.**
From The William A. "Bill" Bond Collection (800-1,200)

12628 Baton Rouge, LA- State of Louisiana $100; $500; $1000 Bonds 1862 Cr. 62; 62c; 62e
These bonds have vignettes of a pelican feeding its young at top and bottom. The 62 grades **Fine** with several tape repairs, the 62c grades **Fine** with a small amout of ink erosion, paper separation at the folds, and small edge notches, and the 62e grades **Fine-VF** with two small tape repairs. All were once mounted with stamp hinges.
From The William A. "Bill" Bond Collection (Total: 3 items)
(900-1,200)

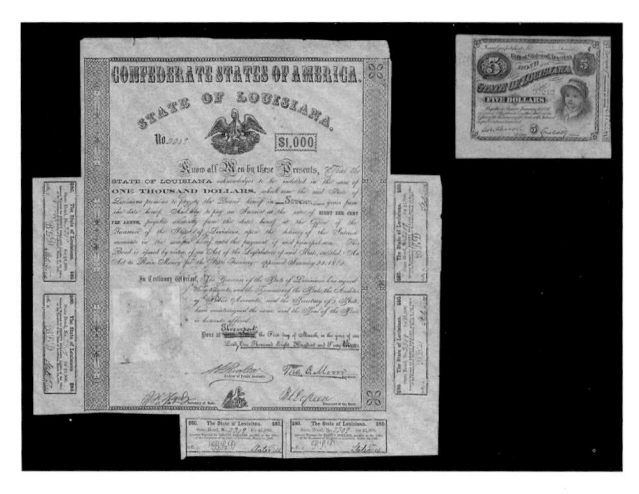

12629 Shreveport, LA- State of Louisiana $1000 Bond Cr. 62F

This bond has coupons at bottom and along the left and right sides. This bond also has the signatures of two Louisiana governors. The signature of Governor Thos. O. Moore, 1862-64 is on the face and on the back is the signature of Governor Henry W. Allen, 1864-65. Bonds signed by two different governors are rare. This bond grades **Fine** with edge splits with the longest being 1.5 inches. There is also ink erosion and some separation of paper at the folds. A couple of repairs are also noticed. A $5 Baby Bond, Cr. 80a, is included. Both were once mounted with stamp hinges.

From The William A. "Bill" Bond Collection (Total: 2 items) **(800-1,200)**

Rare Mississippi 1861 Bond in High Grade

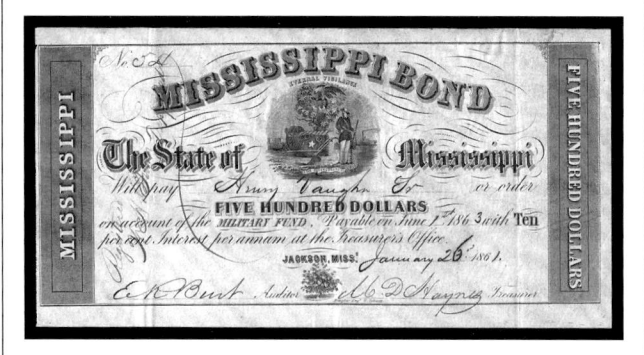

12630 Jackson, MS- State of Mississippi $500 Bond 1861 Cr. 61A

This issued bond has earned Criswell's highest rarity rating, an R11, 2 - 4 known. One edge nick is noticed along with a couple of pinholes and two places that once held stamp hinges. **Very Fine-Extremely Fine.**

From The William A. "Bill" Bond Collection **(800-1,200)**

12631 Jackson, MS- State of Mississippi $500 Bond 1865 Cr. 65A

This Mississippi bond is a R11, too. There is some staining near the right edge. There are also a couple of small right edge notches and a pinhole in the lower right corner of this issued bond. **Very Fine,** hinged.

From The William A. "Bill" Bond Collection **(700-1,000)**

12632 Jackson, MS- State of Mississippi $500 Bond 1874 Cr. 74A

This is a rare bond that was signed by Governor Adelbert Ames, but not issued. Criswell gave this bond a rarity of R11, 2 - 4 known. **Very Fine,** lightly mounted.

From The William A. "Bill" Bond Collection **(1,000-1,500)**

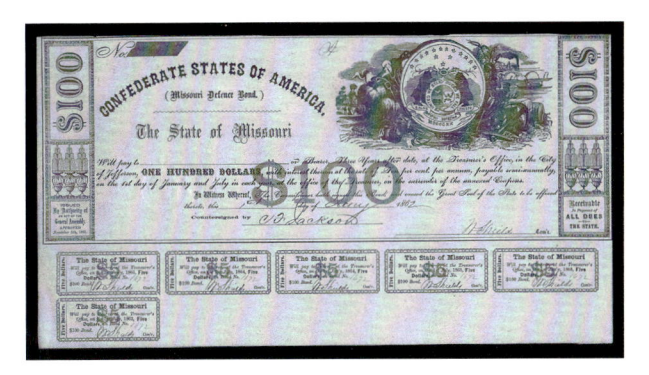

12633 (Jefferson City), MO- State of Missiouri Defence Coupon Bond $100 1862 Cr. 61A
This rare bond has an R9 rarity rating. This unissued bond is signed by Confederate Governor C.F. Jackson. Legislation for this issue was passed while the Rebel state government was in exile. **Uncirculated,** hinged.
From The William A. "Bill" Bond Collection **(700-1,000)**

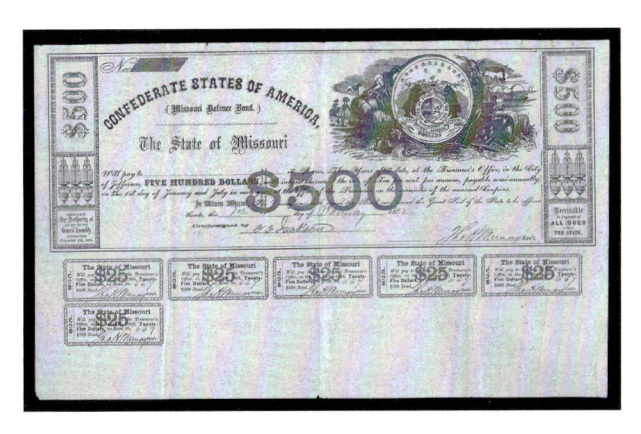

12634 (Jefferson City), MO- State of Missiouri Defence Coupon Bond $500 1862 Cr. 61E
This is another rare bond intended for issuance by the shadow state Confederate government in exile. This bond was also signed by Confederate Governor C.F. Jackson. It was once mounted with stamp hinges. **Very Fine.**
From The William A. "Bill" Bond Collection **(500-800)**

12635 Raleigh, NC- State of North Carolina $1000 Bonds 1862 Cr. 62I; 62K
These unissued bonds show some paper separation along the folds and an approximate two inch edge tear each. Both were once mounted with stamp hinges. **Fine.**
From The William A. "Bill" Bond Collection (Total: 2 items) **(350-500)**

12636 Raleigh, NC- State of North Carolina $1000 Bonds 1862 Cr. 62L; 62O
These unissued bonds are bright and they were once mounted with stamp hinges. **Fine-Very Fine** or better.
From The William A. "Bill" Bond Collection (Total: 2 items) **(400-700)**

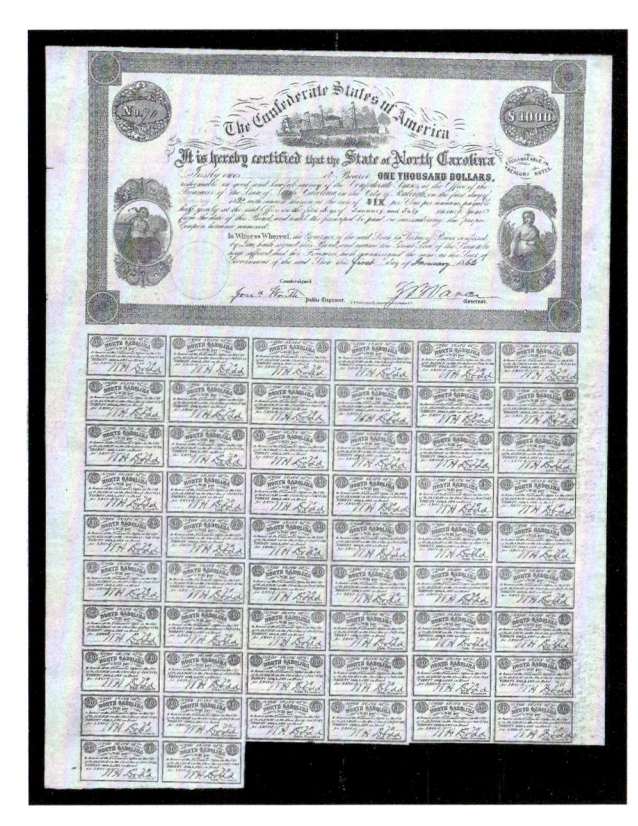

12637 Raleigh, NC- State of North Carolina $1000 Bond 1862 Cr. UNL
This unissued bond has just a few small places of paper separation and edge splits. **Very Fine,** lightly mounted.
From The William A. "Bill" Bond Collection **(700-1,000)**

12638 **Raleigh, NC- State of North Carolina** $500 Bond 1863 Cr. 64T
This unissued **Fine** bond is rare with an R9 rating by Criswell. It has paper separations along the center lateral fold. Aging is also noticed especially in one back quadrant. It was once lightly mounted with stamp hinges.
From The William A. "Bill" Bond Collection **(500-800)**

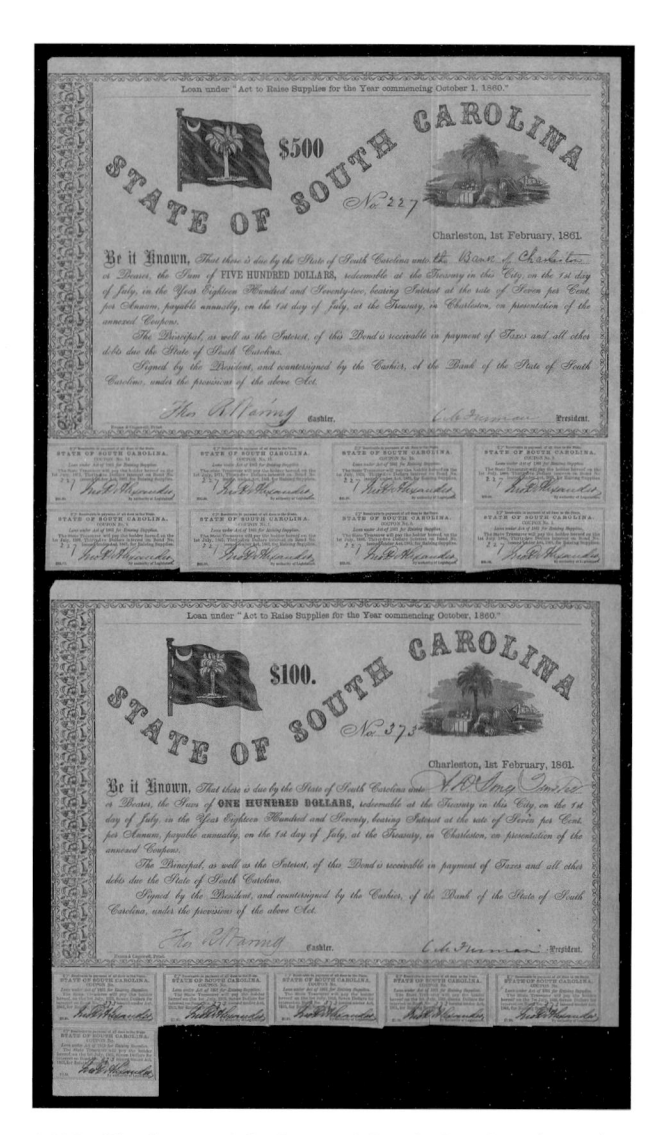

12639 **Charleston, SC- State of South Carolina** $100; $500 Bonds 1861 Cr. 61B; 61C
The 61B grades **XF** with a stamp hinge repair and the 61C grades **VF.** The bonds were once mounted and have the slightest amount of ink erosion. Also, both of these bonds are issued with the $500 going to the Bank of Charleston. These bonds were intended for the raising of supplies for the state militia.
From The William A. "Bill" Bond Collection (Total: 2 items) **(400-600)**

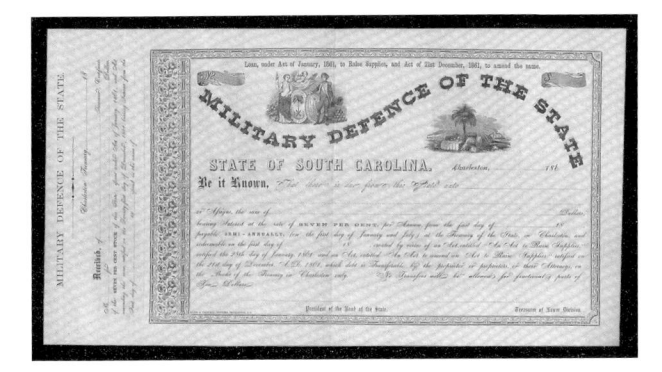

12640 **Charleston, SC- State of South Carolina** Unissued 1861 Bond Cr. 61D
This bond was intended for the "Military Defence of the State." This is an unissued example and the amounts were to be hand-written in. This bond has an R9 rarity rating. **Extremely Fine,** once mounted.
From The William A. "Bill" Bond Collection **(400-700)**

12641 **Charleston, SC-** $5170 Bond 1862 Cr. UNL
This is an unlisted bond in Criswell. It has a tiny bit of ink erosion and it was once mounted with stamp hinges. This "Military Defence of the State" bond was issued to the South Western Rail Road Bank. **Extremely Fine.**
From The William A. "Bill" Bond Collection **(800-1,200)**

12642 **Columbia, SC- State of South Carolina** $1000 Bond 1869 Cr. 69C
This bond has been cut cancelled twice and removed from a bond book. It was once mounted to construction paper with tape. **Extremely Fine.**
From The William A. "Bill" Bond Collection **(300-500)**

12643 **Columbia, SC- State of South Carolina** $1000 Bond 1871 Cr. 71A
This rare bond is unissued and it has a lateral center fold. It and its 39 coupons have each been cut cancelled. Almost every cut cancel has been repaired with tape. Some aging is also noticed on this bond that was once mounted with tape to construction paper. The lower left corner tip is missing, too. It is still attractive with its cotton boll vignette. **Extremely Fine.**
From The William A. "Bill" Bond Collection **(600-900)**

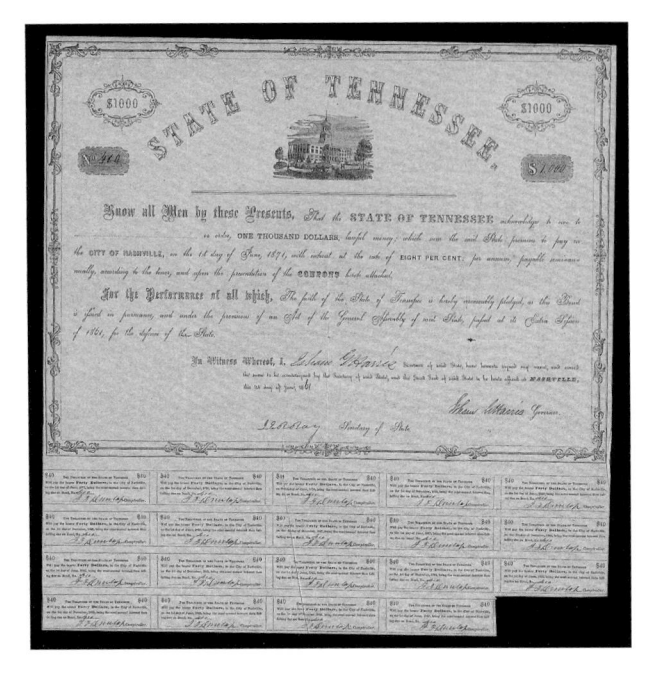

12644 Nashville, TN- State of Tennessee $1000 Bond 1861 Cr. 61A
This is an attractive **Very Fine,** once mounted with a few small paper separations along the folds.
From The William A. "Bill" Bond Collection **(300-500)**

12645 (Nashville), TN- State of Tennessee $1000 Bonds 1862 Cr. 62A; 62B
The 62A grades **VF** and it shows reinforcements of small splits with stamp hinges. It does not have any coupons. The 62B has five coupons and it grades **AU** with an approximate half inch top edge tear. Both were also mounted with stamp hinges and they are unissued.
From The William A. "Bill" Bond Collection (Total: 2 items) **(500-1,000)**

12646 Nashville, TN- State of Tennessee $1000 Bond 1866 Cr. 66B
This carpetbagger bond is bright for the grade. The bond has three large repairs/reinforcements. There is paper separation among some of the folds and an unrepaired two inch top edge split. This bond was once mounted using tape. It was issued to the Louisville & Nashville Railroad. **Fine.**
From The William A. "Bill" Bond Collection **(400-700)**

12647 **Nashville, TN- State of Tennessee** $1000 Bond 1867 Cr. 67A
This is a bright **Fine** bond with four repairs using six pieces of tape. This bond was once mounted. The coupons have a vignette of a train. This post Civil War product was issued by the carpetbagger state government to the Louisville & Nashville Railroad.
From The William A. "Bill" Bond Collection **(500-800)**

12648 **Austin, TX- Public Debt of the Late Republic of Texas** $2300; $126; $25; Remainder Bonds 1849-58 Cr. 37A; UNL; UNL; UNL
The 37A grades **VF**, CC; the Second Class B UNL grades **VF**, CC; the Second Class C UNL grades **VF**, CC, edge splits and pieces missing, and the remainder UNL grades **XF**, and all have been mounted with stamp hinges.
From The William A. "Bill" Bond Collection (Total: 4 items) **(400-700)**

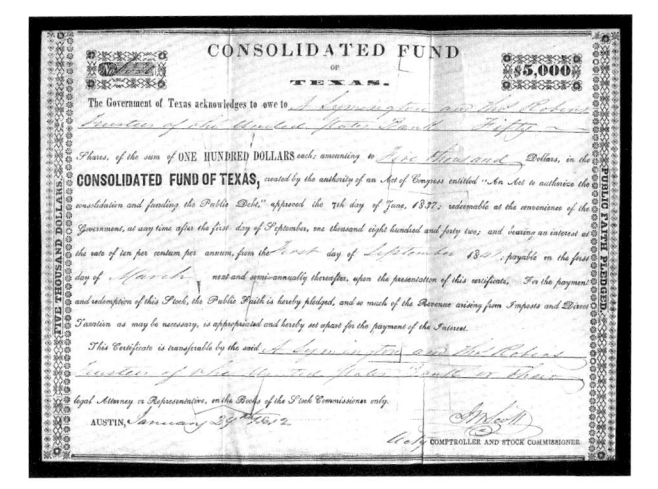

12649 **Austin, TX- Consolidated Fund of Texas** $5000 Bond 1837 Cr. UNL
This unissued bond has several cut cancels and two have been repaired with stamp hinges. Otherwise this is a bright **Extremely Fine-About Uncirculated** example that was once mounted with two more stamp hinges.
From The William A. "Bill" Bond Collection **(500-800)**

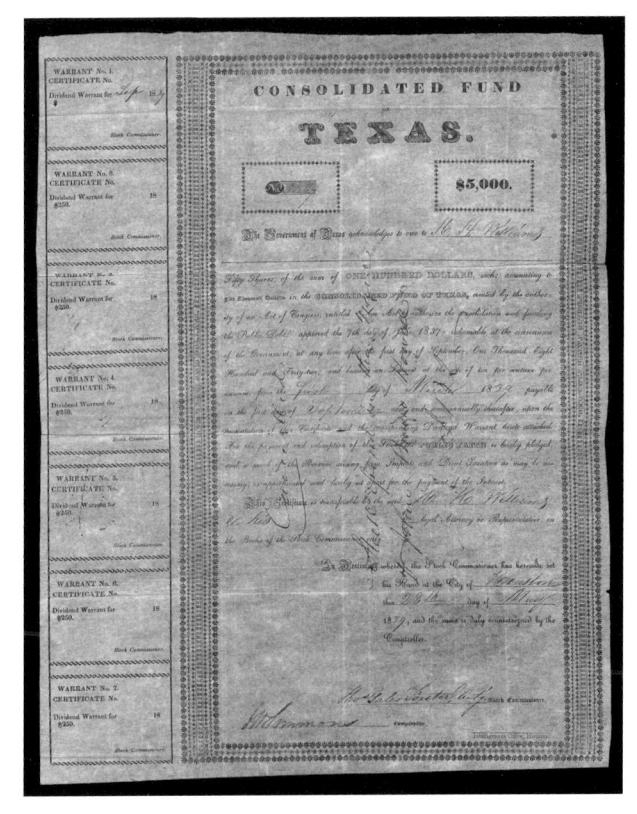

12650 **Austin, TX- Consolidated Fund of Texas** $5000 Bond 1839 Cr. 37F
This rare R10 bond has paper separation that includes an approximate 2.5 inch split. There is also a small amount of ink erosion. **Very Fine**, hinged.
From The William A. "Bill" Bond Collection **(500-800)**

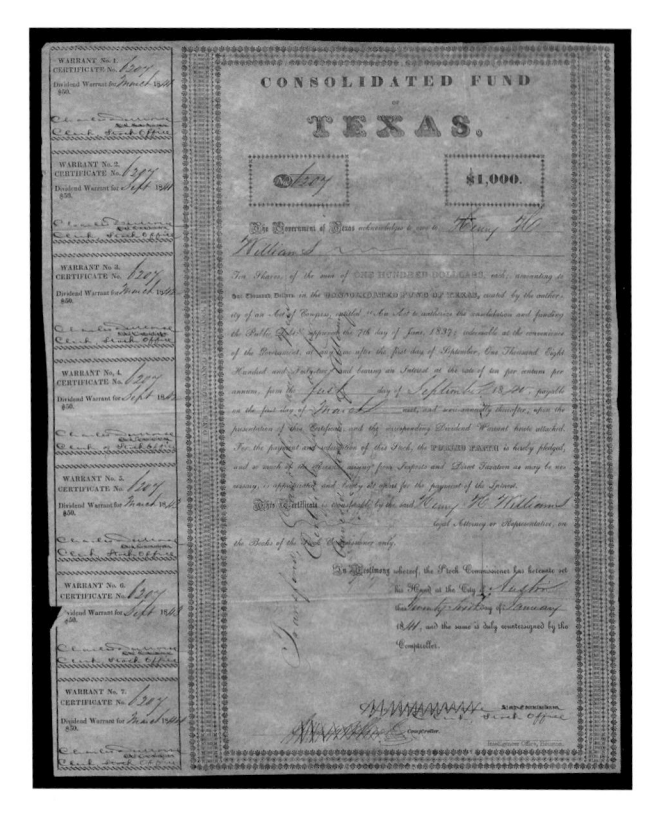

12651 **Austin, TX- Consolidated Fund of Texas** $1000 Bond 1841 Cr. 37E
This bond has a couple of approximate half inch edge tears and also an approximate 2.5 inch internal split. Other small amounts of paper separation are noticed along with ink erosion. This bond was once mounted with two stamp hinges. **Very Fine.**
From The William A. "Bill" Bond Collection **(500-800)**

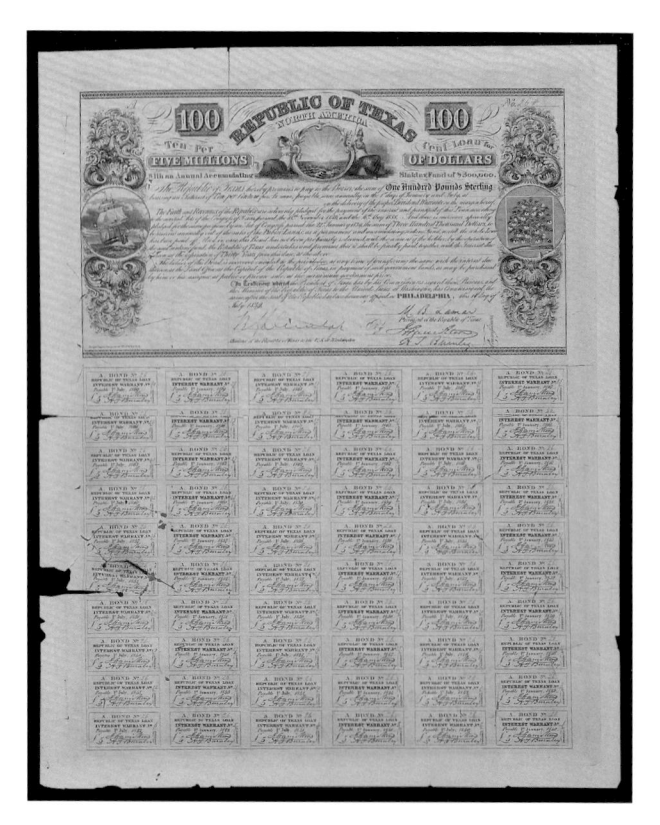

12652 **Austin, TX- Republic of Texas** $100 Bond 1839 Cr. 39B
This bond is signed by the president of the republic, M(irabeau) B(uonaparte) Lamar. This bond has the folds of a **Very Fine,** but numerous cut cancels in the bond itself and the coupons have been repaired with stamp hinges. There are also two 2.5 inch top edge tears. Another 4 inch fold split is found within the body of the bond, there are a couple of pieces missing from the left edge, and it has been mounted.
From The William A. "Bill" Bond Collection **(500-800)**

12653 **Austin, TX- Republic of Texas Government Bond** $100 Bonds 1840-41 Cr. 40B; 40E (2)
The 40B grades **VF,** with cut cancels; and the 40E's grade **XF.** One has cut cancels and the other has toning with a small amount of ink erosion.
From The William A. "Bill" Bond Collection (Total: 3 items) **(900-1,200)**

12654 **Austin, TX- Republic of Texas Government Bond** $500 Bonds 1840-41 Cr. 40A; 40C; 40F; 40G
The 40A grades bright **Fine,** cut cancels and an approximate one inch edge tear; the 40C grades **XF,** COC; the 40F grades **VF,** with cut cancels repaired and some small internal holes due to paper separation or ink erosion; and the 40G grades **XF** with cut cancels and COCs.
From The William A. "Bill" Bond Collection (Total: 4 items) **(1,200-1,700)**

12655 **Austin, TX- Public Debt of the Late Republic of Texas** $135; $67.50; $605; $1681 Bonds 1849-51 Cr. 48A; 48B; 48C; 48D
The 48A grades **VF**, ink erosion, rubber stamp paid; the 48B grades **Fine**, CC; the 48C grades **VF**, soiling, paper splits, edge tears, rubber stamp paid; and the 48D grades **Fine** with orange seal, edge wear that includes an approximate 2.5 inch edge tear, and internal paper separation, and rubber stamp paid. All were once mounted with stamp hinges and they carry endorsements on the back.
From The William A. "Bill" Bond Collection (Total: 4 items)
(400-700)

12656 **Austin, TX- Public Debt of the Late Republic of Texas** $31.50; $25; $140.30 1853-55 Cr. 53A; 53B; 53C
The 53A grades **VF**, CC, edge pieces missing, repair at top center, small holes; the 53B grades **Fine-VF**, paper separation and an approximate half inch internal split; and the 53C grades **XF**, CC with tape residue at top. These were once mounted with stamp hinges and they carry endorsements on the back.
From The William A. "Bill" Bond Collection (Total: 3 items)
(300-500)

12657 **Austin, TX- Texian Loan of One Million Dollars** $1000 Bond 1861 Cr. 61A
A great vignette of a frontiersman adorns this classic Texas bond. It also sports Confederate and Texas flag vignettes. This bond is signed by Governor F(rancis) R. Lubbock. Some aging is noticed with paper separation along the folds. Nearly ten tape repairs have covered most of the paper separation on this once lightly mounted bond. **Fine.**
From The William A. "Bill" Bond Collection **(1,000-1,500)**

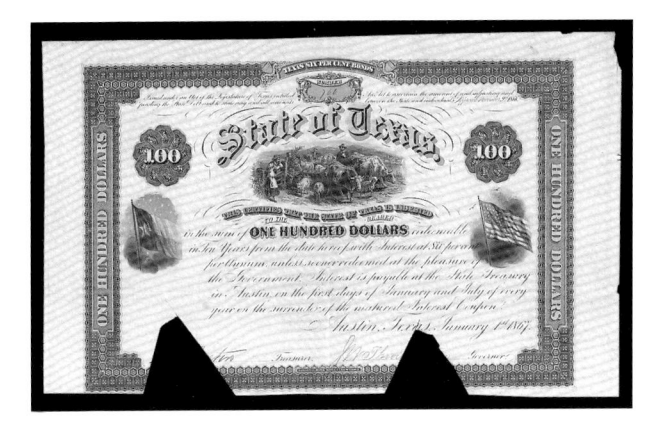

12658 **Austin, TX- State of Texas** $100 Bond 1867 Cr. 66A
This has always been one of the more popular Texas bonds despite its low population numbers. It was printed by the National Bank Note Co and it includes attractive Texas and American flag vignettes. This **Very Fine** once lightly mounted unissued bond has two large cut out cancels. A tiny amount of paper separation is also found along the vertical center fold.
From The William A. "Bill" Bond Collection **(1,000-1,500)**

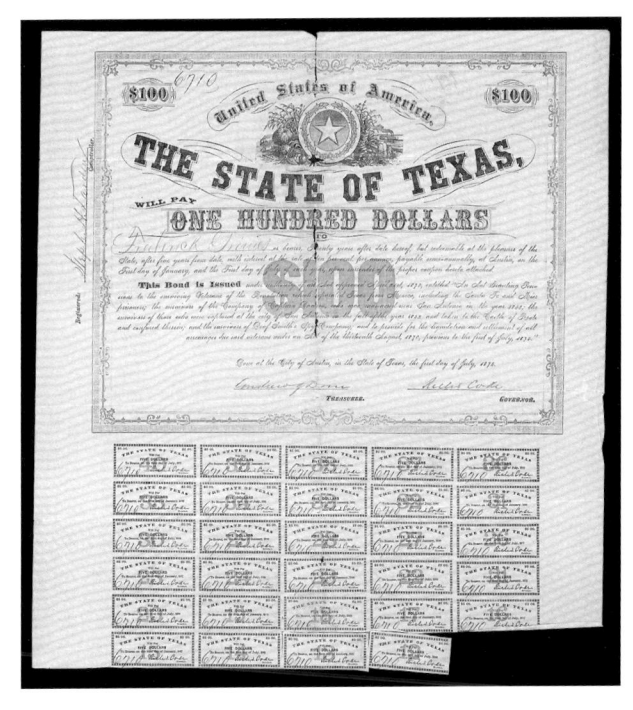

12659 **Austin, TX- State of Texas** $100 Bond 1874 Cr. 74B
This bond has the folds of a **Very Fine,** but it has quite a bit of paper separation among the top 60% of the bond along the vertical center fold. The last two coupons have been reattached with stamp hinges. This bond was also once mounted with stamp hinges. The bond is signed by Governor Richard Coke.
From The William A. "Bill" Bond Collection **(700-1,000)**

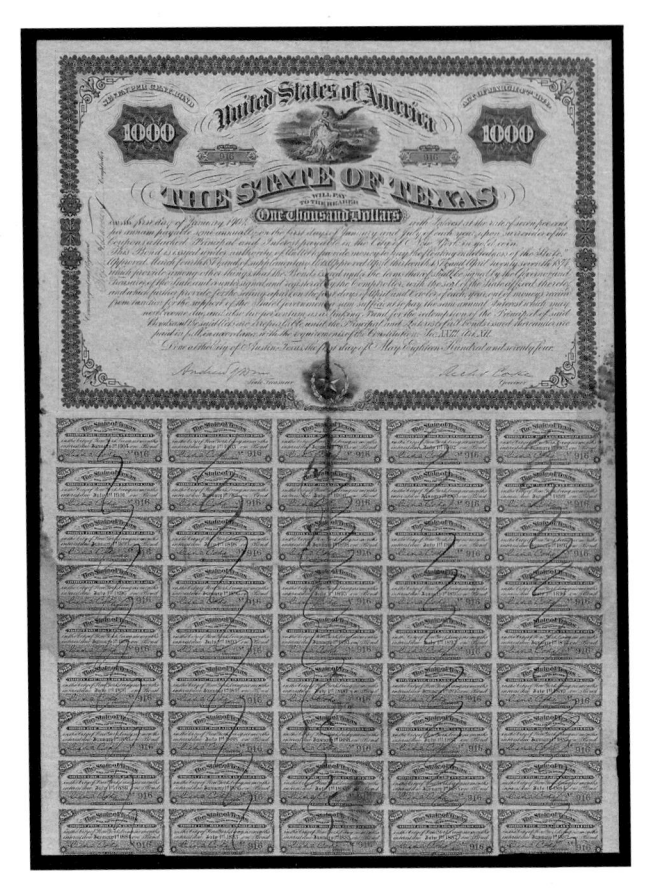

12660 **Austin, TX- State of Texas** $1000 Bond 1874 Cr. 74A
The coupons have been pen cancelled. The bond grades **Very Fine** with several stains including rust at center and along the left and right edges. Still a rare bond that has been mounted. Governor Richard Coke signed this bond.
From The William A. "Bill" Bond Collection **(700-1,000)**

12661 **Austin, TX- State of Texas** $1000 Bond 1879 Cr. 79D
This bond has had red lines printed through the coupons to cancel them. The treasurer is former governor F(rancis) R(ichard) Lubbock and the governor is Oren M(ilo) Roberts. This is a problem-free example that was once mounted with stamp hinges. **Very Fine.**
From The William A. "Bill" Bond Collection **(800-1,200)**

12662 Richmond, VA- Commonwealth of Virginia $3000 Bond 1861 Cr. 61A
This R9 bond has the ABC monogram. It too was once mounted with stamp hinges. There is an approximately one inch tear at top center. **Fine.**
From The William A. "Bill" Bond Collection (500-800)

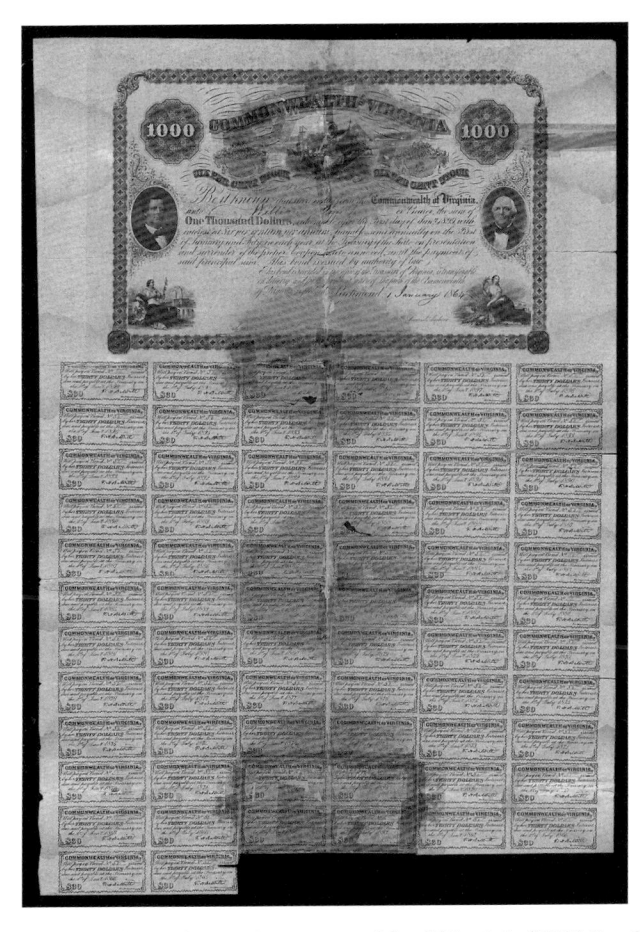

12663 Richmond, VA- Commonwealth of Virginia $1000 Bond 1864 Cr. 64A
Portraits of Virginia governors Floyd and Mason adorn this R9 bond that has had extensive repairs and some loss of paper. It also has several moisture stains and long edge splits. **Good.**
From The William A. "Bill" Bond Collection (200-400)

OBSOLETES BY STATE

ALABAMA

Unlisted Huntsville Issuer

12664 Huntsville, AL- Williams & Long 10¢ June 15, 1862 Rosene UNL
This issuer is unlisted in the Rosene reference, and was not found in our landmark Alabama obsolete collection we sold back in 2001 either. **Very Fine.** (500-800)

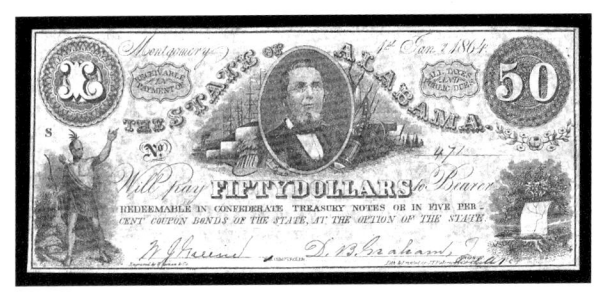

12665 Montgomery, AL - State of Alabama $50 Jan. 1, 1864 Cr.13
Simply a gorgeous **Choice About Uncirculated** example that is a corner fold from being called Gem. Signatures appear to be Greene as Comptroller, and Graham as Treasurer, written over Governor. (250-300)

12666 Montgomery, AL - State of Alabama $100 Jan. 1, 1864 Cr. 12
A very nice, seldom-seen note with an Indian Family vignette at center. A bit of handling keeps this from the gem designation. **Crisp Uncirculated.** (300-400)

ARKANSAS

12667 Fayetteville, AR- Bank of the State of Arkansas $5 Nov. 1, 1838 G152 Rothert 186-6
This note was originally a post note, designed before this bank suspended specie payments after running through funds raised through an issuance of state bonds. The law prohibited the issuance of post notes, and their issue was suspended after judgment was obtained against the bank. That failed to deter the bank, however, which simply hand altered the note removing the interest payment provision, but still leaving the note as a post note payable twelve months after its issue date. **Fine,** and very rare, having sold for $920 in our January, 2006 auction. **(700-1,100)**

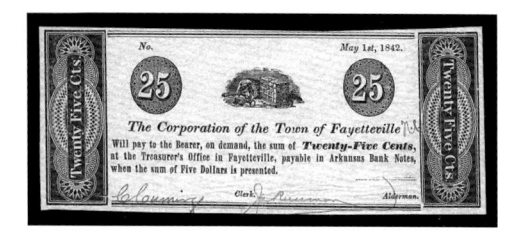

12668 Fayetteville, AR- Corporation of the Town of Fayetteville 25¢ May 1, 1842 Rothert 192-1
There is an as-made sheet fold at the bottom, but this rare early Arkansas municipal issue listed as R-7 in Rothert has clearly never circulated. **Uncirculated. (300-500)**

12669 Fayetteville, AR- Corporation of the Town of Fayetteville 50¢ May 1, 1842 Rothert 192-2
Just as scarce as the 25¢ note above, and just as high grade as well. **Uncirculated. (300-500)**

12670 Fayetteville, AR- Town of Fayetteville 25¢ 1872 Rothert 193-1
A nice example of this post-Civil war issue from Fayetteville, with the two minor denominations using the Fractional Currency size and format. **Uncirculated,** with one small spot on the back. **(250-450)**

12671 Fayetteville, AR- Town of Fayetteville 50¢ 1873 Rothert 193-2
A second fractional denomination with a slightly different face design. **Crisp Uncirculated,** with a mounting spot on the back. **(250-450)**

12672 Fayetteville, AR- Town of Fayetteville $1 1872 Rothert 193-3
A very scarce full size issue in this denomination. **Very Fine-Extremely Fine. (450-650)**

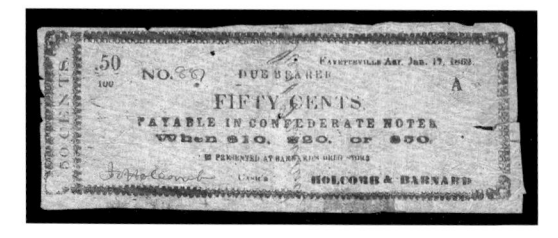

12673 Fayetteville, AR- Holcomb & Barnard 50¢ Jan. 17, 1862 Rothert 198-8
A rare piece of scrip which is the only one we've ever had from this issuer. It's printed on the usual wretched tissue like paper, and shows a few splits and petty holes. **Very Good. (300-500)**

12674 Fayetteville, AR- Stirman & Dickson 50¢ Jan. 25, 1862 Rothert 201-2
An interesting and quite scarce note printed on the backs of the 1842 municipal issue notes due to the severe paper shortage during the Civil War. **Very Good** in appearance, but with a few repairs. **(250-450)**

12675 Helena, AR- Exchange Bank $10 Sept. 2, 1861 Rothert 279-2
This **Fine+** example is solid for the grade and has no visible flaws. The stern visage of John C. Calhoun decorates the lower right corner. **(200-300)**

12676 Helena, AR- Helena Insurance Co. 25¢ July 1, 1861 Rothert 281-1B
The very scarce variety which lacks the words "Confederate Notes" in the obligation. **Fine. (250-450)**

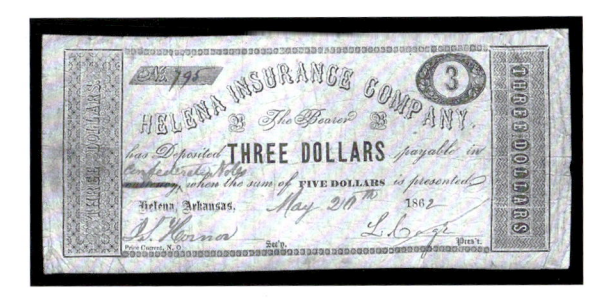

12677 Helena, AR- Helena Insurance Company $3 May 20, 1862 Rothert 281-5
An extremely rare denomination from this issuer, and listed as R-7 in the Rothert reference. Nice **Fine. (350-550)**

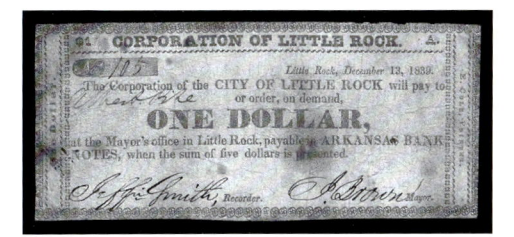

12678 Corporation of Little Rock $1 Dec. 13, 1839 Rothert 420-4
A neat piece of early Arkansas scrip that is seldom seen in any grade. This particular example was made payable to and endorsed on the back by Albert Pike, the well known Arkansas newspaperman and lawyer who later became infamous for his stint as a Brigadier General in the Confederate Army. A regiment of Cherokee troops was under his command during the Battle of Pea Ridge, where they collected about 25 Yankee scalps. Pike quickly lost his command when the scandal became public knowledge. **Very Good-Fine,** with a couple of minor stains that are immaterial to the note's overall appearance. **(400-600)**

12679 Little Rock, AR- Arkansas Treasury Warrants $1, $1 Dec. 1861 Cr. 1, 1b Rothert 375-1, 375-1
The Cr. 1 grades **Fair,** backed and the Cr. 1b grades **Good,** with splits especially along the lateral center fold. Despite their low grades, these are rare notes. In the new Shull, *A Guide Book of Southern States Currency,* for value they are only described as very rare and rare with rarities R10 and R9 respectively. (Total: 2 notes) **(200-400)**

Extremely Rare Arkansas Treasury Warrant

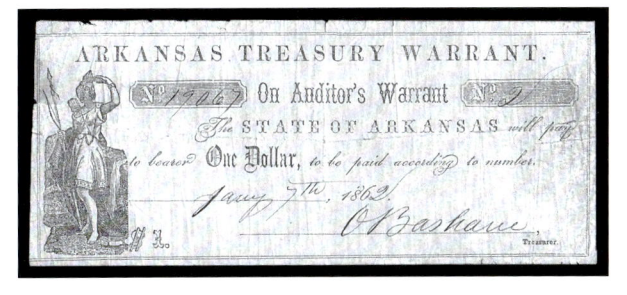

12680 Little Rock, AR- Arkansas Treasury Warrants $1 Jan. 7, 1862 Cr. 4 Rothert 377-1
This is an extremely rare note weighing in at R11, 2 - 4 notes known. An approximate quarter inch left edge split is noticed along with some internal separation of paper. It also is adorned with serial number 2. **Fine. (800-1,200)**

12681 Little Rock, AR- Arkansas Treasury Warrants $1, $3, $10 1861-2 Cr. 8, 10, 15 Rothert 379-1, 379-3, 381-5
The Cr. 8 grades **Very Good** with splits including an approximate 1.5 inch left edge split, the Cr. 10 grades **Fine** with just a few small splits, and the R9 Cr. 15 is a solid **Very Fine.** (Total: 3 notes) **(700-1,000)**

12682 Little Rock, AR- Arkansas Treasury Warrants $1, $2 1861-2 Cr. 8a, 13 Rothert 379-1, 381-2
The Cr. 8a grades **About Good** and it has been backed while also missing its upper left corner. The rare Cr. 9 grades **Fine+.** (Total: 2 notes) **(350-550)**

12683 **Little Rock, AR- Arkansas Treasury Warrants** $1.35, $10 (Uncut Pair), $10 1862 Cr. 26, 54, 55 Rothert 387-1, 393-1, 393-1
The Cr. 26 has a hand-written denomination and it grades **Very Fine,** with pinholes, the Cr. 54 is an uncut pair grading **Fine,** and the Cr. 55 has an inverted back and it grades **Fine.** (Total: 3 notes) (500-800)

12684 **Little Rock, AR- Cincinnati & Little Rock Slate Company** $1, $2, $5 Rothert 409-1, 409-4, 409-7
Three pieces, the $1 **Extremely Fine,** the $2 **Good-Very Good,** and the $5 **Very Fine+.** (Total: 3 notes) (350-550)

12685 **Little Rock, AR- Cincinnati & Little Rock Slate Company** $10 March 1, 1855 Rothert 409-10
A nice example with the engraved reverse. **Uncirculated.** (250-350)

12686 **Little Rock, AR- Cincinnati & Little Rock Slate Company** $1, $2, $2 1854-5 Rothert 409-2, 409-3, 409-4
The 409-2 grades **Very Fine,** the 409-3 grades **Fine,** and the 409-4 grades **Good,** repaired corner. The first two notes have sound edges. (Total: 3 notes) (300-500)

12687 **Little Rock, AR- Cincinnati & Little Rock Slate Company** $3 Dec. 1, 1854 Rothert 409-5, 6
Two pieces of this tougher denomination, the plain back a nice **Very Fine-Extremely Fine,** the engraved back **Very Fine.** (Total: 2 notes) (300-500)

12688 **Little Rock, AR- Haynes' Hotel** 25¢ March 13, 1863 Rothert 416-1
An extremely rare piece of Arkansas scrip which is listed as Rarity-7 in the Rothert reference. It's printed on thin tissue paper, with the usual weak spots and a minor repair or two. **Fine.** (400-600)

12689 **Little Rock, AR- City of Little Rock** $1 Dec. 20, 1872 Rothert 424-2
These city issued "Certificates of Indebtedness" were circulated locally, but were usually discounted to some degree because of the issuer's precarious financial condition. This piece is a solid **Fine** and much nicer than most survivors, which are generally seen in utterly wretched shape. (250-450)

12690 **Peters Landing, AR- Geo. B. Peters** $1 Rothert 550-3
A very scarce piece of full size scrip from this R-7 issuer. **Fine-Very Fine.** (350-550)

12691 **Pine Bluff, AR- City of Pine Bluff** 25¢ Rothert 556-2
A very scarce piece of Pine Bluff municipal scrip which is the only example we've ever had of its type and denomination. **Extremely Fine,** with one small split and a small piece out on the right side. (250-450)

12692 **Pine Bluff, AR- City of Pine Bluff** $5 Rothert 556-7
Just another plain rare Pine Bluff Civil War issue. **Fine.** (350-550)

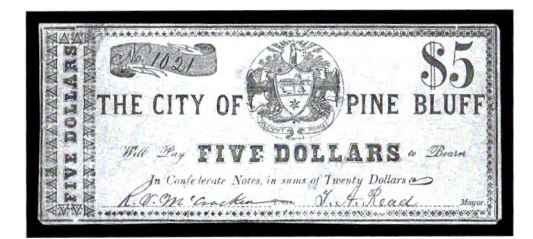

12693 Pine Bluff, AR- City of Pine Bluff $5 Rothert 556-8
This note is different from the example above in design, format and size, although both specimens are listed as R-7 in Rothert. Pleasing **Fine**. (350-550)

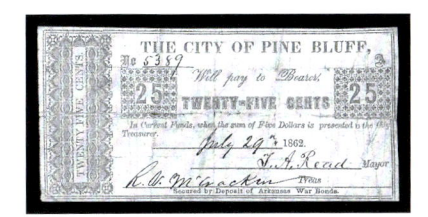

12694 Pine Bluff, AR- City of Pine Bluff 25¢ July 29, 1862 Rothert 557-2
A very scarce Civil War issue with this note listed as R-7 in Rothert. **Fine** in appearance, but with a few reverse repairs. (250-450)

DISTRICT OF COLUMBIA

12695 Washington, DC - Bullion Bank $2 July 4, 1862 G22a
Always a popular example due to the layout and unique green printing on the back. **PMG Choice Uncirculated 63.** (250-300)

FLORIDA

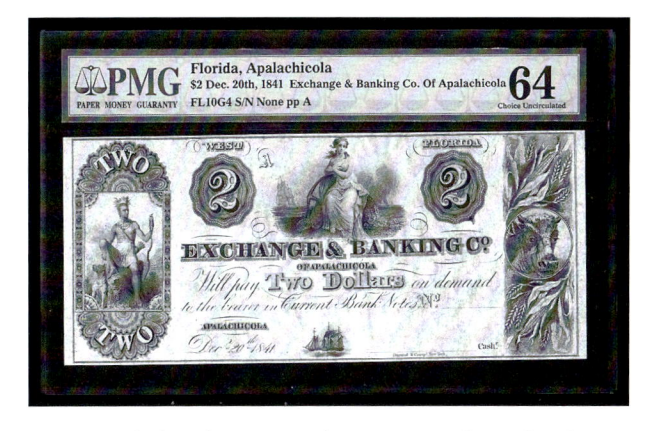

12696 Apalachicola, FL- Exchange & Banking Co. $2 Dec 20th, 1841
This bright remainder boasts solid margins all around, a rarity for many obsolete issues. **PMG Choice Uncirculated 64.** (250-350)

12697 Tallahassee, FL - State of Florida $3 Jan. 1, 1864 Cr.37
Just a little bit of handling is noticed on this gorgeous $3 note that is watermarked. (350-450)

12698 Tallahassee, FL- State of Florida $50 Oct. 10, 1861 Cr. 3
A lone corner tip fold is noted on this nearly perfect **Choice About Uncirculated** $50. (300-400)

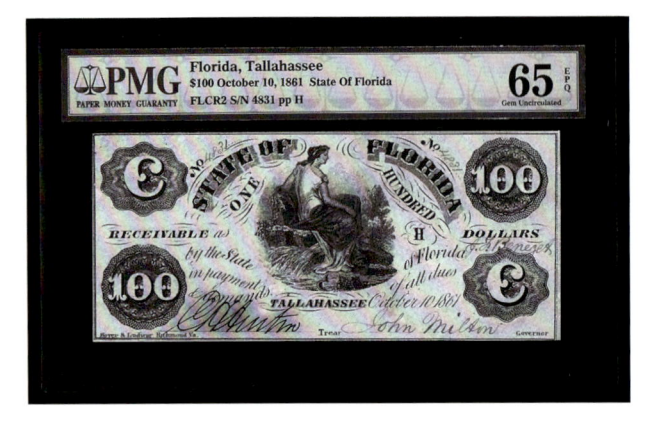

12699 Tallahassee, FL- State of Florida $100 Oct. 10, 1861 Cr. 2
The paper here is exceptional, and while one margin nicks part of the lower border, this note is one of the few that is not missing a border on an entire side. **PMG Gem Uncirculated 65 EPQ.** (300-400)

GEORGIA

12700 Morgan, GA - Bank of Morgan $50 Mar. 9, 1857
This is a scarce denomination from a fraudulent bank that issued six different denominations, and all quite interesting and collectible today. **PMG Choice Uncirculated 64 EPQ.** (400-600)

ILLINOIS

12701 Lockport, IL- State Bank of Illinois $2.50 18__
This proof is stamped "Property of American Bank Note Co." on back and comes with a few paper pulls on the reverse. The face is perfect and faces up well. **PMG Uncirculated 60, Proprietary Proof.** (300-400)

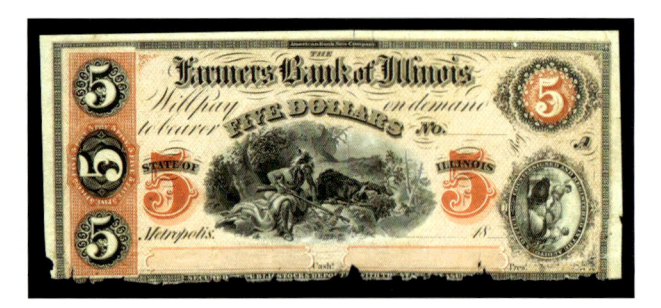

12702 Metropolis, IL- The Farmers Bank of Illinois $5 G6a Proof
A beautiful fully red tinted American Bank Note Company product, although absolutely not part of the ABNCo archives sale of several years ago. There are a few minor splits and a few small pieces missing from the bottom, but this is still a great Illinois item worthy of the finest of collections. **Very Fine.** (400-700)

12703 Metropolis, IL- The Farmers Bank of Illinois $10 G8a Proof
A second red tinted Proof, which is so rare that it is listed in Haxby with the notation "No Description Available." There are a few small repairs, but this is still a beautiful piece which will be a bargain whatever it fetches tonight. **Extremely Fine.** (1,000-1,500)

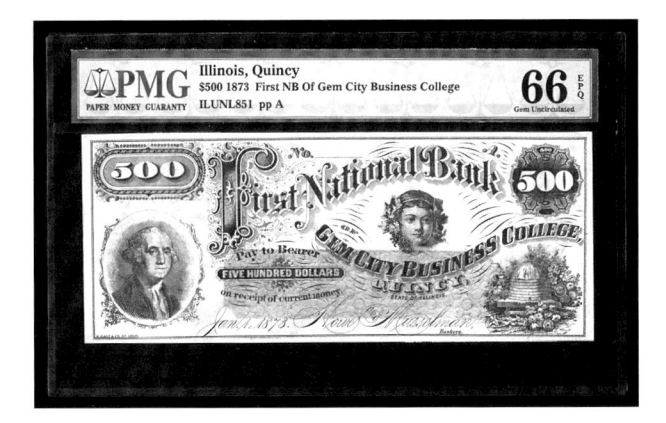

12704 **Quincy, IL- First National Bank of Gem City Business College** Jan. 1, 1873 Schingoethe IL-850 $500
Every usual denomination is listed in Schingoethe for this institution from the $1 to the $1000, except for the $100 and $500 denominations. This $500 is graded **Gem Uncirculated 66 EPQ** by PMG. (300-500)

12705 **Urbana, IL- Grand Prairie Bank** $5 18__ Proof G8a
The paper quality on this piece is exceptional as is the color and printed details. To date, we have handled only one other note from this institution, a ratty VG ace that realized nearly $200. **PCGS Gem New 65PPQ.** (400-600)

INDIANA

12706 **Attica, IN- The Shawnee Bank** $3 July 1, 1854 G4 Wolka 23-2
A very scarce three bearing a classic Indian hunting a buffalo vignette. This piece is listed as Rarity 6 in the Wolka reference. **Fine.** (225-375)

IOWA

12707 **Anamosa, IA- Wapsipinicon Land Co.** $3 March 4, 1858 Oakes 3-2
This issued note boasts perfect paper quality and great remaining signatures. Of the few examples of this issue that we have handled, it is the nicest. **Choice About Uncirculated.** (300-400)

12708 **Burlington, IA- Merchants' Insurance Co. & Burlington Savings Bank** $1 June 1, 1857 Oakes 15-1
This is a scarce financial instrument from Iowa; an R7, or between 1 and 5 surviving notes according to Oakes. In the last seven years, we have handled only one other note from this institution, thus Oakes's rarity ranking is likely very accurate. **Good** with some compromises of the paper. (200-300)

12709 **Dubuque, IA- The Dubuque & Sioux City Rail Road Co.** $1 Feb. 17, 1862 Oakes 52-1
A just plain rare Iowa railroad issue. **Fine,** with a couple of small chips out at the bottom. (500-700)

12710 **Dubuque, IA- Lumberman's Bank** $2 and $3 Sept. 1, 1857 Oakes 55-2a and Oakes 55-3a
This remainder pair is brightly colored, though some light folds account for the grade of **Choice About Uncirculated.** Our archive indicates we have only handled two other examples of this institution's notes, both of which were heavily circulated. **(400-500)**

12711 **Mills County, IA- Onondaga Bank** $2 Apr. 9, 1858 UNL Oakes 100-1
This is the first time for this bank to make an appearance in any of our auctions. This is the only denomination issued for this bank and though good for "Two Dollars in Current Bank Notes," the note has a 1000 counter in the upper left corner. This bank was up to some shenanigans. **Very Good-Fine. (250-350)**

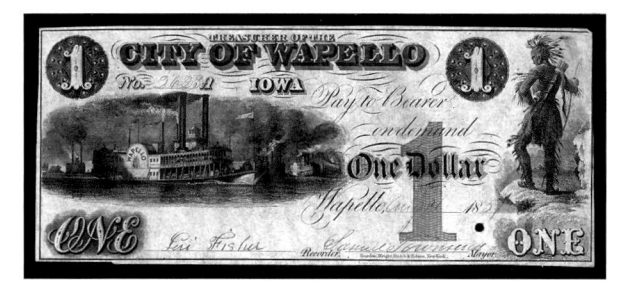

12712 **Wapello, IA- City of Wapello** $1 Aug. 8, 1851 Oakes 109-11
This piece was actually produced as a proof and has one small punch cancellation at lower right. Signatures and a date were filled in, presumably to be passed in circulation. **Choice About Uncirculated. (250-350)**

12713 **Washington, IA- State Bank of Iowa** $1 Oct. 17, 1859 Oakes 110-1
Oakes estimates that only between 1 and 5 examples of this issue are likely to exist. This **About Good** is missing a corner and has some compromises about the edges, but still as nice, or better than the plate note in Oakes's reference. **(200-300)**

KENTUCKY

12714 **Danville, KY- Danville, Lancaster, Nicholasville Turnpike** 50¢ (1862) Hughes 199
This rare note is listed as an R-7, "Description Unknown" in the Hughes reference. The right edge of this note has a contemporary repair with a portion of a page from a spelling primer. The lost paper contained the date and most of the letters for "Lancaster." **Fair. (200-300)**

LOUISIANA

12715 **New Orleans, LA- Citizens' Bank of Louisiana** $10 G26a
A lovely example of the famous "Dix" note. **Crisp Uncirculated,** with a tiny split in the top margin. **(500-700)**

12716 **New Orleans, LA - Canal Bank** $500 remainder G70a
A lovely **PMG Gem Uncirculated 66 EPQ** example of this higher denomination note that is becoming more difficult to find. **(350-450)**

12717 New Orleans, LA - Canal Bank $1,000 Remainder G80a
Like the $500 above, this denomination is becoming more difficult to locate in today's market. **PMG Gem Uncirculated 65 EPQ.** (400-600)

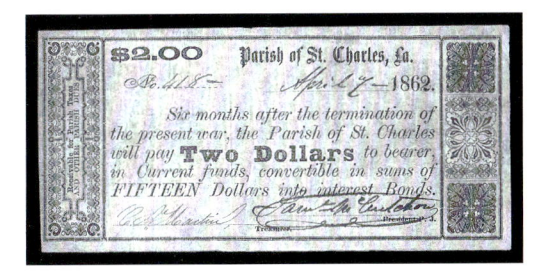

12718 St. Charles Parish, LA- Parish of St. Charles $2 April 7, 1862
An attractive note from this very scarce Parish, with this piece printed on the backs of recycled New Orleans merchant scrip. **Very Fine-Extremely Fine.** (400-600)

MARYLAND

12719 Baltimore, MD- Farmers & Planters Bank $10 G16 Shank 5.66.8 Proof
An extremely rare and likely unique Proof, with the only note known bearing this design a spurious example made from a genuine plate. There are a few repaired splits, and the note is falsely filled in, but this is a truly rare Maryland item worthy of a strong bid. **Extremely Fine.** (500-800)

12720 Port Deposit, MD- Susquehanna Bank $20-$20-$50-$100 18__ G12-G12-G14-G16 Shank 102.11.9-9-10-11 Uncut Sheet
Here is a delightful uncut sheet that is as fresh as the day it was printed more than 150 years ago. **Gem Crisp Uncirculated.** (250-450)

MICHIGAN

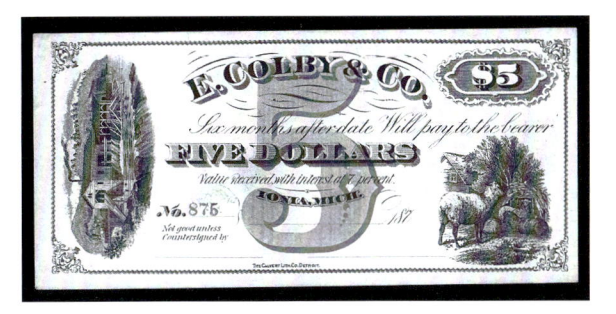

12721 Ionia, MI- E. Colby & Co. $5 Bowen 5
A very scarce piece of scrip from this company, which was in operation from 1868 until 1876. Eastman Colby and his brother C.W. were lumber dealers and manufacturers. **Uncirculated.** (300-500)

MINNESOTA

12722 Minneapolis, MN- Purmont & Steele $5 Hewitt UNL
A newly discovered full size piece of commission scrip that comes from a previously unknown Minnesota issuer, who operated the "Boston One Price Clothing Store." Expect some serious competition before the hammer falls on this bright **Extremely Fine** example. (600-900)

MISSISSIPPI

12723 Jackson, (MS)- Bowman House 25¢ May 26, 1862 Krause UNL
This date is not listed in the Krause reference for this rare issue. This remainder carries a nice portrait of Jefferson Davis. **Fine-Very Fine.**
From The William A. "Bill" Bond Collection **(400-600)**

12724 Port Gibson, MS- The Port Gibson Insurance Co. 50¢ Jan. 1, 1840 Leggett UNL Kraus 23692
An excessively rare and very likely unique note. This denomination is listed as "Not Reported" in the Kraus reference, which notes that only two examples are known from this issuer, a 12 1/2¢ in the Smithsonian and a $3. There are a couple of relatively minor splits, but the color and appearance of this piece is all that one could demand. **Fine,** a great Mississippi item worthy of the finest of collections. **(1,000-1,500)**

MISSOURI

12725 St. Louis, MO-Cairo & St. Louis Railroad 25¢ (1877)
This is a St. Louis Bank Note Co. printer's proof that has been attached to a die card, in this case die 3671. Backs of these notes declare that they are valid for use by company employees only "for meals and lodging." **Choice Crisp Uncirculated.** **(400-600)**

NEBRASKA

12726 Florence, NE- Bank of Florence $1-$2-$3-$5 18__ G2a-G4a-G6a-G8a Uncut Sheet
These remainders are scarce in sheet form. Handling is noticed in the bottom corner selvage far from the notes. A small notch is found in the right edge. We sold one of these sheets in the same grade for $780 in January 2007. **Choice Crisp Uncirculated.** **(400-600)**

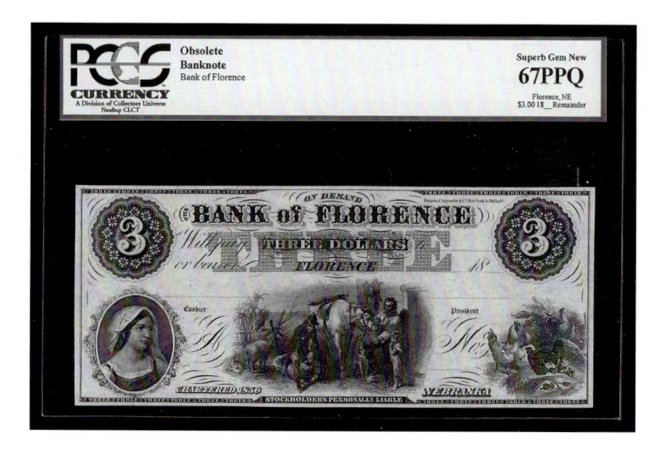

12727 Florence, NE- The Bank of Florence $3 18XX G6a
This well inked piece is graded **Superb Gem New 67PPQ** by PCGS. **(250-350)**

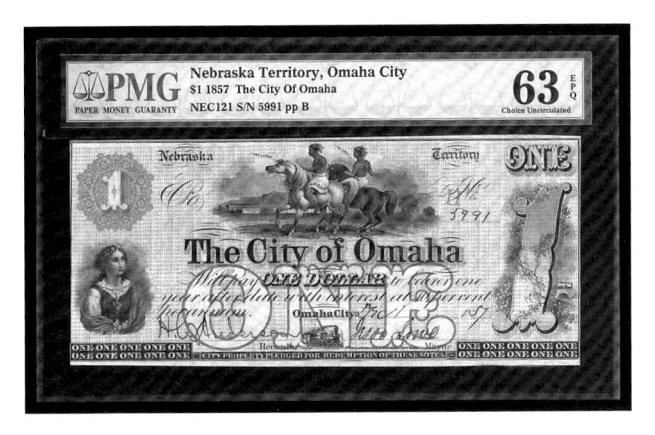

12728 **Omaha, NE - The City of Omaha** $1 Sept. 10, 1857
A well margined example of this scarce and popular denomination, graded **PMG Choice Uncirculated 63 EPQ.** (250-350)

12729 **Omaha, NE - The City of Omaha** $5 Dec. 1, 1857
A pretty note that features a vignette of an elk in the lower right corner. If this note had the bottom frameline, perhaps PMG would have granted a higher grade than **PMG Uncirculated 62 EPQ.** (150-200)

NEW HAMPSHIRE

12730 **Union, NH- Tredick, Swinerton, Gilman** 25¢ Oct. 30, 1862
Prior to this mini-hoard of notes' being offered, we had only handled one example of this trio's scrip. These pieces feature an Indian Head vignette at center and predate their second issue by a mere month and a half. **About Uncirculated to Choice Uncirculated.** (Total: 4 notes) (300-400)

12731 **Union, NH- Tredick, Swinerton, Gilman** 5¢ Dec. 15, 1862
Each of the three denominations offered here is printed in a different color ink, this one being red with the vignette of a miner at left. **About Uncirculated to Choice Uncirculated.** (Total: 5 notes) (300-400)

12732 **Union, NH- Tredick, Swinerton, Gilman** 10¢ Dec. 15, 1862
A farmer stands proudly with his sheath on this blue colored issue. **Choice Crisp Uncirculated.** (Total: 5 notes) (300-400)

12733 **Union, NH- Tredick, Swinerton, Gilman** 25¢ Dec. 15, 1862
At left is a small vignette of a carriage loaded with goods. These pieces vary in grade due to a corner fold on a couple of the pieces. **About Uncirculated to Choice Uncirculated.** (Total: 7 notes) (400-500)

NEW JERSEY

12734 **Garfield, NJ- City of Garfield, Tax Anticipation Note Specimen** $25 Sept. 1, 1933
This large denomination tax anticipation note was issued in the throes of the depression. SPECIMEN is stamped three times at bottom, and the serial number is C0000. The paper is excellent on this **Gem Crisp Uncirculated HOC.** (250-400)

12735 **Newark, NJ- State Bank at Newark** $2 Dec. 15, 1864 G28a Wait UNL
An extremely rare New Jersey note which bears a design which is unlisted in the Wait reference. This late issue piece is an American Bank Note Company product which was this institution's last issue of obsolete currency before it received its national charter in the middle of 1865. **Very Good-Fine.** (600-900)

NEW MEXICO

Rare New Mexico Scrip Note

12736 **Jarilla, NM- Southwestern Mercantile Co.** 10¢
A great piece of obsolete scrip from this little known town, which is now known as Orogrande. This community was located 29 miles north of the Texas border and was named for the Jarilla Mountains. At its peak, between the 1880's and 1920's, it was a gold, silver and copper mining center which boasted a 32 bed hospital, a 63 room hotel, and a newspaper named the Jarilla Enterprise. The town's name was changed in 1905 to Orogrande, due to the discovery of a gold nugget the size of a man's finger, which triggered a short lived gold rush. This is the only piece of scrip we've seen from this location. **Fine-Very Fine.** (1,500-2,500)

NEW YORK

12737 **Albany, NY- The Canal Bank of Albany** $3 May 1, 1838 C6
A decent example of this scarce counterfeit. **Fine.** (100-200)

12738 **Albany, NY- The Canal Bank of Albany** $3 Oct. 1, 1844 G28
A very tough three which is in more than acceptable grade. **Fine-Very Fine.** (200-400)

12739 **Albany, NY- Albany Exchange Bank** $1 May 8, 1840 S5
A nice example of this scarce note. **Fine-Very Fine.** (150-250)

12740 **Albany, NY- Albany Exchange Bank** $2 July 9, 1842 S10
A pleasing **Very Fine** example of this spurious issue. (150-250)

12741 **Angelica, NY- Allegany County Bank** $2 June 1, 1840 G2b
A very scarce note listed as SENC in the Haxby reference. Nice **Fine-Very Fine.** (300-500)

12742 **Angelica, NY- Allegany County Bank** $5 June 1, 1840 G6
A second note from this tough bank which is SENC in Haxby. **Fine.** (250-450)

12743 **Argyle, NY- John C. Rouse** 6 1/4¢ Jany. 8, 1838 Harris 12
A very scarce New York scrip item. Mr. Rouse was a prominent citizen who later served as Argyle's postmaster. **Fine.** (150-250)

12744 **Argyle, NY- John C. Rouse** 12 1/2¢ Jany. 8, 1838 Harris 13
A second piece from this very scarce issuer. **Very Good-Fine.** (150-250)

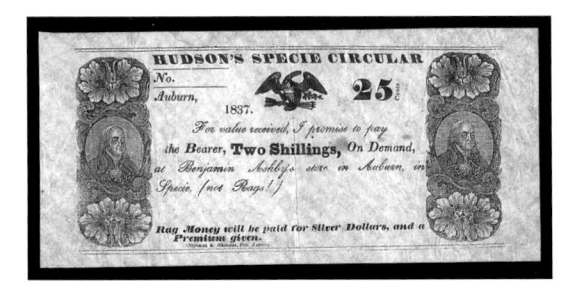

12745 **Auburn, NY- Hudson's Specie Circular** 25¢ 1837 Harris UNL
This is an interesting satirical piece lamenting the use of "Rag Money" in preference to specie. It's unlisted in Harris, with this the first example we've seen. **Very Fine-Extremely Fine.** (250-500)

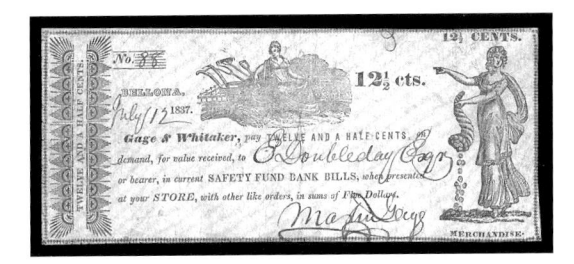

12746 Bellona, NY- Gage & Whitaker 12 1/2¢ July 12, 1837 Harris 6
The first of a set of four different denominations from this very rare issuer. **Fine-Very Fine.** (200-400)

12747 Bellona, NY- Gage & Whitaker 25¢ June 12, 1837 Harris 7
A nice grade piece signed by Martin Gage, one of the two proprietors of this store. Bright **Very Fine.** (200-400)

12748 Bellona, NY- Gage & Whitaker 50¢ June 12, 1837 Harris 8
A third scarce note from this Yates County issuer. **Fine-Very Fine.** (200-400)

12749 Bellona, NY- Gage & Whitaker 75¢ June 8, 1837 Harris 9
The last in this very interesting and scarce set. **Fine-Very Fine.** (200-400)

12750 Binghamton, NY- The Binghamton Bank $20 March 1, 1840 UNL
This post note is the only example of its type from this bank we have ever seen. **Fine-Very Fine.** (250-500)

12751 Brockport, NY- The Bank of Brockport $10 Jan. 1, 1839 Haxby UNL
A rare note from this bank, where all the notes listed from here are SENC. This is an altered example. **Fine.** (200-400)

12752 Brooklyn, NY- W. Richmond 25¢ July 1, 1837 Harris 93
A very rare piece of Brooklyn scrip. This piece is the serial number 1 specimen from this issuer, whose store was on Sands Street at the corner of Pearl. Nice **Very Fine.** (300-500)

12753 Brooklyn, NY- W. Richmond 50¢ July 1 1837 Harris 94
A second serial number 1 example from this rare Brooklyn merchant. **Fine-Very Fine.** (300-500)

12754 Brooklyn, NY- The Atlantic Bank $2 June 20, 1838 S5
A very scarce spurious Brooklyn note which we've not previously handled. **Very Good-Fine.** (175-325)

12755 Buffalo, NY- Bank of America $1 Nov. 1, 1839 G2
A very rare note, with this piece being the Haxby plate example. Sharp **Fine-Very Fine.** (300-500)

12756 Buffalo, NY- Bank of Commerce $5 Oct. 25, 1839 G12
A lovely example of a very rare note. **Very Fine.** (300-500)

12757 **Buffalo, NY- The Commercial Bank of Buffalo** $1 May 1, 1838 G2
An extremely rare note which is listed in the Haxby reference as a Proof only. This piece is signed and issued. **Fine.** (250-450)

12758 **Buffalo, NY- The Commercial Bank of Buffalo** $2 Jan. 1, 1839 G4
Another Haxby plate note, that is a rare piece indeed. **Fine.** (250-450)

12759 **Buffalo, NY- The Commercial Bank of Buffalo** $2 May 1, 1841 A10
A very scarce altered note which is listed in Haxby as SENC. **About Fine,** with a small reverse repair. (175-325)

12760 **Buffalo, NY- Exchange Bank of Buffalo** $1 July 16, 1844 G2
This is the Haxby plate note for this rare bank. **Very Good-Fine.** (250-450)

12761 **Buffalo, NY- The Mechanics Bank** $1 Nov. 1, 1839 G2
Yet another Haxby plate item from this very rare bank. **Fine,** with a few minor repairs. (250-450)

12762 **Buffalo, NY-Tiffany Brothers** $5 Commission Scrip Undated Harris UNL
Close examination of the terms on the back comes up with the location of Buffalo for this firm. **About Good,** with an approximately two inch tear in the upper left corner almost dislodging it. (300-500)

12763 **Canton, NY- R.M. Goddard & Co's. Bank** $5 May 4, 1859 G6
A very scarce item from a bank which was in business from 1859 through 1861. Haxby lists this denomination (and the two others printed) as proofs only, although this is a signed and issued example bearing the signature of Mr. Goddard as President. **Very Good-Fine,** with a few petty holes. (300-500)

12764 **New York, NY- C.L. Van Allen** 50¢
This is a neat Fractional lookalike that has the back printed in green. The back is inverted, and states, rather cryptically, that "This 50¢ stamp will be received at my office on orders for Family Rights." Nice **Fine-Very Fine.** (400-500)

12765 **New York, NY- The City Bank** $20 18__ G114
This proof was removed from some type of collector album or presentation album as there are some paper pulls noted on back. Overall the piece faces up very well, though a bit toned and with a few folds. **Very Fine. (300-400)**

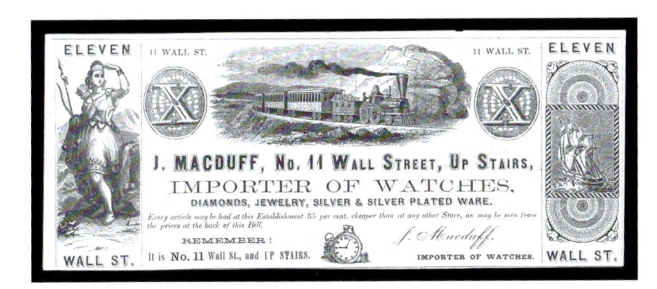

12766 **New York, NY- J. Macduff** Ad Note
This is a lightly circulated New York City Ad Note we've only seen once before. The face has vignettes that remind one of Obsoletes, while Mr. Macduff's price list of watches adorns the back. **Extremely Fine. (300-400)**

12767 **New York, NY- Irish Emigrant Society** 1 Pound June 6, 1878
This is a significant item from an institution which played an important part in the history of nineteenth century New York City. The Irish Emigrant Society was formed in 1841 to "afford advice, information, aid and protection" to emigrants from Ireland. As part of that mission, the society established a Committee on Remittances, which sought to eliminate the more egregious financial abuses perpetrated on recent immigrants, as well as helping finance passage to family members awaiting ticketing in Irish and English ports. This business soon expanded beyond the ability of the society to handle it, and, in 1851, the society helped to organize the Emigrant Savings Bank, which soon became one of New York's leading financial institutions. This note, a 1 Pound Sterling draft, was payable at the Bank of Ireland in Dublin or at any of that bank's offices throughout Ireland or Britain. We have never had any notes of this institution to offer previously, and had never seen any until this attractive **Fine-Very Fine** specimen appeared. **(400-800)**

12768 **Poughkeepsie, NY- Middle District Bank** $2 Oct. 1, 1827 UNL
This denomination and design are unlisted for this issuer in the Haxby reference. **Fine,** with a few small chips out at the bottom. **(200-400)**

12769 **Poughkeepsie, NY- Middle District Bank** $3 Oct. 1, 1827 UNL
A very rare Peter Maverick printed note which is again an unlisted denomination from here in the Haxby reference. **Fine. (300-500)**

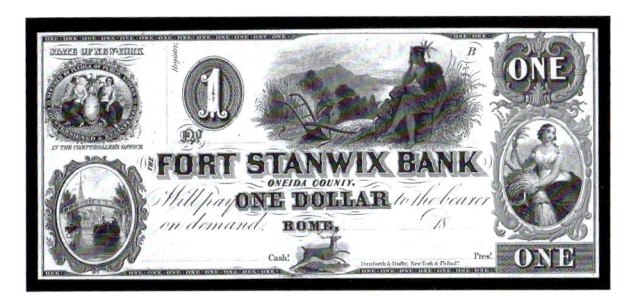

12770 **Rome, NY- Fort Stanwix Bank** $1 18__ G2 SENC
This beautifully engraved issue is likely one of the "Special Proofs" that was printed by the ABNCo. sometime after the originals were printed. The paper is bright white and the margins are solid. This piece is offered without estimate. **Gem Crisp Uncirculated.**

12771 **Utica, NY- Strawberry Grounds of T. Buchanan, Jr.** 10¢ Nov. 1, 1862 Harris 231
We have handled only one other example of this popular note. That piece realized $1,092.50 some four and a half years ago. This **Very Fine** example is attached to an auction catalog description with a hand written date and location, "NY Sale 1882". This hand written notation may be accurate as the catalog description reads, "After great search the owner found the proprietor who says that it is the only one extant." **(750-1,000)**

NORTH CAROLINA

12772 **Asheville, NC- Town of Asheville** 15¢ Nov. 12, 1862
A nice example of this scarce North Carolina municipal issue. **Very Fine. (250-350)**

OHIO

12773 **Eaton, OH- State Bank of Ohio** $10 G696 Wolka 1066-32
A scarce note listed as SENC in Haxby and as Rarity 5 in Wolka. **Very Good. (175-275)**

Signed by J(oseph) Smith

12774 **Kirtland, OH- The Kirtland Safety Society Bank** $10 Mar. 1, 1837 G10 Rust 8 Wolka 1424-12
The signatures on this note are of J(oseph) Smith and S(idney) Rigdon, while the countersignature is of Ovul Pinney. The embossing is deep on this well preserved Mormon issue. **Choice Crisp Uncirculated. (5,000-7,500)**

PENNSYLVANIA

12775 **Hyde Park, PA- Richards & Howell** 10¢ Dec. 18, 1862
We do not often run into notes from this hamlet outside of Pittsburgh. Add the popularity of Fractional lookalikes and this piece should create some bidding interest. **Fine. (300-400)**

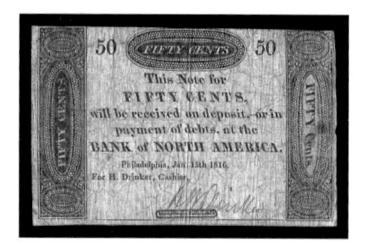

12776 **Philadelphia, PA- Bank of North America** 50¢ Jan. 15, 1816 G54
This is the first example of this denomination that we've handled in quite some time. The paper is perfectly solid and attractive. **Fine. (400-600)**

12777 **Pittsburgh, PA- W.J. Gilmore** $2 Commission Scrip Undated Hoober UNL
This commission scrip for this trunk and valise dealer has its terms in English and German on the back. **Good. (100-200)**

RHODE ISLAND

12778 **Newport, RI- Newport Exchange Bank** $5 Feb. 1, 1854
To date, we have not handled another issue from this Rhode Island institution. The paper is solid for the grade **Very Good.** A small gutter fold is noted at lower right. **(400-500)**

12779 **Providence, RI- Bank of America** $1-$1-$1-$2 Uncut Sheet G4a-G4a-G4a-G8a
This is a gorgeous remainder sheet that is widely margined and printed by the National Bank Note Company. A printer's devil has left a fingerprint on the back of the sheet. **Choice Crisp Uncirculated. (125-175)**

12780 **Wakefield, RI- The Wakefield Bank** $10 April 20, 1847 A15 Durand 2296
A most attractive example of this excessively rare note, which is listed as SENC in Haxby and as R-7 in Durand. **Fine-Very Fine. (300-500)**

SOUTH CAROLINA

12781 **Charleston, SC- The Bank of South Carolina** $20 Feb. 23, 1857
This interesting note carries an additional overprint vertically of the number "1000." We have been unable to determine the reason for this designation. This note grades a pleasing **Fine 12** as awarded by PMG. (200-300)

12782 **Charleston, SC- Bank of the State of South Carolina** $10 Oct. 2, 1861 G60a Sheheen 586
This lovely late issue American Bank Note Company product bears a central vignette entitled "The Rescue," depicting Jasper Newton freeing prisoners from the British in 1781 flanked by vignettes of Generals Morgan and Pickens. The remainder of the note displays a green tint all around. Nice **Very Fine.** (200-300)

12783 **Charleston, SC- The Bank of Charleston** $5 Feb. 2, 1858 G2b Sheheen 51
A scarce and desirable note with a full red tint. There is one small hole and a lightly rounded corner, with the note otherwise grading a pleasing **Fine.** (300-500)

12784 **Charleston, SC- The Bank of Charleston** $20 Dec. 30, 1845 N15 Sheheen 82 (S)
A very rare spurious issue which is listed as Rarity 8 in the estimable new Sheheen South Carolina reference. **Very Good-Fine,** with a couple of corners missing along with a margin chip or two. (250-450)

TENNESSEE

12785 **Chattanooga, TN - Bank of Chattanooga** $3 Jan. 4, 1863 G44c
Just a small corner tip fold keeps this interesting note from Choice. **Choice About Uncirculated.** (200-300)

12786 **Warner, TN- Southern Iron Co.** 5¢ 1893
A well circulated but very rare piece of Tennessee merchant scrip. **Very Good,** with a small hole at the center, rare enough to see bids reach or exceed. . . (250-450)

TEXAS

12787 Austin, TX- Republic of Texas $3 Aug. 1, 1841 Cr. A3, Medlar 23 Olson 756
This is a quality mid-grade Three dollar note. **Fine**, CC. **(400-600)**

12788 Austin, TX - Republic of Texas $10 Jan. 27, 1840 Cr. A5 Medlar 25 Olson 761
This note has great clarity along with fantastic color on the reverse. Low serial # 709 is also noticed on this cut-cancelled example. **Extremely Fine**, CC. **(300-400)**

12789 Austin, TX - Republic of Texas $20 Jany 27, 1840 Cr. A6 Medlar 26 Olson 763
Simply a gorgeous cut-cancelled example that has the following written on the back, "certificate to be issued in the name of Warneken & Kirchhoff" who happened to appear in the 1851 New Orleans City Directory as being commercial merchants located at 15 Bank Place. **Choice About Uncirculated**, CC. **(300-400)**

Key Republic of Texas $500

12790 Austin, TX - Republic of Texas $500 April 26, 1839 Cr. A9 Medlar 29 Olson 772
This is the key denomination for this issue, and should be obtained when the opportunity presents itself. The triangular portion from the cut cancel is missing, which is typical. This note has also been cut in half, which you do find in a majority of the $500's, and has been expertly repaired. The familiar rubber stamp cancel is also noticed on this noble note of the Texas Republic. **Very Fine-Extremely Fine**, COC. **(2,500-3,000)**

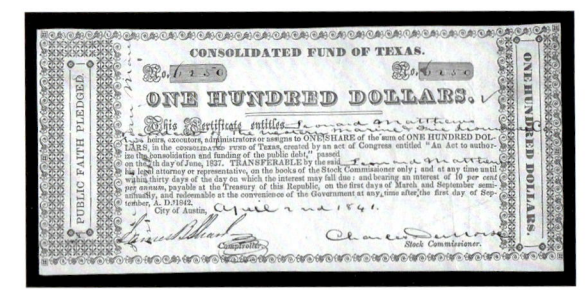

12791 Austin, TX- Consolidated Fund of Texas $100 Apr. 2, 1841 Cr. CF14 Medlar 42
This later Consolidated Fund issue is scarce in all grades. These were issued for only a short time in 1840-41 after Austin became the capital. It is listed as a R6 by Medlar. **Extremely Fine**, CC. **(300-500)**

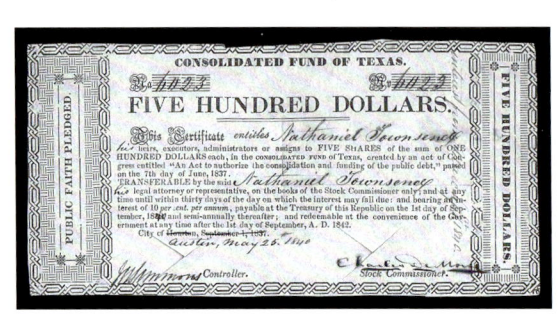

12792 Austin, TX- Consolidated Fund of Texas $500 May 25, 1840 Cr. CF17 Medlar UNL
A lateral fold is found on this example that has Houston and the printed date scratched out. **About Uncirculated**, CC. **(400-600)**

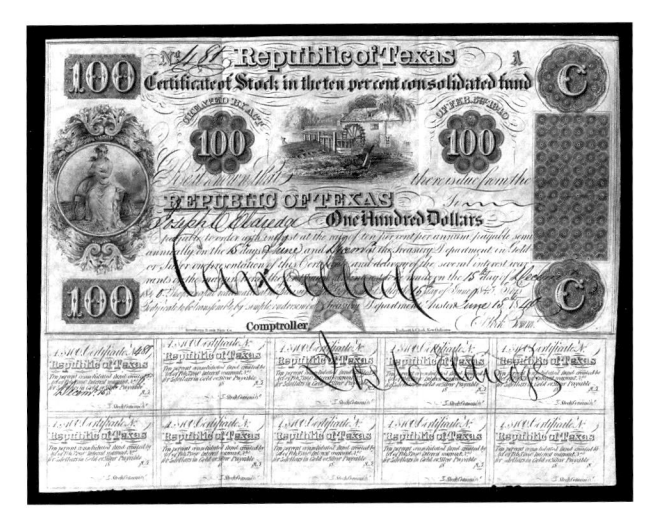

12793 **Austin, TX- Republic of Texas Consolidated Fund Certificate** $100 June 15, 1840 Medlar UNL
This "Certificate of Stock in the ten per cent consolidated fund" is unsigned and unnumbered. Therefore it does not have the usual cut cancels. This **Extremely Fine-About Uncirculated** example has been pen cancelled. There is ink erosion in the "C" of "Cancelled." (500-700)

12794 **Austin, TX- Republic of Texas Consolidated Fund Certificate** $100 June 15, 1840 Medlar UNL
This "Certificate of Stock in the ten per cent consolidated fund" has numerous ink flyspecks on the back. This example is signed and numbered. **Very Fine,** CC. (400-600)

12795 **Austin, TX- Republic of Texas Consolidated Fund Certificate** $500 June 15, 1840 Medlar UNL
This "Certificate of Stock in the ten per cent consolidated fund" has been revalued at eight per cent. Penned statements to this effect have been added to the back. This example has not been cut cancelled, but a little bit of ink erosion is noticed. The $500 denomination from this issue is scarcer than the $100 denomination. **Extremely Fine-About Uncirculated.** (600-800)

Galveston Bay & Texas Land Company

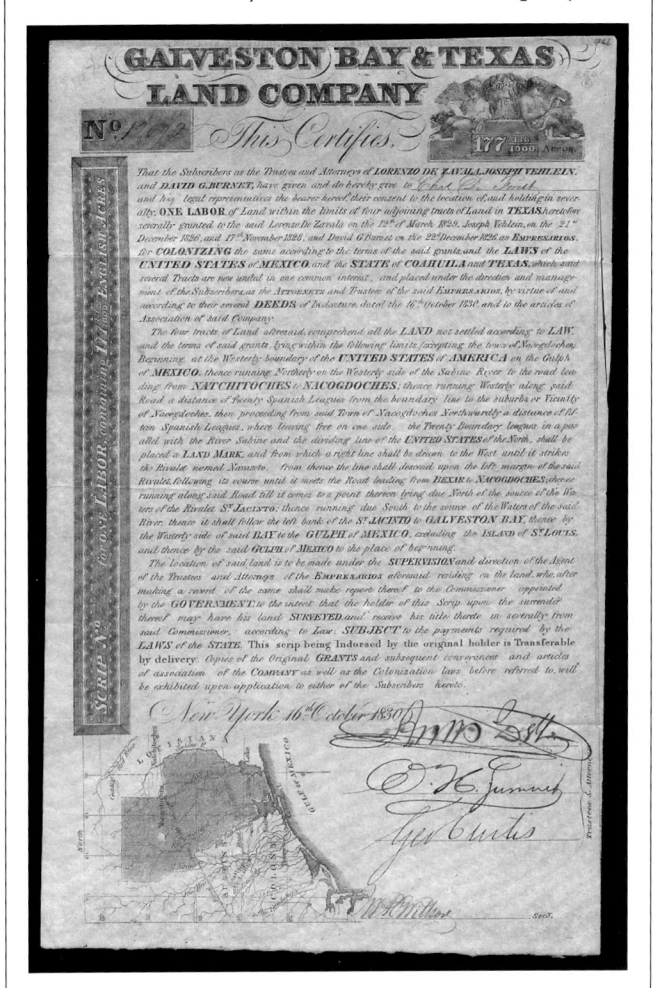

12796 **Galveston Bay & Texas Land Company** Oct. 16, 1830
This is a land certificate good for 177 136/1000 English acres of land in what was then the newly settled area of Texas between the Sabine and San Jacinto Rivers. This land came from grants issued to Lorenzo de Zavala. De Zavala would later become the first vice president of Texas. This is an important historical document that should interest any Texan or collector of Texas currency or historical memorabilia, and also a fascinating document that gives a glimpse into the history of the American settlement of Mexican Texas and the revolution that followed. **Very Fine** or better overall, with just a few folds that are not at all distracting. The top edge shows a thin reinforcement and there is an approximate four inch slit along the right edge. The signatures of the trustees and attorneys of the company are bold and add to the overall appearance. We expect the bidding to reach or exceed. . . (800-1,200)

12797 Galveston, TX- Burgess' Business College $1 Jan. 1, 1875 Schingoethe 210-1
A very scarce Texas college currency issue listed as R-7 in the Schingoethe reference. A nice vignette of General Robert E. Lee graces the left side of the note. **Fine** or better, with a few nicks and splits. **(300-500)**

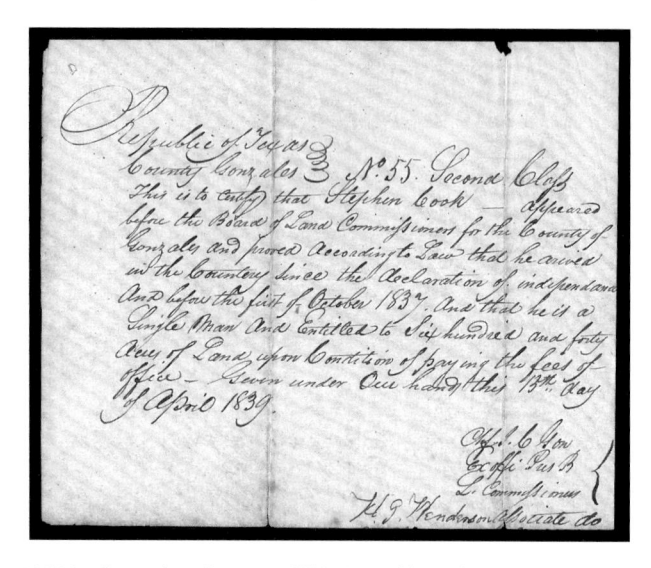

12798 Gonzalez County, TX- Republic of Texas 640 Acres Land Scrip April 13, 1839
This is a holographic document made out to Stephen Cook stating that he had proven that he had arrived in the county since the (Texas) Declaration of Independence and before October 1, 1837 and therefore he was entitled to 640 acres of land. A few small edge splits and notches are noticed on this great Texas item. **Extremely Fine.** **(200-400)**

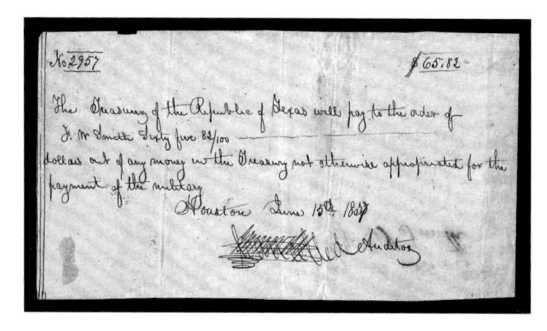

12799 Houston, TX- Audited Draft $65.82 June 15, 1837 Cr. UNL Medlar UNL
This could be Medlar HW1a, but it is missing one penned line along the left edge. It is also similar to Cr. HW1B, but it is handwritten on buff, not white paper. The top edge of this **Very Fine** note is missing a small notch. Still a rare enough note to command a price in the range of... **(400-600)**

12800 Houston, TX- Government of Texas $10 July 1, 1838 Cr. H17 Medlar 60 Olson 550
This note carries serial number 1. This example has been cut in half and reattached with stamp hinges. The pen cancellation has led to ink erosion. Usual rubber stampings are also noted. **Fine, COC. (300-500)**

12801 Houston, TX- Government of Texas $20 Mar. 1, 1838 Cr. H18 Medlar 62 Olson 560
This is the variety with a five-pointed star on the shield at left. The note has been signed by "Sam Houston." Houston's old Creek War wrist injury flared up, so the Texas Congress authorized William G. Cooke to sign notes for Houston. This note has serial number 1. Several pinholes are noted. **Fine, CC. (300-500)**

Extremely Rare $5000 Consolidated Fund

12802 Houston, TX- Consolidated Fund of Texas $5,000 Mar. 1, 1839 Cr. CF6a Medlar 76
Listed as R10 in Medlar, this $5,000 note is the only note of this denomination issued in this series and is extremely rare in all grades. In fact we have handled only one example of this note previously and that was five years ago. A couple of small edge tears are noticed. This is the Criswell plate note. **Very Fine, CC. (1,000-1,500)**

128 Please visit HA.com to view other collectibles auctions.   A 15% Buyer's Premium ($9 min.) Applies To All Lots

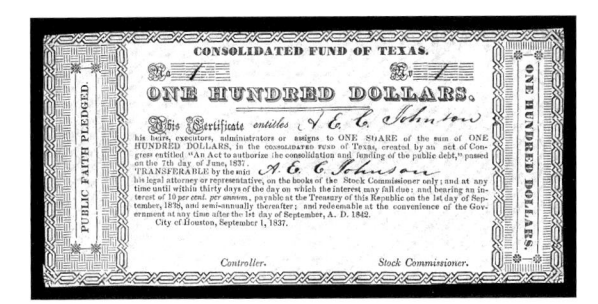

12803　**Houston, TX- Consolidated Fund of Texas** $100 Sep. 1, 1837 Cr. CF7 Medlar 77
Serial number 1 is found on this well preserved **Crisp Uncirculated** remainder. (500-1,000)

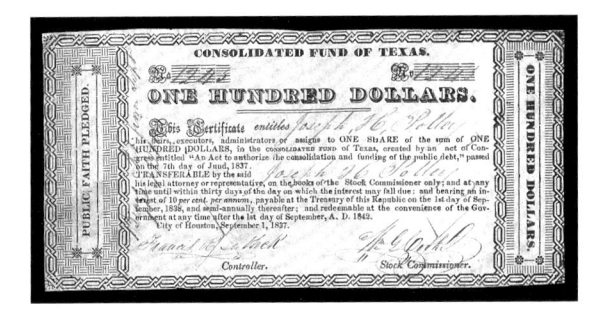

12804　**Houston, TX- Consolidated Fund of Texas** $100 Sep. 1, 1837 Cr. CF7A Medlar 78
Only light handling is found on this bright note that has "June" spelled as "Jund." **Very Fine-Extremely Fine, CC.** (250-450)

12805　**Houston, TX- Consolidated Fund of Texas** $1,000 Sept. 1, 1838 Cr. CF12 Medlar 84
This is a lovely example of this rare high denomination note. This example is not cut cancelled. **About Uncirculated.** (400-600)

12806　**Houston, TX - The City of Houston** 50¢ June 29, 1865 Medlar 95
This item appeared last October at the Stacks sale of the Ford Collection Part XV, and is a piece that not even Bill Bond had acquired in his massive holdings we offered earlier this year. This **Very Good-Fine** note stands out from others is that it is payable in U.S. Currency or City Warrants. (750-1,000)

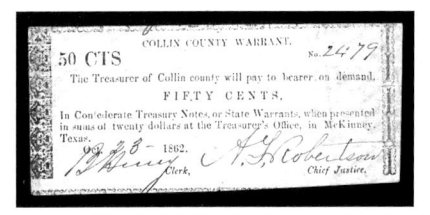

12807　**McKinney, TX - Collin County** 50¢ Oct. 23, 1862
This piece appeared last year in Part XV of the Ford holdings that Stacks is disbursing. This rare item is totally unmolested, and is unlisted in both the Medlar and Olson references. Printed on the back of a legal document. **Fine-Very Fine.** (750-1,000)

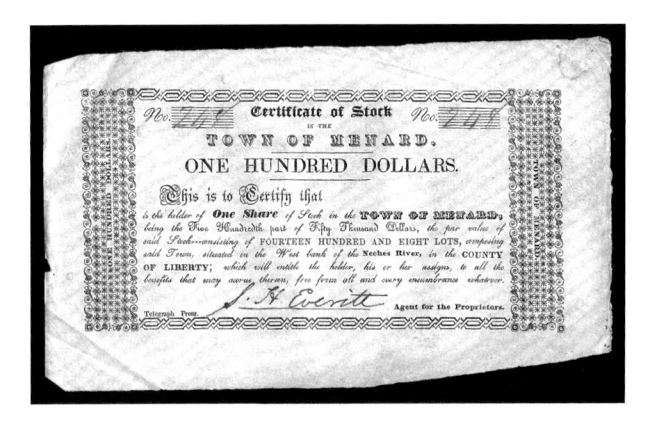

12808　**Menard, TX- Town of Menard** $100 Undated Medlar UNL
This rare stock certificate is for the five hundredth part of $50,000 from this small settlement. Backing for the $50,000 was 1408 town lots. The folds for this **Extremely Fine** note are seen in the corners. The left edge has three small tears and a small notch, too. (200-400)

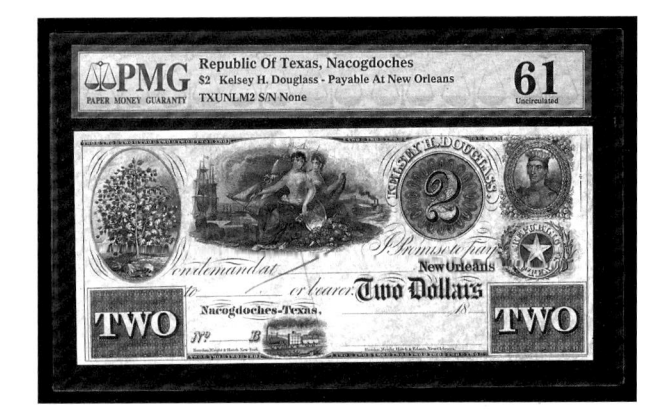

12809　**Nacogdoches, TX- Kelsey H. Douglass** $2 18__ Medlar 2
This merchant's currency circulated locally at par, but he died suddenly, and his widow went bankrupt paying off his obligations. The last example of this issue we handled was a Very Good with serious problems that realized just over $86. This **PMG Uncirculated 61** remainder should reach. . . (300-400)

12810　**Richmond, TX- Fort Bend County** $10 Aug. 1, 1862 Medlar 7
This note is listed as an R-7 in the Medlar reference. This **About Good** $10 has a replaced area along the right edge plus large tape repairs.
From The William A. "Bill" Bond Collection (200-300)

12811 Texana, TX- First Bill of Exchange $3150 Mar. 12, 1840 Medlar UNL
This bill of exchange was signed by Colonel William G. Cooke who also was appointed by the Texas Legislature to sign Sam Houston's name to documents of the Republic. Ink erosion has taken a heavy toll on this document, but it is still presentable. **Fine. (200-300)**

VIRGINIA

12812 Alexandria, VA- Corporation of Alexandria $1 Nov. 9, 1846 Jones TA05-25
A very scarce piece of early Virginia municipal scrip. **Fine. (300-400)**

12813 Alexandria, VA- Bank of Potomac $10 Oct. 24, 1806 G16 Jones UNL
We have chosen to list this excessively rare and very likely unique note under Virginia rather than the District of Columbia, although a good argument could certainly be made for the latter, as Alexandria was part of the District from its formation in 1791 until Congress ceded it back to Virginia in 1846. We have opted for a Virginia listing because notes from this bank from its founding in 1804 through its re-charter as a branch of the Farmers Bank of Virginia in 1847 are illustrated and enumerated in the Jones and Littlefield Virginia reference. This piece is unlisted in that compilation (which lists all other notes from here as Rarity 7), and is listed in Haxby (under the District of Columbia) as SENC, with "No Description Available." Nice **Fine-Very Fine. (1,000-1,500)**

12814 Howardsville, VA - Bank of Howardsville $50 G20a
President Millard Fillmore is depicted on this lovely green overprinted example. An as made diagonal fold is noted on this **Crisp Uncirculated** note, along with "$1.00" written on the back in purple. **(250-300)**

12815 Richmond, VA - Virginia Treasury Note $100 Oct. 15, 1862 Cr. 6
This is a Keatinge & Ball product with a portrait of Civil War era Governor John Letcher. He was governor from 1860-63. **Extremely Fine-About Uncirculated. (200-300)**

WISCONSIN

12816 Hudson, WI- Alfred Goss 5¢-10¢ Nov. 1, 1862 Uncut Pair Kraus UNL, SC2
An uncut pair of these scarce notes, with each exhibiting a small internal split. **Very Fine. (450-650)**

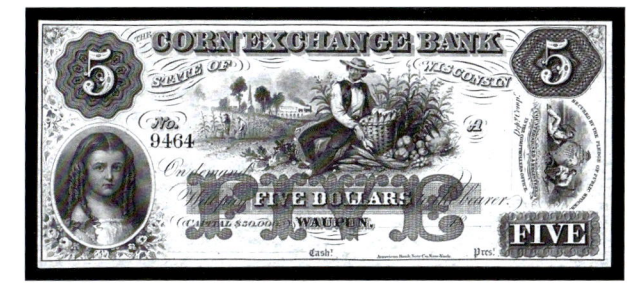

12817 **Waupun, WI- Corn Exchange Bank $5 18__**
This is a well preserved numbered remainder with ample margins. The ABNCo is the printer of this note with detailed vignettes. **Choice Crisp Uncirculated. (275-375)**

12818 **Milwaukee, WI- Bank of Milwaukee $5 G8**
A very scarce early Wisconsin issue which comes as a remainder only. This piece is falsely filled in. **Fine+++**, with a reverse repair that affects little. **(500-800)**

MISCELLANEOUS

12819 **A Large Portrait of Lincoln Framed by a Collage of Currency.** A fascinating, large (approximately 24" by 30") portrait of President Abraham Lincoln, his image framed by portions of approximately sixty pieces of Large Size currency from the early Twentieth Century era. This is a wonderful item for the collector who must have everything. Surprise your spouse and hang this folk art on your living room wall. **(500-up)**

12820 **First Liberty Loan Converted 4 1/4% Gold Bond of 1932-1947** $100 May 9, 1918
This is a rare United States bond that is brilliantly colored with a blue underprint and a red Treasury seal and serial numbers. Thirty-two coupons remain attached. The back is a vivid orange highlighted by a gorgeous patriotic vignette. This bond is crackling fresh as the day it was originally folded with three lateral and one vertical fold. Bold embossing of the serial numbers on the coupons is also noticed. We sold a similar bond in the same grade for over $5000 in September 2003. **Very Fine-Extremely Fine.. (2,000-4,000)**

12821 **First Liberty Loan Converted 4 1/4% Gold Bond of 1932-1947** $100 May 9, 1918
This bond is consecutively numbered to the previous lot and is similar in all respects including the grade and embossing. **Very Fine-Extremely Fine.. (2,000-4,000)**

12822 **Cuban Cane Products Co., Inc. $1000 Bond of 1930. Thirteen Examples. VF, pinholes**
Cuban Cane Products Co., Inc. Stock Certificates. Two Examples. VF, pinholes.
One of the bonds shows signs of once being mounted. One of the stock certificates is for 100 shares and the other certificate is for 30 shares. (Total: 15 items) **(300-400)**

12823 **Ninety Years of Security Printing The Story of the British American Bank Note Company Limited 1866 - 1956.** This is a spiral bound book of 25 pages. There are few pages of engravings. Previous owner's address stamp is on both inside front and back covers. **(50-100)**

12824 **The Story of the American Bank Note Company.** This is the classic reference on the ABNCo written by William H. Griffiths. It covers the time period from 1795 - 1958 within its 92 pages. Many engraved portraits and vignettes are included. What is most helpful to the Obsolete collector is the "family tree" depicting the historical evolution of the ABNCo. Glued inside the front cover is a copy of a book review that appeared in the September 1959 Numismatist. The rare ABNCo announcement card for this book is also tipped in. It has the added inscription, "Commemorating our Siderographers dinner in Washington!" **(100-150)**

12825 **Complete American Bank Note Archive Series.** This is the complete six volume set, which was issued one per year from 1987 through 1992. This annual series of intaglio engravings was printed on acid-free cream-colored paper stock. Each set includes twelve 8 1/2" by 11 1/4" pages of vignettes with four to ten vignettes per page. Important historical information about each vignette is included with each volume. A few titles of the sheets are duplicated among the series, but each of the over 500 vignettes is different. The 1988 set contains the much sought-after brown ABNCo intaglio imprint of a 1919 Czechoslovakian 1000 Korun note that makes it "complete" and original. (Total: 6 books) **(1,000-1,500)**

12826 **ABNCo Opening the West.** This is a complete set of this late 1970s ABNCo classic offering. This set includes the informational booklet and all ten engraving booklets with around 65 proof engravings that include checks and stock certificates. They are housed in a tooled leatherette box with a rawhide tie. Two of the corners of the box have split. **(500-800)**

12827 **BEP 1992 World's Columbian Commission Diploma Proof.** This 1992 BEP offering was printed from the original plate to celebrate the 100th anniversary of the World's Columbian Exposition. The diploma is rolled and it has a moisture stain in the lower left corner. **(100-200)**

12828 **Souvenir Cards.** This lot consists of BEP and ABNCo plus one Krause Publications souvenir cards. Included are the BEP Treasury Department Seal and Great Seal of the United States cards. The time spanned is from the mid-1960s to 2002. There is some duplication and the informational cards that come with some of the souvenir cards are not included in the tally. Almost all of the cards are housed in Avery page holders. (Total: 72 items) **(350-500)**

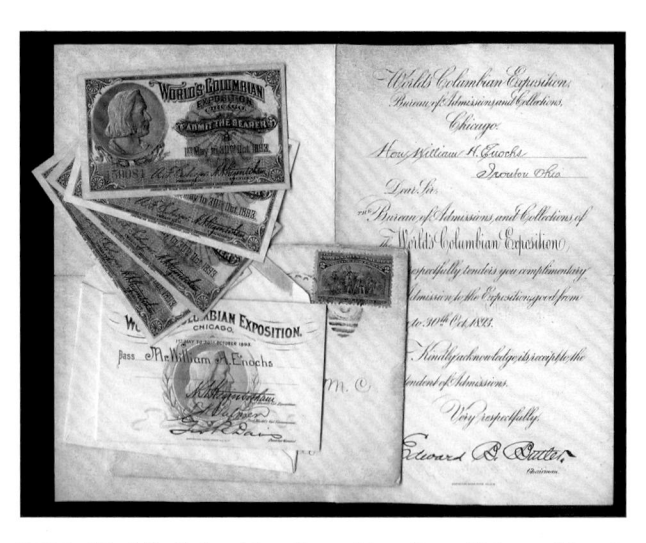

12829 **World's Columbian Exposition Pass Chicago May 1 - Oct. 30, 1893.**
This most interesting lot has a World's Columbian Exposition complimentary pass made out to the Honorable William H. Enochs, US Representative from Ironton, Ohio. The probable reason why this pass exists today is because Mr. Enochs passed away on July 13, 1893. The ABNCo engraved pass is approximately 4 by 2.5 inches and it exhibits a portrait of Columbus that is similar to the Columbus portrait that is found on some regular admission tickets for this expo. Included with this lot is an ABNCo engraved transmittal letter addressed to Mr. Enochs, the original cover with split sides addressed to Mr. Enochs using a 2¢ Landing of Columbus stamp, complimentary pass storage envelope, plus the following ABNCo engraved regular admission tickets of Columbus, Indian with "A" overprint, Washington with "A" overprint, and Lincoln with "A" overprint. The four regular admission tickets were added later to the complimentary pass and associated items. (Total: 8 items) **(400-600)**

12830 **Macerated Currency Hat.** This is a very nice approximate 1 1/2 inch tall macerated hat that has retained its original green ribbon around the crown. This is a solid example of this quaint craft. **(150-250)**

12831 **Sample United States Security Paper 1830.** This approximate 13 by 12 inch sheet has been folded into eighths. The end quarters are blue and the middle half is white. The watermark is "US" in blue. Printed on the paper is, "To the honourable the Senate and House of Representatives of the United States. Gentlemen, The sheet is a sample designed for *Paper Money*. It was manufactured at one operation. It may have any figure, and consist of any number of compositions or qualities of Pulp. The difficulty, expense and exposure attending the manufacture of such paper, will bring infractions to a narrow and responsible compass. Your desire and patronage will furnish an incomparably better specimen. With respect, Daniel Lamborn. Elk Ridge Landing, Anne Arundle Co. Md. May 7th 1830." This looks to be a security paper trial balloon that Mr. Lamborn flew before Congress. Included is a very old auction description. **Very Fine. (1,000-1,500)**

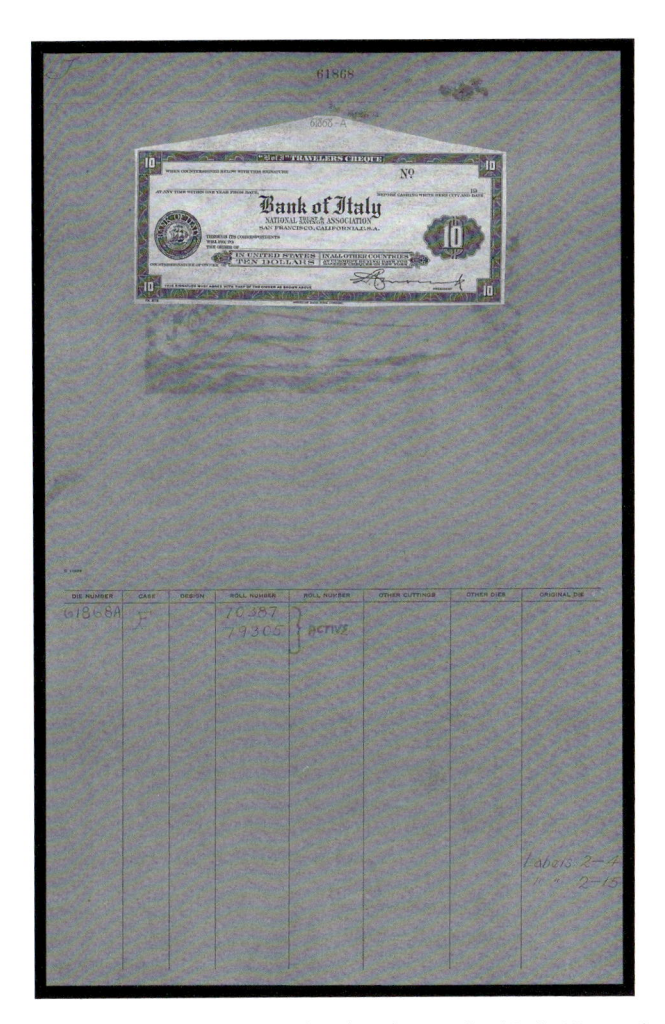

12832 **San Francisco, CA - $10; $20; $50 Bank of Italy National Trust & Savings Assoc** Uniface Travelers Cheque Proofs This lot consists of ABNCo $10; $20; and $50 uniface proofs pasted to tan file folders. Due to this pasting, mucilage is visible through the face of the travelers cheques. These file folders were meant to hold sample printings related to each of these denominations. **Uncirculated.** (Total: 3 items) **(500-750)**

MILITARY PAYMENT CERTIFICATES

12833 **Very Interesting Short Snorter.**
This is one of the very best short snorters we have seen. The main chain consists of 39 notes and there is also a chain of six notes that has broken off plus two single notes. The notes of this short snorter indicate someone who served in both the European and Pacific Theatres of World War II. In fact a North Africa and Hawaii $1 are observed. *There will be no returns on this lot for any reason.* (Total: 47 notes) **(200-400)**

12834 **Japan B Yen.**
10 Sen Original Pack of 100 Schwan-Boling 261 **New**
50 Sen Original Pack of 100 Schwan-Boling 262 **New**
1Yen Original Pack of 100 Schwan-Boling 263 **New**
5 Yen Original pack of 100 Schwan-Boling 264 **New**
10 Yen Original Pack of 100 Schwan-Boling 265 **New**
20 Yen Original Pack of 100 Schwan-Boling 266 **New.**
Each pack is banded in a BEP band. The final 10 Yen note has a spot on the back. (Total: 600 notes) **(4,000-6,000)**

Specimens of Military Yen

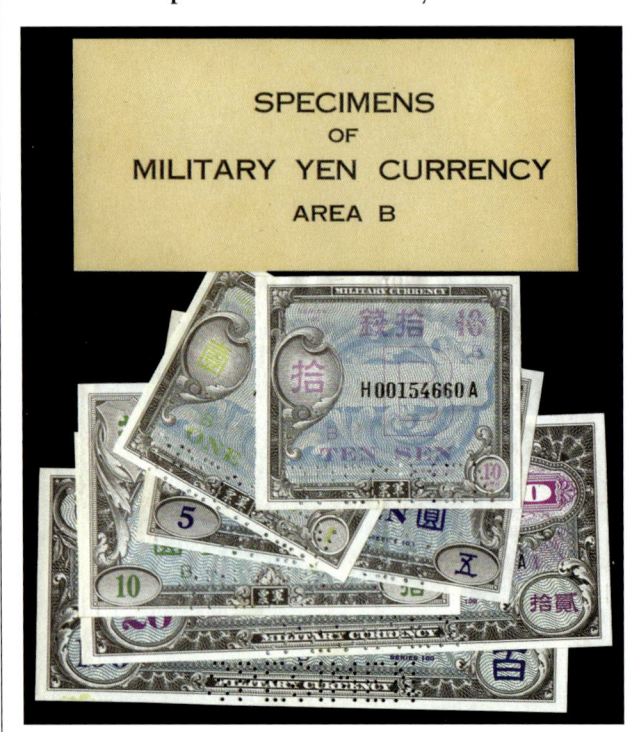

12835 Specimens of Military Japan Supplemental B Yen Currency Schwan-Boling 269. Supplemental B Yen was used in the Japanese home islands from September 6, 1945 through July 15, 1948. On the Ryukyus, it was in use from April 1, 1945 to September 30, 1958. This set consists of six replacement H-A block notes that were perforated with "SPECIMEN" in the field to create the notes for this specimen booklet. The notes are 10 Sen, 1 Yen, 5 Yen, 10 Yen, 20 Yen and 100 Yen. Each of the six notes is **New** and was once mounted within the included specimen booklet cover. Adhesive residue is found at back top and bottom center and also along the right back margin of the six notes. The included cardboard cover of the booklet reads "Specimens of Military Yen Currency Area B." This set once had a 50 Sen specimen note, but that note is missing. Nonetheless, a great item to contend for. **(3,000-up)**

12836 Series 461 $1 PCGS Gem New 65PPQ. This MPC boasts rich original color and ideal paper quality. **(200-up)**

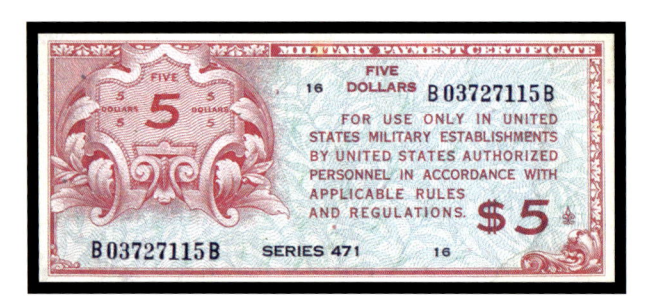

12837 Series 471 $5 About New. This is one of the rarest MPCs in high grade. This $5 has a single center fold, a small paper disturbance at top center, and a couple of pinholes. **(3,250-up)**

12838 Series 481 25¢ PCGS Superb Gem New 67PPQ This bright piece is very well centered. **(400-up)**

12839 Series 481 $10 About New This is a bright pleasing $10 note in a tougher grade for the series. **(500-up)**

12840 Series 521 $5 Fine. This original paper $5 is from the first printing. It has nice edges and color for the grade. **(250-up)**

12841 Series 521 $10 Choice New This is a bright, well margined note which is a touch tight at lower right. The scarcity of this issue cannot be overstated in the higher grades. **(1,750-up)**

Excessively Rare Series 541 $10 Replacement

12842 **Series 541 $10 Replacement Extremely Fine.** This is a very rare replacement from the first printing. The only other known $10 replacement for the first printing of this series is found in the comptroller's book which has made its way into private hands. This attractive example has a center fold plus a little more handling, but is a most appealing high grade piece which is certain to please. It is hard to price such extreme rarities, but in today's market we are certain the hammer will fall somewhere in excess of... **(9,000-up)**

12843 Series 611 25¢ PCGS Gem New 66PPQ This note is nicely margined and quite colorful. (200-300)

12844 **Series 611 $5 Gem New.** This well preserved $5 is nicely margined and centered. We have offered only a half dozen Gem 611 $5s over the last 17+ years. **(1,500-up)**

12845 Series 651 10¢ PCGS Superb Gem New 67PPQ Here is a note rarely seen at this lofty grade level which may be the nicest one known. (750-up)

12846 Series 651 10¢ PCGS Gem New 66PPQ. Here is another stunning beauty of this tough issue that is well margined. (700-up)

12847 Series 651 10¢ PCGS Gem New 66PPQ. Just a gorgeous note in a grade seldom seen for this issue. (700-up)

12848 Series 651 25¢ PCGS Superb Gem New 68PPQ This may well be one of the finest known for this type. Bright inks are surrounded by very large and even margins. (1,250-up)

12849 **Series 651 25¢ PCGS Superb Gem New 67PPQ.** This denomination is a bit scarcer than the others in this small run. **(1,000-up)**

12850 **Series 651 25¢ PCGS Superb Gem New 67PPQ.** Here is another practically flawless example of this popular issue. **(1,000-up)**

12851 **Series 651 5¢, 10¢, 25¢, 50¢ Gem Crisp Uncirculated.** This well matched set varies only slight in margin width, but not quality. One or two pieces may approach Superb in quality. **(1,500-up)**

12852 **Series 651 Complete Denomination Set** This lot contains every issue for the series from fractional through $10. All notes grade **Gem New** or better. (Total: 6 notes) **(2,000-up)**

12853 **Series 661 5¢ PCGS Superb Gem New 69PPQ.** Almost perfect margins surround this piece which may have no equal. **(400-up)**

12854 **Series 661 $1 PCGS Superb Gem New 69PPQ** How close to perfect would you like? This note will undoubtedly find its way to the discerning collector looking for only the best, and for those looking to get a jump on a Registry set... **(1,000-up)**

12855 Series 661 $1 PCGS Superb Gem New 69PPQ. Another lucky collector will benefit from the opportunity to acquire a near perfect example of this pleasing "Clamshell." (1,000-up)

12856 Series 681 $20 PMG Gem Uncirculated 66 EPQ. Full margins and nice centering are highlights of this sharp-corner example. (700-up)

12857 Series 691 $1 PCGS Gem New 66PPQ. This is a gorgeous second printing example from this most attractive, unissued Vietnam Era series. The Five Dollar denomination is proving to be the second scarcest of the four denominations known for this series. (1,000-up)

12858 Series 691 $1 Choice New. A bit more margin at top and this note would certainly grade higher. This ever popular design was never issued and put into service. (300-500)

12859 Series 691 $10 PCGS Superb Gem New 67PPQ. Beautiful color is seen on this MPC issue which never officially saw duty. (1,200-up)

12860 Series 691 $20 PCGS Superb Gem New 68PPQ. This gorgeous example is from the first of two sets that were never officially released. PCGS has bestowed the lofty 68PPQ grade. (800-up)

12861 Series 691 $20 New. A light handling mark is seen on this otherwise vivid example from this Vietnam era series. (500-up)

12862 **Series 692 $20 Extremely Fine-About New Three Consecutive Examples.** This trio, which was held together by a staple at one time, offers vivid color and crisp paper. The holes have been expertly repaired. **(500-up)**

FOREIGN CURRENCY

12863 **Banknotes From Around the World.** This was a Franklin Mint subscription plan during the late 1970s. Each note has a low serial number and is marked "SPECIMEN." In fact all notes for one country will have the same serial number. A list of countries include Bahrain, Botswana, Dominican Republic, Ghana, Gibraltar, Ireland, Jersey, Malta, Philippines, Paraguay, Solomon Islands, Swaziland and Tonga. **Choice Crisp Uncirculated.** (Total: 73 notes) **(800-1,200)**

12864 **Argentina** El Banco Provincial de Santa Fe 10 Centavos 9/1/1874
Serial number embossing remains on this example that has a large left margin. **Very Fine-Extremely Fine.** **(300-500)**

12865 **Bolivia** El Banco de la Nacion Boliviana 1911 Regular Issue 50 Bolivanos Pick 110 Specimen
This is a pleasing example of the engraver's art. There is no listing of this note known in specimen form in the Standard Catalog of World Paper Money values. The lofty grade of **PMG Superb Gem Unc 67** EPQ has been awarded. Any estimate here is but a guess. **(500-800)**

12866 **China** Szechuan-Shensi Prov. Soviet Workers and Farmers Bank 1933 1 Ch'uan Pick S3217
This issue is printed on gray cloth. **Extremely Fine.** **(300-500)**

12867 **China** Manchuria 10, 15, 30 Unlisted in Pick
This trio of issues grade from **Fine** to **Very Fine** (Total: 3 notes) **(400-600)**

12867 **China** Manchuria 10, 15, 30 Unlisted in Pick
This trio of issues grade from **Fine** to **Very Fine** (Total: 3 notes) **(400-600)**

12868 **Costa Rica** 1 Colon El Banco Anglo-Costarricense 1917 Pick S121r 99 Consecutive Examples
This issue started the Colon issue in Costa Rica, but due to the Law of June 23, 1917, however, apparently never was issued to the public, as all examples are either Unsigned Remainders (such as these) or Specimens. The catalog lists these at $20 each in UNC. **Crisp Uncirculated.** **(1,500-2,000)**

12869 **Costa Rica** 5 Colones El Banco Ango-Costarricense 1917 Pick S122r 100 Examples
There are a couple of long consecutive runs in the bundle, strapped with the original Bradberry Wilkinson & Co., Bank Note Manufacturers, London strap. This issue is a simply gorgeous example of why Latin American currency is widely collected. **Crisp Uncirculated.** **(2,000-3,000)**

12870 **El Salvador** El Banco Salvadoreno 100 Pesos (1883-1915) Pick S206p
This face proof is mounted on card stock and it is unpriced in the Krause reference. **PMG Choice About Unc 58.** (300-500)

12871 **Germany** 100,000 Mark Feb. 1, 1923. 60 Examples. Pick 83b.
These German inflation notes will grade **Choice Crisp Uncirculated.** They are contained in three original note bands for 20 notes and a total of 2,000,000 marks each. (Total: 60 notes) (300-500)

12872 **Germany** 20 Reichsmark Specimen 1929 Pick 181a
Serial number A00000000 and "Muster" (Specimen) is overprinted on this note. **Very Fine.** (100-200)

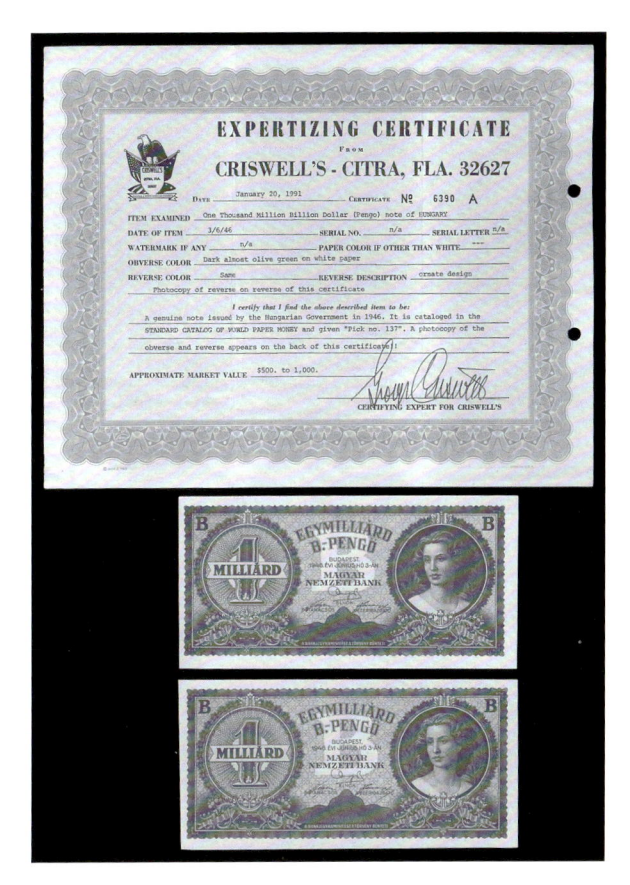

12873 **Hungary** 1 Milliard B.-Pengo (One Thousand Million Billion) 1946 Pick 137 Two Examples
This is by far the key to the post-war Hungarian inflation issues. This pair comes with an expertizing certificate of Criswell's dated January 20, 1991. These are listed singly in the recent Krause reference for $175 in Unc. **Choice Crisp Uncirculated.** (Total: 2 notes) (250-350)

12874 **Jersey** St. Mary's Parochial Bank 1 pound 18XX Pick S327
A corner fold and some light handling are seen on this deeply inked note. **About Uncirculated.** (200-300)

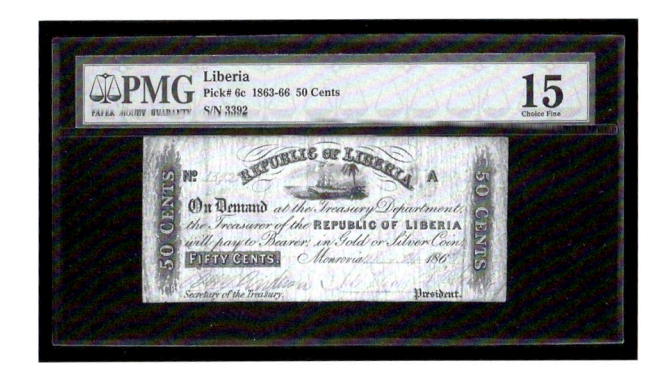

12875 **Liberia** 50¢ Republic of Liberia May 24, 1863 Pick 6c
Liberia issued currency from 1857 through 1880 and did not issue again until 1989, as the US Dollar freely circulated along with British West African currencies. Simply rare in any condition, we offer this **PMG Choice Fine 15** example. (500-700)

12876 **Mexico** Banco Nacional de Mexico ND 1000 Pesos Pick S263r
This is a brightly colored remainder note. **Extremely Fine-About Uncirculated.** (250-350)

12877 **Mexico** El Banco De Jalisco 1902-03 5 Pesos Guadalajara Pick S320a
This lovely specialized-issue unissued remainder from our neighbors to the south has broad margins. Carrying a double zero serial number it is graded **Choice Uncirculated 64 EPQ** by PMG. (800-1,200)

Rare Philippine National Bank Proof

12878 **Philippines** 20 Pesos Philippine National Bank Circulating Note Face Proof 1919 Pick UNL
This is an exciting Proof from a period in United States paper money history when it was decided to reduce the size of Philippine paper money in the second decade of the 1900s. This experiment proved very successful and it led directly to the United States' reducing the size of its own paper money in 1929. This Proof could be considered for a Phillipines or United States collection. The portrait is of Congressman William A. Jones, who was chairman of the Committee on Insular Affairs until his death in office on April 17, 1918. There is a crease running into the "20" counter in the lower right corner and there is a stamped control number on the back. **About Uncirculated.** (750-1,250)

12879 **Philippines** Philippine Islands 1903 2 Pesos Pick 25a
This is an average circulated **Fine** example of a tough red seal. (200-400)

12880 **Philippines** 500 Pesos 1936 Pick 88 Five Consecutive Examples
This issue is unpriced in the Krause reference. It is seldom seen and tonight we have five consecutive notes grading **Fair-AG** which are in rough shape due to numerous punch cancels. Still a scarce note in any condition. Sold with no estimate. *No returns will be allowed on this lot for any reason.*

Rare Filipino Guerilla Culion Leper Colony Notes

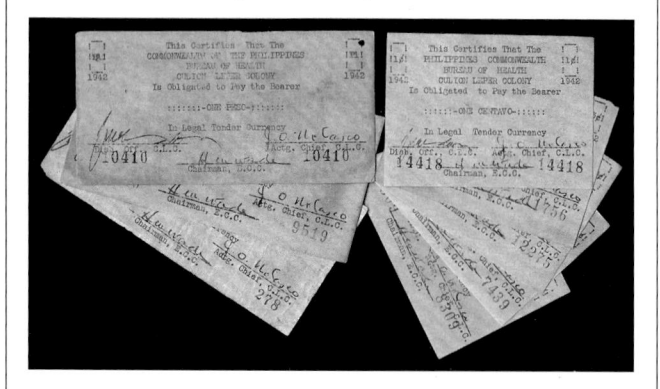

12881 **Philippines Culion Leper Colony.**
First Issue 50 Centavos; 50/20 Centavos Error Note; 1 Peso; 5 Pesos; 20 Pesos 1942 Pick S244; S244x; S245; S246; S247
Second Issue 1 Centavo; 5 Centavos; 20 Centavos 1942 Pick S251; S252; S253.
This is a great set of this scarce World War Two Filipino guerilla paper money. The centavo notes grade **AU** or better, while the 1 Peso grades **XF**, punch cancelled, soiling, tiny hole; the 5 Pesos **AU**, with three small top edge tears; and the 20 Pesos grade **Fine**, shaved lower left corner. The Second Issue Centavos notes have the type-written presidential authority added to the back. None of these notes are priced above XF in the Krause reference. In fact, the 50/20 Centavos error note and the 20 Pesos notes are not priced in any grade. This is an important set of World War Two emergency paper money. (Total: 8 notes) (1,000-1,500)

12882 **Puerto Rico** Ministerio de Ultramar 1895 1 Peso Pick 7a
This note which carries the full "Counterfoil" should see some spirited bidding as the colors are deep and handling light. Graded **Choice About Unc 58EPQ** by PMG. (400-600)

CANADIAN CURRENCY

The "Other Battleship" Note

12883 Montreal, PQ- Royal Bank of Canada $10 Jan. 2, 1913 Ch. 630-12-08
This is a scarce note that is often referred to as the "Other Battleship" note, with the British battleship Bellerophon as the vignette. This is a clean, bright example with a tiny bottom edge tear and a blue "9" on the back. One of the nicest we have handled in years. **Very Fine.** (500-800)

12884 Port of Spain, Trinidad- Canadian Bank of Commerce $20 July 1, 1939 Ch. 75-30-04
This **Very Good** note has a couple of tears due to some skins on the back. (400-600)

12885 DC-8e-ii $1 1878 Very Fine
There are a few tiny margin splits along some of the fold lines on this otherwise crisp issue. (1,250-1,750)

12886 Low Serial Number 0000003 Lawson-Bouey Quartet in Choice Crisp Uncirculated including BC-46a $1; BC-47a $2; $5 BC-48b; and $10 BC-49c. These are well preserved beauties. (Total: 4 notes) (900-1,200)

End of Session One

SESSION TWO

Live, Internet, and Mail Bid Auction 436 • St. Louis, Missouri
Thursday, May 10, 2007, 6:00 PM CT • Lots 12887-13662

A 15% Buyer's Premium ($9 minimum) Will Be Added To All Lots
You can now view full-color images and bid via the Internet at the Heritage website: HA.com

EARLY US BONDS

Likely Unique $5000 Loan of 1846 Bond

12887 Hessler X111I $5000 Loan of 1846 Bond Good. We have not seen anything from this 1846 issue during our many years as professional numismatists, and would not be surprised if this bond was unique in private hands. This issued example printed by Rawdon, Wright and Hatch of New York has a large repair on the back, a repaired cancellation hole with tape, plus several other small repairs along the edges. Still more internal holes and edge tears are found on this rare bond that was redeemed in March 1856. The rarity of this item easily outstrips any grade concerns for this possible one-of-a kind bond as Hessler is unable to provide a photo or a description for any denomination of this issue in his reference, *An Illustrated History of U.S. Loans 1775 - 1898*. **(6,000-up)**

Rare 5-20 1862 Bond

12888 Hessler X130D $1000 Five-Twenties of 1862 Bond Fine. A fantastically rare bond which lacks even a description in the Hessler loan reference. It has been issued and redeemed. There is a cancellation through Register of the Treasury Lucius E. Chittenden's signature. The left and right edges have been reinforced with tape and a couple of other places on this note also once held tape. A moisture stain is noticed in the lower right corner on this bond that was printed by the American Bank Note Company. While the grade is less than perfect, this item may well be unique in private hands, as no one alive today has ever previously seen a bond from this issue. Expect some stiff competition before the hammer falls on this wonderful Civil War item today. **(7,500-up)**

LARGE SIZE TYPE NOTES

DEMAND NOTE

PCGS 45PPQ "for the" Demand Note

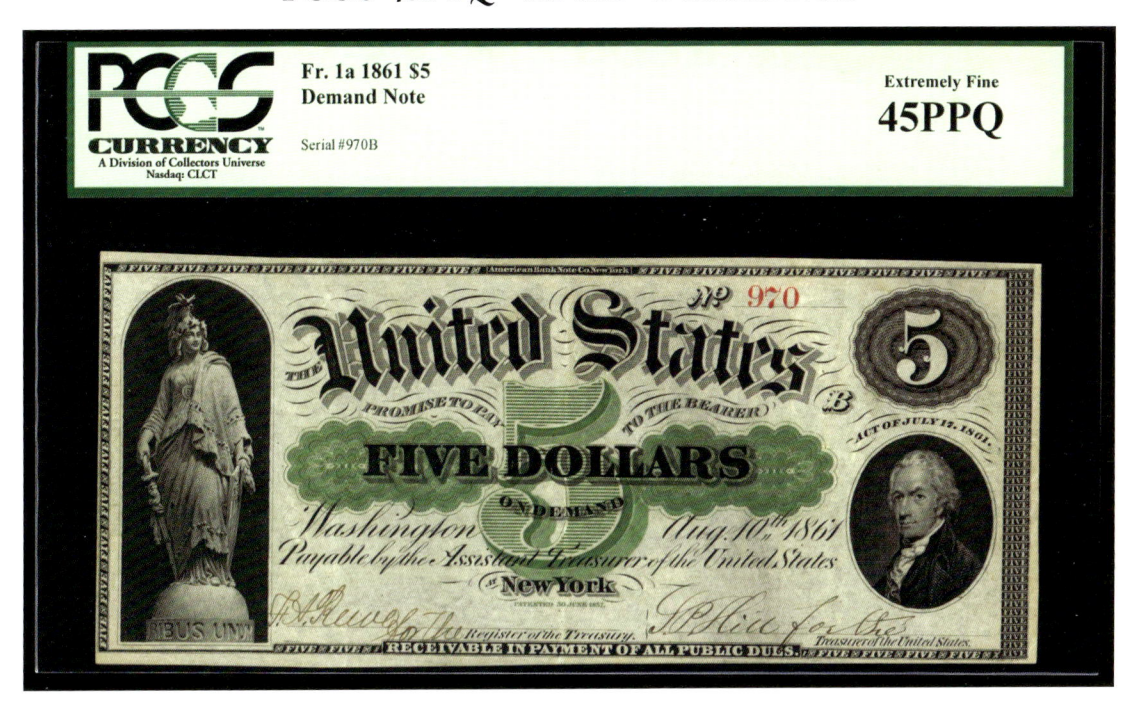

12889 **Fr. 1a $5 1861 "for the" Demand Note PCGS Extremely Fine 45PPQ.** The finest "for the" Demand note and, in our opinion, one of the most historic Large Sized rarities known. When Demand notes were first printed, the words "Register of the Treasury" and "Treasurer of the United States" were printed at the bottom of the note below the signature lines. The Treasury clerks, who were authorized to sign for these officials, added the words "for the" after their signatures. After a short while, it was realized that the words "for the" should be added to the plate in front of "Register of the Treasury" and "Treasurer of the United States" to save a considerable amount of time and effort on the part of the signers. Only eight examples of Fr. 1a are known to exist—this note and one other are EFs, the six others all grade Fine-Very Fine and lower. The last Friedberg 1a that we sold was in April 2006 where it was graded Fine-Very Fine. That piece realized $60,375 after spirited floor bidding. This note is worlds finer. It's a three-fold EF with excellent margins, perfect colors, bold hand signatures, and the "for the" in front of "Register" and "Treasurer" are dark, clean and clear. Even if this were a Fr. 1 (the printed variety with over 100 known), it would be in the top half-dozen known for grade. Old time collectors considered these "for the" Demand notes to be the pinnacle of Large Size currency collecting, and this note is the very best of the Type. **(100,000-up)**

LEGAL TENDER NOTES

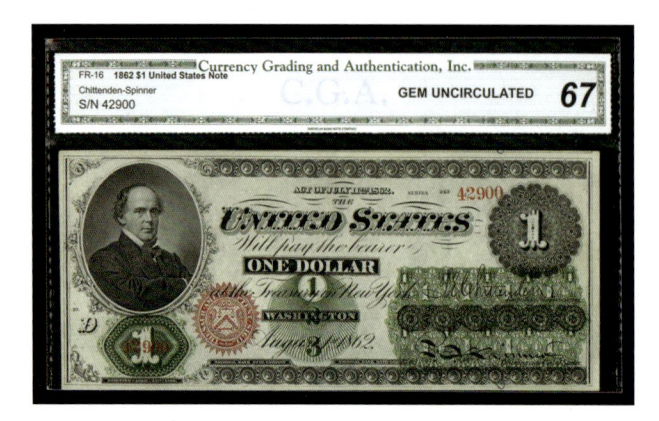

12890 **Fr. 16 $1 1862 Legal Tender CGA Gem Uncirculated 67.** The frameline is complete around this early Legal Ace. The back is centered nicely and some embossing is still visible. **(4,000-up)**

12891 **Fr. 16 $1 1862 Legal Tender Very Choice New.** Incredible color and just about the best original embossing we have seen for a note of this design. The note itself would be a perfect Gem if the adequate margins were a little bit larger. **(2,750-up)**

12892 **Fr. 16 $1 1862 Legal Tender PMG Choice Uncirculated 63 EPQ.** A high end early Ace with terrific paper color. PMG has awarded their Exceptional Paper Quality comment. **(2,000-up)**

12893 **Fr. 16 $1 1862 Legal Tender PCGS New 62PPQ.** A near higher end early Ace with terrific paper color. PCGS has awarded their Premium Paper Quality designation. **(1,750-up)**

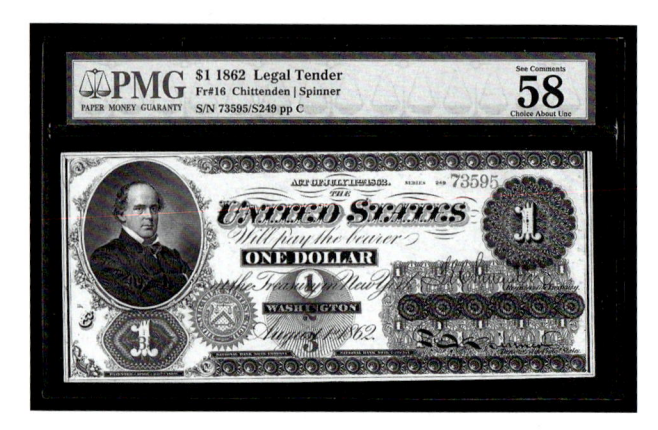

12894 **Fr. 16 $1 1862 Legal Tender PMG Choice About Unc 58 EPQ.** This note, our country's first $1 bill, is apparently separated from the Choice New grade by only a broad corner fold at the bottom right. The piece has earned the "Exceptional Paper Quality" comment. **(1,500-up)**

12895 **Fr. 16 $1 1862 Legal Tender PMG About Uncirculated 50 Net.** The holder mentions the fact that the top margin has endured some split repairs as it is painted on the back. **(1,000-up)**

12896 **Fr. 16 $1 1862 Legal Tender Extremely Fine.** There are a few edge tears into the top on this otherwise very nice, lightly circulated example.
From The Rolling Plains Collection (500-up)

12897 **Fr. 16 $1 1862 Legal Tender CGA Extremely Fine 40.** An inverted plate number of "36" is seen near the top in the center on this lightly handled note. (500-up)

12898 **Fr. 16 $1 1862 Legal Tender Very Fine.** A repaired tear is noticed at lower right on this otherwise bright legal Ace. (450-up)

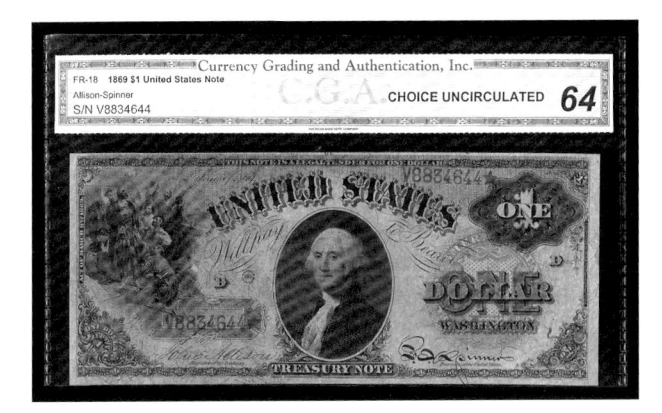

12899 **Fr. 18 $1 1869 Legal Tender CGA Choice Uncirculated 64.** This note is from the highly regarded "Rainbow" issue that uses red, blue, and green inks. (3,250-up)

12900 **Fr. 18 $1 1869 Legal Tender PCGS New 60.** The colors are stong on this Rainbow Ace, but the note has been poorly trimmed with the right-face margin right against the design, and the left-face margin cutting into the design. Hard to estimate, but we would imagine it should realize right around...
From The Collection of Greg Southward (2,250-up)

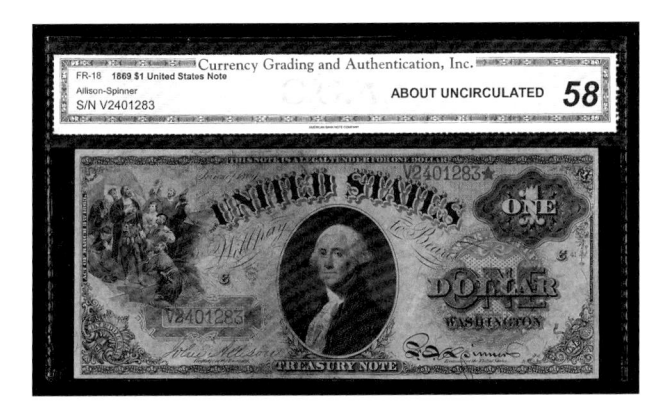

12901 **Fr. 18 $1 1869 Legal Tender CGA About Uncirculated 58.** Bold color and good centering highlight this Rainbow Ace. (2,000-up)

12902 **Fr. 18 $1 1869 Legal Tender CGA Very Fine 35.** We hate to regrade third party graded notes, but can't restrain ourselves from mentioning that 35 seems a bit of a stretch here. (650-up)

12903 **Fr. 18 $1 1869 Legal Tender Fine-Very Fine.** The paper still retains some snap on this Rainbow Ace.
From The Collection of Greg Southward (500-up)

12904 **Fr. 18 $1 1869 Legal Tender Fine.** Great color abounds on this average circulated note that has some splits in the margins. (400-up)

12905 **Fr. 19 $1 1874 Legal Tender Very Fine+.** This is a crisp and colorful note that should easily fit into a collector's mid-grade collection of Large Type. (250-up)

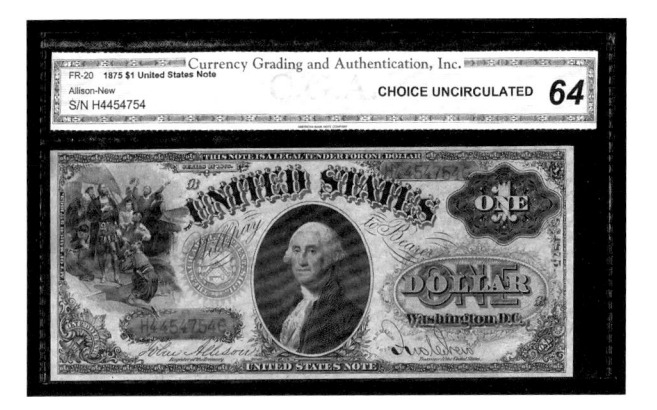

12906 **Fr. 20 $1 1875 Legal Tender CGA Choice Uncirculated 64.** A handsome example of this early Ace that appears to us to have been graded quite accurately. (1,500-up)

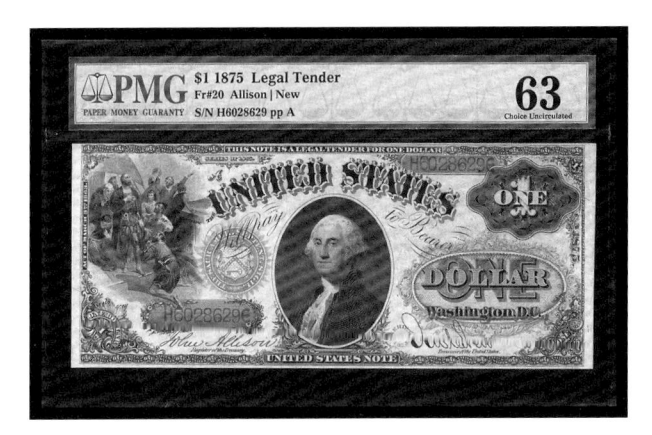

12907 **Fr. 20 $1 1875 Legal Tender PMG Choice Uncirculated 63.** Closely margined across the top, but with excellent color. (1,200-up)

12908 **Fr. 20 $1 1875 Legal New.** This well margined and perfectly original piece has a bit of handling that precludes a higher grade. We must note however that the paper quality is exceptional, as is the embossing. (800-up)

12909 **Fr. 20 $1 1875 Legal Tender PMG About Uncirculated 55 EPQ.** A well margined, brightly colored example of this early Ace. The red overprint is very strong, adding considerably to the eye appeal. (900-up)

12910 **Fr. 26 $1 1875 Legal Tender PCGS Superb Gem New 67PPQ.** A hugely margined example with ideal colors, and perfect printing quality. Fr. 26 is not a particularly scarce note up through the 64 grade. However, 65 and higher pieces will remain forever scarce, and 67PPQ examples will always be rare. At the present levels, we feel that the smallish gap between Green Sheet 65 and 67 is quite unrealistic, and we expect that as time goes by and population figures are gathered, this gap will open considerably. **(3,750-up)**

12911 **Fr. 26 $1 1875 Legal Tender PCGS Superb Gem New 67PPQ.** The PPQ designation from PCGS is the equivalent of the EPQ (Exceptional Paper Quality) comment used by PMG. Both are sought-after positive qualifiers used in addition to the numerical grade, and both add considerable value to any note they are bestowed on. This broadly margined 67PPQ 1875 Ace seems to have every positive attribute that a collector could hope for in a Type note. Expect to see some very active bidding before the hammer falls on this brightly colored beauty. **(3,750-up)**

12912 **Fr. 26 $1 1875 Legal Tender PMG Choice Uncirculated 64 EPQ.** This is the variety of Fr. 26 that is printed on the paper with an extraordinarily heavy profusion of fibers at one end. It is a handsome piece that has earned every point of its 64 EPQ grade. **(1,750-up)**

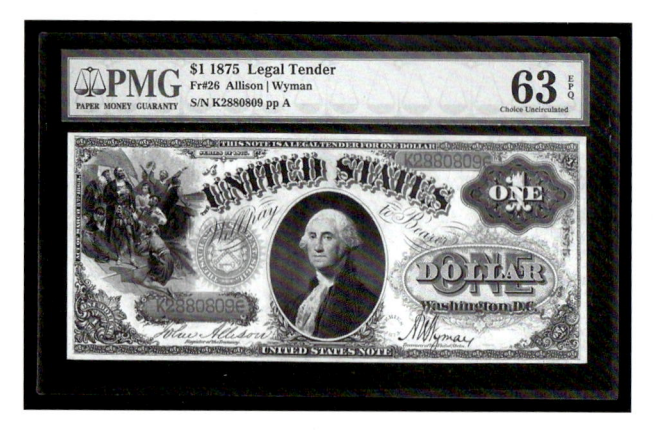

12913 **Fr. 26 $1 1875 Legal Tender PMG Choice Uncirculated 63 EPQ.** Apparently the back centering, which is quite low, caused the 63 grade, as this note sure looks like a 66 from the face. An attractive piece with good originality. **(1,250-up)**

12914 **Fr. 26 $1 1875 Legal Tender Choice About New.** The bottom margin strays very close to the design at its right end, and there is a corner fold that just reaches the design at the upper-left of the note. It's a strictly original piece with bright color and ideal paper surfaces.
From The Collection of Greg Southward **(750-up)**

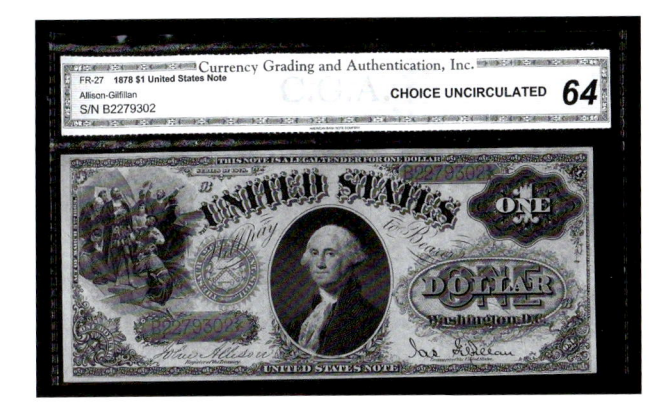

12915 **Fr. 27 $1 1878 Legal Tender CGA Choice Uncirculated 64.** Nicely margined and with simply spectacular color. (1,500-up)

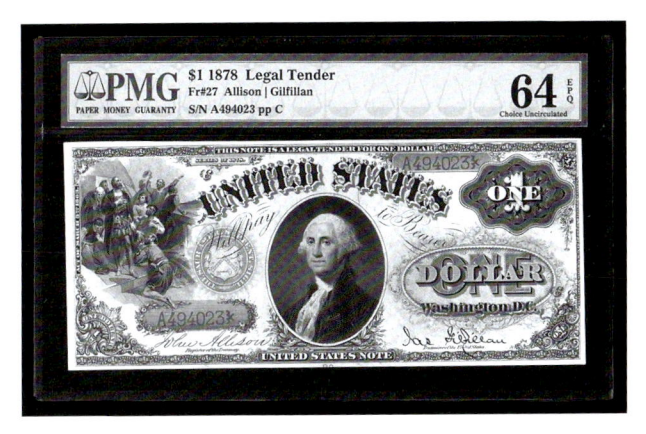

12916 **Fr. 27 $1 1878 Legal Tender PMG Choice Uncirculated 64 EPQ.** The margins, though a touch uneven, are nearly perfect. Most examples of this issue have a weak overprint, though this one is particularly strong. Further examination reveals ideally original paper and perfect eye appeal.
From The Jacob and Heather Dedman Collection (1,500-up)

12917 **Fr. 27 $1 1878 Legal Tender PCGS Choice New 63PPQ.** The original embossing is visible through the PCGS holder on this early Ace. Decently margined and well printed, with a strong red overprint. (1,000-up)

12918 **Fr. 27 $1 1878 Legal Tender Extremely Fine.** This very handsome example spent a touch too much time in a PVC holder. (400-up)

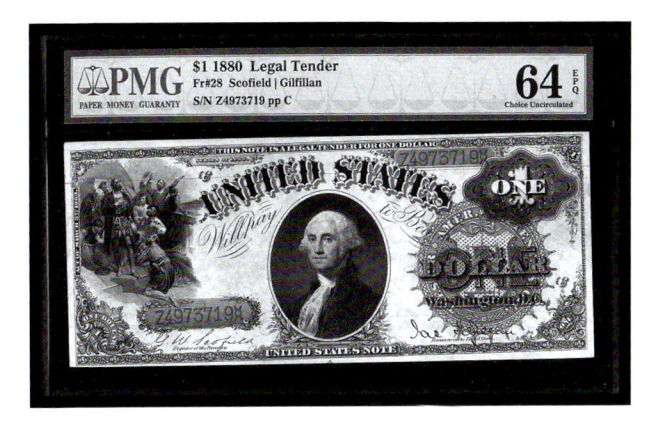

12919 **Fr. 28 $1 1880 Legal Tender PMG Choice Uncirculated 64EPQ.** Just a touch under full Gem quality. (1,250-up)

Serial Number 1 1880 $1 Legal Tender

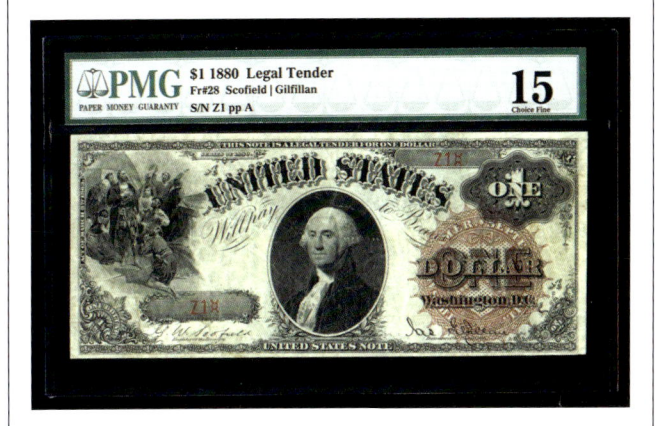

12920 **Fr. 28 $1 1880 Legal Tender PMG Choice Fine 15.** In looking at this note, we think back to the Highlander films where the saying "There can be only one" was used. Such is the case here as this note, which was recently discovered, should prove very popular this evening. Out of a printing of almost 20 million notes, the odds of this #1 note surviving once it entered circulation is comparable to winning the lottery. We are pleased to have the chance to offer this one of a kind item. A few minor repairs are noticed on this well margined example. (12,500-up)

12921 **Fr. 30 $1 1880 Legal Tender Gem New.** The margins are quite attractive as is the well embossed seal on this beautiful Legal. Plate 101 is seen along the top margin of this bright piece that has a touch of handling. (1,750-up)

12922 **Fr. 30 $1 1880 Legal Tender PMG Gem Uncirculated 65.** Treasury Seal embossing is strong on this example. The margins are wide for the issue and they reveal plate number "84" at bottom center. **(1,750-up)**

12923 **Fr. 30 $1 1880 Legal Tender PMG Choice Uncirculated 64.** This 1880 Ace has bold ink color and primarily broad margins. **(1,500-up)**

12924 **Fr. 30 $1 1880 Legal Tender PMG Choice Uncirculated 64 EPQ.** Embossing is noticed on this Ace that has three ample margins. The colors and paper are excellent. **(1,500-up)**

12925 **Fr. 30 $1 1880 Legal Tender PCGS Choice New 63.** Our description of this note before it was third-party graded still rings true today, "Gem paper quality and originality and would have been well within the definition of that grade, but for the fact that the bottom margin lacks just a bit to meet our standard for the higher grade. Overall, as fresh and well embossed a note as one could hope to locate from this attractive and sought after series." **(1,200-up)**

12926 **Fr. 30 $1 1880 Legal Tender Choice New.** This well embossed beauty serves as a lasting reminder as to why Mylar holders are important. There is slight PVC residue along the edges. **(1,200-up)**

12927 **Fr. 31 $1 1880 Legal Tender PMG Very Fine 30.** This is a one-number type, with the large salmon-colored spiked seal and the blue serial numbers. About 100 pieces are known in all grades combined, and this is quite a nice one, with bold color and no problems. **(1,250-up)**

12928 **Fr. 31 $1 1880 Legal Tender PMG Very Fine 25.** This is a scarce $1 Friedberg number type with the Large Red Treasury Seal. (800-up)

12929 **Fr. 34 $1 1880 Legal Tender Extremely Fine-About New.** Wide margins and healthy edges surround this Ace with light folds though some seal bleed is noticed. (600-up)

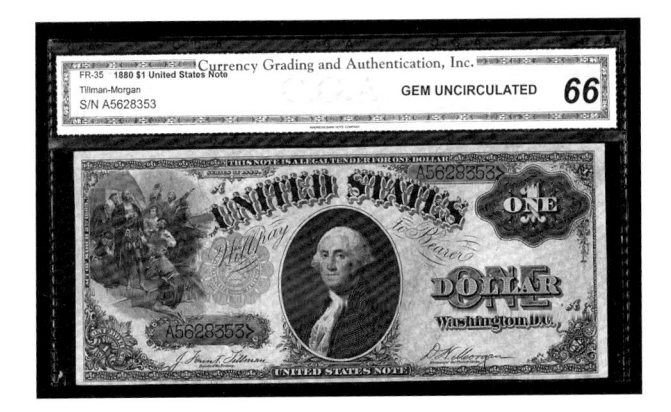

12930 **Fr. 35 $1 1880 Legal Tender CGA Gem Uncirculated 66.** Always a popular type with decent margins seen. (1,750-up)

12931 **Fr. 35 $1 1880 Legal Tender CGA About Uncirculated 58.** There is a little discoloration at the upper corners on this well-margined $1 Legal. (225-up)

12932 **Fr. 36 $1 1917 Legal Tender Superb Gem New.** Huge margins and readily apparent, deep, original embossing highlight this 1917 Ace. It is a very common type, but hard to find when this type of perfection is sought. (600-up)

12933 **Fr. 36 $1 1917 Legal Tender CGA Gem Uncirculated 66.** Broadly margined for the issue and very well centered on both sides. (500-up)

12934 **Fr. 36 $1 1917 Legal Tender Gem New.** This Ace is well preserved with ample margins. (500-up)

12935 **Fr. 36 $1 1917 Legal Tender Very Choice New.** This wholly original three digit Legal Ace is pleasing to the eye. It could have been Gem though a hint of teller handling is noted on either end. (750-up)

12936 **Fr. 36 $1 1917 Legal Tender Two Consecutive Examples.** This is a pair of attractive, original notes. The first note grades **Gem New** while the second note exhibits a light center bend and grades **Choice About New**. (Total: 2 notes) (800-up)

12937 **Fr. 36 $1 1917 Legal Tenders Four Consecutive Examples CGA Crisp Uncirculated 62; Gem Uncirculated 65; Choice Uncirculated 64; Choice Uncirculated 64.** All four of these notes show embossing and natural paper wave. Their plate letters in order are C; D; A; and B. (Total: 4 notes) (1,200-up)

12938 **Fr. 36 $1 1917 Legal Tender Cut Sheet of Four Notes CGA About Uncirculated 55.** All four of these lightly handled notes with original paper wave have the same grade. (Total: 4 notes) (600-up)

12939 **Fr. 36 $1 1917 Legal Tender Two Examples CGA About Uncirculated 50; 55.** These two third-party graded notes are 48 serial numbers apart. The lowest graded note has a thin stripe of red paint on the back. (Total: 2 notes) (250-up)

12940 **Fr. 37 $1 1917 Legal Tender PMG Choice Uncirculated 63.** Dark inks are found on this nicely preserved Ace that is only hindered a little bit by a thin bottom margin. (300-up)

12941 **Fr. 37 $1 1917 Legal Tender CGA Crisp Uncirculated 62.** This bright white piece boasts a rich red overprint. (300-up)

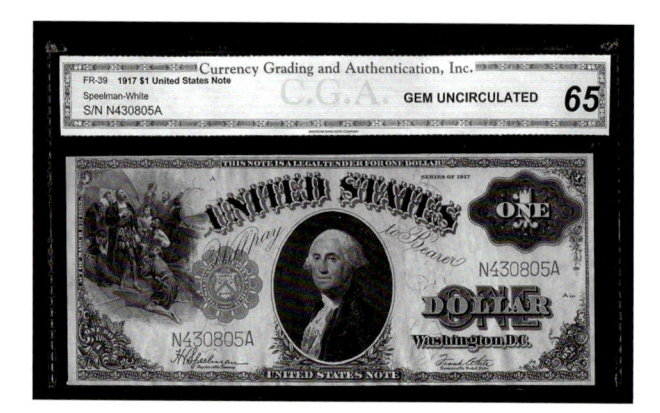

12942 **Fr. 39 $1 1917 Legal Tender CGA Gem Uncirculated 65.** Good original paper surfaces are easily seen through the third party holder. The note is bright and attractive. (550-up)

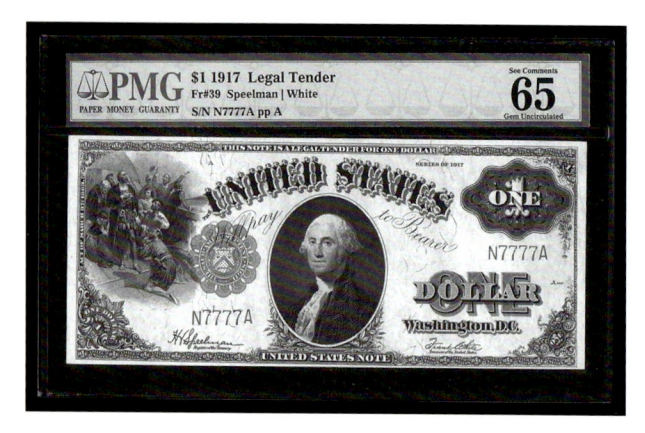

12943 **Fr. 39 $1 1917 Legal Tender PMG Gem Uncirculated 65 EPQ.** This lovely Gem has nice centering, bold colors, and original embossing. The serial number is solid 7s. (1,750-up)

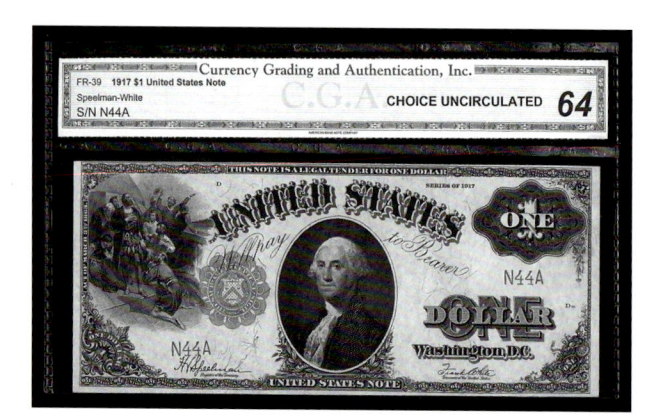

12944 **Fr. 39 $1 1917 Legal Tender CGA Choice Uncirculated 64.** The original embossing of the two-digit N44A serial number can be easily seen through the third party holder. It appears that the tight top margin held this note from Gem, as it seems Gem in every other sense. (750-up)

12945 **Fr. 39 $1 1917 Legal Tender PCGS Choice New 63PPQ.** This is a seven-digit note with a tight bottom margin. (300-up)

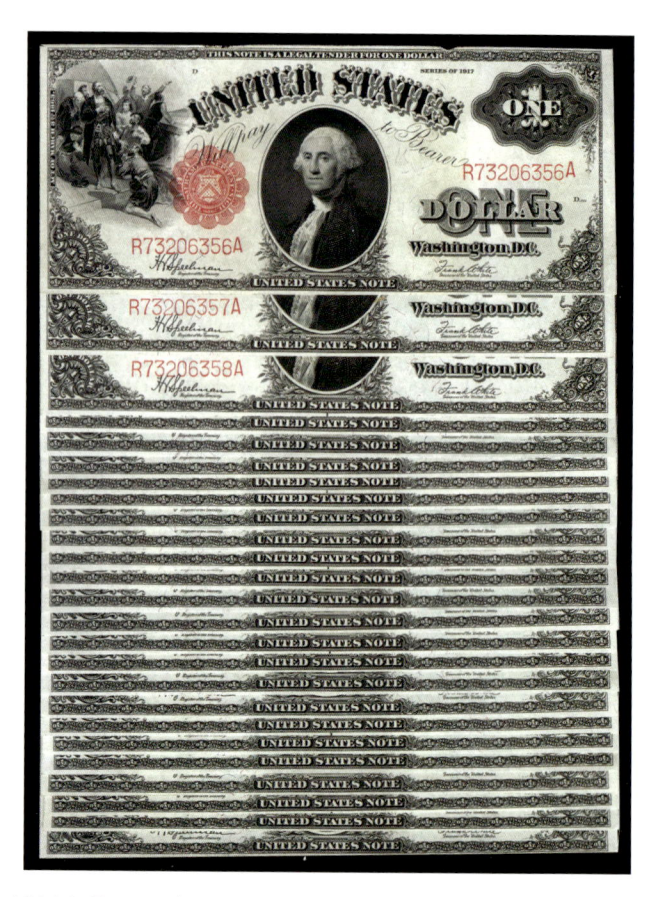

12946 **Fr. 39 $1 1917 Legal Tender Consecutive Run of Twenty-Five Choice New.** The first and last notes from this run have a few minor problems, but the 23 pieces in the middle all grade Choice to Gem. Original runs of Large Size Type Notes have all but disappeared from today's market, and this group is the first of its design type that we've seen in decades. There are six cut sheets in the group. (Total: 25 notes) (6,250-up)

12947 **Fr. 40 $1 1923 Legal Tender PCGS Superb Gem New 67PPQ.** A brightly colored, three-digit example of this very popular Red Seal Twentieth Century Large Size Type Note. With its high third-party grade, along with the PPQ designation and low serial number, you can expect strong competition for this beauty. (2,500-up)

12948 **Fr. 40 $1 1923 Legal Tender Superb Gem New.** An essentially flawless example, with terrific paper originality, broad margins and ideal color. **(2,000-up)**

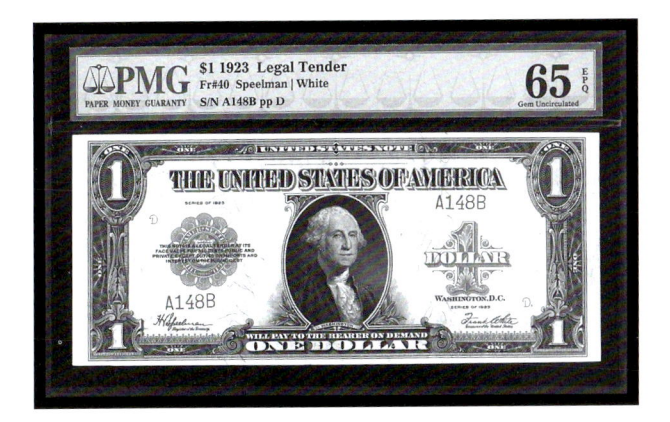

12949 **Fr. 40 $1 1923 Legal Tender PMG Gem Uncirculated 65 EPQ.** This three digit serial numbered Legal is bright and original with perfect depth of embossing and nearly perfect margins. Though a few decent examples exist from this serial number range, they always prove to be popular with bidders. **(1,500-up)**

12950 **Fr. 40 $1 1923 Legal Tender PCGS Very Choice New 64PPQ.** Ample margins and bold embossing are seen through the third-party holder of this delightful note. **(1,100-up)**

12951 **Fr. 40 $1 1923 Legal Tender Choice New.** An attractive note with excellent color and pronounced original embossing. **(600-up)**

12952 **Fr. 40 $1 1923 Legal Tender Choice New.** Mountainous embossing is seen on this note with bright overprints. A counting crinkle is seen at left. **(600-up)**

12953 **Fr. 40 $1 1923 Legal Tender PMG Choice About Unc 58 EPQ.** A well-centered, bright note that has all the visual allure of a Gem. **(450-up)**

12954 **Fr. 40 $1 1923 Legal Tender About New.** There are some minor stains at the edges, as well as a short edge tear confined to the top margin. The note has the three-digit serial number A235B. **(400-up)**

12955 **Fr. 40 $1 1923 Legal Tender CGA Extremely Fine 45.** Deep overprints highlight bright paper that retains a touch of embossing. **(350-up)**

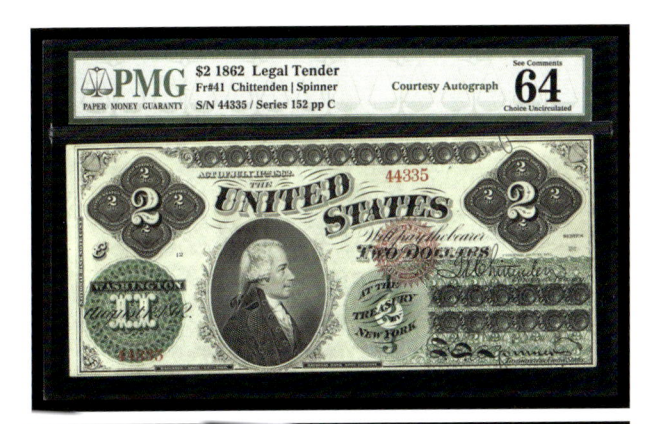

12956 **Fr. 41 $2 1862 Legal Tender Courtesy Autograph PMG Choice Uncirculated 64.** John Burke, who was Treasurer from 1913 until 1921, has courtesy autographed this early Deuce right above Spinner's signature. **(4,000-up)**

12957 **Fr. 41 $2 1862 Legal Tender New.** Three pinholes and a few minor edge tears distract from what is otherwise an extremely nice example of this earliest Legal Deuce. (3,000-up)

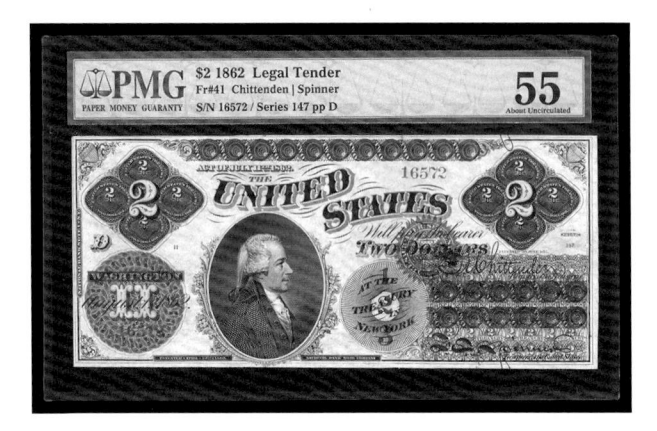

12958 **Fr. 41 $2 1862 Legal Tender PMG About Uncirculated 55.** A solid representative of the series with a touch of handling present and no folds. All the frame lines are visible though a bit tight at top. Simply put a crisp, colorful example. (2,750-up)

12959 **Fr. 41 $2 1862 Legal Tender PMG Choice Extremely Fine 45.** A three-fold XF with strong color and far better-than-average margins for the issue. These early Deuces are particularly handsome and are always very much in demand. A perfect collector grade note. (2,000-up)

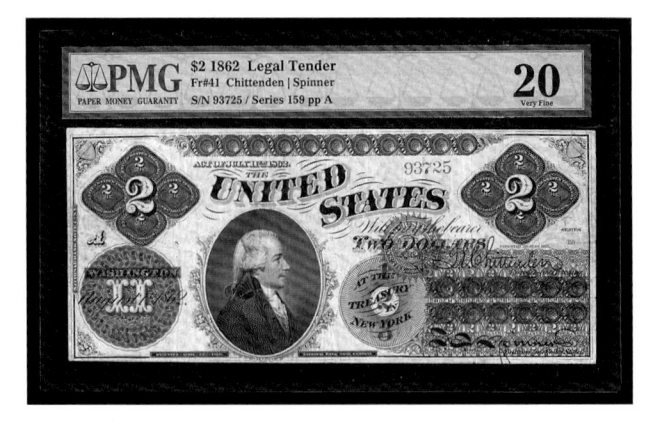

12960 **Fr. 41 $2 1862 Legal Tender PMG Very Fine 20.** This is a most pleasing example that exhibits bold color, but a tear is noticed in the upper right margin, which the grading service also mentions. (1,000-up)

12961 **Fr. 41 $2 1862 Legal Tender Very Fine.** Unusually broadly margined and with bright, bold colors. A handsome example that is sure to please its new owner.
From The Jacob and Heather Dedman Collection (1,200-up)

12962 **Fr. 41 $2 1862 Legal Tender Fine.** The design elements are especially strong given the amount of time this note saw in the channels of commerce. Some margin nicks are the only distractions.
From The Collection of Greg Southward (600-up)

12963 **Fr. 41 $2 1862 Legal Tender CGA Very Good 08.** Decent margins surround this early deuce, but a slight skin is noticed on the back. (300-up)

If Eye Appeal Meant Perfection...

12964 Fr. 42 $2 1869 Legal Tender PCGS About New 53. From the standpoint of appearance, this note is the match of the PCGS 68PPQ which we sold in January 2006 for over $40,000. Clearly, there is a minor fold or two that the PCGS graders saw, but in the holder, this piece is simply spectacular. The margins are huge and even all the way around. The rainbow colors are without equal and the centering of both sides is spectacular. This cataloger has a great deal of faith in the PCGS graders and there is no doubt that the note indeed is an AU, but if appearance is your criteria, you should be willing to step way up on this spectacular piece and pay far more than the technical grade would command. (7,500-up)

12965 Fr. 42 $2 1869 Legal Tender Very Fine-Extremely Fine. This particular example is the somewhat scarcer, though generally unrecognized, variety printed on watermarked paper. Not too many examples of this type are offered with regularity. The colors are pleasing and the folds moderate with a touch of tightness at right. (2,000-up)

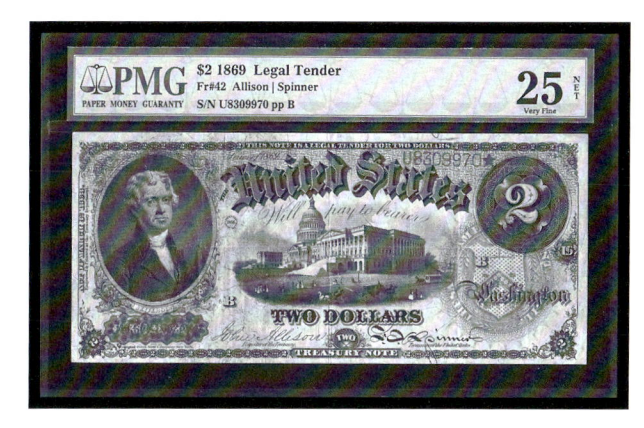

12966 Fr. 42 $2 1869 Legal Tender PMG Very Fine 25 Net. This Rainbow is a new addition to the census, with a repaired hole as the only notable mark. The anti-counterfeiting swath of blue is especially deep. (1,500-up)

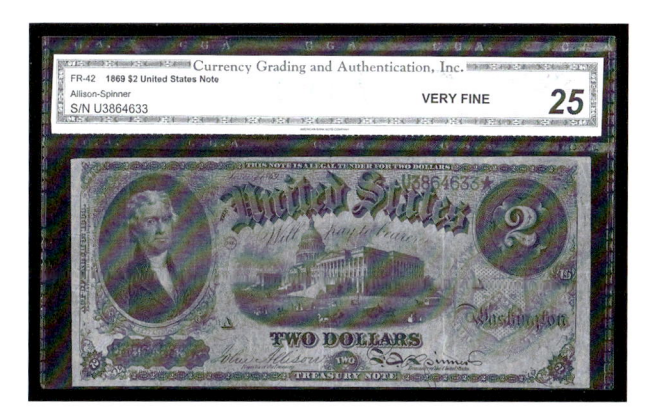

12967 Fr. 42 $2 1869 Legal Tender CGA Very Fine 25. A nice, well margined example with wonderful colors for the grade and sharp corners. A nice note for a circulated type set.
From The Collection of Greg Southward (1,500-up)

12968 Fr. 42 $2 1869 Legal Tender Very Good+. Several margin splits are noticed on this colorful Rainbow deuce. (600-up)

PCGS Superb Gem New 67PPQ 1874 Deuce

12969 Fr. 43 $2 1874 Legal Tender PCGS Superb Gem New 67PPQ. Broadly margined, with impeccable colors and strictly original paper surfaces. Fr. 43 is a scarce one-number type, with only about 85 representatives known in all grades combined, with this being from a small run of original notes. **(7,500-up)**

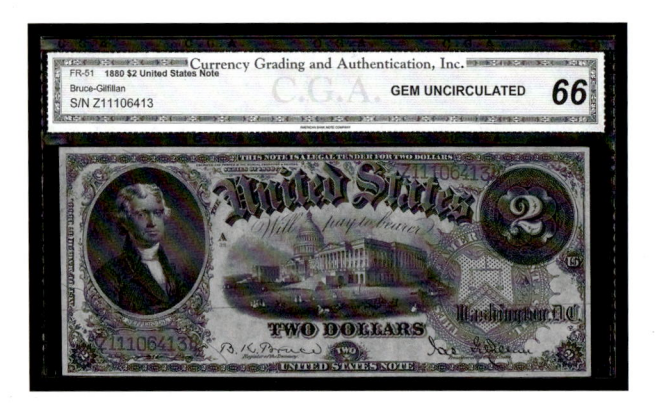

12970 Fr. 51 $2 1880 Legal Tender CGA Gem Uncirculated 66. Paper waves and pleasing color are noted through the holder. **(1,750-up)**

12971 Fr. 51 $2 1880 Legal Tender PMG Very Fine 20. This Deuce exhibits original surfaces. **(400-up)**

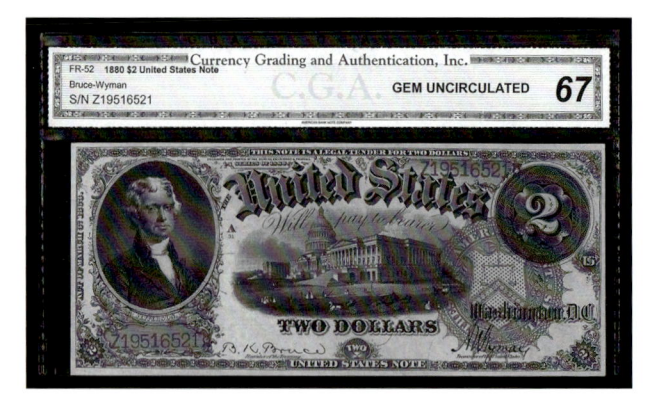

12972 Fr. 52 $2 1880 Legal Tender CGA Gem Uncirculated 67. The seal is deeper in color than usually seen for the type. **(3,500-up)**

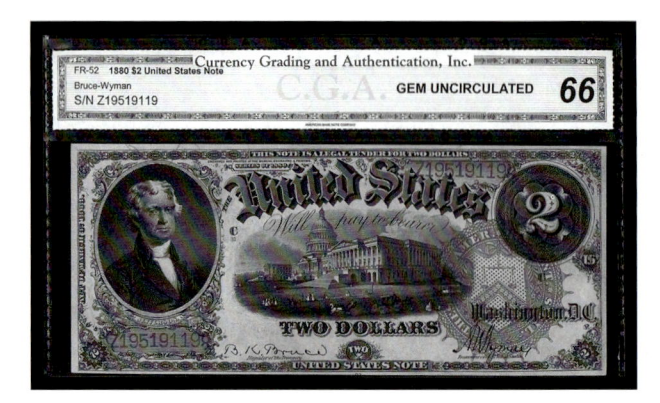

12973 Fr. 52 $2 1880 Legal Tender CGA Gem Uncirculated 66. This Gem has solid margins and bright white paper, though a pinhole is noted. **(3,000-up)**

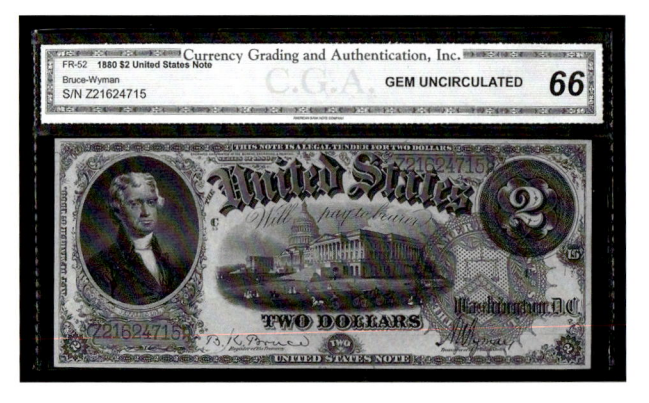

12974 Fr. 52 $2 1880 Legal Tender CGA Gem Uncirculated 66. Here is another pleasing note with plentiful margins and nice color. **(3,000-up)**

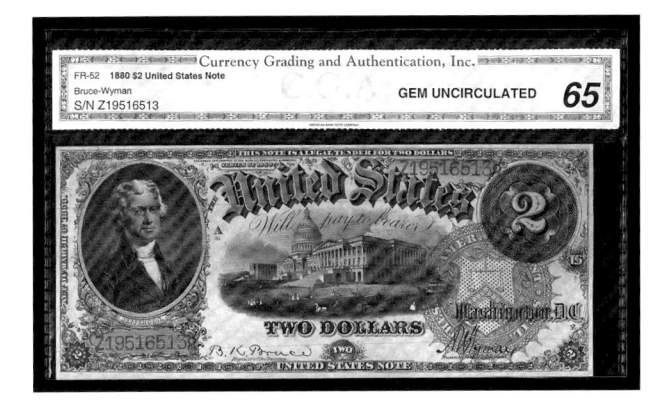

12975 Fr. 52 $2 1880 Legal Tender CGA Gem Uncirculated 65. The print quality is dark on this example from an always popular issue. This note is as deeply printed as one will find, matching the vividly colored brown seal and deep red serial numbers. (2,250-up)

12976 Fr. 52 $2 1880 Legal Tender Very Fine. This example shows even signs of circulation that do not detract from the overall appearance of this early Deuce.
From The Rolling Plains Collection (250-up)

12977 Fr. 53 $2 1880 Legal Tender Fine-Very Fine. A perfect example for the grade, showing even circulation while retaining its bright colors and full eye appeal. This is a rare number in any grade, with the census standing at just thirty six pieces in all grades combined. (2,750-up)

12978 Fr. 53 $2 1880 Legal Tender PCGS Fine 15. Right around three dozen examples of this Friedberg number are known, and it represents a one number type. The large red seal is still bright and the paper solid and problem free. (1,750-up)

12979 Fr. 53 $2 1880 Legal Tender Very Good. A rather scarce note for type with a touch over 35 currently known in all grades. This piece is well circulated but complete. (900-up)

Rare Jefferson Deuce

12980 Fr. 54 $2 1880 Legal Tender Very Good. This is the second rarest Friedberg number for the Jefferson Deuce design. The census contains less than 20 serial numbers and that includes this note. This Friedberg number remains on many, many collectors' want list as there are far too few to go around. Rare numbers command more and more attention, so expect this note to go over any listed value. In fact we sold one of these in the same grade in 1998 for almost $1900. (4,000-up)

12981 Fr. 56 $2 1880 Legal Tender Choice New. This problem-free note is nicely centered on both sides with excellent colors. It is quite close to the full Gem grade. (800-up)

12982 Fr. 57 $2 1917 Legal Tender PMG Choice Uncirculated 64 EPQ. A touch larger bottom margin and this perfectly printed Deuce may have achieved a higher grade. The seal is nearly blood red. (450-up)

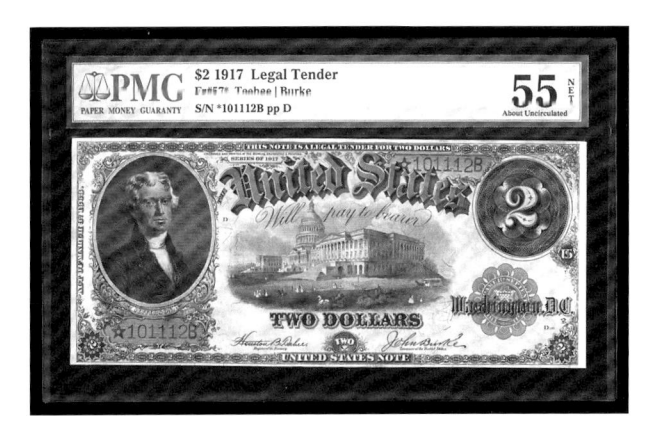

12983 Fr. 57 $2 1917 Legal Tender Star PMG Net About Uncirculated 55. Edge repairs in the top margin keep this note from achieving a full uncirculated grade. Most of the known stars for this issue are in circulated states of preservation. (1,000-up)

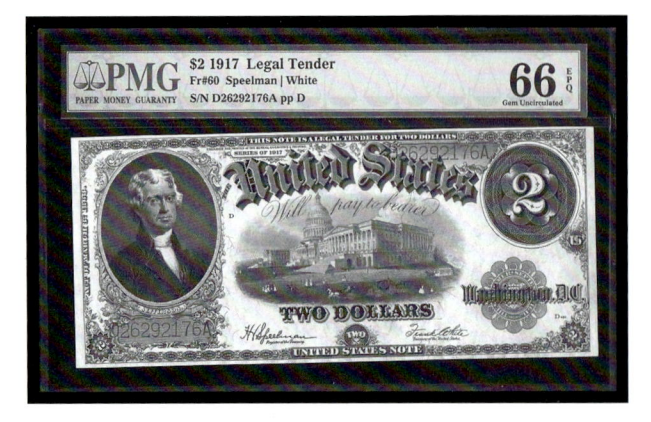

12984 **Fr. 60 $2 1917 Legal Tender PMG Gem Uncirculated 66 EPQ.** A pleasing piece with a cherry red overprint and nice paper originality. **(1,100-up)**

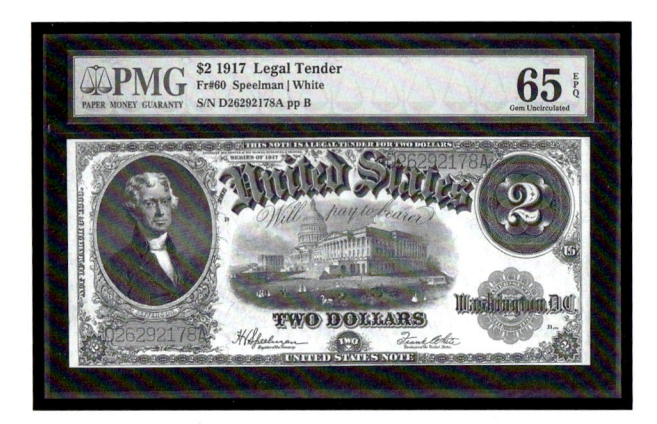

12985 **Fr. 60 $2 1917 Legal Tender PMG Gem Uncirculated 65 EPQ.** This is a near-consecutive note to a PMG 66 EPQ offered here tonight. This piece is as pleasing as the first, though the bottom margin is a touch more lean. **(800-up)**

12986 **Fr. 60 $2 1917 Legal Tender PMG Choice Uncirculated 64.** This is a well preserved Deuce that has top and bottom margins just a little too slender for a higher grade. **(400-up)**

12987 **Fr. 60 $2 1917 Legal Tender PMG Choice Uncirculated 64 EPQ.** The paper quality exhibited here is most pleasing.
From The Jacob and Heather Dedman Collection **(450-up)**

12988 **Fr. 60 $2 1917 Legal Tender Star Very Fine-Extremely Fine.** The surfaces still remain bright with plenty of pleasing color on this early replacement note. **(500-up)**

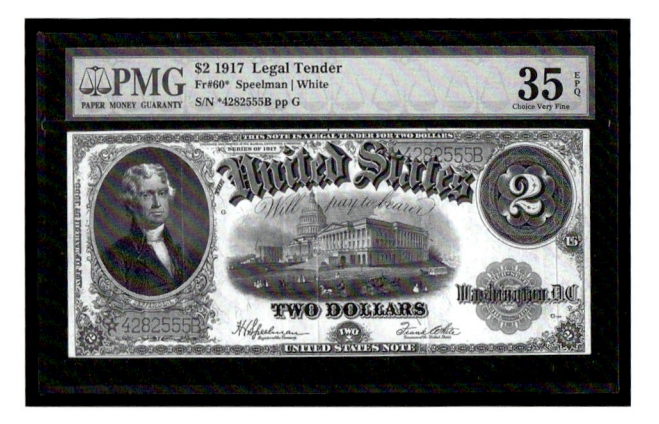

12989 **Fr. 60 $2 1917 Legal Tender Star PMG Choice Very Fine 35 EPQ.** This note circulated for only a short time as the paper is bright and completely free of soiling. **(500-up)**

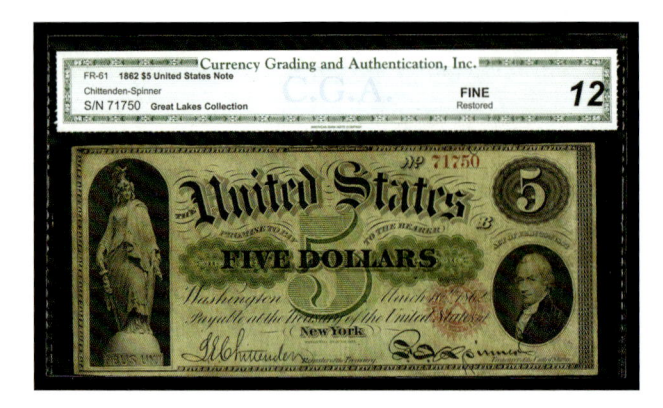

12990 **Fr. 61 $5 1862 Legal Tender CGA Fine 12 Restored.** From our 2006 Central States sale where it was described, "There are only about ten examples known of this number, none of which grades higher than Fine. We sold this piece once before in January of 1998. This note appears to be perfect for the grade, but as noted on the CGA holder, it is restored. It has had minor nicks and edge cuts that have been restored so well that only a well-trained eye can detect their presence. This "No Series" Legal Tender Note is, in effect, Series 1 of the 72 series that were printed. Notes were numbered from 1 through 100,000 and then back to 1 again. To distinguish among serial number runs, notes were marked "Series 2," "Series 3" etc., each time a new run of 100,000 was begun. However, the first run of 100,000 was not marked, hence the existence of the very rare Fr. 61. When we sold this last back in 1998, it was estimated at $3000 and realized $3740." This is a scarce note in a hot market. There is no telling when another example will surface.
From The Lincoln Collection **(6,000-up)**

12991 **Fr. 61a $5 1862 Legal Tender PCGS Very Choice New 64PPQ.** Over-the-top originality is seen on this near-Gem piece. The front to back centering is nearly perfect and save for a tight bottom margin, this would be a full Gem. The original paper wave and embossing are clearly visible through the holder. (3,500-up)

12992 **Fr. 61a $5 1862 Legal Tender PMG Choice Uncirculated 64.** Unusually well margined for this early Type with original embossing that is easily seen through the third party holder. A handsome note that edges right up next to the full Gem grade. (3,500-up)

12993 **Fr. 61a $5 1862 Legal Tender Very Fine.** A single edge split at the bottom is the only flaw on this high-end VF early Five.
From The Collection of Greg Southward (600-up)

Serial Number 1 1862 $5 Legal Tender

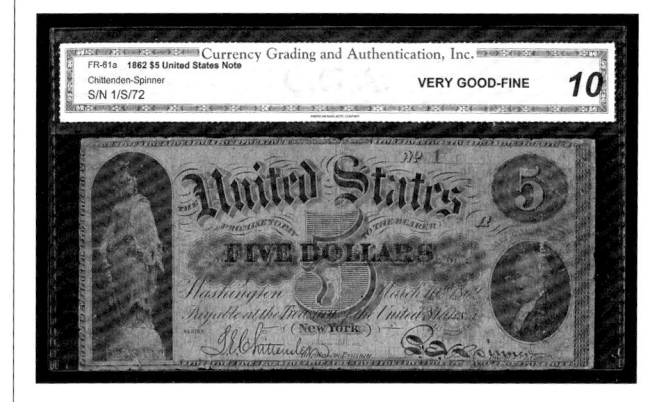

12994 **Fr. 61a $5 1862 Legal Tender CGA Very Good-Fine 10.** This example of a desirable serial number 1 Series 72 issue is mostly complete with a little bit of margin roughness. (2,500-up)

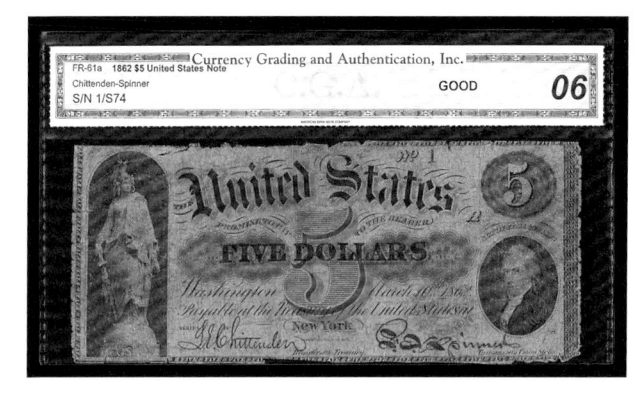

12995 **Fr. 61a $5 1862 Legal Tender CGA Good 06.** From our FUN 2006 auction where it was described, "The edges are considerably worn, and in parts missing, on this serial # 1 Series 71 1862 Legal Tender." (2,000-up)

12996 **Fr. 63 $5 1863 Legal Tender Very Fine.** This $5 has original surfaces despite toning a shade. This example also has nice edges and color. (600-up)

12997 **Fr. 64 $5 1869 Legal Tender PMG Choice Uncirculated 64 EPQ.** Henry Gugler's "Woodchopper" design, formally known as "The Pioneers," is always a collector favorite. The rainbow colors of the 1869 issue give a presentation that is unmatched in the U.S. currency series. Certain to have garnered a higher grade with a little thicker margin at bottom right. (3,500-up)

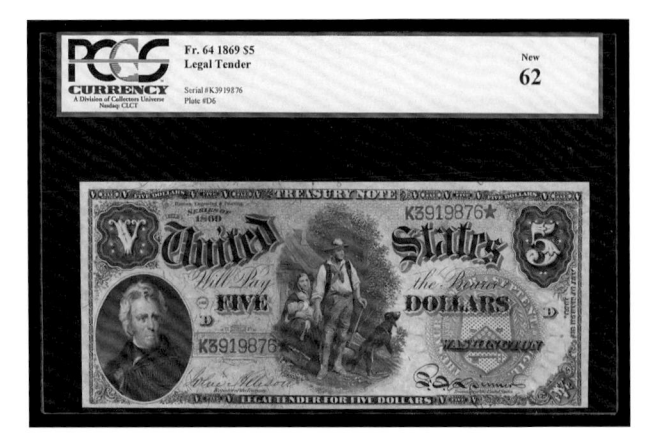

12998 **Fr. 64 $5 1869 Legal Tender PCGS New 62.** Extra broad margins are noted on this $5 Rainbow. Add boldly printed serial numbers, seal, and a pleasing swath of blue and the eye appeal is excellent. In the top margin, a partial sheet number is noted. **(2,500-up)**

12999 **Fr. 64 $5 1869 Legal Tender New.** The note has the appearance of a fully Choice Example, but unfortunately, a small V-shaped piece has been replaced in the top margin. It's not at all conspicuous, and this note will afford some collector the opportunity to spend less than $2000 on a note that looks like a $5000 piece.
From The Jacob and Heather Dedman Collection **(1,750-up)**

13000 **Fr. 64 $5 1869 Legal Tender Choice About New.** A soft center fold is the only circulation this piece has sustained. Bright and crisp with some embossing seen. **(2,000-up)**

13001 **Fr. 64 $5 1869 Legal Tender Choice About New.** A perfectly original note with all the attributes of a full Gem including full margins, original paper waves and bold color. There is unfortunately a light corner fold that precludes the grade. **(2,000-up)**

13002 **Fr. 64 $5 1869 Legal Tender Very Fine.** A broadly margined, brightly colored, evenly circulated example. An ideal collector note.
From The Jacob and Heather Dedman Collection **(600-up)**

13003 **Fr. 64 $5 1869 Legal Tender Fine.** This Rainbow $5 Woodchopper has good margins and color with a few pinholes.
From The Collection of Greg Southward **(400-up)**

13004 **Fr. 68 $5 1875 Legal Tender PCGS Very Choice New 64PPQ.** Bold inks and embossing highlight this early Woodchopper. It is another exquisite note that is not listed in the census, but it comes from a CU run of notes. **(1,900-up)**

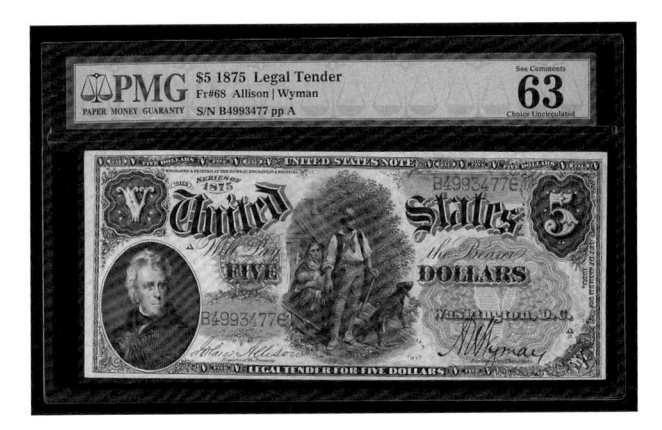

13005 **Fr. 68 $5 1875 Legal Tender PMG Choice Uncirculated 63 EPQ.** The margins are a bit irregular and the lower right corner is rounded on what is otherwise a Gem-quality early Pioneer Legal. (1,100-up)

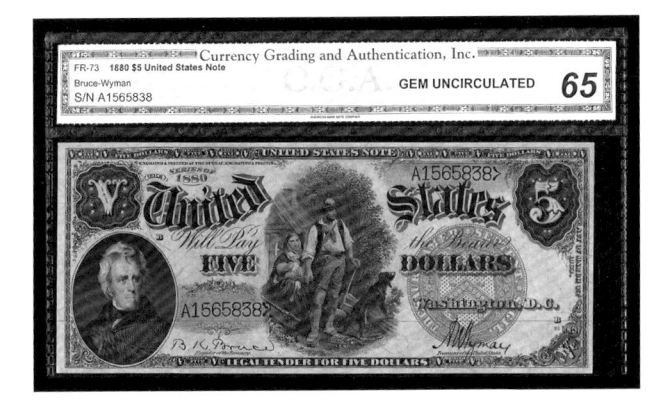

13006 **Fr. 73 $5 1880 Legal Tender CGA Gem Uncirculated 65.** This one certainly appears to be accurately graded. There is a short run of Uncirculated Fr. 73s, but this note has broader margins and better corners than the great majority of those pieces. The original embossing is easy to see on this 1880 Pioneer Family Five. (2,000-up)

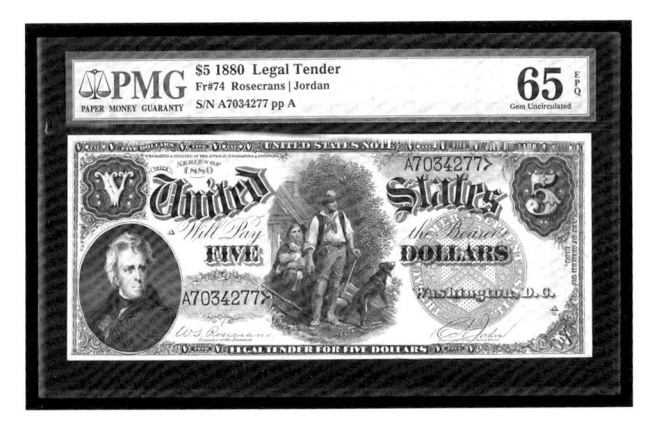

13007 **Fr. 74 $5 1880 Legal Tender PMG Gem Uncirculated 65EPQ.** A very colorful, and clearly originally embossed Large Red Seal 1880 Pioneer Family Legal. The margins are broad and even, and the colors are quite bright. The PMG 65EPQ grade appears to us to be right on the money. (2,000-up)

13008 **Fr. 79 $5 1880 Legal Tender PCGS Choice New 63PPQ.** Natural paper surfaces and embossing make themselves known to the viewer of this colorful $5. It is unreported, but from an early run of CU notes for this design. (700-up)

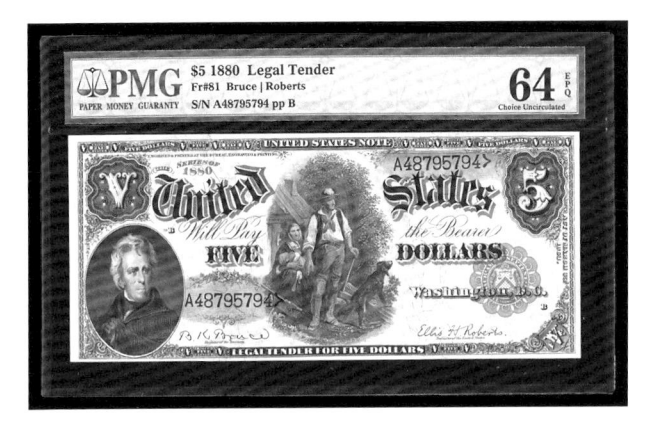

13009 **Fr. 81 $5 1880 Legal Tender PMG Choice Uncirculated 64 EPQ.** An absolutely lovely note which has deep embossing, adequate margins and bright color.
From The Jacob and Heather Dedman Collection (900-up)

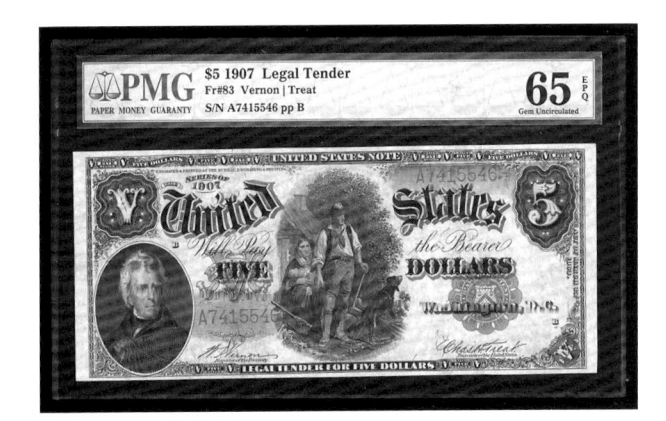

13010 **Fr. 83 $5 1907 Legal Tender PMG Gem Uncirculated 65 EPQ.** A lovely Pioneer Family Five and one of the scarcer series of 1907 Friedberg numbers. The margins are beautiful, as are the colors. (1,200-up)

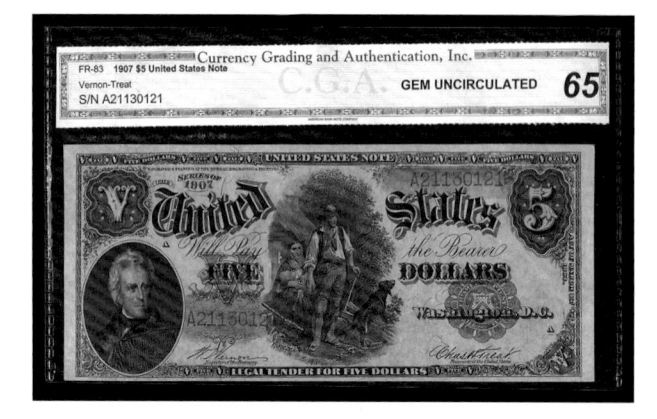

13011 Fr. 83 $5 1907 Legal Tender CGA Gem Uncirculated 65. This lightly toned Woodchopper has large margins for the issue along with a bright red overprint. (1,000-up)

13012 Fr. 87 $5 1907 Legal Tender PCGS Gem New 65PPQ. A pretty Pioneer Five with paper originality visible through the holder. (1,200-up)

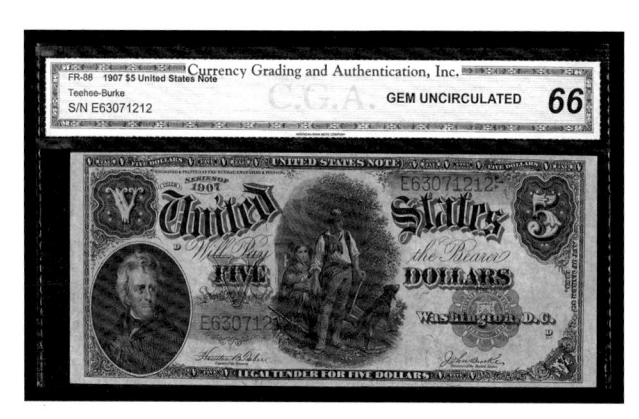

13013 Fr. 88 $5 1907 Legal Tender CGA Gem Uncirculated 66. Very nicely margined with obvious original embossing, and terrific color. (1,250-up)

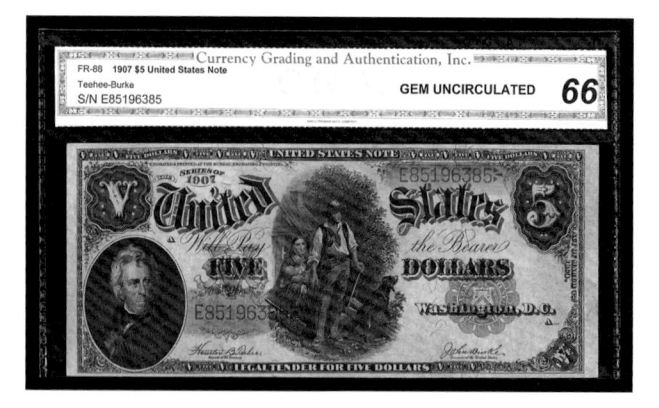

13014 Fr. 88 $5 1907 Legal Tender CGA Gem Uncirculated 66. A pretty Pioneer Five, whose crackling fresh originality can be easily seen through the third-party holder. (1,000-up)

13015 Fr. 88 $5 1907 Legal Tender Choice New. This gorgeous note has deep embossing and is a bit close along the top, but a Gem in every other respect. (500-up)

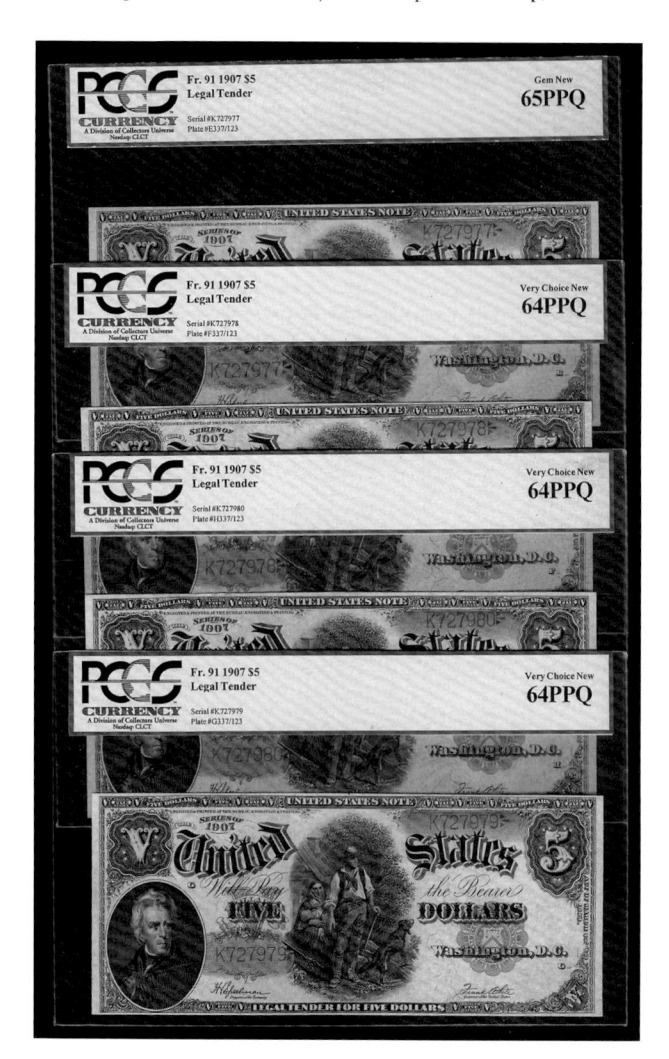

13016 Fr. 91 $5 1907 Legal Tender Cut Sheet of Four PCGS 65PPQ, 64PPQ, 64PPQ, 64PPQ. An amazing cut sheet of flashy Pioneer Fives, encapsulated by PCGS. One note was awarded the grade of 65PPQ, while the remaining notes graded out as 64PPQ. The margins are very nice for the type and, in spite of the fact that Fr. 91 is quite a common number, cut sheets are rarely seen. (3,500-up)

13017 **Engraving Error Fr. 91 $5 1907 Legal Tender PMG Choice Uncirculated 64 EPQ.** This Woodchopper carries the engraving error where "PUBLIC" is engraved "PCBLIC" on line six of the obligation clause that is posted on the back. The error is best seen with a magnifying glass. This error has been known for many years within the hobby. This is the nicest one of these we have seen in quite a while. **(800-up)**

13018 **Fr. 91 $5 1907 Legal Tender PMG Choice About Unc 58.** We suspect a very light center bend accounts for the grade as no corner folds could be found. The embossing is strong as is the color of the printed devices. **(400-up)**

13019 **Fr. 91 $5 1907 Legal Tender PCGS About New 53.** Embossing of the seal and serial numbers is evident through the holder. **(250-up)**

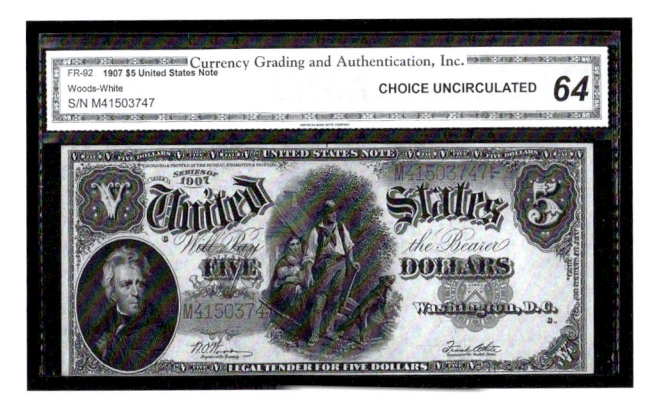

13020 **Fr. 92 $5 1907 Legal Tender CGA Choice Uncirculated 64.** The final signature combination of the Pioneer Family Type, and a much scarcer number. The 64 grade is no doubt the result of the tight bottom margin, as the note appears Gem in all other respects. The paper originality is clearly seen through the third party holder. **(850-up)**

13021 **Fr. 92 $5 1907 Legal Tender About New.** Two center folds millimeters apart separate this note from a full New grade. The overprint is especially bright and well embossed. **(350-up)**

13022 **Fr. 93 $10 1862 Legal Tender PCGS Very Fine 25PPQ.** A tight left hand margin as is most often the case for this issue does little to detract from the appearance of this piece. Deep inks are still present despite a light seal. **(1,500-up)**

CGA Gem Uncirculated 67
1863 $10 Legal Tender

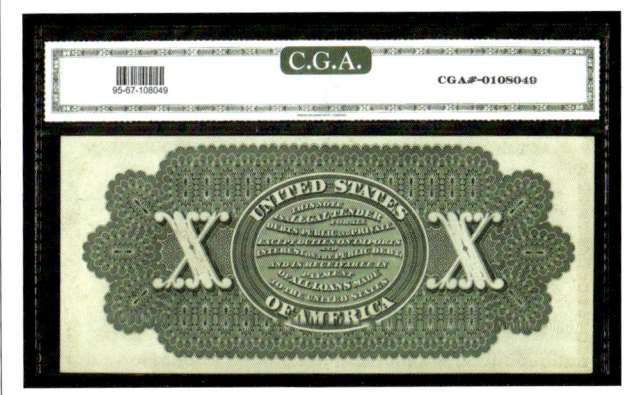

13023 **Fr. 95b $10 1863 Legal Tender CGA Gem Uncirculated 67.** From our 2006 Long Beach Signature sale where the catalog commented, "Beautifully margined, with spectacular color and great eye appeal. The grade would most likely be Superb were it not for a couple of slightly rounded corners. This piece has not been previously reported to the census, though it falls right into a group of notes that has been reported as uncirculated." The note realized $15,525 on an estimate of $7500-up. **(15,000-up)**

13024 **Fr. 95b $10 1863 Legal Tender Very Good.** Although the bottom edge is little frayed, this early $10 Legal is solid for the grade and has plenty of desirability for the budget-conscious collector who doesn't want to spend much more to fill a hole in a type collection.
From The Collection of Greg Southward **(650-up)**

CGA Gem Uncirculated 66
$10 Rainbow Jackass

13025 **Fr. 96 $10 1869 Legal Tender CGA Gem Uncirculated 66.** Very even margins bring a nice balance to the deeply inked surfaces on this wonderfully centered Rainbow. This Webster note should see some spirited bidding as it is also new to the census. **(7,500-up)**

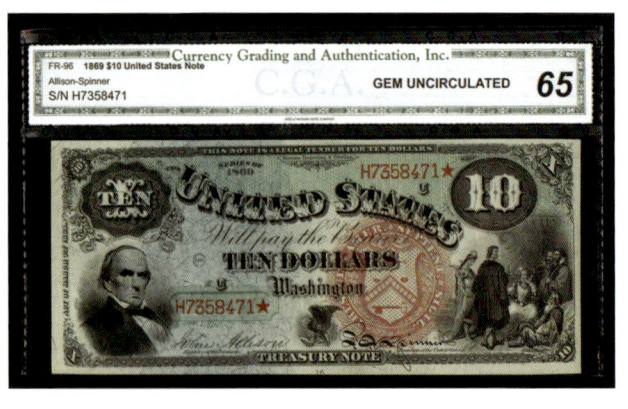

13026 **Fr. 96 $10 1869 Legal Tender CGA Gem Uncirculated 65.** This Rainbow Ten has absolutely spectacular color as well as far larger margins than we're used to seeing on this type. The margins are a bit irregular, but plenty large enough all the way around to support the Gem grade. **(6,500-up)**

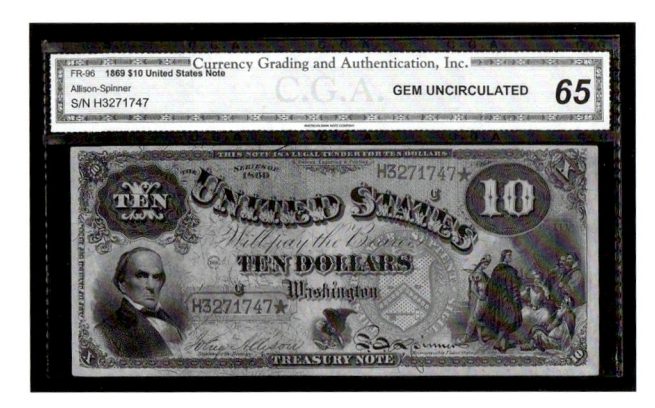

13027 **Fr. 96 $10 1869 Legal Tender CGA Gem Uncirculated 65.** This pleasing Rainbow has a touch of tightness along the top margin otherwise it would have garnered one more point. Wonderful centering is also noticed. **(6,500-up)**

13028 **Fr. 96 $10 1869 Legal Tender Extremely Fine-About New.** This is a pleasing Rainbow that retains much crispness with several folds noticed after much consternation.
From The Collection of Greg Southward **(1,250-up)**

Classically Rare Fr. 97 PMG 30

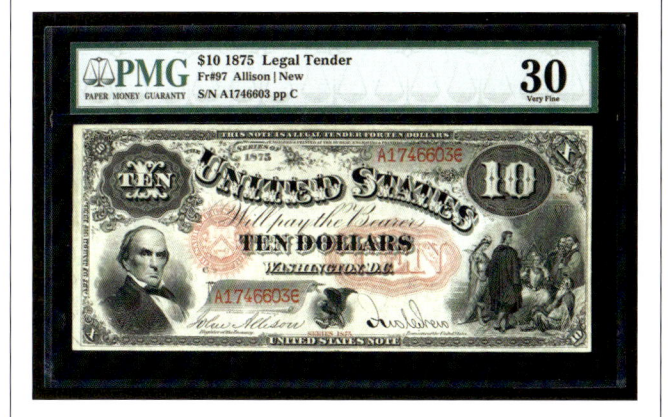

CGA Gem Uncirculated 66 Fr. 99
1878 $10 Legal Tender

13029 **Fr. 97 $10 1875 Legal Tender PMG Very Fine 30.** Fewer than a dozen Fr. 97's are known, and there is not a single uncirculated piece among them. Fr. 97 is a classically rare note. CAA has handled only three examples in our previous 45+ sales, an Extra Fine back in 1992, a Choice About New in September 2003, and another Very Fine. This note is one of only about a dozen examples known to exist, and it is easily within the top half in the census. We sold another Very Fine in January 2006 at our annual FUN auction which realized $25,875. This currently offered piece, which has been sold several times as an XF, and now resides in a PMG VF30 holder, is likely to pass that level.
From The Lincoln Collection **(25,000-up)**

13030 **Fr. 99 $10 1878 Legal Tender CGA Gem Uncirculated 66.** Fr. 99 is the "common" (fewer than 75 known) number of the 1875 and 1878 series, which makes this beauty an ideal representation of the type. This hails from within a known run that has provided numerous gem examples. **(8,500-up)**

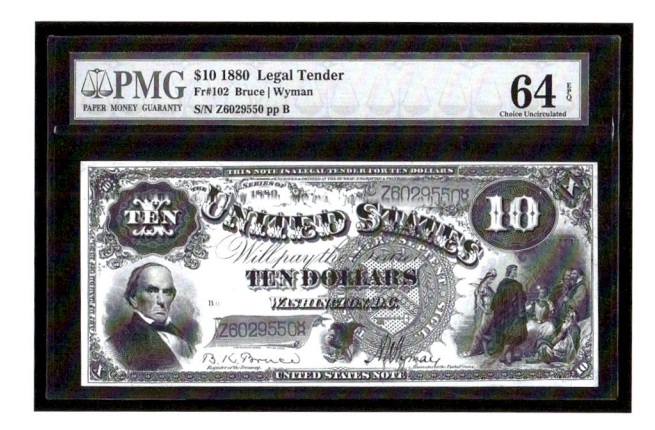

13031 **Fr. 102 $10 1880 Legal Tender PMG Choice Uncirculated 64 EPQ.** The colors are particularly rich on this Large Brown Spiked Seal Red Serial Number 1880 Sawbuck. The "EPQ" designation was clearly earned as the paper originality can be quite easily seen through the holder. **(2,750-up)**

13032 **Fr. 102 $10 1880 Legal Tender Very Fine.** The surfaces are a touch soft, and the paper color is a bit muted on this 1880 Ten.
From The Collection of Greg Southward **(525-up)**

13033 Fr. 102 $10 1880 Legal Tender Very Fine. About twenty small pinholes are found on this Large Brown Seal 1880 Ten. The paper color is somewhat drab, but this well-margined Jackass Ten has good ink color. (475-up)

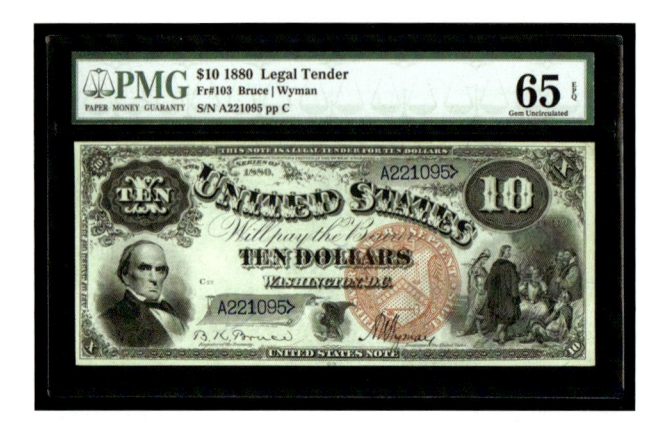

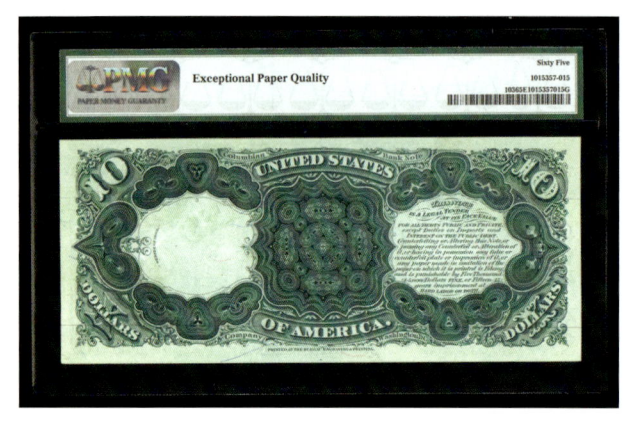

13034 Fr. 103 $10 1880 Legal Tender PMG Gem Uncirculated 65 EPQ. Bright color and deep original embossing highlight this Large Red Seal Jackass Ten. A pretty piece that should knock at the door of a $5,000 realization. (4,500-up)

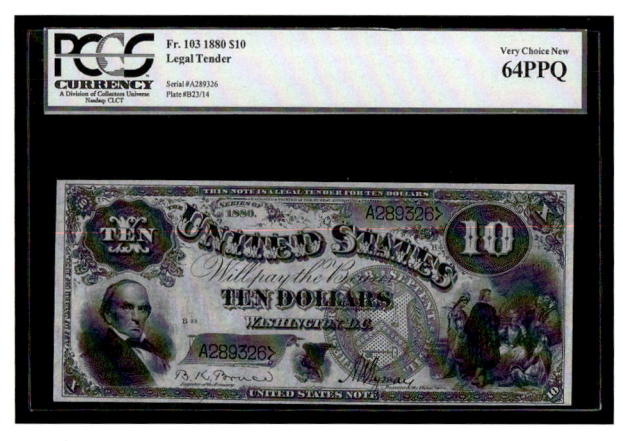

13035 Fr. 103 $10 1880 Legal Tender PCGS Very Choice New 64PPQ. The last auction appearance of this note was in a 1993 CAA sale. It's part of a reasonably long run of very nice examples of this Friedberg number. Our 1993 grade of Very Choice New stood the test of time as PCGS's 64PPQ is its 2007 equivalent.
From The Bill and Kathy Stella Currency Collection
(2,750-up)

13036 Fr. 104 $10 1880 Legal Tender PCGS Extremely Fine 40PPQ. The original embossing remains pronounced on this lightly circulated Large Red Seal 1880 Ten. A handsome example in ideal collector grade. (1,250-up)

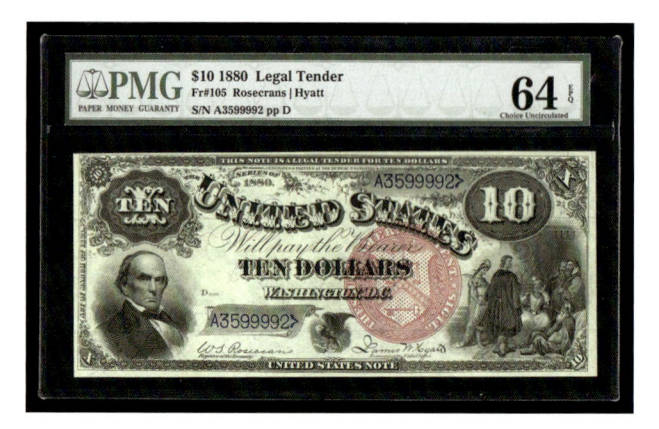

13037 Fr. 105 $10 1880 Legal Tender PMG Choice Uncirculated 64EPQ. The paper originality is bold and easy to see on this much scarcer Large Round Red Seal Jackass Ten. Only about 45 examples of this number are known making it by far the scarcest of the three signature combinations for this Type. This one is a beauty that would likely have earned a far higher grade with a touch more top margin. (7,500-up)

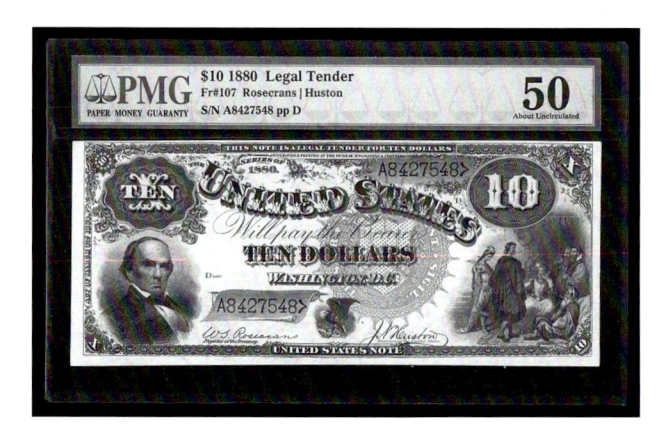

13038 Fr. 107 $10 1880 Legal Tender PMG About Uncirculated 50. A tight top margin is the only distraction on this pleasing, vivid "Jackass." (1,250-up)

13039 **Fr. 108 $10 1880 Legal Tender Choice Extremely Fine.** Three light vertical folds barely interrupt the well-embossed original surfaces of this Large Brown Seal Blue Serial Number Jackass Ten. It's in essence a one-number type, as its type-mate Fr. 109 is represented by only two known examples.
From The Collection of Greg Southward **(1,250-up)**

13040 **Fr. 110 $10 1880 Legal Tender PCGS Gem New 65PPQ.** A strikingly handsome Jackass Ten, and also a somewhat scarcer Friedberg number. The original paper embossing can be easily seen through the third party holder on this 1880 Sawbuck. **(4,000-up)**

13041 **Fr. 110 $10 1880 Legal Tender PMG Gem Uncirculated 65 EPQ.** PMG has commented "Exceptional Paper Quality" as well as "Great Embossing" on this bright and handsome Jackass Ten. **(4,000-up)**

13042 **Fr. 111 $10 1880 Legal Tender PMG Gem Uncirculated 65 EPQ.** This 1880 Ten bears the courtesy autograph of D. N. Morgan directly above his engraved Treasurer signature. Morgan courtesy autographs are often in light gray ink and rather inconspicuous. This bold signature is easily seen and clearly read. PMG has noted the courtesy autograph and has included it in its notations along with the Exceptional Paper Quality comment. **(3,500-up)**

13043 **Fr. 111 $10 1880 Legal Tender PCGS Very Fine 35PPQ.** A pleasingly original note with bright paper and a light amount of soiling seen on the back.
From The Collection of Greg Southward **(750-up)**

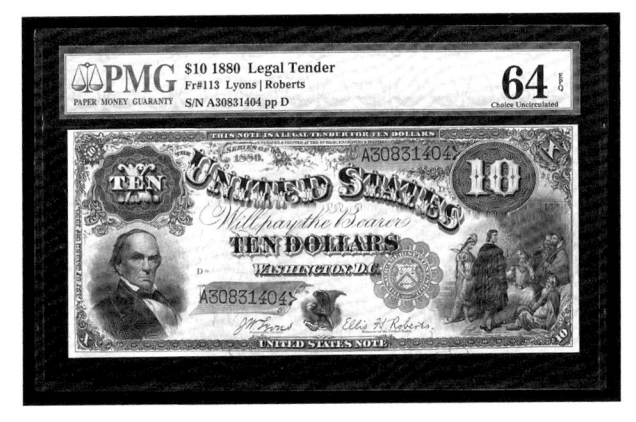

13044 **Fr. 113 $10 1880 Legal Tender PMG Choice Uncirculated 64 EPQ.** Apparently, the top margin held the grade down on this otherwise Superb-appearing 1880 Ten. Pronounced paper originality is easy to see through the third party holder. **(2,500-up)**

13045 Fr. 113 $10 1880 Legal Tender Very Fine. This fully framed $10 has original paper surfaces. This is the last Friedberg number for the popular "Jackass" design. **(550-up)**

13046 Fr. 114 $10 1901 Legal Tender CGA Gem Uncirculated 66. Solid margins are noted on this Gem. This would be a pleasing example for a type set in Gem. **(11,000-up)**

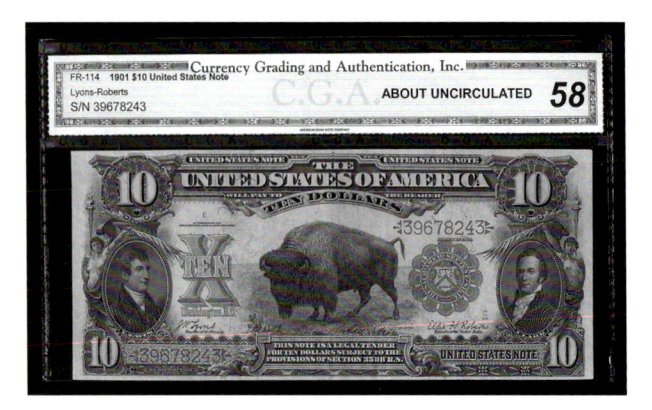

13047 Fr. 114 $10 1901 Legal Tender CGA About Uncirculated 58. A lone center fold is noted on this otherwise new note. **(3,000-up)**

13048 Fr. 114 $10 1901 Legal Tender Very Fine. The paper surfaces are a touch soft, but this Bison boasts unusually broad margins.
From The Collection of Greg Southward **(1,250-up)**

Gorgeous Gem Bison

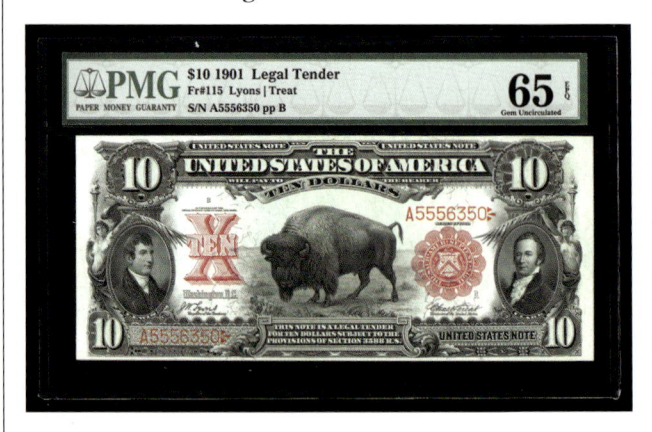

13049 Fr. 115 $10 1901 Legal Tender PMG Gem Uncirculated 65 EPQ. A brightly colored Bison with pronounced originality of the embossing. The margins are excellent, and the PMG 65EPQ grade seems, if anything, a bit conservative. **(10,000-up)**

13050 **Fr. 115 $10 1901 Legal Tender Very Fine.** Well centered with decent color of both the inks and paper. Fr. 115, while not rare, is a somewhat scarcer Bison number.
From The Collection of Greg Southward **(1,250-up)**

13051 **Fr. 115 $10 1901 Legal Tender Fine.** The edges and red overprint are nice for the grade level. **(600-up)**

13052 **Fr. 116 $10 1901 Legal Tender CGA About Uncirculated 50.** This piece boasts fully uncirculated eye appeal, though there are two vertical folds that are noted on either side of the Bison. **(2,600-up)**

13053 **Fr. 116 $10 1901 Legal Tender CGA Very Fine 20.** The moderately circulated paper is solid and free of distractions.
From The Collection of Greg Southward **(800-up)**

13054 **Fr. 118 $10 1901 Legal Tender Very Fine.** This well-margined, fully bright Bison has a minor internal tear that is really not much more than a pinhole. The colors are strong and the note faces up very nicely.
From The Collection of Greg Southward **(1,250-up)**

13055 **Fr. 119 $10 1901 Legal Tender CGA Gem Uncirculated 66.** The margins are perfectly even as are the printed details. **(10,000-up)**

13056 **Fr. 119 $10 1901 Legal Tender PMG Choice Fine 15.** This attractive note still has a solid Bison vignette at center. There are a few pinholes revealed when the note is candled. **(600-up)**

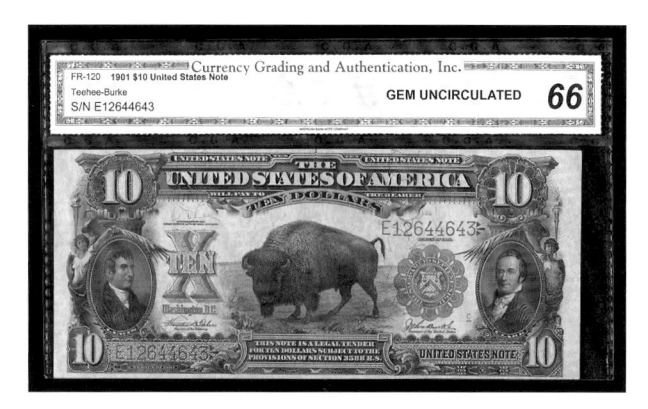

13057 **Fr. 120 $10 1901 Legal Tender CGA Gem Uncirculated 66.** The Friedberg 120 is perhaps 5 to 6 times scarcer than the most common issue of the type, the Friedberg 122. The margins here are ample and the paper is bright. **(9,500-up)**

13058 **Fr. 120 $10 1901 Legal Tender CGA Gem Uncirculated 65.** The margins on this scarcer type note are quite even with pleasing color and print quality throughout. (7,500-up)

13059 **Fr. 120 $10 1901 Legal Tender PCGS Very Fine 35.** This boldly colored Bison appears flawless through the third party holder. (1,250-up)

13060 **Fr. 120 $10 1901 Legal Tender PMG Very Fine 20.** This Bison has bright color and snappy paper. A tiny nick is noticed at left. (900-up)

13061 **Fr. 120 $10 1901 Legal Tender Fine-Very Fine.** This is a lovely mid-grade example of this scarcer Friedberg number that is outnumbered by its Fr. 122 type mate by a count of five to one. This original Bison displays even circulation with nice edges and is problem-free for the grade. This is also the variety with the face plate number found below the plate letter for this Friedberg number. (800-up)

13062 **Fr. 121 $10 1901 Legal Tender Mule Very Fine.** This Bison has back plate number 340 in the mule position for this Friedberg number. It has a dark red overprint and faces up well. The back top margin has a little tape residue from attempting to repair an approximate quarter inch tear.
From The Collection of Greg Southward (900-up)

Fr. 122 Mule in 65 EPQ

13063 **Fr. 122 $10 1901 Legal Tender Mule PMG Gem Uncirculated 65 EPQ.** PMG has added "Great Embossing & Color" to its "Exceptional Paper Quality" comment. They have also noted "John Burke Back Plate #332." Little attention has been paid to these Mule varieties over the years, but now that the third party grading companies are including the information on their holders, a strong market is beginning to coalesce. (12,500-up)

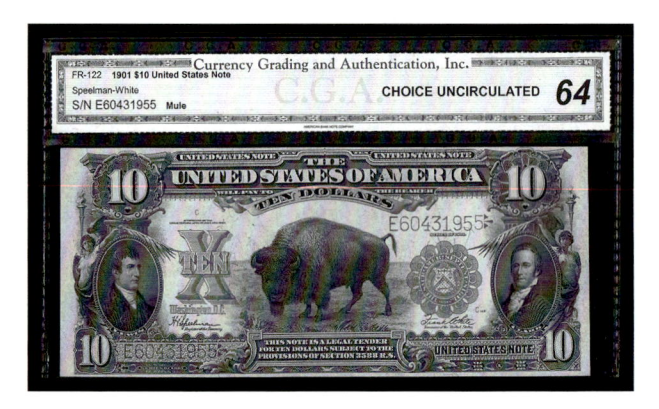

13064 **Fr. 122 $10 1901 Legal Tender Mule CGA Gem Uncirculated 64.** A miniscule corner tip fold is far outside the design, save by the size of the enormous margins on this Mule example. (4,500-up)

13065 Fr. 122 $10 1901 Legal Tender CGA Extremely Fine 40. The all important design is nearly uninterrupted by the folds that account for the grade.
From The Collection of Greg Southward (1,700-up)

13066 Fr. 122 $10 1901 Legal Tender CGA Extremely Fine 40. Three vertical folds and some handling account for the grade on this lightly circulated Bison. (1,700-up)

13067 Fr. 122 $10 1901 Legal Tender Extremely Fine. A lovely collector-grade Bison, with three light folds that can barely be seen, good paper originality, strong color and excellent eye appeal.
From The Jacob and Heather Dedman Collection (2,000-up)

13068 Fr. 122 $10 1901 Legal Tender Very Fine-Extremely Fine. An ideal collector-grade Bison with decent margins, more than acceptable color, original embossing, and a handsome, overall appearance. Strictly problem-free and hard to find this nice.
From The Collection of Greg Southward (1,500-up)

13069 Fr. 122 $10 1901 Legal Tender Mule PMG Very Fine 20. This piece which saw a moderate amount of circulation spent a large amount of time folded as there are some splits noted at the folds. At center there are some paper spots. (750-up)

13070 Fr. 122 $10 1901 Legal Tender Very Fine. Original paper surfaces and healthy edges highlight this Bison with a dark red overprint. (1,300-up)

13071 Fr. 122 $10 1901 Legal Tender Mule Fine-Very Fine. Well circulated, but not at all unattractive. There is a single short split at the top left affecting blank margin area only. (850-up)

13072 Fr. 122 $10 1901 Legal Tender PMG Fine 12. A solid, mid-grade Bison. (600-up)

13073 Fr. 122 $10 1901 Legal Tender Very Good-Fine. This Bison has a little bit of remaining brightness and snap to the paper. (550-up)

13074 Fr. 122 $10 1901 Legal Tender Very Good. The edges and paper are nice for the grade. (500-up)

13075 Fr. 123 $10 1923 Legal Tender Very Fine. This $10 Jackson has toned a shade while the back shows a bleed through of the red third printing.
From The Collection of Greg Southward (2,000-up)

13076 **Fr. 123 $10 1923 Legal Tender Fine-Very Fine.** The sharpness in the overprint is a touch weak.
From The Collection of Greg Southward **(1,700-up)**

13077 **Fr. 123 $10 1923 Legal Tender PMG Choice Fine 15.** A perfectly original and problem free $10 Legal Tender with a bright overprint and solid margins. **(1,700-up)**

13078 **Fr. 123 $10 1923 Legal Tender Very Good.** This note has a faded third printing. Some small rust spots are noticed on the face. **(350-up)**

13079 **Fr. 126b $20 1863 Legal Tender Fine.** The note has extremely good color for the grade and has remained free of the typical edge splits and other problems that generally plague this thin-paper early issue. There is a minor stain at the left of the back and a small penciled number at the top right of the back, but neither of those trivial defects detracts materially from this pleasing early Twenty.
From The Collection of Greg Southward **(2,500-up)**

13080 **Fr. 126b $20 1863 Legal Tender PMG Good 6 Net.** A bit of margin roughness is seen along the top in the form of missing pieces on this example from New Series 26. **(1,000-up)**

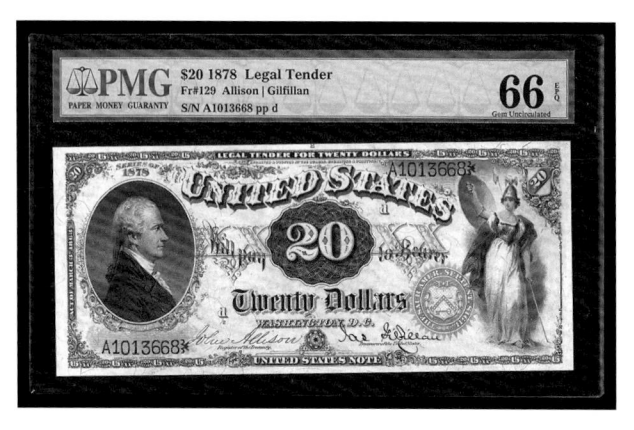

13081 **Fr. 129 $20 1878 Legal Tender PMG Gem Uncirculated 66 EPQ.** This early $20 Legal is hugely margined on the face with excellent color and terrific eye appeal. This type is not terribly rare at this grade level, but the note is so popular that there are never enough available to satisfy collector demand. **(5,500-up)**

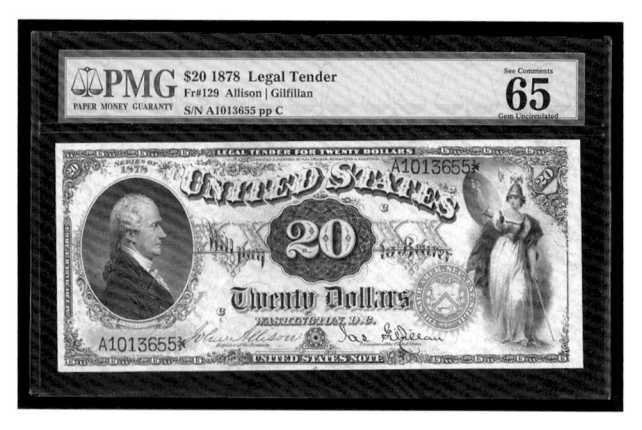

13082 **Fr. 129 $20 1878 Legal Tender PMG Gem Uncirculated 65 EPQ.** A very handsome example, with great color, broad margins and the sought-after EPQ status. This particular example is printed on the same watermarked paper that was used for Fourth Issue Fractional Currency. While certainties are hard to come by in this new world of third-party grading, this hugely margined piece certainly appears to be a possible candidate for a crossover upgrade. (Look at all the new words we've learned.) **(4,500-up)**

13083 **Fr. 133 $20 1880 Legal Tender Very Fine.** Until not long ago, scarcer numbers such as this commanded only very modest premiums above type levels. With the growing availability of information within the collecting fraternity, knowledge of rarity levels has become far more widespread and values for these tougher numbers are experiencing upward pressure. This is an especially scarce signature combination, with a total census fewer than 20. This is a very respectable iteration of a truly scarce number. Plan on spending at least...
From The Collection of Greg Southward **(1,750-up)**

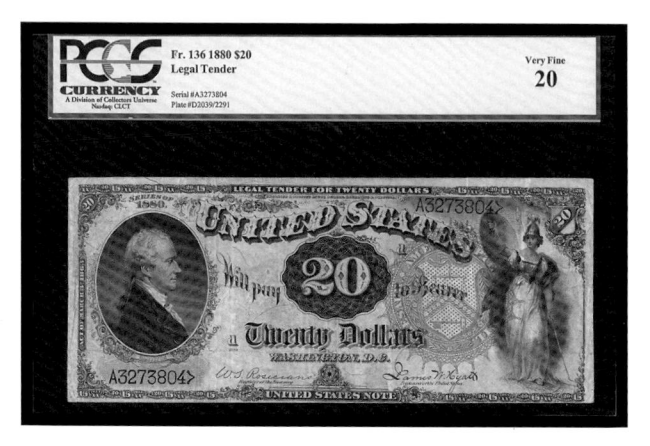

13084 **Fr. 136 $20 1880 Legal Tender PCGS Very Fine 20.** This is our description of this note before it was third-party graded, "This attractive note retains considerable original crispness and the colors are particularly bold and bright." **(1,000-up)**

13085 **Fr. 140 $20 1880 Legal Tender Fine-Very Fine.** It has been over a year since we last had this Friedberg number. This is an evenly circulated example that has one tiny edge tear.
From The Collection of Greg Southward **(1,000-up)**

Superb Bruce-Roberts 1880 Twenty

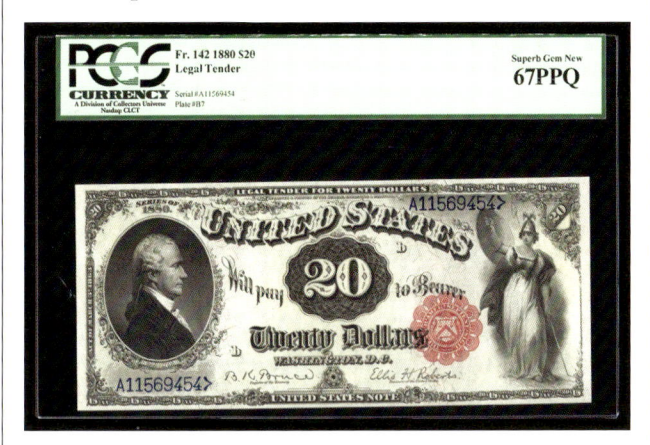

13086 **Fr. 142 $20 1880 Legal Tender PCGS Superb Gem New 67PPQ.** A flawless example of this rather scarce number. About 75 pieces are known, quite a few of which are uncirculated from two short runs, but of the ones we've seen, few if any have the perfect centering, Superb original paper surfaces, deep embossing and the flashy color of this impeccable piece. It's quite simply as nice a representation of the type as any note we have ever seen. Amazing quality. **(5,500-up)**

13087 **Fr. 142 $20 1880 Legal Tender CGA Very Fine 30.** The note has a bit of a washed appearance.
From The Collection of Greg Southward **(350-up)**

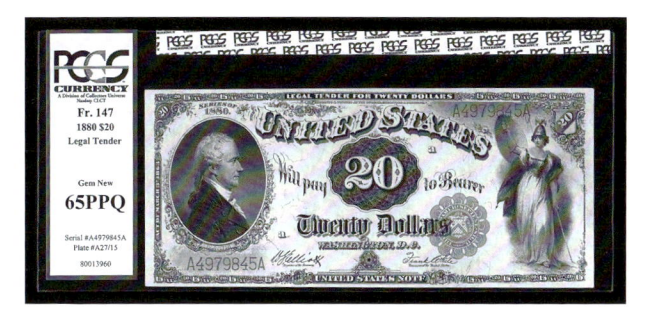

13088 **Fr. 147 $20 1880 Legal Tender PCGS Gem New 65PPQ.** This is a nicely centered $20 that has been lovingly cared for through the years. It is easy to see why this note earned its high grade. The note is from a run of CU notes in the census and the last time it was heard from was when our consignor ordered it from a 1977 fixed price list. **(2,800-up)**

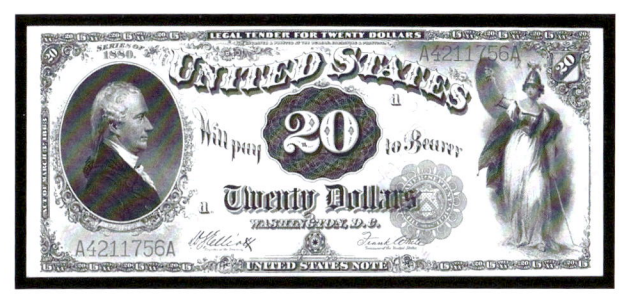

13089 **Fr. 147 $20 1880 Legal Tender Choice About New.** The very lightest of center bends can barely be discerned on this Choice New appearing 1880 Twenty. Don't expect to be able to pick this one up at an AU price—with its only problem being a fold that is almost invisible, it's sure to realize Choice New money. **(2,250-up)**

13090 **Fr. 147 $20 1880 Legal Tender CGA Very Fine 20.** This moderately circulated piece retains a bright red seal and serial numbers and is problem-free. **(500-up)**

13091 **Fr. 147 $20 1880 Legal Tender Fine-Very Fine.** This $20 Legal has original surfaces and sound edges that go hand in hand with the satisfying red overprint. **(1,000-up)**

13092 **Fr. 147 $20 1880 Legal Tender Fine-Very Fine.** Original paper surfaces reveal healthy edges and nice color on this $20 Legal. **(500-up)**

13093 **Fr. 147 $20 1880 Legal Tender PMG Choice Fine 15.** A nice note for the grade with bold color and no noticeable flaws. **(400-up)**

Brightly Colored Rainbow Fifty

13094 Fr. 151 $50 1869 Legal Tender PMG Choice Fine 15. Fr. 151 is a one number type that has always been a challenge to locate in any grade. We offered this note as part of our 1997 FUN sale, grading the note Fine-Very Fine, and describing as follows, "This lovely example is utterly unmolested and completely defect free. It's very well margined and bright for the grade, with full, flashy ink color." Almost ten years later, PMG has concurred noting "Great Color & Margins" listed on the back of the holder. This note sold back in 1997 for $11,500, then Lyn Knight sold it for $24,200 in 2000. In today's market, by what factor will this note pass the previous auction's price? **(32,500-up)**

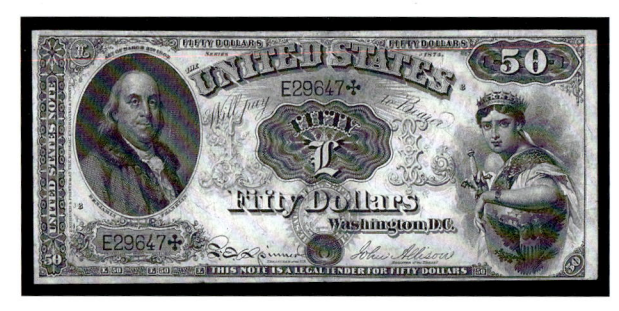

13095 Fr. 152 $50 1874 Legal Tender Fine. The note has the appearance of a solid VF, but there are a number of well done restorations, and a few areas in the center that remain rather thin. About three dozen examples of this One Number Type are known in all grades combined. This piece faces up quite nicely and will likely sell at an affordable level.
From The Collection of Greg Southward **(5,000-up)**

13096 Fr. 159 $50 1880 Legal Tender Very Good. About a dozen and a half examples are known of this number, with two of them grading AU and no others better than Fine. The margins on this piece are tight all the way around, but this note, although very heavily circulated, has no other important problems. There is a sprinkling of very tiny pinholes as one would expect for the grade.
From The Collection of Greg Southward **(2,250-up)**

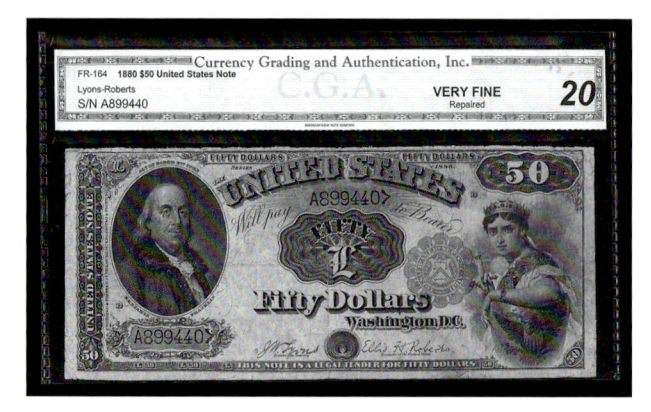

13097 Fr. 164 $50 1880 Legal Tender CGA Very Fine 20 Repaired. Three corner tips have been replaced outside the design area, and there are several repaired splits. Nonetheless, this 1880 Fifty faces up rather well, and should likely prove to be a relatively inexpensive way to represent this challenging Type.
From The Collection of Greg Southward **(2,500-up)**

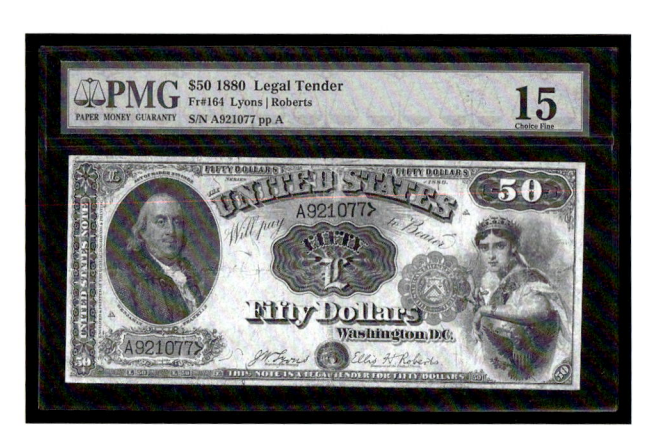

13098 Fr. 164 $50 1880 Legal Tender PMG Choice Fine 15. The majority of the surviving examples from this issue are heavily circulated. This piece shows moderate wear, but the design details are still fairly bold. **(4,000-up)**

REFUNDING CERTIFICATE

PMG Extremely Fine 40 EPQ Fr. 214

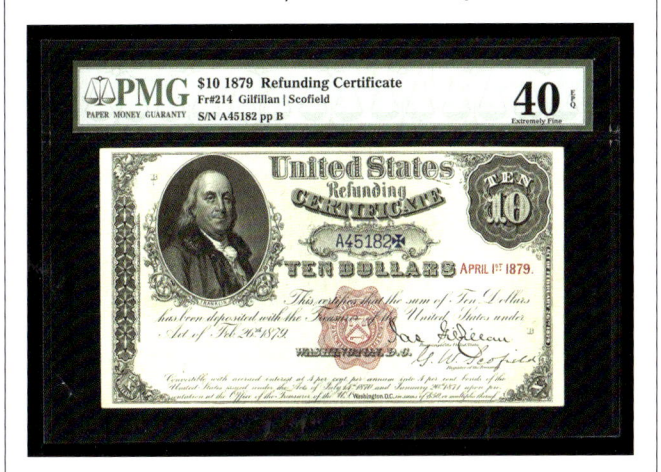

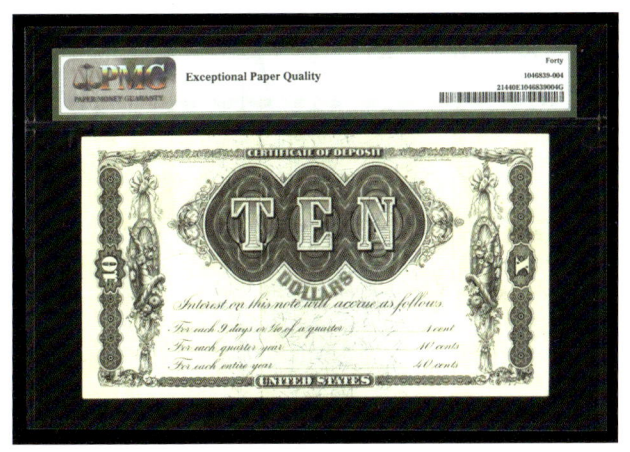

13099 Fr. 214 $10 1879 Refunding Certificate PMG Extremely Fine 40 EPQ. This is a nicely margined example that looks like two hard folds earned this note its third-party grade. This interesting note was issued in an attempt to give the average citizen an opportunity to own government securities. Refunding Certificates were issued with interest accruing at four percent with no definite redemption date stated, providing an inducement to hold the notes and not cash them in. In 1907, the interest was stopped by Congress and the value set at $21.30, causing them to be redeemed quickly. Ironically, the notes were never popular with the citizenry, but were popular with speculators and national banks. **(6,500-up)**

SILVER CERTIFICATES

CGA Gem Uncirculated 67
Fr. 215 $1 Martha

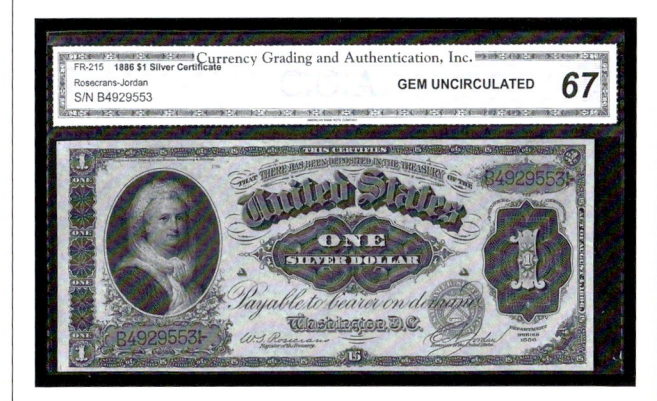

13100 Fr. 215 $1 1886 Silver Certificate CGA Gem Uncirculated 67. The surfaces appear as original as the day this piece was printed. Deep, flashy colors provide a pleasing visual sensation. **(4,000-up)**

13101 Fr. 215 $1 1886 Silver Certificate Very Fine-Extremely Fine. This seven-digit serial number Martha is way closer to the high end of the split grade as it is on the cusp of XF. *From The Collection of Greg Southward* **(500-up)**

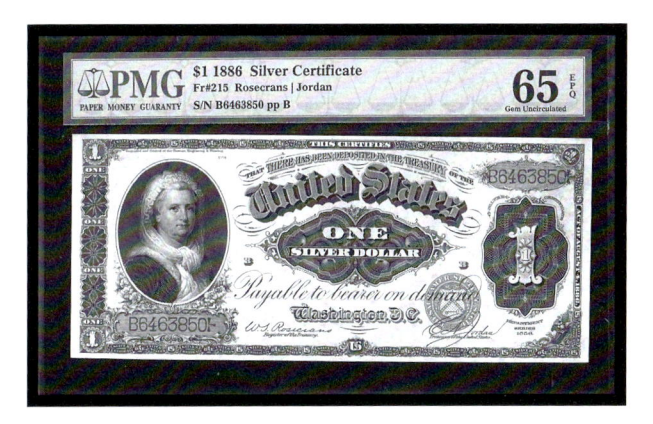

13102 Fr. 215 $1 1886 Silver Certificate PMG Gem Uncirculated 65EPQ. The first of a lovely consecutive pair of this earliest Martha Silver Certificate number. *From The Lincoln Collection* **(4,000-up)**

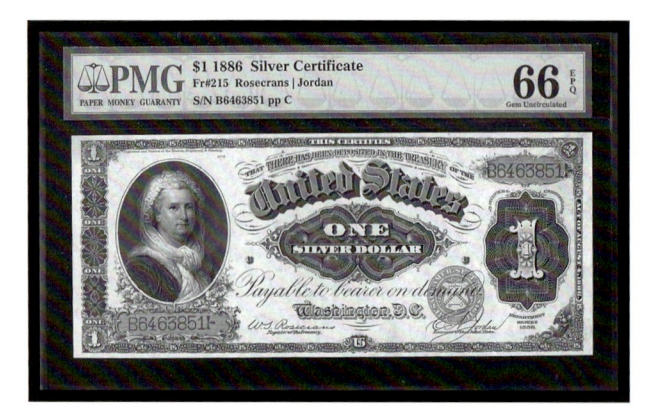

13103 Fr. 215 $1 1886 Silver Certificate PMG Gem Uncirculated 66 EPQ. Perfect colors highlight this second note from the consecutive pair. This one has garnered an extra point from PMG and consequently is worth a considerable premium.
From The Lincoln Collection **(6,500-up)**

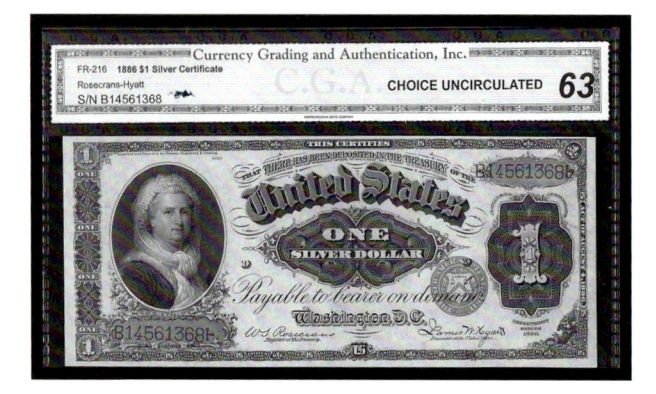

13104 Fr. 216 $1 1886 Silver Certificate CGA Choice Uncirculated 63. A good-looking Martha, likely downgraded to Choice due to its tight top upper right margin. The colors are very nice. **(1,200-up)**

13105 Fr. 219 $1 1886 Silver Certificate Very Fine. Numerous pinholes are visible with a touch of aging around the edges of this still bright Martha. **(500-up)**

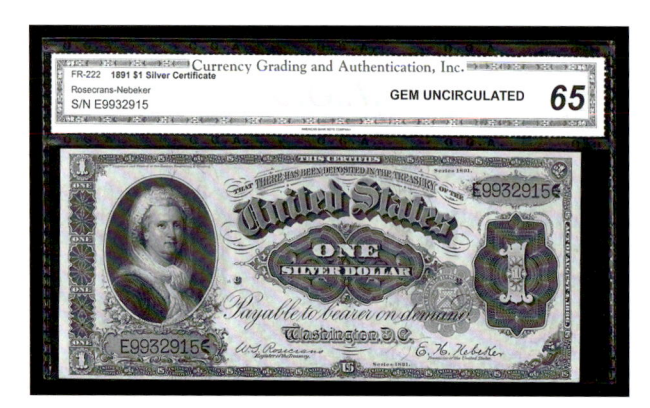

13106 Fr. 222 $1 1891 Silver Certificate CGA Gem Uncirculated 65. Fr. 222 is outnumbered by its type mate, Fr. 223, by more than three to one. This discrepancy grows even larger when only uncirculated notes are considered. Here is a gorgeous example that exhibits embossing, hefty margins, and excellent color. **(2,000-up)**

13107 Fr. 222 $1 1891 Silver Certificate CGA Gem Uncirculated 65. Fr. 222's are outnumbered over three to one by their type mate, Fr. 223. The balance tilts considerably further when uncirculated notes are considered, with 223 being rather common, and 222 decidedly rare. This example has broad margins, and original embossing that can be easily seen through the CGA holder. **(3,500-up)**

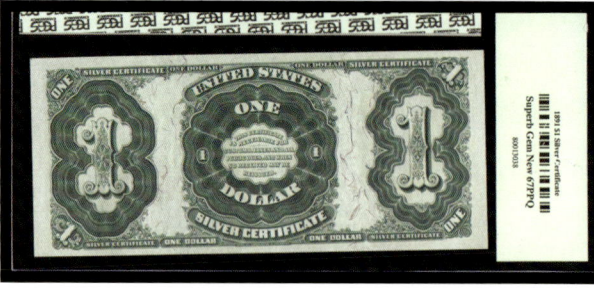

13108 Fr. 223 $1 1891 Silver Certificate PCGS Superb Gem New 67PPQ. A gorgeous Martha, with broad, even margins, bold original embossing, perfect colors and crackling fresh surfaces. This is the quality that has been setting new price records every time a piece reaches the market. **(4,250-up)**

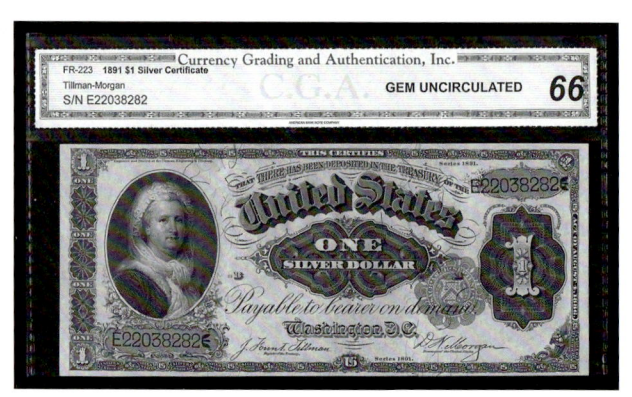

13109 Fr. 223 $1 1891 Silver Certificate CGA Gem Uncirculated 66. This second-back Martha is bright, well margined and has original embossing that is easily seen through the CGA holder. **(2,500-up)**

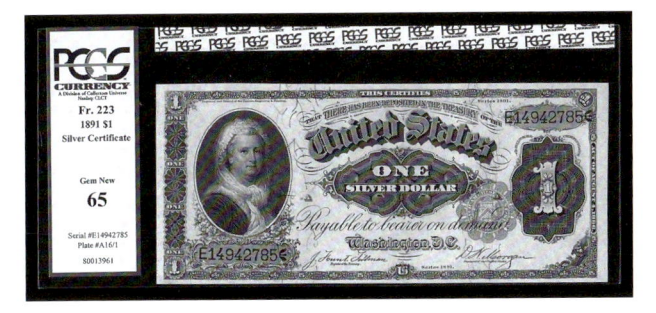

13110 **Fr. 223 $1 1891 Silver Certificate PCGS Gem New 65.** This is a fully margined example with nice colors. Ornate Back designs gave way to Open Backs because silk fibers in two rows for the notes were added to the paper specifications. (2,500-up)

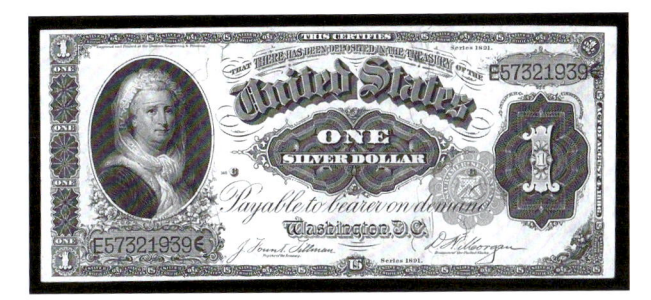

13111 **Fr. 223 $1 1891 Silver Certificate Choice New.** Original embossing remains on this 1891 Martha. The margins are more than adequate. The ink colors are strong, but the paper color is lightly muted. (1,000-up)

13112 **Fr. 223 $1 1891 Silver Certificate Very Fine-Extremely Fine.** This attractive Martha is draped in original paper surfaces and nice color.
From The Collection of Greg Southward (450-up)

13113 **Fr. 223 $1 1891 Silver Certificate Very Fine.** Even circulation is detected on this Martha that retains some crispness. (400-up)

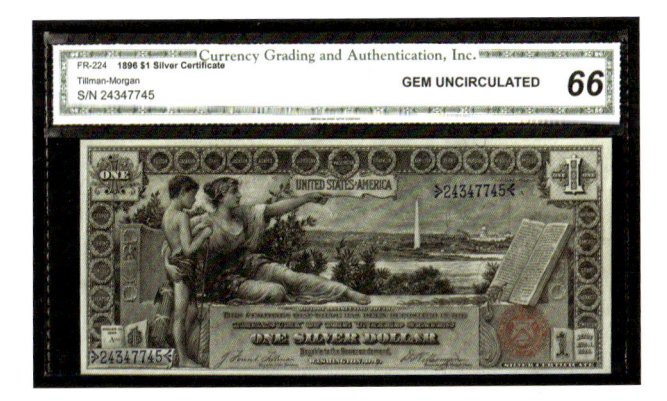

13114 **Fr. 224 $1 1896 Silver Certificate CGA Gem Uncirculated 66.** The $1 Educational remains an enduringly popular note. In this superlative state of preservation the attractive details are especially evident. A premium note well worth a premium price. (5,000-up)

Two Digit Educational Ace

13115 **Fr. 224 $1 1896 Silver Certificate PMG Gem Uncirculated 65 EPQ.** We were privileged to handle this note in our January 2006 Auction before it was sent to a third party grading service. Our description only confirms the third party assessment and read, "Two-digit Educational Aces are seldom seen on the market, and this serial number 98 Tillman-Morgan signed note is a truly nice one. It has broad, even margins, deep original embossing and bold color. Add to that strictly original paper surfaces and you have a very nice overall package..." (6,500-up)

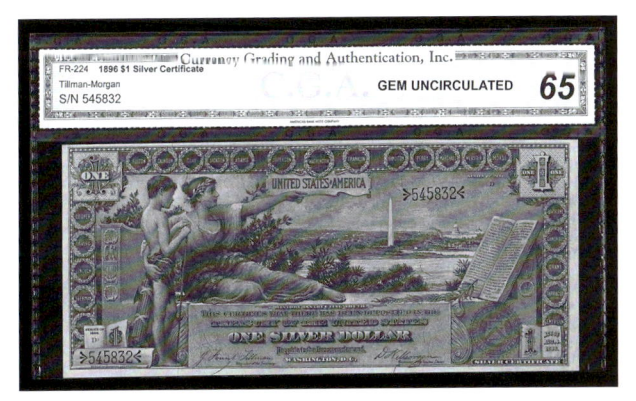

13116 **Fr. 224 $1 1896 Silver Certificate CGA Gem Uncirculated 65.** The embossing on this Educational is deeply impressed, a quality that indicates thorough originality. It is splendidly centered, and the colors are excellent for type. (4,250-up)

13117 Fr. 224 $1 1896 Silver Certificate CGA Gem Uncirculated 65. All the right paper waves are in all the right places. The margins are especially broad for this issue, adding the eye appeal. **(4,250-up)**

13118 Fr. 224 $1 1896 Silver Certificate CGA Gem Uncirculated 65. Nice centering and inks on this ever popular "History Instructing Youth" design. **(4,250-up)**

Four Consecutive $1 Educationals—PMG 64 EPQ, 65 EPQ, 66 EPQ, 65 EPQ

13119 Fr. 224 $1 1896 Silver Certificate PMG Choice Uncirculated 64 EPQ. The first of four consecutive Exceptional Paper Quality $1 Educationals. The four notes are from plate positions: D, A, B, and C—thus, they are not a cut sheet. All four have magnificent color, paper originality that can be clearly seen through the third party holder, and perfect, bright color. They vary slightly in centering and have been graded from 64 to 66 by PMG. They are being offered here as single lots in serial number order.
From The Lincoln Collection **(3,000-up)**

13120 Fr. 224 $1 1896 Silver Certificate PMG Gem Uncirculated 65 EPQ. The second note from the run.
From The Lincoln Collection **(4,250-up)**

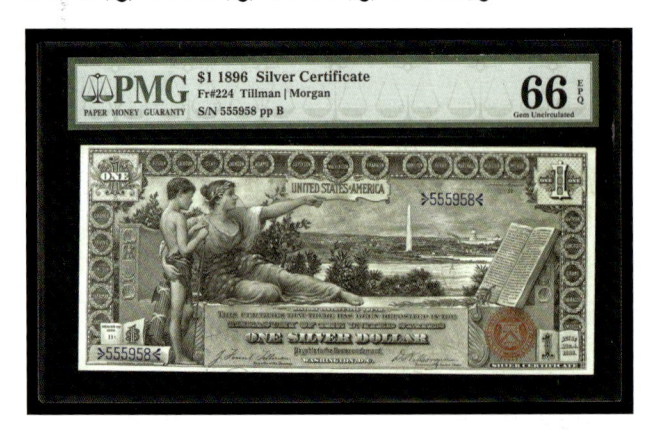

13121 Fr. 224 $1 1896 Silver Certificate PMG Gem Uncirculated 66 EPQ. The third note and the highest grade from this run of four.
From The Lincoln Collection **(5,500-up)**

13122 Fr. 224 $1 1896 Silver Certificate PMG Gem Uncirculated 65 EPQ. The final note from this lovely group.
From The Lincoln Collection **(4,250-up)**

13123 **Fr. 224 $1 1896 Silver Certificate Extremely Fine-About New.** Some light folds can be seen after much searching. Though a few small repairs are noticed, the color is still fabulous.
From The Collection of Greg Southward (750-up)

13124 **Fr. 224 $1 1896 Silver Certificate CGA Extremely Fine 45.** A nice lightly circulated example. (750-up)

13125 **Fr. 224 $1 1896 Silver Certificate Extremely Fine+.** Intersecting light center folds define the grade of this $1 Educational that exhibits great color. (850-up)

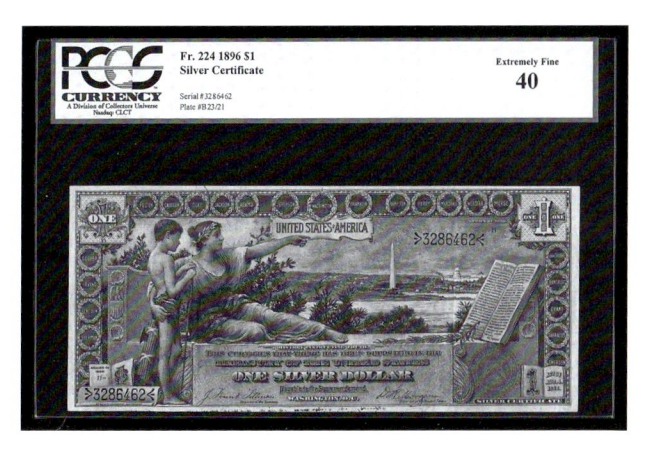

13126 **Fr. 224 $1 1896 Silver Certificate PCGS Extremely Fine 40.** The original embossing is clearly present on this lightly circulated Educational Ace. The PPQ designation was apparently lost due to a bit of stray ink in the bottom face margin. (800-up)

13127 **Fr. 224 $1 1896 Silver Certificate Choice Very Fine.** This pretty Educational Ace has strictly original paper surfaces, broad margins, and considerable claim to the XF grade. An ideal collector piece. (650-up)

13128 **Fr. 224 $1 1896 Silver Certificate Very Fine.** The inks are dark on this $1 Ed that has three wide margins. (550-up)

13129 **Fr. 224 $1 1896 Silver Certificate Very Fine.** An unmolested, problem-free, evenly circulated $1 Educational. (550-up)

13130 **Fr. 224 $1 1896 Silver Certificate Very Fine.** This $1 Ed was folded into eighths. The margins are ample while the edges are sound. It has also kept its original surfaces. (550-up)

Rare Uncut Fr. 226 Sheet

13131 **Fr. 226 $1 1899 Silver Certificates Uncut Sheet of Four PMG Choice Uncirculated 64 EPQ.** This is a lovely uncut sheet of Black Eagle notes, one of less than a half dozen remaining uncut sheets of this Friedberg number. Each note is a Gem by itself, with horizontal folds on the top and bottom that are well into the selvage, and there is a workman's fingerprint on the back at the very top edge of the sheet. The notes are fully original with bold embossing. This is an excellent opportunity for the astute collector to obtain an uncut sheet that is not often offered for sale. (15,000-up)

13132 **Fr. 226 $1 1899 Silver Certificate CGA Gem Uncirculated 67.** Hugely margined all around, with spectacular color and great eye appeal. This is the first number of the extraordinarily popular Black Eagle series, and the only number with the series date above the serial number. **(1,500-up)**

PMG Choice Uncirculated 63 EPQ Sheet

13133 **Fr. 226a $1 1899 Silver Certificates Uncut Sheet of Four PMG Choice Uncirculated 63 EPQ.** All uncut sheets of large size U.S. type notes are quite rare. This Black Eagle sheet is actually one of the more common with around a dozen examples known. The sheet is clean and bright, but there is a fold between each note, and a partial workman's fingerprint is at the bottom edge. With the current popularity of the Black Eagle type combined with the overall rarity of uncut sheets, we would not be surprised to see this sheet reach or exceed ... **(12,000-up)**

13134 **Fr. 226a $1 1899 Silver Certificate Uncut Sheet of Four PMG About Uncirculated 55 EPQ.** This is a perfectly original, problem-free uncut sheet with folds between the notes and one fold in the top margin selvage and another fold in the bottom margin selvage. The face plate number is 12776 and the back plate number is 13192. Workmen initials have been added near the top edge on both sides. This was a practice that was carried over from postage stamp production and was done only during the first decade of the Twentieth Century. One workman has also left behind a fingerprint along the back bottom edge. There are a dozen uncut sheets of this Friedberg number in the census including this sheet. This example has crossed the auction block only twice before in the last thirty years. (9,000-up)

13135 **Fr. 226a $1 1899 Silver Certificate CGA Gem Uncirculated 68.** A hugely margined Black Eagle Ace, with ideal color, good paper surfaces and Superb eye appeal. (1,800-up)

13136 **Fr. 226a $1 1899 Silver Certificate PCGS Superb Gem New 67PPQ.** A simply spectacular example of the earliest of the Black Eagle signature combinations. This is the second variety with the series date below the serial number. Rather common up through the 65 grade, but decidedly rare with these huge margins and strong paper originality. (1,750-up)

13137 **Fr. 226a $1 1899 Silver Certificate CGA Gem Uncirculated 67.** Superb centering, excellent colors, and strong eye appeal all combine on this early issued 1899 Ace. (1,500-up)

13138 **Fr. 226a $1 1899 Silver Certificate CGA Gem Uncirculated 67.** The heavy original embossing is easily seen through the third-party holder on this gorgeous example of the earliest Black Eagle signature combination. (1,500-up)

13139 **Fr. 226a $1 1899 Silver Certificate CGA Gem Uncirculated 67.** Here is yet another pleasing example of this date below variety which looks like it was printed yesterday. (1,500-up)

13140 **Fr. 226a $1 1899 Silver Certificate PMG Gem Uncirculated 66 EPQ.** Broadly margined, bright and handsome with all the visual appeal of a fully Superb piece. (800-up)

13141 **Fr. 226a $1 1899 Silver Certificate CGA Gem Uncirculated 66.** The embossing of the serial numbers is still noted on this well margined Gem. (800-up)

13142 **Fr. 226a $1 1899 Silver Certificate CGA Gem Uncirculated 66.** Nicely margined, with obviously deep, original embossing. (800-up)

13143 **Fr. 226a $1 1899 Silver Certificate CGA Gem Uncirculated 66.** Most pleasing and wholly original. (800-up)

13144 **Fr. 226a $1 1899 Silver Certificate CGA Gem Uncirculated 66.** The margins are broad and the colors quite nice on this Lyons-Roberts signed early Black Eagle. (800-up)

13145 **Fr. 226a $1 1899 Silver Certificate CGA Gem Uncirculated 66.** Perfectly even margins are noted on all four sides of the face, though the back centering is a few millimeters away from Superb. (800-up)

13146 **Fr. 226a $1 1899 Silver Certificate CGA Gem Uncirculated 66.** A beauty, with excellent centering among broad, even margins, lots of color and great eye appeal. This is the first Black Eagle signature combination but the second variety, as the series date appears under the serial number on this "a" type. (800-up)

13147 **Fr. 226a $1 1899 Silver Certificate PMG Gem Uncirculated 65.** Pleasing margins surround this proud Black Eagle that still exhibits some serial number embossing.
From The Collection of Greg Southward (800-up)

13148 **Fr. 226a $1 1899 Silver Certificate PCGS Very Choice New 64.** The margins are solid for the issue and the paper is particularly bright. (600-up)

13149 **Fr. 226a $1 1899 Silver Certificate PMG Choice Extremely Fine 45.** This Black Eagle is adorned with low serial number D40. It has three light folds and original paper surfaces. Don't start singing the *Folsom Prison Blues* if you miss out on this note formerly of the Jhon E. Cash Collection. (1,500-2,000)

13150 **Fr. 228 $1 1899 Silver Certificate PCGS Gem New 66PPQ.** Deep original embossing, broad margins, and strong eye appeal all combine on this handsome Black Eagle. The 66PPQ grade certainly looks accurate to us. (800-up)

13151 **Fr. 228 $1 1899 Silver Certificate CGA Gem Uncirculated 66.** Bold embossing is noted on this evenly margined Gem. (800-up)

13152 **Fr. 228 $1 1899 Silver Certificate PMG Gem Uncirculated 66 EPQ.** Prominent embossing and natural paper ripple are merits of this delightful Black Eagle. **(800-up)**

13153 **Fr. 228 $1 1899 Silver Certificate CGA Gem Uncirculated 65.** Hugely margined with clearly original embossing that can be seen through the third party holder. The "65" grade appears to be conservative to us.
From The Collection of Greg Southward **(750-up)**

13154 **Fr. 228 $1 1899 Silver Certificate PMG Gem Uncirculated 65.** Attempting to second guess third party graded notes after they are sealed is problematic at best. We sure cannot figure out why this note lacks the EPQ designation. The embossing is deep and clearly original, and we are unable to spot even a hint of a defect.
From The Collection of Greg Southward **(750-up)**

13155 **Fr. 228 $1 1899 Silver Certificate PMG Choice Uncirculated 64.** The colors remain vivid on this well embossed example..
From The Collection of Greg Southward **(600-up)**

13156 **Fr. 229 $1 1899 Silver Certificate PCGS Gem New 66PPQ.** Wide margins surround this note which has excellent embossing clearly visible within the holder. **(1,000-up)**

13157 **Fr. 229 $1 1899 Silver Certificate CGA Gem Uncirculated 66.** Bold, original embossing is noticed on this piece with vivid inks. **(1,000-up)**

13158 **Fr. 229 $1 1899 Silver Certificate PCGS Choice New 63PPQ.** A partial up ladder serial number is noticed on this bright example which last appeared for sale 3 years ago. With the demand ever increasing for these fancy serial number notes expect a realization in the area of... **(2,000-up)**

13159 **Fr. 229 $1 1899 Silver Certificate Choice New.** Natural paper wave remains on this handsome Black Eagle from a tougher Friedberg number. **(650-up)**

13160 **Fr. 230 $1 1899 Silver Certificate CGA Gem Uncirculated 67.** The perfectly original paper waves are unhindered by the hint of handling at right. **(1,250-up)**

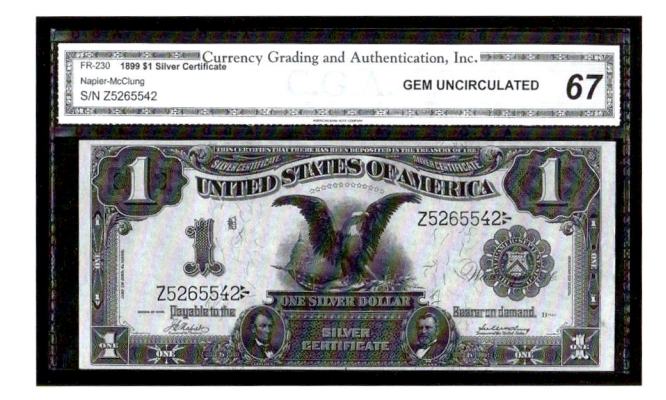

13161 Fr. 230 $1 1899 Silver Certificate CGA Gem Uncirculated 67. Bright, original paper complements the deep blue overprint. (1,250-up)

13162 Fr. 230 $1 1899 Silver Certificate PCGS Gem New 66PPQ. The bold original embossing is easily seen through the third party holder on this two-digit Eagle Ace. (1,750-up)

13163 Fr. 230 $1 1899 Silver Certificate Courtesy Autograph PCGS Gem New 66PPQ. Courtesy autographed vertically to the left of the eagle by an assistant treasurer in a bold hand that appears to be "J. W. Whelps"—in any case, he identifies himself as "Asst Treas US" on one line with the dates "1890-1893" on the next line. (1,000-up)

13164 Fr. 230 $1 1899 Silver Certificate PMG Gem Uncirculated 66. This auction certainly has not realized a shortage of nice Black Eagles and this example is sure to please.
From The Collection of Greg Southward (1,000-up)

13165 Fr. 230 $1 1899 Silver Certificate PCGS Gem New 65PPQ. This two-digit, H16H serial number note, has a counting crinkle on the left-hand side. (1,200-up)

13166 Fr. 230 $1 1899 Silver Certificate PMG Gem Uncirculated 65. This note bears the neat three-digit serial number A100A, and the positive PMG comment "Nice Colors." Although the EPQ comment is missing, the note clearly has deep original embossing. (2,000-up)

13167 Fr. 230 $1 1899 Silver Certificate CGA Gem Uncirculated 65. Deeply printed details are noted on this attractive issue. (500-up)

13168 Fr. 230 $1 1899 Silver Certificate PCGS Very Choice New 64PPQ. The two-digit serial number A32A highlights this nicely margined, strictly original, Eagle Ace. (1,500-up)

13169 Fr. 230 $1 1899 Silver Certificate Choice New. No folds are found on this Black Eagle that has toned a shade. (450-up)

13170 Fr. 231 $1 1899 Silver Certificate Very Fine. This is a much scarcer Black Eagle Friedberg number that carries the Napier-Thompson Treasury signatures. This example possesses original paper surfaces, wholesome edges, and nice color. (300-up)

13171 Fr. 231 $1 1899 Silver Certificate Fine. This scarcer Napier-Thompson note is rarely found in nice circulated grade. Lots of collectors will want this one.
From The Collection of Greg Southward (300-up)

13172 Fr. 232 $1 1899 Silver Certificate CGA Gem Uncirculated 67. One of the more available Black Eagle numbers, but a truly handsome example, with perfect color, margins and embossing. (1,250-up)

13173 Fr. 232 $1 1899 Silver Certificate PCGS Gem New 66PPQ. This is a fresh entrant into the marketplace with deep embossing and dark inks spread deeply onto bright surfaces. (1,000-up)

13174 Fr. 232 $1 1899 Silver Certificate CGA Gem Uncirculated 66. A handsome 1899 Ace and a slightly less commonly seen number in top grade. (900-up)

13175 Fr. 232 $1 1899 Silver Certificate CGA Gem Uncirculated 66. Here is another pleasing Black Eagle which is quite fresh. (900-up)

13176 Fr. 232 $1 1899 Silver Certificate CGA Gem Uncirculated 66. Excellent margins envelope this lovely Black Eagle. (1,000-up)

13177 Fr. 232 $1 1899 Silver Certificate PCGS Very Choice New 64PPQ. A slightly tight top margin is likely what held this note at the 64 level, as it appears Superb in every other sense. (600-up)

13178   Fr. 232 $1 1899 Silver Certificate PMG Choice Uncirculated 64 EPQ. A near Gem originally embossed example that would make that grade but for just a slightly tight bottom margin both face and back. (600-up)

13179   Fr. 232 $1 1899 Silver Certificate PMG Choice About Unc 58. In the holder the eye appeal of this Black Eagle matches that of the Gems offered here. (300-up)

13180   Fr. 233 $1 1899 Silver Certificate PCGS Superb Gem New 68PPQ. Along with its ultra-high third-party-grade and its Premium Paper Quality designation, this gorgeous Black Eagle also boasts the nice two-digit serial number V25V. There are an awful lot of high-grade Black Eagles around, but 99% of them will grade from 63 to 67. 68PPQ two-digit Eagles will never be anything but rare. (2,500-up)

13181   Fr. 233 $1 1899 Silver Certificate CGA Gem Uncirculated 68. Not much can be improved upon as the paper is bright and the surfaces well embossed. Super wide and even margins envelope this beauty. (1,500-up)

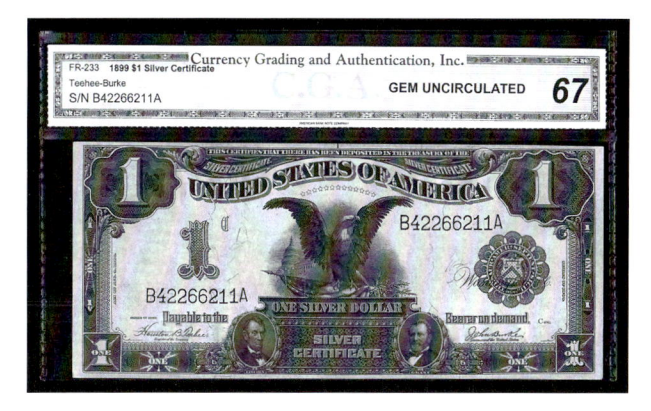

13182   Fr. 233 $1 1899 Silver Certificate CGA Gem Uncirculated 67. Perfectly original paper waves are noted through the third party holder. Additionally the embossing is worthy of mention. (1,250-up)

13183   Fr. 233 $1 1899 Silver Certificate Superb Gem New. A handsome, original Black Eagle, with broad, even margins, excellent embossing, bright colors and the special serial number R77700000R.
From The Jacob and Heather Dedman Collection (1,000-up)

13184   Fr. 233 $1 1899 Silver Certificate PCGS Gem New 66PPQ. Another lovely note, this one carrying serial number B57A. (1,750-up)

13185 **Fr. 233 $1 1899 Silver Certificate PCGS Gem New 66PPQ.** The original embossing is plainly evident through the PCGS holder. The combination of the low serial number T29T, along with the 66 grade and the Premium Paper Quality designation should push this note through the $2,000 mark. **(1,750-up)**

13186 **Fr. 233 $1 1899 Silver Certificate PCGS Gem New 66PPQ.** This Black Eagle is blessed with serial number X50X. It has bold embossing and natural paper wave. **(1,200-up)**

13187 **Fr. 233 $1 1899 Silver Certificate CGA Gem Uncirculated 66.** Embossing is visible through the third-party holder. **(800-up)**

13188 **Fr. 233 $1 1899 Silver Certificate CGA Gem Uncirculated 66.** The perfectly printed details are framed by four sufficient margins. **(800-up)**

13189 **Fr. 233 $1 1899 Silver Certificate CGA Gem Uncirculated 66.** A handsome Black Eagle in a high grade third party holder. **(800-up)**

13190 **Fr. 233 $1 1899 Silver Certificate CGA Gem Uncirculated 66.** The left end of the top margin seems a bit close for the 66 grade, but this note seems extremely nice in every other sense. **(800-up)**

13191 **Fr. 233 $1 1899 Silver Certificate CGA Gem Uncirculated 66.** The face details are about as deeply printed as one will find, the overprint is as deep in color, both of which contrast nicely against the original, wavy paper. **(800-up)**

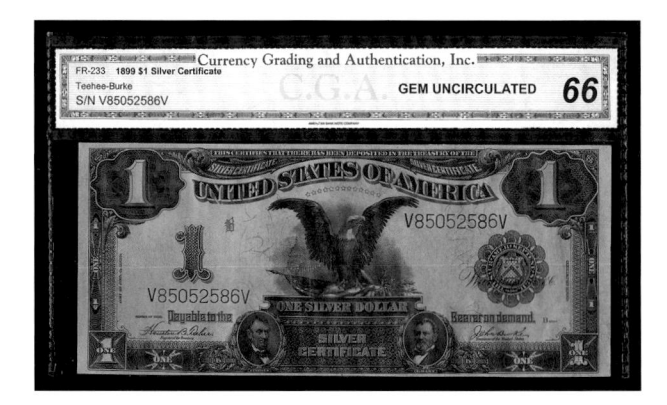

13192 **Fr. 233 $1 1899 Silver Certificate CGA Gem Uncirculated 66.** All the right paper waves are in all the right places on this boldly embossed issue. **(800-up)**

13193 **Fr. 233 $1 1899 Silver Certificate CGA Gem Uncirculated 66.** Here is another typical Black Eagle exhibiting bright color, well inked surfaces, and prominent embossing. (800-up)

13194 **Fr. 233 $1 1899 Silver Certificate CGA Gem Uncirculated 66.** This nice Black Eagle note has great centering, excellent margins for the issue, and decent paper originality. (800-up)

13195 **Fr. 233 $1 1899 Silver Certificate CGA Gem Uncirculated 66.** A wonderful dark blue overprint is found on this Black Eagle that has been third-party graded. (1,000-up)

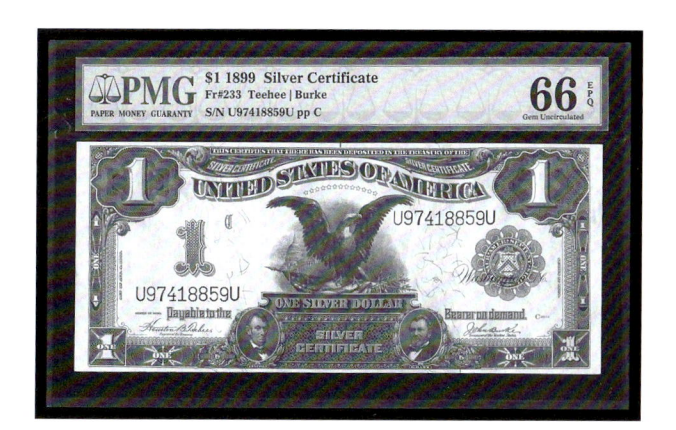

13196 **Fr. 233 $1 1899 Silver Certificate PMG Gem Uncirculated 66 EPQ.** This is one of four near-consecutive notes that recently surfaced in New York. This piece is as pleasing as the others, with original paper waves and bold embossing. (800-up)

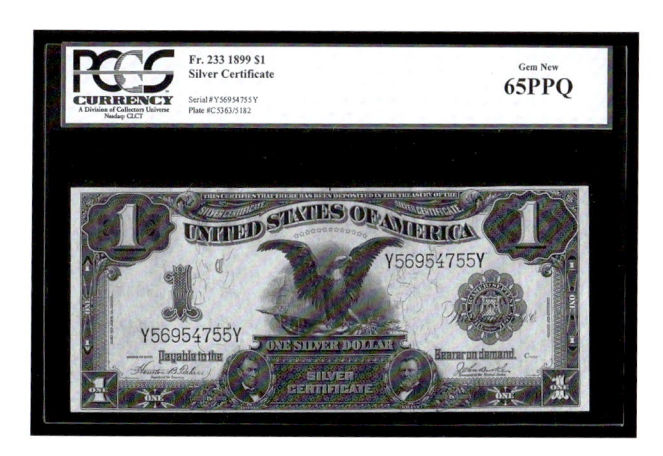

13197 **Fr. 233 $1 1899 Silver Certificate PCGS Gem New 65PPQ.** The margins are ample all around this deeply printed, colorful Black Eagle. (700-up)

13198 **Fr. 233 $1 1899 Silver Certificate PCGS Gem New 65PPQ.** Consecutive to the previous lot this piece exhibits pleasing, natural surfaces. (700-up)

13199 **Fr. 233 $1 1899 Silver Certificate PMG Gem Uncirculated 65 EPQ.** PMG comments "Exceptional Paper Quality, Great Embossing & Color" on this Tehee-Burke signed Black Eagle. (700-up)

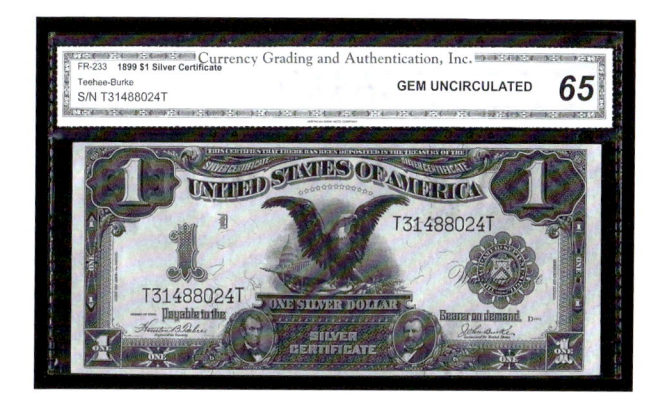

13200 **Fr. 233 $1 1899 Silver Certificate CGA Gem Uncirculated 65.** A tiny corner tip fold is noted well outside of the design on this otherwise boldly original, Superb looking Black Eagle. (700-up)

13201 **Fr. 233 $1 1899 Silver Certificate PMG Gem Uncirculated 65 EPQ.** Perfectly original paper waves are boldly evident through the holder. This piece is as nice as its three partners that are also in this auction. (700-up)

13202 **Fr. 233 $1 1899 Silver Certificate PMG Gem Uncirculated 65 EPQ.** Great front to back centering and bold embossing are noted on this Black Eagle. It is one of a quartet of original, near-consecutive pieces in this auction. (700-up)

13203 **Fr. 233 $1 1899 Silver Certificate PMG Gem Uncirculated 65 EPQ.** This is the first of a quartet of near-consecutive pieces offered here. This piece is boldly original and features adequate margins. (700-up)

13204 **Fr. 233 $1 1899 Silver Certificate Very Choice New.** Natural paper wave and embossing are highlights of this beautiful Black Eagle. (500-up)

13205 **Fr. 233 $1 1899 Silver Certificate Very Choice New.** Complementing the bold blue color is the fresh paper with all the right waves in all the right places. (500-up)

13206 **Fr. 233 $1 1899 Silver Certificate Star PMG Choice Uncirculated 63.** Plenty of embossing is noticed on the serial numbers of this replacement note. Decent margins are noticed for the grade. (1,250-up)

13207 **Fr. 233 $1 1899 Silver Certificate Choice New.** This Black Eagle has original surfaces that exhibit embossing and natural paper paper ripple. (600-up)

13208 **Fr. 233 $1 1899 Silver Certificate Choice New.** Bright and attractive, but a trifle close at the bottom. (400-up)

13209 **Fr. 234 $1 1899 Silver Certificate PCGS Gem New 66PPQ.** This serial number 80 Elliot-Burke signed Black Eagle has excellent margins, good paper originality, and strong eye appeal. (1,750-up)

13210 **Fr. 234 $1 1899 Silver Certificate PMG Choice Uncirculated 64.** This lovely Black Eagle has been designated as a turned digit error. It still has a ways to go before it gets there. Nonetheless, a pleasing well margined, bright representative. (700-up)

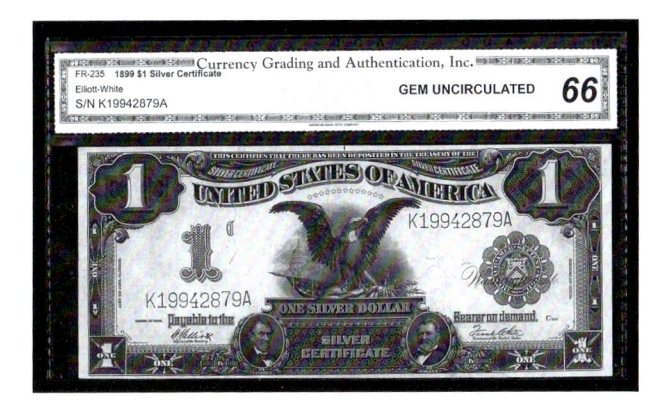

13211 **Fr. 235 $1 1899 Silver Certificate CGA Gem Uncirculated 66.** A very nicely margined example of this extremely popular Black Eagle type. (1,000-up)

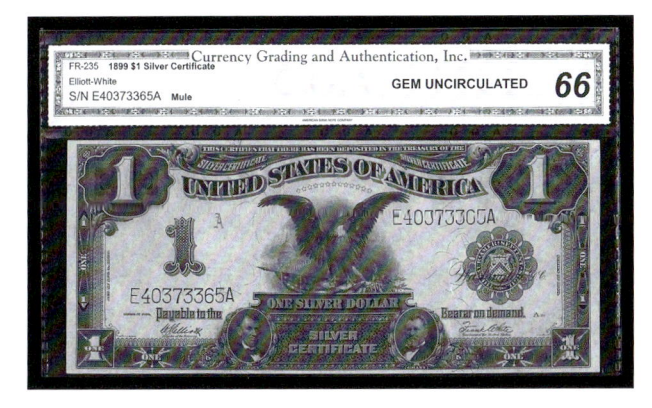

13212 **Fr. 235 $1 1899 Mule Silver Certificate CGA Gem Uncirculated 66.** Nice margins surround this piece with the Mule BP 6090. (1,000-up)

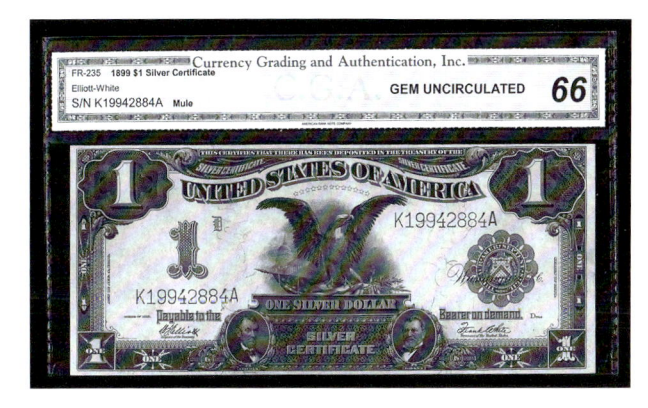

13213 **Fr. 235 $1 1899 Silver Certificate CGA Gem Uncirculated 66.** Some embossing still protrudes on this deeply inked note incorrectly attributed as a Mule. (1,000-up)

13214 **Fr. 235 $1 1899 Silver Certificate CGA Gem Uncirculated 66.** Embossing is noticed on this example. *From The Collection of Greg Southward* (1,000-up)

13215 **Fr. 235 $1 1899 Silver Certificate CGA Gem Uncirculated 66.** Plenty of embossing is noticed on this example that is well margined. (1,000-up)

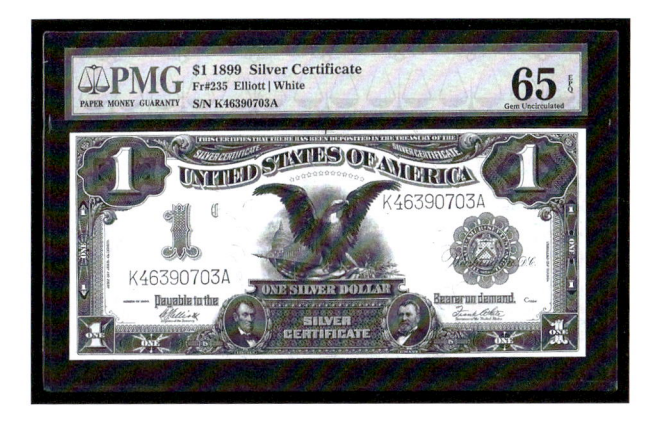

13216 **Fr. 235 $1 1899 Silver Certificate PMG Gem Uncirculated 65 EPQ.** Perfectly even margins are noted as well as ideal front to back centering. (800-up)

13217 **Fr. 235 $1 1899 Silver Certificate Very Choice New.** One of a consecutive trio, all of which are lovely uncirculated examples. (550-up)

13218 **Fr. 235 $1 1899 Silver Certificate Very Choice New.** A fresh and appealing piece which is very close to the full Gem grade. (550-up)

13219 **Fr. 235 $1 1899 Silver Certificate Very Choice New.** Another of the consecutive trio offered here, with bright colors and very close to Gem eye appeal. **(550-up)**

13220 **Fr. 236 $1 1899 Silver Certificate CGA Gem Uncirculated 67.** The margins and appearance of this last of the Black Eagles certainly seem to support the high assigned grade. **(1,000-up)**

13221 **Fr. 236 $1 1899 Silver Certificate CGA Gem Uncirculated 66.** Beautifully margined with bright color and strong eye appeal. This is the final signature combination of the Black Eagles. A design Type that was our basic dollar bill for nearly 30 years. **(800-up)**

13222 **Fr. 236 $1 1899 Silver Certificate CGA Gem Uncirculated 66.** A broadly margined Ace with bright color and broad margins all around. Notes in certified grades higher than 65 continue to be under intense buying pressure.
From The Collection of Greg Southward **(800-up)**

13223 **Fr. 236 $1 1899 Silver Certificate PMG Gem Uncirculated 66.** Paper waves are seen in all the right places and the color is excellent. **(900-up)**

13224 **Fr. 236 $1 1899 Silver Certificate PCGS Gem New 65PPQ.** This note exhibits embossing and it has a serial number that begins with six "9s." **(1,000-up)**

13225 **Fr. 236 $1 1899 Silver Certificate CGA Gem Uncirculated 65.** Solid margins are noted on this piece, though a touch more at top and this note might have been propelled to a Superb grade. **(1,000-up)**

13226 **Fr. 236 $1 1899 Silver Certificate PCGS Very Choice New 64PPQ.** A blazingly original piece with ideal paper quality. **(700-up)**

13227 **Fr. 236 $1 1899 Silver Certificate PCGS Very Choice New 64PPQ.** This pack fresh Black Eagle boasts solid margins and pleasing paper quality. **(700-up)**

13228 **Fr. 236 $1 1899 Silver Certificate PCGS Very Choice New 64PPQ.** Serial number 5555 graces this nicely preserved Black Eagle. **(1,500-up)**

13229 **Fr. 236 $1 1899 Silver Certificate Very Choice New.** The bottom margin is a bit tight on this three-digit solid Black Eagle. The original embossing is pronounced, the note is bright, and the serial number N666A is darkly attractive. **(1,500-up)**

13230 **Fr. 236 $1 1899 Silver Certificate Mule PCGS Choice New 63PPQ.** Solid serial number 55555 is found on this $1 Silver Mule that is not mentioned on the holder. **(2,000-up)**

13231 **Fr. 236 $1 1899 Silver Certificate Choice New.** This glorious example carries the neat two digit serial number of X35A. A little tightness along the upper margin keeps this colorful piece from the gem ranks. Still a desirable low serial number Black Eagle. **(1,500-up)**

13232 Fr. 236 $1 1899 Silver Certificate Choice New. This is yet another glorious two digit serial number X55A Black Eagle that has remained off the market for 15 years. Nicely embossed with a touch too much tightness at upper left. (1,500-up)

13233 Fr. 236 $1 1899 Silver Certificate PCGS New 62PPQ. Serial number 22222 is found on this Black eagle from the R-A block. This Black Eagle has a thin bottom margin (1,700-up)

13234 Fr. 236 $1 1899 Silver Certificate PCGS New 62PPQ. Serial number 6666666 graces this original note from the X-A block. (2,000-up)

13235 Fr. 236 $1 1899 Silver Certificate PMG Uncirculated 62. Embossing and natural paper wave are seen through the third-party holder. (500-up)

13236 Fr. 236 $1 1899 Silver Certificate PMG Uncirculated 62. The third-party holder does not conceal the embossing. (400-up)

13237 Fr. 237 $1 1923 Silver Certificate PMG Gem Uncirculated 66 EPQ. This $1 is well margined with plenty of embossing. (200-up)

13238 Fr. 237 $1 1923 Silver Certificate CGA Gem Uncirculated 66. A nice high-end example of the most common Large Size type. (200-up)

13239 Fr. 237 $1 1923 Silver Certificate CGA Gem Uncirculated 66. A strictly original example of the single most common Large Size number. (200-up)

13240 Fr. 238 $1 1923 Silver Certificates Cut Sheet of Four. This well matched set is graded PMG Gem Uncirculated 65 EPQ, save for a single 64 EPQ. The original paper waves are easily seen through the holders and the margins are consistently even from note to note. (900-up)

13241 **Fr. 238 $1 1923 Star Silver Certificate PMG Gem Uncirculated 65 EPQ.** The margins on this note are solid and surprisingly, there are only a handful of Gem stars known for this issue. What's more, a survey of auction records indicates only two Gem stars have been offered at public auction since 2003. **(1,150-up)**

13242 **Fr. 238/Fr. 237 $1 1923 Silver Certificates Reverse Changeover Pair PCGS Choice New 63.** This neat "Changeback" is one of only three such pairs we have had for auction in five years. Though not uncommon, these by no means are as common as some people may think. **(750-up)**

13243 **Fr. 238 $1 1923 Silver Certificate Choice New.** Bold embossing and natural paper ripple are traits of this $1 Silver that carries a better signature combination. **(200-up)**

13244 **Fr. 238 $1 1923 Silver Certificates Four Consecutive Examples Choice New.** The face plate letters on this consecutive foursome are G-H-E-F. These notes are from the 71,000,000 range of the B-E block. This was the last block for large size $1 Silvers and the serial numbers ended at just before 80,000,000. (Total: 4 notes) **(900-up)**

13245 **Fr. 238 $1 1923 Silver Certificates Cut Sheet of Four Choice New.** This cut sheet crackles with originality, paper wave, and freshness. The B-E block was the final regular block for large size $1 Silvers. (Total: 4 notes) **(900-up)**

13246 **Fr. 239 $1 1923 Silver Certificate Choice New.** While certainly not rare in any real sense, with almost 200 examples known, this is by far the rarest of the 1923 Ones. There are over 2,500 Fr. 237's and just over a thousand Fr 238's. This number, while outnumbered ten to one by Fr. 237, does not have its true scarcity reflected in its price. **(400-up)**

PMG 67EPQ Hancock Two

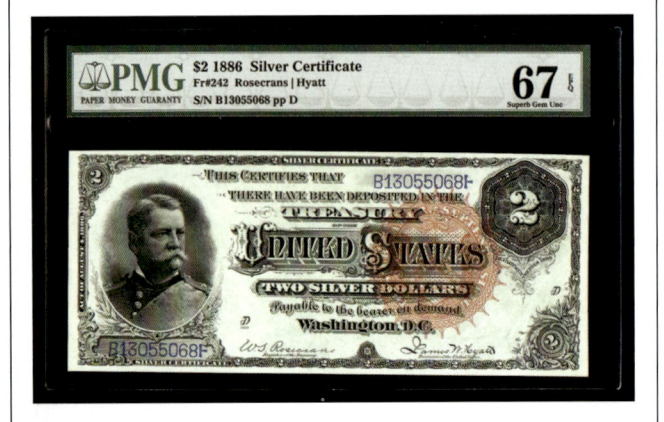

13247 Fr. 242 $2 1886 Silver Certificate PMG Superb Gem Unc 67 EPQ. Fr. 242 is a note that comes quite nice due to two runs of uncirculated pieces that have made their way into the 21st century in basically as-issued condition. PMG recently released population report is indicative of the quantity of nice pieces that have survived. A total of 23 notes have been graded either 65 or 66 by PMG for Fr. 242, but only this piece and three others have been graded at the 67 level. While we are sure that number will increase over the years, we expect that the proportions will hold fairly true, and EPQ 67s will remain quite elusive. **(10,000-up)**

13248 Fr. 242 $2 1886 Silver Certificate PCGS Gem New 65. This unreported high-end Hancock falls into a run of CU notes for this Friedberg number. This example exhibits perfect paper color and inks. If the top margin didn't dip the slightest bit towards the right corner, a higher grade would have been easily attained. **(5,500-up)**

13249 Fr. 242 $2 1886 Silver Certificate PCGS Very Choice New 64PPQ. This wonderfully original Hancock remains attractive and bright. Overall, the eye appeal is most pleasing. **(3,000-up)**

13250 Fr. 242 $2 1886 Silver Certificate Very Choice New. This deuce boasts all the attributes worthy of a Gem including perfectly adequate margins, bright white and wavy paper, and bold embossing. There is a bit of residue noticed from stamp hinges.
From The Jacob and Heather Dedman Collection **(2,000-up)**

13251 **Fr. 242 $2 1886 Silver Certificate PMG Very Fine 20.** This Hancock Deuce shows even circulation and is problem free for the grade. **(800-up)**

13252 **Fr. 242 $2 1886 Silver Certificate Very Fine.** The surfaces are original on this well-margined Hancock Deuce. It would be a Choice VF were it not for some translucent staining at the very outer edges apparently from a prior mounting. **(700-up)**

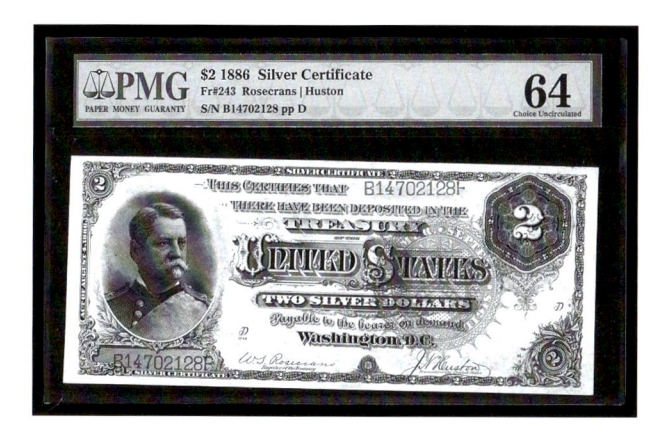

13253 **Fr. 243 $2 1886 Silver Certificate PMG Choice Uncirculated 64.** A gorgeous Hancock Deuce that appears to be a far higher grade than the 64 that it was assigned. The note carries the comment, "Hinged." While nothing is a certainty in this Brave New Third Party World, it seems to us that a little minor repair would be greatly rewarded on resubmission. **(3,500-up)**

13254 **Fr. 243 $2 1886 Silver Certificate Very Fine.** This mid-grade Hancock Deuce shows uniform handling that has left this note with bright paper and wholesome edges. *From The Collection of Greg Southward* **(900-up)**

13255 **Fr. 243 $2 1886 Silver Certificate PMG Fine 12.** Fr. 243 is right behind Fr. 241 as the scarcest of the Hancock Deuces. **(500-up)**

PMG Gem Uncirculated 66 EPQ
Fr. 246 $2 1891 Windom

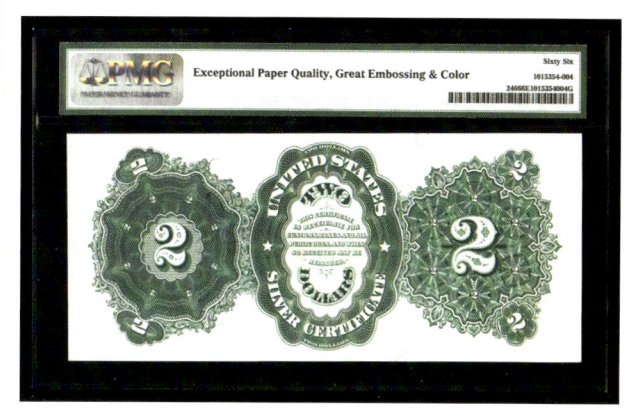

13256 **Fr. 246 $2 1891 Silver Certificate PMG Gem Uncirculated 66 EPQ.** This is a beautiful Windom, with nice centering of both sides, great color, and easily seen bold, original serial number embossing. This two-number type has always been a favorite of collectors and it is quite difficult to locate in gem or above. PMG mentions exceptional paper quality, great embossing and color. **(11,000-up)**

13257 **Fr. 246 $2 1891 Silver Certificate CGA Extremely Fine 45.** This Windom is nicely margined yet suffers from some heavy fold lines which have split along the bottom margin. Expert repairs have minimized the effects of the damage. *From The Collection of Greg Southward* **(1,500-up)**

13258 Fr. 246 $2 1891 Silver Certificate Extremely Fine. Very broadly margined with three light folds and some minor rippling at the left edge. A handsome Windom Deuce that should realize... (1,500-up)

13259 Fr. 246 $2 1891 Silver Certificate Fine-Very Fine. Terrific color remains for the grade—particularly from the face. The back shows a few areas of soil. (550-up)

13260 Fr. 246 $2 1891 Silver Certificate Fine-Very Fine. This nicely margined Windom appears to have been wet at one time which has faded the treasury seal a bit. (550-up)

PMG 66 EPQ Educational Deuce

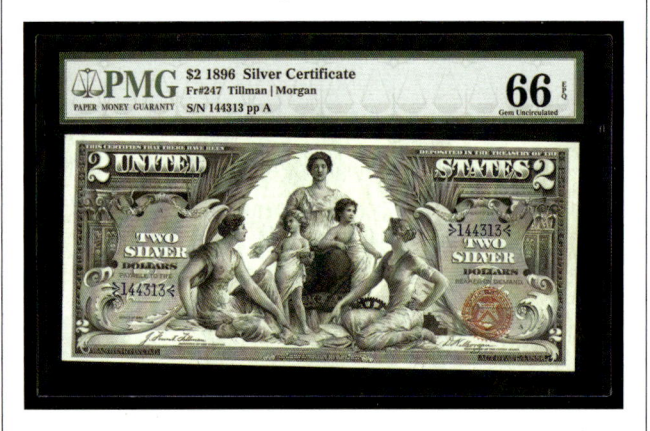

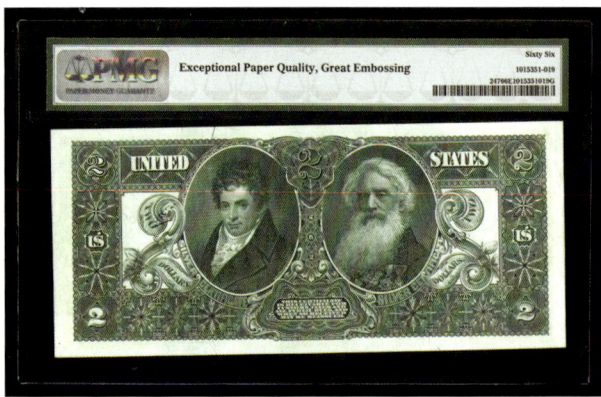

13261 Fr. 247 $2 1896 Silver Certificate PMG Gem Uncirculated 66EPQ. This two dollar Educational certainly seems to have earned every point of its 66EPQ grade. The original embossing is easy to see through the holder, the margins are exceptional and the colors are perfect. PMG liked this one as much as we do...they comment "Exceptional Paper Quality" as well as "Great Embossing." (12,500-up)

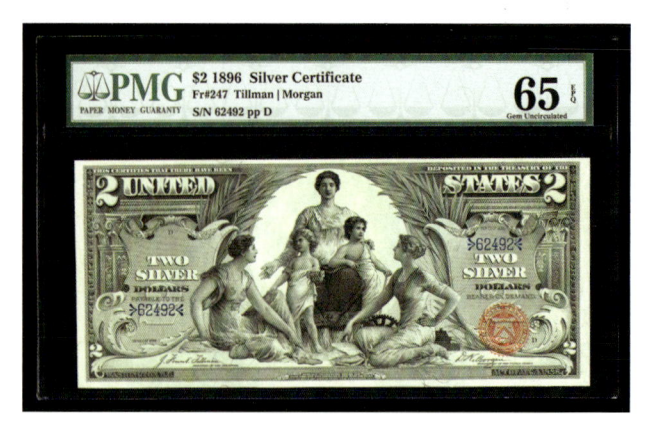

13262 Fr. 247 $2 1896 Silver Certificate PMG Gem Uncirculated 65 EPQ. This $2 Educational is hugely margined on the face with excellent color and terrific eye appeal. This type is not terribly rare at this grade level, but the note is so popular that there are never enough available to supply collector demand. The original embossing of the five-digit serial number is deep enough to be easily seen through the third party holder. (10,000-up)

13263 Fr. 247 $2 1896 Silver Certificate New. Immediately this piece faces up as a full Gem with bright serial numbers and a bright red seal. The design is perfectly executed and the paper is bright. However, there are some repairs along the edges, including both side margins. (7,500-up)

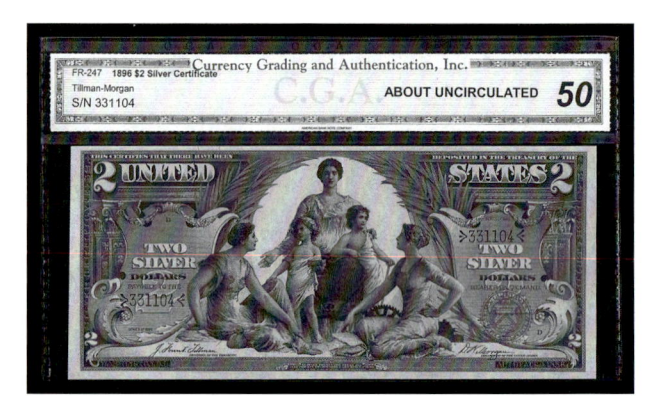

13264 Fr. 247 $2 1896 Silver Certificate CGA About Uncirculated 50. Well margined and bright, with the appearance of a piece in higher grade. (5,000-up)

13265 Fr. 247 $2 1896 Silver Certificate PMG Extremely Fine 40. A very nice three fold XF with plenty of eye appeal. The PMG grade seems quite conservative when the note is looked at from the face, but the folds are a bit easier to see from the back. A solid piece worth a strong bid. (3,500-up)

13266 Fr. 247 $2 1896 Silver Certificate PCGS Very Fine 35PPQ. Nicely margined with good color and an attractive overall appearance. (1,750-up)

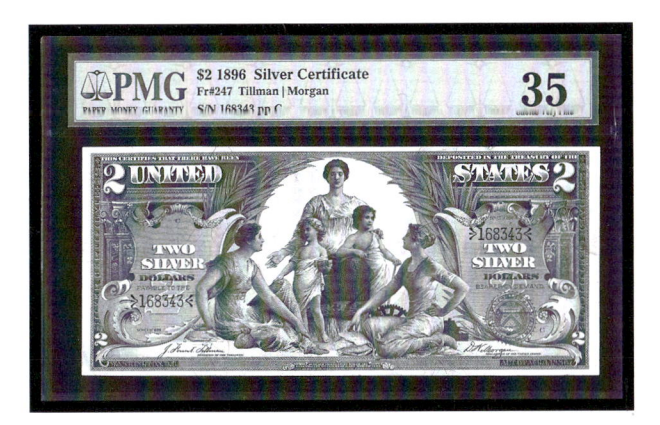

13267 Fr. 247 $2 1896 Silver Certificate PMG Choice Very Fine 35. Serial number embossing can clearly be seen through the holder on this glorious Educational Deuce. Plenty of eye appeal is coupled with vibrant inking. (1,750-up)

13268 Fr. 247 $2 1896 Silver Certificate PMG Very Fine 25. This broadly margined Educational Deuce faces up very well for the grade, with bold five digit serial numbers and a cherry red seal. (1,500-up)

13269 Fr. 247 $2 1896 Silver Certificate CGA Very Good 08. Solid for the grade, this piece will fill that hole. (400-up)

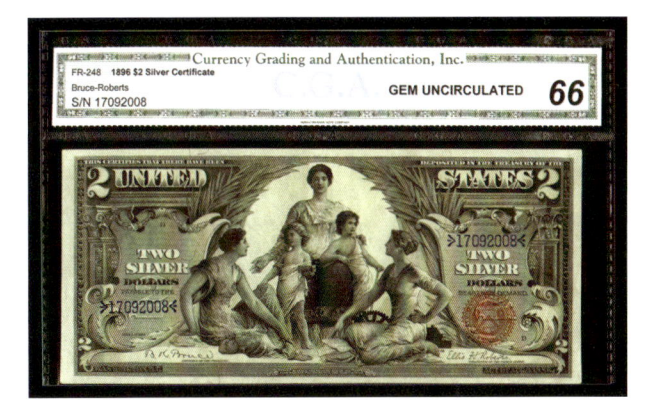

13270 Fr. 248 $2 1896 Silver Certificate CGA Gem Uncirculated 66. This Educational Deuce features enormous margins for the issue, which only adds to the overall eye appeal of the design and bright white paper. A couple of corner bumps are noted, perhaps limiting the grade by a point. (10,000-up)

13271 Fr. 248 $2 1896 Silver Certificate CGA Very Fine 25. A popular design with all the guess work taken out of the grading equation by CGA. (1,750-up)

13272 Fr. 248 $2 1896 Silver Certificate Very Fine. Lightly aged with some staining at the outer edges. This is a very well-margined Educational Deuce that should do quite well in spite of its minor problems. (1,750-up)

13273 **Fr. 248 $2 1896 Silver Certificate Fine.** This $2 Ed has toned over the years.
From The Collection of Greg Southward **(700-up)**

13274 **Fr. 248 $2 1896 Silver Certificate Very Good.** This $2 Ed must have fallen into the starch and left a note that is not unattractive for the grade. **(200-up)**

13275 **Fr. 253 $2 1899 Silver Certificate PCGS Superb Gem New 67PPQ.** One of the highest grade 1899 Silver Two's that we have yet seen in a third party holder. The note is broadly margined with terrific color, easily seen paper originality, great centering of the design on both sides, and all the eye appeal one would expect from a Superb note. **(4,000-up)**

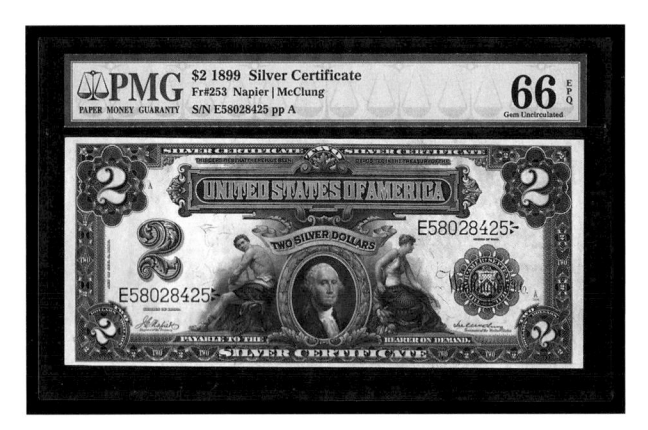

13276 **Fr. 253 $2 1899 Silver Certificate PMG Gem Uncirculated 66 EPQ.** Huge margins, ideal centering and embossing that's visible through the holder are all highlights of this perfect looking turn-of-the-century Deuce.
From The Jacob and Heather Dedman Collection **(3,000-up)**

13277 **Fr. 253 $2 1899 Silver Certificate Extremely Fine.** This bright Deuce was once folded into fourths leaving it with three verical folds. **(500-up)**

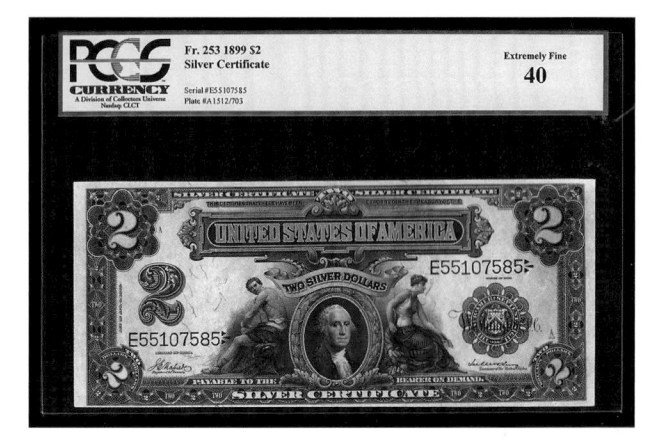

13278 **Fr. 253 $2 1899 Silver Certificate PCGS Extremely Fine 40.** A handsome Silver Deuce that faces up beautifully in the TPG holder. **(500-up)**

13279 **Fr. 255 $2 1899 Silver Certificate PCGS New 62PPQ.** The bold embossing and natural paper wave jump out at you from this Washington Deuce. It is not listed in the census, but the next two serial numbers are, and those notes are CU. **(1,000-up)**

13280 **Fr. 255 $2 1899 Silver Certificate Choice About New.** A soft crease along the right side is the only circulation this note has endured. The margins are pleasing and the colors bright. **(800-up)**

13281 **Fr. 255 $2 1899 Silver Certificate CGA Extremely Fine 45.** A nice lightly circulated Deuce which is quite bright. **(500-up)**

13282 **Fr. 256 $2 1899 Silver Certificate PMG Uncirculated 66 EPQ.** This seven-digit serial number note with great color has "exceptional paper quality." **(3,500-up)**

13283 **Fr. 256 $2 1899 Silver Certificate PMG Choice About Unc 58.** This beauty appears fully uncirculated and has sufficient margins and bright white paper. **(850-up)**

13284 **Fr. 258 $2 1899 Silver Certificate CGA Gem Uncirculated 66.** From our FUN 2007 auction where this was from a cut sheet. Even margins frame this bright white issue. **(3,000-up)**

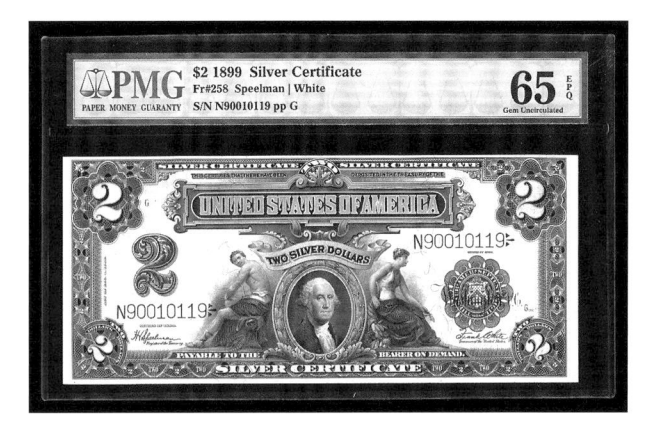

13285 **Fr. 258 $2 1899 Silver Certificate PMG Gem Uncirculated 65 EPQ.** 1899 Deuces are far from a rare type, but it's a bit of a challenge to find a well margined, fully bright, strictly uncirculated example. This embossed one meets all those requirements and then some. It is nicely centered on both sides and has all the eye appeal in the world. **(3,000-up)**

13286 **Fr. 258 $2 1899 Silver Certificate PMG Choice Uncirculated 64 EPQ.** This boldly printed 1899 Deuce bumps right up against the margin of the full Gem grade. It's a handsome piece with pronounced original embossing and perfect color. **(1,750-up)**

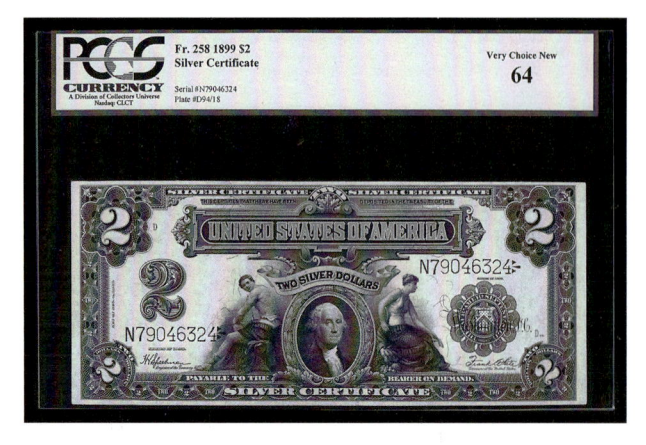

13287 **Fr. 258 $2 1899 Silver Certificate PCGS Very Choice New 64.** With better margins on the front this pristine example would most certainly have been Gem. Nice colors are present as well. (1,250-up)

13288 **Fr. 258 $2 1899 Silver Certificate CGA Extremely Fine 45.** Very nice centering, original embossing and pleasing color are all present on this nice XF note.
From The Collection of Greg Southward (500-up)

13289 **Fr. 258 $2 1899 Silver Certificate Very Fine.** This Deuce was evenly circulated before being put aside. (400-up)

13290 **Fr. 259 $5 1886 Silver Certificate PMG Very Fine 25.** This issue is of the highly sought after "Silver Dollar Back" due to the five Morgan Dollars depicted on the reverse. There are currently less than 35 examples listed in the Gengerke census, including this note. (3,500-up)

13291 **Fr. 260 $5 1886 Silver Certificate PCGS Apparent Fine 15.** The seals and serial numbers are faded on this Silver Dollar Back which also has a few margin splits.
From The Collection of Greg Southward (500-up)

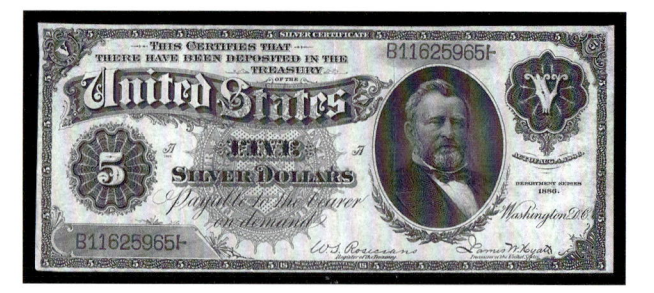

13292 **Fr. 261 $5 1886 Silver Certificate Very Fine.** This is a solid representative for the grade with the back centered a touch low.
From The Collection of Greg Southward (2,500-up)

PMG 65EPQ Silver Dollar Back

13293 **Fr. 263 $5 1886 Silver Certificate PMG Gem Uncirculated 65 EPQ.** PMG has given its coveted "Exceptional Paper Quality" comment to this brightly colored Gem Silver Dollar Back. Fr. 263 is the most common of the 1886 Fives in Gem condition—making it an ideal piece to represent the type. (20,000-up)

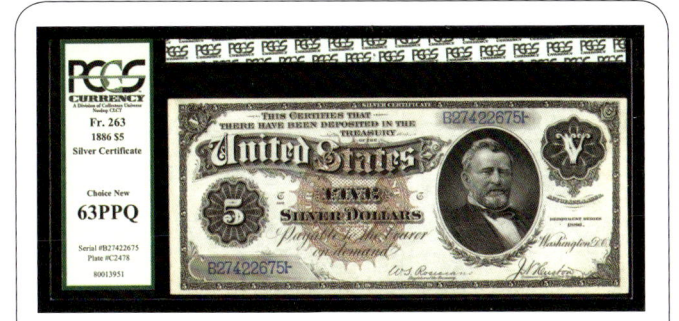

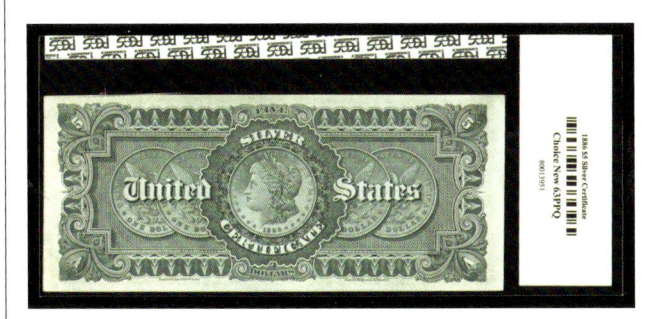

13294 **Fr. 263 $5 1886 Silver Certificate PCGS Choice New 63PPQ.** The famous "Silver Dollar" back graces this design that also is the earliest portraying of "In God We Trust" on our nation's paper money. The paper is bright while the portrait of Grant and the silver dollar at center on the back each display large silk fibers as-made that could be mistaken at first for handling. This note was first recorded when it appeared in a late 1970s auction. (8,000-up)

13295 **Fr. 263 $5 1886 Silver Certificate PMG Very Good 8.** A few splits are seen along the top margin and have been reported by PMG. (600-up)

13297 **Fr. 264 $5 1886 Silver Certificate Fine.** The back of this note displays a nice rendition for the grade of the Silver Dollar Back. The paper is crisp while the top edge shows some wear on this example. This note becomes the new low serial number by a large margin in the census. (750-up)

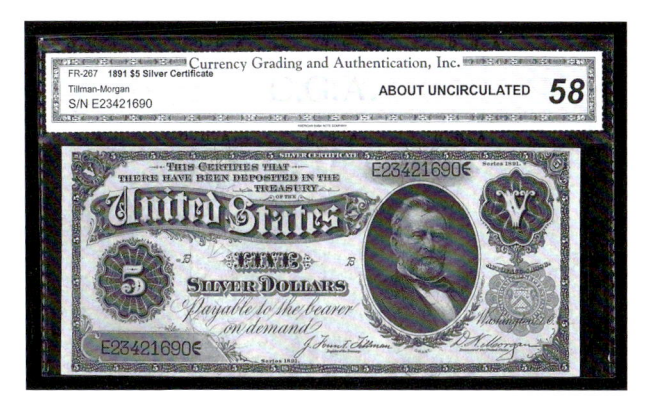

13298 **Fr. 267 $5 1891 Silver Certificate CGA About Uncirculated 58.** This pleasing Open Back design definitely looks better and it is difficult to see what may be the reason for the grade. Nice margins and pleasing centering on both sides along with bright colors produces a piece with excellent eye appeal. (2,000-up)

13299 **Fr. 267 $5 1891 Silver Certificate Fine-Very Fine.** This is a moderately circulated Open Back example that retains crisp paper, nice colors, and eye appeal. This design type is scarcer than the more popular Silver Dollar Back and as such perhaps represents great value for the next purchaser. A small spot of lost ink is noticed on the back.
From The Collection of Greg Southward (1,000-up)

Near Gem PMG 64 Silver Dollar Back

13296 **Fr. 264 $5 1886 Silver Certificate PMG Choice Uncirculated 64.** Minor aging of the upper corners appears to be what has held the grade down on this otherwise Gem appearing Large Brown Seal Silver Dollar Back. Fr. 264 is a much scarcer number of the type—particularly in high grade. (10,000-up)

CGA Gem Uncirculated 66 $5 Educational

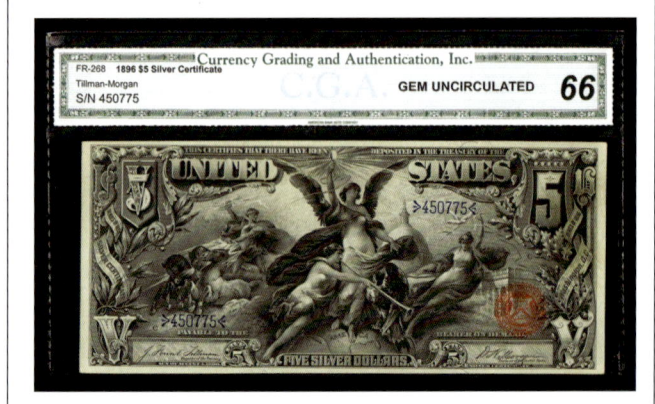

13300 Fr. 268 $5 1896 Silver Certificate CGA Gem Uncirculated 66. A beauty of a Five Dollar Ed, with great centering, broad, even margins and flashy bright colors. This type is always in tremendous demand, and this one appears to be as nice as any we've seen in quite some time. A lovely note made lovelier by a six digit serial number. **(20,000-up)**

CGA Gem Uncirculated 66 $5 Educational

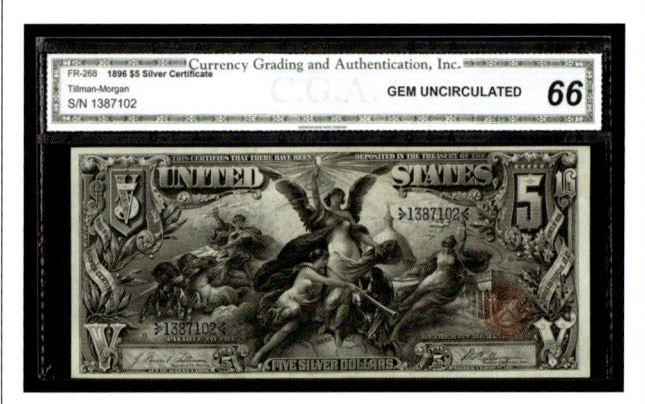

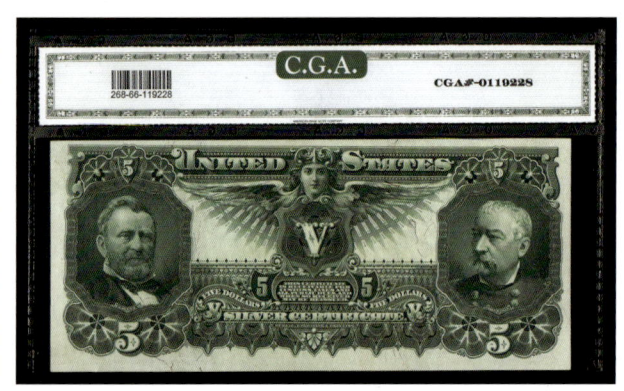

13301 Fr. 268 $5 1896 Silver Certificate CGA Gem Uncirculated 66. The margins, color, and eye appeal of this note are seldom encountered for the series. Simply a gorgeous example that is widely regarded by collectors as one of the highlights in the designs of US currency. This note is new to census and should see some spirited bidding. **(20,000-up)**

Five Dollar Educational Graded PMG 65EPQ

13302 Fr. 268 $5 1896 Silver Certificate PMG Gem Uncirculated 65 EPQ. PMG has commented "Exceptional Paper Quality, Great Embossing" on this broadly margined and very handsome $5 Educational. The note is enhanced by a five-digit serial number. An ideal piece for a Gem Educational set. **(20,000-up)**

13303 Fr. 268 $5 1896 Silver Certificate PMG Choice Extremely Fine 45. A very handsome $5 Educational with the margins, color, and eye appeal of a perfect Gem. Once holdered, nice XFs, which generally have three light folds, are impossible to decipher from far higher grade examples. There is absolutely no difference in appearance between this super piece and a note that would grade 20+ points higher. A terrific buy for the collector who values Superb appearance over technical grade.
From The Bill and Kathy Stella Currency Collection
(5,000-up)

13304 **Fr. 268 $5 1896 Silver Certificate CGA Very Fine 20.** CGA has mentioned a repair on this popular design. Further examination detects numerous margin issues. (2,000-up)

13305 **Fr. 268 $5 1896 Silver Certificate Fine.** This $5 Ed has soft surfaces and the back reveals some discoloration.
From The Collection of Greg Southward (1,200-up)

13306 **Fr. 269 $5 1896 Silver Certificate Fine.** A bit soft and with a little of the green back beginning to turn slightly blue. From the face, this decently margined $5 Ed has the appearance of a Very Fine.
From The Collection of Greg Southward (1,500-up)

PMG 64 Fr. 270—The Rarest of the $5 Eds

13307 **Fr. 270 $5 1896 Silver Certificate PMG Choice Uncirculated 64.** Over 650 $5 Educationals are known, but only 20% of them are Fr. 270s. This PMG 64 comes right up to the very edge of the full Gem grade. Fr. 270 is the scarcest $5 Ed number by count, but in high grade, it is disproportionately scarcer. We would not be at all surprised to see this handsome and classically designed note reach or exceed... (12,500-up)

13308 **Fr. 270 $5 1896 Silver Certificate Good-Very Good.** This is the scarcest Friedberg number for the $5 Educationals. This example shows more wear on the back than on the face. (400-up)

13309 **Fr. 271 $5 1899 Silver Certificate PMG Gem Uncirculated 65 EPQ.** The original embossing is easily viewed through the third party holder on this well margined, brightly colored Chief. This piece has earned PMG's EPQ designation and that, along with its terrific eye appeal, should carry it to or beyond... (6,500-up)

13310 **Fr. 271 $5 1899 Silver Certificate PMG Gem Uncirculated 65 EPQ.** Exceptionally broad margins, as well as pronounced original embossing, are features of this handsome Chief. This is the earliest of the 11 signature combinations issued during the first few years of this design's 29-year run as our Workhorse $5 bill. (6,500-up)

13311 **Fr. 271 $5 1899 Silver Certificate Very Fine.** This note is from the first Friedberg number for this design. The edges are nice for the grade while the blue ink has remained dark. (800-up)

13312 **Fr. 271 $5 1899 Silver Certificate PMG Very Fine 20.** A solid, problem free example that has garnered the full VF grade. (800-up)

13313 **Fr. 272 $5 1899 Silver Certificate CGA Gem Uncirculated 65.** A touch of handling is noted on this otherwise Superb Gem. The embossing is bold as are the printed devices. (5,500-up)

13314 **Fr. 274 $5 1899 Silver Certificate PCGS Very Choice New 64PPQ.** This delightful, embossed Chief is not listed in the census, but it is only three serial numbers removed from a CU listed note. Fr. 274 is the second scarcest Chief and they have always been tough notes to find in top grade. (4,000-up)

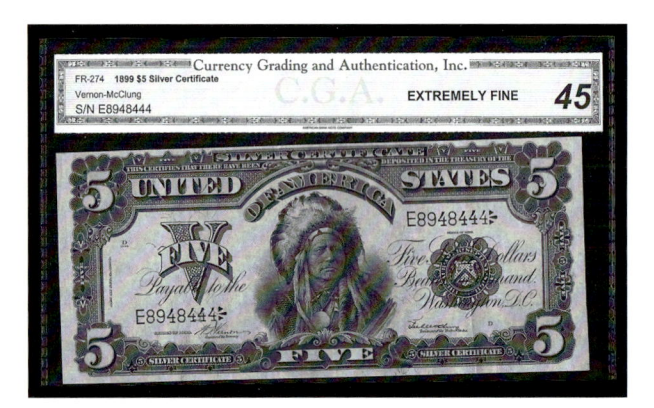

13315 **Fr. 274 $5 1899 Silver Certificate CGA Extremely Fine 45.** Three folds are seen within the holder on this note's otherwise natural surfaces. This premium Chief is likely to see spirited bidding. (1,250-up)

13316 **Fr. 274 $5 1899 Silver Certificate CGA Very Fine 35.** A bright and crisp moderately circulated Indian Chief that is just about perfect for the grade.
From The Collection of Greg Southward (750-up)

13317 **Fr. 274 $5 1899 Silver Certificate PCGS Very Fine 25.** This example was 100 notes removed from a radar. The paper looks to be quite crisp with the usual folds associated with the grade.
From The Collection of Greg Southward (700-up)

13318 **Fr. 275 $5 1899 Silver Certificate PMG Gem Uncirculated 65 EPQ.** PMG has given this lovely Chief a trio of positive comments: "Exceptional Paper Quality" and "Great Embossing & Color." The note appears to have all that and more. A very handsome Chief and a less common number in high grade. (7,000-up)

13319 **Fr. 275 $5 1899 Silver Certificate Choice About New.** This Chief has terrific margins, bright colors and most all of the hallmarks of a perfect Gem. It's held from that grade by a single very light centerfold.
From The Collection of Greg Southward (1,500-up)

13320 **Fr. 275 $5 1899 Silver Certificate PMG Very Fine 25.** A touch of light soiling affects the back of this pleasing Chief. (850-up)

13321 **Fr. 275 $5 1899 Silver Certificate PMG Very Fine 25.** Plenty of embossing is noticed on this problem-free Chief. (850-up)

13322 Fr. 275 $5 1899 Silver Certificate PMG Very Fine 20. A light amount of staining at upper left does little to detract from the brightness of this Chief. (850-up)

13323 Fr. 277 $5 1899 Silver Certificate PMG About Uncirculated 50. A very nicely margined example, which, save for one heavy fold in the left margin, carries the full appearance of a Gem. (2,000-up)

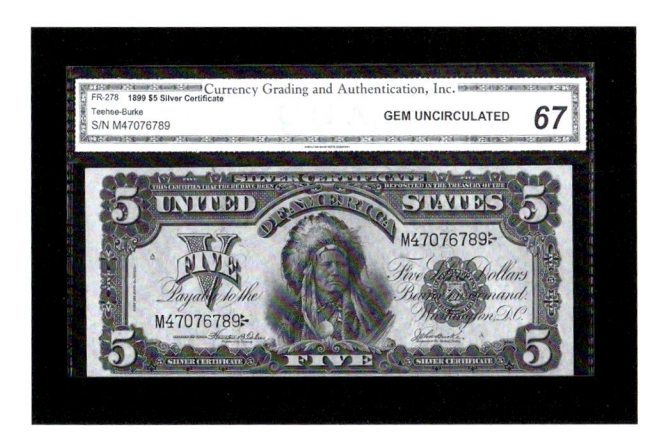

13324 Fr. 278 $5 1899 Silver Certificate CGA Gem Uncirculated 67. Excellent original embossing - that can be seen through the CGA encasement - on top of strict uncirculated condition make this a fine choice for the collector of this staple type as well as for the hobbyist looking to add a Chief to his collection. (7,250-up)

13325 Fr. 278 $5 1899 Silver Certificate CGA Gem Uncirculated 66. This is a pleasing note for type which is well embossed and is a solid, original, problem-free Chief with broad margins and good eye appeal. (6,000-up)

13326 Fr. 278 $5 1899 Silver Certificate PMG Gem Uncirculated 66 EPQ. The EPQ designation was clearly earned by this deeply embossed, beautifully centered, fully bright Chief. It's a note that has the right-off-the-press appearance that is so much in demand by today's condition conscious collectors. (8,500-up)

13327 **Fr. 278 $5 1899 Silver Certificate PMG Gem Uncirculated 65 EPQ.** Sixty Five EPQ is a coveted Type Note grade, but in spite of that grade having been assigned to this note, it still strikes us as a bit conservative. The margins are broad, the colors are spectacular, and the note has the type of magnetic eye appeal usually associated with the Superb grade. (7,500-up)

13328 **Fr. 278 $5 1899 Silver Certificate CGA Extremely Fine 40.** Nicely centered on both sides, with good colors and no problems.
From The Collection of Greg Southward (1,200-up)

13329 **Fr. 279 $5 1899 Silver Certificate CGA Extremely Fine 45.** Three folds are plainly visible on this bright Chief.
From The Collection of Greg Southward (1,200-up)

13330 **Fr. 279 $5 1899 Silver Certificate Very Fine.** This is a solid note for the grade that sports sound edges and even handling. (800-up)

13331 **Fr. 279 $5 1899 Silver Certificate Fine.** This is a much tougher Friedberg number for Chiefs. The edges are nice for the grade. (600-up)

PCGS Gem 66PPQ Fr. 280 Mule

13332 **Fr. 280 $5 1899 Silver Certificate Mule PCGS Gem New 66PPQ.** A broadly margined and brilliantly colored example of this second to last Chief signature combination, with the back plate in the Burke position, thus the Mule designation. Both sides of the note are beautifully centered, and in spite of its high third party grade, it looks to us like one more point might have been warranted. (8,500-up)

CGA Gem Uncirculated 66 $5 Chief

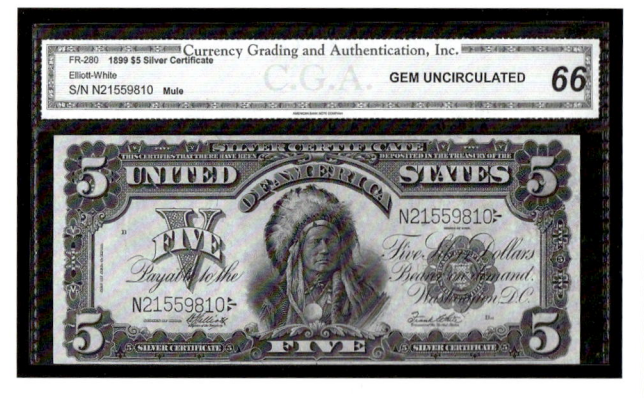

13333 **Fr. 280 $5 1899 Silver Certificate Mule CGA Gem Uncirculated 66.** This is a wonderful opportunity to acquire a Gem example of the popular "Running Antelope" note. This piece is vividly printed and neatly centered. (6,000-up)

13334 **Fr. 280 $5 1899 Silver Certificate Mule Very Fine-Extremely Fine.** Sound edges and paper are highlights of this attractive Chief. The back is centered a little high. (1,300-up)

13335 **Fr. 280 $5 1899 Silver Certificate Mule Very Fine-Extremely Fine.** Dark inks and light folds are observed on this Chief.
From The Collection of Greg Southward (1,300-up)

13336 **Fr. 280 $5 1899 Silver Certificate PCGS Very Fine 25.** A little embossing remains on this Chief graced with solid margins and plenty of eye appeal. (800-up)

13337 **Fr. 280 $5 1899 Silver Certificate Mule PMG Very Fine 25.** This is a large size Mule with the back plate number 1251 located to the left of the 5 counter in the right-hand corner instead of the normal position to the right of the 5 counter in the left-hand corner. Large size Mules are an area in paper money collecting that is rarely explored and should gain momentum in coming years. (850-up)

13338 **Fr. 281 $5 1899 Silver Certificate PMG Choice Uncirculated 64.** This final signature combination of Chief Silver Certificate has bright colors and tremendous eye appeal. The margins are also excellent, and the note certainly appears to be at least the 64 that it has been designated as.
From The Jacob and Heather Dedman Collection (3,250-up)

13339 **Fr. 281 $5 1899 Silver Certificate PMG Choice Extremely Fine 45 EPQ.** Another lovely Type note whose appearance far exceeds its technical grade. This note has the visual impact of a perfect Gem, and as its EPQ designation implies, its original embossing can still be easily seen. A lovely collector grade note that will likely push the upper limits of its price category.
From The Collection of Greg Southward (2,000-up)

13340 **Fr. 281 $5 1899 Silver Certificate Very Fine.** The paper surfaces are a touch soft, but this well-centered Chief has retained a handsome appearance.
From The Collection of Greg Southward (800-up)

13341 **Fr. 281 $5 1899 Silver Certificate Very Good-Fine.** This Chief has retained some snap. (500-up)

PMG 67 EPQ Porthole

13342 **Fr. 282 $5 1923 Silver Certificate PMG Superb Gem Unc 67 EPQ.** Deep original embossing is easily seen on this hugely margined, 100% fully bright, ideally centered Porthole. Most third party graded 67s tend to meet with some scepticism, but this Porthole Five should please the most critical buyer as it appears to us to have earned every point of its 67 EPQ grade. (12,500-up)

CGA Gem 66 Fr. 282 1923
$5 Silver Certificate

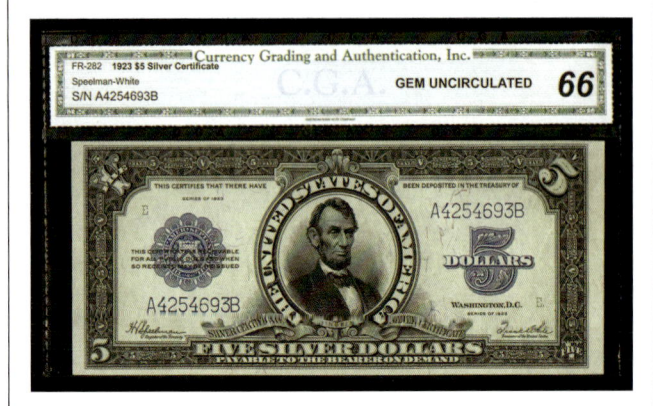

13343 Fr. 282 $5 1923 Silver Certificate CGA Gem Uncirculated 66. This note, which is new to the census, comes from a small run of known uncirculated examples. Bright and pleasing, this specimen surely will add some flair to any collection. **(8,500-up)**

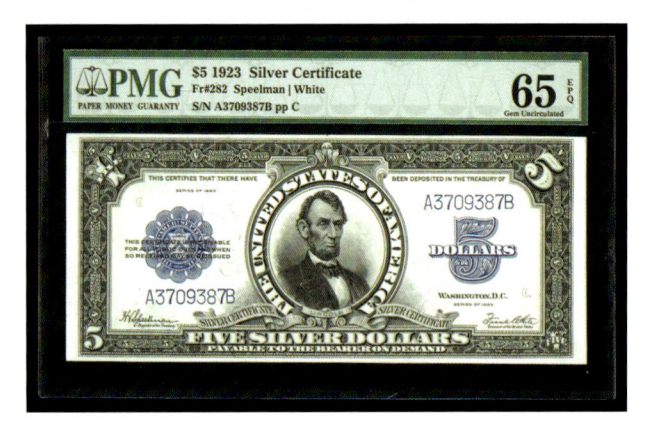

13344 Fr. 282 $5 1923 Silver Certificate PMG Gem Uncirculated 65. Examination of this Gem reveals a perfectly printed design and overprint set against wholly original and deeply embossed paper. An as made crinkle is noted and does not hinder the overall eye appeal of this solidly margined issue.
From The Jacob and Heather Dedman Collection **(7,000-up)**

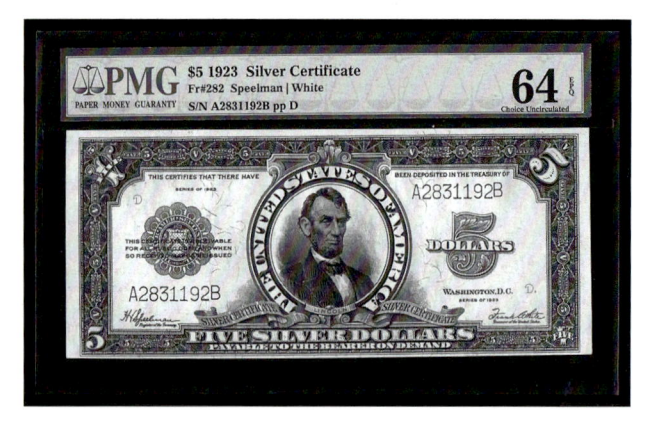

13345 Fr. 282 $5 1923 Silver Certificate PMG Choice Uncirculated 64 EPQ. The bottom margin is a bit tight on this boldly original, brilliantly colored Porthole. Save for that, the note has all the appearance of a truly Superb piece. Nice Portholes are notoriously difficult to locate, and, at the current price levels, this cataloger thinks they may be the best Type note buy in premium 64 holders. **(4,000-up)**

13346 Fr. 282 $5 1923 Silver Certificate CGA Choice Uncirculated 64. A beautiful "Porthole" note with bold colors, great embossing, original paper wave, and decent centering. This note would look terrific in any collection, and should command a premium bid. **(4,000-up)**

13347 Fr. 282 $5 1923 Silver Certificate PCGS Choice New 63. This note was put away long before the census takers began their activities. This original surface Porthole falls neatly within a CU run of notes. Only the tight top margin keeps this appealing $5 from climbing higher on the grading scale. **(3,000-up)**

13348 **Fr. 282 $5 1923 Silver Certificate CGA Crisp Uncirculated 62.** This broadly margined issue was likely used in a couple bank to bank transactions as there is a touch of handling, but no signs of wear. A minor repaired split is noted in the bottom margin, but was only noticed upon careful examination of the note. (2,500-up)

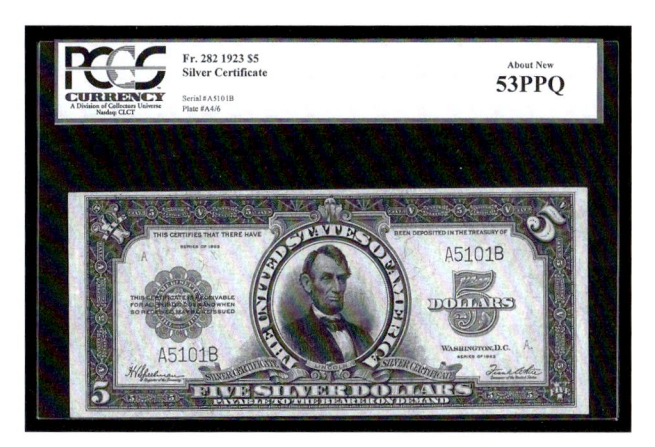

13349 **Fr. 282 $5 1923 Silver Certificate PCGS About New 53PPQ.** Terrific originality and exceptional centering, along with a four-digit serial number, all highlight this strikingly handsome Porthole. An ideal collector-grade with all the appearance of a note ten points higher. (2,750-up)

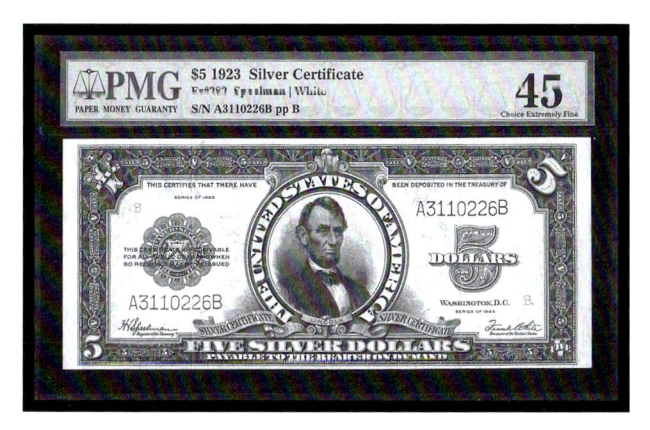

13350 **Fr. 282 $5 1923 Silver Certificate PMG Choice Extremely Fine 45.** A totally natural Porthole, with a bright blue overprint and original paper surfaces. (2,000-up)

13351 **Fr. 282 $5 1923 Silver Certificate Very Fine-Extremely Fine.** This high end Very Fine has a fair amount of claim to the Extra Fine grade. It's a wholly unmolested piece with good color, ideal paper originality, and broad margins. An ideal collector grade Porthole.
From The Collection of Greg Southward (1,500-up)

13352 **Fr. 282 $5 1923 Silver Certificate Very Fine.** At a glance, this Porthole appears far higher grade. The surfaces are a hair soft, but it is clean and most attractive.
From The Collection of Greg Southward (1,250-up)

13353 **Fr. 282 $5 1923 Silver Certificate Very Fine.** This original note is consecutive to the previous lot and it shares a similar circulation pattern. (1,200-up)

13354 **Fr. 282 $5 1923 Silver Certificate Very Fine.** Good original paper surfaces remain on this note, which has a number of heavy folds, but few traces of actual circulation. (1,200-up)

PMG 64 EPQ 1880 Ten Dollar Silver

13355 Fr. 288 $10 1880 Silver Certificate PMG Choice Uncirculated 64 EPQ. Good paper originality is easily seen through the PMG holder on this well-margined, black back Robert Morris 1880 Silver. PMG has commented "Exceptional Paper Quality, Great Embossing & Color." This is a difficult Type to find in this high grade—particularly with these important positive qualifiers. **(14,500-up)**

13356 Fr. 288 $10 1880 Silver Certificate Good-Very Good. While this note has definitely seen its share of use in the channels of commerce, this type is difficult to locate, and only about five dozen examples are known to exist in any grade. This is a decent looking piece to fill a hole in a type set. A blue "4" is found on the face along with some edge wear. **(700-up)**

Beautifully Original 1880 Ten Dollar Silver

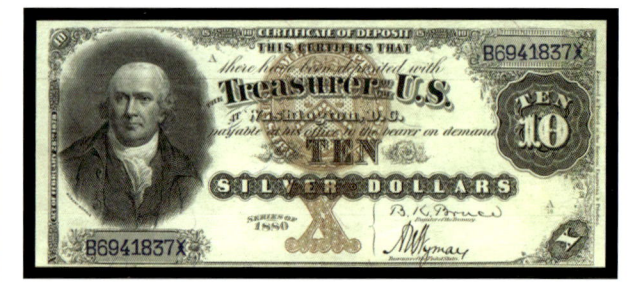

13357 Fr. 289 $10 1880 Silver Certificate Very Choice New. This is one of the very few uncirculated Fr. 289's to be found outside of the B71133XX run of approximately 50 notes. It's strictly original, with terrific embossing, extraordinary color and three extra-large margins. This handsome note would be a Superb Gem if the adequate but somewhat tight bottom margin were the size of the other three. The back centering is virtually perfect.
From The Jacob and Heather Dedman Collection
(10,000-up)

13358 Fr. 289 $10 1880 Silver Certificate PCGS Very Fine 35. These 1880 Silvers are tough notes to find in attractive, evenly circulated mid grades. This one is a real beauty.
From The Collection of Greg Southward **(2,500-up)**

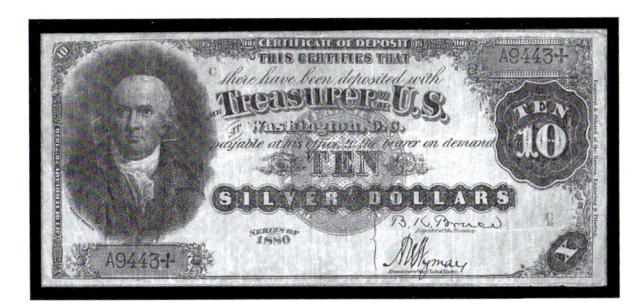

13359 **Fr. 290 $10 1880 Silver Certificate Very Fine.** When we last sold this note in April 2006, we used the following description, "We sold this very note in our 1996 Florida United Numismatists auction, where it went for $440, a figure it will handily surpass tonight. Silked, in the style of notes which are *ex-Farouk*, and with a tiny chip in the top margin." It did indeed well surpass that figure, realizing $2,990. It should do about that well again.
From The Collection of Greg Southward (2,500-up)

13360 **Fr. 293 $10 1886 Silver Certificate Very Fine.** There is some very light staining and a tiny repaired edge split on this scarce Early Back Tombstone. The overall appearance of the note is quite nice, and it has some claims to a higher grade.
From The Collection of Greg Southward (2,000-up)

13361 **Fr. 294 $10 1886 Silver Certificate Fine.** This early Tombstone has seen a great deal of circulation, but it has withstood the test of time by retaining its snappy paper. This is a very difficult type to find in any grade and a note that will still attract quite a number of bids. (850-up)

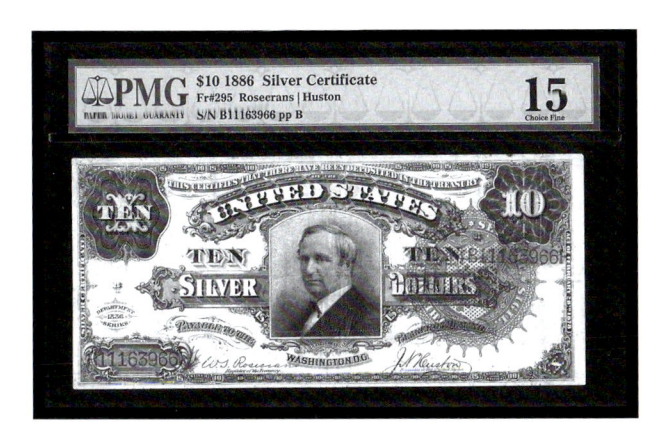

13362 **Fr. 295 $10 1886 Silver Certificate PMG Choice Fine 15.** As of the catalog print date, only one other example of this relatively scarce Friedberg number has appeared at auction; a paltry Good with problems. This piece is solid with a seal boasting most of its original brown color. (2,000-up)

CGA Gem Uncirculated 66 Fr. 296
1886 $10 Tombstone

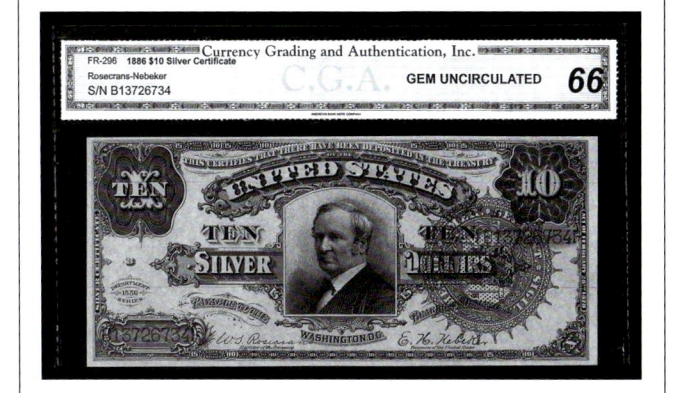

13363 **Fr. 296 $10 1886 Silver Certificate CGA Gem Uncirculated 66.** Broadly margined and beautifully bright, this is new to the census of a touch over 50 examples of this number known to exist and one of only about 20 uncirculated examples. The margins are broad, the important Early Back design is beautifully centered and the note has tremendous eye appeal. 1886 Ten Dollar Silvers are one of the more challenging lower-denomination types to obtain in top grade, and this is a truly nice example. (12,500-up)

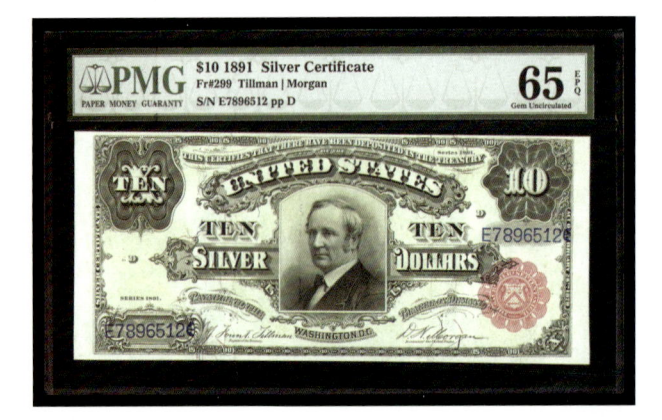

13364 **Fr. 299 $10 1891 Silver Certificate PMG Gem Uncirculated 65 EPQ.** The Exceptional Paper Quality designation, which is given to this note by PMG, along with its Gem numerical grade will quite likely carry the piece to just below the 5-figure mark. A lovely Tombstone for your high-end Type set. **(8,000-up)**

13365 **Fr. 299 $10 1891 Silver Certificate Very Fine.** A perfect collector-grade note with strictly original paper surfaces, bright colors, and no problems of any kind. While certainly a technical VF, the note has many of the attributes of an EF and will likely sell closer to that value level. A fresh and pretty note.
From The Jacob and Heather Dedman Collection **(1,250-up)**

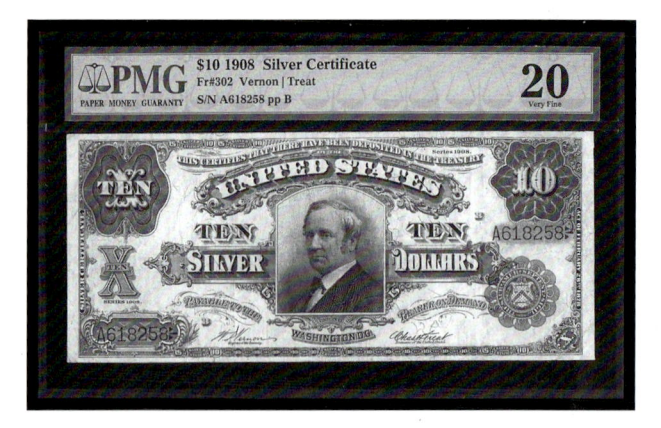

13366 **Fr. 302 $10 1908 Silver Certificate PMG Very Fine 20.** This bright "Tombstone" note displays solid margins, and a solid blue overprint. **(1,000-up)**

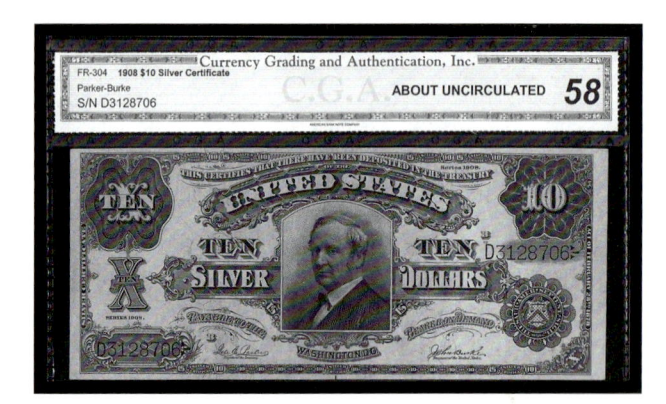

13367 **Fr. 304 $10 1908 Silver Certificate CGA About Uncirculated 58.** A lone center bend is noted on this AU note, but is really only visible from the back. The margins on the face are bold for the issue. **(2,250-up)**

13368 **Fr. 304 $10 1908 Silver Certificate Very Fine-Extremely Fine.** This is an attractive Tombstone and it is ideal for a type collection. The inks are dark and the paper is bright. **(1,400-up)**

13369 **Fr. 304 $10 1908 Silver Certificate PCGS Fine 15.** A solid Blue Seal Tombstone, with strong ink color and no problems save for the normal circulation soil that one would expect for this grade. This is the last Friedberg number for the Tombstones with the blue "X" counter. **(900-up)**

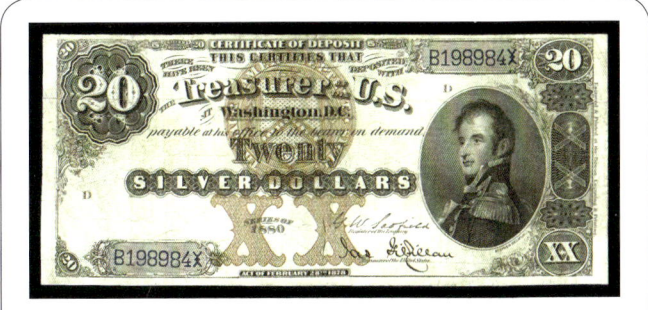

13370 **Fr. 309 $20 1880 Silver Certificate Fine.** There are a few repaired edge splits, but this scarce number has retained good color and is quite well margined. About fifty examples are known in all grades combined. These Stephen Decatur 1880 Silver Certificates have the striking dark brown back that distinguishes this entire series, the only series of U.S. currency that used this color. It's a rather rare number in any grade and very rare in high grade, with not a single uncirculated example reported.
From The Collection of Greg Southward **(5,000-up)**

Lovely 1880 $20 Silver

13371 **Fr. 311 $20 1880 Silver Certificate PMG Choice Very Fine 35.** A handsome example of this popular Silver Certificate type. The Stephen Decatur portrait is particularly lifelike, and that, along with the vivid brown seal and "XX", bring to the note the appearance of a higher grade piece. Although about 125 Fr. 311's are known, only ten of those have been graded AU or better, several of which are impounded; in all likelihood, not many of that number are - in actuality - nicer than this note. **(12,000-up)**

PMG Very Fine 30 Fr. 311

13372 Fr. 311 $20 1880 Silver Certificate PMG Very Fine 30. This high-end VF has retained its original embossing, which can be easily seen through the third party holder. It's a well margined, bright note that is only a hair off the quality of the piece in the previous lot. **(10,500-up)**

Serial Number E10 $20 1891 Silver PMG 65 EPQ

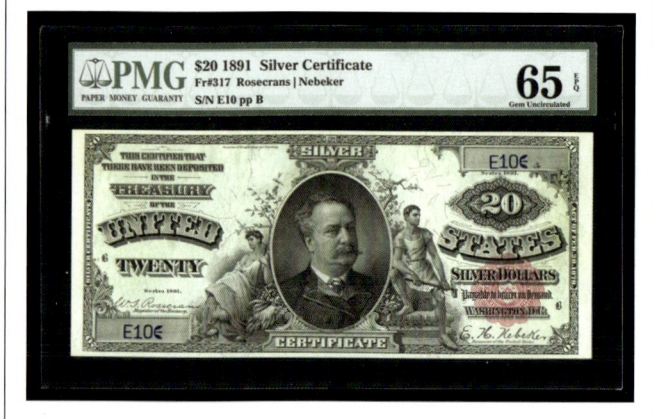

13373 Fr. 317 $20 1891 Silver Certificate PMG Gem Uncirculated 65 EPQ. Only about a half dozen Uncirculated examples are known for this number, and this E10 is currently far and away the finest graded by PMG. At least as significant as the Gem numerical classification is the "Exceptional Paper Quality" comment, which PMG has included on this holder. Low number notes have been extremely popular of late, and this gorgeous piece with its low number, Type rarity, and condition rarity, could move into record territory for the Friedberg Number. **(20,000-up)**

13374 Fr. 318 $20 1891 Silver Certificate Extremely Fine. Light handling is found on this $20 Silver with natural paper ripple. The paper is bright and the colors are excellent. The professional repair in the right margin is best seen when the note is "candled," i.e. held up to a light source.
From The Bill and Kathy Stella Currency Collection
(2,000-up)

13375 **Fr. 318 $20 1891 Silver Certificate Courtesy Autograph PCGS Very Fine 35.** Daniel Morgan has signed this handsome $20 Silver Certificate immediately above his engraved signature as treasurer. Although quite scarce, Courtesy Autograph notes have never come into their own as a sub-speciality, and consequently, they can be purchased for just a small premium over the normal Type. (2,500-up)

$20 1891 Silver Certificate PMG Choice Uncirculated 64

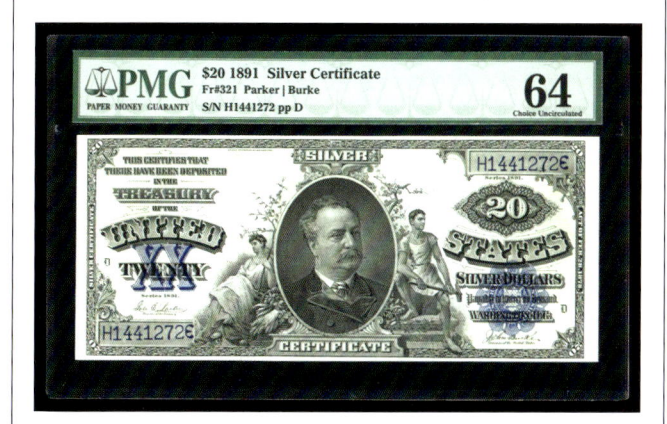

13376 **Fr. 321 $20 1891 Silver Certificate PMG Choice Uncirculated 64.** Though a handful of uncirculated examples of this type are known to exist, their auction appearances are fairly infrequent, perhaps one or two a year on average. Additionally, many of those so-called uncirculated issues barely make the grade with thin margins. This piece is perfectly margined with great back to front centering and a vibrant bright blue overprint.
From The Jacob and Heather Dedman Collection (10,000-up)

13377 **Fr. 321 $20 1891 Silver Certificate Very Fine.** A nice evenly circulated example with no problems of any kind. These Blue Seal Daniel Manning Silver Certificates are always in demand and this nice natural example should prove to be a popular lot.
From The Collection of Greg Southward (1,750-up)

13378 **Fr. 321 $20 1891 Silver Certificate Very Fine.** Excellent color remains on this popular Silver Certificate Type. It is nicely centered on both sides, and has much of the look of a piece in higher grade.
From The Collection of Greg Southward (2,000-up)

13379 **Fr. 321 $20 1891 Silver Certificate Fine.** This Manning has some remaining snap. An edge tear of approximately a quarter of an inch is noticed. (1,200-up)

13380 **Fr. 322 $20 1891 Silver Certificate Extremely Fine.** This is by far the scarcer of this two signature type, with a little over 100 known versus over 230 for the more available Fr. 321. Tonight's offering would fit well visually with any collection of Choice CU or better notes. It has superior color, nice centering, and it is simply far better than most typically encountered examples of this number, most of which are clustered at the low end of the grading scale. **(2,500-up)**

13381 **Fr. 322 $20 1891 Silver Certificate Fine-Very Fine.** Nice, natural paper surfaces on this blue seal Manning that has a fair amount of claim to the Very Fine grade. About a dozen very tiny pinholes are present.
From The Collection of Greg Southward **(1,400-up)**

13382 **Fr. 322 $20 1891 Silver Certificate PMG Choice Fine 15.** This is a solid mid-grade example of this design that has the added blue "XX" counters, and is a new note to the census. **(1,500-up)**

Rare 1880 $50 Silver Certificate

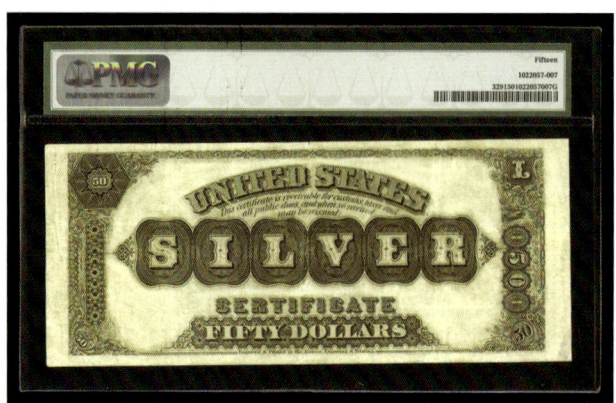

13383 **Fr. 329 $50 1880 Silver Certificate PMG Choice Fine 15.** Fewer than 30 examples of this number are known—most of which are right around this grade. The PMG Fine 15 grade appears to us to be right on the money. The note is well margined, reasonably clean for the grade, and free of meaningful defects. **(12,500-up)**

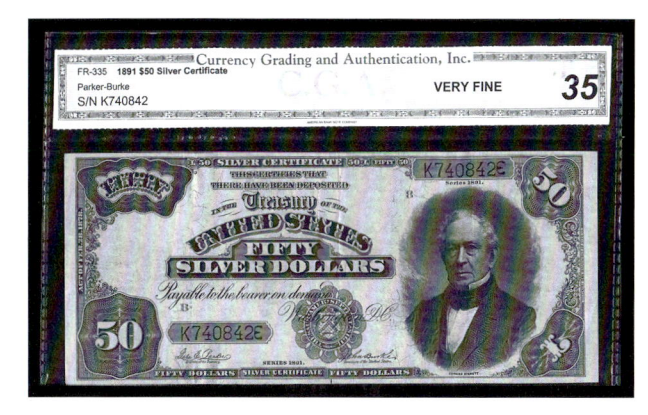

13384 **Fr. 335 $50 1891 Silver Certificate CGA Very Fine 35.** This piece last appeared in our 2006 FUN auction where it was described, "An extremely nice example, with strictly original paper surfaces whose embossing can be clearly seen through the third-party holder. It's also beautifully margined, with bright paper and ink colors. A stately example of this Edward Everett Fifty Dollar Silver."
From The Collection of Greg Southward **(4,000-up)**

13385 **Fr. 335 $50 1891 Silver Certificate Fine.** There are a few minor edge nicks in the top margin, and the paper is somewhat soft, but this very scarce Blue Seal Silver Certificate Fifty is rather pleasing-looking for the Fine grade.
From The Collection of Greg Southward **(2,250-up)**

TREASURY NOTES

High-Grade Low Serial Number Stanton Ace

13386 **Fr. 347 $1 1890 Treasury Note Very Choice New.** Low serial number 749 adorns this delightful Stanton with an Ornate Back design. The note exhibits originality and three oversized margins. With a little more bottom margin this $1 Coin Note would step up to the next grade level. **(5,000-up)**

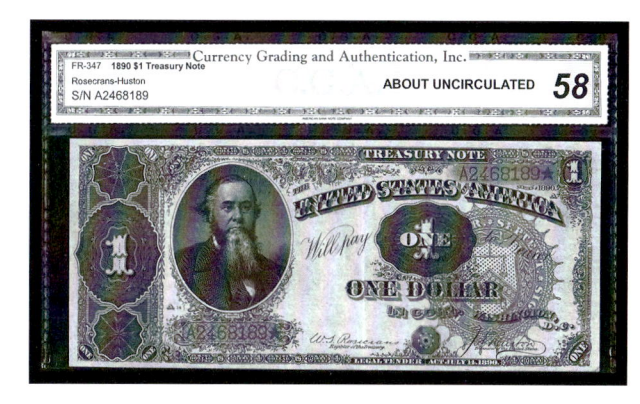

13387 **Fr. 347 $1 1890 Treasury Note CGA About Uncirculated 58.** A very nicely margined 1890 Treasury Ace with bold color, and good eye appeal. **(2,500-up)**

13388 **Fr. 348 $1 1890 Treasury Note Very Fine+.** This is by far the rarest of the 1890 Treasury Aces, with only about 40 examples known, as compared to nearly 250 Fr. 347s and just under a hundred Fr. 349s. The paper is crackling fresh and the note has the appearance of a higher grade. A tiny imperfection in the paper is noticed on the back. **(800-up)**

PCGS Gem New 65PPQ 1890 Fr. 349 $1 Coin Note

13389 Fr. 349 $1 1890 Treasury Note PCGS Gem New 65PPQ. Ample margins and great color highlight this well preserved Ornate Back Stanton Ace. It will be added to a run of CU notes already listed in the census. For Coin Notes, a serial number with an "A" prefix tells you that you have an Ornate Back note, while a serial number with a "B" prefix tells you that you have an Open Back note. (7,500-up)

13390 Fr. 349 $1 1890 Treasury Note Very Fine-Extremely Fine. A half-dozen or so light folds make this note technically a VF, but its lovely appearance cries out for the higher grade. We've seen pieces inferior to this called About New or better. A very attractive 1890 Treasury Ace.
From The Collection of Greg Southward (1,250-up)

13391 Fr. 350 $1 1891 Treasury Note PCGS Gem New 66PPQ. Rolling paper wave and punch-through embossing make this Open Back $1 Coin Note a joy to behold. The margins are also full for the design, while the inks are excellent. Friedberg 350 is by far the scarcest signature combination of the three 1891 numbers. This is another note that was previously missing from a run of CU notes in the census. (2,800-up)

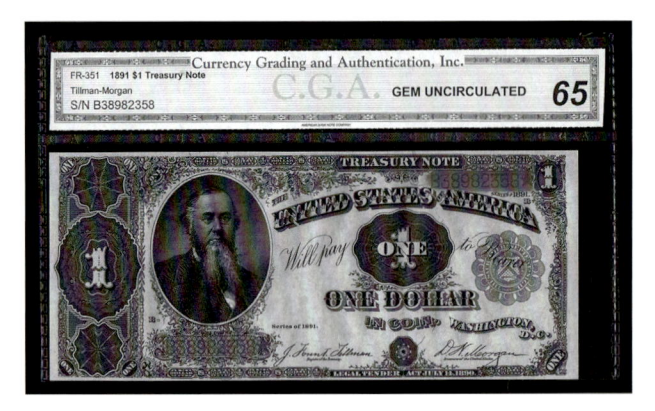

13392 Fr. 351 $1 1891 Treasury Note CGA Gem Uncirculated 65. Pronounced original embossing is easily seen through the third party holder on this brightly colored, nicely margined, Stanton Ace. (2,000-up)

13393 Fr. 351 $1 1891 Treasury Note CGA Extremely Fine 45. This is a nice looking example with good color. The usual trifold is seen in the encasement. (500-up)

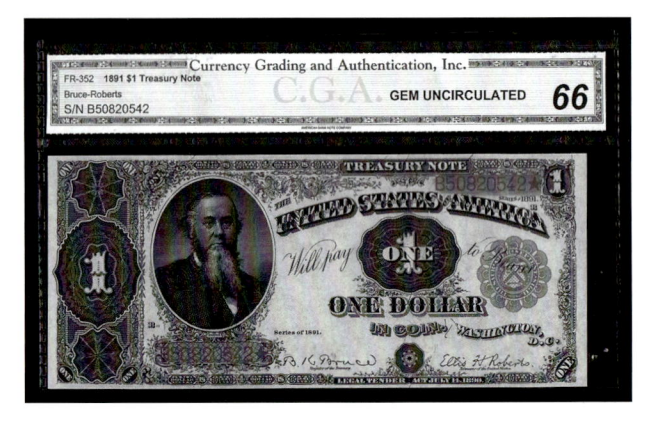

13394 Fr. 352 $1 1891 Treasury Note CGA Gem Uncirculated 66. The original embossing is easily seen on this bright, well-centered Stanton Ace. (3,000-up)

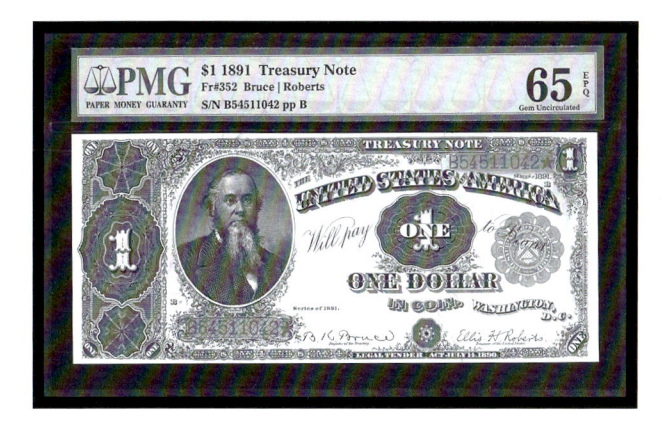

13395 **Fr. 352 $1 1891 Treasury Note PMG Gem Uncirculated 65 EPQ.** Bold embossing of the serial numbers is noted when viewing the back. The margins are ample and the printed details bright. **(2,000-up)**

13396 **Fr. 352 $1 1891 Treasury Note Extremely Fine.** A three-fold XF with strong eye appeal and excellent centering.
From The Collection of Greg Southward **(450-up)**

13397 **Fr. 353 $2 1890 Treasury Note Fine.** The Deuce for this issue carries the portrait of Union Major General James Birdseye McPherson, who was killed in action by Confederate pickets during the Battle of Atlanta. There is a street named for McPherson in Atlanta with a marker near where he fell. McPherson was the highest-ranking officer in the Union Army to be killed in battle during the Civil War. This $2 has a repaired lower right corner tip starting at the edge of the "2" counter.
From The Collection of Greg Southward **(600-up)**

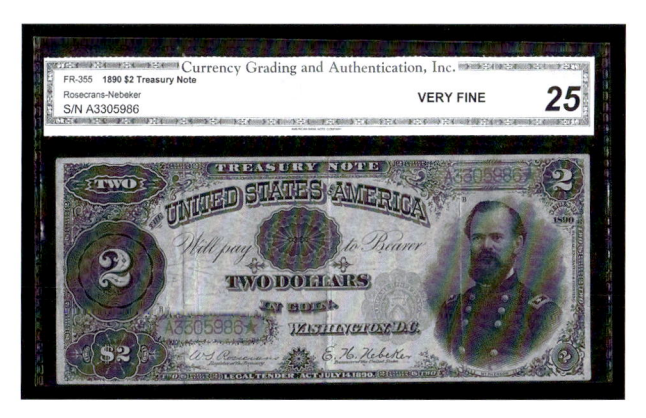

13398 **Fr. 355 $2 1890 Treasury Note CGA Very Fine 25.** Greg purchased this mid-grade example out of our 2005 Long Beach sale.
From The Collection of Greg Southward **(2,000-up)**

PMG 66 EPQ 1891 $2 McPherson

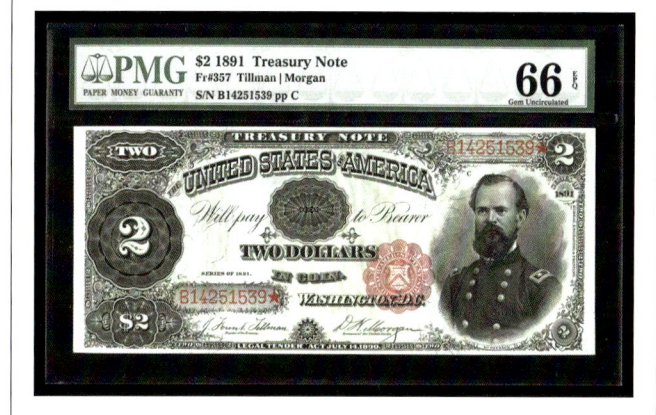

13399 **Fr. 357 $2 1891 Treasury Note PMG Gem Uncirculated 66 EPQ.** The original embossing on this high end McPherson Deuce can be very easily seen through the third party holder. The margins are as broad as one would expect on a 66 and the colors are simply perfect. **(6,500-up)**

13400 **Fr. 357 $2 1891 Treasury Note PCGS Gem New 65.** A very nicely margined McPherson Deuce with super color and tremendous eye appeal. Union General McPherson was a hero of the Battle of Vicksburg, and was killed near Atlanta in 1864. **(5,750-up)**

13401 **Fr. 357 $2 1891 Treasury Note Very Fine+.** This is an attractive $2 Coin Note that has fewer folds than a typical VF, but it also reveals two approximate quarter inch top edge tears.
From The Collection of Greg Southward **(800-up)**

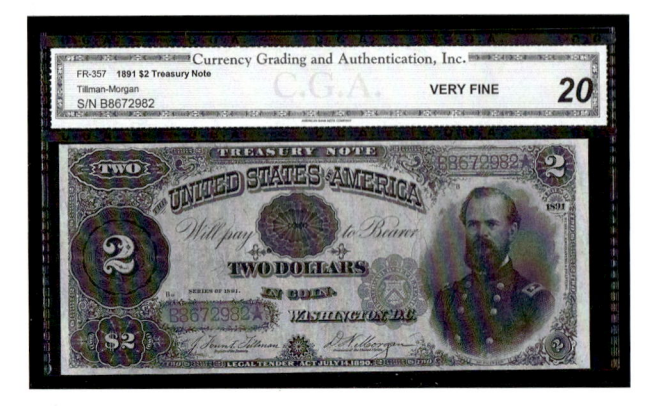

13402 **Fr. 357 $2 1891 Treasury Note CGA Very Fine 20.** Well margined with excellent color for the grade. (850-up)

13403 **Fr. 358 $2 1891 Treasury Note Fine-Very Fine.** The "Star" at the end of the serial number for Coin Notes does not indicate a replacement, but it is a printer's embellishment mark to signify the end of the serial number. This Deuce has nice edges.
From The Collection of Greg Southward **(900-up)**

13404 **Fr. 363 $5 1891 Treasury Note PCGS New 62.** The margins are a bit irregular on what is otherwise a most attractive Treasury Five.
From The Collection of Greg Southward **(1,750-up)**

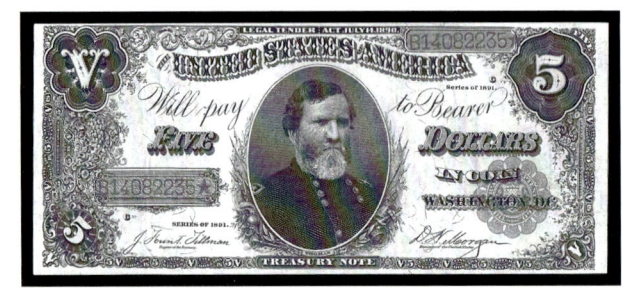

13405 **Fr. 363 $5 1891 Treasury Note Very Fine.** This $5 Coin Note has the appearance of a higher grade as a few of the folds are hard to see unless the note is closely inspected.
From The Collection of Greg Southward **(700-up)**

13406 **Fr. 366 $10 1890 Treasury Note Fine-Very Fine.** Last appearing in our 2005 Long Beach sale, and described as follows, "Totally problem-free example, with perfectly natural surfaces, good margins and bold color for the grade. 1890 Tens are an underrated type in our opinion, with fewer than 250 examples known for all three numbers combined. This number is represented by only about 90 pieces" Both census products now list less than 100 pieces for this number.
From The Collection of Greg Southward **(1,300-up)**

13407 **Fr. 368 $10 1890 Treasury Note PCGS Choice New 63.** This is a charming $10 Sheridan Ornate Back with razor-sharp printing quality and dark inks. Margins are the only restriction on one of the nicest 63s you will ever see without a PPQ modifier. **(5,000-up)**

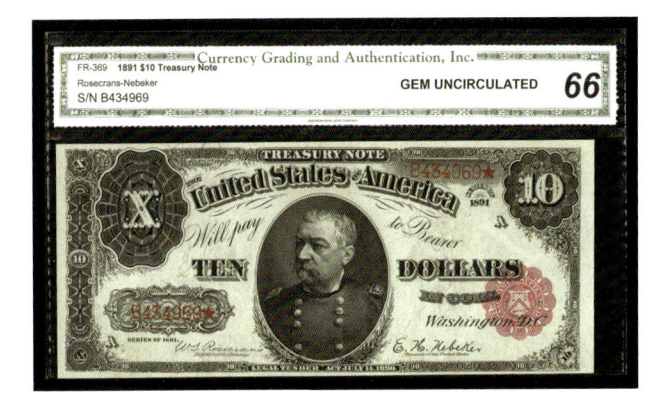

13408 **Fr. 369 $10 1891 Treasury Note CGA Gem Uncirculated 66.** The original embossing is easily seen through the third party holder. Treasury Tens in high grade seem to be disproportionately inexpensive in today's market. **(6,000-up)**

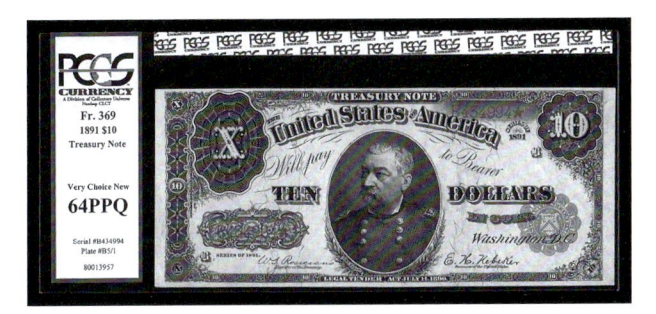

13409 **Fr. 369 $10 1891 Treasury Note PCGS Very Choice New 64PPQ.** This $10 Coin Note is well preserved thus saving its strong embossing and original surfaces. This note is not listed in the census, but it falls neatly within a run of CU notes. **(4,500-up)**

13410 **Fr. 370 $10 1891 Treasury Note Extremely Fine.** This Sheridan $10 is problem-free with its nice edges, color, and paper surfaces. General Sheridan scored his greatest successes defeating Confederate forces in the Shenandoah Valley during 1864.
From The Collection of Greg Southward **(1,500-up)**

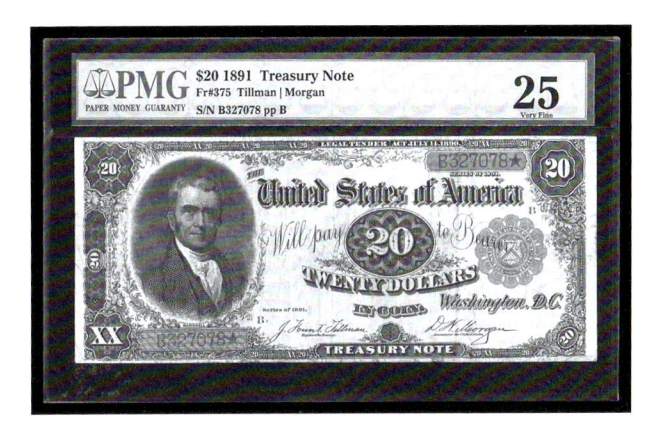

13411 **Fr. 375 $20 1891 Treasury Note PMG Very Fine 25.** Good paper originality, and better color than one would expect for the grade, highlight this 1891 $20 Treasury. **(4,250-up)**

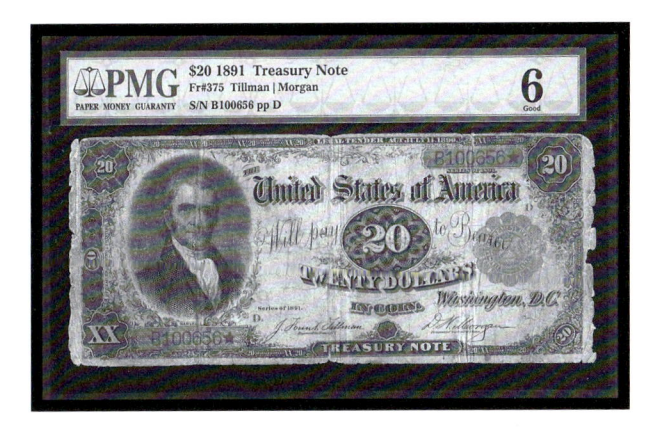

13412 **Fr. 375 $20 1891 Treasury Note PMG Good 6.** This is likely one of the most affordable $20 Treasury notes that will ever find its way to the marketplace. While it does have some minor missing edge pieces (which are duly noted on the PMG holder) they affect only the blank side margins and do not touch the design. Internally, the note grades a solid VG. **(1,250-up)**

Handsome Mid-Grade Watermelon Hundred

13413 Fr. 377 $100 1890 Treasury Note PMG Very Fine 30. This Watermelon Hundred is one of fewer than three dozen examples of its type in existence, and one of fewer than two dozen that have ever appeared on the market. Eight pieces are permanently in government hands, and several others are known by serial number only, having never reached the numismatic marketplace. The back, from which the nickname of this note is derived, is beautifully clean, and the "Watermelon" effect of the large zeros remains pronounced, as the ink quality is razor sharp. This piece is beautifully margined, with the only place even questionably close being the lower right of the face where the margin approaches but does not touch the frameline. With the current tremendous emphasis on paper money collecting, it is a shame that only two dozen collectors are in the exclusive group that may possess this stately type. **(150,000-up)**

FEDERAL RESERVE BANK NOTES

13414 Fr. 708 $1 1918 Federal Reserve Bank Note PCGS Gem New 66PPQ. A handsome note with broad margins and pronounced paper originality. (900-up)

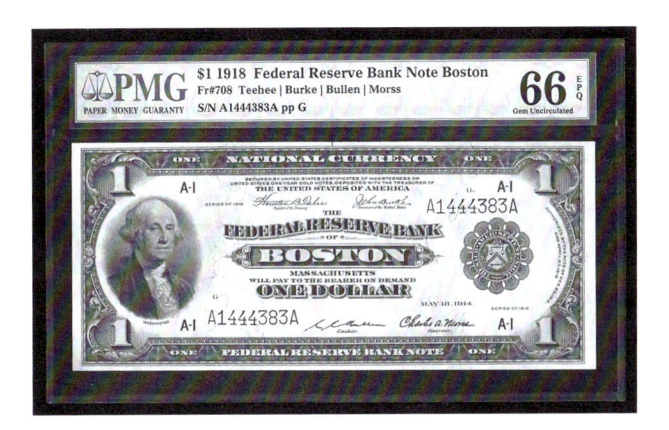

13415 Fr. 708 $1 1918 Federal Reserve Bank Note PMG Gem Uncirculated 66 EPQ. The original embossing can be easily seen through the PMG holder on this broadly margined Boston FRBN. (800-up)

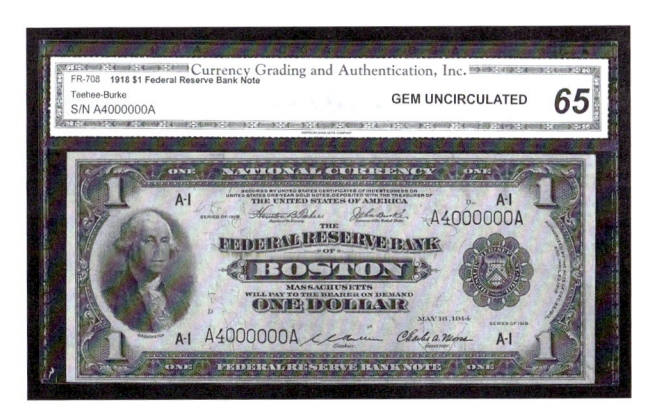

13416 Fr. 708 $1 1918 Federal Reserve Bank Note CGA Gem Uncirculated 65. This fancy serial numbered ace is the four millionth note printed with the serial number A4000000A. The embossing is bold and the paper waves original. (1,200-up)

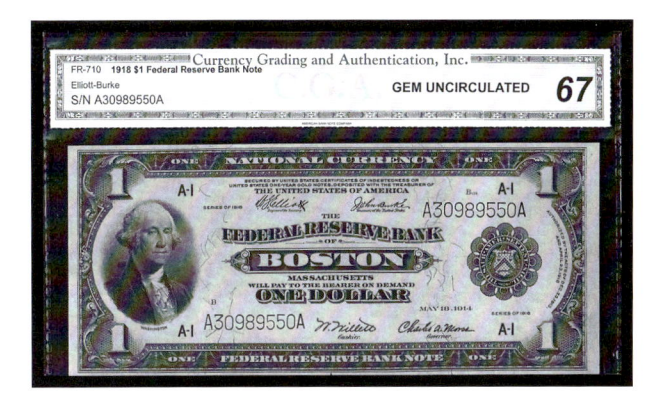

13417 Fr. 710 $1 1918 Federal Reserve Bank Note CGA Gem Uncirculated 67. This widely margined issue is a near-consecutive mate to a CGA 66 also offered here. (800-up)

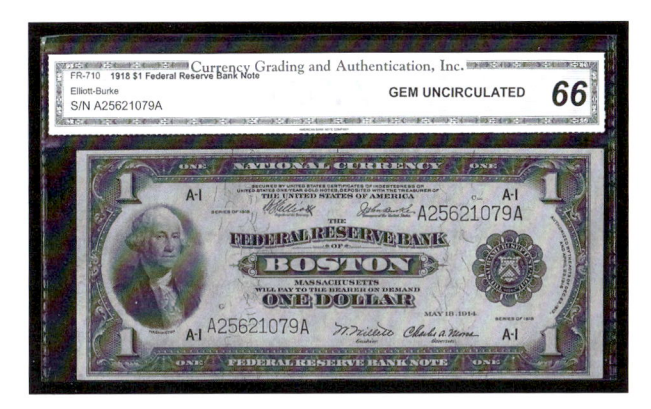

13418 Fr. 710 $1 1918 Federal Reserve Bank Note CGA Gem Uncirculated 66. This Ace exhibits serial number embossing. (600-up)

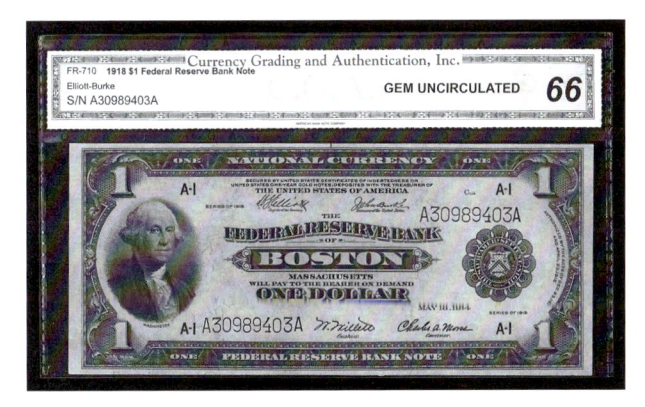

13419 Fr. 710 $1 1918 Federal Reserve Bank Note CGA Gem Uncirculated 66. This is a nice note for a high-grade type collection. (600-up)

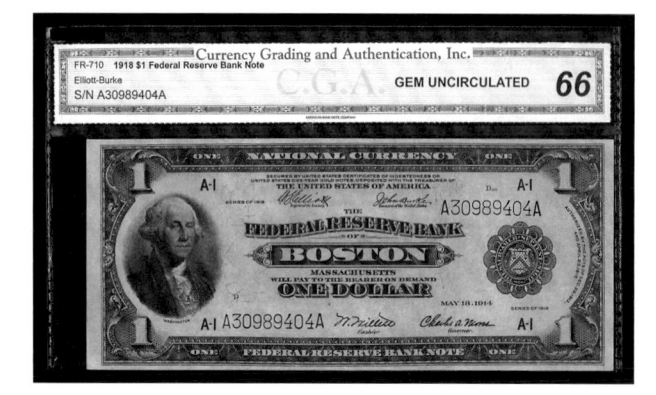

13420 **Fr. 710 $1 1918 Federal Reserve Bank Note CGA Gem Uncirculated 66.** Wide margins and nice centering combine with the natural paper surfaces of this Boston Deuce. **(600-up)**

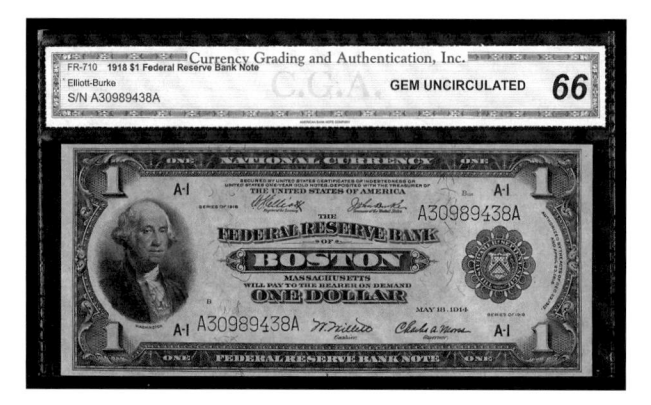

13421 **Fr. 710 $1 1918 Federal Reserve Bank Note CGA Gem Uncirculated 66.** Perfectly even margins are noted all around. **(600-up)**

13422 **Fr. 710 $1 1918 Federal Reserve Bank Note CGA Gem Uncirculated 65.** Broad margins, ideal colors, and lots of eye appeal grace this Boston FRBN. **(450-up)**

13423 **Fr. 710 $1 1918 Federal Reserve Bank Note PMG Choice Uncirculated 64.** A handsome Boston Ace.
From The Collection of Greg Southward **(400-up)**

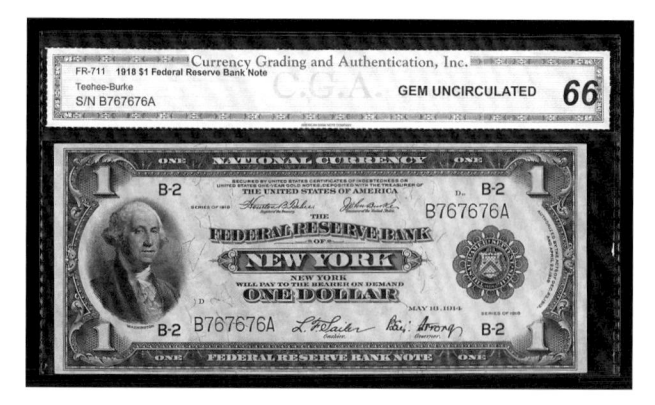

13424 **Fr. 711 $1 1918 Federal Reserve Bank Note CGA Gem Uncirculated 66.** The last time this note with special serial number B767676A crossed the auction block was in 1989. This Ace displays embossing and natural paper ripple. **(2,000-up)**

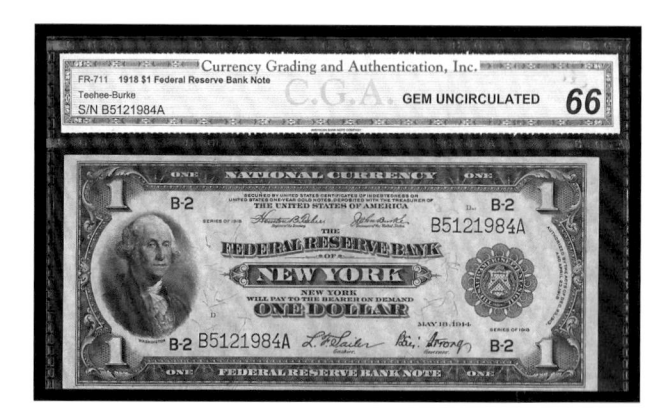

13425 **Fr. 711 $1 1918 Federal Reserve Bank Note CGA Gem Uncirculated 66.** Beautifully centered on both sides, with bright colors and a surplus of attractiveness.
From The Collection of Greg Southward **(600-up)**

13426 **Fr. 711 $1 1918 Federal Reserve Bank Note PMG Choice Uncirculated 64.** PMG has properly identified what appears to be a corner fold as an "As Made Paper Defect Top Left Corner." **(400-up)**

13427 **Fr. 711 $1 1918 Federal Reserve Bank Note Very Choice New.** Hints of handling are noted on this deeply embossed and original note. What's more, the three digit serial number is solid 9s. **(750-up)**

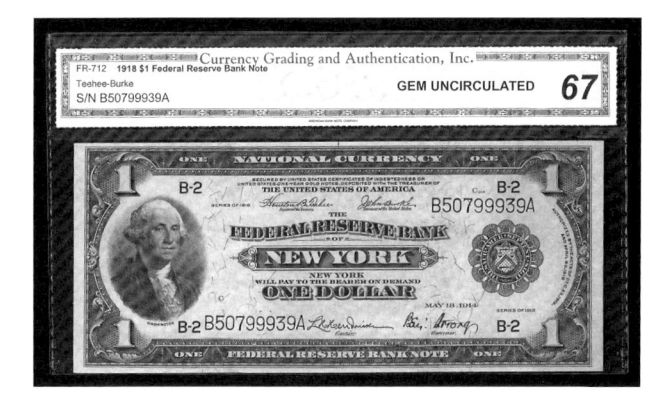

13428 Fr. 712 $1 1918 Federal Reserve Bank Note CGA Gem Uncirculated 67. Perfect margins and great front to back centering add to the eye appeal of this well embossed note. (800-up)

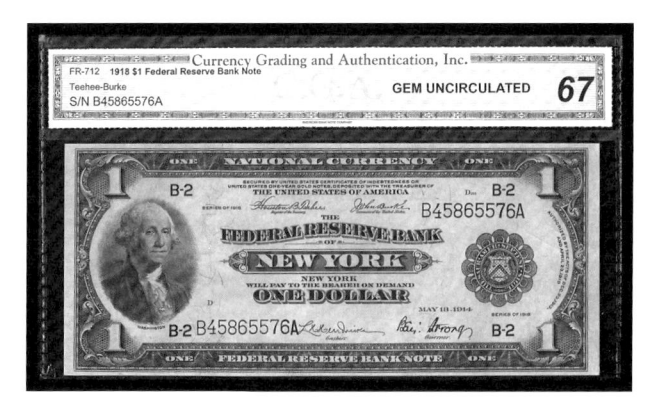

13429 Fr. 712 $1 1918 Federal Reserve Bank Note CGA Gem Uncirculated 67. A touch of teller handling is noted on this bright white issue. (800-up)

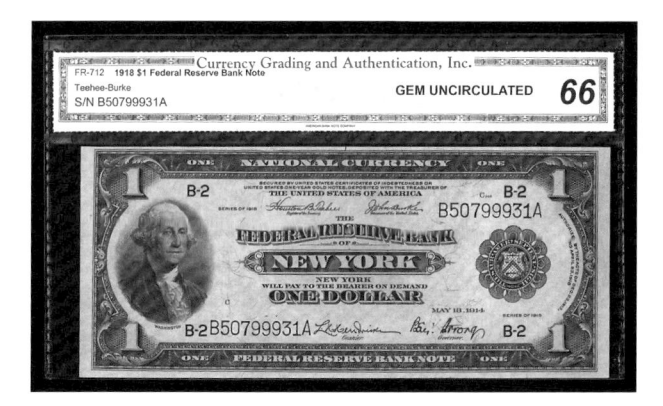

13430 Fr. 712 $1 1918 Federal Reserve Bank Note CGA Gem Uncirculated 66. The embossing of the serial numbers is easy to see through the third-party holder. (600-up)

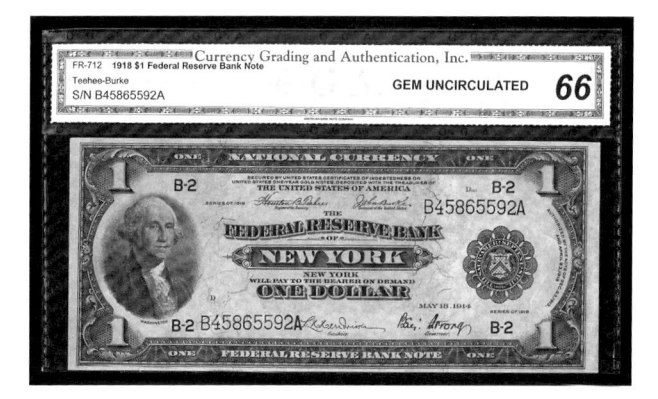

13431 Fr. 712 $1 1918 Federal Reserve Bank Note CGA Gem Uncirculated 66. This New York $1 has strong embossing. (600-up)

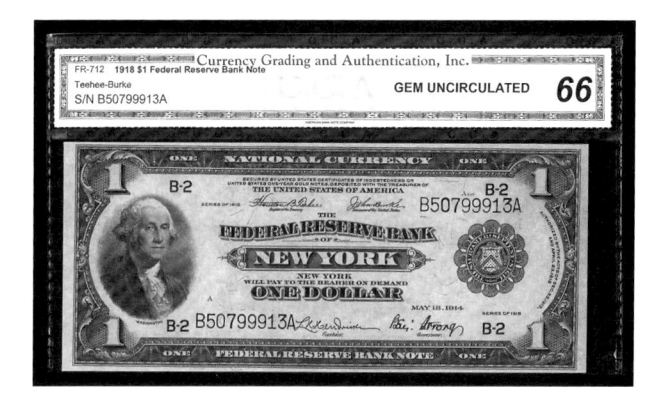

13432 Fr. 712 $1 1918 Federal Reserve Bank Note CGA Gem Uncirculated 66. Embossing includes the district designators on this note. (600-up)

13433 Fr. 712 $1 1918 Federal Reserve Bank Note CGA Gem Uncirculated 66. This $1 is highlighted by original surfaces and embossing. (600-up)

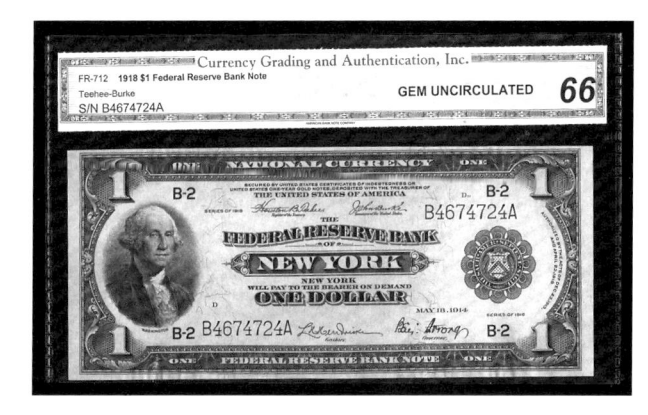

13434 Fr. 712 $1 1918 Federal Reserve Bank Note CGA Gem Uncirculated 66. This bright, well margined note seems to have a bit of embossing that can be seen through the holder. (600-up)

13435 Fr. 712 $1 1918 Federal Reserve Bank Note CGA Gem Uncirculated 65. The finely detailed design is deeply printed and boasts a bold blue overprint. (450-up)

13436 **Fr. 712 $1 1918 Federal Reserve Bank Note CGA Choice Uncirculated 64.** A nicely margined example from the New York district.
From The Collection of Greg Southward **(400-up)**

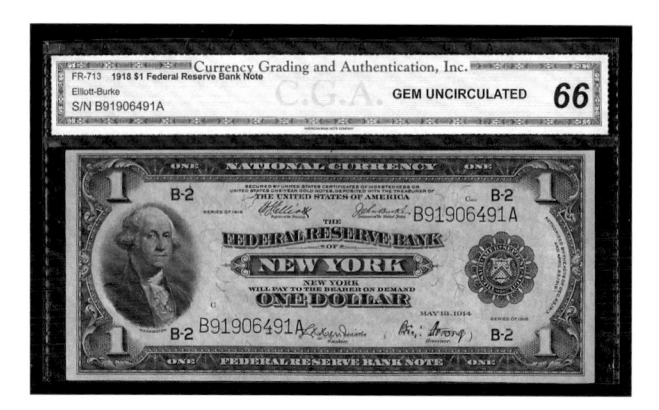

13437 **Fr. 713 $1 1918 Federal Reserve Bank Note CGA Gem Uncirculated 66.** Natural paper quality is observed on this $1. **(600-up)**

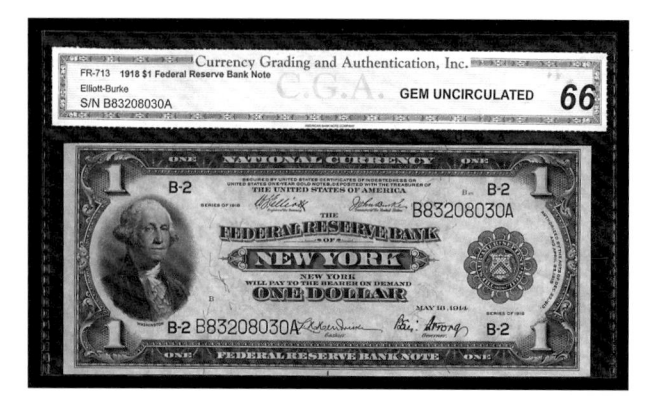

13438 **Fr. 713 $1 1918 Federal Reserve Bank Note CGA Gem Uncirculated 66.** Spacious margins grace this New York ace.
From The Collection of Greg Southward **(500-up)**

13439 **Fr. 713 $1 1918 Federal Reserve Bank Note Gem New.** Dark inks and embossing are traits of this handsome note.
From The Collection of Greg Southward **(600-up)**

13440 **Fr. 714 $1 1918 Federal Reserve Bank Note PMG Choice Uncirculated 63.** This Philadelphia FRBN Ace has the neat solid serial number C1000000A. It is a very pretty note that carries the PMG comment, "Great Embossing." Two and three-digit special serial number notes are not that hard to locate from this series, but special numbers of this ilk are very hard to come by. **(1,000-up)**

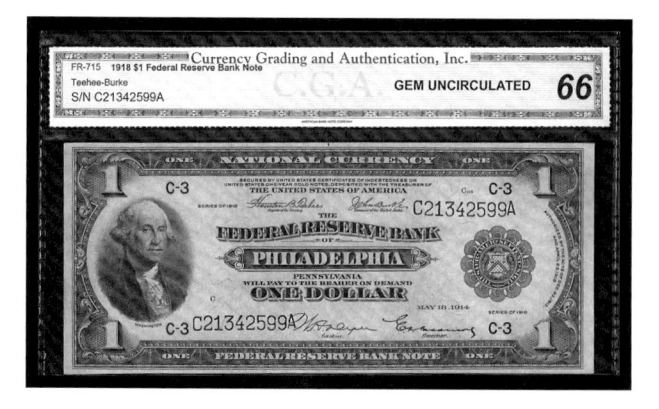

13441 **Fr. 715 $1 1918 Federal Reserve Bank Note CGA Gem Uncirculated 66.** Four solid margins frame this Gem Ace. **(600-up)**

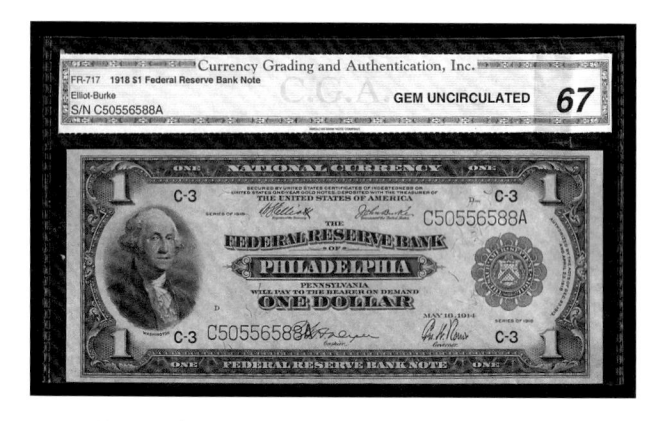

13442 **Fr. 717 $1 1918 Federal Reserve Bank Note CGA Gem Uncirculated 67.** Broad margins and natural paper wave are in tandem on this Philly Ace. **(800-up)**

13443 **Fr. 717 $1 1918 Federal Reserve Bank Note CGA Gem Uncirculated 67.** Pleasing paper waves and bold embossing are noted on this bright white piece. **(800-up)**

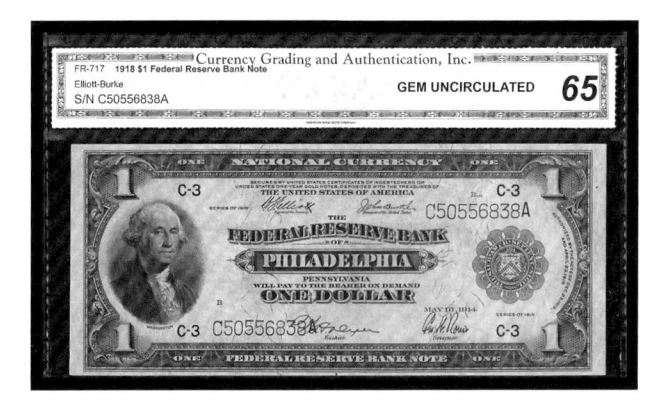

13444 **Fr. 717 $1 1918 Federal Reserve Bank Note CGA Gem Uncirculated 65.** Some as made paper crinkles are noted on the right hand side of this note, but they fail to interrupt the design or aesthetic continuity. **(450-up)**

13445 **Fr. 717 $1 1918 Federal Reserve Bank Note PMG Gem Uncirculated 65 EPQ.** Exceptionally well margined for a Federal Reserve Bank Note.
From The Collection of Greg Southward **(750-up)**

13446 **Fr. 717 $1 1918 Federal Reserve Bank Star Note Fine.** The last time this Star note was available was when we sold it in October 1998. **(350-up)**

13447 **Fr. 718 $1 1918 Federal Reserve Bank Note Choice About New.** Low serial number D22A graces the surfaces of this splendid piece which has a soft horizontal fold visible after much inspection. **(1,000-up)**

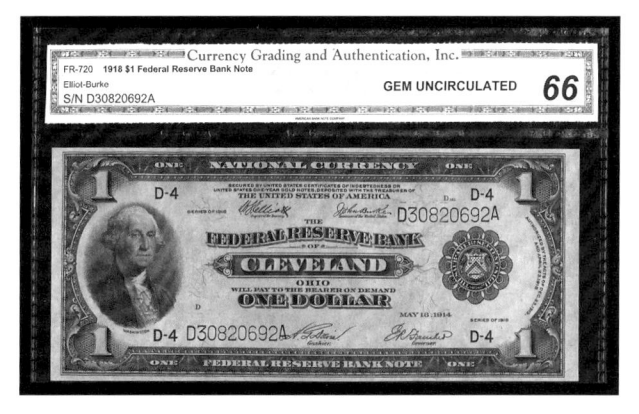

13448 **Fr. 720 $1 1918 Federal Reserve Bank Note CGA Gem Uncirculated 66.** Broad, even margins, ideal colors of the inks and paper plus deep, original embossing all combine on this flawless Cleveland $1. **(700-up)**

13449 **Fr. 720* $1 1918 Federal Reserve Bank Star Note Good-Very Good.** There are only around ten star serial numbers documented in the census for this signature combination. This is only the third one we have encountered since 1990. This Star will not win any beauty contests, but it is so rare. **(400-up)**

13450 **Fr. 722 $1 1918 Federal Reserve Bank Note CGA Choice Uncirculated 63.** A third-party encapsulated Richmond District FRBN Ace which last appeared in our September 2005 Signature sale.
From The Collection of Greg Southward **(400-up)**

13451 **Fr. 723 $1 1918 Federal Reserve Bank Note Very Choice New.** This $1 Atlanta FRBN has traces of embossing and nice color. **(400-up)**

13452 **Fr. 727 $1 1918 Federal Reserve Bank Note CGA Gem Uncirculated 66.** Here is another well embossed "Green Eagle" from Chicago. **(600-up)**

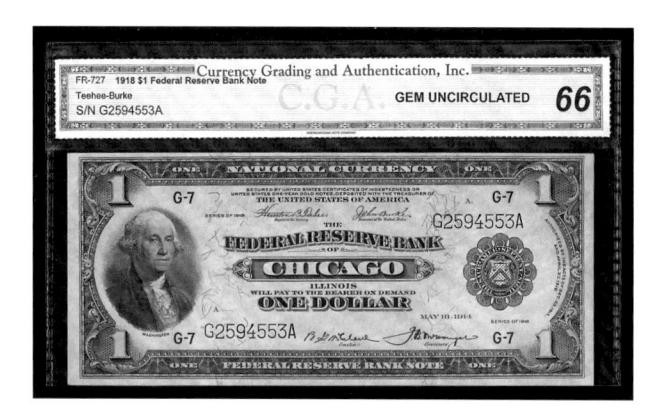

13453 **Fr. 727 $1 1918 Federal Reserve Bank Note CGA Gem Uncirculated 66.** This is a well preserved Chicago $1. **(600-up)**

13454 **Fr. 727 $1 1918 Federal Reserve Bank Note CGA Gem Uncirculated 66.** Serial number and district designator embossing are found on this Ace with natural paper wave. **(600-up)**

13455 **Fr. 727 $1 1918 Federal Reserve Bank Note CGA Gem Uncirculated 66.** Here is yet another lovely example of this ever popular design. **(600-up)**

13456 **Fr. 727 $1 1918 Federal Reserve Bank Note CGA Gem Uncirculated 66.** A nice example of this Chicago District Federal Reserve Bank Note. **(600-up)**

13457 **Fr. 727 $1 1918 Federal Reserve Bank Note CGA Gem Uncirculated 66.** Great paper originality, broad margins, strong color, and great eye appeal. **(600-up)**

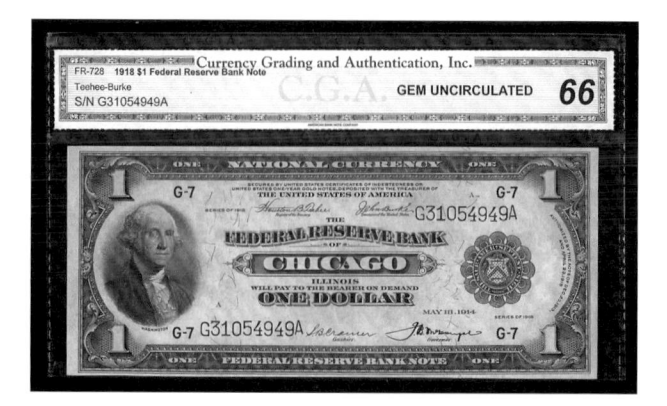

13458 **Fr. 728 $1 1918 Federal Reserve Bank Note CGA Gem Uncirculated 66.** The embossed serial numbers are about to punch through the paper on this example. **(600-up)**

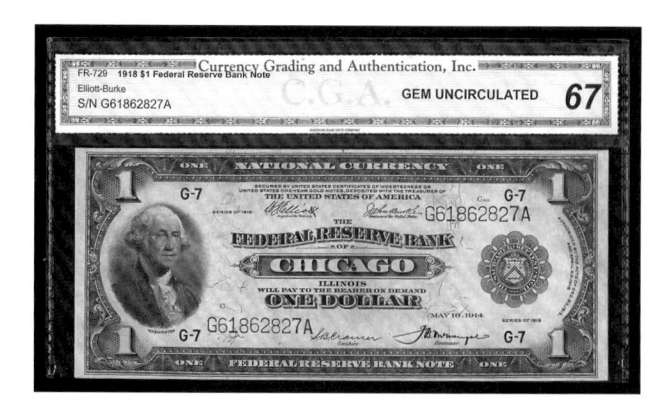

13459 **Fr. 729 $1 1918 Federal Reserve Bank Note CGA Gem Uncirculated 67.** Natural paper wave is noticed on this note. **(800-up)**

13460 **Fr. 729 $1 1918 Federal Reserve Bank Note CGA Gem Uncirculated 66.** Prominent embossing is found on this $1 FRBN. **(600-up)**

13461 Fr. 729 $1 1918 Federal Reserve Bank Note CGA Gem Uncirculated 66. The back upper left corner shows some green inking. (600-up)

13462 Fr. 729 $1 1918 Federal Reserve Bank Note CGA Gem Uncirculated 66. Natural paper wave adorns this Ace. (600-up)

13463 Fr. 729 $1 1918 Federal Reserve Bank Note CGA Gem Uncirculated 66. Bright white paper complements the deep blue overprint. (600-up)

13464 Fr. 729 $1 1918 Federal Reserve Bank Note PCGS Gem New 65PPQ. A beautifully embossed Chicago District FRBN Single that clearly makes the Gem grade. (550-up)

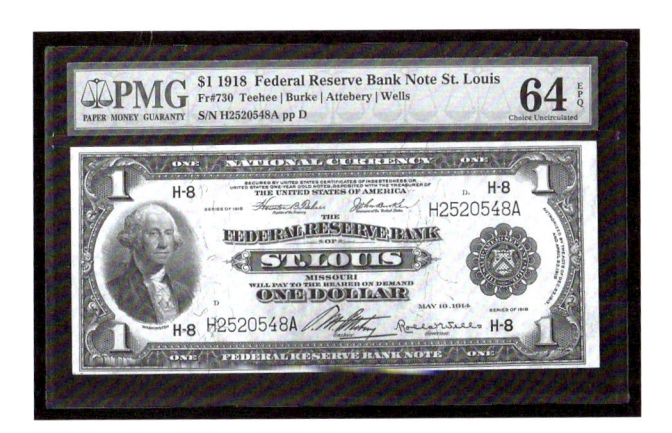

13465 Fr. 730 $1 1918 Federal Reserve Bank Note PMG Choice Uncirculated 64 EPQ. A handsome $1 FRBN that has garnered the EPQ designation, and comes quite close to being a full Gem. (500-up)

13466 Fr. 734 $1 1918 Federal Reserve Bank Note Extremely Fine-About New. This embossed Minneapolis $1 has a couple of light folds.
From The Collection of Greg Southward (200-up)

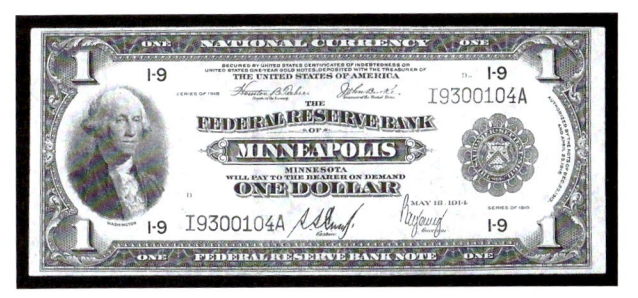

13467 Fr. 735 $1 1918 Federal Reserve Bank Note Very Fine. Of the three Minneapolis Friedberg numbers for this design, this is by far the scarcest. In fact Fr. 735 was long considered the scarcest $1 FRBN. With the census data of today, several other $1 FRBN Friedberg numbers are known to be scarcer. Nonetheless, this is still a scarce note. The surfaces are soft on this example.
From The Collection of Greg Southward (500-up)

13468 Fr. 737 $1 1918 Federal Reserve Bank Note CGA Gem Uncirculated 66. This $1 has strong embossing. (600-up)

13469 Fr. 737 $1 1918 Federal Reserve Bank Note CGA Gem Uncirculated 65. A well centered Gem with sharp corners and excellent eye appeal for the grade. Plenty of embossing is seen. (500-up)

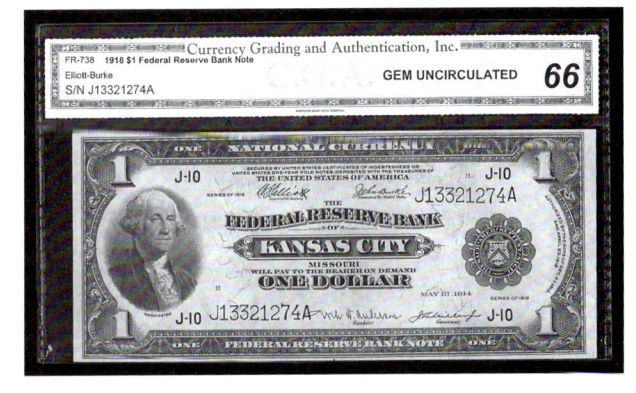

13470 Fr. 738 $1 1918 Federal Reserve Bank Note CGA Gem Uncirculated 66. The embossing is more defined on the bottom serial number of this $1. (600-up)

13471 Fr. 738 $1 1918 Federal Reserve Bank Note CGA Gem Uncirculated 66. Embossing is noticed on this KC Ace. (600-up)

13472 Fr. 738 $1 1918 Federal Reserve Bank Note CGA Gem Uncirculated 66. Each digit of the serial number is embossed on this example. (600-up)

13473 Fr. 738 $1 1918 Federal Reserve Bank Note CGA Gem Uncirculated 66. A bright and lovely, well-margined example that is a trifle flat. Not a rare number, but an exceptionally high-grade note. (600-up)

13474 Fr. 738 $1 1918 Federal Reserve Bank Note CGA Gem Uncirculated 66. A glorious "Eagle Holding Flag" that is surrounded by huge margins and exhibits original paper surfaces through the holder.
From The Collection of Greg Southward (600-up)

13475 Fr. 738 $1 1918 Federal Reserve Bank Note Gem New. Centering and face to back registration is pretty near bull's-eye perfect on this note.
From The Collection of Greg Southward (550-up)

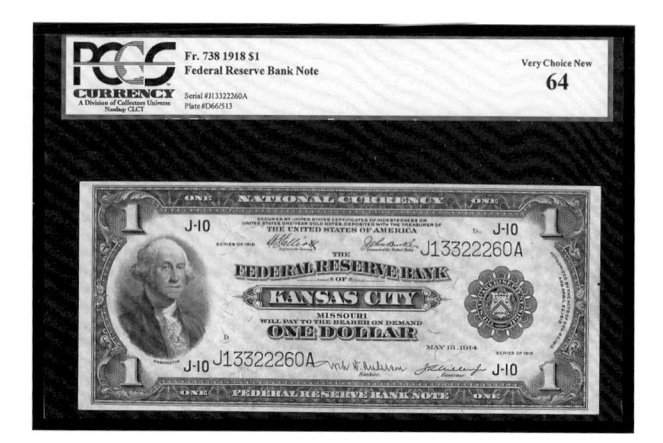

13476 Fr. 738 $1 1918 Federal Reserve Bank Note PCGS Very Choice New 64. A nicely centered "Eagle Holding Flag" note off the tougher KC district.
From The Collection of Greg Southward (500-up)

13477 Fr. 738 $1 1918 Federal Reserve Bank Note Choice New. This embossed note falls neatly within a run of CU notes in the census. (350-up)

13478 Fr. 738 $1 1918 Federal Reserve Bank Note Choice New. A decent Kansas City FRBN Ace. (400-up)

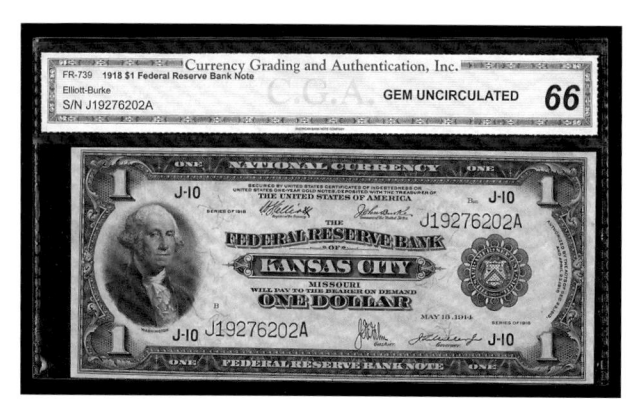

13479 Fr. 739 $1 1918 Federal Reserve Bank Note CGA Gem Uncirculated 66. Bold embossing adorns this $1. (600-up)

13480 Fr. 739 $1 1918 Federal Reserve Bank Note CGA Gem Uncirculated 66. Strong punch through embossing is on this well margined note. (600-up)

13481 Fr. 739 $1 1918 Federal Reserve Bank Note CGA Gem Uncirculated 66. A beautifully centered, fully bright, well embossed strictly original Kansas City FRBN Ace. (600-up)

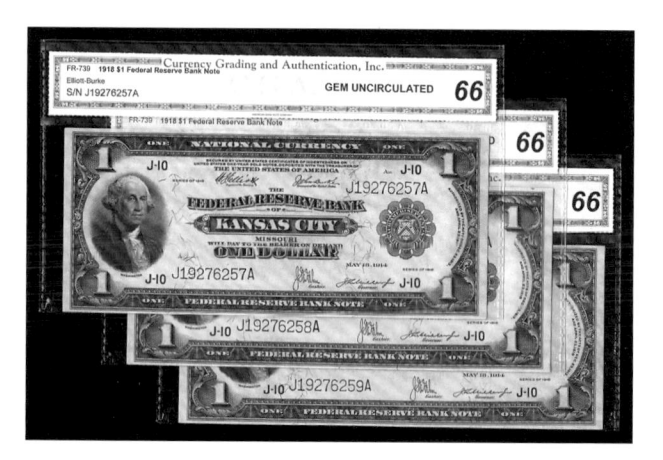

13482 Fr. 739 $1 1918 Federal Reserve Bank Notes Three Consecutive Examples CGA Gem Uncirculated 66. This wonderful trio was separated from the D position note. Pleasing surfaces can be seen beneath the holders. (Total: 3 notes) (1,750-up)

13483 Fr. 739 $1 1918 Federal Reserve Bank Note CGA Gem Uncirculated 65. The punch through embossing on the district seal is quite pronounced. (500-up)

13484 Fr. 739 $1 1918 Federal Reserve Bank Note CGA Gem Uncirculated 65. A touch of tightness along the top margin holds this deeply inked example from a higher grade. (500-up)

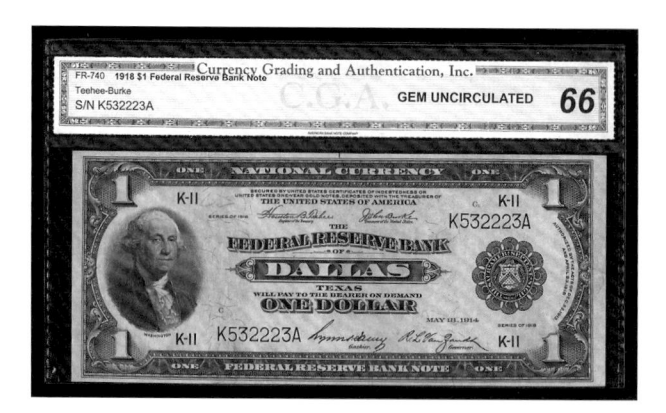

13485 Fr. 740 $1 1918 Federal Reserve Bank Note CGA Gem Uncirculated 66. Embossing of the serial numbers and paper waves are noted through the third party holder. The overprint is bold on this Dallas Ace. (600-up)

13486 Fr. 740 $1 1918 Federal Reserve Bank Note PCGS Very Choice New 64PPQ. A well embossed, strictly original near Gem example. (450-up)

13487 Fr. 741 $1 1918 Federal Reserve Bank Note PMG Choice Extremely Fine 45. Two light folds account for the grade on this note which boasts uncirculated attributes such as perfect paper waves and embossing.
From The Collection of Greg Southward (400-up)

13488 **Fr. 743 $1 1918 Federal Reserve Bank Note CGA Gem Uncirculated 66.** Unusually broad margins for the type combined with excellent color and deep original embossing. A very nice San Francisco FRBN Ace.
From The Collection of Greg Southward **(650-up)**

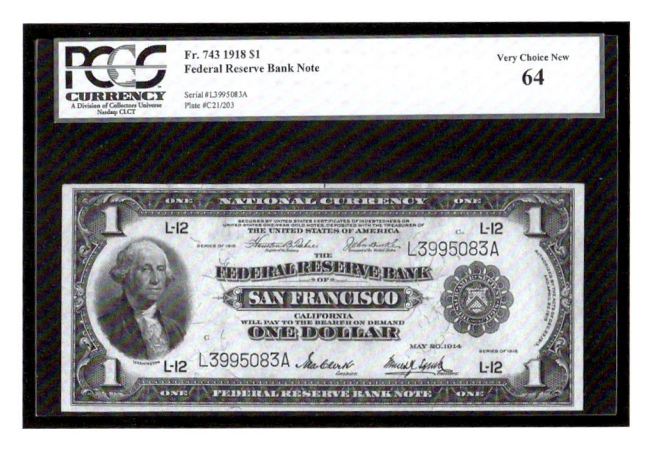

13489 **Fr. 743 $1 1918 Federal Reserve Bank Note PCGS Very Choice New 64.** The most common of the San Francisco FRBN's, but a real beauty that would be a perfect Gem with just a touch more bottom margin at lower right. **(400-up)**

13490 **Fr. 749 $2 1918 Federal Reserve Bank Note Very Fine.** This Deuce evenly circulated and it has two pinholes at top center just inside the frame line.
From The Collection of Greg Southward **(500-up)**

13491 **Fr. 751 $2 1918 Federal Reserve Bank Note CGA Gem Uncirculated 67.** The margins here are broad for the issue and the paper is bright with sharp corners, complementing the deep blue overprint. **(4,500-up)**

13492 **Fr. 751 $2 1918 Federal Reserve Bank Note Very Fine-Extremely Fine.** Bright white paper still exists on this lightly folded Big Apple Battleship. **(650-up)**

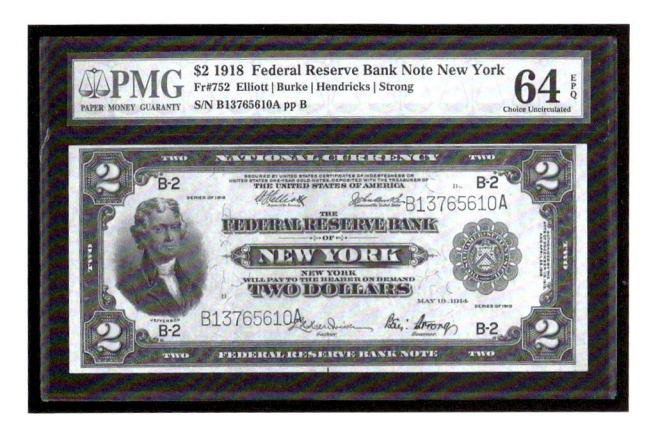

13493 **Fr. 752 $2 1918 Federal Reserve Bank Note PMG Choice Uncirculated 64 EPQ.** Strong embossing has earned this Battleship its EPQ modifier. **(2,750-up)**

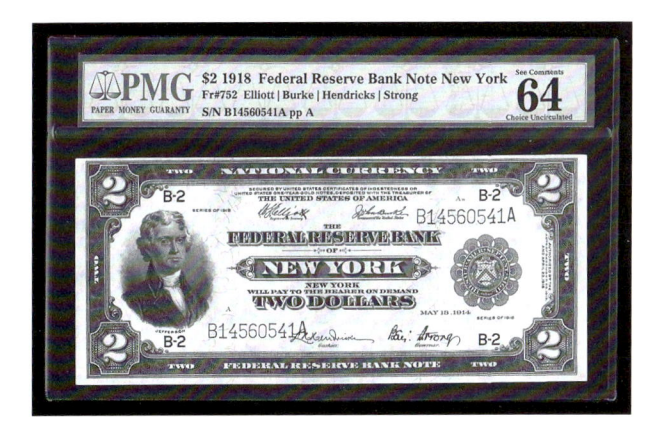

13494 **Fr. 752 $2 1918 Federal Reserve Bank Note PMG Choice Uncirculated 64 EPQ.** Embossing is easily viewed through the third-party holder. **(2,750-up)**

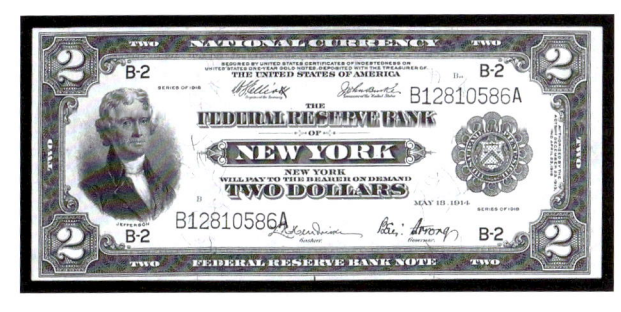

13495 **Fr. 752 $2 1918 Federal Reserve Bank Note Choice New.** Good original embossing and broad margins carry this New York District Battleship quite close to the full Gem grade. **(2,750-up)**

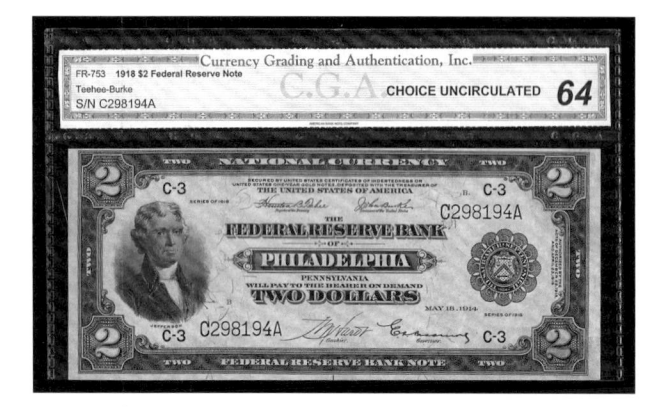

13496 **Fr. 753 $2 1918 Federal Reserve Bank Note CGA Choice Uncirculated 64.** This good looking Battleship appears to be even higher in grade and downgraded due solely to the tight top margin. **(2,250-up)**

13497 **Fr. 756 $2 1918 Federal Reserve Bank Note Fine-Very Fine.** The face is bright while the back shows some light soiling. **(475-up)**

13498 **Fr. 757 $2 1918 Federal Reserve Bank Note PCGS Gem New 66PPQ.** This appealing Battleship boasts a three digit serial number, D303A. The embossing is strong and the paper waves are unmistakably original. **(3,750-up)**

13499 **Fr. 765 $2 1918 Federal Reserve Bank Note Choice About New.** The tiniest of corner folds is noted on this issue. Its intrusion into the design is minimal and fails to interrupt any of the details on this popular type note. **(1,000-up)**

13500 **Fr. 767 $2 1918 Federal Reserve Bank Note CGA Gem Uncirculated 65.** Upper serial number embossing is strong on this Battleship. **(4,000-up)**

13501 **Fr. 767 $2 1918 Federal Reserve Bank Note PCGS Very Choice New 64PPQ.** This Battleship cruises through the natural paper waves of this lovely Deuce. This note was last available in May 1981 during a Steve Ivy auction of the Royce Samuels Collection. **(2,750-up)**

13502 **Fr. 767 $2 1918 Federal Reserve Bank Note Very Fine-Extremely Fine.** The seas of circulation have left this Battleship with light handling and a little soil at the back right quarter panel.
From The Collection of Greg Southward **(550-up)**

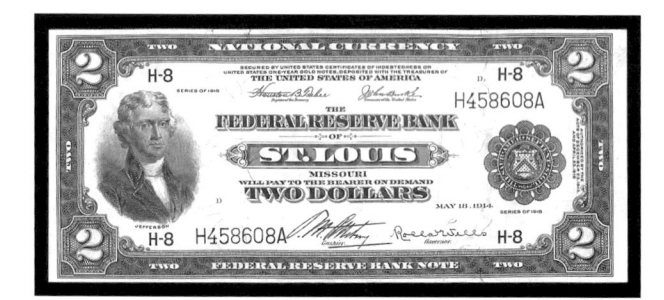

13503 **Fr. 768 $2 1918 Federal Reserve Bank Note Very Fine-Extremely Fine.** "Federal Reserve Bank" still maintains embossing on this Battleship from a tougher district. **(1,000-up)**

13504 **Fr. 769 $2 1918 Federal Reserve Bank Note CGA Very Good 08.** The census of eleven known notes makes this one of the rarest Battleship Friedberg numbers. That figure does not include this note. The note is well circulated to be sure, but it exhibits no problems that are not wholly commensurate with its assigned grade. **(1,250-up)**

13505 **Fr. 772 $2 1918 Federal Reserve Bank Note CGA Gem Uncirculated 65.** The certified grade of 65 appears to be right on the money. This note falls within a run of about 75 mostly consecutive notes, almost all of which are listed in the Gengerke census as CU.
From The Collection of Greg Southward **(2,250-up)**

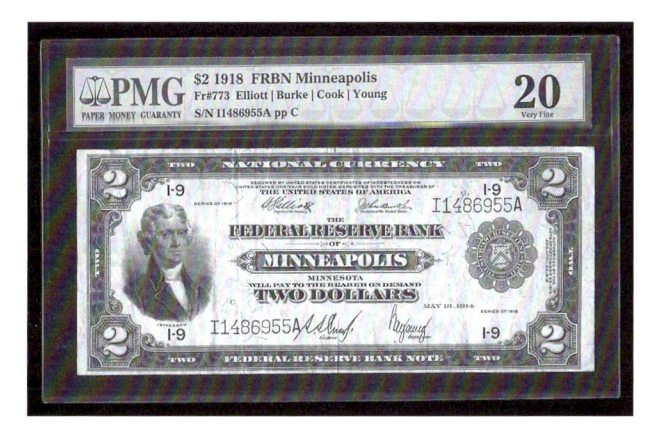

13506 **Fr. 773 $2 1918 Federal Reserve Bank Note PMG Very Fine 20.** The face of this Battleship is a little brighter than its back. **(450-up)**

13507 **Fr. 774 $2 1918 Federal Reserve Bank Note PCGS Very Fine 30.** This Battleship is evenly circulated save for one heavier than average fold.
From The Collection of Greg Southward **(400-up)**

13508 **Fr. 776 $2 1918 Federal Reserve Bank Note Gem New.** The colors on this Battleship Deuce are gorgeous, and the value is considerably enhanced by the clearly evident deep, original embossing. High-end Battleships, particularly from the scarcer Dallas district, are not at all easy to come by, and this piece will likely bring very near or slightly over...
From The Jacob and Heather Dedman Collection **(4,000-up)**

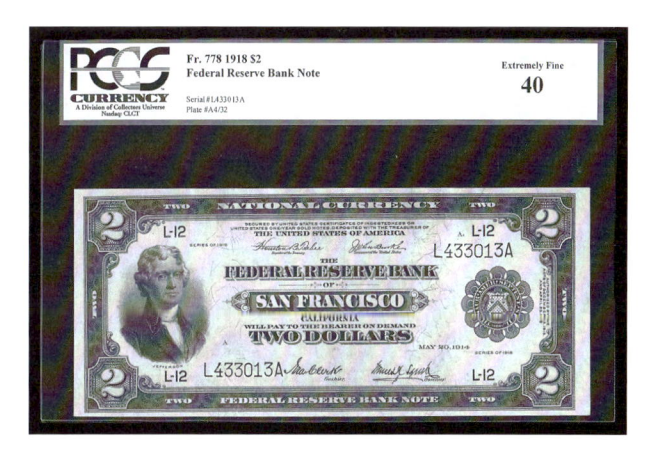

13509 **Fr. 778 $2 1918 Federal Reserve Bank Note PCGS Extremely Fine 40.** A very broadly margined San Francisco Battleship Deuce with strong color. **(750-up)**

13510   **Fr. 779 $2 1918 Federal Reserve Bank Note CGA Extremely Fine 40.** This is only the fifth one of this Friedberg number that we have offered over the years. It also has the lowest serial number in the census for this Friedberg number out of a total population of around 20.
From The Collection of Greg Southward **(750-up)**

13511   **Fr. 779 $2 1918 Federal Reserve Bank Note PCGS Extremely Fine 40.** The folds are light on this San Fran Battleship.
From The Collection of Greg Southward **(750-up)**

13512   **Fr. 782 $5 1918 Federal Reserve Bank Note Very Fine.** Embossing is seen behind "Federal Reserve Bank" and "Five Dollars" at center on this New York $5.
From The Collection of Greg Southward **(600-up)**

13513   **Fr. 782 $5 1918 Federal Reserve Bank Note Very Fine.** This is an evenly circulated New York $5 that shows a little paper disturbance in the back bottom margin. **(550-up)**

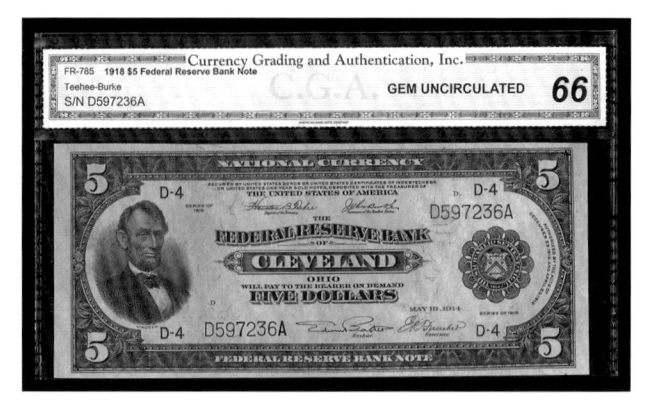

13514   **Fr. 785 $5 1918 Federal Reserve Bank Note CGA Gem Uncirculated 66.** Broad margins for the issue are noted on this bright Cleveland FRBN. This note comes from a run of uncirculated notes that are Gem or better. **(1,750-up)**

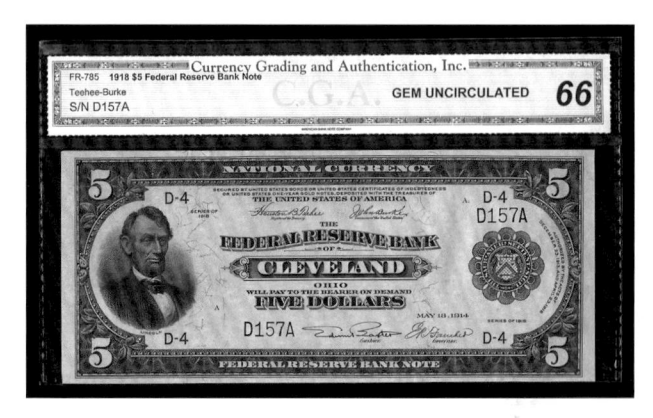

13515   **Fr. 785 $5 1918 Federal Reserve Bank Note CGA Gem Uncirculated 66.** An attractive Cleveland FRBN with a three digit serial number. The paper is blazing white and the margins boardwalk in width for the issue. **(2,500-up)**

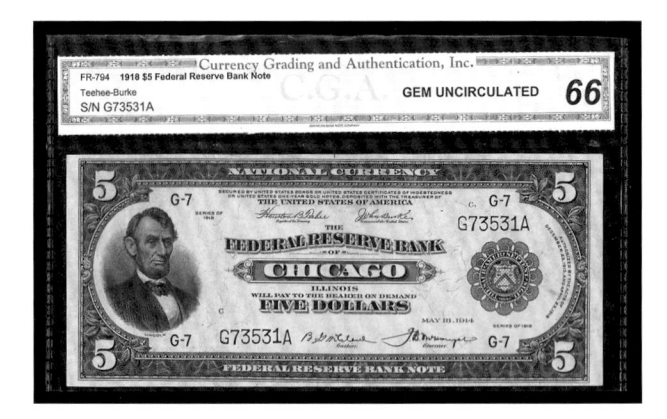

13516   **Fr. 794 $5 1918 Federal Reserve Bank Note CGA Gem Uncirculated 66.** A touch of handling is noted at the left end of this fully margined Chicago issue.
From The Collection of Greg Southward **(3,500-up)**

FEDERAL RESERVE NOTES

13517 **Fr. 832b $5 1914 Red Seal Federal Reserve Note Very Fine-Extremely Fine.** Nice color is found on this unreported $5 that is from near the end of the print run for Boston. Only around 20 serial numbers have been documented for this Friedberg number in the census. The paper is bright and the red overprint is delightful.
From The Bill and Kathy Stella Currency Collection
(550-up)

13518 **Fr. 833a $5 1914 Red Seal Federal Reserve Note Fine.** A's are outnumbered by b's for this Friedberg number by around three to one. The red overprint is bold on this $5 that has two small holes. The back has a 1911 inscription penned in a margin and there is also a penned phrase in a face margin that has mostly faded away. **(450-up)**

13519 **Fr. 833b $5 1914 Red Seal Federal Reserve Note CGA Gem Uncirculated 67.** The bright red seal and serial numbers complement the perfectly white paper. The margins are particularly broad for a FRN. **(3,500-up)**

13520 **Fr. 833b $5 1914 Red Seal Federal Reserve Note CGA Gem Uncirculated 66.** The margins are almost perfectly even, with only a millimeter of variance throughout their entire lengths. Add vivid, white paper and a well embossed overprint and the note is certainly worthy of a Gem grade. **(3,250-up)**

13521 **Fr. 833b $5 1914 Red Seal Federal Reserve Note Very Fine.** This Red Seal $5 is dressed in original surfaces. The upper serial number still exhibits some embossing, too. The paper is also bright and the red overprint complements it greatly. There is an approximate quarter inch tear at bottom center of this attractive mid-grade note.
From The Bill and Kathy Stella Currency Collection
(400-up)

13522 **Fr. 834a $5 1914 Red Seal Federal Reserve Note Very Fine.** This example has original surfaces, sound edges, and a dark red overprint. Red Seal a's are outnumbered by b's for this Friedberg number by almost three to one. Overall a nice mid-grade representative. **(800-up)**

13523 **Fr. 834b $5 1914 Red Seal Federal Reserve Note Extremely Fine-About New.** This is a lovely high end circulated example which displays bold colors, great paper quality, and immaculate centering. Expect this Red Seal to realize far more than your average EF-AU specimen. **(900-up)**

13524 **Fr. 835b $5 1914 Red Seal Federal Reserve Note CGA Very Fine 20.** This moderately circulated Red Seal retains most of its original color. To date only about 45 examples of this issue have been reported. **(1,000-up)**

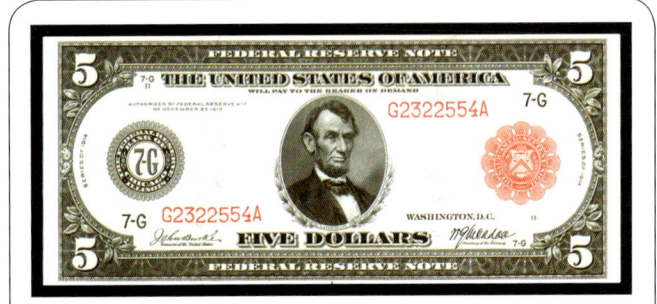

13525 **Fr. 838b $5 1914 Red Seal Federal Reserve Note Gem New.** Last seen in our 2006 Long Beach sale, described as, "This note was last sold by CAA in 2000 and not much has changed over the years. Perfect centering, monster margins, vibrant color, and plenty of eye appeal are noticed. Definitely a type note that will be put away again for many years by its new owner." In today's market, years are replaced by months... **(4,000-up)**

13526 **Fr. 839b $5 1914 Red Seal Federal Reserve Note Very Good.** This is a scarce note on St. Louis. Low grade Red Seal FRNs are the rule, not the exception. **(250-up)**

13527 **Fr. 843b $5 1914 Red Seal Federal Reserve Note Very Good.** This is a well circulated $5 San Fran Red Seal that has been able to retain some snap to its paper. **(300-up)**

13528 **Fr. 845 $5 1914 Federal Reserve Note Very Fine.** A perfectly natural note, and a very scarce one at that, with fewer than twenty five pieces known in all grades combined. **(400-up)**

13529 **Fr. 847a $5 1914 Federal Reserve Note CGA Gem Uncirculated 66.** Some light handling is noted on this otherwise fully original issue. **(350-up)**

13530 **Fr. 847a $5 1914 Federal Reserve Note Gem New.** Dark inks, embossing, and original paper ripple are highlights of this attractive Boston $5. **(500-up)**

13531 **Fr. 850 $5 1914 Federal Reserve Note CGA Gem Uncirculated 65.** A great-looking New York-district Five Dollar Fed, with the scarcer Burke-Houston signature combination. **(400-up)**

13532 **Fr. 850 $5 1914 Federal Reserve Note Very Choice New.** The margins are a touch skewed keeping this piece from the Gem grade. **(350-up)**

13533 **Fr. 851a $5 1914 Federal Reserve Note Gem New.** Although this is the more common "a" variety for this type, the quality is excellent. The margins are very plentiful and there is embossing, natural paper wave, and bright dark blue ink. **(400-up)**

13534 **Fr. 859c $5 1914 Federal Reserve Note Extremely Fine.** The seals are moved closer to the portrait on the "c" varieties. William Philpott and Tom Bain's research pinned the dates down for the printing of the "c" varieties from January to June 1928. This example has nice color and inks while the handling is concentrated at center. **(350-up)**

13535 Fr. 863a $5 1914 Federal Reserve Note Extremely Fine-About New. Original surfaces that include serial number embossing are highlights of this Richmond $5. (350-up)

13536 Fr. 868 $5 1914 Federal Reserve Note PMG Superb Gem Unc 67 EPQ. The label tells us that this $5 note has "Exceptional Paper Quality and Great Margins." It is not a particularly rare note, but certainly not common at this upper grade level. In fact this is the highest graded note we have had from this issue. (750-up)

13537 Fr. 869 $5 1914 Federal Reserve Note About New. A high end Burke-Glass example that appears Choice New or better until very closely examined. (400-up)

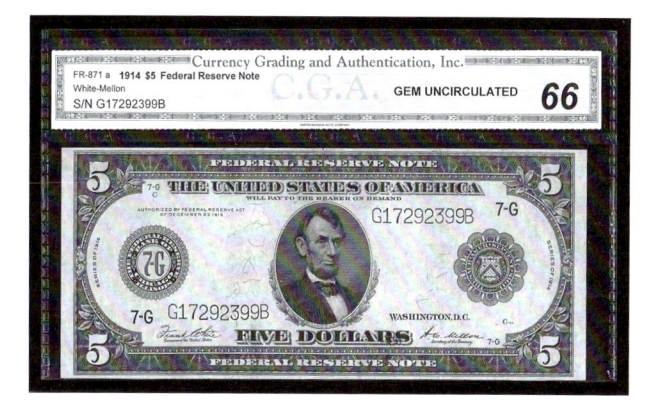

13538 Fr. 871a $5 1914 Federal Reserve Note CGA Gem Uncirculated 66. Original paper surfaces are viewed through the third-party holder. (400-up)

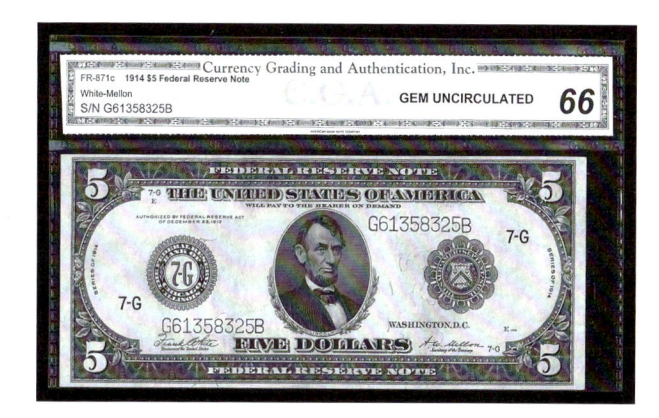

13539 Fr. 871c $5 1914 Federal Reserve Note CGA Gem Uncirculated 66. A somewhat challenging number with excellent eye appeal. The example we offer this evening has pack fresh paper surfaces and enjoys the status of a Gem. (600-up)

13540 Fr. 879a $5 1914 Federal Reserve Note PMG Choice Uncirculated 64 EPQ. A plethora of circulated examples of this issue are known to collectors. However, uncirculated notes are a bit scarcer with only one other appearance of an uncirculated issue in the last year and half. This piece shows fairly even margins and excellent paper quality. (600-up)

13541 **Fr. 881 $5 1914 Federal Reserve Note Very Choice New.** Embossing, nice centering, and natural paper wave are highlights of this scarce KC $5. We sold the preceding serial number note that is a carbon copy of this note in May 2002 for over $500. In fact this and the other note discussed are the highest graded examples we have ever sold of this Friedberg number. This Kansas City Burke-Glass $5 is represented in the census with less than 20 recorded serial numbers. **(500-up)**

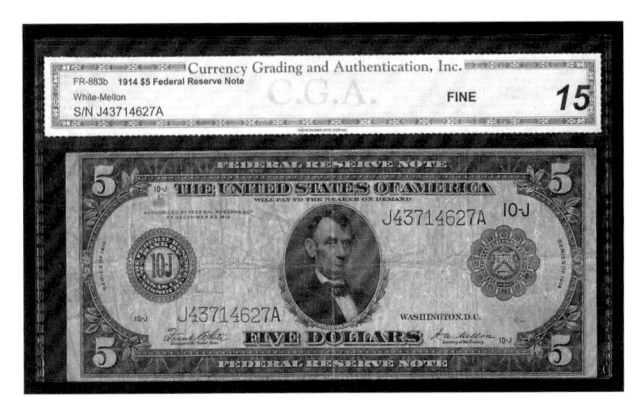

13542 **Fr. 883b $5 1914 Federal Reserve Note CGA Fine 15.** A mere 12 survivors are recorded for this "B" variety, all of which are circulated. This piece is the first of those to be offered at public auction since 2005. The paper shows signs of moderate wear and is likely original. **(500-up)**

Rare $5 Fr. 891c

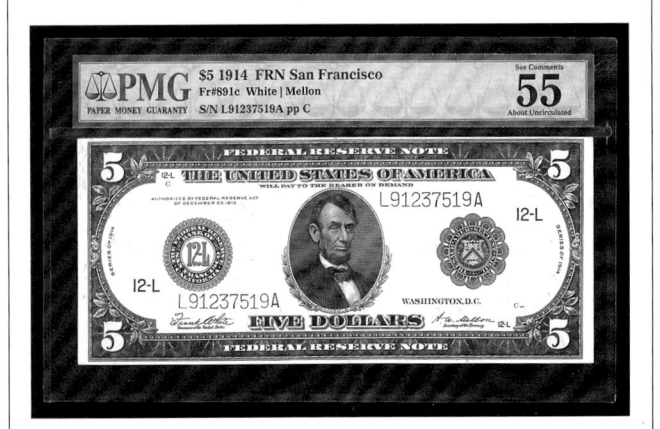

13543 **Fr. 891c $5 1914 Federal Reserve Note PMG About Uncirculated 55 EPQ.** This is a rare Friedberg number with only around ten serial numbers in the census and one of those notes is in the Smithsonian Institution. The current example is a new addition to the census with it possibly being the nicest known. **(1,200-up)**

13544 **Fr. 893b $10 1914 Red Seal Federal Reserve Note PMG Choice Fine 15.** Despite the moderate amounts of circulation, the seal and serial numbers remain bold. **(450-up)**

13545 **Fr. 893b $10 1914 Red Seal Federal Reserve Note PCGS Fine 15.** This is a pleasingly original note with a bold red overprint. We must mention for accuracy's sake that there is a bit of light showing through the intersection of the vertical fold and center fold. **(350-up)**

13546 **Fr. 898b $10 1914 Red Seal Federal Reserve Note PMG Choice Very Fine 35.** The overprint has avoided the ravages of age and remains deep red.
From The Collection of Greg Southward **(750-up)**

13547 **Fr. 898b $10 1914 Red Seal Federal Reserve Note Fine.** The Chicago "b's" are a little scarcer than the "a's" for this Friedberg number. The BEP got its red ink from Germany at this time. The start of World War I cut this trade off, necessitating the switch to blue ink for FRNs. **(400-up)**

Rare $10 San Fran Red Seal

13548 **Fr. 903a $10 1914 Red Seal Federal Reserve Note Fine.** This is a new addition to the census for this rare Friedberg number. It also becomes the new low serial number and the first four-digit serial number note for this Friedberg number. There are around 15 notes documented with one note residing in the collection of the Smithsonian. Also, the last auction offering was almost four years ago. This example has a brighter face than back and the edges are nice for the grade. The red overprint is darker than what is usually seen at this grade level, too. **(1,000-up)**

13549 **Fr. 905 $10 1914 Federal Reserve Note Very Fine.** A nice Burke-Glass example which is definitely in the top half of the reported population. **(350-up)**

13550 **Fr. 907a $10 1914 Federal Reserve Note CGA Gem Uncirculated 66.** This brilliantly white issue boasts particularly large margins for the issue. **(500-up)**

13551 **Fr. 907b $10 1914 Federal Reserve Note Very Choice New.** A very scarce note in this grade, with only a literal handful of examples reported. This bright and beautifully margined piece is certainly one of the best, if not the best. **(900-up)**

13552 **Fr. 907b $10 1914 Federal Reserve Note Choice Crisp Uncirculated.** This is a well preserved note that is blessed with embossing and natural paper surfaces. This scarce note is unreported, but it falls neatly within a range of a mini-run of CU notes in the census. **(750-up)**

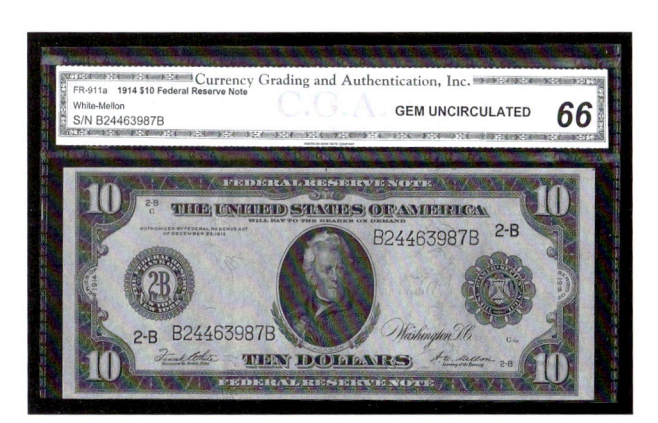

13553 **Fr. 911a $10 1914 Federal Reserve Note CGA Gem Uncirculated 66.** Solid margins are noted all around the face design and the front to back centering is ideal. When viewed from the back, embossing is noted on the serial numbers. For those aficionados of minor errors, the right serial number is so irregular that is appears to be printed on a curve. **(700-up)**

13554 **Fr. 911b $10 1914 Federal Reserve Note PMG Gem Uncirculated 65 EPQ.** Broad margins and original paper surfaces highlight this New York $10. **(550-up)**

13555 **Fr. 915a $10 1914 Federal Reserve Note CGA About Uncirculated 58.** Though the paper is a touch toned, it is fully New with the exception of a lone center fold. **(250-up)**

13556 **Fr. 918 $10 1914 Federal Reserve Note Very Choice New.** A little too much handling for the Gem designation is noticed on this vibrantly hued note. Purchased by our consignor for $119 many years ago. **(600-up)**

13557 **Fr. 933 $10 1914 Federal Reserve Note Fine.** An honest and unmolested example of this better Burke-Glass number. **(350-up)**

High Grade Kansas City $10 Star

13558 **Fr. 942 $10 1914 Federal Reserve Star Note Very Fine-Extremely Fine.** A lovely fully natural piece which is new to the census and offered here to the collecting fraternity for the first time. The inks are bright and the margins full and even, giving this star great eye appeal to go along with its scarcity. **(1,250-up)**

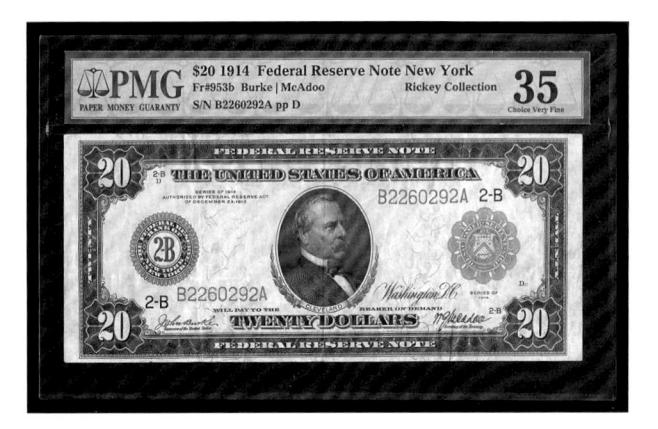

13559 **Fr. 953b $20 1914 Red Seal Federal Reserve Note PMG Choice Very Fine 35.** A bold red seal contrasts nicely against the perfectly original and bright white paper on this moderately circulated issue. Not even a hint of soil is noted making this the ideal VF for any collection.
From The Collection of Greg Southward **(1,500-up)**

13560 **Fr. 958b $20 1914 Red Seal Federal Reserve Note Fine.** The "b" variety is more than twice as scarce as the "a" variety for this Friedberg number with less than 20 serial numbers recorded. This note exhibits even wear with an approximate quarter inch top edge tear. **(1,000-up)**

13561 **Fr. 959a $20 1914 Red Seal Federal Reserve Note Very Good-Fine.** We see on the average about one of this Friedberg number per year. The Treasury Seal has faded some on this example. **(250-up)**

13562 **Fr. 959b $20 1914 Red Seal Federal Reserve Note Very Fine-Extremely Fine.** This is a rare note in all grades, with the census showing just one dozen examples extant. This piece is on that short list, and is the only one without any sales history. It is bright for the grade, and comes with plenty of eye appeal as well. If rarity is any guide, expect this note to surprise before the hammer falls this evening. **(2,000-up)**

13563 **Fr. 962 $20 1914 Red Seal Federal Reserve Note Choice About New.** After much coaxing a very soft horizontal fold makes its presence known. This piece is Gem quality with behemoth margins and pristine surfaces. Great eye appeal is derived from the deep red overprint on this piece which lists 18 known in the census. **(4,000-up)**

13564 **Fr. 975 $20 1914 Federal Reserve Note CGA Gem Uncirculated 65.** Only one variety is known for this Friedberg number. **(450-up)**

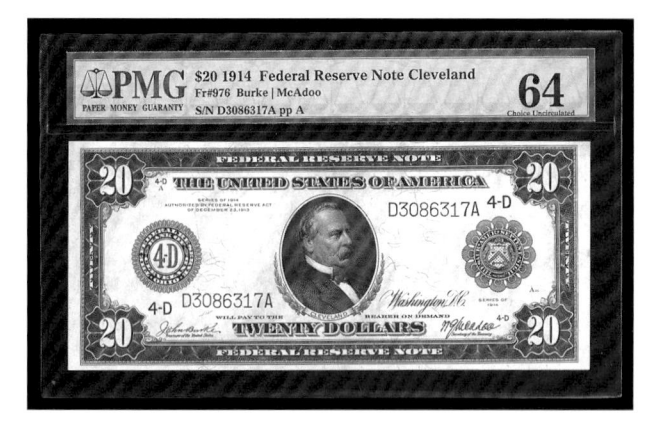

13565 **Fr. 976 $20 1914 Federal Reserve Note PMG Choice Uncirculated 64.** A somewhat scarcer Fed number. **(400-up)**

13566 **Fr. 977 $20 1914 Federal Reserve Note Extremely Fine-About New.** A lovely Burke-Glass note which appears new until closely examined and which is far above the average grade for this scarce Friedberg number. (700-up)

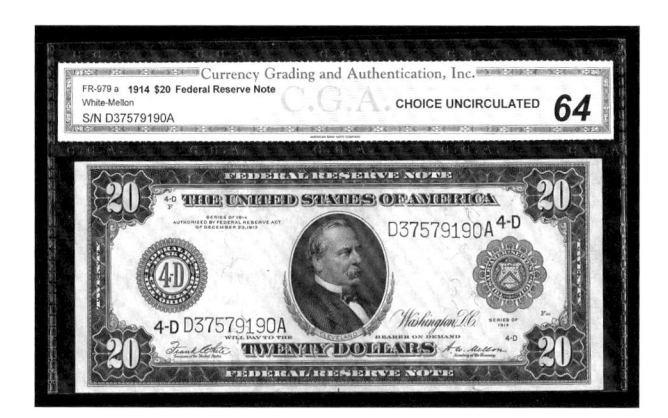

13567 **Fr. 979a $20 1914 Federal Reserve Note CGA Choice Uncirculated 64.** We have had only a couple of notes of this Friedberg number as nice as this example over the last six years. (350-up)

13568 **Fr. 979a $20 1914 Federal Reserve Note Extremely Fine.** This $20 looks to be of a higher grade at first glance. However, light handling can be observed with diligence. (200-up)

13569 **Fr. 980 $20 1914 Federal Reserve Note Fine.** A scarce note, with only eleven pieces reported in Fine or better grade. (350-up)

13570 **Fr. 982 $20 1914 Federal Reserve Star Note Very Fine.** This discovery piece brings the total of known Stars for this issue to five and according to the census it rivals one other for finest known. The paper is solid and bright for a moderately circulated piece. There is however a lone ink mark hidden in the details of the face design. (2,500-up)

13571 **Fr. 990 $20 1914 Federal Reserve Star Note PMG Very Fine 25.** This attractive Star boasts wholly original paper, and a vividly colored overprint. A mere two pinholes are noted, but do nothing to detract from the overall appearance. (500-up)

13572 **Fr. 991b $20 1914 Federal Reserve Note Extremely Fine.** A bright and fresh example which displays perfect centering, considerably above average for this Friedberg number. (350-up)

13573 **Fr. 995 $20 1914 Federal Reserve Note Gem New.** Broadly margined, bright and strictly original. Twenty Dollar Feds are quite common, but few are as nice as this one. The face margins are those of a Superb example, and the back only slightly less so. A very handsome note.
From The Jacob and Heather Dedman Collection (500-up)

13574 **Fr. 1002 $20 1914 Federal Reserve Note Choice About New.** This is an embossed KC $20 with original surfaces. It is also one of the nicest examples of this Friedberg number that has around 40 reported in the census. **(300-up)**

Rare Dallas $20 FRN

13575 **Fr. 1005 $20 1914 Federal Reserve Note Very Fine.** This Dallas Burke-Glass $20 is an extremely rare note in all grades, as the census shows just seven examples reported to date and that does not include this note. With the demand for better Friedberg numbers continuing unabated, expect to see some strong bidding on this lot. **(700-up)**

13576 **Fr. 1007 $20 1914 Federal Reserve Note PCGS Very Choice New 64PPQ.** This piece is from a cut sheet that we auctioned over ten years ago. **(500-up)**

13577 **Fr. 1007 $20 1914 Federal Reserve Note Choice New.** This note and the next come from a Dallas district cut sheet which we sold almost ten years ago. Both notes are crackling fresh and gem but for the close trim at the bottom. **(400-up)**

13578 **Fr. 1007 $20 1914 Federal Reserve Note Choice New.** A second fresh and attractive Dallas district example. **(400-up)**

13579 **Fr. 1011a $20 1914 Federal Reserve Note Choice About New.** Plenty of embossing remains on this example that has a soft horizontal fold. **(350-up)**

13580 **Fr. 1025 $50 1914 Federal Reserve Note Very Fine-Extremely Fine.** A Burke-Glass fifty from the Boston district, a scarce note in all grades but particularly so in the higher grade ranges, where the census is under ten examples. **(1,000-up)**

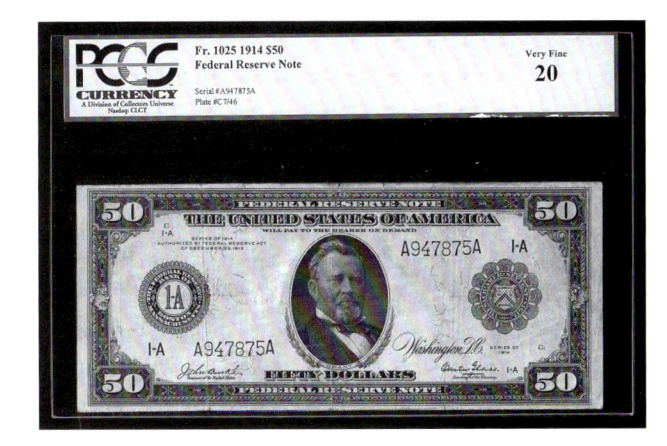

13581 **Fr. 1025 $50 1914 Federal Reserve Note PCGS Very Fine 20.** We are fortunate to have two examples of this type from the Boston district. Burke-Glass notes have fueled interest in the series, making this a desirable issue. **(900-up)**

13582 **Fr. 1029 $50 1914 Federal Reserve Note CGA Very Good-Fine 10.** There are less than 30 examples of this Friedberg number, with this a new number to both the Gengerke and Track & Price census tools. **(400-up)**

13583 **Fr. 1038 $50 1914 Federal Reserve Note CGA Very Fine 25.** The paper on this note is still crisp with nice margins all the way around. The holder mistakenly lists this as a Fr. 1036. **(400-up)**

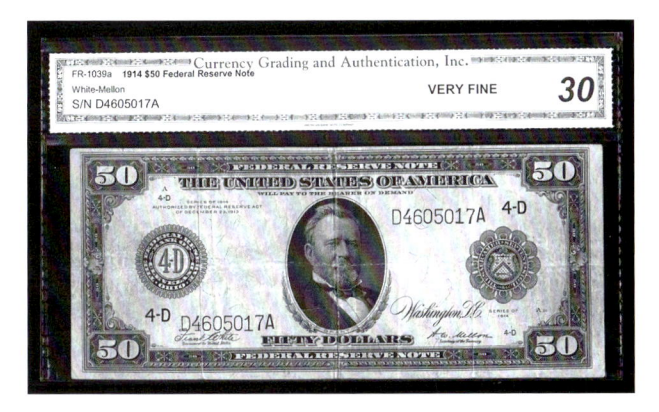

13584 **Fr. 1039a $50 1914 Federal Reserve Note CGA Very Fine 30.** This is a nicer example than usually encountered. **(500-up)**

13585 **Fr. 1039b $50 1914 Federal Reserve Note Fine.** Cleveland "b's" are more than twice as scarce as Cleveland "a's." **(300-up)**

13586 **Fr. 1044 $50 1914 Federal Reserve Note PMG Gem Uncirculated 66 EPQ.** Originally embossed Gem $50 Feds are a rare breed, and this 66 EPQ is one of the nicer examples we've seen over the years. The original embossing is easily deep enough to be seen through the third party holder, and the note is beautifully margined and well-printed. Of the fewer than twenty pieces known for this number, only a half dozen are high grade. This is likely the finest of them. **(7,500-up)**

13587 **Fr. 1048 $50 1914 Federal Reserve Note PCGS Choice New 63PPQ.** Plenty of embossing is spotted beneath the holder of this note which is one of the finest for this Friedberg number we have handled. **(1,500-up)**

13588 **Fr. 1050 $50 1914 Federal Reserve Notes. Two Consecutive Examples. Very Fine.** This consecutive pair of Chicago $50s exhibit similar wear patterns and original paper surfaces. (Total: 2 notes) **(700-up)**

13589 **Fr. 1052 $50 1914 Federal Reserve Note PCGS Very Fine 20.** Fewer than two dozen examples of this $50 are known to collectors. Expect to see some spirited bidding as few of this type seldom turn up. **(800-up)**

13590 **Fr. 1054 $50 1914 Federal Reserve Note Very Fine-Extremely Fine.** This elusive FRN is only a couple horizontal folds away from the higher of the split grades. **(500-up)**

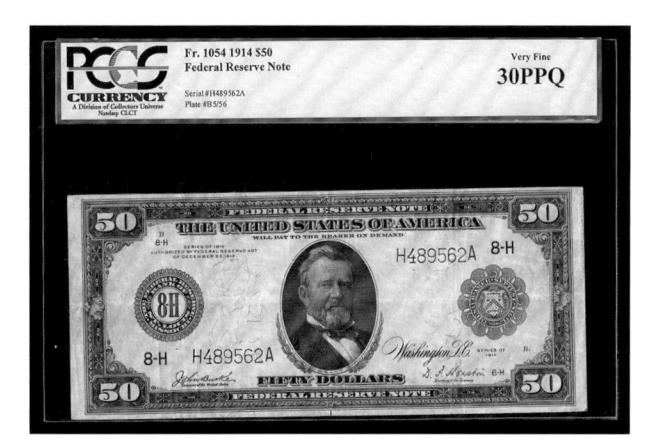

13591 **Fr. 1054 $50 1914 Federal Reserve Note PCGS Very Fine 30PPQ.** A little more than two dozen examples of this Burke-Houston $50 are known in currency circles. This note appears completely original and problem free. **(500-up)**

13592 **Fr. 1084 $100 1914 Federal Reserve Note PCGS Apparent Very Fine 25.** Less than twenty examples are known for this Boston piece. PCGS has printed "Rust Stain on Back" to alert us to the unfortunate problem this piece has. **(600-up)**

13593 **Fr. 1098 $100 1914 Federal Reserve Note Extremely Fine.** This piece appears more AU than EF and has pleasing paper to boot. To date only about 30 examples of this Cleveland issue have been reported according to Track & Price. Though this isn't the highest graded issue known, it is the finest to appear at auction in nearly two years. **(1,500-up)**

CGA Gem 67 $100 Atlanta FRN

13594 **Fr. 1104 $100 1914 Federal Reserve Note CGA Gem Uncirculated 67.** The note's original embossing can be easily seen through the third party holder. A beautifully margined, handsome Atlanta District C-note. This is a very hard type to find in this high a grade. The centering of both sides, as well as the margin size, is terrific. **(4,500-up)**

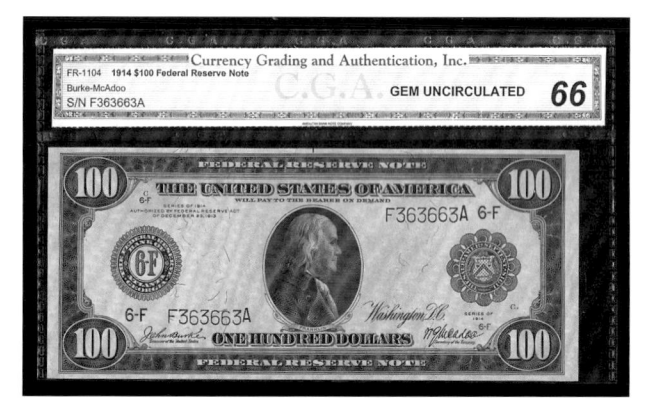

13595 **Fr. 1104 $100 1914 Federal Reserve Note CGA Gem Uncirculated 66.** This Atlanta District $100 Fed has beautifully broad margins, clearly evident original embossing, good color, and the eye appeal that easily carries it to the assigned grade. **(3,500-up)**

13596 **Fr. 1104 $100 1914 Federal Reserve Note PMG Very Fine 25.** Pleasing surfaces are noticed on this Atlanta C-note.
From The Collection of Greg Southward (600-up)

13597 **Fr. 1108 $100 1914 Federal Reserve Note CGA Gem Uncirculated 66.** This note is near a small run of CU examples broken up long ago. Nice margins and decent centering are seen. (2,000-up)

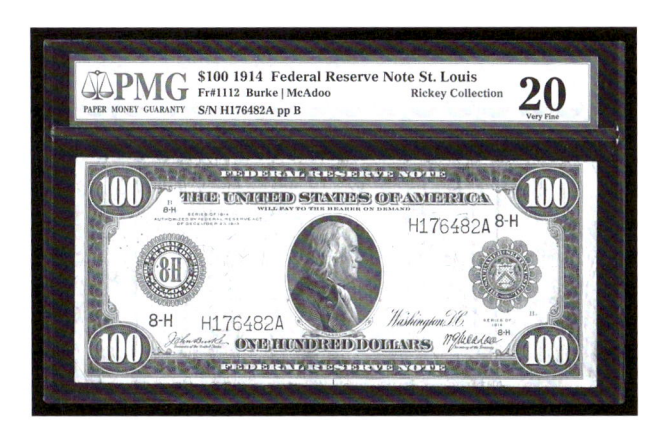

13598 **Fr. 1112 $100 1914 Federal Reserve Note PMG Very Fine 20.** A very pleasing example of this very scarce number which is bright and crisp with good eye appeal and bold printing. There are also a scattering of pinholes throughout mentioned for accuracy's sake. In our 2006 FUN Sale a Very Fine with pinholes sold for $1,265 and we believe this example is strikingly similar in quality. (1,250-up)

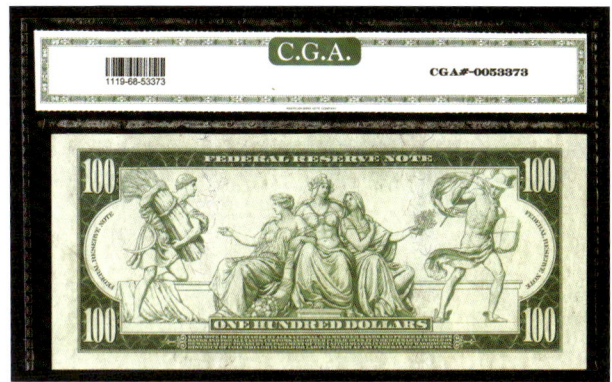

13599 **Fr. 1119 $100 1914 Federal Reserve Note CGA Gem Uncirculated 68.** To date, only nine examples of this Minneapolis $100 are known to currency collectors, this being the finest. It has been off the market for a couple of years and last realized more than $12,000. Broad margins are present on this bright white and original issue. When viewed from the back, embossing of the serial numbers and seal is noted as well as good front to back centering. (15,000-up)

13600 **Fr. 1124 $100 1914 Federal Reserve Note Very Good-Fine.** Dallas is a very scarce district for $100 Feds, and even though this Friedberg number is by far the more common of the two, it's still represented by only around 20 examples. This note shows some edge tears with the longest being approximately a quarter of an inch. The back reveals two paper clip rust outlines and there is a small carbon spot. This note will become the new low serial number in the census. (700-up)

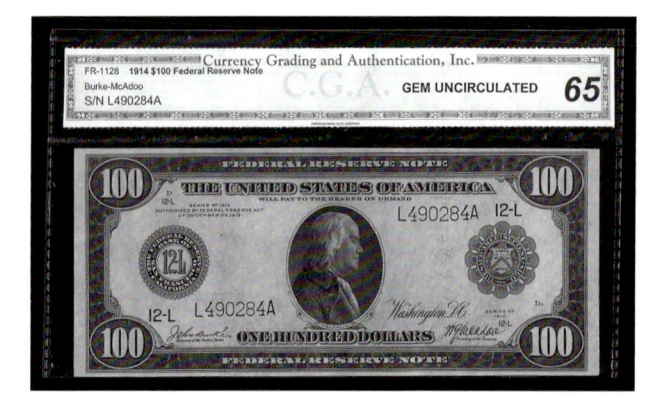

13601 Fr. 1128 $100 1914 Federal Reserve Note CGA Gem Uncirculated 65. A broadly margined $100 Fed that shows bright inks and colors. It appears to have fully earned its Gem 3rd party designation. (2,500-up)

Cleveland $500

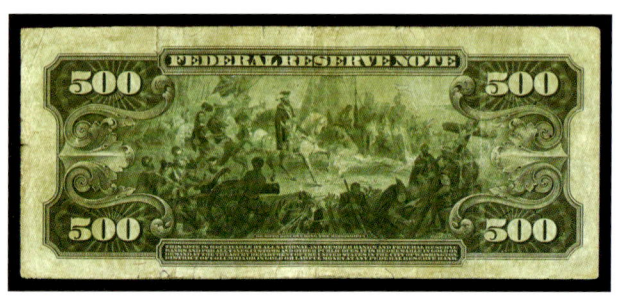

13602 Fr. 1132 $500 1918 Federal Reserve Note Fine. This is a new find on this district that is blessed with low serial number D134A. The overall appearance is nice for a mid-grade note while several pinholes are noticed. The three districts of New York, Chicago, and San Francisco are more plentiful than Cleveland in the census, so this Cleveland $500 carries a little more rarity with it.
From The Lincoln Collection (8,000-up)

PCGS 64 San Francisco 1918 $1000

13603 Fr. 1133 $1000 1918 Federal Reserve Note PCGS Very Choice New 64. A broadly margined, strikingly handsome $1000 Fed from the San Francisco district. This well-printed note, which PCGS pedigreed to the Rickey Collection, falls just short of the full Gem grade. This is the highest grade San Francisco Fed $1000 that is not part of the short run of AU and CU notes. With high-grade rarities being snapped up with regularity in today's market, now could be your last chance to acquire a beauty such as this for some time to come. **(50,000-up)**

Evenly Circulated 1918 $1000

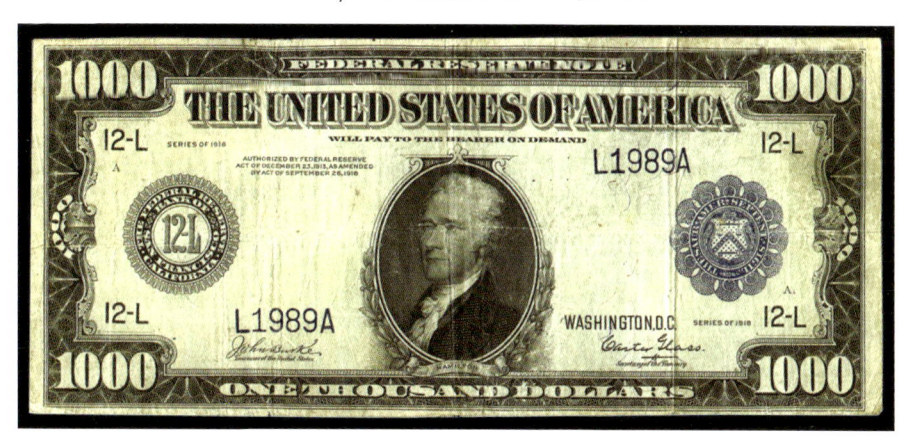

13604 Fr. 1133-L $1000 1918 Federal Reserve Note Fine+. This is very similar in appearance to the note which sold in our September 2006 Long Beach auction for over $18,000. This note is bright for the grade and has retained considerable eye appeal. Even at current price levels, these rare items are still remarkably inexpensive relative to their true scarcity, a situation which likely will not last forever. **(15,000-up)**

The Finest Known of Four San Francisco Fr. 1133b's

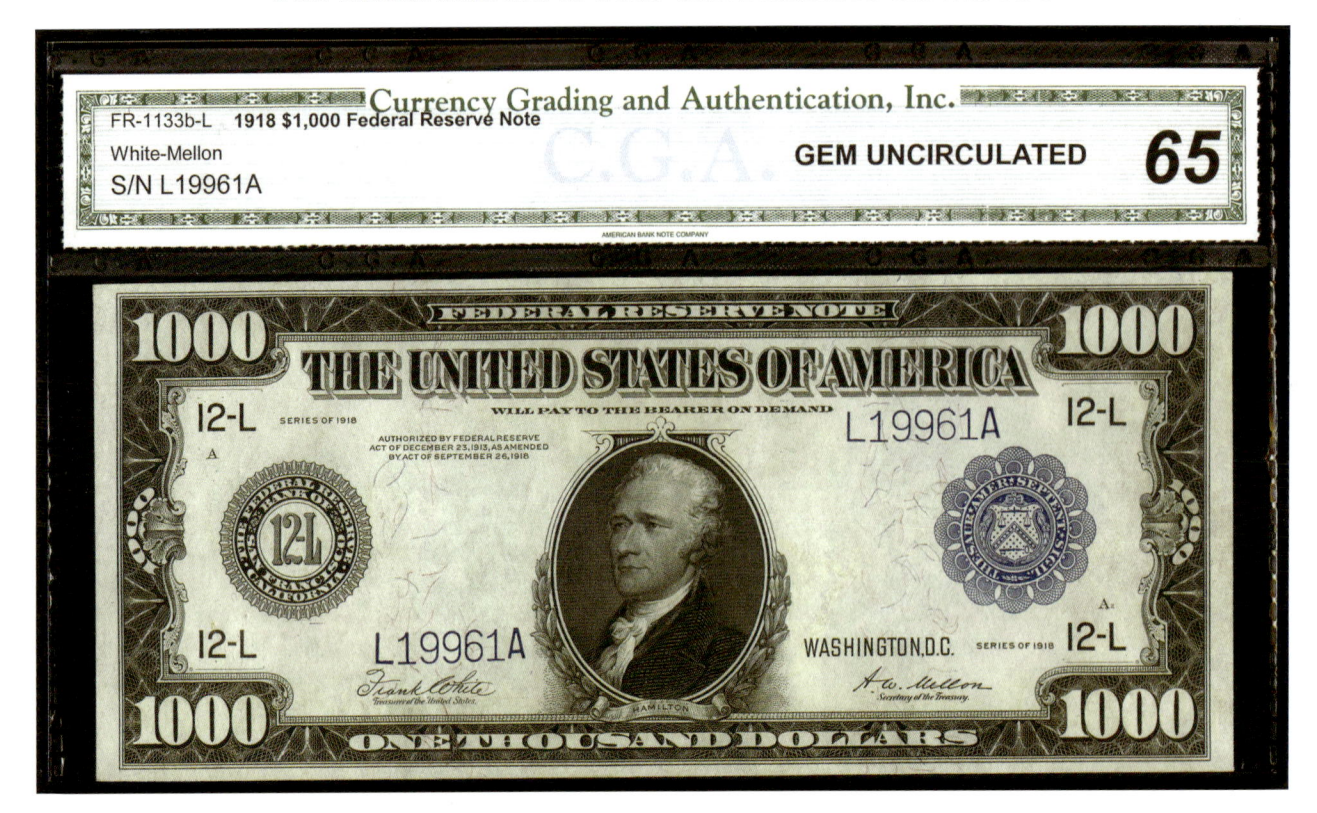

13605 Fr. 1133bL $1000 1918 Federal Reserve Note CGA Gem Uncirculated 65. When we first offered this note in May 1993, we described it as: "Only four $1000s are known from this district with the White-Mellon signature combination, and this is the finest of them. Well centered on both sides with excellent colors, margins, and paper surfaces, this beauty is just a breath away from being Superb." The Census has not changed in the intervening years and there are still only four San Francisco Fr. 1133b's known. Those four, plus five pieces from the Atlanta District, make up the total Census for Fr. 1133b's. As with the equally rare Fr. 1133a's, the value of these notes is held down simply because it does not have its own Friedberg number. This oversight in 1953 is still being felt in today's market. Were this note a separate Friedberg number, as it certainly should be, its value would be significantly higher. This note would be a $60,000 item as a simple Fr. 1133. As the infinitely rarer White-Mellon signature combination Fr. 1133b, it should certainly double that number. (100,000-up)

GOLD CERTIFICATES

13606 **Fr. 1167 $10 1907 Gold Certificate CGA Extremely Fine 40.** A pleasing well margined note, with good color, but with a few too many folds. **(400-up)**

13607 **Fr. 1170a $10 1907 Gold Certificate PMG Choice Extremely Fine 45.** Three folds preclude this otherwise New note from a full CU grade. The paper is blazingly original as is the overprint and back design. Around 40 examples are known of this Napier-Thompson signed Ten Dollar Gold number.
From The Collection of Greg Southward **(500-up)**

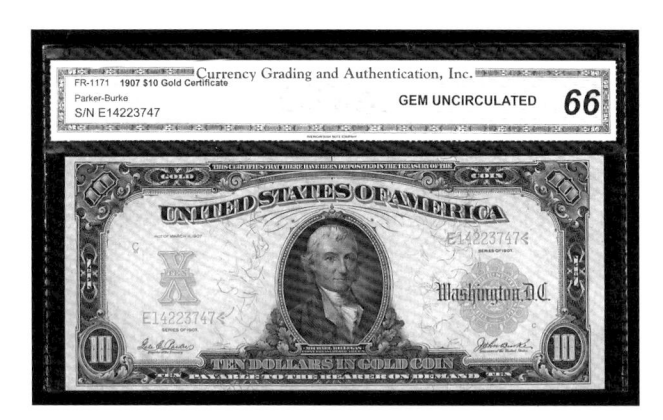

13608 **Fr. 1171 $10 1907 Gold Certificate CGA Gem Uncirculated 66.** A well margined, nicely centered example with vibrant overprints awaits the high bidder. **(2,250-up)**

13609 **Fr. 1171 $10 1907 Gold Certificate CGA Gem Uncirculated 65.** Beautifully bright with broad even margins all the way around on both sides. Second guessing third party holders is unwise at best, but we can't help but mention that this beauty appears to be somewhat under graded. **(3,500-up)**

13610 **Fr. 1172 $10 1907 Gold Certificate PMG About Uncirculated 55.** Both the overprint and back printing are bright and most pleasing in appearance. **(800-up)**

13611 **Fr. 1173 $10 1922 Gold Certificate CGA Gem Uncirculated 67.** This is a nicely margined well preserved $10 Gold with striking orange ink. **(3,000-up)**

13612 **Fr. 1173 $10 1922 Gold Certificate CGA Gem Uncirculated 65.** Beautifully margined with bright colors and lots of eye appeal. **(2,250-up)**

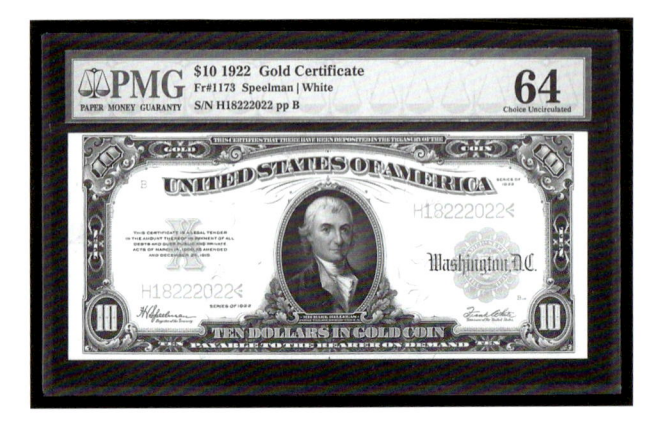

13613 Fr. 1173 $10 1922 Gold Certificate PMG Choice Uncirculated 64. The color is terrific on this $10 Gold. The original embossing is easy to see through the holder. (1,500-up)

13614 Fr. 1173 $10 1922 Gold Certificate Very Choice New. The margins fall just short of the full Gem grade on this strictly original Ten Dollar Gold. The colors are lovely, and the piece has terrific eye appeal.
From The Jacob and Heather Dedman Collection (1,500-up)

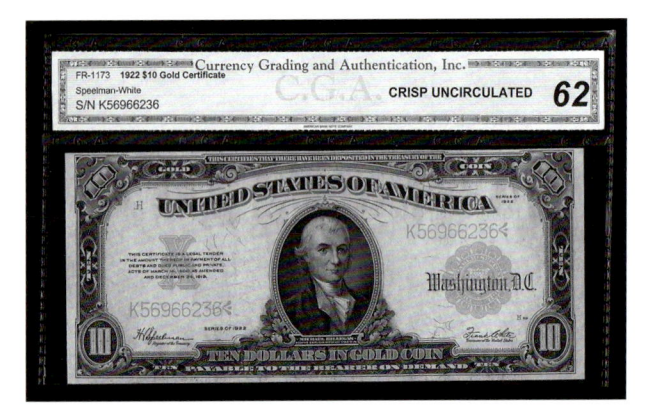

13615 Fr. 1173 $10 1922 Gold Certificate CGA Crisp Uncirculated 62. While hardly scarce in lower grades, large Gold Certificates are quite scarce in this state of preservation. With a broader top margin, this piece would likely have been graded considerably higher (1,100-up)

13616 Fr. 1173 $10 1922 Gold Certificate PMG Choice About Unc 58. An examination of the brightly printed back design reveals embossing of the serial numbers.
From The Collection of Greg Southward (600-up)

13617 Fr. 1173 $10 1922 Gold Certificate Choice About New. Good original surfaces and perfect color make this Gold Ten a desirable addition to any collection. A single broad soft corner fold holds it from the Choice New grade. (600-up)

13618 Fr. 1173 $10 1922 Gold Certificate PCGS Choice About New 55PPQ. Plenty of embossing remains visible on this brightly inked, lightly handled piece.
From The Collection of Greg Southward (900-up)

13619 Fr. 1173 $10 1922 Gold Certificate CGA About Uncirculated 55. A fold is seen through the portrait area on this note with creamy white surfaces. (900-up)

13620 Fr. 1173 $10 1922 Gold Certificate Extremely Fine. The original embossing is absent, but this well-margined $10 Gold retains a strong visual appeal. (400-up)

13621 Fr. 1173 $10 1922 Gold Certificate Extremely Fine. A bit tight along the bottom, but with great color and a handsome appearance. (500-up)

13622 Fr. 1173 $10 1922 Gold Certificate Star Fine+. The edges are sound and the paper is without pinholes on this evenly circulated $10 Gold star. (450-up)

Mid-Grade Fr. 1174

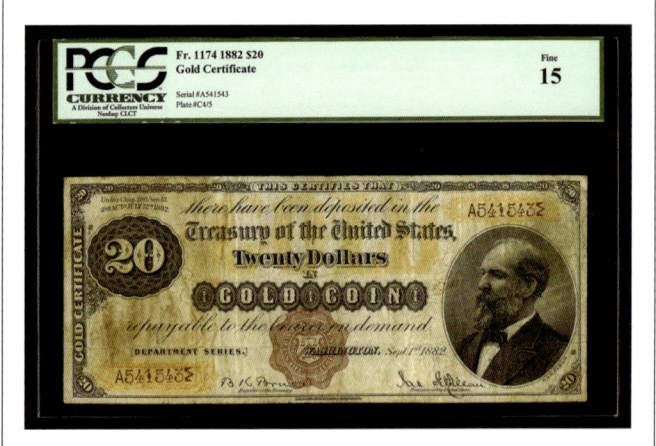

13623 Fr. 1174 $20 1882 Gold Certificate PCGS Fine 15. This note is a solid, well-margined, attractive piece that has some claims to the Very Fine grade. The left third of the note is lightly stained, but it's not a serious detraction, and the overall appearance is quite handsome. Only a few more than dozen examples are known for this number. (12,500-up)

Premium Paper Quality Triple-Signature Gold Certificate

13624 Fr. 1175a $20 1882 Gold Certificate PCGS Very Fine 25PPQ. Full margins, sound edges, and good color go hand-in-hand with this nice mid-grade note from one of the heralded issues in United States paper money. This is one of approximately 30 serial numbers reported in the census, with this much in demand variety having the engraved countersignature of Thomas C. Acton. Also, scrutiny reveals a natural note that has not been repaired, and is sure to bring a smile to the face of its next guardian. (20,000-up)

13625 Fr. 1176 $20 1882 Gold Certificate PCGS Fine 15. The full census for this number is 20 pieces, several of which are permanently impounded. The note has retained excellent color, giving the appearance of a full Very Fine from the face, although the brightly colored back shows a touch more wear. There is also a very tiny split at the top center. A rare note that will attract multiple bids and will likely go home with a new collector in the range of . . . (7,500-up)

Superb Gem 1882 Twenty Dollar Gold

13626 Fr. 1178 $20 1882 Gold Certificate Superb Gem New. A fabulous Gold Twenty from this popular series, the most common issue of the design and ideal for a high grade type set. In this grade, however, this note is anything but common. The colors are unimpeachable, the paper is flawless, and the original embossing is easily evident. The margins are incredibly broad and the design is perfectly centered on both sides. It is likely that very few other notes could match this example in terms of technical or aesthetic merit, and even the fussiest collector would be pleased with the overall quality. A note that is worth every bit of our estimate of...
From The Jacob and Heather Dedman Collection
(25,000-up)

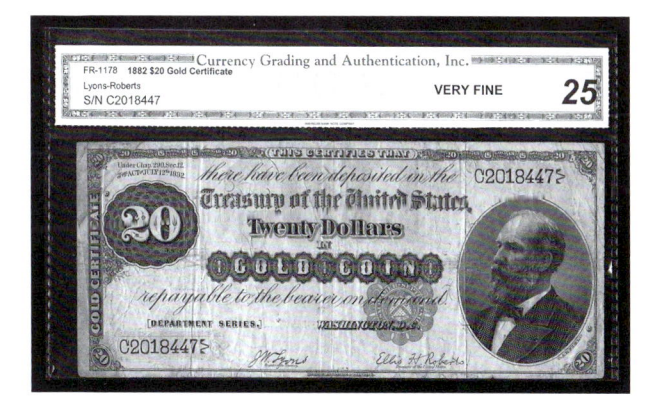

13627 Fr. 1178 $20 1882 Gold Certificate CGA Very Fine 25. This problem-free Gold Certificate appears to be an ideal mid-grade type note through the holder. This note is not easy to locate in this grade, and original examples such as this are always snapped up by eager collectors. (1,500-up)

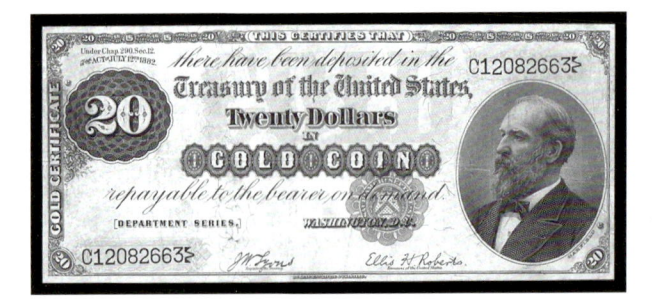

13628 **Fr. 1178 $20 1882 Gold Certificate Very Fine.** A perfect VF from the face, but the back is strangely overinked. The ink is so thick and heavy on the paper that it can be felt. It's also badly smeared toward the right end, creating somewhat of an Error Note. Hard to evaluate, but this strikes us as the type of "error" that lowers rather than raises the value.
From The Jacob and Heather Dedman Collection **(1,500-up)**

13629 **Fr. 1178 $20 1882 Gold Certificate Fine.** A few pinholes and a bit of soil on the back, but the note has kept all its ink color and looks rather nice.
From The Collection of Greg Southward **(800-up)**

13630 **Fr. 1178 $20 1882 Gold Certificate Very Good.** This is a good note for type as it has nice edges and paper for the grade.
From The Collection of Greg Southward **(450-up)**

13631 **Fr. 1179 $20 1905 Gold Certificate PCGS Apparent Very Fine 20.** PCGS notes "minor edge repairs" to this mid-grade Technicolor. Most importantly, the color of the design is still bright and the back fully golden-orange. **(3,500-up)**

13632 **Fr. 1180 $20 1905 Gold Certificate Very Good.** This well circulated but fully intact Technicolor Twenty has an attractive face, but a typically weakly printed reverse. **(800-up)**

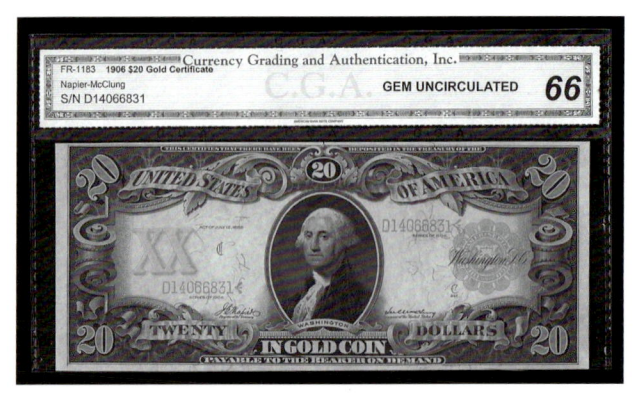

13633 **Fr. 1183 $20 1906 Gold Certificate CGA Gem Uncirculated 66.** Pleasing paper waves and bright white paper are noted on this Gem $20 Gold. **(4,000-up)**

13634 **Fr. 1187 $20 1922 Mule Gold Certificate PMG Gem Uncirculated 66 EPQ.** A gorgeous Gold Certificate Twenty with the important EPQ qualifier. This note is also the much scarcer Mule variety. PMG notes in their comment "John Burke Back Plate #138." **(5,000-up)**

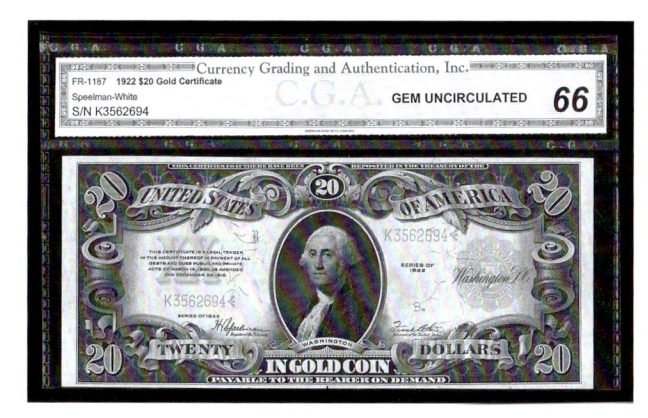

13635 **Fr. 1187 $20 1922 Gold Certificate CGA Gem Uncirculated 66.** A very handsome $20 Gold with bold colors, sharp print quality, and embossing that can be easily seen through the third party holder. (4,000-up)

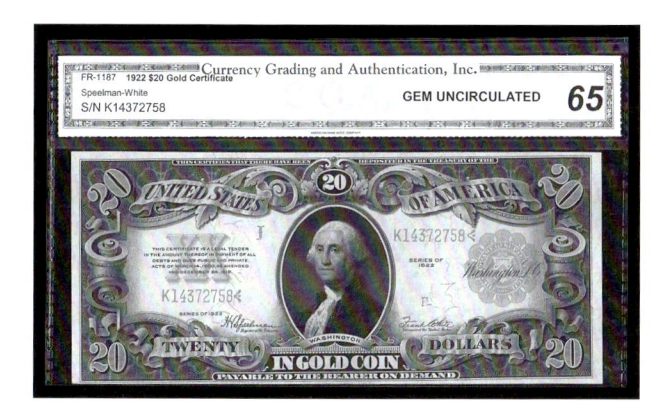

13636 **Fr. 1187 $20 1922 Gold Certificate CGA Gem Uncirculated 65.** The back design is blazing orange as are the seal, serial numbers, and two X's signifying the denomination. (3,500-up)

13637 **Fr. 1187 $20 1922 Gold Certificate CGA Choice Uncirculated 64.** Embossing of the golden-orange overprint is noted on the back of this note. The paper is bright and the details finely executed. (1,750-up)

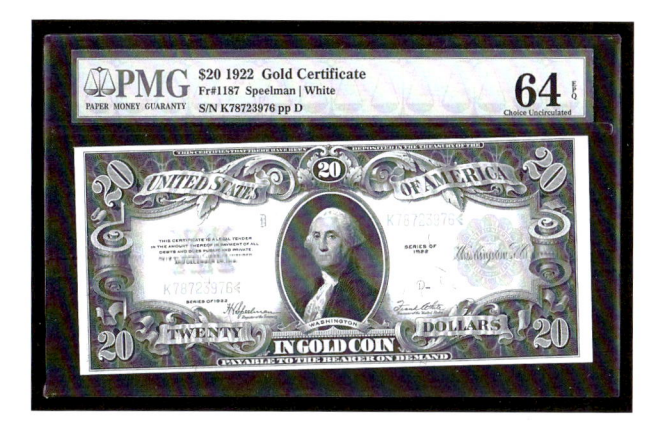

13638 **Fr. 1187 $20 1922 Gold Certificate PMG Choice Uncirculated 64 EPQ.** An attractive $20 gold with perfectly original paper waves, embossing and a richly colored overprint. (2,000-up)

13639 **Fr. 1187 $20 1922 Gold Certificate CGA About Uncirculated 58.** One fold and a light bend account for the grade on this otherwise original and colorful note. (600-up)

13640 **Fr. 1187 $20 1922 Gold Certificate Very Fine.** Dark orange ink is a highlight of this $20 Gold that has a partial paper clip rust outline on both sides at top center. The back also exhibits a little counting soil. (450-up)

13641 **Fr. 1187 $20 1922 Gold Certificate Very Fine.** Original surfaces and nice color highlight this mid-grade $20 Gold, (450-up)

13642 **Fr. 1187 $20 1922 Gold Certificate Very Fine.** Even wear and just a trace of serial number embossing are found on this $20. (450-up)

Fr. 1192 - Recent Discovery

13643 Fr. 1192 $50 1882 Gold Certificate Very Fine. This recently discovered issue brings the total of known examples to seventeen. The sum is a bit misleading to hopeful collectors as four of the pieces are permanently impounded in institutional collections and seven more haven't been offered publicly in six years or longer. Pleasing, original paper and bold printed details add to the appeal of this $50 which ranks as one of the finest known examples. Frankly, only one other piece can lay claim to a higher grade, an EF that last appeared in 2003 and sold for $57,500. More recently, we sold the Dr. Edward and Joanne Dauer PMG VF30 EPQ example for $74,750 in September of last year. With the recent increase in interest for scarce, original rarities and a proven history of auction prices realized, we fully expect this piece to exceed... **(60,000-up)**

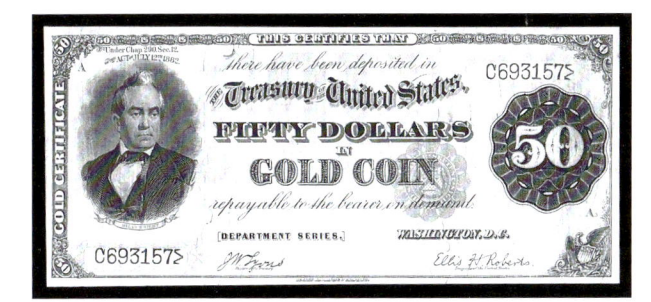

13644 **Fr. 1193 $50 1882 Gold Certificate Fine-Very Fine.** Fully Very Fine from the face, but the back is somewhat weaker. About 80 examples are known in all grades combined—many of which are far lower grade than this problem-free Fifty.
From The Collection of Greg Southward (2,500-up)

13645 **Fr. 1193 $50 1882 Gold Certificate PMG Choice Fine 15.** An unmolested, strictly original example that is perfect for the grade. The margins are broad, the colors bright, and the note is completely free of the defects normally associated with this grade and denomination. (1,700-up)

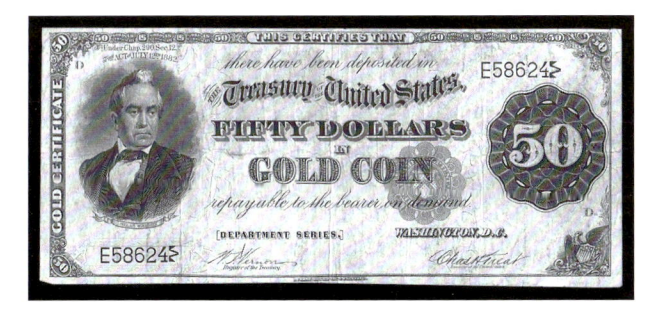

13646 **Fr. 1195 $50 1882 Gold Certificate Fine.** There is a small tear at the right end of the top of this very scarce $50 Gold Certificate. Fewer than 50 examples are known in all grades combined, as compared to well over 125 Fr. 1197's, the most common example of the same type. The color is excellent on the face of the note, and only slightly weaker on the back.
From The Collection of Greg Southward (2,500-up)

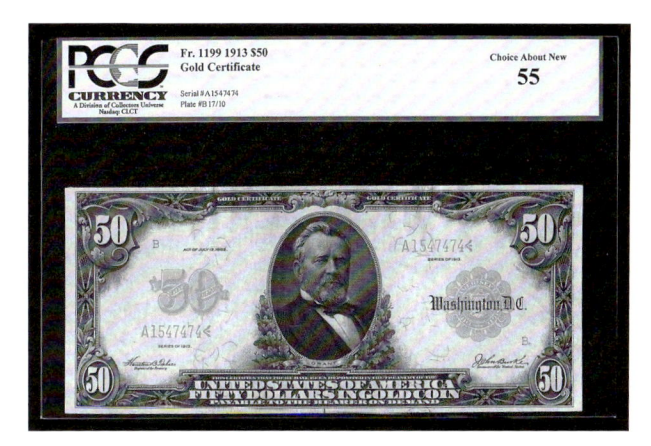

13647 **Fr. 1199 $50 1913 Gold Certificate PCGS Choice About New 55.** This lightly circulated beauty has broad margins, perfect colors and original embossing which are all featured elements of this gorgeous 1913 high-denomination Gold Certificate. Even the back color, which fades rather easily, is spectacularly bright. A lovely example that creates the initial visual effect of a Superb Gem. (2,750-up)

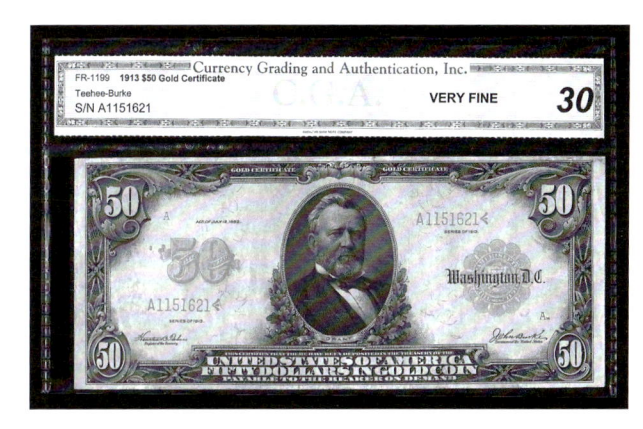

13648 **Fr. 1199 $50 1913 Gold Certificate CGA Very Fine 30.** This is the scarcer of the two signature combinations on Series 1913 $50's. The note boasts pleasing color of the overprint and the back design. (1,400-up)

13649 **Fr. 1200 $50 1922 Gold Certificate Very Fine.** Nice inks and clean paper define this pleasing mid-grade $50 Gold.
From The Collection of Greg Southward (1,400-up)

13650 **Fr. 1200 $50 1922 Gold Certificate Fine-Very Fine.** This $50 Gold looks a full VF at first, but a few more folds are revealed by closer study.
From The Collection of Greg Southward **(1,100-up)**

13651 **Fr. 1200 $50 1922 Gold Certificate Fine.** A solid, problem-free Fine with strictly original paper surfaces and good color. **(800-up)**

13652 **Fr. 1200a $50 1922 Mule Gold Certificate Very Fine.** All Fr. 1200a's are Mules, with this note having back plate number 8 positioned at lower right of center up next to the finely detailed scroll work. Fr. 1200a's were issued before Fr. 1200's, and 1200's outnumber 1200a's by more than five to one in the census. Fr. 1200a's were not added to the Friedberg reference until the 1992 13th edition. This example has a deep orange back and healthy edges.
From The Collection of Greg Southward **(1,500-up)**

13653 **Fr. 1211 $100 1882 Gold Certificate Very Fine.** This Napier-Thompson signed Hundred is hugely margined and it appears fully XF from the face. The back has retained its fully bright orange color, but it's a little soiled. This is a scarce Friedberg number and a perusal through the census places this note easily in the top half for appearance.
From The Collection of Greg Southward **(2,250-up)**

1882 $100 Gold Certificate PMG 65EPQ

13654 **Fr. 1214 $100 1882 Gold Certificate PMG Gem Uncirculated 65 EPQ.** A very pretty note with lots of positive qualifiers. PMG has commented "Exceptional Paper Quality, Great Embossing & Color." This beauty is just a hair of margin away from the Superb grade. **(17,500-up)**

PCGS 65PPQ 1922 Hundred Dollar Gold

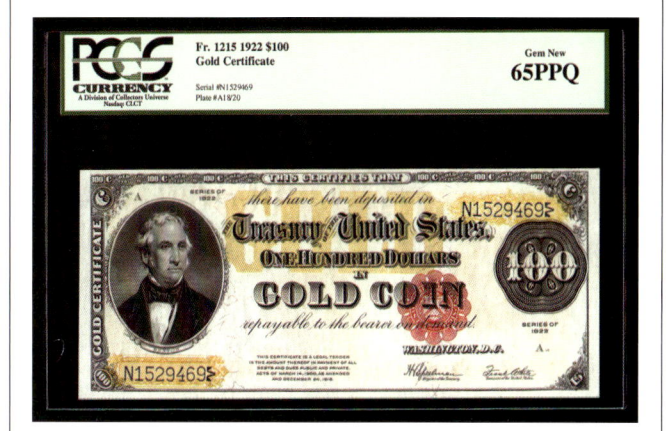

13655 **Fr. 1215 $100 1922 Gold Certificate PCGS Gem New 65PPQ.** One of the nicest $100 Gold Certificates we've had the pleasure of handling. The colors are simply spectacular, and the original embossing easily seen. If the top margin were as broad as the other three, this note could have easily graded 68. An exceptional piece. (15,000-up)

13656 **Fr. 1215 $100 1922 Gold Certificate Very Fine.** This is a bright $100 Gold with ample margins, original surfaces, and nice color. Half of the folds are located near the center and they are in turn flanked by two folds on both sides.
From The Collection of Greg Southward (1,400-up)

13657 **Fr. 1215 $100 1922 Gold Certificate Very Fine.** A bit soft and with a minor ink stain, as well as a few short edge splits. (1,000-up)

13658 **Fr. 1215 $100 1922 Gold Certificate Fine.** This $100 Gold has nice color for the grade while the edges show some tiny nicks. However, there are no traits outside of the assigned grade. (900-up)

High Grade 1882 $500 Gold Certificate

13659 **Fr. 1216b $500 1882 Gold Certificate CGA Extremely Fine 45.** Brightly colored and very nicely centered on both sides. The total census for this number is about 40 pieces. No uncirculated note is known, and to our knowledge, there is only one About New. This note grades in the top ten for technical merit, and far above that for eye appeal. It has the look of an About New note from the face. The back has retained all its bright orange color, but it does show a number of light folds. This is an important high-end example of this popular high-denomination Gold Certificate. (25,000-up)

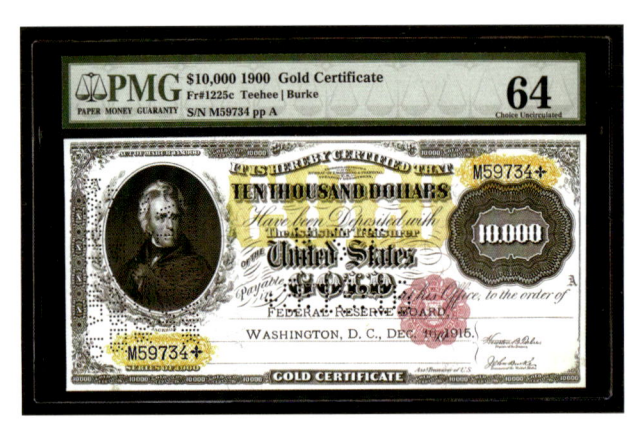

13660 **Fr. 1225 $10000 1900 Gold Certificate PMG Choice Uncirculated 64.** These non redeemable series 1900 Gold notes are relatively common in lower grade, but very few are near as nice as this note. It's a broadly margined, beautifully bright example. **(6,000-up)**

13661 **Fr. 1225 $10000 1900 Gold Certificate Extremely Fine.** This note was not intended for circulation, but it was used within the Federal Reserve System. Unlike other notes of this Friedberg number, the back is blank and there are perforation cancellations at the left in the portrait that says this note is payable only to the Treasurer or a Federal Reserve Bank. There are some splits where the folds meet the edges plus a couple of other scattered small splits. **(2,500-up)**

13662 **Fr. 1225 $10000 1900 Gold Certificate Fine-Very Fine.** These notes exist because of a fire in a government post office in Washington, D.C. in 1935. Firefighters tossed stacks of these cancelled notes out onto the streets, and passersby picked up examples and took them home. They, of course, are no longer legal tender, and are rumored to be illegal to own or possess. No one has made a test case out of one, however, and they often sell in public auctions, coin and currency shows and in coin shops. This example has some paper clip rust visible which has degraded the paper, but comes without the normal punch cancels. **(1,000-up)**

End of Session Two

SESSION THREE

Live, Internet, and Mail Bid Auction 436 • St. Louis, Missouri
Friday, May 11, 2007, 1:00 PM CT • Lots 13663-14262

A 15% Buyer's Premium ($9 minimum) Will Be Added To All Lots
You can now view full-color images and bid via the Internet at the Heritage website: HA.com

SMALL SIZE TYPE NOTES

13663 **Fr. 1500 $1 1928 Legal Tender Note. CGA Gem Uncirculated 67.**
This note bucks the usual trend for Fr. 1500 as it has a larger than normal fourth margin to go along with three other broad margins. Embossing and natural paper wave are easily seen through the third-party holder. (900-1,200)

13664 **Fr. 1500 $1 1928 Legal Tender Note. PCGS Gem New 66PPQ.**
Natural paper ripple and embossing are seen through the PCGS holder. The margins for this note are wider and straighter than usually found. (700-900)

13665 **Fr. 1500 $1 1928 Legal Tender Note. Gem Crisp Uncirculated.**
Crackling fresh, fully embossed, and exceptionally well centered, a real peach of a note. (500-700)

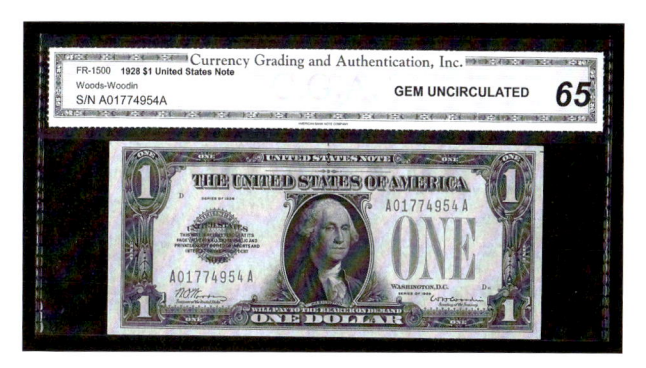

13666 **Fr. 1500 $1 1928 Legal Tender Note. CGA Gem Uncirculated 65.**
Solid, almost perfectly even margins frame this Legal Tender Ace. A quick look at the back design reveals bold embossing of the serial numbers and seal, and great front to back centering. (500-700)

13667 **Fr. 1500 $1 1928 Legal Tender Note. PMG Choice Uncirculated 64 EPQ.**
An exquisite example of this sub-5000 serial numbered note that PMG has bestowed their EPQ designation. (350-450)

13668 **Fr. 1500 $1 1928 Legal Tender Notes. Three Consecutive Examples. Choice Crisp Uncirculated.**
This handsome trio has three wide and one thin margin as is customary with the vast majority of $1 Legals. Most of this series was kept in storage until 1948-49 when the notes were issued in Puerto Rico so that this odd issue would not cause sorting problems with the Federal Reserve Banks on the mainland. These notes come from that Puerto Rico release. (Total: 3 notes) (750-1,000)

13669 **Fr. 1500 $1 1928 Legal Tender Notes. Two Consecutive Examples. Choice Crisp Uncirculated.**
This twosome has strong paper wave and embossing. The thin bottom margin is recognized along with a counting crinkle on this pair. The serial numbers are 1778 and 1779. (Total: 2 notes) (600-900)

13670 **Eight Consecutive Fr. 1500 $1 1928 Legal Tender Notes. Crisp Uncirculated to Very Choice Crisp Uncirculated.**
This exquisite run of eight consecutive notes boasts wholly original paper, deep embossing, and four digit serial numbers. The first 5000 notes were released in and around Washington, DC. The margins vary a bit from note to note, but are all solid. (Total: 8 notes) (2,500-3,500)

13671 **Four Consecutive Fr. 1500 $1 1928 Legal Tender Notes. Choice Crisp Uncirculated.**
This is one of a couple of runs of Legal Tender Aces in this auction. This group boasts the same original paper quality and bold colors. (Total: 4 notes) (1,000-1,500)

13672 **Fr. 1500 $1 1928 Legal Tender Note. Choice Crisp Uncirculated.**
Bold embossing, natural paper wave, and the classic "fire engine red overprint" are exhibited by this note with serial number 944. (750-1,000)

13673 **Fr. 1500 $1 1928 Legal Tender Notes. Three Consecutive Examples. Choice Crisp Uncirculated.**
Serial numbers 1794-1796 are found on this trio that also has a counting crinkle. The second two notes have the thin bottom margin, while the first note has a thin top margin. (Total: 3 notes) (900-1,200)

13674 **Fr. 1500 $1 1928 Legal Tender Notes. Two Consecutive Examples. Choice Crisp Uncirculated.**
This $1 Legal pair with natural paper wave is adorned with serial numbers 1526 and 1527. Notes from the initial Washington, DC release of 5000 in 1933 have always been heavily pursued by collectors. This duo shows the usual trait for these of a thin bottom margin. (Total: 2 notes) (600-900)

13675 **Fr. 1500 $1 1928 Legal Tender Note. CGA Choice Uncirculated 63.**
The paper is bright with well embossed overprint elements contrasting very nicely against it. (300-400)

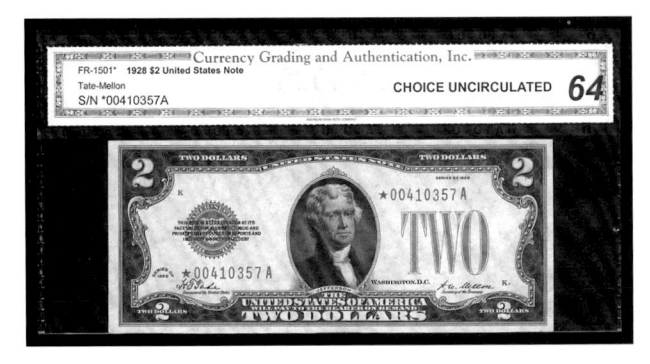

13676 **Fr. 1501★ $2 1928 Legal Tender Note. CGA Choice Uncirculated 64.**
This is a brightly overprinted example of an ever popular replacement issue that is well margined with plenty of embossing visible. Auction appearances of high grade examples are few and far between.
From The Lincoln Collection (1,750-2,250)

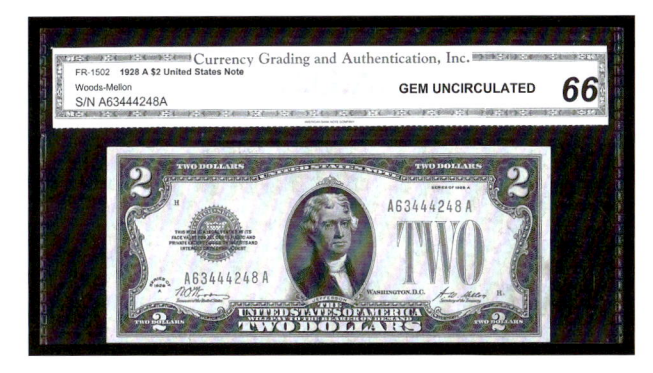

13677 **Fr. 1502 $2 1928A Legal Tender Note. CGA Gem Uncirculated 66.**
Pleasing waves of originality are noted on the paper, even through the holder. The margins are ample all around for a full Gem grade, though two are slighter larger than the rest. (500-600)

13678 **Fr. 1503 $2 1928B Legal Tender Note. Gem Crisp Uncirculated.**
A nicely centered and very bright example of the scarcer A-A block in this key to the series note. (1,500-2,000)

13679 **Fr. 1503 $2 1928B Legal Tender Note. Very Choice Crisp Uncirculated.**
Original paper waves are noted on this pleasing Legal Deuce. Were the margins a bit large on two sides, the piece would surely grade Gem or better. (900-1,100)

13680 **Fr. 1503 $2 1928B Legal Tender Note. PCGS Choice About New 55PPQ.**
The surfaces are quite bright on this elusive example for the issue. (600-800)

13681 **Fr. 1503 $2 1928B Legal Tender Note. PMG About Uncirculated 55.**
A center fold and some counting soil at back top center define this key to the $2 Legals. (600-800)

13682 **Fr. 1504★ $2 1928C Legal Tender Note. PMG Very Fine 30.**
This is a collectible example of a tough star. The note is bright and problem-free with several folds seen. (800-1,200)

13683 **Fr. 1505 $2 1928D Legal Tender Note. Very Good-Fine.**
A well circulated but fully intact example of the very scarce non-mule B-B block, valued at $1000 in Very Fine (and unpriced in higher grade) in the latest Schwartz reference. (400-600)

13684 Fr. 1505★ $2 1928D Mule Legal Tender Note. PMG Gem Uncirculated 66 EPQ.
Micro back check number 279 can be seen on the back of this lovely replacement note whose condition may have no equal. Blazing overprints and deep embossing are seen beneath the third party holder. This is a gorgeous, full Gem destined for the finest of small size collections. (1,500-2,000)

13685 Fr. 1508 $2 1928G Legal Tender Notes. Uncut Sheet of 12. Choice Crisp Uncirculated.
This is an attractive sheet. The right edge has a tiny nick and the top right note has a counting crinkle.
From The Jacob and Heather Dedman Collection
(900-1,200)

13686 Fr. 1509 $2 1953 Specimen Legal Tender Note. PCGS Gem New 65PPQ.
This perfectly margined note is the first of a quartet of Legal Tender Deuce Specimens in this auction. We have handled one other Small Size Legal Tender Specimen, a $100 which is also part of this auction. Opportunities in currency to view a progression of notes from one series to another provides collectors with information about practices in the BEP. This set, all of which boast H-G block 8 digit ladder serial numbers, reveals a change in the SPECIMEN overprint used between the Series 1953B and Series 1953C. At some point in the early 1960's while these two series were printed, the font used to designate the word Specimen was changed from measurements of 23mm down to 15mm beginning with Series 1953C. The style of the letters were changed slightly from blocklike with serifs to simply small and blocklike. Also starting with Series 1953C the word SPECIMEN was stamped twice on both sides, horizontally and vertical on the face and then twice vertically on the back. This practice was continued on for Series 1966 Legal Tender $100's and even into the 1970's as illustrated on the denomination set of Specimens that we handled for Series 1974. Since we cannot confirm the existence of any other $2 Legal Tender Specimens, a likely realization for this piece may be... **(10,000-15,000)**

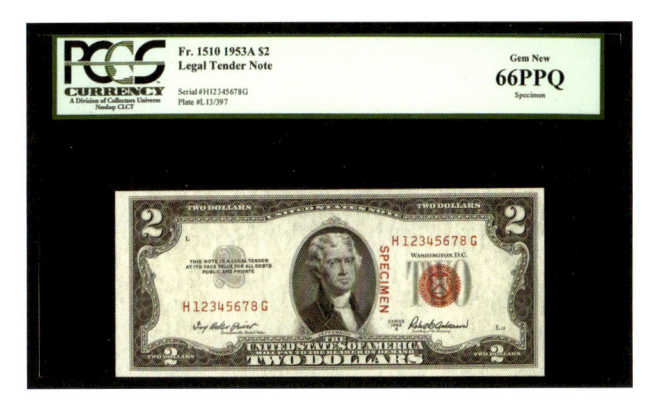

13687 **Fr. 1510 $2 1953A Legal Tender Note. PCGS Gem New 66PPQ.**
This is the second of four different $2 Legal Tender Specimens, each of which is similar in grade and technical merit. SPECIMEN is printed twice, vertically to the right of Jefferson's portrait and again on the back vertically to the right of Monticello. Bold embossing of the serial numbers, seal and SPECIMEN overprints is noted. (10,000-15,000)

13689 **Fr. 1512 $2 1953C Specimen Legal Tender Note. PCGS Gem New 65PPQ.**
It is likely that sometime shortly after Kathryn O. Granahan took office in January of 1963 specimens were printed to display the new Series 1953C notes bearing her signature. This SPECIMEN was different from the Series that preceded it in that the font for the word SPECIMEN was changed and the word was used twice on either side of the note. Though this is the lowest graded of the four different Legal Tender Specimen Deuces offered here, it is no slouch. The paper is exceptional as is the bright red and deeply embossed overprint. (10,000-15,000)

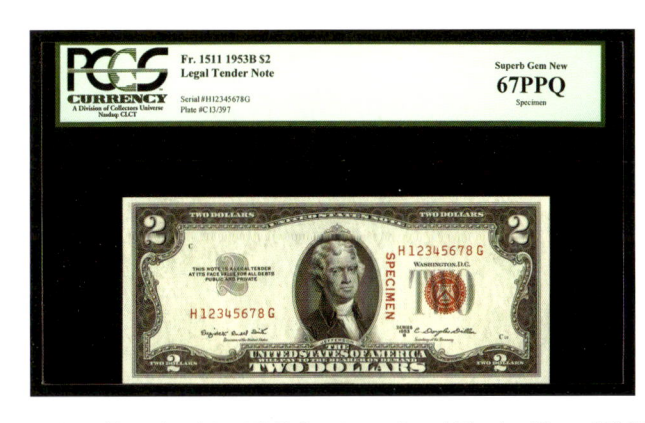

13688 **Fr. 1511 $2 1953B Specimen Legal Tender Note. PCGS Superb Gem New 67PPQ.**
The third installment of this quartet of Legal Tender Specimens boasts the most evenly sized margins of the group. The word SPECIMEN appears twice in the font with serifs. Embossing is noted on the ladder serial number and the paper is perfectly original. (10,000-15,000)

13690 **Fr. 1509★ $2 1953 Legal Tender Notes. Twenty Consecutive Examples Very Choice Crisp Uncirculated.**
Prominent embossing and bright colors are the mainstays of these pieces. Some gems are also seen in this lot of original replacement notes. (Total: 20 notes) (1,200-1,800)

13691 **Fr. 1511 $2 1953B Legal Tender Notes. Original Pack of 100. Choice Crisp Uncirculated.**
This BEP banded pack has 42 Star notes within its confines. The bank band has this number written in pencil on it. The regular notes catalog for $15 a piece and the Stars for $75 a piece in CU in the latest Schwartz reference. This is the most Stars we have seen in a pack from the 1953B Series. (Total: 100 notes) (2,000-3,000)

13692 **Fr. 1511 $2 1953B Legal Tender Notes. Fifty Consecutive Examples. Choice Crisp Uncirculated.**
Teller 2 stamped the bank band for this run on Mar 27, 1963. The notes are nicely centered and embossed. A few of the outside notes show handling with the remaining notes gem quality or certainly close to it. (Total: 50 notes) (500-750)

13693 **Fr. 1511 $2 1953B Legal Tender Notes. Original Pack of 100 Choice Crisp Uncirculated.**
Thirty-six replacement notes are contained within this original pack. The inks are fresh and the paper crisp. We are pleased to offer yet another interesting, seldom seen item to the collecting community. (Total: 100 notes) (2,000-3,000)

13694 **Fr. 1511 $2 1953B Legal Tender Notes. Original Pack of 100 Choice Crisp Uncirculated.**
Complete packs of red seals are no longer seen with any regularity. We are fortunate to offer several tonight. (Total: 100 notes) (1,000-1,500)

13695 **Fr. 1511 $2 1953B Legal Tender Notes. 94 Examples Crisp Uncirculated.**
Some notes have some light handling while others have a light corner bump not into the design. One note shows a vertical fold. (Total: 94 notes) (900-1,200)

13696 **Fr. 1511 $2 1953B Legal Tender Notes. Original Pack of 100. Choice Crisp Uncirculated.**
Prominent embossing and crackling paper are traits of this delightful pack. (Total: 100 notes) (1,000-1,500)

13697 **Fr. 1511 $2 1953B Legal Tender Notes. Original Pack of 100. Choice Crisp Uncirculated.**
This pack is consecutive to the previous lot and it is nearly its identical twin. (Total: 100 notes) (1,000-1,500)

Original $2 1953B Star Note Pack

13698 **Fr. 1511★ $2 1953B Legal Tender Notes. Original Pack of 100 Choice Crisp Uncirculated.**
This scarce star note pack had star notes inserted to replace other star notes. These notes are as crisp and fresh as the day they left the BEP. There is writing on the strap that lists an acquired date of April 3, 1962. Over 45 years have done little to affect these beauties. The first couple notes have a touch of handling at upper left.
(Total: 100 notes) (4,500-6,500)

13699 **Fr. 1512 $2 1953C Legal Tender Notes. 75 Examples Choice Crisp Uncirculated.**
This partial pack is comprised of many beautiful pieces which are well embossed and well inked. Several notes exhibit a few corner bumps and light handling, especially the last note. (Total: 75 notes) (1,000-1,500)

13700 **Fr. 1512★ $2 1953C Legal Tender Note. Gem Crisp Uncirculated.**
A quintet of consecutive star examples, with each of the five pieces a bright and original well centered gem. (Total: 5 notes) (400-500)

13701 **Fr. 1513 $2 1963 Legal Tender Notes. Pack of 100. Gem Crisp Uncirculated.**
The first couple of notes show handling, but nothing great enough to derail the Gem designation from this pack that also has a homemade bank band. (Total: 100 notes) (1,000-1,500)

13702 **Fr. 1513 $2 1963 Legal Tender Notes. Original Pack of 100 Gem Crisp Uncirculated.**
The margins are quite even and embossing prominent on this strap of red seals. (800-1,200)

13703 **Fr. 1513 $2 1963 Legal Tender Notes. Fifty Consecutive Examples. Choice Crisp Uncirculated.**
The bank band has been stamped by G. Fox & Co. Embossing is easy to see while the right-hand margin is slender. (500-750)

13704 **Fr. 1513 $2 1963 Legal Tender Note. Near-Complete Pack. Choice Crisp Uncirculated.**
This partial pack consists of 83 pieces in two runs. The notes are all bright and crisp, with only the last note showing some light folds. (Total: 83 notes) (800-1,000)

13705 **Fr. 1513 $2 1963 Legal Tender Notes. Original Pack of 100. Crisp Uncirculated.**
The edges show some soiling on this pack. (Total: 100 notes) (400-600)

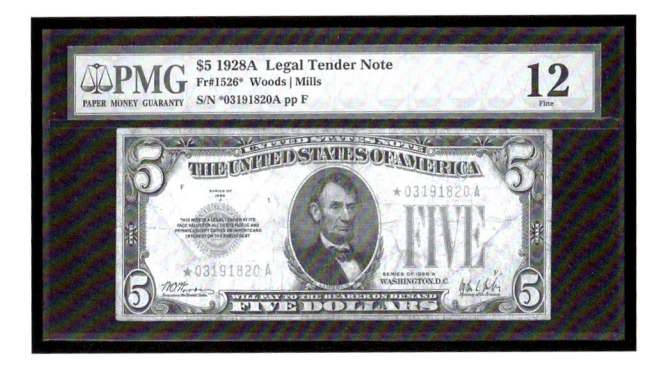

13706 Fr. 1526★ $5 1928A Legal Tender Note. PMG Fine 12.
This is the scarcest of the non-mule red seal stars which should see strong bidding in order to complete someone's collection. The VG/F value in Schwartz is $800 and we would not be surprised to see that amount surpassed tonight. (600-900)

13707 Fr. 1527★ $5 1928B Legal Tender Note. Fine+.
This nicely margined replacement has a touch of discoloration along the top margin. (250-350)

13708 Fr. 1528/Fr. 1529 $5 1928C/1928D Legal Tender Notes. Changeover Pair Crisp Uncirculated.
This becomes the highest recorded serial number for this occurrence in the Schwartz tome. The 1928D exhibits some embossing, grading Choice while the 1928C is a touch flat perhaps from storage. This is only the second such pair we have had the pleasure to auction in the past five years. (Total: 2 notes) (850-1,250)

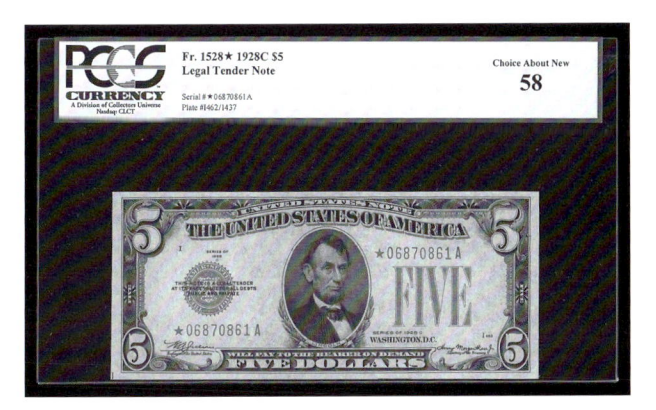

13709 Fr. 1528★ $5 1928C Legal Tender Note. PCGS Choice About New 58.
Red seal replacement notes have always fascinated collectors due to their low print runs. This note is vividly crimson hued with adequate margins. (500-700)

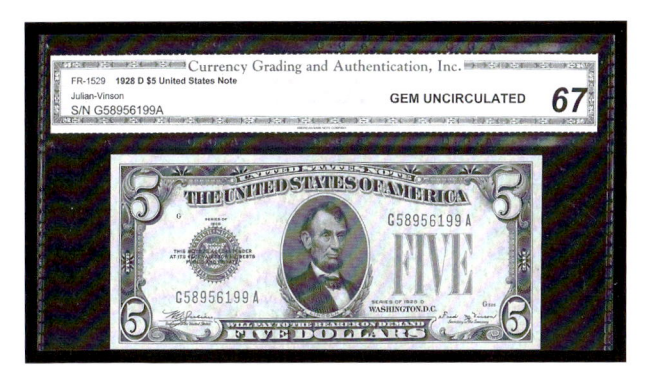

13710 Fr. 1529 $5 1928D Legal Tender Note. CGA Gem Uncirculated 67.
This is a pleasing example of the key to the regular issue of $5 Legals. Wide margins are noticed along with bright, creamy surfaces. (600-800)

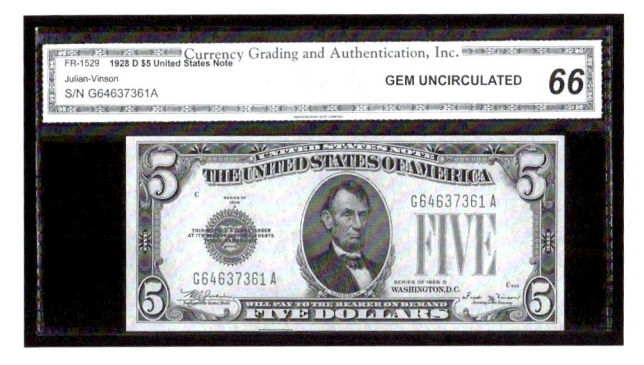

13711 Fr. 1529 $5 1928D Legal Tender Note. CGA Gem Uncirculated 66.
Utter originality is seen on this key Legal Five that has superb embossing, especially upon the treasury seal. With so many unoriginal gems from this series floating around the marketplace this beauty will be a breath of fresh air to one lucky bidder. (600-900)

13712 Fr. 1529 $5 1928D Legal Tender Note. Gem Crisp Uncirculated.
A beautiful example of this key note featuring bright colors and great centering. (350-550)

13713 **Fr. 1530★ $5 1928E Legal Tender Note. Gem Crisp Uncirculated.**
A broadly margined brightly colored Gem with great eye appeal and excellent centering. (900-1,100)

Rare Wide II Star

13714 **Fr. 1531★ $5 1928F Wide II Legal Tender Note. Fine.**
This Star is a member of the rare Wide II family that has only around twenty serial numbers recorded for this variety. In fact this newcomer becomes the new low serial number for this elusive variety. In February 2005 we sold a VF that was formerly of the Taylor Family Collection for nearly $7500. We don't expect this evenly circulated example to go that high, but if true rarity is any type of measure, we could easily see... (2,000-4,000)

13715 **Fr. 1534★ $5 1953B Legal Tender Note. PMG Superb Gem Unc 67 EPQ.**
A pleasingly original piece with broad margins.
From The Bill and Kathy Stella Currency Collection
(300-400)

13716 **Fr. 1535★ $5 1953C Legal Tender Notes. Two Consecutive Examples. PMG Choice Uncirculated 64.**
These stars show Treasury seal embossing. (Total: 2 notes) (600-900)

13717 **Fr. 1535★ $5 1953C Legal Tender Note. Very Choice Crisp Uncirculated.**
The side margins on this pleasing replacement are huge.
From The Bill and Kathy Stella Currency Collection
(350-500)

13718 **Fr. 1550 $100 1966 Legal Tender Note. PCGS Gem New 66PPQ.**
Huge margins and lavish paper surfaces lend credence to the grade for this wonderfully centered Red Seal note. (700-900)

13719 **Fr. 1550 $100 1966 Legal Tender Note. Gem Crisp Uncirculated.**
Ample margins and a dark red overprint add up to a winning note with embossing.
From The Rolling Plains Collection (650-850)

1966 $100 Legal Tender Specimen

13720 **Fr. 1550 $100 1966 Legal Tender Note. Very Fine-Extremely Fine.**
From our January 2006 FUN auction where the description read, "Bold red vertical stamps on both sides of Franklin and at each end of the back denote this C-note as a Specimen as does the serial number H12345678G. While Federal Reserve Note Specimens are seen with some regularity, this note is a rare sight indeed, we have not seen another example of a $100 Legal Tender Specimen in our many years of work." (5,000-7,000)

High Grade $100 Legal Star

13721 Fr. 1550★ $100 1966 Legal Tender Note. PCGS Superb Gem New 68PPQ.
This $100 Legal has the proverbial board walk margins to go along with its sharp corners, embossing, and deep red third printing. This is a fantastic note that is just one grading point shy of the 69PPQ we sold in April 2006 for $13,800. This one point grading difference may enable you to get this note at half the price of a 69PPQ.. **(6,000-9,000)**

13722 Fr. 1550★ $100 1966 Legal Tender Note. PCGS New 62.
This is a modern day rarity from the late 1960s and extremely tough in the uncirculated grades.
From The Rolling Plains Collection **(1,500-2,000)**

13723 Fr. 1551 $100 1966A Legal Tender Note. PMG Gem Uncirculated 66 EPQ.
The overprints are deep on this legal from the tougher of the two series. **(1,500-1,750)**

13724 Fr. 1551 $100 1966A Legal Tender Note. PMG Choice Uncirculated 64.
A bold red overprint is seen on this note that is a touch thin at left. **(800-1,200)**

13725 Fr. 1551 $100 1966A Legal Tender Note. Crisp Uncirculated.
Gem quality margins and a bright red overprint are noted. **(650-850)**

13726 Fr. 1551 $100 1966A Legal Tender Note. PCGS Choice About New 58.
This example of this popular high denomination has vivid red overprints and faces up very well. **(400-600)**

13727 Fr. 1551 $100 1966A Legal Tender Note. PMG Choice About Unc 58.
Excellent margins and fire engine red inks are found on this magnificent example from the much scarcer "A" series. If there is a fold in the paper it must be very faint. **(400-600)**

13728 Fr. 1600★ $1 1928 Silver Certificate. PMG Choice Uncirculated 63 EPQ.
The embossing is quite pronounced on this bright replacement ace. (650-850)

13729 Fr. 1600★ $1 1928 Silver Certificate. PCGS Choice New 63.
A bright and well printed example of our first small Silver Certificate star. (600-800)

13730 Fr. 1600★ $1 1928 Silver Certificate. About Uncirculated.
Full margins encircle this darkly inked star that has a faint center fold.
From The Rolling Plains Collection (250-350)

13731 Fr. 1601 $1 1928A Silver Certificates. Two Examples. Gem Crisp Uncirculated.
These notes come from the K-A and S-A blocks with the same serial number - 178. They exhibit wide margins and embossing. (Total: 2 notes) (300-400)

13732 Fr. 1601 $1 1928A Silver Certificate. Choice Crisp Uncirculated.
Three digit serial number 111 graces this bright Funnyback with a touch of teller handling. (350-550)

Solid 9's

13733 Fr. 1601 $1 1928A Silver Certificate. Choice Crisp Uncirculated.
This is a great note which bears serial number R99999999A, by far the rarest of solid serial numbers to obtain. It has been several years since we've had even one of these rare small size solid 9s to offer in any grade, let alone an uncirculated piece from an early series. The all-important serial number is strongly embossed while a couple of minor counting crinkles are noticed. Great rarities are hard to estimate, but our best guess is... (5,000-10,000)

13734 Fr. 1601★ $1 1928A Silver Certificate. CGA Gem Uncirculated 66.
This well centered example displays bold embossing through the third party holder and boasts solid margins. (700-800)

13735 Fr. 1602 $1 1928B Silver Certificates. X-B, Y-B, Z-B Experimentals.
This is a group of these popular experimental notes used to test changes in linen content of the paper. The X-B block 50% linen and 50% cotton note is housed in a CGA **Gem Uncirculated 65** holder, the Y-B block 75% linen 25% cotton note grades **Crisp Uncirculated,** with adhesive residue in each of the back corners, and the Z-B block control note rounds out the trio at a grade of **Choice CU** with a counting crinkle.
From The Bill and Kathy Stella Currency Collection (Total: 3 notes) (400-600)

13736 **Fr. 1603 $1 1928C Silver Certificate. PMG Gem Uncirculated 65 EPQ.**
Bold blue inks and plenty of embossing are found on this crackling fresh semi-key ace. Gem type notes in holders have been selling for all the money as demand has not abated for such items. **(800-1,200)**

13737 **Fr. 1605 $1 1928E Silver Certificate. Very Fine-Extremely Fine.**
Light folds and handling appear on this well embossed original mid-grade key note from the I-B block. **(600-900)**

13738 **Fr. 1605 $1 1928E Silver Certificate. Very Good.**
The edges are much nicer for the grade than usually found at this level.
From The Rolling Plains Collection **(200-300)**

13739 **Fr. 1606★ $1 1934 Silver Certificate. Crisp Gem Uncirculated.**
This is a pleasing example of this Funnyback replacement. **(850-1,250)**

13740 **Fr. 1607★ $1 1935 Silver Certificate. CGA Gem Uncirculated 65.**
This is a scarce star in Gem and has excellent color and paper quality. **(500-700)**

13741 **Fr. 1608 $1 1935A Mule Silver Certificates. Ten Consecutive Examples. Choice Crisp Uncirculated.**
Original paper wave and embossing are merits of this crackling fresh mule mini-run. (Total: 10 notes) **(300-400)**

13742 **Fr. 1609 $1 1935A R Silver Certificate. PMG Gem Uncirculated 66 EPQ.**
A splendid example of this "R" Experimental note which is always coveted in these high grades. The margins are huge with bright ink colors and embossing clearly visible through the holder. **(800-1,200)**

13743 **Fr. 1609, Fr. 1610 $1 1935A R & S Silver Certificates. Very Choice Crisp Uncirculated to Gem Crisp Uncirculated.**
This well matched pair has sizeable, perfectly matched margins and great color. (Total: 2 notes) **(800-1,000)**

13744 Fr. 1610 $1 1935A S Silver Certificate. PMG Superb Gem Unc 67 EPQ.
This perfectly margined Experimental is one of the finest we've seen. As noted by PMG, the paper quality is second to none, as are the bold colors of the printed design, seal, serial numbers, and all important red S. **(800-1,000)**

13745 Fr. 1610 $1 1935A S Silver Certificate. PMG Choice Uncirculated 64 EPQ.
Due to the tight bottom right this note just misses gem. Strong embossing is readily seen. **(400-600)**

13746 Fr. 1610★ $1 1935A S Silver Certificate. CGA Choice Uncirculated 64.
Pleasing paper quality is noted through the third party holder as is the embossing. **(400-600)**

13747 Fr. 1613N/W $1 1935D Silver Certificates. Original Pack of 100 with Changeover Pairs. Choice Crisp Uncirculated.
This crackly fresh pack is most interesting as it contains both Wide and Narrow varieties. With unused back plate number 5016 as the dividing point, Wides have numbers below and Narrows have numbers above. A quick perusal of this pack finds two Narrow/Wide Reverse Changeover pairs and three Wide/Narrow Changeover pairs. This is a great pack that will yield much study and enjoyment. Pencilled writing and a small white sticker is found on the BEP band. (Total: 100 notes) **(800-1,000)**

13748 Fr. 1614 $1 1935E Silver Certificates. Fifty Consecutive Examples. Choice Crisp Uncirculated.
This first half of a pack has three broad margins and a tight top margin. Many of the notes exhibit a portion of a paper guide line marker in the lower right-hand corner. (Total: 50 notes) **(300-400)**

13749 Fr. 1614 $1 1935E Silver Certificates. 99 Consecutive Examples Choice Crisp Uncirculated.
The first piece has been pulled from this almost complete pack of notes. A few bumps and bruises are seen on original surfaces. (Total: 99 notes) **(800-1,200)**

High Grade B71-J Note

13750 Fr. 1615 $1 1935F Silver Certificate. About Uncirculated.
A high grade example of the scarce B71-J block, which had a print run of just 360,0000 pieces. These notes, which were printed after the start of the 1935G series, were stored until officials decided to release them some time after their printing. New Orleans was chosen as the release point, and just about the entire issue disappeared into circulation before collectors discovered their existence. The result was that few were saved in any grade, with uncirculated specimens truly rare. **(500-800)**

13751 Fr. 1617 $1 1935G With Motto Silver Certificates. Ninety-eight Consecutive Examples. Choice Crisp Uncirculated.
The "With Motto" variety of this series had a print run of only about one-sixth that of the "No Motto" variety. This fact is not truly reflected in the current price relationship between the two. In January 2006 we sold a pack of 99 notes on this Friedberg number in the same grade for almost $3000 The left margin is overly broad on this particular run of notes. (Total: 98 notes) **(2,750-3,250)**

13752 Fr. 1618 $1 1935H Silver Certificates. Original Pack of 100. Very Choice Crisp Uncirculated.
The margins improve greatly beyond the first couple of notes. (Total: 100 notes) **(1,000-1,250)**

13753 Fr. 1618 $1 1935H Silver Certificates. Forty-nine Consecutive Examples. Choice Crisp Uncirculated.
These notes are the back half of an original pack. They have resided quietly in a safe deposit box since 1963. A homemade band keeps these well preserved notes in place. The penned number of notes on the band is one less than it should be. (Total: 49 notes) **(350-550)**

13754 Fr. 1618 $1 1935H Silver Certificates. Fifty Consecutive Examples. Choice Crisp Uncirculated.
A bank band is found on this run that has a few of the outside notes showing a little handling. (Total: 50 notes) (350-550)

13755 Fr. 1618 $1 1935H Silver Certificate. Fifty Consecutive Notes. Choice Crisp Uncirculated to Gem Crisp Uncirculated.
This pleasing pack is fresh and bright, with only minor variances in margin width through the run. (Total: 50 notes) (500-750)

13756 Fr. 1619 $1 1957 Silver Certificate. CGA Gem Uncirculated 67.
Broad, even margins surround this low serial number 54 Silver Certificate. (300-400)

13757 Fr. 1619 $1 1957 Silver Certificate. CGA Gem Uncirculated 67.
This boldly colored Silver Certificate boasts the low, two-digit serial number 97. (250-350)

13758 Fr. 1619 $1 1957 Silver Certificate. Original Pack of 100. Gem Crisp Uncirculated.
A total of 13 star notes is sprinkled through this exquisite pack. The original strap is included and is stamped *National Bank of Detroit, Jan. ?2 1964*. A couple of notes have some minor bumps, and the first note shows a touch of the teller stamp. (Total: 100 notes) (1,250-1,500)

13759 Fr. 1619 $1 1957 Silver Certificates. Thirty-two Examples. Treasury Presentation Set # 17 Gem Crisp Uncirculated.
This was the sixteenth sheet printed for the 1957 Series. Then it was cut up at the BEP and deposited in a Treasury Department envelope. Notes on a 32 subject sheet are not numbered consecutively and in this case each note advances by 20,000. The notes are beautiful and were originally intended for a dignitary. The blue Treasury Seal on the first note shows light smearing. It must be remembered that distribution of uncut sheets ended on January 6, 1954. Therefore, this explains why these first few sheets for the 1957 Series were cut up and prepared for distribution in this form. (Total: 32 notes) (900-1,200)

13760 Fr. 1619 $1 1957 Silver Certificates. Pack of 100. Gem Crisp Uncirculated.
This handsome pack is held by a bank band instead of a BEP band. A couple of the notes show handling (Total: 100 notes) (800-1,000)

13761 Fr. 1619 $1 1957 Silver Certificates. Original Pack of 100. Very Choice Crisp Uncirculated.
Fifteen Star notes are sprinkled throughout this crackling fresh strap of Silvers. (Total: 100 notes) (1,250-1,500)

13762 Fr. 1619★ $1 1957 Silver Certificate. Seventy Four Consecutive Stars. Choice Crisp Uncirculated.
A single note is missing from this original run of star notes. (Total: 74 notes) (1,000-1,250)

13763 Fr. 1619 $1 1957 Silver Certificates. Original Pack of 100 Choice Crisp Uncirculated.
The first and last notes in this pack have some issues with a corner tip fold affecting a few notes. There is also a bit of rubber band residue affecting the back of the last piece. (Total: 100 notes) (800-1,200)

13764 Fr. 1619 $1 1957 Silver Certificate. CGA Choice Uncirculated 63 Stained.
From our 2006 FUN auction where it was described, "From the Taylor Family Collection comes this note, which is an otherwise attractive piece with some light brown staining evident on the face and considerably more on the back. Solid serial number Silver Certificates are especially elusive, as this is a collecting specialty that did not become widely popular until after the period of their printing was well past." (1,250-1,750)

13765 Fr. 1619 $1 1957 Silver Certificates. Original Pack of 100 Choice Crisp Uncirculated.
Twelve star notes are inserted within this original pack of blue seals. (Total: 100 notes) (1,000-1,250)

13766 Fr. 1619★ $1 1957 Silver Certificates. Two Examples. Gem CU
Fr. 1620 $1 1957A Silver Certificates. Fourteen Examples. Gem CU
Fr. 1620★ $1 1957A Silver Certificates. Thirty-eight Examples. Gem CU
Fr. 1621★ $1 1957B Silver Certificate. Gem CU.
One of the Fr. 1620 notes grades no better than VF and all but one of the Fr. 1620★'s is consecutive. (Total: 55 notes) (400-700)

13767 Fr. 1620 $1 1957A Silver Certificates. Original Pack of 100. Choice Crisp Uncirculated.
A few of the outside notes show handling plus a corner bump is found on the approximate first half of the pack. (Total: 100 notes) (500-700)

Matching Serial Number 8 Pair

13768   **Fr. 1621 $1 1957B Silver Certificate. PMG Gem Uncirculated 66.**
This pair boasts matching, single digit serial numbers, R00000008A and S00000008A. Both notes display solid margins and bold blue overprints. (Total: 2 notes) (1,500-2,000)

13769   **Fr. 1613N $1 1935D Silver Certificate. Courtesy Autograph CH AU.**
Fr. 1617 $1 1935G No Motto Silver Certificate Courtesy Autograph CH CU.
Fr. 1619 $1 1957 Silver Certificate Courtesy Autograph VF-XF
Fr. 1621 $1 1957B Silver Certificate Courtesy Autograph Gem CU
This pleasing lot carries the autographs of six different people. A nice way to begin a collection of courtesy Autograph notes.
From The Rolling Plains Collection (Total: 4 notes) (400-600)

13770   **Fr. 1651 $5 1934A Silver Certificates. Ten Consecutive Examples. CGA Choice Uncirculated 64 or Better.**
Seven notes weigh in at 66; two at 67; and one at 64. A cut half sheet is found within this lot. (Total: 10 notes) (400-600)

13771   **Fr. 1651 $5 1934A Silver Certificates. Six Consecutive Examples. CGA Gem Uncirculated 65 or Better.**
This is a cut half sheet with one 65; four 66s; and one 67. (Total: 6 notes) (250-350)

13772   **Fr. 1651 $5 1934A Silver Certificates. Four Consecutive Examples. CGA Choice Uncirculated 63 or Better.**
The first note is a 63 and the last three notes tip the scales at 65. (Total: 4 notes) (150-250)

13773   **Fr. 1651★ $5 1934A Silver Certificate. CGA Gem Uncirculated 67.**
A broadly margined and very well embossed example of this popular early blue seal star. Radiant ink colors are complemented by bold printing to give this silver Five a lot of aesthetic appeal. (500-700)

13774   **Fr. 1653 $5 1934C Silver Certificates. Ninety-two Examples. About Uncirculated.**
Counting these notes produces the crackling sound that is associated with freshness. This grouping lacks a few serial numbers from being consecutive. A few of the notes will be above and a few below the assigned grade of AU. (Total: 92 notes) (900-1,200)

13775   **Fr. 1654 $5 1934D Narrow Silver Certificate. PMG Superb Gem Unc 67 EPQ.**
This note boasts a serial number from the scarcer V-A Block.
From The Bill and Kathy Stella Currency Collection (300-400)

13776   **Fr. 1654 $5 1934D Silver Certificates. Twenty Consecutive Examples Very Choice Crisp Uncirculated.**
Great embossing, wide margins, and deep inks are seen on these notes with some that are true Gems. (600-1,000)

13777   **Fr. 1654★ $5 1934D Wide Silver Certificate. Choice Crisp Uncirculated.**
Embossing is noticed along with a tiny paper imperfection in the back upper corner.
From The Bill and Kathy Stella Currency Collection (200-250)

13778 Fr. 1655 $5 1953 Silver Certificates. Uncut Sheet of 18. Choice Crisp Uncirculated.
This exceptionally attractive sheet would clearly be a full Gem but for the presence of a few scattered handling wrinkles, all of which are so trivial and unimportant that they are hardly worth mentioning. This ex-Irving Moskovitz Collection piece was sold as Lot 1630 of the dispersal of that fabled holding by Bowers and Ruddy in 1977 and bears the original lot tag as documentation of its pedigree. It is attractively matted next to an inscribed copy of Lincoln's Gettysburg Address with hand lettering and illumination above. The upper left note of the sheet bears serial A00000052A and the serials advance by 8000 per note vertically down the columns. The lower right note bears the autographs of Treasurer of the United States Ivy Baker Priest and Secretary of the Treasury George Humphrey, both of whose engraved signatures adorn this lovely sheet. While the Priest autograph is fresh and vivid, the Humphrey autograph has faded almost entirely. Given the growing popularity of Treasury official autographed currency, the allure of items pedigreed to major collections, the attractive display and the overall superior aesthetics of this appealing item, it is likely that bidding will reach no less than...
From The Rolling Plains Collection (2,500-3,500)

13779 Fr. 1655 $5 1953 Silver Certificates. Thirty-five Examples. Choice Crisp Uncirculated.
These notes are crackling fresh and nicely embossed. This grouping is just a few serial numbers short of a consecutive run. (Total: 35 notes) (550-750)

13780 Fr. 1655 $5 1953 Silver Certificates. Forty Consecutive Examples. Choice Crisp Uncirculated.
This grouping has been bank wrapped. Hand-written in blue ink on the band is, "Save in rotation June 1954 $200." In another hand is the Friedberg number and "20." These have been nicely preserved for almost 53 years since then. This is the most of this Friedberg number that we have ever offered in one lot. (Total: 40 notes) (600-900)

13781 Fr. 1655 $5 1953 Silver Certificates. Twenty Consecutive Examples. Choice Crisp Uncirculated.
This partial pack of notes was plucked from the First Wisconsin National Bank of Milwaukee on 6/18/54 and has finally been found over 50 years later. Uncompromised, original surfaces are seen throughout the run. (350-500)

13782 Fr. 1655 $5 1953 Silver Certificates. Twenty Consecutive Examples. Choice Crisp Uncirculated.
Here is another pleasing, original mini-run of notes put away long ago. (Total: 20 notes) (350-500)

13783 Fr. 1655 $5 1953 Silver Certificates. Twenty Consecutive Examples. Choice Crisp Uncirculated.
We are lucky to have another batch of consecutive notes from the First Wisconsin National Bank of Milwaukee per the strap. (Total: 20 notes) (350-500)

13784 Fr. 1655 $5 1953 Silver Certificates. Twenty Consecutive Examples. Choice Crisp Uncirculated.
The First Wisconsin National Bank of Milwaukee bank band has written in blue pencil, "Save in rotation." We are glad that they were because of their prominent embossing and freshness. (Total: 20 notes) (350-500)

13785 Fr. 1655★ $5 1953 Silver Certificates. Thirty-nine Consecutive Examples. Crisp Uncirculated.
This is the first time that we have had a consecutive run of this star. They are listed at $120 individually in Ch CU in the Schwartz reference. Many of the notes are Choice CU, but several have an edge pinch or extreme corner tip bend. One note near the center of the grouping has teller graffiti. (Total: 39 notes) (1,500-2,000)

Late Finished FP #87

13786 Fr. 1702 $10 1934A Silver Certificate. PMG About Uncirculated 55 EPQ. Late Finished Plate # 87.
A lone horizontal fold is noted on this issue. The margins are solid and the overprint remains bright. PMG has endowed this beauty with their comment of "Exceptional Paper Quality" and we certainly concur with that assessment. The latest Schwartz reference quotes $3,000 for Choice CU. (1,500-2,500)

13787 Fr. 1705 $10 1934D Wide Silver Certificate. PMG Gem Uncirculated 65 EPQ.
The overprint is vivid on this Wide variety Silver Five.
From The Bill and Kathy Stella Currency Collection (300-350)

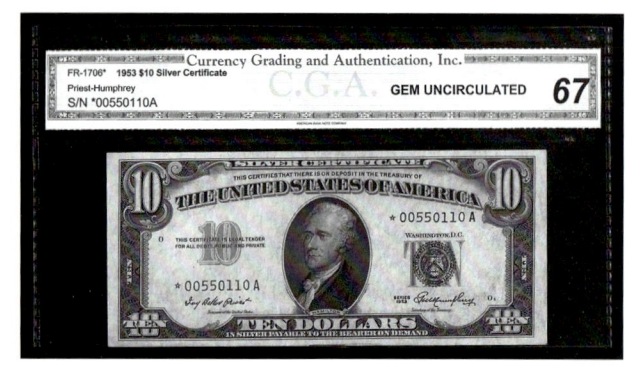

13788 **Fr. 1706★ $10 1953 Silver Certificate. CGA Gem Uncirculated 67.**
A well centered example of this in demand star which has been graded as Gem Uncirculated 67 by CGA. (900-1,200)

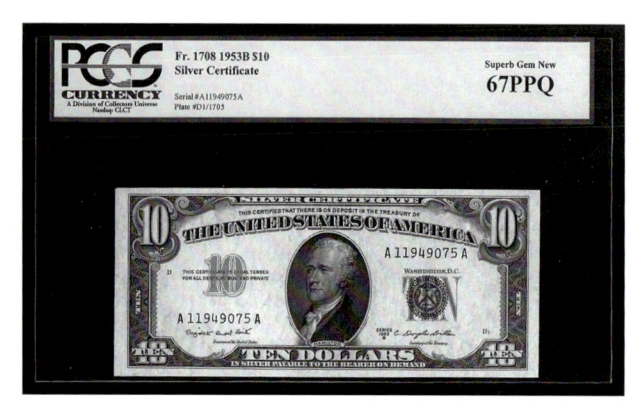

13789 **Fr. 1708 $10 1953B Silver Certificate. PCGS Superb Gem New 67PPQ.**
As perfect a note as one could hope to locate enhanced by the PCGS decree of "nihil obstat." (400-600)

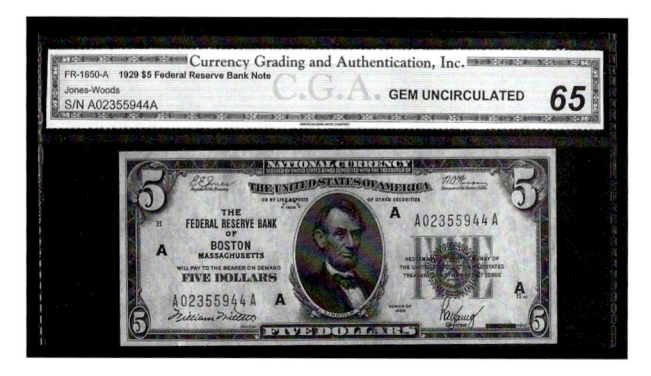

13790 **Fr. 1850-A $5 1929 Federal Reserve Bank Note. CGA Gem Uncirculated 65.**
This is a pleasing piece with plenty of embossing visible. (400-600)

13791 **Fr. 1850-B $5 1929 Federal Reserve Bank Note. PMG Gem Uncirculated 65.**
Superb original embossing and the PMG comment "Vivid Details" is found on this totally original New York FRBN. The note clearly is deserving of the EPQ designation and it would be our guess that this is an old PMG holder before they used to affix the EPQ designation. (200-300)

13792 **Fr. 1850-D $5 1929 Federal Reserve Bank Note. Choice Crisp Uncirculated.**
A bit of handling on the right side takes this low serial number D00000046A example from the Gem class. (450-650)

13793 **Fr. 1850-F $5 1929 Federal Reserve Bank Note. PMG Choice Uncirculated 64.**
This is a clean example from the tougher Atlanta district. (350-450)

One of Only Four CU Stars from KC

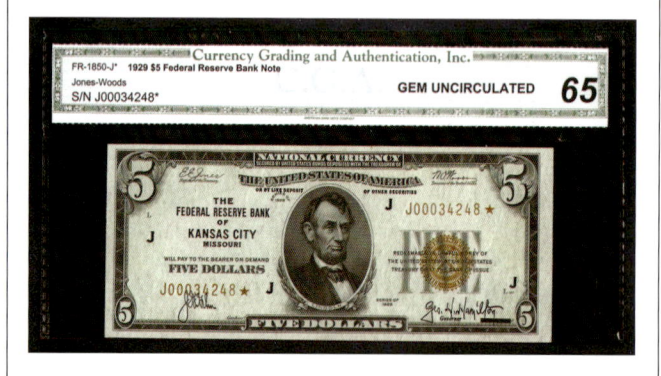

13794 **Fr. 1850-J★ $5 1929 Federal Reserve Bank Note. CGA Gem Uncirculated 65.**
Last seen in our 2004 Central States sale, "A nicely centered star example which is one of a short (4 note) Uncirculated run. These four pieces are the only CU stars listed for the district. This note has been encapsulated by CGA and graded as Gem Uncirculated 65. The Cookson example, which graded only Choice, realized $3680, and this piece will likely do even better." With the recent release of the Jhon E. Cash FRBN Star Census, this is still one of only four CU $5 stars from KC. (5,000-7,500)

13795 Cut Half Sheet. Fr. 1850-K $5 1929 Federal Reserve Bank Notes. CGA Choice Uncirculated 64 to CGA Gem Uncirculated 65.
This pleasing half sheet was kept together for posterity. The notes show some minor differences in margin size, but are well matched. Deep embossing is noted even through the holders on each of the notes. (1,250-1,750)

13796 Fr. 1850-K $5 1929 Federal Reserve Bank Note. CGA Gem Uncirculated 65.
From our 2005 Long Beach sale, "This Dallas FRBN appears fully original and beautifully embossed through the CGA holder, and is well-centered and boldly printed. A lovely Gem example from this popular district." (400-600)

13797 Fr. 1850-K $5 1929 Federal Reserve Bank Note. PMG Choice Uncirculated 64 EPQ.
The collectors of today are fortunate that William Philpott was able to discover a nice supply of these $5 FRBNs through his contacts with Texas bankers, or Dallas would be the scarcest $5 FRBN. This example carries fresh, white paper, and bold bank title embossing as noted by the EPQ designation. (300-400)

Serial # 15 Boston $10 FRBN

13798 Fr. 1860-A $10 1929 Federal Reserve Bank Note. CGA Very Fine 35.
Low serial number "15" graces this Boston $10 FRBN. (400-600)

One of Only Five Known CU Stars

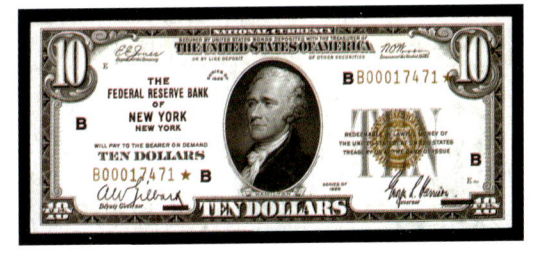

13799 Fr. 1860-B★ $10 1929 Federal Reserve Bank Star Note. Very Choice Crisp Uncirculated.
Last appearing in our 2004 FUN sale of Dr. Cookson's FRBN Notes, this example is one of only five known CU notes, out of the 101 recorded stars in the Jhon E. Cash census. This is still the finest example we have had the pleasure of handling, and look forward to finding a new home for the next collector. (2,000-3,000)

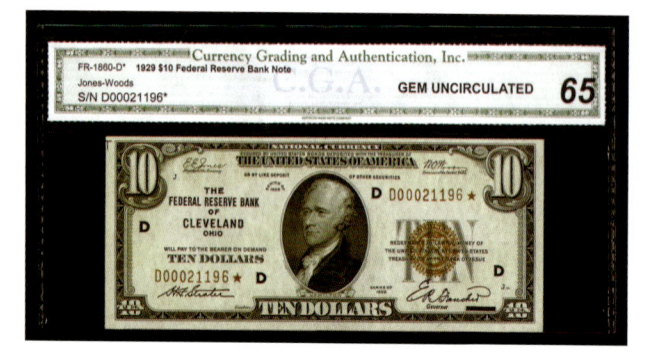

13800 Fr. 1860-D★ $10 1929 Federal Reserve Bank Note. CGA Gem Uncirculated 65.
Bold original embossing is found on this bright and colorful star. In the past half decade we have only handled four of these stars and this one is the finest. (2,250-2,750)

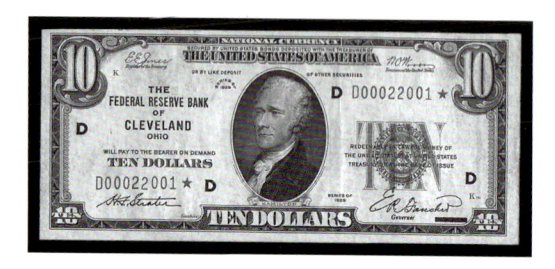

13801 Fr. 1860-D★ $10 1929 Federal Reserve Bank Star Note. Extremely Fine-About Uncirculated.
One of the nicest of the survivors of the original issue of just 24,000 pieces some seventy years ago. This is the kind of Extremely Fine-About Uncirculated note every collector craves, with this example displaying only two light folds that are barely visible without close inspection. Utterly original and problem free, and one of the finest five or six pieces known, this is a note which would fit perfectly into any high grade star set. (750-1,000)

Gorgeous Atlanta 1929 $10 FRBN Star Note

13802 Fr. 1860-F★ $10 1929 Federal Reserve Bank Note. Extremely Fine-About Uncirculated.
From our Taylor Family Sale where the description read, "This piece is easily the finest known of any of the eight reported $10 Richmond district stars, and by a considerable margin at that. It's got an illustrious pedigree, coming from the Oakes collection and, prior to that, from the Jim Thompson holdings." It's listed in the Cybuski and Oakes censuses as uncirculated, and indeed was sold as "Gem CU" in the Oakes collection sale, but there are a pair of hard to miss folds which make it impossible for this cataloguer to adhere to that previously assigned grade. Expect this example to now realize somewhere in the vicinity of... (4,000-6,000)

Key to the Series

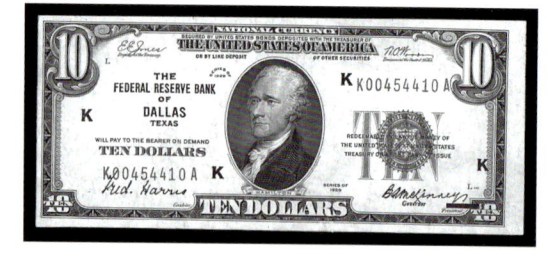

13803 Fr. 1860-K $10 1929 Federal Reserve Bank Note. About Uncirculated.
While appearing UNC, this Dallas beauty does have a very faint center fold, along with a tiny, tiny tear at top center and a scuff mark along the lower margin. (1,500-2,000)

13804 Fr. 1860-K $10 1929 Federal Reserve Bank Note. PMG Fine 12.
These have long been recognized as the key to the $10 FRBN issue. This example is free of pinholes and any undue soiling for the grade. (400-600)

13805 Fr. 1860-L★ $10 1929 Federal Reserve Bank Note. Fine.
This is a tough star to find in any grade, with the new census compiled by Jhon Cybuski showing just seventeen examples, with only one grading higher than Very Fine. This piece shows a couple of tiny separations at the folds, along with a bit of soil on one section of the reverse. (700-1,200)

Serial # 20 on a $20

13806 Fr. 1870-D $20 1929 Federal Reserve Bank Note. Gem Crisp Uncirculated.
Another example last seen in our 2004 FUN sale, where we described, "What could be better than serial number D00000020A on a $20 bill, especially when that note is a crackling fresh well centered gem." (1,000-1,500)

13807 **Fr. 1870-G★ $20 1929 Federal Reserve Bank Note. Very Fine+.**
This note, which is in the Cybuski census, brings the number known to 16. It is the second nicest known as the paper is bright, with no problems of any kind. Expect to see heated competition on this possible upgrade piece. (1,750-2,250)

13808 **Fr. 1870-H★ $20 1929 Federal Reserve Bank Note. PCGS New 62.**
According to the Jhon E. Cash Official Census of 1929 FRBN Star notes, of the 24,000 examples printed only 38 examples have been documented to date. This may prove to be the finest known example as only one other note carries the grade of CU. (1,500-2,500)

13809 **Fr. 1870-J★ $20 1929 Federal Reserve Bank Note. Fine-Very Fine.**
This piece, which retains some crispness, is lightly stained with a touch of soiling on the back. Only 24 survivors are enumerated in the Cybuski census out of a print run of 24,000. (600-800)

High Grade Dallas $20

13810 **Fr. 1870-K $20 1929 Federal Reserve Bank Note. About Uncirculated.**
A totally original example, with great embossing in what some people say is the real key to this series, versus the Ten. Our consignor claims to have obtained this beauty from his Dallas branch bank some 10 years ago. How it can pay off to befriend your bank teller! (1,000-1,500)

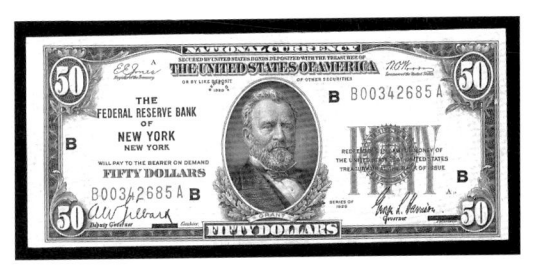

13811 **Fr. 1880-B $50 1929 Federal Reserve Bank Note. Choice Crisp Uncirculated.**
This note is Gem, but for slight centering imperfections, as the design is positioned too low and to the right. (350-450)

13812 **Fr. 1880-B $50 1929 Federal Reserve Bank Note. Choice Crisp Uncirculated.**
Bold embossing and natural paper surfaces are highlights of this $50 that has a counting crinkle. (350-450)

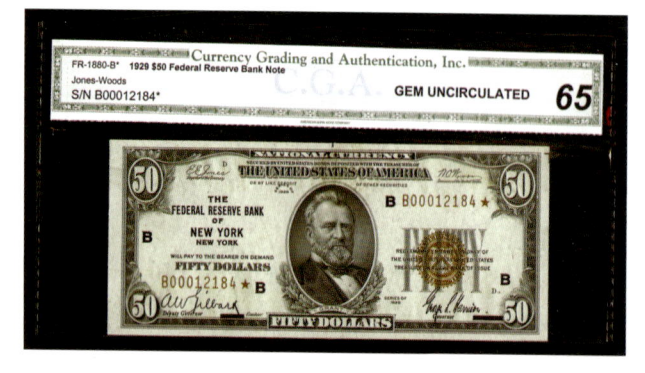

13813 Fr. 1880-B★ $50 1929 Federal Reserve Bank Note. CGA Gem Uncirculated 65.
Solid margins are met by bright white paper. Remnants of a teller's fingerprint are noted, but do little to detract from the overall eye appeal of the note. (3,000-4,000)

13814 Fr. 1880-B★ $50 1929 Federal Reserve Bank Note. Fine.
New York is the most common star $50, with 63 currently recorded in the Cash census. This note reappears from our 2004 FUN sale minus the ink on the face, as the ink is also noted in the Cash reference. (400-600)

13815 Fr. 1880-D $50 1929 Federal Reserve Bank Note. CGA Gem Uncirculated 66.
Low serial number D00005805A is found on this bright and well embossed Cleveland FRBN, the first of six consecutive notes. (600-900)

13816 Fr. 1880-D $50 1929 Federal Reserve Bank Note. CGA Gem Uncirculated 66.
A broadly margined and crackling fresh gem that has good embossing and a low four digit number D00005806A. (600-900)

13817 Fr. 1880-D $50 1929 Federal Reserve Bank Note. CGA Gem Uncirculated 66.
This four digit FRBN with serial number D00005807A is consecutive to the previous lot and virtually identical in appearance. (600-900)

13818 Fr. 1880-D $50 1929 Federal Reserve Bank Note. CGA Gem Uncirculated 66.
Broad margins and decent paper quality are noted on this Cleveland $50. (600-900)

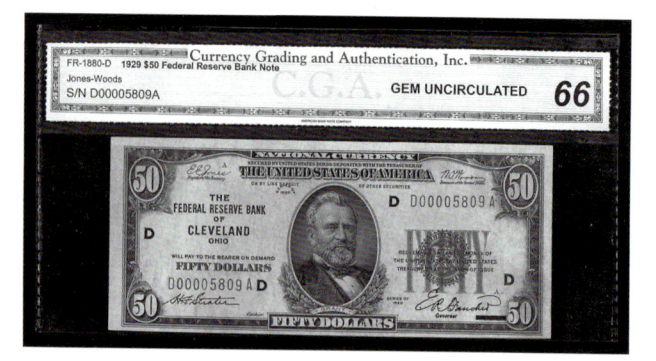

13819 Fr. 1880-D $50 1929 Federal Reserve Bank Note. CGA Gem Uncirculated 66.
This is the fifth note of the consecutive group offered here, and like the third has a little tighter margins than the first. (600-900)

13820 Fr. 1880-D $50 1929 Federal Reserve Bank Note. CGA Gem Uncirculated 66.
While this piece is not the most broadly margined of the three Gem examples offered here, its paper quality is certainly worthy of note. (600-900)

13821 Fr. 1880-G $50 1929 Federal Reserve Bank Note. Choice Crisp Uncirculated.
Embossing and natural surfaces are found on this Chicago $50. The bottom margin is thin while a counting crinkle is noticed. (300-400)

13822 Fr. 1880-J★ $50 1929 Federal Reserve Bank Note. Extremely Fine.
This broadly margined Star appears Gem, though there are three soft folds as is the case with many EF's. (1,750-2,250)

13823 Fr. 1880-K $50 1929 Federal Reserve Bank Note. Choice About Uncirculated.
The $50 and $100 Dallas FRBN's are the keys to their respective series. This attractive piece has a light horizontal bend that precludes a Gem grade. The paper is bright and the margins sizeable. (3,000-4,000)

13824 **Fr. 1880-K $50 1929 Federal Reserve Bank Note. About Uncirculated.**
Soft surfaces are noted on this bright and pleasing $50 that has a light center fold. Our lucky consignor put together his set of Dallas FRBN's by acquiring them through his bank over ten years ago, but, don't let his teller know. (3,000-4,000)

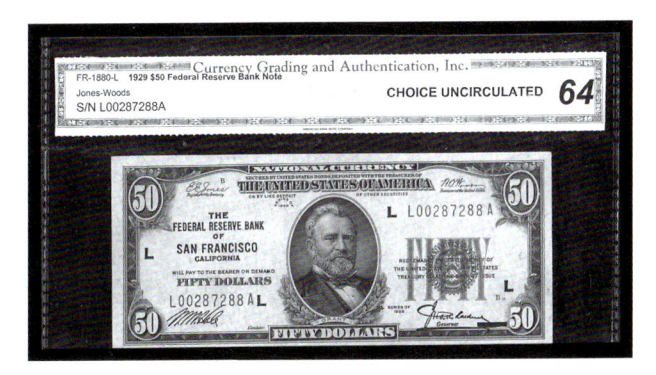

13825 **Fr. 1880-L $50 1929 Federal Reserve Bank Note. CGA Choice Uncirculated 64.**
Two broad margins are matched with two other sufficient margins. The embossing from the serial numbers and seal are noted on the back. (500-600)

13826 **Fr. 1890-D $100 1929 Federal Reserve Bank Note. Very Choice Crisp Uncirculated.**
Crackling fresh and fully embossed, but the centering is just not up to Gem standards. (350-450)

13827 **Fr. 1890-D $100 1929 Federal Reserve Bank Note. Very Choice Crisp Uncirculated.**
Fully embossed and very close to the full Gem grade, but the back centering takes it from that classification. (350-450)

13828 **Fr. 1890-E $100 1929 Federal Reserve Bank Note. PMG Choice Uncirculated 63 EPQ.**
Plenty of embossing remains on this note that needed a thicker bottom margin for a higher grade. It lists for $800 in the Schwartz tome. (600-800)

Three Consecutive $100 FRBN's

13829 **Fr. 1890-G $100 1929 Federal Reserve Bank Notes. Three Consecutive Examples (2) PCGS Very Choice New 64PPQ (1) Gem New 65PPQ**
This is simply a marvelous trio of original brown seals off the Chicago district. The colors are quite vivid and the embossing pronounced. (Total: 3 notes) (1,250-1,750)

13830 **Fr. 1890-G $100 1929 Federal Reserve Bank Note. Crisp Uncirculated.**
A bright note with a bit too much handling for the higher grade. (350-450)

13831 **Fr. 1890-G $100 1929 Federal Reserve Bank Notes. Two Consecutive Examples. About Uncirculated.**
Both of these embossed notes have a center fold and a very little bit of staining at top center. The first note has it more on the face, while the second note has it more on the back. (Total: 2 notes) (400-600)

13832 **Fr. 1890-I $100 1929 Federal Reserve Bank Note. Choice About Uncirculated.**
Gem margins and paper quality are present here, though there is a bit too much handling to be called New. (500-600)

Fr. 1890-I★ - One of Three Known

13833 **Fr. 1890-I★ $100 1929 Federal Reserve Bank Note. PMG Very Fine 20.**
This is a newly discovered piece and it increases the census of this rare Friedberg number up to a mere three. In February 2005 we sold the Taylor Family Collection example that is a full grade lower for almost $11,000. The PMG label states "Margin Tear." We see the tear and it barely penetrates the bottom frame line. Though we have had two in the last two years of this number, when will another opportunity arise? (11,000-14,000)

13834 **Fr. 1890-J★ $100 1929 Federal Reserve Bank Note. Fine.**
We average about one of this Friedberg number every two years, making it the most available $100 FRBN star and perfect for a type collection. This example spent time as a wallet piece, yet the edges are better than normally found on similarly housed pieces. (450-650)

13835 **Fr. 1890-K $100 1929 Federal Reserve Bank Note. PMG Choice Uncirculated 63 EPQ.**
A slim, but sufficient top margin prevented a full Gem grade for this attractive and obviously original C-note. According to our archives, two years have passed since we last offered an example of this key in Uncirculated condition or better. We expect the Oakes premium may be conservative given the drought of quality pieces. (2,500-3,500)

13836 **Fr. 1890-K $100 1929 Federal Reserve Bank Note. Very Fine-Extremely Fine.**
Here is the last of our lucky consignor's Dallas FRBN collection, each acquired over 10 years ago from a Dallas bank. This note is wholly original, with excellent embossing, and should tip the third-party scales more towards a grade of 40 than 35, provided it is submitted one day. (600-900)

13837 **Fr. 1890-K $100 1929 Federal Reserve Bank Note. PCGS Very Fine 20.**
A scarce note in any grade from the ever popular Dallas district. (400-600)

13838 **Fr. 1901-G★ $1 1963A Federal Reserve Notes. Original Pack of 100. Gem Crisp Uncirculated.**
This well preserved pack starts off with 47 Stars and finishes with 53 regular notes. (Total: 100 notes) (300-500)

13839 **Fr. 1902-B $1 1963B Federal Reserve Notes. Original Pack of 100. Gem Crisp Uncirculated.**
Wide margins are found on this pack of Barr notes that has handling restricted to a few of the outside notes. (Total: 100 notes) (250-350)

13840 **Fr. 1902-B $1 1963B Federal Reserve Notes. Original Pack of 100. Gem Crisp Uncirculated.**
This pack went straight from the teller to the bank patron's safe deposit box where it reposed for nearly 40 years. (Total: 100 notes) (250-350)

13841 **Fr. 1902-G $1 1963B Federal Reserve Notes. Original Pack of 100. Gem Crisp Uncirculated.**
The packs we offer in this auction were put away by our consignor's parents at the time of issue. (Total: 100 notes) (250-350)

13842 **Fr. 1902-G $1 1963B Federal Reserve Notes. Original Pack of 100. Gem Crisp Uncirculated.**
Only a couple of the notes show handling in this pack that was put away in the late 1960s. (Total: 100 notes) (250-350)

13843 **Fr. 1902-G $1 1963B Federal Reserve Notes. Original pack of 100. Choice Crisp Uncirculated.**
The first third of the notes in this pack has an indentation at the bottom edge. (Total: 100 notes) (200-300)

13844 **Fr. 1903-D $1 1969 Federal Reserve Note. Choice About Uncirculated.**
Serial number 10000000 should stir up some interest. (250-450)

13845 Fr. 1905-C★ $1 1969B Federal Reserve Notes. Original Pack of 100. Gem Crisp Uncirculated.
Wide margins and nice centering are found on the Stars in this pack. They are held by a dark blue BEP band with a date stamp of May 3, 1972. Other teller writings are noted on the band, too. (Total: 100 notes) (350-450)

13846 Fr. 1905-C★ $1 1969B Federal Reserve Notes. Original Pack of 100. Choice Crisp Uncirculated.
Teller writing is found on the BEP band for this pack of Stars that begins with three zeros in the serial number. (Total: 100 notes) (300-400)

13847 Fr. 1911-A★, B★, E★, J★, K★ $1 1981 Federal Reserve Notes. Fine Changeover Pair Sets Gem Crisp Uncirculated.
Each set contains a regular star and a mule star which carries a high numbered 1977A back. (Total: 10 notes) (800-1,200)

Elusive Dallas $1 FRN Star

13848 Fr. 1912-K★ $1 1981A Federal Reserve Note. Gem Crisp Uncirculated.
In the Robert Azpiazu reference, *Collectors Guide to $1 FRNs Series 1963 - 2003A*, he lists this star as the second rarest at $1300 in CU.
From The Rolling Plains Collection (1,100-1,600)

13849 Fr. 1913-H★ $1 1985 Federal Reserve Note. PMG Gem Uncirculated 65.
The Series 1985 $1 St. Louis Star is a modern rarity. A mere 640,000 notes were printed but most succumbed immediately to attrition. This example escaped circulation, boasting broad margins and solid embossing. (1,500-2,000)

Rare St. Louis $1 FRN

13850 Fr. 1913-H★ $1 1985 Federal Reserve Note. Crisp Uncirculated.
This star weighs in at number three on the Azpiazu star listing at $1500 in CU. This example has a pre-printing paper crinkle just inside the top edge.
From The Rolling Plains Collection (1,000-1,500)

Rarest $1 FRN Star

13851 Fr. 1914-F★ $1 1988 Federal Reserve Note. Choice Crisp Uncirculated.
In the Azpiazu reference he list this star as the rarest $1 FRN star at $1500 in CU.
From The Rolling Plains Collection (1,200-1,700)

13852 Fr. 1918-C★ $1 1993 Federal Reserve Note. Gem Crisp Uncirculated.
This star comes in sixth place on Azpiazu's Top Ten Star listing. Four broad margins frame this lovely example.
From The Rolling Plains Collection (150-250)

13853 Fr. 1924-A★ $1 1999 Federal Reserve Notes. Original Pack of 100. Gem Crisp Uncirculated.
This is the first time for us to a have a pack on this Friedberg number. The top note shows handling.
From The Rolling Plains Collection (Total: 100 notes) (300-500)

13854 Fr. 1924-C★ $1 1999 Federal Reserve Notes. Ten Examples. Gem Crisp Uncirculated.
The 1924-C★ notes are priced in the Azpiazu reference at $75 a piece. This broad margined grouping has been well preserved. (Total: 10 notes) (400-600)

13855 Fr. 1924-E★ $1 1999 Federal Reserve Notes. Original Pack of 100. Gem Crisp Uncirculated.
Wide margins are a highlight of this pack that has a couple of characters rubber-stamped on the left edge.
From The Rolling Plains Collection (Total: 100 notes) (300-500)

13856 Fr. 1925-H★ $1 1999 Federal Reserve Notes. Two Original Packs of 100. Gem Crisp Uncirculated.
One pack has a Banco Nacional de Panama bank band along with its BEP band.
From The Rolling Plains Collection (Total: 200 notes) (800-1,000)

13857 Fr. 1925-L★ $1 1999 Federal Reserve Notes. Original Pack of 100. Gem CU
Fr. 1927-L★ $1 2001 Federal Reserve Notes. Original Pack of 100. Gem CU.
Both of these packs have been pampered.
From The Rolling Plains Collection (Total: 200 notes) (800-1,000)

13858 Fr. 1928-A★ $1 2003 Federal Reserve Notes. Original Pack of 100. Gem Crisp Uncirculated.
This is a well preserved pack with wide margins. The final note shows some handling.
From The Rolling Plains Collection (Total: 100 notes) (400-600)

13859 Fr. 1928-E $1 2003 Federal Reserve Notes. Original Pack of 100 Choice Crisp Uncirculated.
These notes are from a run not listed in the new edition of the Schwartz-Lindquist Small Size Guide. The last five pieces have a bump into the design in the upper left margin. (Total: 100 notes) (400-600)

13860 Fr. 1929-K★ $1 2003 Federal Reserve Note. PCGS Perfect New 70PPQ.
This broadly margined note has garnered the ultimate grade at PCGS. (500-700)

13861 Fr. 1935-A-L★ $2 1976 Federal Reserve Notes. Complete Issue Set 29 Examples Gem Crisp Uncirculated.
A group such as this is no longer seen with regularity. It includes the ever elusive I-★ and J-★ along with every sheet only issue for the series. All notes are well margined with excellent embossing. A quick way to add to you small size collection.
From The Rolling Plains Collection (Total: 29 notes) (800-1,200)

13862 Fr. 1935-A-L Complete District Set $2 1976 Federal Reserve Notes. Choice CU
Fr. 1935-A★-L★ Complete District Set $2 1976 Federal Reserve Notes. Choice CU.
Many of the notes are better than Choice, except for the G★ which grades **XF-AU**. (Total: 24 notes) (700-1,000)

Star Pack of Bicentennial Deuces

13863 Fr. 1935-G★ $2 1976 Federal Reserve Notes. Original Pack of 100. Gem Crisp Uncirculated.
This is the first time that we have handled a full pack of Chicago stars for the Bicentennial series. Chicago is one of the scarcer districts for stars as the Schwartz-Lindquist reference lists the notes at $60 a piece in CU. Ample margins and nice centering are found on the notes of this pack. The BEP band has been hand-dated with blue pencil. (Total: 100 notes) (4,500-5,500)

13864 Fr. 1935-I★ $2 1976 Federal Reserve Note. Gem Crisp Uncirculated.
The paper quality is blazingly original and the embossing bold on this scarce star. (300-350)

Serial #4 1976 $2 FRN

13865 Fr. 1935-L $2 1976 Federal Reserve Note. Choice Crisp Uncirculated.
This pleasing note carries the single digit serial number four. Plenty of embossing remains on this example which was most likely a presentation piece. (500-1,000)

13866 Fr. 1935-L $2 1976 Federal Reserve Note. Choice Crisp Uncirculated.
Another example which would make a good mate to the note above. This original beauty is graced with serial number five. (500-1,000)

13867 **Premium Millennium Federal Reserve $2 Set Fr. 1936-A★-L★ $2 1995 Federal Reserve Notes. Choice Crisp Uncirculated.**
All twelve of these Stars have serial number 200001754★ and this limited BEP product quickly sold out. All of the twelve notes have a thin stain of varying degrees along the bottom margin. This is a common phenomena found on notes of this set. Speculation is that the stains are oil from a cutting blade within the Western Currency Facility. Only the F★ was made for general circulation. Included with this set is a **Fr. 1935-A★ $2 1976 Federal Reserve Notes Uncut Sheet of Four in Gem CU.** (Total: 2 items) (550-750)

13868 **Courtesy Autographed Fr. 1936-F★ $2 1995 Federal Reserve Note. PCGS Superb Gem New 69PPQ.**
Treasurer Mary Ellen Withrow signed this near-perfect note above her signature. (400-500)

13869 **Fr. 1936-F★ $2 1995 Federal Reserve Notes. Original Pack of 100 Gem Crisp Uncirculated.**
For being the only replacement released for general circulation there are not many packs around. This one is a beauty with little handling and excellent margins. (Total: 100 notes) (800-1,200)

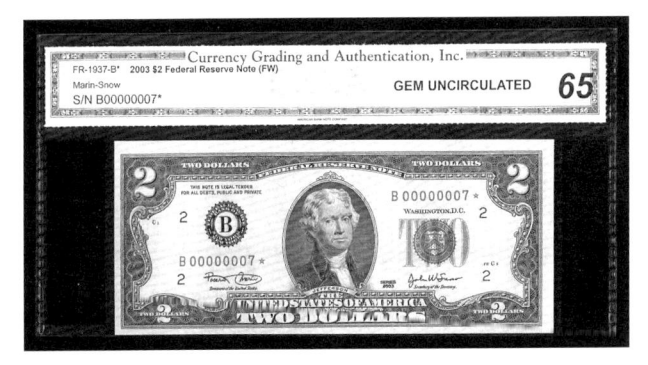

13870 **Fr. 1937-B★ $2 2003 Federal Reserve Note. CGA Gem Uncirculated 65.**
Just 8,000 of these notes were printed for the special use Bureau products sold by the government, with this the second single digit example we've ever had to offer. Based on what the serial number B00000004★ example realized in our 2005 Long Beach sale we would expect in today's more sophisticated marketplace a price that will likely reach or exceed... (2,250-2,750)

13871 **Fr. 1937-C★ $2 2003 Federal Reserve Note. CGA Gem Uncirculated 65.**
This now makes the third single digit example we have offered. (2,250-2,750)

13872 **Fr. 1937-J $2 2003 Federal Reserve Note. PCGS Perfect New 70PPQ.**
Jumbo margins are noted on all four sides of this Perfect Deuce. (500-700)

13873 **Fr. 1950-I $5 1928 Federal Reserve Note. Crisp Uncirculated.**
The margins are broad on three sides and the paper is bright. The Minneapolis issue is the key to this series, and is not easy to find in grades above circulated. (1,250-1,500)

13874 **Fr. 1950-J $5 1928 Federal Reserve Note. Choice Crisp Uncirculated.**
Strong embossing is found on this KC $5. We have seen this Friedberg number in all of our auctions in the last six years only a half dozen times. (300-400)

13875 **Fr. 1951-G Pack of Twenty Consecutive $5 1928A Federal Reserve Notes. Choice Crisp Uncirculated.**
This is a splendid, original pack of notes from this daunting numbered district series. Each is well margined with excellent embossing and that "pack fresh" smell. If it were not for handling at the right this would undoubtedly be a gem pack as every note is lovely in its own right. (Total: 20 notes) (3,000-4,000)

13876 **Fr. 1953-F $5 1928C Federal Reserve Notes. Three Examples. Very Fine.**
This is a dealer's lot of three pieces of this scarce note. One note has a couple of blue ink drops on the back, while all three notes show aging. Viewing is especially advised. (Total: 3 notes) (1,400-1,800)

13877 **Fr. 1960-F $5 1934D Federal Reserve Note. PMG Gem Uncirculated 66 EPQ.**
Nearly 9.6 million notes were printed for the Atlanta Series 1934D, more than the totals for five other different districts, yet it remains the key. Uncirculated notes are especially scarce after attrition depleted the majority of the issue. This piece features broad borders and original surfaces. (1,000-2,000)

13878 **Fr. 1960-I $5 1934D Federal Reserve Note. CGA Gem Uncirculated 68.**
Titanic margins and good embossing are seen on this very scarce district note that lists for $600 in CU in Schwartz. It has been almost five years since we offered an example of this district and this one is about ten points its superior on the grading scale. (800-1,200)

13879 **Forty One Fr. 1962-G $5 1950A Federal Reserve Notes. Choice Crisp Uncirculated to Gem Crisp Uncirculated.**
This pack includes two consecutive runs of 20 each and a lone note. The two 20 note runs are wrapped in a strap labeled $100 and are either from the First Wisconsin National Bank of Milwaukee or Marine National Exchange Bank of Milwaukee. The teller stamp on the later pack's strap is dated Nov. 11, 1960. (Total: 41 notes) (800-1,000)

13880 **Fr. 1963-G $5 1950B Federal Reserve Notes. Forty Examples. Gem Crisp Uncirculated.**
Two consecutive runs of well preserved notes are found within this homemade bank band. (Total: 40 notes) (1,000-1,500)

13881 **Fr. 1964-G $5 1950C Federal Reserve Notes. Twenty-six Examples. Choice Crisp Uncirculated.**
Two Stars are mixed in with the regular notes. There are two separate runs of notes from the same original pack in this lot. All of the notes are crackly fresh and have recently been paroled from the safe deposit box. A homemade band embraces these notes. (Total: 26 notes) (900-1,200)

13882 **Twenty Consecutive Fr. 1964-G $5 1950C Federal Reserve Notes. Choice Crisp Uncirculated.**
This pleasing group is bound by a strap indicating the face value of $100. The notes are crisp with margins ranging from Choice to Gem in quality. (Total: 20 notes) (400-600)

13883 **Fr. 1965-G $5 1950D Federal Reserve Notes. Twenty Examples. Gem Crisp Uncirculated.**
This coterie consist of five Star notes mixed in with fifteen regular notes. This well preserved score of notes beam with originality and freshness. It is held by a homemade bank band with numismatic information written on it about the notes. (Total: 20 notes) (400-700)

13884 **Fr. 1969-I★ $5 1969 Federal Reserve Note. PMG Gem Uncirculated 66EPQ.**
With only 640,000 printed, the Minneapolis district is the key to the series. This example has been blessed with great margins, superb embossing and healthy paper surfaces. This Minneapolis star has a two digit serial number I00000031★ and it is unlikely that there are many surviving examples with lower numbers than this one. (400-600)

13885 **Fr. 1971-F★ $5 1969B Federal Reserve Note. PMG Superb Gem Unc 68.**
This is what appears to be as perfect a star as one could hope to obtain. Four hulking margins are complemented by cavernous embossing and resplendent ink colors. Stars from this issue are very tough to obtain but are rarely ever found in this state of preservation. PMG has graded two in this grade with only a single note graded higher. Expect fireworks before the hammer falls on this treasure. (400-600)

13886 **Fr. 1978-G $5 1985 Federal Reserve Notes. Original pack of 100. Gem Crisp Uncirculated.**
A BEP band with "FO" penned on it is included in this lot. The first couple of notes show edge handling. A homemade bank band is also employed to hold this pack in place. (Total: 100 notes) (800-1,200)

13887 **Fr. 1985-G★ $5 1995 Federal Reserve Notes. Original Pack of 100 Gem Crisp Uncirculated.**
The first note in the pack has a corner fold at upper left, but the rest are as fresh as the driven snow. These catalog for $25 each. (Total: 100 notes) (1,500-2,500)

13888 **Twenty Consecutive Fr. 1985-G★ $5 1985 Federal Reserve Notes. Choice Crisp Uncirculated to Gem Crisp Uncirculated.**
The Chicago Stars are the key to this Series with a premium of $150 per note. The notes range in quality only because of the variances in margin width. (Total: 20 notes) (2,500-3,500)

13889 **Fr. 1987-J $5 1999 Federal Reserve Note. PMG Gem Uncirculated 65 EPQ.**
Pleasing low serial number 20 exhibits great eye appeal with all those zeroes. (400-600)

13890 **Fr. 1989-G★ $5 2003 Federal Reserve Notes. Uncut Sheet of 16. Gem Crisp Uncirculated.**
The 2003 Series $5s are no longer available in uncut form from the BEP. (150-250)

13891 **Fr. 2000-I $10 1928 Federal Reserve Note. PCGS Gem New 66.**
Near perfect margins and front to back centering add to the eye appeal of this piece. (750-1,000)

13892 **Fr. 2000-I $10 1928 Federal Reserve Note. PCGS Very Choice New 64PPQ.**
Bold original embossing and crackling fresh paper are clearly visible through the holder. The Minneapolis district is really quite scarce for this numbered district issue and high grade examples are particularly difficult to locate. The new Schwartz value of $600 in CU could likely prove to be conservative before the hammer falls tonight. (600-900)

13893 **Fr. 2000-K $10 1928 Federal Reserve Note. Gem Crisp Uncirculated.**
This rare beauty returns to us, last seen in our 2004 FUN sale, "An extremely rare note in this grade which is on the want lists of many collectors, as Dallas district examples are virtually never available this nice. This is an attractively centered and crackling fresh beauty which is certain to please." (650-950)

13894 **Fr. 2002-G $10 1928B Light Green Seal Federal Reserve Note. CGA Gem Uncirculated 66.**
Boardwalk margins and embossing are traits of this LGS $10. (100-150)

13895 **Fr. 2002-G★ $10 1928B Federal Reserve Note. CGA Gem Uncirculated 67.**
The margins are nearly perfect as is the front to back centering. The bright white paper contrasts nicely against the deep, dark green seal and serial numbers. Though stars were issued for nearly all the districts in this issue, the printing totals of only the Kansas City and Atlanta districts were released. (900-1,100)

13896 **Fr. 2002-G★ $10 1928B Federal Reserve Note. Crisp Uncirculated.**
This replacement note at first glance looks Choice, but further scrutiny reveals some edge repairs. (400-600)

13897 **Fr. 2002-G★ $10 1928B Federal Reserve Note. Choice About Uncirculated.**
This is a pleasing DGS star with a faint center fold. (300-500)

Rare 1928-C $10 Cleveland

13898 **Fr. 2003-D $10 1928C Federal Reserve Note. CGA Gem Uncirculated 65.**
A very rare note in this grade, with this piece graded and encapsulated by CGA. (5,000-7,000)

13899 **Fr. 2003-D $10 1928C Federal Reserve Note. PMG Very Fine 30 EPQ.**
This is a moderately circulated example of the much scarcer Cleveland district of this key early date. The margins are solid with the PMG comment "Exceptional Paper Quality" and the eye appeal is also exceptional for a circulated note. (600-800)

13900 **Fr. 2003-D $10 1928C Federal Reserve Note. CGA Very Fine 20.**
An evenly circulated example of this scarcer Cleveland district that appears less handled from the back. (500-700)

13901 **Fr. 2003-G $10 1928C Federal Reserve Note. Choice Crisp Uncirculated.**
Embossing and original surfaces grace this Chicago $10 from a scarce series. The latest Schwartz lists this note at $625 in Ch CU. (400-600)

13902 **Fr. 2006-B $10 1934A Federal Reserve Notes. Twenty-four Examples. Crisp Uncirculated.**
Original paper quality and embossing are joined by pinholes on each note. (Total: 24 notes) (350-450)

13903 Fr. 2006-C/2007-C $10 1934A/1934B Federal Reserve Notes. Changeover Pair. Choice Crisp Uncirculated.
This discovery will raise the changeover listing for this series combination to only two in the Schwartz-Lindquist reference.
From The Lincoln Collection (Total: 2 notes) (500-700)

13904 Fr. 2006-G★ $10 1934A Mule Federal Reserve Note. PMG Choice Uncirculated 64 EPQ.
The label for this third-party graded note sums it up quite well, "Exceptional Paper Quality, Great Embossing." (500-700)

13905 Fr. 2006-G★ $10 1934A Mule Federal Reserve Note. PMG Choice Uncirculated 64 EPQ.
This note is consecutive to the previous lot and it has an identical grade. This is also a new high serial number for the Schwartz-Lindquist reference. (500-700)

13906 Fr. 2007-C/2006-C $10 1934B/1934A Federal Reserve Notes. Reverse Changeover Pair. Choice Crisp Uncirculated.
This duo will become the fifth changeover pair in the census listing, but the first in this serial number range. A tiny imperfection is noticed in the paper of the 1934B $10.
From The Lincoln Collection (Total: 2 notes) (300-500)

13907 Fr. 2007-K★ $10 1934B Federal Reserve Note. Crisp Uncirculated.
This is the first appearance for this Friedberg with us in the last five years. A hard teller counting mark along Hamilton's head accounts for the grade on this bright piece. (1,250-1,750)

Star Reverse Changeover Pair

13908 Fr. 2009-C★/Fr. 2008-C★ $10 1934D/1934C Federal Reserve Notes. Reverse Changeover Pair. Gem Crisp Uncirculated.
This is a most attractive star reverse changeover pair, featuring two crackling fresh and most desirable examples. Only eight of these star pairs are recorded for the 1934D to 1934C combination in the new Schwartz-Lindquist reference. This does not include this exciting find that will become the pair with the lowest serial number. (Total: 2 notes) (500-800)

13909 Fr. 2009-D $10 1934D Federal Reserve Note. CGA Gem Uncirculated 68.
Behemoth margins are found on this Cleveland FRN which was printed from this more challenging issue. Bold embossing is seen through the holder and in today's market one never knows how high this could go. (100-200)

13910 Fr. 2010-A★ $10 1950 Federal Reserve Note. Extremely Fine-About Uncirculated.
Nice centering and original surfaces highlight this star. (200-300)

13911 Fr. 2010-C★ $10 1950 Wide Federal Reserve Note. PMG Choice Uncirculated 64 EPQ.
A well margined and wonderfully embossed example of this somewhat challenging district which had a printing of just over one million. (400-600)

13912 **Fr. 2010-K★ $10 1950 Federal Reserve Note. PCGS Very Choice New 64PPQ.**
We have handled only two other uncirculated examples of this scarce star note. This piece is centered a touch high, though the paper quality is unmistakable. (600-800)

13913 **Fr. 2011-G $10 1950A Federal Reserve Notes. Thirty Examples. Gem Crisp Uncirculated.**
First ten and then twenty notes are consecutive within this grouping of fresh notes. A homemade band comes with this lot plus a bank band date stamped, "Sep 29 1960." (Total: 30 notes) (1,000-1,500)

13914 **Fr. 2011-J★ $10 1950A Federal Reserve Note. Choice Crisp Uncirculated.**
Ample margins are found on this pack fresh KC star that has the third printing shifted to the right enough so that the "★" is just outside the scrollwork. A minor counting pinch at upper right is mentioned for cataloging accuracy. (200-300)

13915 **Four Consecutive Fr. 2012-G★ $10 1950B Federal Reserve Notes. Choice Crisp Uncirculated.**
The tiniest of corner bumps prevent these perfectly margined pieces from receiving a full Gem grade. (Total: 4 notes) (500-700)

13916 **Fr. 2013-C $10 1950C Federal Reserve Notes. Ten Consecutive Examples. Gem Crisp Uncirculated.**
Basic facts of this issue are written in black ink on the First Wisconsin National Bank of Milwaukee bank band. These original notes have strong embossing. This is only the third time that we have handled this Friedberg number in an auction. (Total: 10 notes) (500-750)

13917 **Fr. 2013-F★ $10 1950C Federal Reserve Note. PMG Choice Uncirculated 64 EPQ.**
This is one of four examples of this scarce issued offered here. The four pieces are two consecutive pairs separated by about thirty notes. (325-425)

13918 **Fr. 2013-F★ $10 1950C Federal Reserve Note. PMG Gem Uncirculated 65 EPQ.**
This is the second of the quartet offered here, with this piece boasting a bit better margins and equally as nice paper quality. (350-450)

13919 **Fr. 2013-F★ $10 1950C Federal Reserve Note. PMG Gem Uncirculated 66 EPQ.**
The margins on this issue are near perfect, and is consecutive to the next lot. (375-475)

13920 **Fr. 2013-F★ $10 1950C Federal Reserve Note. PMG Choice Uncirculated 64 EPQ.**
This is the last of the quartet offered here and the margins are as nice as the two Gems offered above. (325-425)

13921 **Fr. 2013-L★ $10 1950C Federal Reserve Notes. Two Examples. PCGS Gem New 66PPQ.**
We have had very few of this Friedberg number over the years. The originality of these notes that are separated by one serial number is seen through the third-party holders. (Total: 2 notes) (400-600)

13922 **Fr. 2017-J $10 1963A Federal Reserve Note. Gem Crisp Uncirculated.**
Fancy serial number 20000000 graces this early FRN. Wide margins and deep embossing are noticed. (600-800)

13923 **Fr. 2027-A★ $10 1985 Federal Reserve Notes. Eight Consecutive Examples. Gem Crisp Uncirculated.**
Bold embossing and broad margins are found on these well preserved Boston stars. (Total: 8 notes) (300-400)

13924 **Fr. 2027-A★ $10 1985 Federal Reserve Notes. Seven Consecutive Examples. Gem Crisp Uncirculated.**
Original paper surfaces and nice centering highlight this mini-run of stars. (Total: 7 notes) (275-375)

13925 **Fr. 2034-K★ $10 1999 Federal Reserve Notes. 100 Consecutive Examples. Choice Crisp Uncirculated.**
A corner bump is noticed on the stars of this grouping.
From The Rolling Plains Collection (Total: 100 notes) (1,500-2,000)

13926 **Fr. 2040-L★ $10 2004A Federal Reserve Note. PCGS Superb Gem New 70PPQ.**
The third party grade is the ideal description for all of this note's attributes. The margins are perfect, the printing is perfect, and the paper quality is perfect. (600-700)

13927 **Fr. 2050-A $20 1928 Federal Reserve Note. Very Choice Crisp Uncirculated.**
A nice example from one of the scarcer districts in this series. The new Schwartz catalogue valuation is $375. (300-500)

13928 **Fr. 2050-A $20 1928 Federal Reserve Note. PCGS Extremely Fine 40PPQ.**
The Boston $20 issue carries a substantial premium in the Oakes reference and nice mid-grade examples are very elusive. (500-1,000)

Gem Cleveland 1928 $20 Star Note

13929 **Fr. 2050-D★ $20 1928 Federal Reserve Note. Gem Crisp Uncirculated.**
From our 2004 FUN sale where it was described, "This perfectly centered star Twenty from the Cleveland district is gorgeous on both sides and has deep, dark inks that add to its considerable eye appeal. The Oakes & Schwartz reference lists this note at $1,500, and we expect that to be just the jumping off point tonight." All the attributes described remain the same. (1,500-2,000)

13930 **Fr. 2050-E★ $20 1928 Federal Reserve Note. Choice Crisp Uncirculated.**
From our 2004 Long Beach sale, "A lovely example of this very rare early star, which is valued in the new Oakes reference at $3000. We seriously doubt that figure could buy even one note as it's quite probable that years could pass without the offering of any other $20 1928 Richmond star in anywhere near this grade." The Oakes reference is now referred as the Schwartz reference, and, we have not handled another Uncirculated Richmond Star since that sale. (2,500-3,500)

13931 **Fr. 2050-G $20 1928 Federal Reserve Note. Gem Crisp Uncirculated.**
A consecutive trio of well centered Chicago district notes. (Total: 3 notes) (375-525)

13932 **Fr. 2050-G★ $20 1928 Federal Reserve Notes. Five Examples.**
These replacement notes grade **F-VF** with a couple exhibiting problems such as teller stamps and a one inch tear. (Total: 5 notes) (400-600)

13933 **Fr. 2050-I★ $20 1928 Federal Reserve Note. Very Choice Crisp Uncirculated.**
A very rare star note in any grade, and exceptionally rare this nice. The centering is not perfect, and there is a touch of light handling, but this important star rarity is clearly destined for a major holding. We previously called this note Gem in our 2004 Long Beach sale, however in today's market a more accurate representation would be Very Choice. (2,500-3,500)

13934 **Fr. 2050-J $20 1928 Federal Reserve Note. PMG Gem Uncirculated 66 EPQ.**
Exceptionally bright paper, original paper waves, and a deep green overprint add to the appeal of this piece.
From The Lincoln Collection (300-400)

13935 **Fr. 2050-L★ $20 1928 Federal Reserve Note. Extremely Fine.**
This note exhibits a bit of toning, but remains crisp. It now becomes the lowest serial number reported in the Schwartz-Lindquist reference. An ashtray pen mark is noticed. (500-800)

13936 **Fr. 2051-K $20 1928A Federal Reserve Note. Very Choice Crisp Uncirculated.**
While not displaying enough side margins for the Gem grade in our opinion, perhaps a grading service will overlook that in favor of the embossing to grant the coveted "65". (400-600)

13937 **Fr. 2053-G $20 1928C Federal Reserve Note. Fine.**
This is a classic Small Size rarity that came out of the depths of the Great Depression. Chicago and San Francisco were the only two districts to issue this series and denomination. This example displays uniform circulation and a small pencil mark on the back. (400-600)

Rare CU 1928-C SFO District

13938 **Fr. 2053-L $20 1928C Federal Reserve Note. Choice Crisp Uncirculated.**
From our 2005 Dallas sale, "The San Francisco district is by far the scarcer of the pair which issued, and this piece is by a considerable margin the finest 1928C $20 we've had the privilege of offering. It's bright and exceptionally well centered, truly a note worthy of a place in any fine collection of small size currency." To this day, we have yet to handle a nicer example from SFO. (6,000-9,000)

13939 **Fr. 2053-L $20 1928C Federal Reserve Note. Very Fine.**
These are scarce due to their release during the depths of the Great Depression. Sound edges frame this mid-grade San Fran $20. (650-850)

13940 **Fr. 2053-L $20 1928C Federal Reserve Note. CGA Fine 15.**
A problem free circulated example of a note which is seldom available in any grade. (500-700)

13941 **Fr. 2053-L $20 1928C Federal Reserve Note. Fine.**
This tough note exhibits a tiny margin split, but otherwise retains decent color. (450-650)

13942 **Fr. 2054-B★ $20 1934 Light Green Seal Federal Reserve Note. Choice Crisp Uncirculated.**
Gorgeous inks highlight this New York star. The Schwartz reference lists these at $800 each. (750-1,000)

13943 Fr. 2054-C★ $20 1934 Mule Federal Reserve Note. PCGS Very Choice New 64.
Large margins surround this very bright replacement note from the Philadelphia district. (400-600)

13944 Fr. 2054-D $20 1934 Non-Mule/Mule Federal Reserve Notes. Changeover Pair.
Schwartz does not list any changeover pairs of this persuasion for this denomination and series. The first note of the pair is a Non-mule with micro back plate number 312 and the second note is a Mule with macro back plate number 320.
From The Lincoln Collection (Total: 2 notes) (600-900)

13945 Fr. 2054-D★ $20 1934 Federal Reserve Note. Choice Crisp Uncirculated.
This nicely preserved Cleveland LGS star is kept from Gem by light handling. (900-1,200)

13946 Fr. 2054-F★ $20 1934 Mule DGS Federal Reserve Note. PCGS Choice New 63.
The Schwartz value is $600 in CU for this enormously margined Atlanta star. This cataloger still is not quite sure as to why the grade is what it is since it appears to be a broadly margined gem. (500-700)

13947 Fr. 2054-F★ $20 1934 Federal Reserve Note. Choice Crisp Uncirculated.
A vivid LGS is noticed on this Atlanta star. (1,000-1,500)

13948 Fr. 2054-I★ $20 1934 Light Green Seal Federal Reserve Note. Choice Crisp Uncirculated.
This is the toughest star within this series, with this example displaying original paper wave and embossing. (1,500-2,000)

13949 Fr. 2055-B $20 1934A Federal Reserve Notes. Eight Examples. Choice CU
Fr. 2057-B $20 1934C Federal Reserve Notes. Five Examples. Choice CU.
(Total: 13 notes) (550-750)

13950 Ten Consecutive Fr. 2055-B $20 1934A Federal Reserve Notes. Choice Crisp Uncirculated to Gem Crisp Uncirculated.
Perfect paper waves and bold embossing are noted on the run of 10 pieces. (Total: 10 notes) (500-750)

13951 Fr. 2055-D★ $20 1934A Federal Reserve Note. PCGS Choice New 63.
Three broad margins and solid embossing are seen on this Cleveland star twenty. The top margin is smaller than the others but the eye appeal is really quite nice for an early FRN star. The Schwartz value of $500 in CU seems right on the note for a quality example from this issue. (400-600)

13952 Fr. 2055-G $20 1934A Federal Reserve Notes. Nineteen Consecutive Examples. About Uncirculated or Better.
Many of the notes show handling near the district seal. (Total: 19 notes) (500-700)

13953 **Fr. 2055-G★ $20 1934A Mule Federal Reserve Note. PCGS Gem New 65PPQ.**
From our 2006 Central States Sale where this piece was described, "An exceptionally fresh example of an extremely scarce star. With the imprimatur of PCGS attesting to its quality, this premium item should sell comfortably in the range of..." **(1,500-2,000)**

13954 **Old and New Back Design Dallas $20 Stars.**
Fr. 2057-K★ $20 1934C Federal Reserve Notes. Two Examples. Gem Crisp Uncirculated.
Both of these embossed stars have ample margins and they are neatly centered. The "New Back" star is also the listed high in Schwartz. Of the two designs, we've only handled an "Old Back" Dallas star before and that was when we sold the massive Taylor Family Collection. (Total: 2 notes) **(1,000-1,500)**

13955 **Fr. 2058-C★ $20 1934D Federal Reserve Note. Gem Crisp Uncirculated.**
In the latest Schwartz reference, there is no price listed, due to the recently discovered Wide and Narrow back variety, of which this is a Wide. This note did realize $517 in our 2005 FUN sale, so, we'll use that as a reference point. **(600-900)**

13956 **Fr. 2064-B★ $20 1950E Federal Reserve Note. About Uncirculated.**
Original paper surfaces and a center fold are found on this Star. It is also a new low serial number for the Schwartz-Lindquist reference. **(350-550)**

13957 **Fr. 2066-G★ Five Consecutive $20 1963A Federal Reserve Notes. Gem Crisp Uncirculated.**
A lovely quintet of Chicago stars that are all as crisp and crackling fresh as the day they were printed. Technically the right margin is too small to qualify for the gem grade but the paper surfaces are so nice that it would be a travesty not to do so. (Total: 5 notes) **(500-700)**

13958 **Fr. 2089/2090-A-L $20 2004 and Fr. 2128-A-L $50 2004 Federal Reserve Notes. Gem Crisp Uncirculated.**
This is the Federal Reserve Evolutions Collection Series and it quickly sold out after being released on June 30, 2005 at a subscription price of $1700. This collection was limited to only 500 sets from each of the twelve Federal Reserve Banks. Each district features a 2004 $20 and $50 note with matching low serial nubmers (in the 2100-2200 range for this set) and a beautifully illustrated booklet detailing the Federal Reserve System, the particular Federal Reserve Bank, plus other pertinent facts. Each set in this collection is housed in a velvet-lined, leatherette presentation case. This is the first complete set of these we have seen.
From The Rolling Plains Collection (Total: 12 items) **(2,000-3,000)**

PCGS Gem 65PPQ Boston 1928 $50 FRN

13959 **Fr. 2100-A $50 1928 Federal Reserve Note. PCGS Gem New 65PPQ.**
This certainly is one of the keys to completing a set of notes for all districts within the series. Our offerings in the past five years number only ten with this bright example being one of the nicest. Throw the price guides away on this one. **(4,000-6,000)**

13960 **Fr. 2100-G $50 1928 Federal Reserve Note. PMG About Uncirculated 55.**
Some minor handling is noted through the holder and is responsible for the grade. This note likely never entered circulation, rather sat in an original pack and held for cash reserves by a bank in the Midwest. **(300-400)**

13961 **Fr. 2100-G★ $50 1928 Federal Reserve Note. Crisp Uncirculated.**
From our auction of the Taylor Family Collection where it was described, "While Chicago is not one of the tougher districts for stars in this series, this example bears the lowest serial number reported to date from this district." It remains the lowest serial number reported. (1,300-1,600)

13962 **Fr. 2101-A $50 1928A Federal Reserve Note. CGA Gem Uncirculated 66.**
Solid margins surround boldly printed, deep black and green inked details. (400-600)

13963 **Fr. 2101-D $50 1928A Federal Reserve Note. Choice Crisp Uncirculated.**
Natural paper ripple is a merit of this $50. (350-450)

13964 **Fr. 2101-D $50 1928A Federal Reserve Note. Choice Crisp Uncirculated.**
The first of a small group of these notes, all bright and new but not up to the gem standard. (300-400)

13965 **Fr. 2101-D $50 1928A Federal Reserve Notes. Two consecutive examples. Choice Crisp Uncirculated.**
A well centered and very attractive consecutive pair. (Total: 2 notes) (550-650)

13966 **Fr. 2101-D $50 1928A Federal Reserve Notes. Two consecutive examples. Choice Crisp Uncirculated.**
A second consecutive pair. (Total: 2 notes) (550-650)

13967 **Fr. 2101-G $50 1928A Federal Reserve Note. PMG Gem Uncirculated 66.**
Here is a nice well centered example in an undervalued series. (500-700)

13968 **Fr. 2101-H $50 1928A Federal Reserve Note. PMG Choice Uncirculated 64.**
This example has the grading guesswork eliminated. (400-600)

13969 **Fr. 2101-H $50 1928A Federal Reserve Note. Very Choice Crisp Uncirculated.**
A fresh and brightly colored example of this very tough note which catalogues for $500 in CU. (400-600)

13970 **Fr. 2101-H $50 1928 Federal Reserve Note. PCGS Choice New 63PPQ.**
This is a broadly margined and well embossed example of this somewhat scarcer district that certainly looks closer to the Gem grade than Choice. The holder indicates the wrong Friedberg number. (600-900)

13971 **Fr. 2101-H $50 1928A Federal Reserve Note. Very Choice Crisp Uncirculated.**
Consecutive to the note above and just as attractive. (400-600)

13972 **Fr. 2101-K $50 1928A Federal Reserve Note. Choice Crisp Uncirculated.**
Dallas is a very scarce district in this series, with the new Schwartz & Lindquist reference valuing this note at $800. (700-900)

13973 **Fr. 2102-G/Fr. 2103 $50 1934/1934A Federal Reserve Notes. Changeover Pair PMG Choice Uncirculated 64 EPQ.**
Here is a new changeover pair that only makes the second we have sold. Currently this issue from Chicago does not have any listed in the Schwartz tome. (Total: 2 notes) (750-1,000)

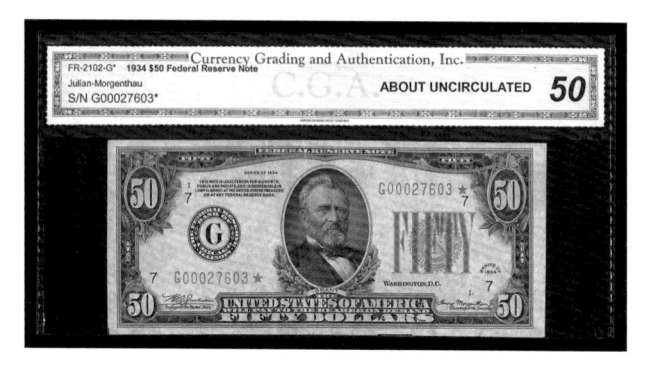

13974 **Fr. 2102-G★ $50 1934 Federal Reserve Note. CGA About Uncirculated 50.**
Vibrant color still shows through the CGA encasement. (350-500)

13975 **Fr. 2102-H $50 1934 Light Green Seal Federal Reserve Note. Gem Crisp Uncirculated.**
The first of a gorgeous consecutive pair, with this piece displaying full originality and pinpoint centering. (350-550)

13976 **Fr. 2102-H $50 1934 Light Green Seal Federal Reserve Note. Gem Crisp Uncirculated.**
Consecutive to the last and its equal in very way, a well nigh perfect Light Green Seal fifty. (350-550)

13977 **Fr. 2102-H★ $50 1934 Federal Reserve Note. PMG Choice Uncirculated 63.**
According to our archives, we have handled only two other examples of this scarce star, both of which were moderately circulated. This piece is fully uncirculated with solid margins and great eye appeal. (1,250-1,500)

13978 **Fr. 2102-I★ $50 1934 Federal Reserve Note. PMG Choice Uncirculated 63 EPQ.**
Gem margins and bold embossing are noted on this piece which shows some light handling. The Oakes premium listed may prove to be conservative as we have only one other example of this Star. (1,500-2,000)

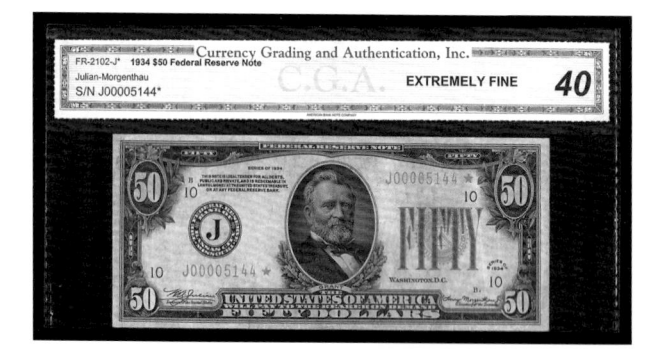

13979 **Fr. 2102-J★ $50 1934 Federal Reserve Note. CGA Extremely Fine 40.**
This replacement exhibits even circulation. (300-500)

13980 Fr. 2102-K★ $50 1934 Light Green Star Federal Reserve Note. Extremely Fine.
This Dallas LGS star is blessed with serial number 482 and some natural paper ripple. It is also the highest graded LGS $50 star we have handled on this Friedberg number. (900-1,200)

13981 Fr. 2102-L★ $50 1934 Federal Reserve Note. PMG Choice Uncirculated 64 EPQ.
Original embossing of the seal is noted through the holder and the margins are sufficient for some to call this example a Gem. (750-1,250)

Scarce St. Louis Star

13982 Fr. 2103-H★ $50 1934A Federal Reserve Note. PMG Choice Uncirculated 64.
This is a very scarce series for stars, with examples in this grade range almost never available. In fact, this is the only example that we have handled. It was previously offered as part of the Taylor Family Collection in 2005 where it realized just shy of $3,000. We expect that price may prove conservative in today's market. (3,000-3,500)

13983 Fr. 2105-H $50 1934C Federal Reserve Notes. Two Consecutive Examples Choice About Uncirculated.
This St. Louis pair possesses plenty of embossing and deep ink, but each has suffered a light center bend. The first note becomes the lowest serial by one in the Schwartz/Lindquist guide. (Total: 2 notes) (300-500)

Finest Known

13984 Fr. 2106-E★ $50 1934D Federal Reserve Note. PMG Choice Uncirculated 64 EPQ.
When we first sold this note, we presumed it may have been unique, though one other piece surfaced in 2005. That piece, a VF, realized $5,175. We expect this piece may realize twice that amount as the finest known piece by a considerable margin. (8,000-10,000)

Scarce 1934D $50 Green Seal Star

13985 Fr. 2106-E★ $50 1934D Federal Reserve Note. Very Fine.
The recently released seventh edition of Schwartz-Lindquist shows this note as the new low serial number as another note claims the high serial number spot. All 1934D $50 Stars are scarce with this evenly circulated and problem free piece probably capable of reaching or exceeding... (5,000-7,500)

13986 Fr. 2107-C $50 1950 Federal Reserve Note. PCGS Gem New 65PPQ.
This issue is fairly scarce in uncirculated grades, thus there is a healthy premium according to Oakes. (800-1,000)

13987 **Fr. 2109-G★ $50 1950B Federal Reserve Note. Choice About Uncirculated.**
Bold embossing and natural paper surfaces overshadow a corner fold on this scarce Star. (200-300)

13988 **Fr. 2111-C★ $50 1950D Federal Reserve Note. CGA Gem Uncirculated 67.**
Razor sharp corners and bold white paper are present. (400-500)

13989 **Fr. 2111-D★ $50 1950D Federal Reserve Note. Choice Crisp Uncirculated.**
Original surfaces grace this $50 that has two broad and two slender margins. (250-350)

13990 **Fr. 2112-B★ $50 1950E Federal Reserve Note. CGA Gem Uncirculated 66.**
This pleasing replacement has garnered a high grade from CGA. (1,250-1,750)

13991 **Fr. 2112-B★ $50 1950E Federal Reserve Note. PCGS Choice About New 58.**
A very nice example of this just plain scarce star that barely misses the uncirculated grade. (850-1,050)

13992 **Fr. 2112-B★ $50 1950E Federal Reserve Note. PCGS Choice About New 58.**
Another lucky collector will have an opportunity to obtain this tough issue that just misses. (850-1,050)

13993 **Fr. 2112-B★ $50 1950E Federal Reserve Note. CGA About Uncirculated 58.**
The faintest of center bends is noted on this 1950E star. While the bottom portion of the third party holder is still sealed, the top is open. Clearly the note belongs to the insert as the serial number is listed. (600-800)

13994 **Fr. 2113-C★ $50 1963A Federal Reserve Star Note. PMG Gem Uncirculated 66 EPQ.**
This is a perfectly original, fully embossed Gem example of this scarce Star Fifty. (450-550)

13995 **Fr. 2116-K $50 1969B Federal Reserve Note. Extremely Fine.**
Huge margins and bright paper are found on this lightly circulated Dallas Fifty. This series is always a great challenge to locate in any grade and this example should fit the bill for the budget-minded collector. (400-600)

13996 **Fr. 2150-A $100 1928 Federal Reserve Note. CGA Gem Uncirculated 65.**
This example is from the very tough Boston district, and has been encapsulated and graded Gem Uncirculated 65 by CGA. (900-1,200)

13997 **Fr. 2151-G $100 1928A Federal Reserve Note. CGA Gem Uncirculated 67.**
A very high grade example of this underrated early FRN series. The ink colors are robust and the paper surfaces fresh and bright. (500-700)

13998 **Fr. 2151-G $100 1928A DGS Federal Reserve Note. CGA Gem Uncirculated 66.**
This C-note boasts large margins and bright paper. (350-500)

13999 **Fr. 2151-G $100 1928A Federal Reserve Note. CGA Gem Uncirculated 65.**
The centering is somewhat off on this early Chicago FRN that has vibrant green inks and superb print quality. (400-600)

14000 **Fr. 2152-D $100 1934 LGS Federal Reserve Note. PMG Gem Uncirculated 66EPQ.**
This is an abundantly margined example of this much scarcer Light Green Seal variety from this issue. The PMG designation of "Exceptional Paper Quality" appears to be well deserved. We would expect the Schwartz value of $500 in CU to be on the low side for a note of this quality and scarcity. (500-700)

14001 **Fr. 2152-E★ $100 1934 Mule Federal Reserve Note. Very Fine.**
This is an important Star for the collecting fraternity. It is listed as the high serial number in the just released seventh edition of the Schwartz-Lindquist reference. Only three districts now have reported Mule Stars for the 1934 Series - Richmond, Chicago, and Kansas City. Notes like this are notoriously difficult to estimate. Specialists realize just how truly rare the notes are, and then they stoke the impetus for bidding. (1,750-2,500)

14002 **Fr. 2152-G★ $100 1934 Federal Reserve Note. About Uncirculated.**
This pleasing star has a light bend at center but appears fully Uncirculated. The overprint is bright and the margins are sizeable. (750-1,000)

Only Known KC 1934 Mule $100 Star Note

14003 **Fr. 2152-J★ $100 1934 Mule Federal Reserve Note. Fine-Very Fine.**
This is the sole 1934 Mule Star $100 listed from any district outside of Richmond and Chicago. It is unpriced in the Schwartz reference, which simply states "Extremely Rare." The bidders will determine the price level tonight for this great Small Size rarity. (4,000-8,000)

14004 **Fr. 2153-A-L $100 1934A Federal Reserve Notes. Fine or Better.**
The New York note is of the Light Green Seal Variety. Of the other 11 notes, all are Mules except for the Atlanta $100. Each of the remaining ten notes sets a new low serial number for the 1934A Mules in the Schwartz reference. The Minneapolis $100 has several pinholes. (Total: 12 notes) (1,800-2,400)

14005 **Fr. 2153-B★ $100 1934A Mule Federal Reserve Note. CGA Extremely Fine 45.**
This is a tougher replacement note as reflected in the Schwartz tome of $350 in VF. (400-600)

14006 **Fr. 2153-G $100 1934A Mule Federal Reserve Notes. Six Consecutive Examples. Very Choice Crisp Uncirculated.**
These $100s possess wide margins and nice centering. The extreme upper right corner tip on each has a minute purple ink dot. (Total: 6 notes) (1,000-1,500)

14007 **Fr. 2152-G★ $100 1934 Federal Reserve Note. PCGS Very Choice New 64PPQ.**
This is a scarce star note which is not found in upper grade ranges with regularity. The note looks pack fresh with plenty of embossing present. (1,250-1,750)

14008 **Fr. 2153-G★ $100 1934A Mule Federal Reserve Note. PCGS Choice New 63PPQ.**
This is only the third example in this grade we have offered at auction. With a touch better back centering this note certainly goes higher. (800-1,200)

14009 **Fr. 2153-G★ $100 1934A Mule Federal Reserve Note. CGA About Uncirculated 55.**
The colors remain bright on this once lightly folded example. (600-800)

14010 Fr. 2154-K★ $100 1934B Federal Reserve Note. Choice Crisp Uncirculated.
Over the last half decade, we have seen only three other examples of this issue. This deeply printed example is fully and evenly margined and appears Gem or better. There is however a touch of handling that precludes the grade, which will not discourage the collector of rare and desirable star notes. (4,000-5,000)

14011 Fr. 2155-G★ $100 1934C Federal Reserve Note. About Uncirculated.
According to a couple of different references, this is the most common star note for this Series. We must note that auction appearances tell another story as we have only handled two examples of this issue in the last eight or so years. This piece shows a light center fold and corner fold. The margins are solid on this piece that appears fully Uncirculated. (2,000-2,500)

14012 Fr. 2157-G★ $100 1950 Federal Reserve Note. Gem Crisp Uncirculated.
An attractive example of this popular Star displaying more than adequate centering to merit the full Gem grade. (900-1,200)

14013 Fr. 2158-D★ $100 1950A Federal Reserve Note. Gem Crisp Uncirculated.
Solid margins are noted, as is wholly original paper. (1,000-1,200)

14014 Fr. 2159-L★ $100 1950B Federal Reserve Note. PMG Choice Uncirculated 64 EPQ.
The paper quality is exceptional, with the eggshell texture associated with this and some of the other 1950's Series. *From The Lincoln Collection* (350-450)

14015 Fr. 2161-D★ $100 1950D Federal Reserve Notes. Four Consecutive Examples Crisp Uncirculated.
These early high denomination replacements have plenty of embossing, paper wave, and snap. Unfortunately they are quite tight along the bottom. (Total: 4 notes) (1,500-2,000)

14016 Fr. 2161-G★ $100 1950D Federal Reserve Note. CGA Gem Uncirculated 66.
Solid margins surround this issue. (500-700)

14017　Fr. 2161-L★ $100 1950D Federal Reserve Note. Extremely Fine+.
This is a none too common replacement from a tougher district. (300-500)

14018　Fr. 2162-B★ $100 1950E Federal Reserve Note. CGA Crisp Uncirculated 62.
Star notes are seldom seen from this very scarce series, especially in high grades. This nice-looking example from the New York district appears conservatively graded to us, as the centering is indicative of a grade a point or two higher. The CGA holder has been cut along the right side, but the note remains the same. A great Star note rarity that is likely to inspire spirited bidding that will end somewhere in the range of. . . (2,250-2,750)

14019　Fr. 2163-C★ $100 1963A Federal Reserve Notes. Four Consecutive Examples.
These notes are nicely centered with wide margins. The first note grades **XF-AU**, while the other three notes grade **Gem Crisp Uncirculated**. (Total: 4 notes) (1,200-1,600)

14020　Fr. 2163-G $100 1963A Federal Reserve Notes. Twelve Consecutive Examples. Choice Crisp Uncirculated.
We have not had a run of this Friedberg number in the past. The top margin is a little thin on these examples. (Total: 12 notes) (1,500-2,000)

14021　Fr. 2163-L★ $100 1963A Federal Reserve Note. Gem Crisp Uncirculated.
Overly broad margins frame this San Fran Star that is a few serial numbers less than the recorded high serial number in Schwartz. (400-600)

14022　Fr. 2164-G★ $100 1969 Federal Reserve Note. PMG Gem Uncirculated 66 EPQ.
As described by PMG, the paper quality is exceptional and framed perfectly by broad margins.
From The Lincoln Collection (400-500)

1985 San Francisco Specimen $100 FRN

14023　Fr. 2171-L $100 1985 Federal Reserve Note. CGA Choice Uncirculated 64.
This note originally sold in our 2004 Long Beach sale where the description read, "A specimen which is overstamped twice with that word on each side and bears serial number L23456789A. We've had several lower denomination examples, but this is our first hundred. It's been slabbed by CGA and given the grade Choice Uncirculated 64." (2,500-4,500)

14024　Fr. 2178-B $100 2003 Federal Reserve Note. CGA Gem Uncirculated 66.
Superb punch through embossing and bright colors are found on this unusual low serial number note DB00002003B, with the serial number and the series date a perfect match. (300-500)

CGA 65 1928 $500 Cleveland FRN

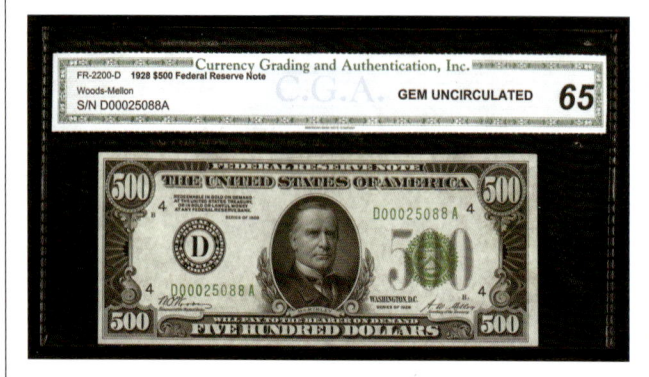

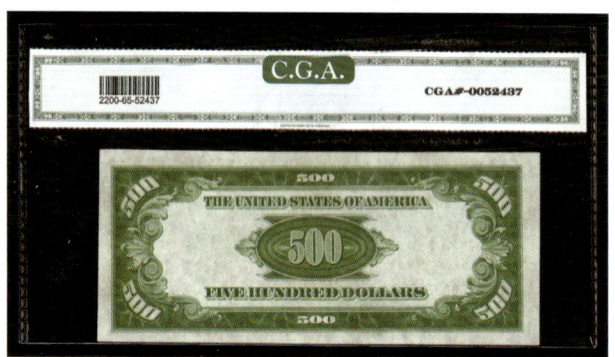

14025 Fr. 2200-D $500 1928 Federal Reserve Note. CGA Gem Uncirculated 65.
Here is a bright series 1928 example given the Gem 65 designation by CGA. Plenty of serial number embossing protrudes from the surfaces of this bright, well inked example. (4,250-5,250)

14026 Fr. 2200-G $500 1928 Federal Reserve Note. PMG About Uncirculated 55.
A perfect example for the collector who wants a nice high end lightly circulated 1928 $500. (1,400-1,800)

CGA Gem 66 1928 St. Louis $500

14027 Fr. 2200-H $500 1928 Federal Reserve Note. CGA Gem Uncirculated 66.
The paper is quite bright on this crackling fresh, well margined St. Louis note. (5,000-7,500)

14028 Fr. 2200-H $500 1928 Federal Reserve Note. PCGS New 62.
Natural paper wave is sighted on this note. (2,000-2,500)

CGA Gem 66 1928 Dallas $500

14029 Fr. 2200-K $500 1928 Federal Reserve Note. CGA Gem Uncirculated 66.
This well centered and bright example is easily the highest grade Series 1928 $500 note we've seen or had to offer from the much collected Dallas district. It combines true rarity and great condition, something that usually results in considerable demand and very strong prices, as it likely will do here as well. Any estimate is but a guess, as we know of no Series 1928 Dallas $500 example in better grade, but our best surmise here is… (9,000-12,000)

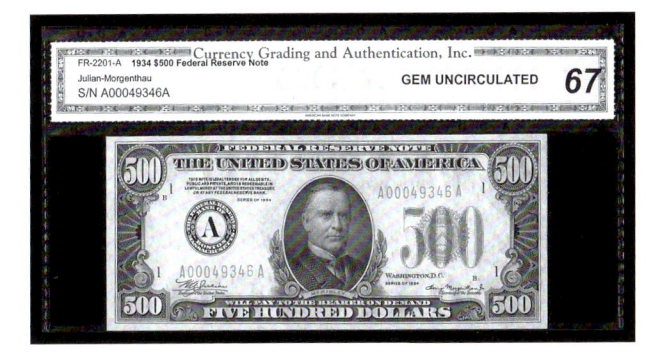

14030 **Fr. 2201-A $500 1934 Federal Reserve Note. CGA Gem Uncirculated 67.**
Deep embossing of the serial numbers and seal are noted through the third party holder. Add four, near-even margins and bright paper and the result is great eye appeal. (2,500-3,500)

14031 **Fr. 2201-A $500 1934 Federal Reserve Note. PMG Choice Uncirculated 63 EPQ.**
A scarcer district, with only 56,628 pieces printed. Were it not for a tight margin at lower right it would have achieved a higher grade. (1,750-2,250)

14032 **Fr. 2201-B $500 1934 Federal Reserve Note. Very Fine.**
The only distraction on this solid example is a tiny stain on the back. (950-1,150)

14033 **Fr. 2201-B $500 1934 Federal Reserve Note. Very Fine.**
Several pinholes are seen to the left of the portrait area on this New York high denomination. (900-1,100)

14034 **Fr. 2201-D $500 1934 Federal Reserve Note. CGA Choice Uncirculated 64.**
Serial number embossing is a merit of this $500. (1,800-2,300)

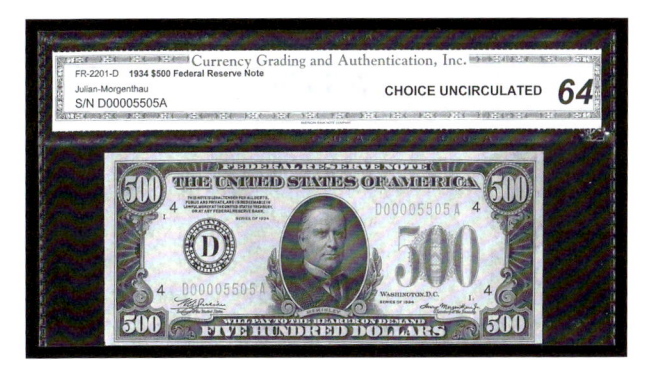

14035 **Fr. 2201-D $500 1934 Light Green Seal Federal Reserve Note. CGA Choice Uncirculated 64.**
Despite a tight margin at bottom right, this note remains bright with some serial number embossing. (1,800-2,300)

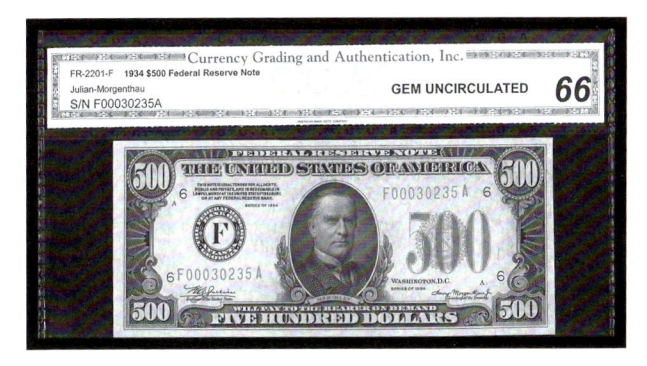

14036 **Fr. 2201-F $500 1934 Federal Reserve Note. CGA Gem Uncirculated 66.**
Perfectly even margins and a dark, boldly printed overprint add to the eye appeal of this Gem. (2,600-3,000)

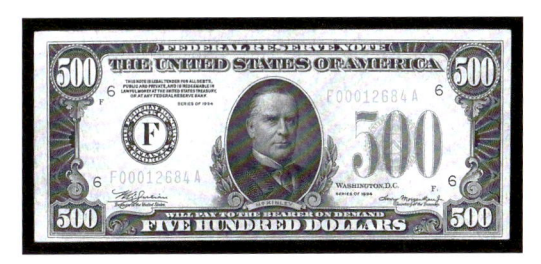

14037 **Fr. 2201-F $500 1934 Light Green Seal Federal Reserve Note. Crisp Uncirculated.**
The back is centered nicely, but the face is centered just a touch low on this $500 from the scarcer LGS variety. (2,000-2,500)

14038 **Fr. 2201-F $500 1934 Federal Reserve Note. CGA Extremely Fine 45.**
The only fold of consequence is the center fold. The others blend nicely into the design giving the note the appearance of an AU. (1,000-1,200)

14039 **Fr. 2201-G $500 1934 Federal Reserve Note. PCGS New 62.**
The holder states that this is a Light Green Seal variety, but it truly is a Dark Green Seal. The right side margin is a bit tight, which is the cause for the grade on this deeply inked example. (1,500-1,750)

14040 **Fr. 2201-G $500 1934 Light Green Seal Federal Reserve Note. Crisp Uncirculated.**
This is a well-centered example which shows a few paper ripples and light handling, but it displays no folds whatever. It's a bright LGS example, and worthy of a premium if only for that reason, as the LGS high denominations are vastly more scarce than their DGS counterparts. (2,000-2,500)

14041 **Fr. 2201-G $500 1934 Federal Reserve Note. PMG Choice About Unc 58.**
This attractive example just misses the New designation. (1,150-1,350)

14042 **Fr. 2201-G $500 1934 Federal Reserve Note. PMG About Uncirculated 55.**
A vertical fold and corner bend are detected on this bright, well margined example. (1,100-1,300)

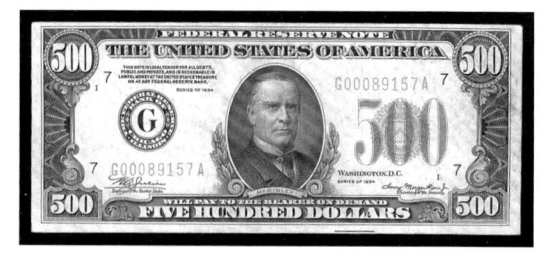

14043 **Fr. 2201-G $500 1934 Federal Reserve Note. About Uncirculated.**
An attractive piece with one barely discernible center fold. (1,250-1,450)

14044 **Fr. 2201-G $500 1934 Federal Reserve Note. About Uncirculated.**
Plenty of embossing remains on this note of which the only real distraction is a hard center fold. (1,100-1,300)

14045 **Fr. 2201-G $500 1934 Federal Reserve Note. PMG About Uncirculated 50.**
This note, which appears Choice Uncirculated has a faint fold at center. (1,200-1,400)

14046 **Fr. 2201-G $500 1934 Federal Reserve Note. Extremely Fine-About Uncirculated.**
A couple of light folds criss-cross the surfaces of this bright, pleasant looking note.
From The Collection of Greg Southward (1,000-1,250)

14047 **Fr. 2201-G $500 1934 Federal Reserve Note. Very Fine-Extremely Fine.**
A problem-free example which is perfect for the grade. (900-1,000)

14048 **Fr. 2201-G $500 1934 Federal Reserve Note. Very Fine+.**
Sound edges and even wear adorn this Chicago $500. (900-1,000)

14049 **Fr. 2201-G $500 1934 Light Green Seal Federal Reserve Note. Very Fine.**
Solid margins surround this note which remains quite colorful. (1,000-1,200)

14050 **Fr. 2201-G $500 1934 Light Green Seal Federal Reserve Note. Fine-Very Fine.**
This is a decent problem-free example of an LGS variety off Chicago. (900-1,000)

14051 **Fr. 2201-G $500 1934 Light Green Seal Federal Reserve Note. Fine.**
A small paper skin is seen on the back along with a pinhole on this still crisp Chicago note. (850-950)

14052 **Fr. 2201-G★ $500 1934 Federal Reserve Note. CGA Extremely Fine 40.**
This lightly circulated star was pulled out of circulation very quickly. The colors remain bright as does the paper, though there was an attempt to cover up some minor paper clip rust. (4,000-6,000)

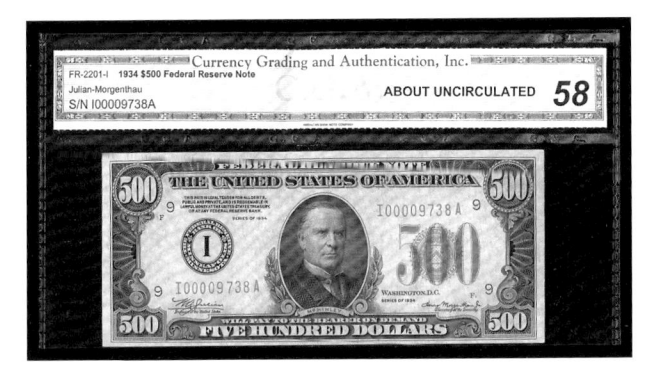

14053 **Fr. 2201-I $500 1934 Federal Reserve Note. CGA About Uncirculated 58.**
In the holder, this note appears to be fully uncirculated. After some examination, we were unable to locate the grade limiting factor. (3,000-3,250)

14054 **Fr. 2201-I $500 1934 Light Green Seal Federal Reserve Note. CGA Extremely Fine 40.**
This three digit Minneapolis $500 has solid paper, though there are a few more light folds and bends than your regular three-fold XF. (750-900)

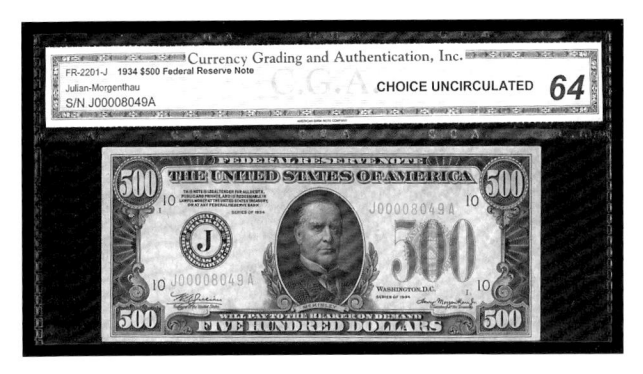

14055 **Fr. 2201-J $500 1934 Light Green Seal Federal Reserve Note. CGA Choice Uncirculated 64.**
On average, two to three examples of this Kansas City issue pass through our auction in a given year. Tonight we are privileged to offer three, with this piece outranking the others in quality. The four digit serial number adds to the eye appeal of the light green overprint and complements the perfect white paper. (1,750-2,000)

14056 **Fr. 2201-J $500 1934 Light Green Seal Federal Reserve Note. About Uncirculated.**
This $500 has original paper surfaces and embossing. Add nice centering to the mix and you have a delightful high denomination note. A center fold is detected plus the back upper left margin has a small mark of black ink. (1,500-2,000)

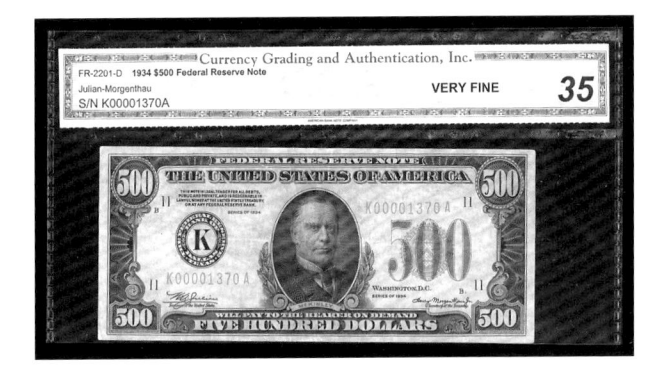

14057 **Fr. 2201-K $500 1934 Federal Reserve Note. CGA Very Fine 35.**
Bright lime green overprints are noticed on this piece that has had some margin repairs done. (1,250-1,500)

Newly Discovered $500 Changeover Pair- One of Two Known

14058 Fr. 2201-L/2202-L $500 1934/1934A Federal Reserve Notes. Changeover Pair. Gem Crisp Uncirculated.

A simply spectacular new discovery which brings the number of known $500 changeover pairs to two. Each of the two notes is a crackling fresh and utterly original Gem, with both pieces displaying full original embossing and totally unmolested paper surfaces. We have never had the opportunity of offering any $500 changeover pair in any previous sale, and, if rarity, grade and desirability are any indication, our estimate could well prove extremely conservative. (17,500-32,500)

14059 Fr. 2201-L $500 1934 Light Green Seal Federal Reserve Note. PCGS Choice About New 55.
This is a brightly inked, lightly circulated example that is sure to please. (1,800-2,200)

14060 Fr. 2202-B $500 1934A Federal Reserve Note. PCGS Gem New 65.
The centering is quite pleasing on this New York high denomination. (1,800-2,200)

14061 Fr. 2202-B $500 1934A Federal Reserve Note. PMG Choice Uncirculated 64.
Nice margins surround this bright note from the Big Apple. (1,600-2,000)

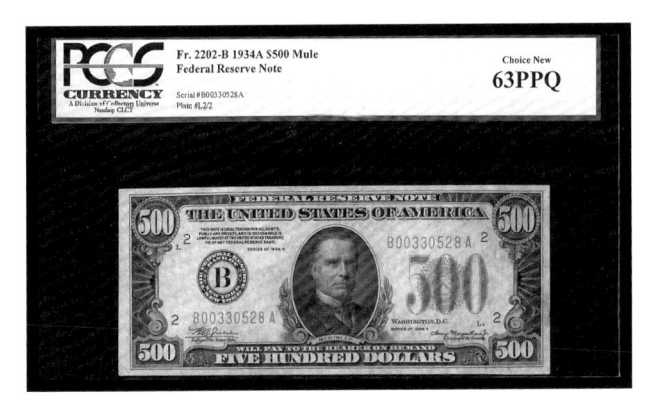

14062 Fr. 2202-B $500 1934A Federal Reserve Note. PCGS Choice New 63PPQ.
A touch of light teller handling is seen on an otherwise nicely margined and well inked note. The back centering is a touch out of register. (1,500-1,800)

14063 Fr. 2202-B $500 1934A Federal Reserve Note. CGA Choice Uncirculated 63.
The margins are surely ample for even a point more in grade, though it is not readily apparent what limited this note to a Choice. (1,500-1,800)

14064 Fr. 2202-B $500 1934A Federal Reserve Note. PMG Uncirculated 62.
Treasury Seal embossing is noted on this broadly margined $500, though a bit of handling has precluded this note from a higher grade. (1,400-1,600)

14065 Fr. 2202-B $500 1934A Federal Reserve Note. About Uncirculated.
An attractively centered example that appears new until closely examined. (1,200-1,400)

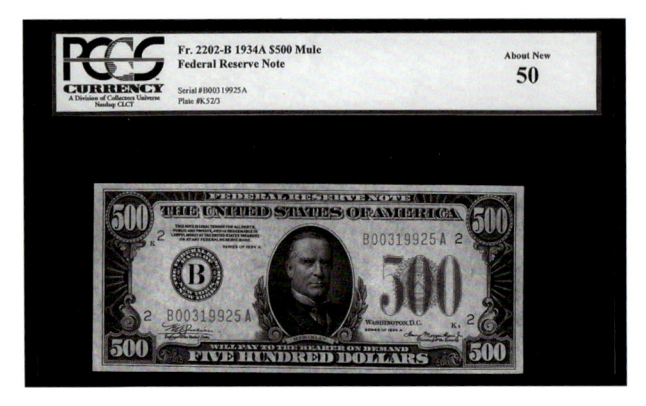

14066 Fr. 2202-B $500 1934A Federal Reserve Note. PCGS About New 50.

In the holder, this piece looks to have all the attributes of a full Gem. The margins are broad and even and the paper is bright. (1,200-1,400)

High Grade New York $500 Star

14067 Fr. 2202-B★ $500 1934A Federal Reserve Note. About Uncirculated.

This attractive high grade $500 star is consecutive to the only known uncirculated star example from this district, which we sold last year for over $25,000. It's only the sixth Star to surface from the New York district in this series, with four pieces in middle road circulated grades and one the aforementioned CU example. This piece displays some handling and minor surface wrinkling, but is unmolested and fully original, with excellent color and broad even margins. (10,000-14,000)

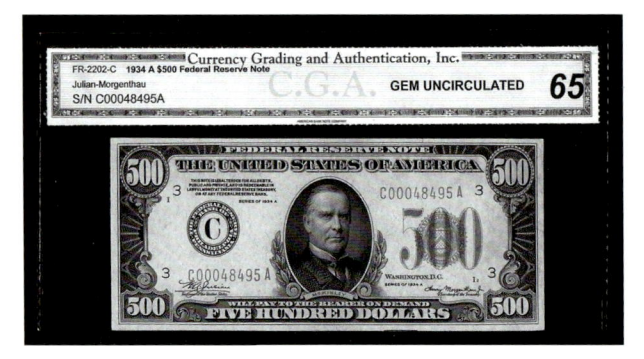

14068 Fr. 2202-C $500 1934A Federal Reserve Note. CGA Gem Uncirculated 65.

The original surfaces are visible through the third-party holder. (2,500-2,750)

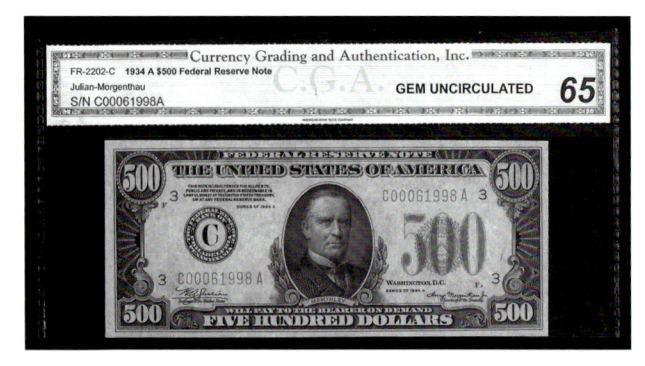

14069 Fr. 2202-C $500 1934A Federal Reserve Note. CGA Gem Uncirculated 65.

A touch better front to back centering and this well margined note may have achieved a better grade. (2,500-2,750)

14070 Fr. 2202-C $500 1934A Federal Reserve Note. Very Fine.

A touch of flatness is noticed on this Philly issue. (900-1,100)

14071 Fr. 2202-D $500 1934A Mule Federal Reserve Note. PCGS Apparent Very Choice New 64.

A slight teller mark and some rust on the back have caused this Cleveland note to be placed in a red holder. The overall eye appeal is commensurate with the grade. (1,500-2,000)

14072 Fr. 2202-D $500 1934A Federal Reserve Note. CGA Choice Uncirculated 63.

An as made wrinkle transects the top and bottom margins to the left of the treasury seal. A tiny margin split that affects nothing is also seen. (1,300-1,600)

14073 Fr. 2202-E $500 1934A Federal Reserve Note. PMG Extremely Fine 40.

An evenly circulated issue with the typical three folds seen on EF's. (1,000-1,200)

14074 **Fr. 2202-G $500 1934A Federal Reserve Note. PCGS Very Choice New 64.**
Here is a perfect type note which exhibits good centering, bright colors and natural paper ripple. (2,000-2,500)

14075 **Fr. 2202-G $500 1934A Federal Reserve Note. PCGS Choice New 63.**
Here is yet another bright representative from Chicago with even margins. (1,800-2,200)

14076 **Fr. 2202-G $500 1934A Federal Reserve Note. Choice Crisp Uncirculated.**
An attractive note, but the centering is a touch off on the face. (1,800-2,200)

14077 **Fr. 2202-G $500 1934A Federal Reserve Note. Fine-Very Fine.**
A light erasure of the number 16 is seen to the left of the portrait on this otherwise crisp example. (800-950)

14078 **Fr. 2202-H $500 1934A Federal Reserve Note. CGA Choice Uncirculated 64.**
Embossing of the seal is easily seen when the note is viewed from the back. (1,600-1,900)

14079 **Fr. 2202-H $500 1934A Federal Reserve Note. Very Fine+.**
A touch of light teller soiling is seen on this bright, crisp St. Louis note. (950-1,000)

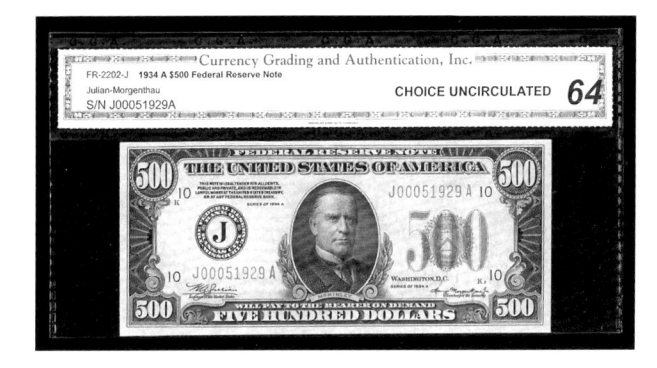

14080 **Fr. 2202-J $500 1934A Federal Reserve Note. CGA Choice Uncirculated 64.**
Nice margins and embossing are highlights of this $500. (1,800-2,300)

14081 **Fr. 2202-J $500 1934A Mule Federal Reserve Note. PMG About Uncirculated 55.**
A diagonal fold can be seen on this bright example which is sure to please. (1,250-1,500)

14082 **Fr. 2202-K $500 1934A Federal Reserve Note. Extremely Fine.**
Dallas is a tougher district for high denominations. This lightly handled note will cause several collectors to take notice.
From The Rolling Plains Collection (1,300-1,800)

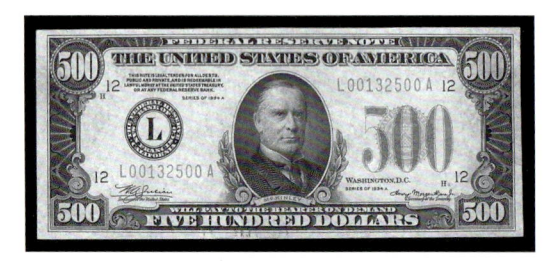

14083 **Fr. 2202-L $500 1934A Federal Reserve Note. Choice About Uncirculated.**
This $500 is nicely centered and it has a center bend. The right-hand margin reveals some counting soil. (1,300-1,500)

Consecutive Pair San Francisco $500 FRN's

14084 **Fr. 2202-L $500 1934A Federal Reserve Notes. Two Consecutive Examples PMG About Uncirculated 50 and About Uncirculated 55.**
Consecutive survivors certainly are not seen with regularity for this series as this is the first time we have the pleasure to offer a pair. Plenty of original embossing remains visible within the holders on each piece. (2,500-3,000)

14085 **Fr. 2202-L $500 1934A Federal Reserve Note. Fine-Very Fine.**
Despite the surfaces of this note falling victim to some wetness it still remains snappy. (800-1,000)

CGA 66 1928 Chicago $1000

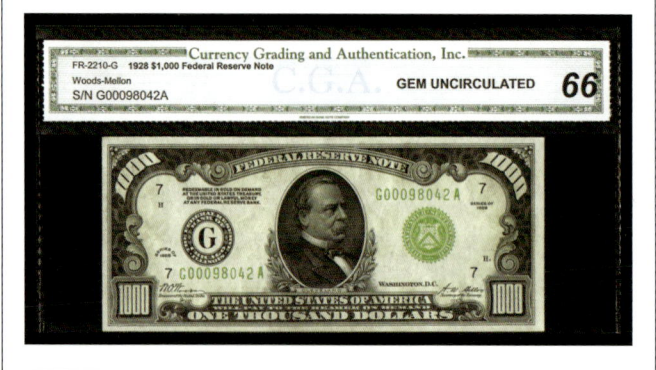

14086 **Fr. 2210-G $1000 1928 Federal Reserve Note. CGA Gem Uncirculated 66.**
Beneath the holder this piece looks crackling fresh, well embossed, beautifully bright, and very well centered. A perfect type example of this rare note awaits the high bidder. (7,000-9,000)

PMG Gem Uncirculated 65 EPQ
1928 $1000 Chicago FRN

14087 Fr. 2210-G $1000 1928 Federal Reserve Note. PMG Gem Uncirculated 65 EPQ.
This note, which hails from the "Dearborn Hoard," is as nice as this series has to offer. Prominent embossing shows through quite nicely. The paper surfaces remain bright white. With the interest towards quality and the strong market reaction notes as this create expect this beauty to easily reach or exceed bidding in the range of. . . (6,500-8,500)

14088 Fr. 2210-G $1000 1928 Federal Reserve Note. PMG Choice Uncirculated 64.
PMG informs us via their label that this note has "Great Color." From our vantage point we also see embossed serial numbers and Treasury Seal. This is a perfect example for type, as this 1928 $1000 is simply lovely. (5,000-7,000)

14089 Fr. 2210-G $1000 1928 Federal Reserve Note. Crisp Uncirculated.
Bright and displaying excellent color, this 1928 series example is just a handling mark and a bit of bottom margin from the full Choice grade. (3,200-3,700)

CGA 63 1928 Dallas $1000

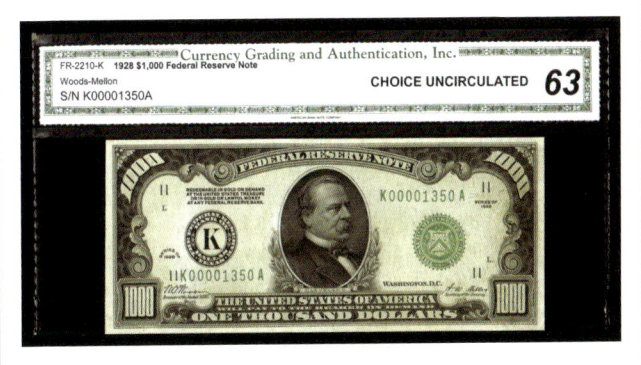

14090 Fr. 2210-K $1000 1928 Federal Reserve Note. CGA Choice Uncirculated 63.
This is a nice piece from the ever elusive Dallas district. Were it not for a few corner tip folds and a pinhole in the margin it surely would have graded higher. (15,000-20,000)

14091 Fr. 2211-A $1000 1934 Light Green Seal Federal Reserve Note. CGA Choice Uncirculated 64.
This Boston $1000 has bright white paper. (3,700-4,200)

14092 **Fr. 2211-B $1000 1934 Light Green Seal Federal Reserve Note. Crisp Uncirculated.**
A bright and attractive high denomination example with some teller handling at right that barely distracts. (2,700-2,900)

14093 **Fr. 2211-B $1000 1934 Light Green Seal Federal Reserve Note. PMG Very Fine 30 EPQ.**
Light Green Seals are especially attractive on the high denomination notes. This example displays much embossing and honest even wear. (2,000-2,500)

14094 **Fr. 2211-B $1000 1934 Federal Reserve Note. Fine-Very Fine.**
A repaired margin split is in the upper left margin on this Big Apple high denomination. (1,650-1,950)

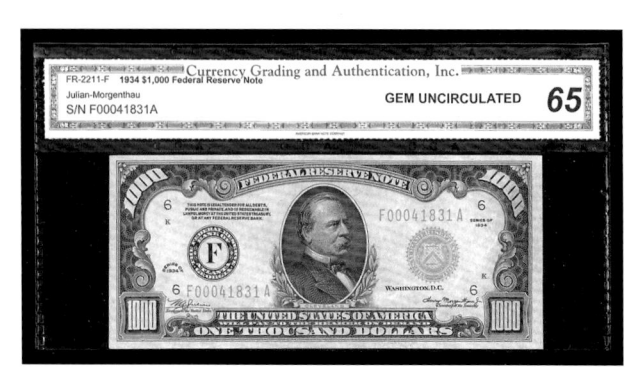

14095 **Fr. 2211-F $1000 1934 Federal Reserve Note. CGA Gem Uncirculated 65.**
Serial number embossing is noticed on this nicely margined example. (3,750-4,250)

14096 **Fr. 2211-F $1000 1934 Light Green Seal Federal Reserve Note. PCGS Extremely Fine 40PPQ.**
The lime green seals certainly have more eye appeal than their deep pine green seal counterparts. Some embossing still can be seen on bright surfaces. (3,250-3,750)

14097 **Fr. 2211-G $1000 1934 Federal Reserve Note. PMG Gem Uncirculated 65 EPQ.**
The first in a consecutive pair of original Chicago notes. The margins are even and the embossing pronounced. (4,000-5,000)

14098 **Fr. 2211-G $1000 1934 Federal Reserve Note. PMG Gem Uncirculated 65 EPQ.**
Bright paper and solid embossing are the hallmarks of this Chicago note. (4,000-5,000)

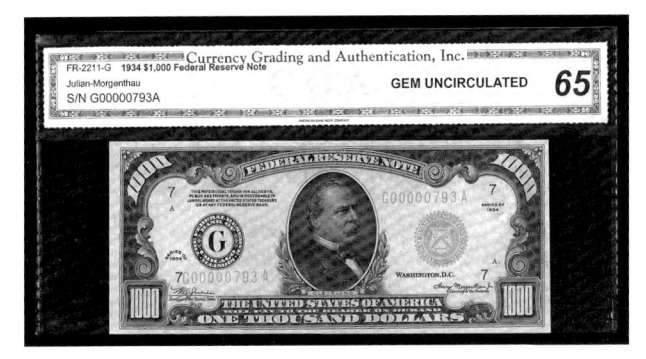

14099 Fr. 2211-G $1000 1934 Federal Reserve Note. CGA Gem Uncirculated 65.
A deep green seal and serial number add to the eye appeal of this bright white note. (3,500-4,500)

14100 Fr. 2211-G $1000 1934 Federal Reserve Note. Very Fine.
A tiny rust spot affects the bottom margin along with several pinholes near the top on this well margined Chicago high denomination. Some scuffiness is also seen to the left of the portrait for full disclosure. (1,650-1,950)

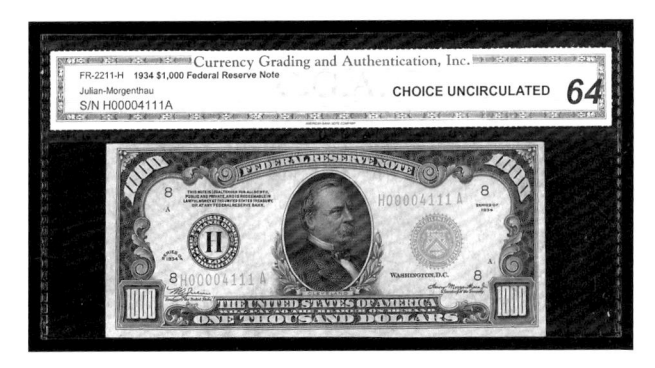

14101 Fr. 2211-H $1000 1934 Light Green Seal Federal Reserve Note. CGA Choice Uncirculated 64.
This is a bright, attractive example of the scarcer LGS that falls just short of gem. (3,700-4,200)

14102 Fr. 2211-H $1000 1934 Light Green Seal Federal Reserve Note. CGA Choice Uncirculated 64.
Pleasing colors are seen on this attractive note which had a nominal printing of 22,440 notes. (3,700-4,200)

14103 Fr. 2211-H $1000 1934 Federal Reserve Note. PMG Choice About Unc 58.
A lone corner fold is noted at bottom right, though the note faces up as a fully uncirculated piece with embossing on the serial numbers and seal. (2,800-3,200)

14104 Fr. 2211-I $1000 1934 Federal Reserve Note. PMG Choice Very Fine 35.
From the lowest print run of only 12,000 notes for this series, this Minneapolis note displays bright colors and solid margins. (1,750-2,250)

14105 Fr. 2211-J $1000 1934 Federal Reserve Note. Crisp Uncirculated.
A bright note with plenty of appeal lacking the centering on both the face and back to support a higher grade. (2,500-2,700)

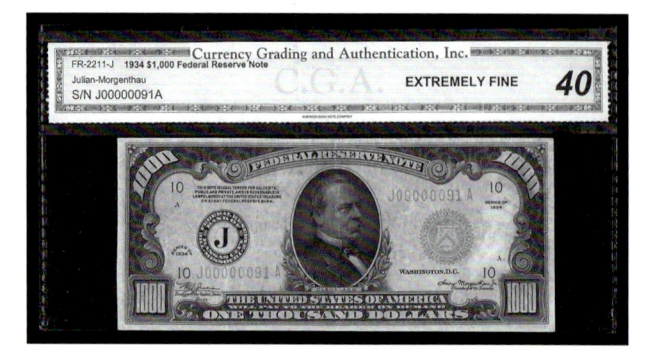

14106 Fr. 2211-J $1000 1934 Federal Reserve Note. CGA Extremely Fine 40.
The three heaviest folds leave the face printing mostly uninterrupted. (1,750-2,000)

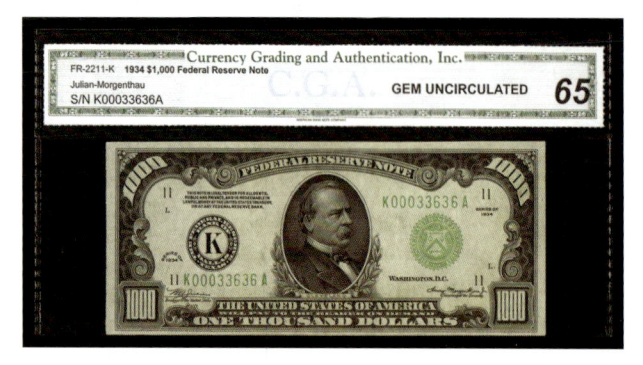

14107 Fr. 2211-K $1000 1934 Federal Reserve Note. CGA Gem Uncirculated 65.
The Dallas district is the key to this series in Uncirculated grades. Currently most price guides list the premium to be nearly three times that of any other district. This piece is deeply printed with a bright overprint. (6,000-9,000)

14108 Fr. 2211-L $1000 1934 Federal Reserve Note. PMG About Uncirculated 50.
A lovely example which is just the lightest of center and corner folds from New. (2,750-3,250)

1934 San Francisco Star

14109 Fr. 2211-L★ $1000 1934 Mule Federal Reserve Note. PCGS Extremely Fine 45.
In a market driven by new discoveries, this note will be sure to please as it is new to the census. A neat serial number complements deeply inked, bright surfaces. (8,000-12,000)

14110 Fr. 2211-L★ $1000 1934 Federal Reserve Note. CGA Fine 12.
The paper has a bit of life despite breaks in its continuity at the heaviest of the folds that account for the grade. This is now the fourteenth known example of this issue with the two discoveries here in this auction. (2,500-4,000)

14111 Fr. 2212-C $1000 1934A Federal Reserve Note. CGA Gem Uncirculated 65.
This bright piece still exhibits some strong embossing. We have not offered many of this type in the higher grade ranges. (3,250-3,750)

14112 Fr. 2212-D $1000 1934A Mule Federal Reserve Note. PCGS Choice About New 58.
Some serial number embossing is visible on this well margined M-note from the Cleveland district. (2,500-3,000)

14113 Fr. 2212-D $1000 1934A Federal Reserve Note. PMG Choice About Unc 58.
A light center fold and natural paper wave can be seen on this Cleveland $1000. (2,500-3,000)

14114 Fr. 2212-D $1000 1934A Federal Reserve Note. PMG About Uncirculated 55.
Ample margins surround this Cleveland district piece that has a light center fold visible. (2,250-2,750)

14115 Fr. 2212-D $1000 1934A Federal Reserve Note. PMG Very Fine 25.
The holder mentions a minor top margin tear. (1,500-1,800)

14116 Fr. 2212-E $1000 1934A Federal Reserve Note. Choice About Uncirculated.
A center fold and one minor corner fold account for the grade on this original and attractive $1000. (2,500-3,000)

14117 Fr. 2212-F $1000 1934A Federal Reserve Note. CGA Gem Uncirculated 67.
Nearly perfect, even margins are noted top to bottom and side to side. As is the case with many of the "Florida Find" $1000's, the embossing is evident through the third party holder. (5,000-6,000)

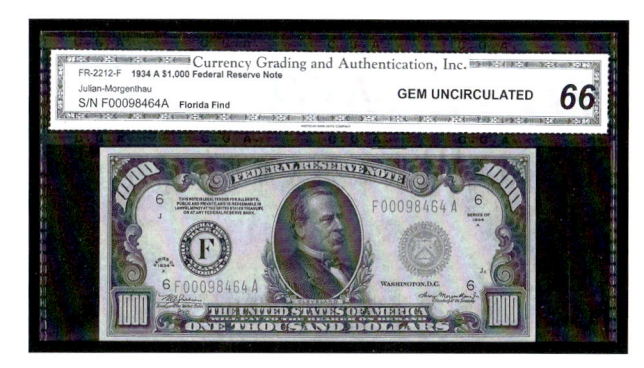

14118 Fr. 2212-F $1000 1934A Federal Reserve Note. CGA Gem Uncirculated 66.
This note, which was part of the fabled "Florida Find," is well margined with wonderful color throughout. (4,000-5,000)

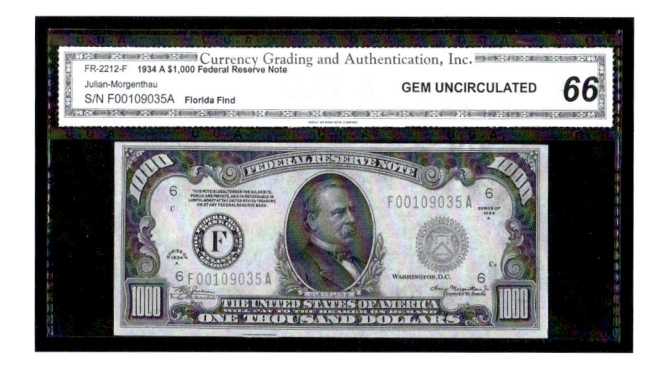

14119 Fr. 2212-F $1000 1934A Federal Reserve Note. CGA Gem Uncirculated 66.
Two of the margins on this "Florida Find" note are much bigger than seen on most $1000's. (4,000-5,000)

14120 Fr. 2212-F $1000 1934A Federal Reserve Note. CGA Gem Uncirculated 65.
A lovely, well centered Gem example of this Atlanta Thousand. It has plenty of eye appeal and appears to have fully earned its third party "65" grade. (3,250-3,750)

PMG Gem 66 EPQ 1934A Chicago $1000 FRN

14121 Fr. 2212-G $1000 1934A Federal Reserve Note. PMG Gem Uncirculated 66 EPQ.
Not much can be improved on as this high denomination note has wonderful margins and plenty of punch through embossing of the seals and serials. (4,000-5,000)

14122 Fr. 2212-G $1000 1934A Federal Reserve Note. CGA Gem Uncirculated 65.
A well centered and bright example graded Gem Uncirculated 65 by CGA. (3,500-4,000)

14123 Fr. 2212-G $1000 1934A Federal Reserve Note. PMG Choice Uncirculated 64.
This is a pleasing, attractive example with vibrant inks from the Chicago district. (3,250-3,750)

14124 Fr. 2212-G $1000 1934A Mule Federal Reserve Note. PCGS Choice New 63.
This is a boldly colored example which is just a wider top margin shy of an even higher grade. (2,750-3,250)

14125 Fr. 2212-G $1000 1934A Federal Reserve Note. PMG Choice About Unc 58.
An attractive well centered note that is just a corner fold from grading Choice Crisp Uncirculated. (2,000-2,500)

The Only Known $1000 Changeover Pair

14126 Fr. 2212-J/2211-J $1000 1934A/1934 Federal Reserve Notes. Changeover Pair. PMG Gem Uncirculated 66 EPQ/65 EPQ.

This reverse changeover pair is the only known changeover pair in the $1000 denomination. The pair has long been listed in the Oakes/Schwartz (now Schwartz/Lindquist) small size reference, and has now been graded by PMG, with the first note grading Gem Uncirculated 66 and the second Gem Uncirculated 65, with both pieces receiving the EPQ (Exceptional Paper Quality) designation. Any estimate here is but mere speculation, as this pair is unique and likely to remain that way for years to come, but the opportunity is now open for one collector to buy both the $500 and $1000 changeover pairs offered in this sale and have a set that might well remain unique forever. **(30,000-50,000)**

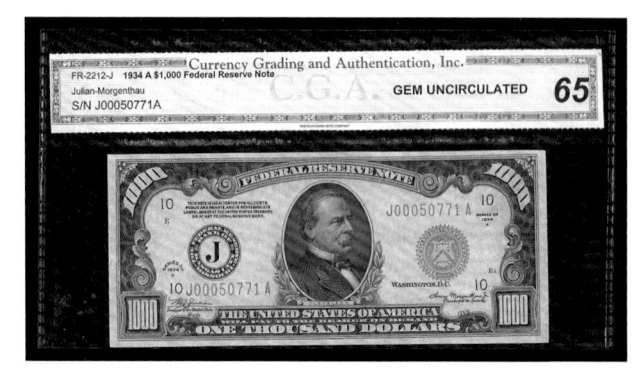

14127 **Fr. 2212-J $1000 1934A Federal Reserve Note. CGA Gem Uncirculated 65.**
This note is quite colorful and plenty of serial number embossing remains visible. (3,500-4,250)

14128 **Fr. 2212-J $1000 1934A Mule Federal Reserve Note. PCGS New 62.**
Here is a pleasing example from a district where high grade high denomination notes do not turn up with much regularity. Uneven margins preclude a higher grade. An interesting minor BEP ink smear is seen on the back. (3,250-3,750)

14129 **Fr. 2212-J $1000 1934A Federal Reserve Note. About Uncirculated.**
This bright note is one of but 21,600 printed from here in this series. A light center fold and handling are seen. (2,800-3,300)

14130 **Fr. 2212-L $1000 1934A Federal Reserve Note. Choice Crisp Uncirculated.**
This is a well preserved and attractive $1000 with nice margins. (3,700-4,200)

New to the Census 1928 Atlanta $10000

14131 Fr. 2230-F $10000 1928 Federal Reserve Note. PMG Choice Extremely Fine 45.
This serial number F00000016A $10,000 note increases the census to only nine for all districts for the 1928 Series. Two of those enumerated notes are locked away in the San Francisco Federal Reserve Bank Collection, reducing the number available to collectors to just seven in all grades combined. We had the privilege of selling the finest of the seven, a Choice CU Richmond example, which realized over $241,000 in our February 2005 auction of the Taylor Family Collection. The example presented here is not quite that nice, but it is only lightly circulated and is a strong contender for second finest known for this type and denomination. Offered here to the numismatic community for the first time, a true trophy item that is certain to become the centerpiece of the collection it enters. In a market where truly rare items of all kinds sell for record prices whenever they are offered, expect this prize to easily reach and likely considerably exceed our conservative estimate of... (150,000-200,000)

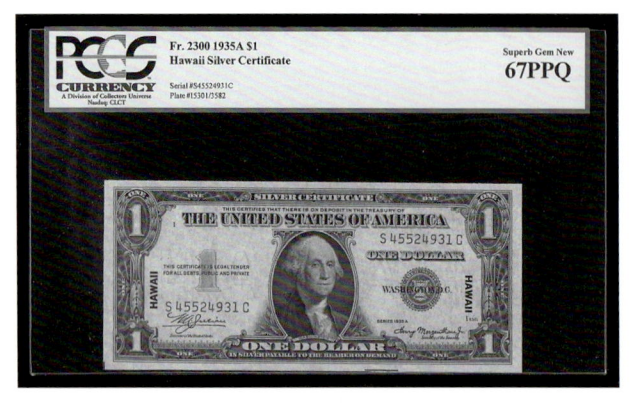

14132 Fr. 2300 $1 1935A Hawaii Silver Certificate. PCGS Superb Gem New 67PPQ.
Huge margins and very bright inks are the pleasing features of this note. (400-600)

14133 Fr. 2300 $1 1935A Hawaii Silver Certificate. PCGS Superb Gem New 67PPQ.
Here is yet another well margined and deeply embossed beauty. (400-600)

Pack of $1 Hawaiis

14134 Fr. 2300 $1 1935A Hawaii Silver Certificates. Original Pack of 100. Choice Crisp Uncirculated.
It has been quite awhile since we last saw a pack of Hawaii $1s. This nicely margined and centered pack is crackling fresh. The top note shows light handling. The BEP band also shows pencilled writing. (Total: 100 notes) (10,000-15,000)

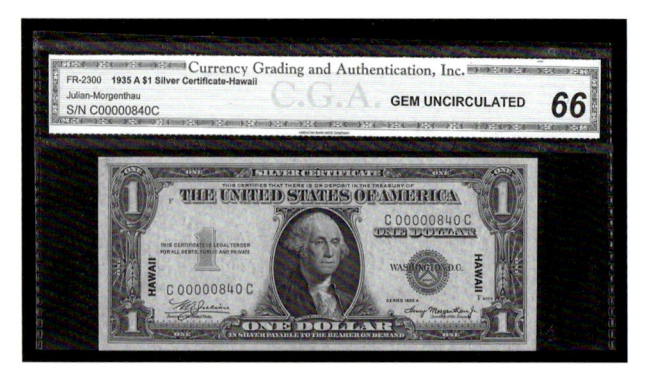

14135 Fr. 2300 $1 1935A Hawaii Silver Certificate. CGA Gem Uncirculated 66.
This three digit serial numbered Hawaiian boasts nearly perfect margins. The embossing from both overprints is visible through the holder. (1,000-1,250)

14136 Fr. 2300 $1 1935A Hawaii Silver Certificate. PMG Gem Uncirculated 65 EPQ.
With a print run of only 12,000 notes, fewer F-C block Hawaii's were printed than star notes. This piece which is perfectly margined boasts great embossing and color as noted by PMG. (800-1,000)

14137 Fr. 2300 $1 1935A Hawaii Silver Certificates. Ninety-eight Examples. Choice Crisp Uncirculated.
This nicely margined pack is two notes short of being complete. The centering is also nice while the paper is crackling fresh. Pencilled writing is found on the BEP band. (Total: 98 notes) (10,000-15,000)

14138 **Fr. 2300★ $1 1935A Hawaii Silver Certificate. PMG Gem Uncirculated 66 EPQ.**
The last PMG 66 we handled sold for a touch more than $4,000 in 2006. Since that time, the market for certified Small Size Type, including Hawaiian Stars has shown no sign of slowing down. We expect this boldly original and attractive issue to exceed that price. **(4,000-5,000)**

14139 **Fr. 2301 $5 1934 Hawaii Federal Reserve Note. Choice About Uncirculated.**
This scarce non-mule rarely shows up with regularity, though we are privileged to have two in this auction. The paper here is bright and the margins are sufficient for a Gem. **(1,000-1,500)**

14140 **Fr. 2301 $5 1934 Mule Hawaii Federal Reserve Note. PMG Choice About Unc 58.**
Bright paper and deep inks are seen on this example which there never seem to be enough of. **(400-600)**

14141 **Fr. 2301 $5 1934 Hawaii Federal Reserve Note. About Uncirculated.**
The very rare non-mule 1934 Hawaii $5, a vastly underpriced note considering its true scarcity. It is outnumbered, using a conservative estimate, at least 20 to 1 by its mule sibling. This piece may well surprise, as collectors who have been looking for a high grade example appreciate how difficult it is to locate one. **(1,000-1,500)**

14142 **Fr. 2301★ $5 1934 Mule Hawaii Federal Reserve Note. Very Good.**
Only 48,000 replacement notes were printed for this series. Until now we could count on one hand how many times an example has appeared with us in the past five years. The note is complete with decent margins for the grade. **(1,200-1,600)**

14143 **Fr. 2302 $5 1934A Hawaii Federal Reserve Note. CGA Gem Uncirculated 66.**
A well margined Hawaii Five that appears to have earned its grade. **(800-1,200)**

14144 **Fr. 2303 $10 1934A Hawaii Federal Reserve Note. PMG Gem Uncirculated 66 EPQ.**
This piece is a couple dozen serial numbers away from one of the other fully uncirculated Hawaii $10's offered here. It's likely they were well cared for and ultimately came from the same source. The margins are nearly even and the paper quality is as nice as its twin. **(1,750-2,000)**

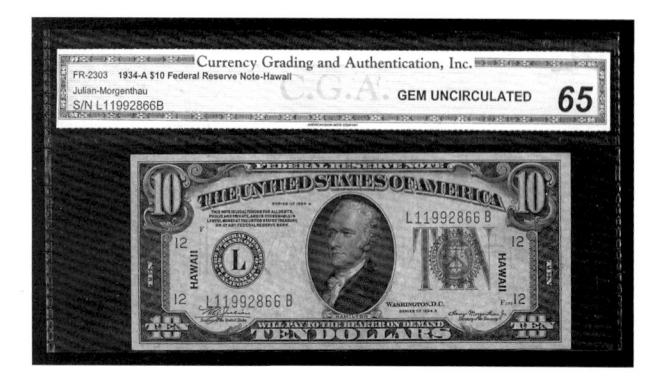

14145 **Fr. 2303 $10 1934A Hawaii Federal Reserve Note. CGA Gem Uncirculated 65.**
Pleasing paper quality is noted, and there is still a faint amount of embossing noted from the Hawaii overprint on back. (1,500-1,750)

14146 **Fr. 2303 $10 1934A Hawaii Federal Reserve Note. PMG Choice Uncirculated 64 EPQ.**
This unadulterated note boasts pack-fresh paper waves and embossing. (750-1,000)

14147 **Fr. 2303★ $10 1934A Hawaii Federal Reserve Note. CGA Very Fine 20.**
A very scarce star with a total printing of only 108,000 pieces. This example is from the last run of only 8,000 pieces. While the $1 and $20 Hawaii stars are often available, the $5 and $10 Hawaii stars are all either very scarce or just plain rare. (1,500-2,000)

14148 **Fr. 2303★ $10 1934A Hawaii Federal Reserve Note. Fine+.**
Sound edges for the grade and a bit of paper snap highlight this tough Star that is near the beginning of the second printing of only 4000 notes. This is by far the scarcest of the three printings. (1,000-1,500)

14149 **Fr. 2303★ $10 1934A Hawaii Federal Reserve Note. Fine.**
A very scarce star which had a printing of only 108,000 pieces. There is a paper clip mark on the reverse, and some staining which affects the front of the note as well. (800-1,200)

14150 **Fr. 2304 $20 1934 Mule Hawaii Federal Reserve Note. About Uncirculated.**
A lone center fold is noted on this exceptionally scarce Mule. Though we have seen some movement in the price for the CU grade range, we still do not think it reflects the true rarity of this issue. (2,500-4,000)

14151 **Fr. 2304★ $20 1934 Mule Hawaii Federal Reserve Note. CGA Fine 15.**
A moderately circulated example of this Hawaii Mule star which can only be termed as rare since we have only handled half a dozen or so. Not many more are listed in the census. Examples in this grade are representative of what is available as high grade pieces are virtually unknown. (1,500-2,000)

14152 **Fr. 2305 $20 1934A Hawaii Federal Reserve Note. PMG Choice Uncirculated 64.**
The margins here are Gem in size and the front to back centering is nearly perfect. (900-1,100)

14153 **Fr. 2305★ $20 1934A Hawaii Federal Reserve Note. Fine.**
This was once a relatively available star, but the supply has been cut virtually to nothing in recent years, which is why the new Schwartz and Lindquist small size catalogue values this piece at $1750 in Very Fine. This example is not quite that nice, but will likely see a realization of near that figure nevertheless. (1,250-1,750)

14154 **Fr. 2306 $1 1935A North Africa Silver Certificate. PMG Gem Uncirculated 65 EPQ.**
Similar to the Hawaiian Ace, the North Africa F-C block also had a print run of only 12,000 notes. This Gem boasts larger than normal margins all around and a deep yellow seal to complement the rich blue serial numbers. (500-750)

Rare $1 North Africa Sheet

14155 **Fr. 2306 $1 1935A North Africa Silver Certificates. Uncut Sheet of 12. Choice Crisp Uncirculated.**
North Africa uncut sheets are always exciting to see. The yellow and blue inks of this sheet are dark. There are also no folds. The margins show some aging especially around the top two and bottom two notes. The top edge has a tiny nick. Still a great World War Two item. (10,000-15,000)

14156 **Fr. 2306★ $1 1935A North Africa Silver Certificate. Choice About Uncirculated.**
While having the appearance of a Gem note, a light center fold is detected on this scarce World War II star note. (1,000-1,500)

14157 **Fr. 2307 $5 1934A North Africa Silver Certificate. PCGS Gem New 66PPQ.**
Wide margins and natural surfaces are merits of this World War Two veteran. (500-700)

14158 **Fr. 2307 $5 1934A North Africa Silver Certificates. Late Finished Plate 307 Changeover Sextet. Very Fine-Extremely Fine.**
The first three notes of this grouping were printed from the fabled late finished face plate 307 and the last three notes are from face plate 1605. Face plate 307 was begun on April 6, 1936. Then it was stored in the plate vault until being discovered in 1942. It was finished on July 3, 1942 and it was then put to use from July 9, 1942 to June 3, 1943. All six of these lightly handled notes have close to matching handling. (Total: 6 notes) (2,500-3,500)

14159 Fr. 2308 $10 1934 Mule North Africa Silver Certificate. Fine-Very Fine.
This Friedberg number is a tough hurdle for the small size collector. This is an evenly circulated example that sports nice edges. An erased "72" is noticed to the left of the portrait and will help you clear that hurdle for a lot less than you anticipated.
From The Bill and Kathy Stella Currency Collection
(2,000-3,000)

14160 Fr. 2309 $10 1934A North Africa Silver Certificates. Very Choice Crisp Uncirculated.
An attractive and well centered consecutive pair with each note displaying better than average centering. (Total: 2 notes) (450-650)

14161 Fr. 2309★ $10 1934A North Africa Silver Certificate. PCGS Gem New 65.
Our description from Central States 2006 read, "This piece is an extraordinary note and a major star note rarity. We have seen numerous examples of this star in the low to middle grades, and a fair number of "wannabe uncirculated" examples or notes that claimed to be uncirculated, but this example is the first $10 North Africa star that has been labeled as gem. It is vividly colored. As a star, it is a major rarity, and the only piece we know of with all of the attributes for true gem status. Expect our estimate to be quickly surpassed by the ranks of star collectors who appreciate just how important this example is..." (2,500-3,500)

PMG 64 $10 1934A North Africa Star Note

14162 Fr. 2309★ $10 1934A North Africa Silver Certificate. PMG Choice Uncirculated 64.
It has been a few auctions since we have had the opportunity to offer this elusive replacement issue. The colors are dazzling with pleasing margins all the way around. (2,000-2,500)

14163 Fr. 2309★ $10 1934A North Africa Silver Certificate. Very Fine.
This is a pleasing, bright North Africa star example exhibiting the usual folds for the grade. (300-400)

14164 Fr. 2400 $10 1928 Gold Certificate. PMG Choice Uncirculated 64.
The overprints are stunning on this piece that is a touch tight in the upper left margin for Gem. (700-900)

14165 Fr. 2400 $10 1928 Gold Certificate. Choice Crisp Uncirculated.
Plenty of original embossing is seen on lightly handled surfaces that keep the piece from a higher grade. (600-800)

PCGS Very Choice New 64PPQ
$10 Gold Certificate Star

14166 Fr. 2400★ $10 1928 Gold Certificate. PCGS Very Choice New 64PPQ.
High grade replacements for this series are relegated to a few surviving notes. The originality and brightness have not been compromised on this glorious type note. (4,000-6,000)

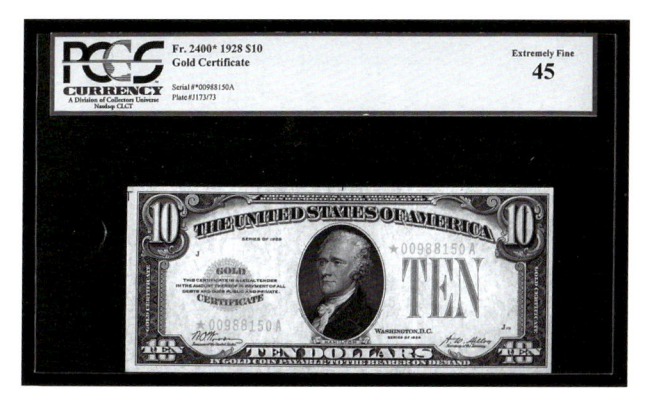

14167 Fr. 2400★ $10 1928 Gold Certificate Star. PCGS Extremely Fine 45.
This is a truly rare Star in the higher circulated grades and beyond. This Star exhibits a nice yellow-orange overprint and bright paper. The margins exhibit two paper guide line markers. Overall a great note in a preserved state seldom seen. (2,000-3,000)

14168 Fr. 2400★ $10 1928 Gold Certificate. Extremely Fine.
This replacement note appears at first glance to be a higher grade, but several light folds and some foxing at right are noticed. (600-1,000)

14169 Fr. 2400★ $10 1928 Gold Certificate. Fine.
This replacement Gold will not break the bank. A light cleansing has removed contaminants from its surface. (300-400)

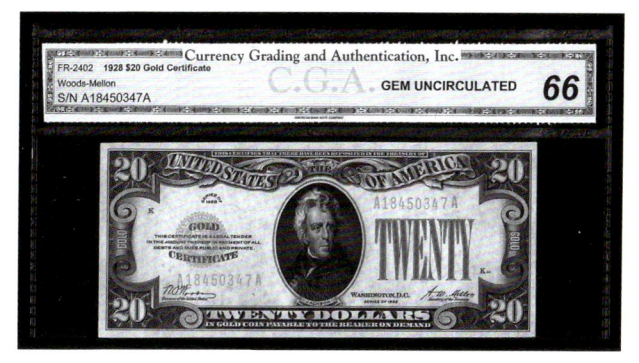

14170 Fr. 2402 $20 1928 Gold Certificate. CGA Gem Uncirculated 66.
Rich golden color and pleasing paper waves are noted on this $20 Gold. (1,500-2,000)

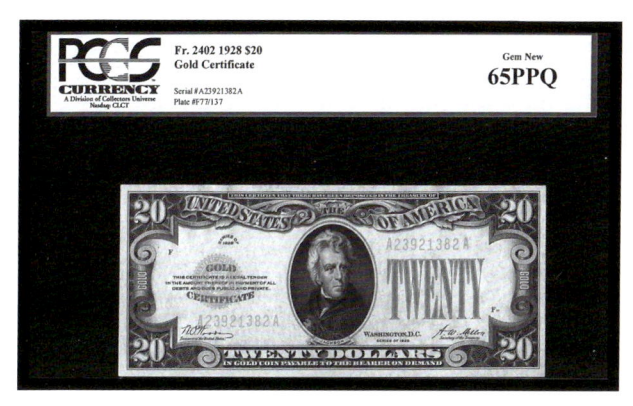

14171 Fr. 2402 $20 1928 Gold Certificate. PCGS Gem New 65PPQ.
Natural paper wave is easily viewed on this high-grade $20 Gold that possesses dark inks and embossing. (1,250-1,500)

Six Consecutive $20 Golds

14172 Fr. 2402 $20 1928 Gold Certificates. Six Consecutive Examples. PCGS Very Choice New 64PPQ (3); Gem New 65PPQ (3).
This is the first time that we have had such an especially nice run of $20 Gold notes. Ample margins, embossing, deep orange third printing, and natural paper wave are merits of each note. This is not a cut half sheet as the plate letters are B, C, D, E, F, and A. Multiples of this Friedberg number have been thoroughly dispersed over the years making this offering that much more special. A trivial spot is seen on the first note below the portrait. (Total: 6 notes) (10,000-12,500)

14173 Fr. 2402 $20 1928 Gold Certificate. Choice Crisp Uncirculated.
The eye appeal of this note is exemplary with deep color in the overprint. Plenty of embossing demonstrates originality while an as made vertical paper wrinkle transects the portrait. (600-800)

Gem Gold Star

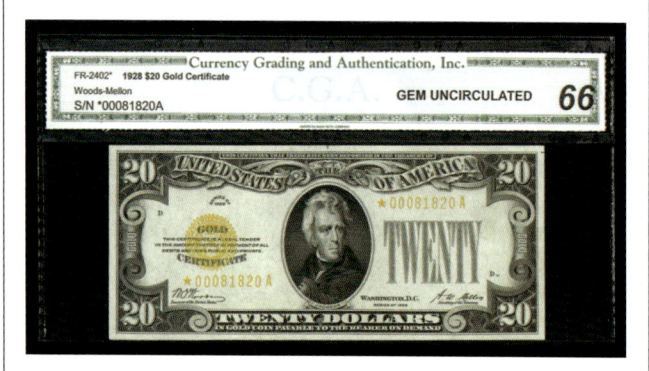

14174 Fr. 2402★ $20 1928 Gold Certificate. CGA Gem Uncirculated 66.
Four ample margins reveal parts of two paper guide line markers on this star. The paper is exceptionally bright while traces of embossing are viewed through the third-party holder. This is the highest graded third-party note we have seen for this Friedberg number. (7,500-12,500)

$20 Star Note

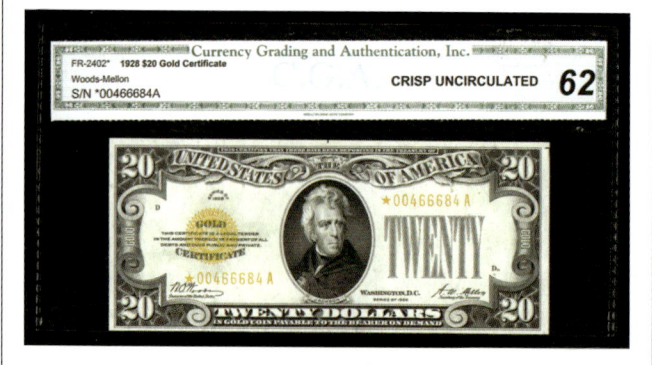

14175 Fr. 2402★ $20 1928 Gold Certificate. CGA Crisp Uncirculated 62.
The $20 Small Size Gold star is an easy note to find in grades through Fine-Very Fine or so, but higher grade examples become progressively more scarce until they simply disappear once the Uncirculated grade is reached. This piece, which has been encapsulated and graded as Crisp Uncirculated 62 by CGA, most likely is kept from a higher grade by a small closed hole at upper right. (6,000-9,000)

14176 Fr. 2402★ $20 1928 Gold Certificate. PMG Very Fine 30.
A trace of embossing and even handling are noticed on this elusive $20 Gold Star. Gold Stars continue their upward ride. (700-1,000)

14177 Fr. 2402★ $20 1928 Gold Certificate. PMG Very Fine 30.
The all important overprint on this Star note is still bold. The lightly circulated but bright paper is complementary to the overall eye appeal. (700-1,000)

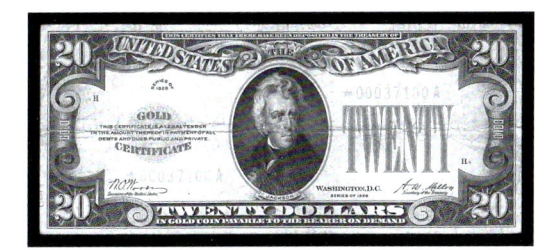

14178 Fr. 2402★ $20 1928 Gold Certificate. Fine+.
This is an evenly circulated and problem free star. These $20 Gold stars are scarcer than is commonly realized. (400-600)

14179 Fr. 2404 $50 1928 Gold Certificate. PMG Gem Uncirculated 66 EPQ.
We are privileged to have a wide selection of $50 Gold Certificates in this auction in a wide range of grades. This piece is by far the best and will garner considerable interest. Perfectly original paper waves are visible through the third party holder and the deep golden overprint adds to the eye appeal. (6,000-7,500)

14180 Fr. 2404 $50 1928 Gold Certificate. PCGS Very Choice New 64PPQ.
Prominent embossing and natural paper wave are just two of the many merits of this spectacular $50 Gold. Pinpoint back centering is also noticed, while the orange overprint is as strong as you will ever see. The only humbling statement to be made about this $50 Gold is that the face is centered just a smidgen too low, thus its third-party grade. (3,500-4,500)

14181 Fr. 2404 $50 1928 Gold Certificates. Two Consecutive Examples.
It is unusual to find consecutive notes of this design. The first note grades VF and has a paper clip indentation. The second note grades XF with a paper clip indentation plus two partial paper clip rust outlines. The paper clipping of these notes to a document probably accounts for their survival. (Total: 2 notes) (1,000-1,300)

14182 Fr. 2404 $50 1928 Gold Certificate. Extremely Fine.
A nice high-end circulated example of this popular note. (700-900)

14183 Fr. 2404 $50 1928 Gold Certificate. Very Fine+.
A nice circulated Small Size $50 Gold. A couple of tiny bank stamp lines barely detract. (550-750)

14184 Fr. 2404 $50 1928 Gold Certificate. Very Fine-Extremely Fine.
The overprints on this note remain bold and the paper bright despite a touch of flatness. (550-750)

14185 Fr. 2404 $50 1928 Gold Certificate. Very Fine.
A couple of stray marks on the back affect nothing on this bright representative. (500-700)

14186 Fr. 2404 $50 1928 Gold Certificate. Very Fine.
The perfect golden-yellow overprint complements the wholly original paper. (500-700)

14187 Fr. 2404 $50 1928 Gold Certificate. Very Fine.
This is a tough note in all grades, with this example exhibiting solid edges. (500-700)

14188 Fr. 2404 $50 1928 Gold Certificate. Fine-Very Fine.
Original surfaces and ample margins are merits of this evenly circulated $50 Gold. (450-650)

14189 Fr. 2404 $50 1928 Gold Certificate. Fine.
The overprint is still bold on this sound edge example. (400-600)

PCGS Choice New 63 $100 Gold Certificate

14190 Fr. 2405 $100 1928 Gold Certificate. PCGS Choice New 63.
This is a well margined and nicely centered note that is tougher in this grade range. The overprint remains bright. Expect to see demand push the final hammer up and over our conservative estimate of. . . (4,000-6,000)

14191 Fr. 2405 $100 1928 Gold Certificate. PMG Uncirculated 62.
The overprint and paper quality are suggestive of a Choice grade, though the bottom margin is a little tight. (2,500-3,500)

14192 Fr. 2405 $100 1928 Gold Certificate. Choice About Uncirculated.
A light center fold is noted on this otherwise Gem looking Gold Certificate. The overprint is bright as is the paper. (2,200-2,500)

14193 Fr. 2405 $100 1928 Gold Certificate. Extremely Fine+++.
There are three light folds, but this note has the appearance of a gem until examined very closely. (1,500-2,000)

14194 Fr. 2405 $100 1928 Gold Certificate. PCGS Extremely Fine 40.
Bountiful margins and bright ink colors are seen on this lightly circulated Gold note. Higher denomination Gold Certificates are more popular than ever and are bringing very strong prices at auction. (1,400-1,800)

14195 Fr. 2405 $100 1928 Gold Certificate. PMG Extremely Fine 40.
This $100 Gold appears fully About New as not a single fold is readily visible through the holder or even when the note is candled. (1,400-1,800)

14196 Fr. 2405 $100 1928 Gold Certificate. Extremely Fine.
An attractive high end $100 Gold, a note which is very difficult to obtain in this grade. (1,400-1,800)

14197 Fr. 2405 $100 1928 Gold Certificate. Very Fine.
A bright representative from a popular issue exhibiting a heavy horizontal fold and some repaired pinholes. (650-950)

14198 Fr. 2405 $100 1928 Gold Certificate. Fine+.
The edges and overprint are nice for the grade on this $100 Gold. The upper right corner has a small moisture spot. A tiny spot is seen on the back, too. (500-800)

Pleasing PCGS About New 55 $500 Gold

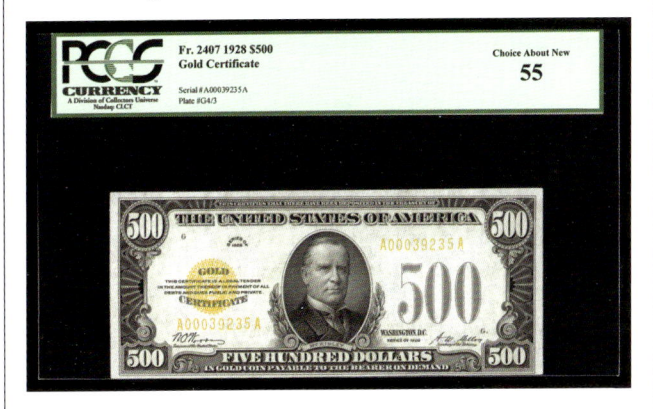

14199 Fr. 2407 $500 1928 Gold Certificate. PCGS Choice About New 55.
The popularity of this type note has increased substantially in the past 24 months, and it shows no sign of slowing. This spectacular note boasts bright white paper, a deep golden-yellow overprint and appears fully Uncirculated. Even close scrutiny of the note fails to reveal the grade limiting fold or bend that is invisible in the third party holder. (20,000-25,000)

$500 Gold Certificate PMG Very Fine 30

14200 Fr. 2407 $500 1928 Gold Certificate. PMG Very Fine 30.
This is a nice, bright high grade circulated example with a very pleasing overall appearance. There are a pair of tiny pinholes near the portrait area which are virtually undetectable but otherwise this much in demand type example is free of any other distractions. (7,000-10,000)

14201 Fr. 2407 $500 1928 Gold Certificate. PMG Very Fine 25.
The overprint is bright on this example which has plenty of body remaining. The eye appeal certainly is there, which makes this affordable example of a scarce high denomination Gold Certificate desirable. (5,000-7,000)

14202 Fr. 2407 $500 1928 Gold Certificate. Fine.
This is a much in demand type and denomination which is almost never offered in this grade. There are a few pinholes, a pencil mark or two and some soil typical for the grade, but the color is good, and there are no real distractions worthy of mention. With so few of these notes available in affordable condition, expect this example to easily surpass our likely conservative estimate of. . . (3,000-4,000)

Solid $1000 Gold

14203 Fr. 2408 $1000 1928 Gold Certificate. PCGS Choice About New 55.
Through the third party holder some embossing of the serial numbers is still visible. Add the pleasing color and attractive appearance of the paper, and this is a note certainly worth chasing. No single fold can be located on this issue, leading us to conclude that it was a bit of handling that accounted for the grade. A lone pinhole must be noted for accuracy's sake. (22,500-27,500)

Bright White $1000 Gold

14204 **Fr. 2408 $1000 1928 Gold Certificate. PCGS About New 50.**
The overprint and paper remain quite bright. This piece offers great eye appeal and the back centering is near perfect. The eye appeal is exceptional and rivals the About New 55 graded piece also offered here. Expect our estimate to prove conservative as so few of these issues appear on the market with a realization of. . . (20,000-30,000)

Pleasing $1000 Gold Certificate

14205 **Fr. 2408 $1000 1928 Gold Certificate. PCGS Extremely Fine 45.**
This is a bright note on a series and denomination seldom encountered with regularity. What this example lacks in centering is made up for in rarity. (12,500-17,500)

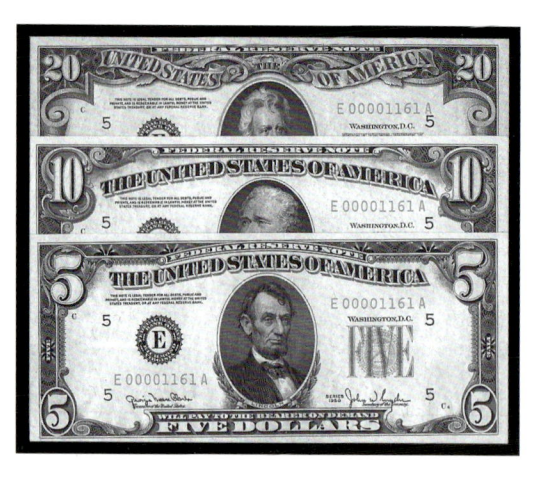

14206 **1950 Matching Serial Number Set.**
This set last appeared at our 2004 FUN sale, where we described, "Three 1950 Federal Reserve Notes that form a neat and hard-to-replicate set, a Fr. 2059-E $5, Fr. 2010-E $10, and Fr. 1961-E $20, each bearing the matching serial number E00001161A. All three notes have a single light vertical storage fold and thus grade **Choice About Uncirculated**."
From The Bill and Kathy Stella Currency Collection
(800-1,200)

14207 **$20 FRN Chicago Stars** including 1934 LGS; 1934A; 1934C; 1950A (2); 1950B; 1963A; 1969A; 1969C; 1981; and 1988A (2). A couple of these **Fine to AU** notes show partial teller rubber stampings.
From The Bill and Kathy Stella Currency Collection (Total: 12 notes) (600-800)

14208 **Collection of Eight Chicago Star $50 FRNs** including 1934; 1963A (2); 1969; 1969C; 1974; 1985; and 1990. All of the stars grade in the **Fine to VF-XF** neighborhood. A couple of the notes have pinholes.
From The Bill and Kathy Stella Currency Collection (Total: 8 notes) (700-900)

14209 **Thirteen Chicago $100 FRNs** including 1934A Mule; 1950A; 1950B; 1950D; 1963A (2); 1969; 1969A; 1969C; 1974; 1981; 1988; and 1990★. Grade ranges are from **VF to Choice CU**.
From The Bill and Kathy Stella Currency Collection (Total: 13 notes) (1,600-2,000)

ERROR NOTES

14210 **Fr. 232 $1 1899 Silver Certificate Very Good.** Here is a new entrant for the census. The bottom margin is bit rough at center, but it is complete. (800-1,200)

Excessively Rare 1928B $2 Legal Invert

14211 **Fr. 1503 $2 1928B Legal Tender. Fine-Very Fine.** This example of the key to the Small Size $2 notes has something we have never previously seen or heard of on any $2 1928B Legal...an Inverted Reverse. Even the massive Taylor Collection, which had a huge number of inverts, lacked a 1928B $2 legal invert. Any estimate here is just a total guess, but if rarity and desirability are any guide, expect the hammer to fall in the range of... (1,500-2,500)

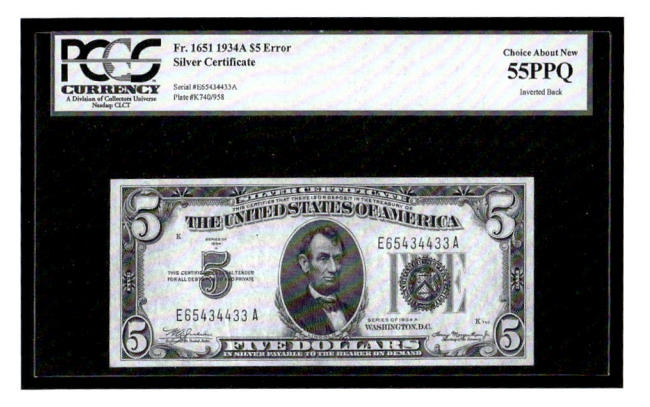

14212 **Fr. 1651 $5 1934A Inverted Reverse Silver Certificate. PCGS Choice About New 55PPQ.** This is a very rare note in this grade. The massive collection of inverts we sold seven years ago had only one 1934A $5 Silver, which graded only About Fine. In fact, that collection had only three $5 Silvers in all series, the nicest of which graded Fine-VF. Expect this outstanding invert to reach or even exceed... (1,000-1,500)

14213 **Fr. 1909-D $1 1977 Federal Reserve Note. PCGS Choice About New 55.**
The light center fold is seen on this example that totally missed the first print. (350-500)

14214 Fr. 1908-J $1 1974 Federal Reserve Note. PCGS Gem New 66PPQ.
This type 1 inverted third printing example is simply stunning. The margins are huge, the embossing deep, and the visual effect marvelous. (500-700)

14215 Fr. 2077-H $20 1990 Federal Reserve Notes. Three Examples PMG Gem Uncirculated 66, Superb Gem Unc 67.
This interesting trio consists of a neat Type II invert error sandwiched between bookends. (Total: 3 notes) (800-1,200)

14216 Fr. 2168-J $100 1977 Federal Reserve Note. CGA Choice Uncirculated 64.
This is a pleasing error which really catches your eye. A bit of light foxing is seen at upper right. (800-1,200)

14217 Fr. 1921-A $1 1995 Federal Reserve Note. Very Choice Crisp Uncirculated.
This piece totally bypassed the third printing. A touch too much handling keeps it from Gem. (400-600)

14218 Fr. 2071-B $20 1974 Federal Reserve Note. Extremely Fine.
This note has traces of a New York district seal and district numbers while the serial numbers were never laid down. (200-400)

14219 Fr. 1909-L $1 1977 Federal Reserve Note. PCGS Choice About New 58.
This is the first San Francisco district issue for this Friedberg number we have the pleasure to auction. Wide margins and decent back centering leave their mark. (400-600)

14220 Fr. 1614 $1 1935E Silver Certificate. Choice Crisp Uncirculated.
This is a pristine example of a mismatch on a tougher series. (650-850)

14221 Fr. 1621 $1 1957B Silver Certificate. Superb Gem Crisp Uncirculated.
This is a nicely margined example with plenty of embossing on crackling fresh paper of the popular U37/U47 mismatch. (450-650)

14222 Fr. 1621 $1 1957B Silver Certificate. Gem Crisp Uncirculated.
This note carries a neat two digit mismatch of x50A/x46A on the lesser encountered S-A block. The margins are very large and the surfaces pristine. (600-750)

14223 Fr. 1903-F $1 1969 Federal Reserve Note. PCGS Gem New 65PPQ.
Besides being a tough mismatch to acquire, this example is one of the nicest to grace our auctions. Sizeable margins and bright inks grace this note from the famed F68/F67 block. (600-800)

14224 Fr. 1907-B $1 1969D Federal Reserve Note. Extremely Fine.
This three fold example carries the B44/B43 mismatch for the series. (300-500)

14225 Fr. 1926-B $1 2001 Federal Reserve Note. PMG Gem Uncirculated 66.
This is a neat two interior digit mismatch on a Series 2001 note. This example of this error is the only one we've seen. It has been encapsulated by PMG and it appears to be a hugely margined beauty that well deserves its 66 grade. With the popularity of mismatched serial number notes at an all time high, expect this exciting new discovery double digit mismatch to realize... (500-800)

14226 Fr. 1935-B $2 1976 Federal Reserve Note. PCGS Very Choice New 64PPQ.
This is a nifty mismatch that no longer appears with regularity. In fact a few Signature auctions have passed since our last. (600-800)

14227 Fr. 1973-J $5 1974 Federal Reserve Note. Very Fine-Extremely Fine.
Only five of these type errors have appeared in any of our sales in the past five years attesting to the scarcity of the J36/J35 mismatch error. (400-600)

14228 Fr. 2074-B $20 1981A Federal Reserve Note. PMG Gem Uncirculated 65 EPQ.
The B1/0 mismatch is quite scarce. The last example we were fortunate to auction was a CGA 65 which sold for almost $1100. This note is only three serial numbers removed from that one and has been awarded the EPQ designation from PMG. This note is exceptionally well embossed with decent face margins and excellent back centering. (1,000-1,250)

14229 Fr. 1935-B $2 1976 Federal Reserve Note. PCGS Gem New 66PPQ.
This is a wonderful example of this ever popular H/B prefix error. Is it from New York or is it from St. Louis? (600-800)

14230 Fr. 1935-B $2 1976 Federal Reserve Note. CGA Gem Uncirculated 66.
The serial number of this note is very close to the other example of this popular H/B prefix error in our sale. $2 error notes continue to realize strong prices. (600-800)

14231 Fr. 1935-B $2 1976 Federal Reserve Note. PMG Gem Uncirculated 66 EPQ.
Solid margins frame this popular mismatched prefix issue. The left serial number begins with an H and the right serial number beginning with a B. (600-800)

14232 Fr. 1935-B $2 1976 Federal Reserve Note. Choice About Uncirculated.
This pleasing example of the H/B prefix error has a light corner fold at left into the design. (300-500)

14233 Fr. 1915-H $1 1988A Federal Reserve Note. Choice Crisp Uncirculated.
The district seal is printed on top of Ms. Villalpando's engraved signature. (150-200)

14234 Fr. 1962-G $5 1950A Federal Reserve Note. PMG Choice Uncirculated 64 EPQ.
The third printing is shifted to the right and into the portrait area on this well preserved $5. (300-400)

14235 Fr. 2081-F $20 1995 Federal Reserve Note. PMG Choice Extremely Fine 45 EPQ.
The black portion of the overprint is shifted into the serial number. (250-350)

14236 Fr. 2121-B $50 1981A Federal Reserve Note. Extremely Fine. A really neat shift error where the third printing goes right off the note on the right side. (350-550)

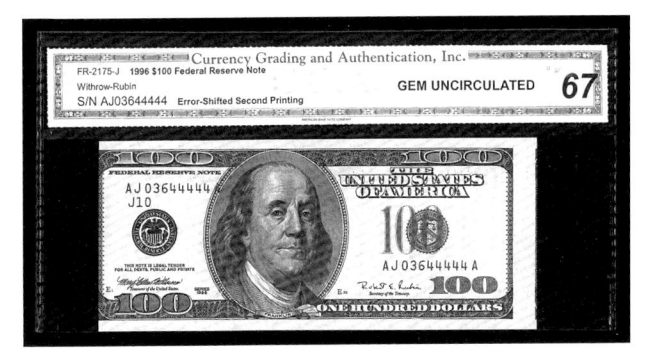

14237 **Fr. 2175-J $100 1996 Federal Reserve Note. CGA Gem Uncirculated 67.**
The third printing is shifted enough to the right so that the suffix letter of the left serial number is on the portrait frame. Also, a sliver of the next note on the sheet shows at right. (250-350)

14238 **Fr. 2011-G $10 1950A Federal Reserve Note. PMG Gem Uncirculated 65 EPQ.**
This is a visually exciting error which happened prior to the third print. (750-1,250)

14239 **Fr. 2028-B $10 1988A Federal Reserve Notes. Two Examples PMG Gem Uncirculated 66 EPQ.**
This pair of massive foldovers, which occurred after the second printing, is simply amazing. The first note actually sustained an obstruction of some type as no printing is noticed at left as on the other. Quite an intriguing pair that leaves a couple of questions unanswered.
(Total: 2 notes) (3,500-4,500)

14240 **Fr. 2076-L $20 1988A Federal Reserve Note. Extremely Fine-About Uncirculated.** A very impressive foldover and associated cutting error. (300-500)

14241 **Fr. 2107-G $50 1950 Federal Reserve Note. Choice Crisp Uncirculated.**
This is a neat cut and fold error on a tough denomination for any errors. (500-750)

$500 Gutter Fold Error

14242 **Fr. 2201-H $500 1934 Light Green Seal Federal Reserve Note. Very Fine.**
A neat gutter fold runs along the bottom of this St. Louis LGS high denomination note. This is a very scarce and desirable error on a $500 note.
(1,250-1,750)

14243 Fr. 1619 $1 1957 Silver Certificate. Gem CU
Fr. 1901-G $1 1963A Federal Reserve Note. Gem CU.
Both of these notes have a dark back to face offset that covers approximately the bottom half of the note. Back to face offsets are scarcer than face to back offsets. (Total: 2 notes) (200-400)

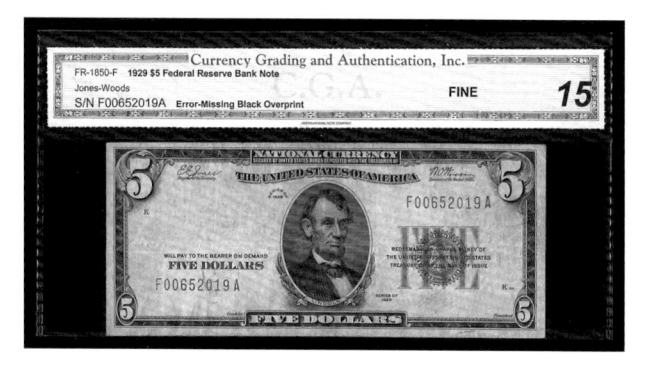

14244 Fr. 1850-F $5 1929 Federal Reserve Bank Note. CGA Fine 15.
The first of a pair of interesting missing black overprint errors on Federal Reserve Bank Notes from Atlanta. We have closely examined these pieces and they look good to us. This note is bright and inspection of the surfaces shows no chemical residue or erasure marks as the whole overprint and all four district letter designators are missing. A neat type for the error specialist. (1,000-2,000)

14245 Fr. 1850-F $5 1929 Federal Reserve Bank Note. CGA Fine 15.
From what we can tell there seems to be no apparent manipulation to remove the overprint that listed the Atlanta Federal Reserve Bank name in black along with the four black district letters. In our opinion we feel this error certainly could have occurred. A tough error on an FRBN. (1,000-2,000)

14246 Fr. 1935-K $2 1976 Federal Reserve Note. Gem Crisp Uncirculated. Excess inking has caused the city and state designation to just about disappear in the district seal, an interesting and rather scarce $2 error. (200-400)

14247 Fr. 1984-E $5 1995 Federal Reserve Note. PMG Gem Uncirculated 66 EPQ.
This is an eye catching mistake with only "68" visible in both serial numbers of the green overprint. (400-600)

14248 Fr. 2073-E $20 1981 Federal Reserve Notes. Three Consecuitve Notes. PCGS Gem New 65PPQ; 66PPQ; 66PPQ.
The left two-thirds of this high-grade trio has been inadequately inked. (Total: 3 notes) (500-700)

14249 **Fr. 2077-B $20 1990 Federal Reserve Note. Fine.**
The usual black Treasury Seal and district numbers are green on this note. Fountain ink contamination is the culprit of this according to Secret Service letters discussing other notes with this type of error. A red spot of ATM ink tightropes the top edge. (300-500)

14250 **Fr. 2079-B $20 1993 Federal Reserve Notes. Two Consecutive Notes. PCGS Very Choice New 64PPQ and PCGS Gem New 65PPQ.**
Ink jet failure has left about 40% of the back of this New York pair unprinted. (Total: 2 notes) (300-500)

14251 **Fr. 2081-B $20 1993 Federal Reserve Note. Gem Crisp Uncirculated.** A striking example of the magnetic ink from the first face printing failing to adhere to the paper and flaking off during printing, a problem that plagued the Bureau's early efforts to use this printing process. This fully embossed Gem is about as nice as these errors ever come, and is a virtual twin to the example we sold for $920 in our April, 2006 Central States sale. (700-1,100)

14252 **Fr. 1601 $1 1928A Silver Certificate. Very Fine.**
An obstruction caused the top serial number to miss having its last six characters printed. However, their embossing can be seen. (200-400)

14253 **Fr. 1608 $1 1935A Silver Certificate. Extremely Fine.**
An obstruction caused the final seven characters of the lower serial number not to print on this wide margined $1 Silver. (300-500)

14254 **Fr. 2080-L $20 1993 Federal Reserve Note. Very Fine+.**
This note has its magnetic ink, but it is missing its non-magnetic ink. This is a scarce and dramatic error. A small red spot of ATM ink is found along the top edge. We saw a similar item in a higher grade go for over $2700 in our February 2005 auction. (800-1,200)

Interesting Multiple Error

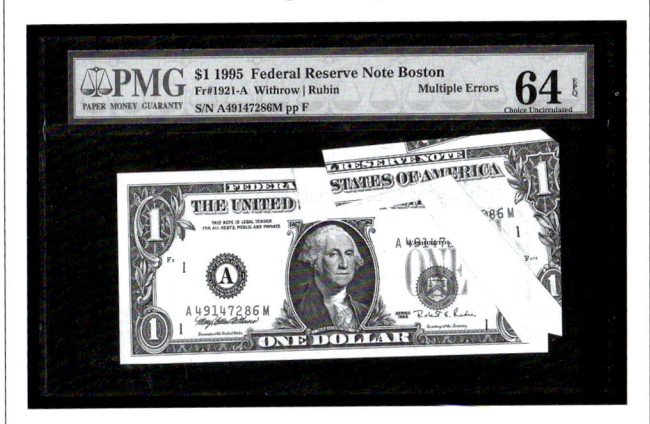

14255 **Fr. 1921-A $1 1995 Federal Reserve Note. PMG Choice Uncirculated 64 EPQ.**
This note suffers from a couple different issues that creates a visually interesting display. A large gutter coupled with a neat cut and fold error affecting all three prints makes you wonder how this escaped detection at the BEP. (1,750-2,250)

14256 **Fr. 2011-C $10 1950A Federal Reserve Note. Choice Crisp Uncirculated.**
A dramatic misaligned back print error is seen on this embossed $10. (200-300)

14257 **Fr. 2169-I $100 1981 Federal Reserve Note. About Uncirculated.**
This is a neat error which has affected a seldom seen high denomination. The classification would fall between moderate to major. (1,500-2,000)

Scarce $1 Hawaii Error

14258 **Fr. 2300 $1 1935A Hawaii Silver Certificate. Gem Crisp Uncirculated.**
The Hawaii overprint on the front is shifted left into the design elements. The back centering on the note may preclude a superb designation. Hawaii errors do not turn up often, but when they do bidding is sure to be heated. (400-600)

One of Two Nationals Known with Mismatched Prefix Letters

14259 **Fort Branch, IN - $10 1929 Ty. 1 The Farmers & Merchants NB Ch. # 9077**
This is an evenly circulated example with mismatched prefix letters, the left serial number being B000164A and the right serial number being A000164A. This is one of only two Nationals known to exist with mismatched prefix letters. Nice **Fine+**, with a few pinholes mentioned solely for the sake of total accuracy in cataloging. This is a great note that is worthy of the finest of collections. It is also plated in Kelly on page 546 of the Fourth Edition. (15,000-20,000)

Fantastic Double Printing $20 Face

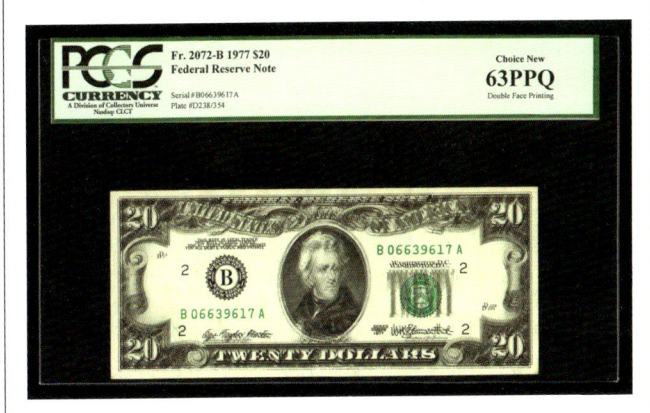

14260 Fr. 2072-B $20 1977 Federal Reserve Note. PCGS Choice New 63PPQ.
This is a fantastic double printing $20. The doubling is pronounced across the entire note, showing doubled signatures, a pair of separate and distinct plate positions and numbers, and Jackson's facial features. This is a great error destined for a great collection. (3,000-5,000)

Near Gem End of Roll Splice Error

14261 Fr. 2073-A $20 1981 Federal Reserve Note. PCGS Very Choice New 64PPQ.
This great end of roll splice error covers almost 50% of the bottom half of the note. The grade clearly qualifies this note as one of the finest known of these type errors. Our last splice error sold for over $5000 in April of 2006. This example is more attractive and offers better margins than the previous note. (5,000-8,000)

14262 Fr. ? $20 ? Federal Reserve Note. Choice Crisp Uncirculated.
This is a partially printed fragment of a "New" $20 Federal Reserve Note which lacks any evidence of a third printing. It is clearly genuine and was obviously not cut from a sheet. This is a dramatic enough error to entice bidding into the range of... (700-1,200)

End of Session Three

SESSION FOUR

Live, Internet, and Mail Bid Auction 436 • St. Louis, Missouri
Friday, May 11, 2007, 6:00 PM CT • Lots 14263-15474

A 15% Buyer's Premium ($9 minimum) Will Be Added To All Lots
You can now view full-color images and bid via the Internet at the Heritage website: HA.com

NATIONAL BANK NOTES

ALABAMA

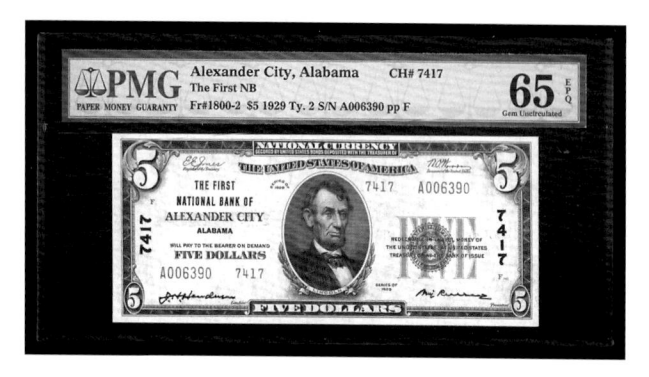

14263 Alexander City, AL - $5 1929 Ty. 2 **The First NB** Ch. # 7417
A well centered beauty which shows its full original embossing through its third party encapsulation. PMG has graded this piece **Gem Uncirculated 65** and given it the much desired "Exceptional Paper Quality" designation as well. (600-900)

14264 Andalusia, AL - $10 1929 Ty. 1 **The First NB** Ch. # 5970
This bank is even harder to find in small than large, with a scant three examples now documented from the 1929 Series in the census. Notes of this scarcity are more highly sought after than ever in today's rarity driven National marketplace. **Very Good-Fine.** (800-1,200)

14265 Huntsville, AL - $20 1929 Ty. 2 **The Henderson NB** Ch. # 8765
A lovely example with evident original embossing. PMG has graded it **Choice Uncirculated 64** and awarded the note its coveted "Exceptional Paper Quality" designation. (500-700)

14266 Jacksonville, AL - $10 1929 Ty. 1 **The Tredegar NB** Ch. # 4319
This is a very scarce bank in both large and small, with the census now documenting seven 1929 survivors from here. While this example has an inked notation on the face, its overall appearance is quite attractive. **Fine-Very Fine.** (600-900)

ARKANSAS

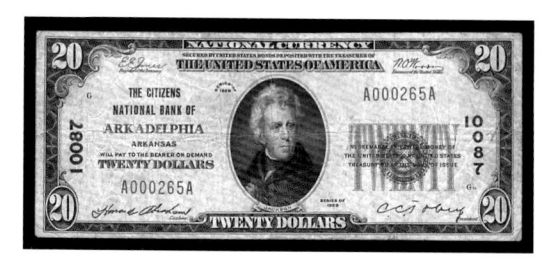

14267 Arkadelphia, AR - $20 1929 Ty. 1 **The Citizens NB** Ch. # 10087
A tougher note from the only bank in this community to issue. **Fine.** (500-700)

14268 Batesville, AR - $10 1902 Date Back Fr. 616 **The First NB** Ch. # (S)7556
A high grade large example. **Extremely Fine+,** with purple signatures.
From The Jacob and Heather Dedman Collection (700-900)

14269 Batesville, AR - $20 1929 Ty. 1 **The First NB** Ch. # 7556
Common enough in large size, but not so in small, with this one of only five Series 1929 examples reported in the census, not surprising as only a relative handful of small notes were issued from here before the bank was liquidated in May of 1930. **Fine. (750-1,250)**

14270 Bentonville, AR - $10 1929 Ty. 1 **The Benton County NB** Ch. # 8135
While large notes from this bank are fairly plentiful, series 1929 examples are downright rare, with the census showing just four specimens reported to date. This piece is tied with one other for the "finest known" designation. **Fine-Very Fine. (1,000-1,500)**

14271 Camden, AR - $5 1929 Ty. 1 **The First NB** Ch. # 4066
A decent example of the only denomination issued by this bank. Camden was the home of Matt Rothert, who, in addition to authoring the reference work on Arkansas obsoletes, had an award winning collection of Fractional Currency and was the person most responsible for the legislation passed by Congress adding the motto "In God We Trust" to U.S. currency. **Fine-Very Fine.**
From The Jacob and Heather Dedman Collection **(500-700)**

14272 Camden, AR - $10 1929 Ty. 2 **The Citizens NB** Ch. # 14096
Our records indicate just four offerings from this rare 14000 charter bank during the past sixty years, with three of those notes grading Very Good and one Fine. This piece, which is new to the census, is a happy exception, grading a strong **Extremely Fine-About Uncirculated** and sporting single digit serial number A000004 as a bonus.
From The Jacob and Heather Dedman Collection
(1,500-2,500)

14273 Clarksville, AR - $10 1929 Ty. 2 **The Farmers NB** Ch. # 11580
This is not a terribly rare bank, but offerings from here have been few and far between in recent years. **Fine-Very Fine,** with a couple of teller stamp remainders on the front. **(450-750)**

14274 DeWitt, AR - $10 1902 Plain Back Fr. 628 **The First NB** Ch. # (S)10178
A scarce large size note with bold signatures, from a bank that is represented by less than ten notes in the census. Pleasing **Fine-Very Fine. (1,200-1,600)**

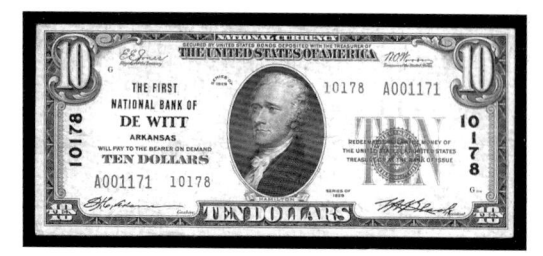

14275 **DeWitt, AR** - $10 1929 Ty. 2 **The First NB** Ch. # 10178
A nice, evenly circulated example from this none too common bank. **Very Fine.** (350-550)

14276 **El Dorado, AR** - $20 1929 Ty. 2 **The First NB** Ch. # 7046
A beautifully centered and crackling fresh example bearing low serial number A000003. **Gem Crisp Uncirculated.** (1,250-1,750)

14277 **Fayetteville, AR** - $20 1902 Date Back Fr. 642 **The First NB** Ch. # (S)7346
An evenly circulated piece which is one of just two $20 Date Backs enumerated in the census. **Fine.** (400-600)

14278 **Fayetteville, AR** - $5 1929 Ty. 2 **The First NB** Ch. # 7346
A very attractive high grade small example. **About Uncirculated.** (500-700)

14279 **Fayetteville, AR** - $20 1929 Ty. 1 **The First NB** Ch. # 7346
A high grade small example from this well collected community. **Extremely Fine.** (400-600)

14280 **Fordyce, AR** - $20 1929 Ty. 1 **The First NB** Ch. # 9501
This **Very Fine-Extremely Fine** $20 has a minimum of folds for the grade and some soiling.
From The Jacob and Heather Dedman Collection (400-600)

14281 **Forrest City, AR** - $20 1929 Ty. 1 **The NB of Eastern Arkansas** Ch. # 13637
This bank may offer the greatest disparity between the number of notes recorded in the census and the availability of notes for collectors. Ninety six notes are listed in the census, but their whereabouts of the vast majority are clearly unknown, as our records show just seven offerings from here during the past sixty years. When the remainder of the listed notes will appear we do not know, but for collectors in the real world this specimen is available here and now. **About Fine,** with a couple of stray blue pencil marks on the right side. (450-750)

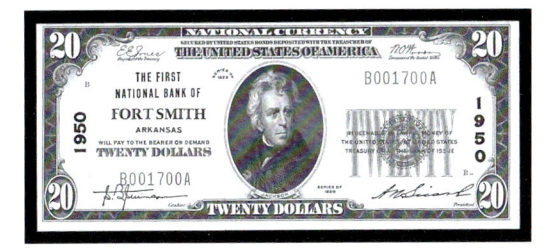

14282 **Fort Smith, AR** - $20 1929 Ty. 1 **The First NB** Ch. # 1950
There is the barest trace of a center bend, but to label this crackling fresh and fully embossed beauty anything less than **Choice Crisp Uncirculated** would be a travesty. (400-600)

14283 **Fort Smith, AR** - $5 1902 Red Seal Fr. 589 **The American NB** Ch. # (S)3634
While quite well circulated and certainly well worn, this is the only Red Seal extant from this rather scarce bank which liquidated in 1916. **Very Good**, definitely rare enough to realize... (2,500-4,500)

14284 **Fort Smith, AR** - $10 1902 Date Back Fr. 618 **The American NB** Ch. # (S)3634
A decent Third Charter Date Back from this less often seen Fort Smith bank. **Fine.** (600-900)

14285 **Fort Smith, AR** - $20 1929 Ty. 1 **The Merchants NB** Ch. # 7240
A very common bank, but few notes from here are available in this state of preservation. **About Uncirculated.** (250-450)

14286 **Fort Smith, AR** - $10 1902 Plain Back Fr. 631 **The City NB** Ch. # (S)10609
Nice red stamp signatures and decent margins enhance the appeal of this attractive ten from this less common Fort Smith bank. **Very Fine-Extremely Fine.** (600-900)

14287 **Gravette, AR** - $20 1929 Ty. 1 **The First NB** Ch. # 8237
A more than acceptable example from this tougher one bank community. **Fine.** (500-700)

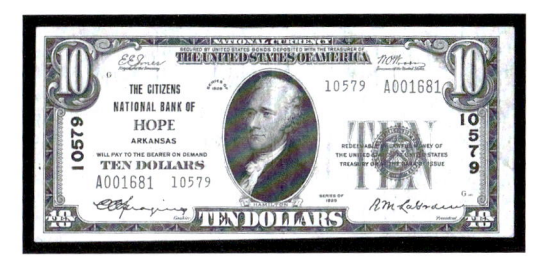

14288 **Hope, AR** - $10 1929 Ty. 2 **The Citizens NB** Ch. # 10579
An above average small example from this bank. **Very Fine.** (300-500)

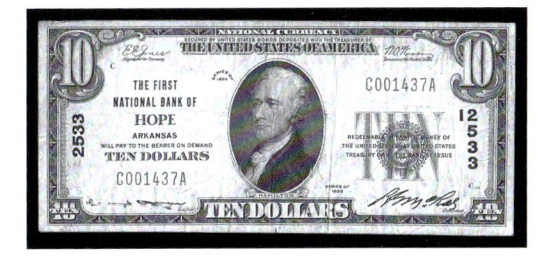

14289 **Hope, AR** - $10 1929 Ty. 1 **The First NB** Ch. # 12533
An evenly circulated example from Hope's last issuing bank, which circulated Series 1929 notes only. **Fine-Very Fine.** (300-400)

14290 Hot Springs, AR - $5 1929 Ty. 1 **The Arkansas NB** Ch. # 2832
A scarce type and denomination from here, and in considerably higher grade than most examples from this bank. Nice **Very Fine. (400-600)**

14291 Hot Springs, AR - $10 1929 Ty. 2 **The Arkansas NB** Ch. # 2832
A nice grade Type 2 example from this always sought after location. **Very Fine+. (700-900)**

14292 Hot Springs, AR - $10 1929 Ty. 2 **The Arkansas NB** Ch. # 2832
A nice evenly circulated example from this well collected resort community. **Fine-Very Fine. (400-600)**

14293 Lake Village, AR - $5 1929 Ty. 1 **The First NB** Ch. # 11262
By far the scarcer of this location's two issuers. Pleasing **Fine-Very Fine. (600-800)**

14294 Lake Village, AR - $5 1929 Ty. 1 **The First NB** Ch. # 11262
An evenly circulated **About Fine** example from by far the scarcer of Lake Village's two banks. (450-650)

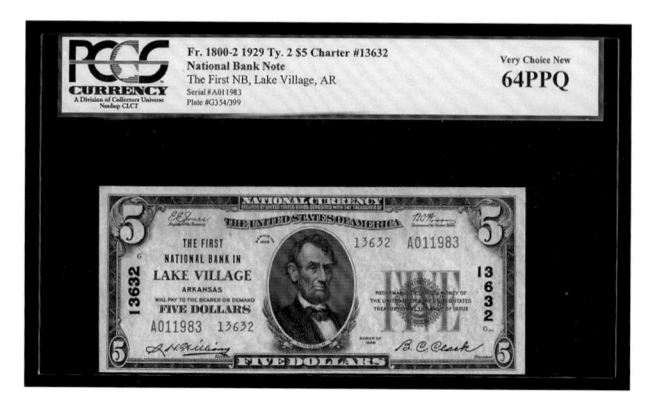

14295 Lake Village, AR - $5 1929 Ty. 2 **The First NB** Ch. # 13632
Embossing, dark inks, and natural paper wave enhance the desirability of this well preserved note. **PCGS Very Choice New 64PPQ. (500-800)**

14296 Little Rock, AR - $10 1902 Plain Back Fr. 624 **The Exchange NB** Ch. # (S)3300
Large notes only from this tougher Little Rock bank. **Fine**, with the top margin a trifle close. (300-400)

Perhaps Finest Known Arkansas Red Seal

14297 Little Rock, AR - $10 1902 Red Seal Fr. 613 **The State NB** Ch. # (S)6902
Red Seals are among the very rarest types from Arkansas, with the reported population from the entire state totaling a mere twenty five pieces. This example is considerably nicer than the Red Seal from here we sold back in January, which, despite being lower grade and close cut on the bottom realized $5462.50. This example, grading **Extremely Fine,** is at least tied for the honor of being the "finest known" Red Seal from any Arkansas issuer and certainly may, in a head to head competition, indeed be the finest. Expect some serious competition before the hammer falls on this rarity tonight. (8,000-12,000)

14298 Malvern, AR - $5 1929 Ty. 1 **The First NB** Ch. # 7634
A scarce note from this elusive one bank location. Nice **Fine-Very Fine.** (600-900)

14299 Mansfield, AR - $5 1902 Plain Back Fr. 606 **The First NB** Ch. # (S)11195
A high quality large example which has been off the market since our consignor obtained it back in 2000. This is the only large note from here to be offered in the past fifteen years, and is as nice as any example, large or small, we've ever seen from this institution. Bright **Very Fine+.** (1,750-2,250)

14300 Mansfield, AR - $5 1929 Ty. 1 **The First NB** Ch. # 11195
This small community's two banks must have engaged in an interesting rivalry, having received successive charters and likely opened virtually simultaneously with each other. This institution was the larger and more successful of the two, outstripping its sibling with more than twice the circulation and twice the capital of its slightly younger rival. **Fine,** with a couple of inconsequential spots. (500-800)

14301 McGehee, AR - $5 1929 Ty. 1 **The First NB** Ch. # 13280
This was McGehee's only bank, with fives the sole denomination issued. Just four large and seven small notes make up the entire census, with offerings few and far between. **About Fine.** (600-800)

Serial Number 1 Newark Note

14302 **Newark, AR** - $5 1929 Ty. 1 **The First NB** Ch. # 9022
An attractive serial number 1 example which has been off the market since our consignor obtained it at the Byron Stuart collection sale back in November of 1993. **Choice Crisp Uncirculated,** very nearly as nice as the number 1 example from here we sold back in January for $2990. (2,500-3,500)

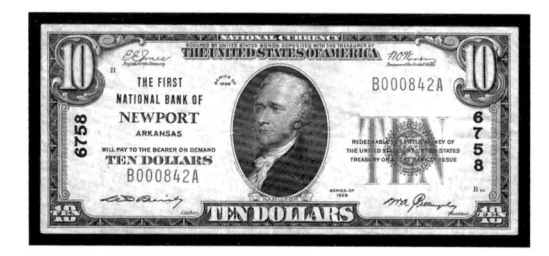

14303 **Newport, AR** - $10 1929 Ty. 1 **The First NB** Ch. # 6758
This is somewhat of a hoard note in large size, but Series 1929 examples from here are quite scarce, with this piece nicer than most any listed to date in the census. Nice **Very Fine.** (600-800)

14304 **Newport, AR** - $20 1929 Ty. 1 **The First NB** Ch. # 6758
The paper here is solid for the grade. An attractive example of this scarce small size note. **Very Fine.** (600-800)

14305 **Paragould, AR** - $10 1902 Plain Back Fr. 627 **NB of Commerce** Ch. # (S)10004
A decent circulated large example from this none too common bank. Pen signed **Fine.** (500-700)

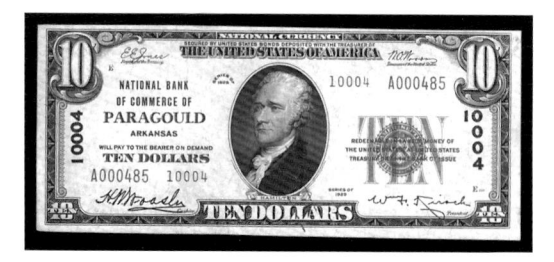

14306 **Paragould, AR** - $10 1929 Ty. 2 **NB of Commerce** Ch. # 10004
A high grade series 1929 note which is far above the average for this location. **Extremely Fine-About Uncirculated,** with a tiny bit of paper clip residue below the portrait. (350-550)

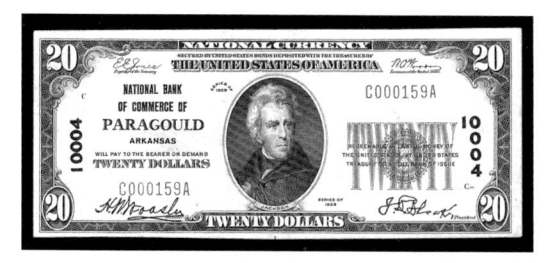

14307 **Paragould, AR** - $20 1929 Ty. 1 **NB of Commerce** Ch. # 10004
This is one of the highest grade Series 1929 examples from this bank reported to date. **Extremely Fine.** (450-650)

14308 **Paragould, AR** - $20 1902 Plain Back Fr. 662 **The New First NB** Ch. # 13155
Low grade but very rare, with this bank issuing large examples for only a year and a half before the advent of small size currency. Just three large notes from here are listed in the census, with this piece the only one we've ever seen at public sale. **Very Good,** with a few stains and problems, most of which are actually quite minor. (2,000-3,000)

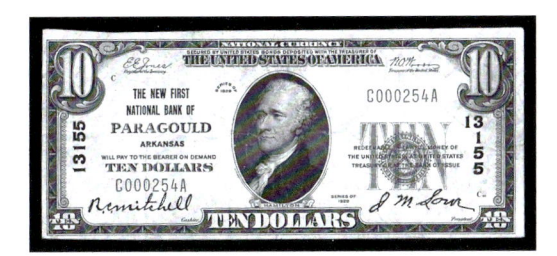

14309 **Paragould, AR** - $10 1929 Ty. 1 **The New First NB** Ch. # 13155
A nice companion piece to the large note from here offered above. Pleasing **Fine-Very Fine.** (400-600)

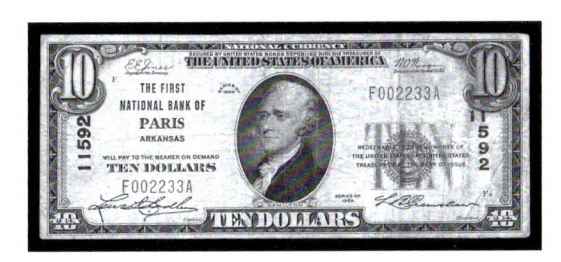

14310 **Paris, AR** - $10 1929 Ty. 1 **The First NB** Ch. # 11592
The sole denomination issued by this bank in both large and small size. **Fine.** (300-400)

14311 **Pine Bluff, AR** - $10 1902 Plain Back Fr. 624 **The Simmons NB** Ch. # 6680
A decent large size note from this community's most prolific issuer. **Fine,** with the signatures faded. (350-550)

14312 **Pine Bluff, AR** - $20 1902 Plain Back Fr. 650 **The Simmons NB** Ch. # 6680
This note is pen signed by woman assistant cashier Cora Niven. President Nichol has also pen signed his name. This note has acquired a purple hue to its face and back. **Very Fine.**
From The Jacob and Heather Dedman Collection (400-600)

14313 **Pine Bluff, AR** - $20 1929 Ty. 1 **The Simmons NB** Ch. # 6680 Two Examples
This is a private named bank with the two notes represented in this lot having acquired a light purplish hue especially in the face margins and back. **Very Fine.**
From The Jacob and Heather Dedman Collection (Total: 2 notes) (300-500)

14314 **Pine Bluff, AR** - $10 1902 Plain Back Fr. 632 **The NB of Arkansas at Pine Bluff** Ch. # (S)10768
Other than one bank which is yet unreported, this is Pine Bluff's scarcest large issuer, with the census listing just six large examples not including this note. Our records show just two offerings of large notes from here since 1980, with one coming in a 1983 Hickman-Oakes auction and the other an appearance in one of our auctions in 1999. The pen signed signatures are of the cashier and vice president. The tombstone also displays an interesting layout that includes the state name. There is some staining, mostly near the Treasury Seal. **Fine.**
From The Jacob and Heather Dedman Collection (1,500-2,500)

14315 Rector, AR - $10 1929 Ty. 1 **The First NB** Ch. # 10853
A just plain scarce bank which had a miniscule small size issue before it entered receivership in December of 1930. Nice **Fine+,** and scarce enough to see bidding reach or exceed... **(1,500-2,000)**

14316 Rogers, AR - $10 1929 Ty. 1 **The American NB** Ch. # 10750
While not an exceptionally rare bank, this new to the census example is one of the nicest Series 1929 specimens reported to date. Bright **Very Fine-Extremely Fine. (400-600)**

14317 Siloam Springs, AR - $5 1902 Plain Back Fr. 602 **The First NB** Ch. # (S)9871
The second title used by this bank, which issued large notes only. **Very Good-Fine,** a very typical grade for notes from this scarce issuer. **(1,000-1,500)**

14318 Siloam Springs, AR - $5 1929 Ty. 1 **The First NB** Ch. # 13274
This is actually a considerably more difficult to obtain bank in small size than large, as a group of cut sheets skew the large census upward. The count for series 1929 examples remains at just a literal handful, with this one of that number. **Very Good+. (1,000-1,400)**

14319 Springdale, AR - $10 1902 Plain Back Fr. 626 **The First NB** Ch. # 8763
The signatures are printed nicely on this example. A Plain Back $10 on this bank in the same grade went for almost $2400 in September 2005. **Very Fine. (1,500-2,000)**

14320 Springdale, AR - $10 1929 Ty. 2 **The First NB** Ch. # 8763
A tough to find small note from the only bank to issue here. Bright **Very Fine,** with a couple of small ink spots which barely detract. **(500-800)**

14321 Stuttgart, AR - $5 1929 Ty. 1 **The First NB** Ch. # 10459
A high grade example from this by no means common bank, although the paper is considerably toned. **Crisp Uncirculated. (1,500-2,500)**

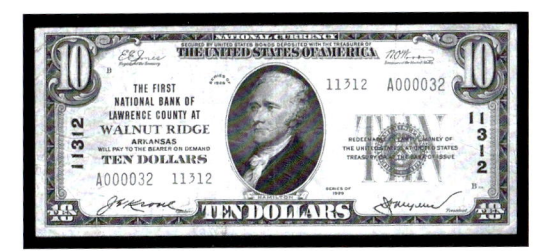

14322 **Walnut Ridge, AR** - $10 1929 Ty. 2 **The First NB of Lawrence County** Ch. # 11312
Although chartered in 1919 as the First National Bank of Black Rock (what a marvelous note that would have made) this bank elected to issue only Type 2 examples after it adopted this issuing title in September of 1933. A paltry four notes are known, one five, one ten, one fifty and one hundred. The fifty and hundred both represent the only specimens of their denomination known from the state, while the five and ten have never been previously offered to collectors at public sale. In fact, this note is listed in the census lacking both a serial number and a grade. We sold the $50 example from here back in January for $20,125. This piece, although just as rare, will bring considerably less. Sharp **Fine-Very Fine,** a most significant Arkansas small size rarity. (3,000-5,000)

One of Two Known

14323 **Walnut Ridge, AR** - $5 1929 Ty. 1 **The Planters NB** Ch. # 12083
This piece bears one of the great names in Arkansas Nationals, and is excessively rare to boot, as it is one of just two Series 1929 examples extant from this bank. The other example reported from here has been off the market since we last sold it in 1994, making this attractive specimen the sole small note available to collectors from this rare bank. Sharp **Fine-Very Fine,** a true Arkansas small size trophy item. (3,500-5,500)

CALIFORNIA

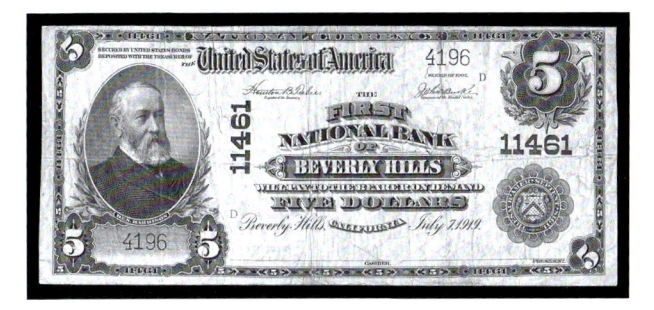

14324 **Beverly Hills, CA** - $5 1902 Plain Back Fr. 606 **The First NB** Ch. # 11461
A new to the census example from this always much in demand issuer. Evenly circulated **Fine+.** (1,750-2,250)

Newly Discovered Brawley Note

14325 **Brawley, CA** - $5 1902 Plain Back Fr. 601 **The First NB** Ch. # (P)9673
This new discovery comes from an extremely rare Imperial County community whose only bank issued large notes only before liquidating in 1922. Only two examples are known from here, a damaged piece which was the only note from here that Charley Colver could find in more than three decades of searching, and the Fine-Very Fine example we offered as part of the Lowell Horwedel's California collection in September of 2004. Colver's impaired example sold for $3300, while the Horwedel piece realized $9200. This example, which is offered here for the first time to the collecting community, is an evenly circulated and problem free specimen which will allow one more fortunate California collector to add this prohibitively rare town to his holdings. **Fine.** (7,500-10,500)

14326 Brea, CA - $5 1929 Ty. 2 **Oilfields NB** Ch. # 13877
While this is hardly a rare bank, notes from this Orange County community are avidly collected and seldom available. Bright **Very Fine**. (800-1,200)

14327 Los Angeles, CA - $50 1902 Plain Back Fr. 683 **Los Angeles-First National Trust & Savings Bank** Ch. # 2491
The edges are nice for the grade, while the signatures are darkly printed. **Very Good**. (900-1,200)

14328 Los Angeles, CA - $5 1882 Brown Back Fr. 471 **The NB of California** Ch. # (P)4096
This is a bright $5 Brown Back for the grade that also sports sound edges. **Fine**. (900-1,200)

14329 Napa, CA - $20 1929 Ty. 1 **The First NB** Ch. # 7176
Spacious margins all around have earned this piece from California's wine country a grade of **Gem Uncirculated 66** from PMG. (800-1,200)

14330 Orange Cove, CA - $10 1929 Ty. 1 **The First NB** Ch. # 11616
A mid-grade small example from this popular location which unfortunately is trimmed slightly into the design at the top. **Fine-Very Fine**. (800-1,200)

14331 Pasadena, CA - $5 1902 Plain Back Fr. 609 **Pasadena NB** Ch. # 12385
Fives only from this sought after Los Angeles County issuer, with this piece easily in the top third of the grade census from here. **Very Fine,** with engraved signatures. (750-950)

14332 Petaluma, CA - $20 1902 Plain Back Fr. 653 **The Sonoma County NB** Ch. # 9918
Large notes only from this northern California bank. **Very Good-Fine**. (750-950)

All Serial Number 1 Uncut Pleasanton Sheet

14333 **Pleasanton, CA** - $20 1929 Ty. 1 **The First NB** Ch. # 9897 Uncut Sheet
A beautiful all serial number 1 sheet from this much in demand Alameda County community. The sheet displays no folds whatever, and the tiny amount of handling is at a minimum for these large items. **Gem Crisp Uncirculated,** a premium uncut sheet. (22,500-32,500)

14334 **Redlands, CA** - $20 1902 Date Back Fr. 642 **The Redlands NB** Ch. # (P)7259
A new discovery from this rare San Bernardino County bank. Only seven notes comprise the entire census population from here, with this bank having liquidated in 1922. This is only the second Date Back reported, and the first twenty. **Very Good+,** with clear signatures and no problems save for the normal wear associated with this grade. (3,000-4,000)

14335 **Richmond, CA** - $5 1902 Plain Back Fr. 609 **The First NB** Ch. # (P)12341
Evenly circulated **Fine** northern California example, with the signatures a bit faded. (600-800)

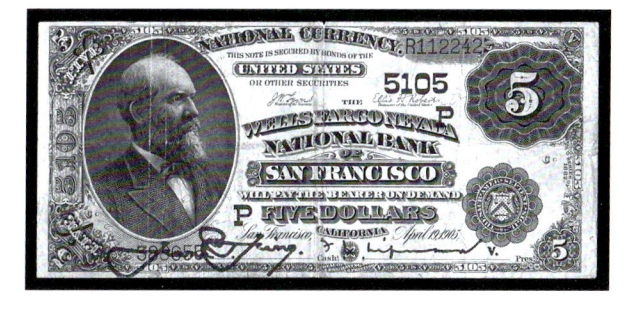

14336 **San Francisco, CA** - $5 1882 Date Back Fr. 537 **Wells-Fargo Nevada NB** Ch. # (P)5105
This is a snappy $5 with darkly printed officers' signatures including that of the vice president. This bank title always conjures up romantic Old West memories based on the exploits of Hollywood. A small nick is at top center. **Fine.** (550-750)

14337 San Francisco, CA - $100 1929 Ty. 1 **Bank of America National Trust & Savings Assoc** Ch. # 13044
Bank title embossing is seen through the **PCGS Choice About New 58** holder. (600-900)

14338 San Mateo, CA - $5 1929 Ty. 1 **The NB of San Mateo** Ch. # 9424
A better type and denomination from the only bank to issue in this bay area location. This newly discovered specimen is one of just four Type 1 fives recorded from here to date. **Fine.** (450-650)

14339 Santa Barbara, CA - $5 1929 Ty. 2 **First NT&SB** Ch. # 2104
A high grade example from this always in demand bank. Fully embossed **Choice Crisp Uncirculated,** with some handling at the right end taking this from the Gem class. (600-900)

14340 Ukiah, CA - $5 1902 Plain Back Fr. 606 **The First NB** Ch. # 10977
Nine large size are known on this sole Mendocino County issuer. The paper quality is that of a **Very Good** with some heavy wallet staining visible on the back. (1,500-2,500)

COLORADO

14341 Central City, CO - $10 1929 Ty. 1 **The First NB** Ch. # 2129
While Black Charter territorial examples abound from this institution, later issues are quite difficult to obtain. Small size specimens are especially scarce, with the census standing at just four pieces, none of which have been offered at public sale for many years. This piece is a fortuitous new discovery. Expect this evenly circulated and problem free **About Fine** example to easily reach and likely exceed our estimate of... (3,000-5,000)

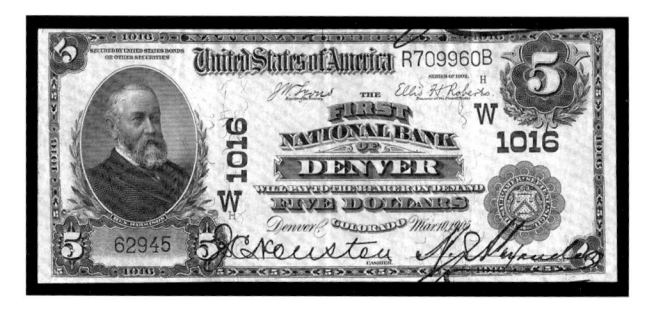

14342 Denver, CO - $5 1902 Plain Back Fr. 598 **The First NB** Ch. # (W)1016
A high grade large example from the first bank chartered in what was then the Colorado Territory. Bright **Extremely Fine,** with a miniscule repair at the bottom. (600-900)

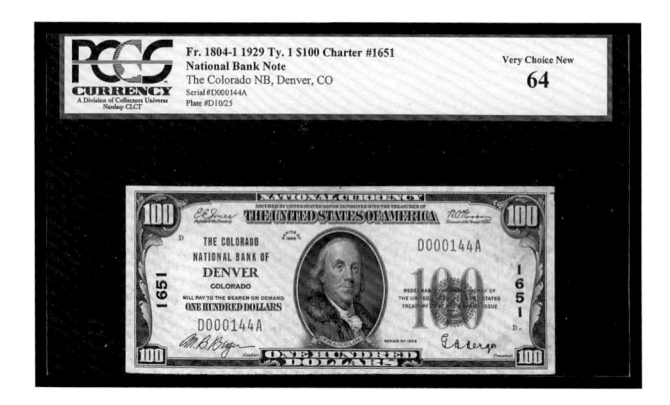

14343 Denver, CO - $100 1929 Ty. 1 **The Colorado NB** Ch. # 1651
Although there were no less than 20 issuing banks in Denver only three issued the $100 denomination in the 1929 series. This **PCGS Very Choice New 64** example is from the 144th of only 420 sheets printed. (1,000-1,250)

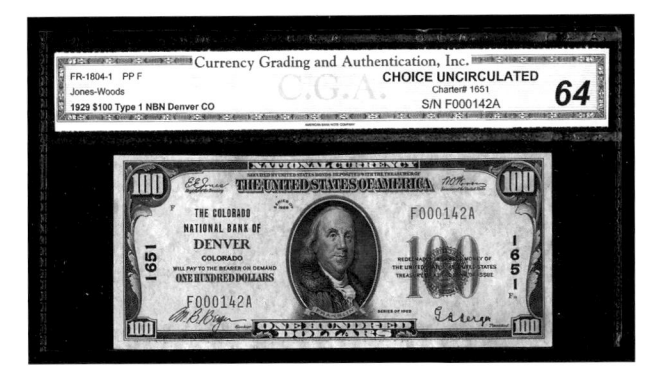

14344 **Denver, CO** - $100 1929 Ty. 1 **The Colorado NB** Ch. # 1651
This is a nice $100 for type. This note is **CGA Choice Uncirculated 64** due to a bank employee not being diligent enough during the cutting of this note from its parent sheet. This left only the top margin not ample enough for a higher grade. (600-800)

Serial #1 Eads, CO

14345 **Eads, CO** - $10 1929 Ty. 1 **The First NB** Ch. # 8412
A fresh and attractive serial number 1 example. **About Uncirculated.** (3,000-4,000)

Lovely 14000 Charter Eads Note

14346 **Eads, CO** - $5 1929 Ty. 2 **First NB** Ch. # 14213
A great note from this very rare 14000 charter Eads bank. It is by far the nicest example from here we've ever seen for sale, and is light years nicer than the Very Fine-Extremely Fine example from here we sold for $6600 back in January of 2005. Crackling fresh **Choice Crisp Uncirculated,** a monster of a Colorado small size note. (5,000-8,000)

14347 **Fleming, CO** - $10 1902 Plain Back Fr. 633 **The First NB** Ch. # (W)11571
This note is one of only six large enumerated in the census on this one bank town in Logan County. It has nice signatures of the cashier and vice president. A tiny tear is noticed at top center. Bright **Fine.** (2,000-3,000)

14348 **Fountain, CO** - $10 1902 Red Seal Fr. 613 **The First NB** Ch. # (W)6772
A just plain rare El Paso County bank with only four large examples in the census, with this example the sole Red Seal. This piece, which has been heavily restored, is in a CGA **Very Good-Fine 10** holder, which bears the notation "Repaired." (4,000-6,000)

14349 **Greeley, CO** - $5 1929 Ty. 1 **The Greeley Union NB** Ch. # 4437
This nicely centered $5 is well embossed with wide margins. **CGA Choice Uncirculated 63.** (250-450)

Excessively Rare Fr. 408a- One of Two Known

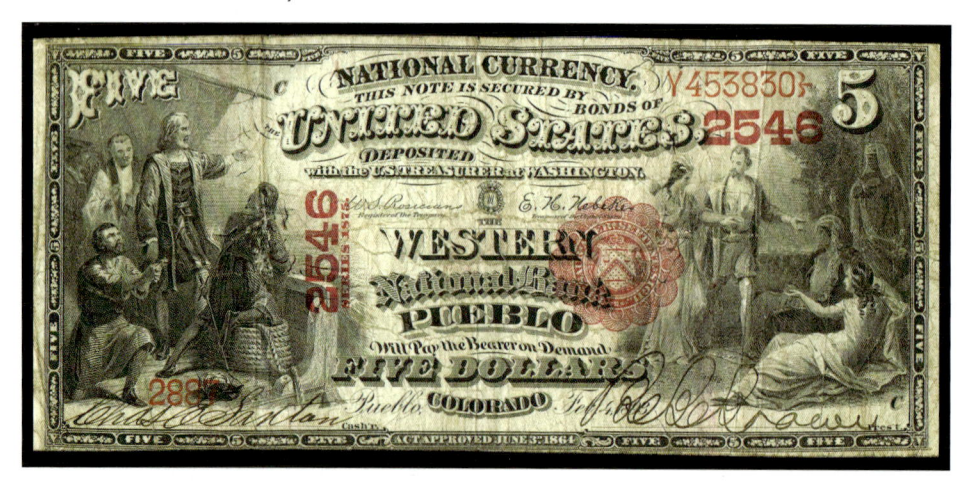

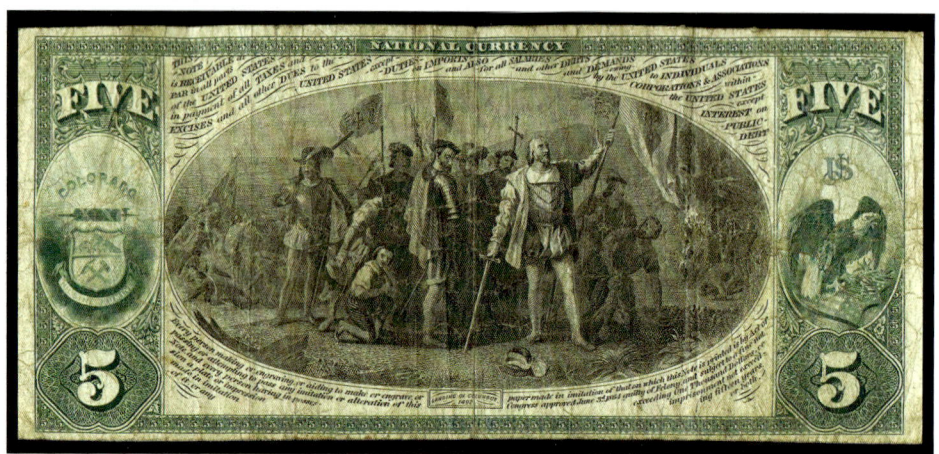

14350 Pueblo, CO - $5 1875 Fr. 408a The Western NB Ch. # 2546
A title change on this First Charter example has produced both a major Colorado rarity as well as a major signature rarity, with this piece only the second Series 1875 $5 note discovered bearing the Rosecrans-Nebeker signature combination. This institution changed its issuing location from South Pueblo to Pueblo in February of 1893. Five First Charter examples are known from the South Pueblo issue, but this is the first First Charter example of any denomination reported bearing the second issuing title. After the title was changed in early 1893, new First Charter plates had to be prepared bearing the revised title. Although the 1875 issue was long over for newly chartered banks, the new plates for this bank had to be Series 1875 plates as this bank's twenty year 1875 issue would not conclude until 1901, twenty years after it was originally chartered. Therefore, the signatures of the then serving Treasury officials, W.S. Rosecrans and E.H. Nebeker, were placed on the newly prepared plates. Of course, the Rosecrans-Nebeker signatures would appear on Series 1875 plates only if a previously chartered bank changed either its title or location, or elected to issue a hitherto unissued denomination. Only one such note has ever been previously discovered, a $5 example from The United States National Bank of the City of New York, which, although chartered in 1881, decided for some unknown reason a decade later to issue $5 notes instead of fifties and hundreds. That note, although quite well circulated, resided in your cataloguer's personal collection of New York City Nationals until sold to researcher Doug Walcutt, and now, after Doug's untimely passing, resides in a major New York holding. This note grades a bright **Fine,** with one small hole that does nothing to disturb its evident eye appeal. Expect this excessively rare item to see demand from both Colorado and signature collectors, and it would not surprise us at all to see a five figure realization before the hammer falls on this lot tonight. **(12,500-22,500)**

14351 Pueblo, CO - $10 1929 Ty. 1 **The Western NB** Ch. # 2546
Even wear and sound edges are hallmarks of this National. **Very Fine-Extremely Fine.** (500-700)

14352 Pueblo, CO - $20 1929 Ty. 1 **The Western NB** Ch. # 2546
This colorful note from a tough state is lightly soiled. **Fine-Very Fine.** (400-600)

14353 Salida, CO - $20 1929 Ty. 1 **The First NB** Ch. # 4172
One of a pair of consecutively numbered high grade examples from this Chaffee County institution. Bright **Extremely Fine-About Uncirculated.** (450-650)

14354 Salida, CO - $20 1929 Ty. 1 **The First NB** Ch. # 4172
A second lovely example. Like its predecessor, it too bears the signatures of Reeves and Preston. **Extremely Fine-About Uncirculated.** (450-650)

14355 Salida, CO - $20 1929 Ty. 1 **The First NB** Ch. # 4172
This evenly circulated $20 bears the first signature combination found from here, with Reeves and Sandusky the two officers. **Fine-Very Fine.** (350-450)

14356 Salida, CO - $20 1929 Ty. 2 **The First NB** Ch. # 4172
This note bears the last bank signature combination used from here, with two completely new officers, J. Ford White and Lewis N. Uenbech. It's also one of just two Type 2 twenties known from here as well. **Fine+,** with a couple of pinholes. (350-450)

14357 Trinidad, CO - $50 1902 Date Back Fr. 674a **The First NB** Ch. # (W)2300
This $50 is from a very tough Friedberg number and it is nicely pen signed by the assistant cashier and vice president. Unusual scroll work is also noticed on the tombstone. Only $50s and $100s were issued by this bank after the First Charter Period. **PCGS Very Good 08.** (1,500-2,500)

CONNECTICUT

14358 Bridgeport, CT - $2 Original Fr. 387 **The First NB** Ch. # 335
Before this note showed up, there were no reported First Charters on this bank, even though it was chartered in March 1864 and it lasted through the National Bank Note era. The bank officer signatures have nearly faded completely away. The back shows several large repairs and a reinforcement of the top edge. **CGA Very Good 08.** (1,500-2,500)

Gorgeous PCGS Gem New 66PPQ Connecticut Ace

14359 Stamford, CT - $1 1875 Fr. 383 **The First NB** Ch. # 4
An absolutely gorgeous note from this low charter bank that may well be the finest First Charter ace we've ever had the privilege of offering. The note displays spectacular colors, bold signatures, and margins that are unusually broad and even for this issue. PCGS has graded this item **Gem New 66PPQ,** and we expect that it will be one of the very few aces to ever gain that (or any higher) grade. (8,000-10,000)

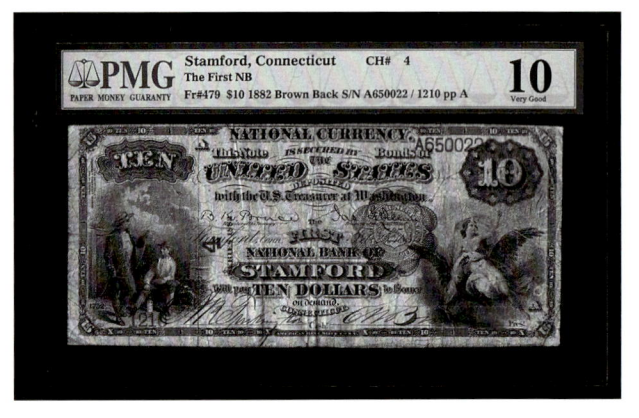

14360 Stamford, CT - $10 1882 Brown Back Fr. 479 **The First NB** Ch. # 4
Nice brown-ink pen signatures add to the charm of this $10 from Fairfield County. **PMG Very Good 10.** (3,000-5,000)

DELAWARE

14361 Delaware City, DE - $5 1902 Plain Back Fr. 598 **The Delaware City NB** Ch. # 1332
This nice **Fine-Very Fine** note enjoys ample margins, clean unmolested surfaces, and legible printed officers' signatures. The only distraction is a miniscule stain just below the left serial number. Delaware is one of those states where collectors far outnumber the available material, especially when it comes to large size nationals. (2,000-3,000)

14362 Wilmington, DE - $20 1929 Ty. 1 **The Central NB** Ch. # 3395
Delaware notes are always in demand due to state collectors. This is an evenly circulated $20 with officers Howard F. McCall and Robt. P. Robinson. A couple of small margin tears are noticed. **Fine-Very Fine.** (250-350)

FLORIDA

Dual Office Holder Note

14363 Lakeland, FL - $10 1929 Ty. 1 **The Florida NB** Ch. # 13370
This note has the signature of J.W. Gressing as both cashier and president. National Bank laws did not prohibit this situation, which in most cases appears to have been done as a Depression era cost saving measure, and your cataloger has documented twelve different charter number dual office holder situations like this during the 1929-35 era. **Fine.** (500-700)

14364 Pensacola, FL - $20 1929 Ty. 2 **The American NB** Ch. # 5603
The gargantuan margins on this **PMG Gem Crisp Uncirculated 66 EPQ** embossed $20 leads credence to the fact that this note was cut from its parent sheet with great care. (700-900)

14365 Pensacola, FL - $20 1929 Ty. 2 **The American NB** Ch. # 5603
While hardly from a scarce bank, the collecting fraternity is indebted to the foresight of a previous generation that preserved high-grade notes such as this in order to satisfy the demand for quality uncirculated material today. **PCGS Very Choice New 64.** (400-600)

Spectacular Serial Number 1 Florida Brown Back

14366 Tampa, FL - $5 1882 Brown Back Fr. 469 **The First NB** Ch. # 3497
A simply wonderful new discovery that has everything a collector could ever wish for. This lovely item is the only serial number 1 $5 Brown Back reported to date from any Florida bank, and is by far the highest grade of any $5 Brown Back known from Florida as well. It's a beautiful high grade example with no trace whatever of any real circulation, and bears a great layout found only on $5 Brown Backs as well. If ever there was a Florida trophy item, this is it. A liberal bid is suggested to bring home this monster note tonight. Pen signed **About Uncirculated. (40,000-60,000)**

GEORGIA

One of Two Known

14367 Albany, GA - $10 1882 Brown Back Fr. 483 **The First NB** Ch. # 3872
Low grade but excessively rare, with the census showing only one other note extant with this title, which was used by the bank only until 1908. With the one other Brown Back bearing this nomenclature in very tight hands, this may well be the only opportunity for collectors to add this title to their collections for many years. Well circulated but intact **Very Good,** with a neat and quite scarce title layout displaying the city and state together in the tombstone. (3,000-5,000)

14368 Marietta, GA - $20 1929 Ty. 2 **The First NB** Ch. # 3830
Only seven small were documented in the census including two Type 2s before the emergence of this note on this much sought after Cobb County bank. **Good-Very Good.** (300-500)

14369 Statesboro, GA - $20 1929 Ty. 1 **The First NB** Ch. # 7468
You can add this $20 to the list of only five known Series 1929 notes on this scarce bank. Officers Groover and Simmons closed the doors on this bank for the last time on December 19, 1931. **Very Good.** (600-900)

HAWAII

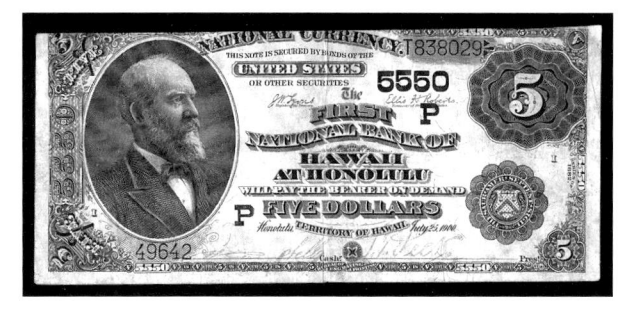

14370 Honolulu, HI - $5 1882 Value Back Fr. 574 **The First NB** Ch. # (P)5550
While territorial examples from this bank are hardly rare, any Hawaii Territory Value Back is a scarce and desirable item indeed. This piece shows even wear and is problem free for the grade, save for its typically trimmed in top margin. Nice **Fine+.** (3,500-4,500)

14371 Honolulu, HI - $5 1902 Plain Back Fr. 607 **The First NB of Hawaii at Honolulu** Ch. # 5550
A pleasing evenly circulated example of the only truly affordable large size Territorial issue. **Fine-Very Fine,** with the typical close top margin more than offset by the strong signatures and good paper surfaces. (2,500-3,500)

14372 Honolulu, HI - $10 1929 Ty. 1 **Bishop First NB** Ch. # 5550
An evenly circulated example bearing the second title used by this always in demand bank. **About Fine.** (500-700)

14373 **Honolulu, HI - $50 1929 Ty. 1 Bishop First NB** Ch. # 5550
A tougher high denomination example from this always sought after bank. **Very Fine,** with a small rust spot at the top right margin that does not enter the design. **(1,000-1,400)**

14374 **Honolulu, HI - $50 1929 Ty. 1 Bishop First NB** Ch. # 5550
PCGS informs us on the red label that there is a "minor tape repair at top center." This tape repair is approximately a quarter inch. **PCGS Apparent Fine 12. (700-900)**

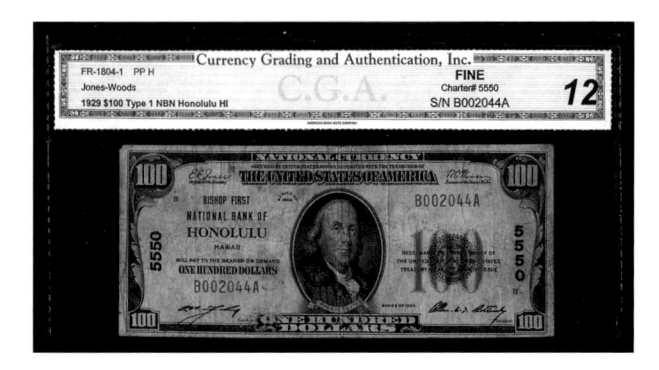

14375 **Honolulu, HI - $100 1929 Ty. 1 Bishop First NB** Ch. # 5550
Here's a chance to add a $100 Territorial to your collection even if the note does not say "Territory." The face shows some discoloration. **CGA Fine 12. (400-600)**

14376 **Honolulu, HI - $5 1929 Ty. 2 Bishop NB of Hawaii at Honolulu** Ch. # 5550
The last of the three titles used here, and the scarcest as well. **Fine. (550-750)**

IDAHO

14377 **Boise, ID - $10 1929 Ty. 2 The First NB of Idaho** Ch. # 1668
This is an evenly circulated **Fine** $10 from the state capital. It is also from the first national bank to be chartered in the state. **(700-900)**

14378 **Lewiston, ID - $50 1902 Date Back Fr. 667 The First NB** Ch. # 2972
The bold signatures of Hawkinson and Clarke are complementary to the white paper on this high denomination example. A bright blue overprint also adds to the eye appeal. **Very Fine. (2,500-3,500)**

ILLINOIS

14379 **Abingdon, IL - $10 1902 Red Seal Fr. 614 The First NB** Ch. # (M)3377
A very scarce Red Seal from a bank which issued large notes only. **Very Good+,** ex-Lynn Shaw collection.
From The Lincoln Collection **(1,500-2,000)**

14380 **Abingdon, IL - $10 1902 Plain Back Fr. 625 The First NB** Ch. # (M)3377
This institution was the only issuing bank located in this Knox County locale and entered receivership in 1927. Kelly has traced twelve survivors. The example we offer here is an attractive **Fine** with dark ink signatures, albeit a touch flat.
From The Lincoln Collection **(600-800)**

14381 Aledo, IL - $10 1902 Plain Back Fr. 624 **The First NB** Ch. # 7145
Bold signatures highlight this note which comes from the more common issuer of two in town for large size examples. The cut is a touch askew with an errant blue mark near the left side charter number. **Fine.**
From The Lincoln Collection (500-800)

14382 Aledo, IL - $5 1902 Plain Back Fr. 601 **The Farmers NB** Ch. # 9649
This is the first of a series of Illinois notes offered in this sale which bear the word "Farmers" or some close agricultural equivalent as part of their title. This piece, while well worn, is one of only three recorded large notes in the Kelly census. **Very Good.**
From The Lincoln Collection (1,000-1,500)

14383 Alton, IL - $10 1902 Plain Back Fr. 632 **The Citizens NB** Ch. # 5188
Although three federally chartered banks were at one time or another located here, all had failed by the end of the National Bank Note era. In fact, this institution and its sole competitor at the time, the Alton National Bank, both ceased operations on May 17, 1930. The note we offer here is a bright **Choice About Uncirculated.**
From The Lincoln Collection (500-700)

14384 Alton, IL - $10 1902 Plain Back Fr. 632 **The Citizens NB** Ch. # (M)5188
This note has the appearance of a higher grade, but the folds are light. The signatures have faded. **Very Fine-Extremely Fine.** (300-500)

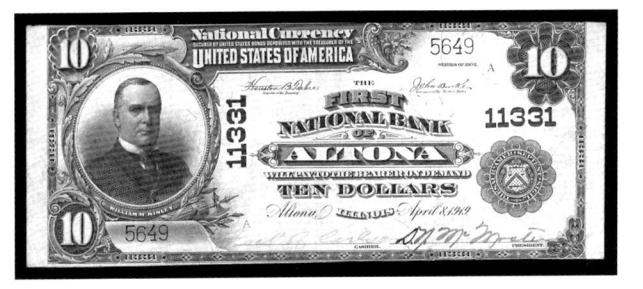

14385 Altona, IL - $10 1902 Plain Back Fr. 632 **The First NB** Ch. # 11331
Plenty of embossing is seen on this piece that remains quite bright. Only six large size are extant on this Knox County issuer which was liquidated in 1932. **Very Fine+.**
From The Lincoln Collection (1,000-1,500)

14386 Amboy, IL - $20 1902 Plain Back Fr. 658 **The First NB** Ch. # 5223
Another old friend returns as this note was last sold by CAA in 2001. **Fine.**
From The Lincoln Collection (300-500)

14387 Annapolis, IL - $10 1902 Plain Back Fr. 628 **The First NB** Ch. # (M)10257
Six large notes are known on this Crawford County institution. This **Fine-Very Fine** example hails from a CAA sale in September 2000.
From The Lincoln Collection (1,250-1,750)

$100 Brown Back

14388 Arcola, IL - $100 1882 Brown Back Fr. 527 **The First NB** Ch. # (M)2204
This example and one other $100 Brown Back are the only two early notes known from this one bank town, with this the finer of the pair. It's a pleasing **Very Fine** specimen, with the margins trimmed close all around. Expect bidding to easily reach and possibly well exceed...
From The Lincoln Collection (5,500-6,500)

14389 Arcola, IL - $10 1902 Plain Back Fr. 631 **The First NB** Ch. # 2204
This note, which is new to the census, has pleasing pen signatures. **Very Fine.**
From The Lincoln Collection **(500-800)**

14390 Arenzville, IL - $20 1902 Plain Back Fr. 652 **The First NB** Ch. # 9183
Here is a piece from the only bank to issue in this Cass County location. **Very Good+,** with clear signatures of Fred Engelbach and H. Engelbach.
From The Lincoln Collection **(400-600)**

14391 Atlanta, IL - $20 1902 Plain Back Fr. 652 **The Atlanta NB** Ch. # (M)3711
This is the only example for type known with a total population of seven large size notes accounted for. CAA last handled this **Fine+** piece in Jan. 2001.
From The Lincoln Collection **(1,000-1,500)**

14392 Augusta, IL - $10 1902 Date Back Fr. 616 **The First NB** Ch. # (M)6751
A few tears into the design at top mar this otherwise bright example with nice pen signatures. **Fine.**
From The Lincoln Collection **(500-750)**

14393 Barry, IL - $20 1902 Plain Back Fr. 659 **The First NB** Ch. # 5771
Dark signatures grace the surface of this Pike County issuer. **Very Fine.**
From The Lincoln Collection **(400-600)**

14394 Batavia, IL - $10 1902 Plain Back Fr. 628 **The First NB** Ch. # 4646
This lightly circulated and well margined issue is one of the nicer surviving large size notes from this bank. **Very Fine++.**
From The Lincoln Collection **(500-700)**

14395 Batavia, IL - $10 1902 Plain Back Fr. 626 **The Batavia NB** Ch. # 9500
This **Fine-Very Fine** is closer to the latter grade in quality and eye appeal.
From The Lincoln Collection **(500-700)**

14396 Beardstown, IL - $20 1882 Brown Back Fr. 496 **The First NB** Ch. # (M)3640
A lovely Brown Back with great color and nice pen signatures. We know of no finer note from this small Cass County town. **Choice Crisp Uncirculated,** the margin just a bit tight at the top on the reverse, ex-Lynn Shaw collection.
From The Lincoln Collection **(3,000-3,500)**

14397 **Belvidere, IL** - $10 1902 Plain Back Fr. 624 **The First NB** Ch. # 1097
This **Extremely Fine** example is one of six $10 Plain Backs documented in the census from here and displays fully legible stamped officers' signatures.
From The Lincoln Collection (500-1,000)

14398 **Belvidere, IL** - $10 1902 Plain Back Fr. 624 **The Second NB** Ch. # (M)3190
From our 2002 FUN sale where it was described, "One of two National Banks in this Boone County town and a scarce bank in Large Size, one of just six reported. This is a nicely centered **Fine** with heavy quarter folds that result in an edge split at top center."
From The Lincoln Collection (500-750)

14399 **Biggsville, IL** - $10 1902 Date Back Fr. 616 **The First NB** Ch. # (M)3003
Even circulation and a few pinholes with most of this **Good-Very Good** note intact. Only eight large are known from this Henderson County issuer.
From The Lincoln Collection (400-600)

14400 **Blandinsville, IL** - $10 1902 Plain Back Fr. 626 **The First NB** Ch. # 8908
This previously unreported note raises the count of large size survivors from this town to four, all of which are moderately to heavily circulated. This piece is solid save for a missing corner. **Very Good.**
From The Lincoln Collection (1,000-1,250)

14401 **Bloomington, IL** - $5 1902 Plain Back Fr. 598 **The First NB** Ch. # 819
The printed signatures of Frank M. Rice and Wilber M. Carter are noted on this mid-grade issue. **Fine.**
From The Lincoln Collection (500-700)

Grace Butterworth, Assistant Cashier

14402 **Brookport, IL** - $10 1902 Date Back Fr. 616 **The Brookport NB** Ch. # (M)6713
This note is one of only four large enumerated on this charter number. Of the other three, only one has been publicly available, and that was by us in January 2000. That note was signed by members of the Holifield family as cashier and president. This nicely pen signed $10 still has H.W. Holifield as president, but Grace Butterworth joins him as assistant cashier. **Fine**, pinholes.
From The Lincoln Collection (1,250-1,750)

14403 **Brownstown, IL** - $5 1902 Plain Back Fr. 603 **The First NB** Ch. # 10397
Just four large notes make up the census from this Fayette County issuer, the sole National Bank chartered in this community. As one might imagine, offerings from here have been rather sparse, with our records showing only one other large example available at public sale during the past decade. **Very Good+**, with clear pen signatures of C.A. Griffith and M.J. Griffith.
From The Lincoln Collection (1,500-2,000)

14404 Bushnell, IL - $10 1882 Brown Back Fr. 485 The First NB Ch. # (M)4709
The corner has been clipped on this otherwise pleasing note from this McDonough County issuer which served the community for 40 years. **Very Good-Fine.**
From The Lincoln Collection **(700-1,000)**

14405 Bushnell, IL - $5 1902 Plain Back Fr. 602 The First NB Ch. # 4709
This is the highest graded note, large or small, in the census for this charter number. Natural paper ripple is observed along with the blue-green stamped signature of the cashier and the purple stamped signature of the president. **Extremely Fine-About Uncirculated.**
From The Lincoln Collection **(500-800)**

14406 Cambridge, IL - $20 1882 Date Back Fr. 555 The First NB Ch. # (M)2540
The pen signatures remain sharp on this **Fine-Very Fine** example that has a few spots mainly in the corners. Eleven large size are recorded in the Kelly census, with this the sole $20 Date Back.
From The Lincoln Collection **(1,000-1,500)**

14407 Cambridge, IL - $10 1882 Value Back Fr. 577 The First NB Ch. # (M)2540
The pen signatures are still visible on this tougher type and denomination. This is the only $10 Value Back in the census from here. **Very Good** with edge roughness and pinholes.
From The Lincoln Collection **(750-1,250)**

14408 Cambridge, IL - $20 1882 Value Back Fr. 581 The Farmers NB Ch. # (M)2572
This ex-Lynn Shaw collection note grades **Very Fine+** and is a scarce type and denomination from this Henry County bank. A small tear at the top doesn't distract.
From The Lincoln Collection **(1,000-1,500)**

14409 Canton, IL - $50 1902 Date Back Fr. 667 The First NB Ch. # 415
Only 14 large size are known from this Fulton County issuer with this piece being quite scarce for type. The signatures have faded on this **Fine** note though it is generally problem free with a touch of aging.
From The Lincoln Collection **(1,000-1,500)**

14410 Canton, IL - $50 1902 Plain Back Fr. 675 The First NB Ch. # 415
Here is another high denomination example from this location. The margins are solid though the surfaces are a bit soft. **Fine+.**
From The Lincoln Collection **(1,000-1,500)**

14411 Canton, IL - $100 1902 Date Back Fr. 689 The First NB Ch. # 415
Only two examples of this type are currently known. Pleasing eye appeal is noticed on this **Fine-Very Fine** with decent color though a pinhole has pierced the portrait area.
From The Lincoln Collection **(1,250-1,750)**

14412 Canton, IL - $20 1902 Plain Back Fr. 652 **The Canton NB** Ch. # (M)3593

This institution went into receivership in 1933, but not before issuing more than $1.5 Million in National Currency. This piece is solid for the grade and features strong remaining signatures. **Very Good-Fine.**
From The Lincoln Collection **(600-800)**

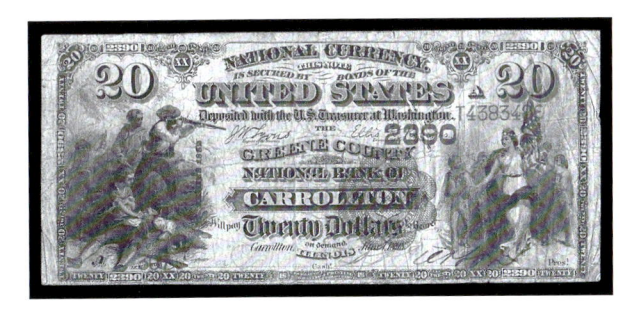

14413 Carrollton, IL - $20 1882 Brown Back Fr. 504 **The Greene County NB** Ch. # 2390

A tough note from this Greene County bank, with this the only $20 Brown Back in the census from here. A hole at center doesn't distract too much from this average circulated piece. **Very Good.**
From The Lincoln Collection **(700-1,000)**

14414 Carrollton, IL - $5 1882 Date Back Fr. 537 **The Greene County NB** Ch. # (M)2390

This bank was in operation for 40 years before being liquidated. Bright signatures on this tougher type from here. **Fine.**
From The Lincoln Collection **(750-1,000)**

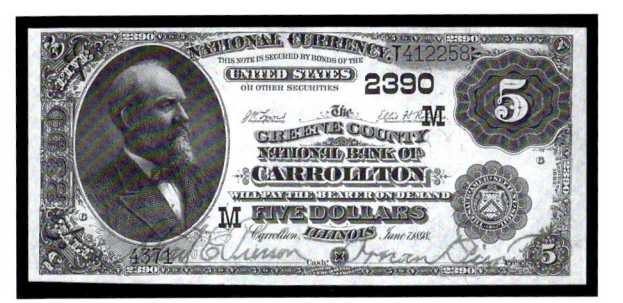

14415 Carrollton, IL - $5 1882 Value Back Fr. 574 **The Greene County NB** Ch. # (M)2390

A perfect type example, with great color, signatures, and eye appeal. There is a very well hidden centerfold, but this is superior to many if not most of the examples from here that we've seen called Choice New or better. **Choice About Uncirculated.**
From The Lincoln Collection **(1,750-2,250)**

14416 Carrollton, IL - $20 1882 Value Back Fr. 581 **The Greene County NB** Ch. # (M)2390

A perfect circulated example of this scarcer type and denomination. Bright **Fine-Very Fine,** far above average for a $20 Value Back. **(1,100-1,400)**

14417 Casey, IL - $20 1902 Plain Back Fr. 660 **The First NB** Ch. # 6026

This **Fine-Very Fine** piece from one of three issuers in this Clark County community sports dark signatures. Strong margins add to the overall appearance of this lightly worn piece of which Kelly reports eight large size.
From The Lincoln Collection **(750-1,250)**

14418 Centralia, IL - $10 1902 Plain Back Fr. 633 **The Centralia NB** Ch. # (M)11904
A just plain rare bank which was in business for barely three years between 1921 and 1924. Our records show only three appearances of notes from here at public sale during the past sixty years. This one comes back after a seven year hiatus. **Fine.**
From The Lincoln Collection **(600-900)**

14419 Centralia, IL - $20 1902 Plain Back Fr. 659 **The Centralia NB** Ch. # (M)11904
Only four notes from this institution have been offered at public auction. This piece retains the signatures and is solid for a **Very Good.** Some pinholes are noted, but do not distract from the overall appearance.
From The Lincoln Collection **(500-700)**

14420 Charleston, IL - $10 1902 Red Seal Fr. 613 **The First NB** Ch. # (M)763
A very attractive Red Seal which is the only such example from this bank in the census. Bright **Fine+++,** ex-Lynn Shaw holdings.
From The Lincoln Collection **(1,200-1,600)**

14421 Charleston, IL - $10 1882 Brown Back Fr. 485 **The Second NB** Ch. # (M)1851
Only a dozen large notes are reported from this Coles County institution. Pleasing signatures are seen on this problem free **Very Good+** note.
From The Lincoln Collection **(500-800)**

14422 Charleston, IL - $5 1902 Plain Back Fr. 602 **The Second NB** Ch. # (M)1851
This is a most attractive piece for the grade. The overprint is bright and the paper is unadulterated. **Fine.**
From The Lincoln Collection **(500-750)**

14423 Charleston, IL - $5 1902 Plain Back Fr. 606 **National Trust Bank** Ch. # 11358
This is a bright **Extremely Fine-About Uncirculated** example whose signatures have long since faded away.
From The Lincoln Collection **(350-550)**

14424 Chatsworth, IL - $10 1882 Date Back Fr. 545 **The Commercial NB** Ch. # (M)5519
Great pen signatures are seen on this **Fine** ex-Lynn Shaw collection note. Seven large notes are traced in the Kelly census, but despite the rough margin at left this is still a tough note, as it is the only $10 Date Back known from here.
From The Lincoln Collection **(1,250-1,500)**

14425 Chatsworth, IL - $10 1902 Plain Back Fr. 633 **The Commercial NB** Ch. # 5519
Auction appearances of notes from here are measured in years. Cashier John Brosnahan's signature captures your attention on this bright and crisp piece from Livingston County. **Very Fine-Extremely Fine.**
From The Lincoln Collection **(750-1,250)**

14426 Chatsworth, IL - $20 1902 Plain Back Fr. 659 **The Commercial NB** Ch. # 5519
Tonight we offer another denomination from this Livingston County issuer. Bright **Very Fine** with strong pen signatures.
From The Lincoln Collection **(750-1,250)**

14427 Chicago, IL - $10 1902 Red Seal Fr. 613 **The Commercial NB** Ch. # (M)713
This picture perfect **Very Fine** boasts bright paper, large margins, and a bold red overprint.
From The Lincoln Collection **(800-1,000)**

Chicago Large Size Uncut Sheet

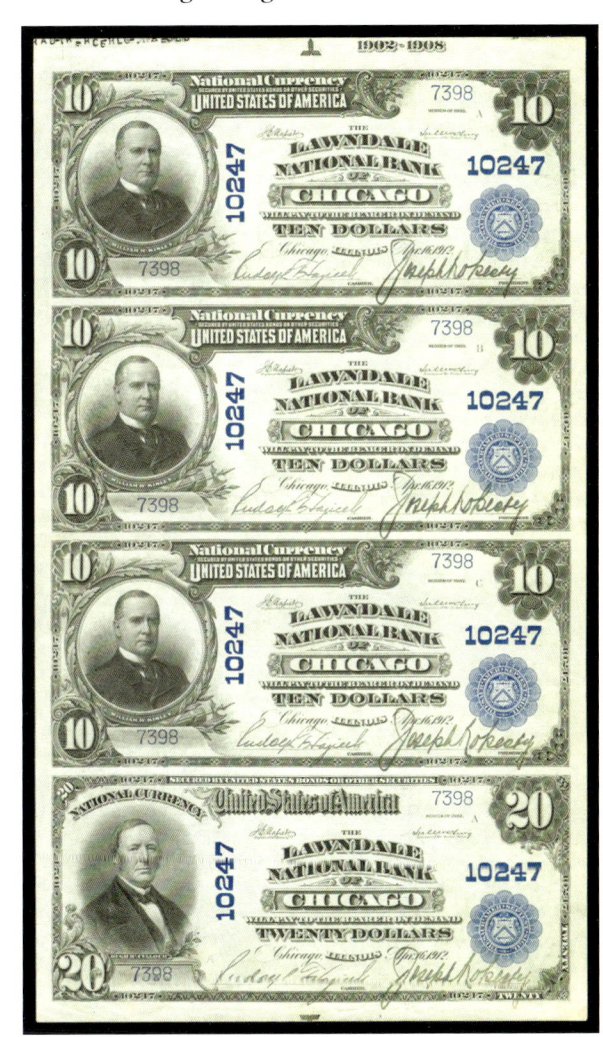

14428 Chicago, IL - $10-$10-$10-$20 1902 Plain Back Fr. 628/654 **The Lawndale NB** Ch. # 10247 Uncut Sheet
This Plain Back sheet was printed from plates that were originally intended to print Date Backs. The "1902-1908" at the top of the sheet and the "or other securities" phrase on the notes tell us this. The signatures are bold on this embossed sheet. The top and bottom notes show traces of handling and there is a center fold along the bottom of the second note. Still **Choice Crisp Uncirculated** in appearance. **(7,000-10,000)**

14429 Chicago, IL - $5 1902 Plain Back Fr. 609 **The Lawrence Avenue NB** Ch. # 12873
Original paper surfaces and charter number embossing are found on this attractive $5 from a seldom seen Chicago bank. **Very Fine-Extremely Fine.** **(250-350)**

14430 Chillicothe, IL - $10 1882 Brown Back Fr. 490 **The First NB** Ch. # (M)5584
This is the sole Brown Back known from this scarce Peoria County issuer, which shows a large size census of just a half dozen pieces of all types and denominations combined. **Fine+.**
From The Lincoln Collection **(1,500-2,500)**

14431 Chrisman, IL - $20 1902 Plain Back Fr. 650 **The First NB** Ch. # 7111
Only three large size notes are known from this scarce one bank location. It last appeared in a September 2000 CAA sale. Pleasing **Fine-Very Fine** with interesting dual color signatures. **(1,000-1,500)**

14432 **Christopher, IL** - $20 1902 Plain Back Fr. 651 **The First NB** Ch. # (M)8260
Here is a lovely note that would make a great gift for that special "Christopher" in your life. Solid margins and bright colors remain. **Fine+.** (1,250-1,750)

14433 **Cicero, IL** - $5-$5-$5-$5 1902 Plain Back Fr. 607 **The First NB** Ch. # (M)11662 Uncut Sheet
This is a fresh and original $5 uncut sheet from this better northern Illinois bank. Dark pen signatures of members of the Kaspar family further enhance this sheet that is the only one known on this bank. There is a lateral fold in the fully present top and bottom selvage, but the notes themselves are letter perfect. **Choice Crisp Uncirculated.** (9,000-12,000)

14434 **Clinton, IL** - $10 1902 Plain Back Fr. 628 **The DeWitt County NB** Ch. # 1926
The paper quality is wholly original and still boasts original embossing. Though the signatures have faded a bit, the overall eye appeal of the note is exceptional. **Extremely Fine.**
From The Lincoln Collection (600-800)

14435 **Cobden, IL** - $10 1882 Value Back Fr. 577 **The First NB** Ch. # (M)5630
A rare Value Back from the only bank chartered in this rural community. Only seven large notes are known from here, with this one of just two Value Backs. Pen signed **Fine-Very Fine,** with unusually nice margins for this issue, ex-Lonnon and Shaw collections.
From The Lincoln Collection (1,500-2,000)

14436 **Cobden, IL** - $20 1902 Plain Back Fr. 659 **The First NB** Ch. # 5630
A very scarce note from the sole bank to issue here. Nice **Fine,** with strong pen signatures.
From The Lincoln Collection (750-1,250)

14437 **Colchester, IL** - $20 1902 Plain Back Fr. 652 **The NB of Colchester** Ch. # (M)8485
This was the sole bank to issue from this small farming community in west-central Illinois. Only eight large notes are listed in the census, and we've seen none finer than this handsome example, which formerly was a part of the Lynn Shaw collection. **Extremely Fine,** with two color pen signatures.
From The Lincoln Collection **(1,500-2,000)**

14438 **Columbia, IL** - $20 1902 Plain Back Fr. 650 **The First NB** Ch. # 7717
The pleasing paper here boasts bold embossing and perfectly printed devices. As the only **Choice Crisp Uncirculated** it is perhaps the finest known.
From The Lincoln Collection **(2,000-2,500)**

14439 **Cuba, IL** - $5 1902 Plain Back Fr. 606 **The First NB** Ch. # 11144
Over ten years have passed since CAA crossed paths with this piece in 1996. The signatures have faded though the note is all there. **Very Good+.**
From The Lincoln Collection **(350-500)**

14440 **Dallas City, IL** - $20 1882 Brown Back Fr. 504 **The First NB** Ch. # (M)5609
This bank remained in operation for exactly 33 years to the day. Pleasing signatures remain on this somewhat soft but brightly printed **Very Good** piece.
From The Lincoln Collection **(500-1,000)**

14441 **Danville, IL** - $50 1902 Date Back Fr. 667 **The First NB** Ch. # (M)113
A couple pinholes are seen at left on this **Very Good-Fine** note with bi-color signatures.
From The Lincoln Collection **(750-1,250)**

14442 **Danville, IL** - $100 1929 Ty. 1 **The First NB** Ch. # 113
Deep brown overprints are seen on this lightly circulated note. A few stray pinholes are noticed to the left of the portrait. **Very Fine-Extremely Fine.** **(400-600)**

14443 **Danville, IL** - $50 1902 Plain Back Fr. 684 **The Second NB** Ch. # (M)2584
Lovely pen signatures grace the surfaces of this desirable example whose issues consisted mainly of high denominations. No problems are noticed on this **Very Fine** note that is cut a bit tight into the bottom.
From The Lincoln Collection **(750-1,250)**

14444 **Danville, IL** - $50 1902 Plain Back Fr. 684 **The Second NB** Ch. # 2584
Great signatures are seen on this **Very Fine** high denomination. A slight wallet stain is seen at left on the back and a few pinholes have left their mark.
From The Lincoln Collection **(750-1,250)**

14445 **Danville, IL** - $50 1929 Ty. 1 **The Second NB** Ch. # 2584
When it comes to Type One Nationals on this town, all three national banks in Danville only issued $50s and $100s. **About Uncirculated.** **(500-700)**

14446 **Danville, IL** - $100 1929 Ty. 1 **The Second NB** Ch. # 2584
In the Series 1929 era, this bank elected to issue only Type One Fifties and Hundreds. Officers are H.E. Douglas and C.V. McClenathan. Graded **PCGS Very Fine 35.** (650-950)

14447 **Danville, IL** - $100 1902 Date Back Fr. 693 **The Palmer NB** Ch. # (M)4731
Auction appearances of high denomination notes from here are sparse. This is perhaps the nicest survivor with signatures still visible and plenty of crispness remaining. A few pinholes are noticed on this bright **Very Fine+** example.
From The Lincoln Collection (1,000-1,500)

14448 **Danville, IL** - $100 1902 Plain Back Fr. 702 **The Palmer NB** Ch. # 4731
A nice high denomination example which is perfect for type. **Fine-Very Fine.**
From The Lincoln Collection (1,000-1,500)

14449 **Danville, IL** - $10 1882 Date Back Fr. 545 **The Danville NB** Ch. # (M)5812
Certainly the scarcest of the Danville issuers as Kelly only lists nine large survivors from here. Problem free and bright, the only blemish on this lovely **Very Fine** note is a small pencilled "M" on the back right margin which affects nothing.
From The Lincoln Collection (1,000-1,500)

14450 **De Kalb, IL** - $10 1902 Plain Back Fr. 624 **The First NB** Ch. # 2702
Crackling fresh and fully embossed, a real beauty which appears to have left the press this very morning. If a finer note exists from here, we certainly haven't seen it. **Gem Crisp Uncirculated.**
From The Lincoln Collection (2,000-3,000)

14451 **De Kalb, IL** - $10 1902 Plain Back Fr. 624 **The First NB** Ch. # 2702
Pleasing pen signatures are found on this piece from this farming community two hours west of Chicago. **Very Fine.**
From The Lincoln Collection (750-1,250)

14452 **De Land, IL** - $5 1902 Plain Back Fr. 607 **The First NB** Ch. # 5699
Eight large notes are known from here. Some softness is noticed to the touch. **Fine.**
From The Lincoln Collection (500-800)

14453 **Decatur, IL - $10 1902 Plain Back Fr. 627 The Citizens NB** Ch. # 4576
A nicely margined, bright and crispy $10 Plain Back from De Witt County. The stamped signatures are still quite strong and there are no distractions to impair the overall attractive eye appeal of this premium circulated example. **Extremely Fine.**
From The Lincoln Collection (500-750)

14454 **Decatur, IL - $10 1882 Value Back Fr. 576 The Millikin NB** Ch. # (M)5089
The paper here is bright for the grade. A repaired split and retraced signatures are noted for accuracy's sake. **Fine.**
From The Lincoln Collection (750-1,000)

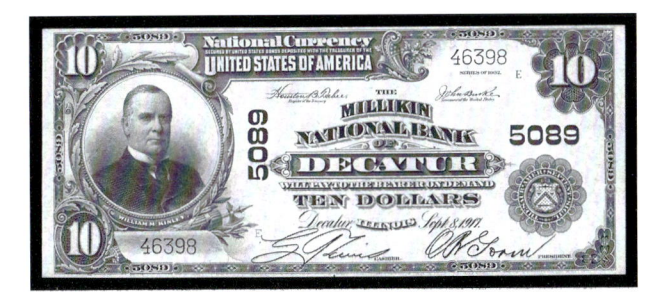

14455 **Decatur, IL - $10 1902 Plain Back Fr. 632 The Millikin NB** Ch. # 5089
This beauty was last sold by us in 2001. The margins are very nice though the embossing is a bit subdued. **Choice Crisp Uncirculated.**
From The Lincoln Collection (400-600)

14456 **Dieterich, IL - $20 1902 Plain Back Fr. 653 The First NB** Ch. # (M)9582
The signatures have faded from this piece which was well used before it entered this collection. **Very Good.**
From The Lincoln Collection (400-700)

14457 **Divernon, IL - $10 1902 Date Back Fr. 621 The First NB** Ch. # (M)10296
This is a truly rare note from the only bank to issue in this tiny Sangamon County locale. While four notes are known from here, all save one have been closely held for many years. Our records show just one public offering during the past six decades, with that coming when we sold the Shaw holdings bank in January of 2001. That piece was far lower grade than this, and still realized $2420 over six years ago. Pen signed **Extremely Fine,** and bearing low serial number 2 as a bonus, a great item fit for the finest of collections.
From The Lincoln Collection (3,000-5,000)

14458 **Dundee, IL - $20 1902 Plain Back Fr. 659 The First NB** Ch. # 5638
This is a nice, attractive example from this popular Kane County locale. **Fine-Very Fine.**
From The Lincoln Collection (500-800)

14459 **DuQuoin, IL - $20 1902 Plain Back Fr. 654 The First NB** Ch. # 4737
While two dozen Series 1929 examples are known from this one bank community, large examples are quite scarce, with the census showing only four such notes extant from here. This is one of that small group, having been sold by us back in January of 2002. **Fine,** with pen signatures.
From The Lincoln Collection (1,250-1,750)

14460 East Peoria, IL - $5 1902 Plain Back Fr. 598 **First NB** Ch. # 6724
A well-centered and problem-free **Fine** with lightly stamped blue officers' signatures still visible. The majority of the 17 large size survivors extant from here are of this denomination and design type. Despite the fact that the grades listed in the census for the ten $5 1902 Plain Backs known cover quite a range, the serial number range of the known examples is quite narrow. When this institution was liquidated in 1934 and its circulation assumed by the First National Bank in East Peoria, a scant $335 survived in large. We sold this same note in our January 2001, FUN Signature Sale for $385. This should approach if not surpass that figure.
From The Lincoln Collection **(400-600)**

14461 East Peoria, IL - $20 1902 Plain Back Fr. 650 **First NB** Ch. # (M)6724
Three examples of this type and denomination are in the Kelly census. **Very Fine.**
From The Lincoln Collection **(400-600)**

14462 El Paso, IL - $10 1902 Plain Back Fr. 624 **The First NB** Ch. # (M)2997
A pleasing misplaced town name example that has deep stamped signatures remaining. **Very Fine.**
From The Lincoln Collection **(500-750)**

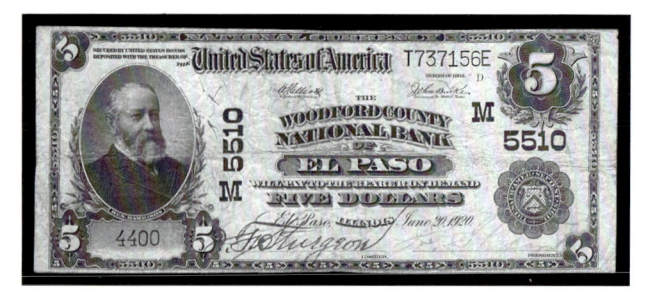

14463 El Paso, IL - $5 1902 Plain Back Fr. 607 **The Woodford County NB** Ch. # (M)5510
From a community with a skyline dominated by grain elevators, El Paso was the birthplace of Bishop Fulton J. Sheen, who hosted a popular religiously oriented television show during the 1950's. Only ten large are known with this **Fine** problem-free example being off the market for several years.
From The Lincoln Collection **(750-1,000)**

CGA Graded Gem Uncirculated $100 Elgin Brown Back

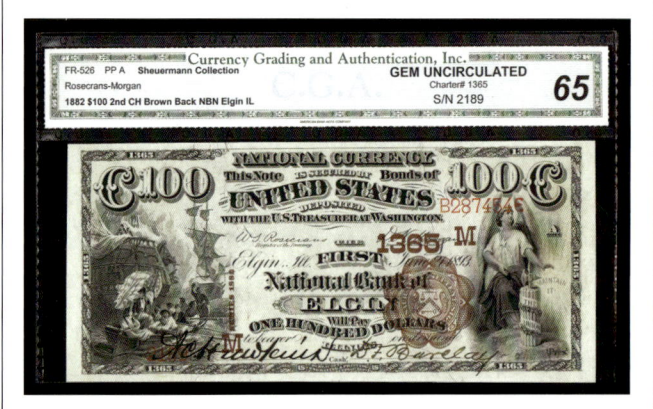

14464 Elgin, IL - $100 1882 Brown Back Fr. 526 **The First NB** Ch. # (M)1365
A hugely margined example which has an impeccable pedigree, coming from the Henry Scheuermann collection, which we sold back in January of 2001. It is a beautiful $100 Brown Back which is perfect for type, and which has been encapsulated and graded as **Gem Uncirculated 65** by CGA. Expect to see bidding easily reach and perhaps well exceed...
From The Lincoln Collection **(25,000-45,000)**

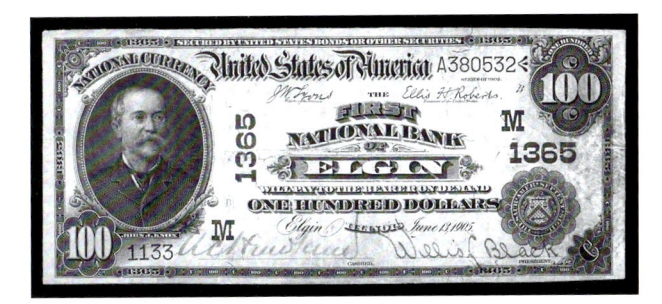

14465 **Elgin, IL** - $100 1902 Date Back Fr. 689 **The First NB** Ch. # (M)1365
A nice high denomination example from this well collected Kane County location. Evenly circulated dual color pen signed **Fine-Very Fine,** considerably closer to the higher rather than the lower grade.
From The Lincoln Collection **(1,000-1,500)**

14466 **Elgin, IL** - $50 1902 Date Back Fr. 671 **The Home NB** Ch. # (M)2016
2016
This Third Charter Date Back Fifty has bright paper and strong signatures, but the paper is lacking in crispness and there are some margin nicks along the edges. Still an attractive **Fine** representative of the type and bank.
From The Lincoln Collection **(1,000-1,500)**

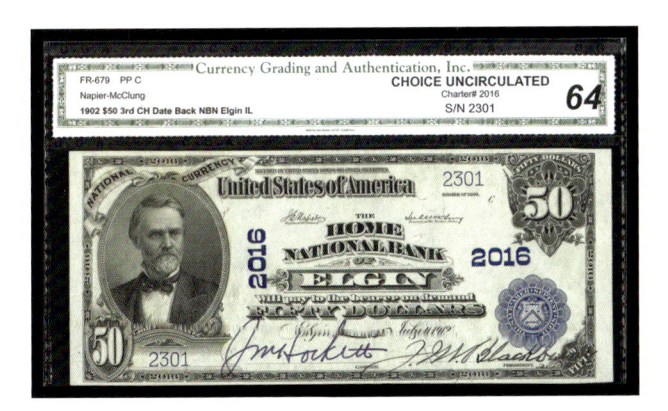

14467 **Elgin, IL** - $50 1902 Plain Back Fr. 679 **The Home NB** Ch. # 2016
A lovely high grade piece which CGA has encapsulated and assigned a grade of **Choice Uncirculated 64.** It certainly appears to justify that grade through the holder, with bright white paper contrasting with two color pen signatures. Expect the hammer to fall in the range of...
From The Lincoln Collection **(4,250-6,250)**

14468 **Elgin, IL** - $10 1902 Date Back Fr. 620 **The Elgin NB** Ch. # (M)4735
This river town along the Fox River is in the midst of a rebirth as an All-American city. Glorious pen signatures grace the circulated surfaces with some margin issues visible on this tough note. **Very Good.**
From The Lincoln Collection **(600-900)**

14469 **Enfield, IL** - $10 1902 Date Back Fr. 617 **The First NB** Ch. # (M)7948
October 17, 1905 saw the bank receive its charter and assume the obligations of the Bank of Enfield which commenced operations in this White County locale in 1889. U.B. Barnett's name as president and C.W. Crawford's as cashier grace the note in blue pen. Barnett served as president for a total of 13 years. It has been 14 years since we have seen this piece. **Fine.**
From The Lincoln Collection **(800-1,100)**

14470 **Farmer City, IL** - $10 1902 Plain Back Fr. 625 **The John Weedman NB** Ch. # 3407
This bank is always in demand due to its status as a private name bank. **Fine.**
From The Lincoln Collection **(600-800)**

14471 Farmer City, IL - $10 1902 Plain Back Fr. 631 The Old First NB Ch. # (M)4958
The last time any note from this institution was offered at public auction was more than two years ago, and this piece has been off the market for nearly six years. The paper is solid and the overprint bright. **Fine.**
From The Lincoln Collection (600-800)

14472 Farmersville, IL - $10 1902 Date Back Fr. 619 The First NB Ch. # (M)10057
A very scarce note from the only bank chartered here. This institution issued large notes only before disappearing in 1927. Only five notes make up the entire population from here, with our records showing just one offering during the past ten years. This example is the sole Date Back reported. Pen signed **Fine.**
From The Lincoln Collection (1,500-2,000)

14473 Findlay, IL - $20 1902 Plain Back Fr. 650 The First NB Ch. # 6861
This Shelby County issuer was liquidated in 1927 leaving this town with no bank. The other bank in town closed in 1907 leaving this as the only collectible institution here as the other is unreported. Pleasing **Fine-Very Fine** with stamped signatures remaining.
From The Lincoln Collection (1,000-1,500)

14474 Flora, IL - $20 1902 Plain Back Fr. 654 The First NB Ch. # 1961
This bank received its charter on April 18, 1872 and during the National banking period issued a touch over $1.2 million. Only $5150 remained outstanding in large size. **Fine** with rounded corners.
From The Lincoln Collection (500-750)

14475 Freeport, IL - $20 1902 Plain Back Fr. 650 The First NB Ch. # (M)2875
This attractive issue was last offered as part of of the Lynn Shaw Collection in our January 2000 Auction. The piece boasts solid margins, the dark signatures of J.M. Clark, and A.Bidwell, and solid paper. **Fine.**
From The Lincoln Collection (400-500)

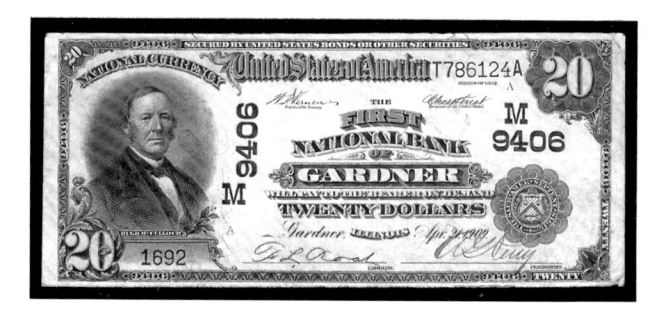

14476 Gardner, IL - $20 1902 Date Back Fr. 644 The First NB Ch. # (M)9406
This **Extremely Fine** note certainly could be the finest example available to collectors. It last appeared at auction in 2001 where it realized over $2000. The color is deep and the pen signatures remain strong on surfaces affected by three folds..
From The Lincoln Collection (1,000-2,000)

14477 Gardner, IL - $20 1902 Plain Back Fr. 652 The First NB Ch. # 9406
This Grundy County issuer fell on hard times and closed in 1932. Strong signatures remain visible with no major distractions seen on this **Fine** note.
From The Lincoln Collection (750-1,000)

14478 Geneva, IL - $10 1902 Plain Back Fr. 626 **The First NB** Ch. # 8740
This note last appeared in CAA's May 2001 sale. Only $690 remained outstanding from this very scarce Kane County bank with only five large size documented. **Very Good-Fine.**
From The Lincoln Collection **(750-1,250)**

14479 Gibson, IL - $10 1902 Red Seal Fr. 614 **The First NB** Ch. # (M)8174
A very scarce type from this small one bank Ford County community. This is one of just two Red Seals known from here, with both in just about the same grade. This example is completely natural and utterly unmolested, with bright colors and bold pen signatures. Pleasing **Fine+**.
From The Lincoln Collection **(1,500-2,000)**

14480 Gibson, IL - $10 1902 Plain Back Fr. 625 **The First NB** Ch. # (M)8174
Just $4380 was left outstanding for the sole issuer in town. The signatures are barely there and a pinhole or two are spotted. **Fine.**
From The Lincoln Collection **(500-750)**

14481 Gillespie, IL - $10 1902 Plain Back Fr. 625 **The Gillespie NB** Ch. # (M)7903
This piece faces up like a full Fine, though the paper firmness is more consistent with a **Very Good.** Only five examples are reported from this bank, with this the sole $10 Plain Back.
From The Lincoln Collection **(600-800)**

14482 Gillespie, IL - $5 1902 Plain Back Fr. 609 **The American NB** Ch. # 12314
This Macoupin County bank survived only seven years, failing during the Depression in 1930 after issuing only $5 Plain Backs in large size. Of these Kelly documents but seven survivors. Stamped purple officers' signatures. **Fine.**
From The Lincoln Collection **(500-750)**

14483 Gilman, IL - $10 1902 Plain Back Fr. 633 **The First NB** Ch. # 5856
A lovely example with everything one could want in a National, including bank rarity, full originality, blazing fresh colors, and bold pen signatures of Marie W. Hausmann, Asst. Cashier. **Gem Crisp Uncirculated.**
From The Lincoln Collection **(1,750-2,250)**

14484 Gilman, IL - $20 1902 Plain Back Fr. 659 **The First NB** Ch. # 5856
Of the Series 1902 notes known to collectors from this institution, this piece boasts the highest serial number, only about 80 notes from the end of the issue. The paper is bright thought the signatures have faded. **Fine.**
From The Lincoln Collection **(400-500)**

14485 Golconda, IL - $10 1902 Plain Back Fr. 624 **The First NB** Ch. # (M)7385
All of the large size survivors from this Pope County issuer are heavily circulated. This piece shows strong original signatures and fairly solid paper. **Very Good,** with a few pinholes.
From The Lincoln Collection **(400-500)**

14486 **Granite City, IL** - $10 1902 Plain Back Fr. 633 **The First NB** Ch. # 5433
This attractive and original issue boasts perfectly bright blue penned signatures. **Fine+.**
From The Lincoln Collection **(350-450)**

14487 **Grant Park, IL** - $10 1902 Plain Back Fr. 633 **The First NB** Ch. # 11952
Only four large size notes from this bank are known to collectors. Though two banks were located in Grant Park, no survivors are known from the town's other bank. This piece is wholly original and moderately circulated. **Fine,** ex-Lynn Shaw collection.
From The Lincoln Collection **(1,500-1,750)**

Rare Friedberg Number

14488 **Grayville, IL** - $10 1902 Date Back Fr. 623a **The First NB** Ch. # (M)4999
This is a very scarce Friedberg number, with fewer than ten pieces known from all banks combined. It comes from a much in demand Illinois bank, and is one of just two 1902 Date Backs recorded, with this the nicer of the pair. Pleasing **Fine.**
From The Lincoln Collection **(1,250-1,750)**

One of Two Known

14489 **Greenfield, IL** - $10 1902 Plain Back Fr. 626 **The First NB** Ch. # (M)8473
An excessively rare note from the only bank to issue in this tiny Greene County hamlet. This is one of only two large examples known, with the other never having been available to collectors, having been ensconced in a major Illinois collection for a full generation. Pen signed **Fine**, a true Illinois trophy item likely to reach or exceed...
From The Lincoln Collection **(4,000-6,000)**

14490 **Greenup, IL** - $20 1902 Plain Back Fr. 651 **The Greenup NB** Ch. # (M)8115
Every reported survivor from this bank is circulated, and the large size survivors are especially well circulated. This piece boasts solid paper and remaining signatures. **Very Good-Fine.**
From The Lincoln Collection **(400-600)**

14491 **Greenville, IL** - $10 1902 Date Back Fr. 619 **The Bradford NB** Ch. # (M)9734
This scarce issue faces up well, though there is a hidden paper clip stain which could escape even the best eyes. The signatures remain bold. **Fine.**
From The Lincoln Collection **(400-600)**

Myrtle T. Bradford, President

14492 Greenville, IL - $20 1902 Plain Back Fr. 653 **The Bradford NB** Ch. # 9734

This private named bank was started in 1867 by James and Samuel Bradford. It was organized as a national bank in April 1910 by John S. Bradford. It is still in business today with its original national bank name. Today the main bank is located on property originally owned by Samuel Bradford. This **Very Fine** $20 with original surfaces displays a large bottom selvage that exhibits BEP workmen's initials and a large portion of the paper guide line arrow. The added bonus of this note is that it is pen signed by Myrtle T. Bradford as president. She was the widow of John S. Bradford and she was the president only from July 1925 to January 1926. She was succeeded by Nancy Rogers Bradford, the widow of Samuel Bradford.
From The Lincoln Collection **(700-1,000)**

14493 Griggsville, IL - $10 1882 Brown Back Fr. 486 **The Griggsville NB** Ch. # (M)2116

A rather scarce Brown Back with the rare Rosecrans-Morgan Treasury signatures. **Very Good+**.
From The Lincoln Collection **(1,200-1,600)**

14494 Hamilton, IL - $5 1902 Plain Back Fr. 601 **The First NB** Ch. # 9883

Two years ago marked the last appearance of a note from this bank appearing at public auction. The entire surviving population of this bank is well circulated, thus this piece with an attractive overprint, solid paper and the remaining signatures of Wallace and Piggot should not be ignored. A couple of pinholes are noted for accuracy's sake. **Fine+**.
From The Lincoln Collection **(400-600)**

14495 Hamilton, IL - $10 1902 Plain Back Fr. 627 **The First NB** Ch. # (M)9883

This newly discovered piece is bright, with bold signatures. **Fine**.
From The Lincoln Collection **(400-600)**

14496 Harrisburg, IL - $10 1902 Plain Back Fr. 626 **The First NB** Ch. # (M)4003

The last large size note from this bank appeared at auction in 2004. This piece which features wholly intact paper shows retraced signatures. **Fine**.
From The Lincoln Collection **(500-700)**

14497 Harrisburg, IL - $5 1902 Plain Back Fr. 606 **The City NB** Ch. # 5153

This Saline County institution issued nearly $2 Million in National Currency. Of the few reported survivors, this deeply embossed and attractive $5 is the finest, making it worthy of even the finest collection of Illinois Nationals. **Choice Crisp Uncirculated**.
From The Lincoln Collection **(1,500-2,000)**

14498 **Havana, IL** - $10 1882 Date Back Fr. 542 **The Havana NB** Ch. # (M)2242
A very tough early note from this one bank town. This is a common enough bank in small size, but large notes from here are just plain rare, with this one of only four of all types listed in the census. **Very Fine,** ex-Walter Herget collection.
From The Lincoln Collection **(2,250-3,250)**

14499 **Havana, IL** - $20 1929 Ty. 1 **The Havana NB** Ch. # 2242
This is an attractive mid-grade $20 from this elusive bank. The cashier is P.D. Dieffenbacher. **Very Fine+. (250-350)**

14500 **Henry, IL** - $50 1902 Date Back Fr. 667 **The First NB** Ch. # 1482
This note last appeared in CAA's January 2000 FUN sale. This is a very scarce bank which only issued high denominations during the second charter period. Six large are currently on the Kelly roster with this being the only $50 DB known. It is a pleasing **Fine** with the signatures still visible and some trivial aging on the back. **(1,250-1,750)**

14501 **Herrin, IL** - $50 1902 Plain Back Fr. 683 **The First NB** Ch. # 5303
High denominations only in Third Charters, with this pen signed example carrying the Shaw collection pedigree. Nice **Fine,** and bearing the signature of the town's namesake John Herrin as Cashier.
From The Lincoln Collection **(1,400-1,800)**

14502 **Hillsboro, IL** - $5 1902 Plain Back Fr. 599 **The Peoples NB** Ch. # 8006
Bold signatures remain on this moderately circulated issue. The center fold is a bit heavy and results in splits in the margins. **Fine.**
From The Lincoln Collection **(400-600)**

14503 **Hillsboro, IL** - $10 1902 Date Back Fr. 617 **The Peoples NB** Ch. # (M)8006
Nine large size examples are reported for this institution from this two bank town. It is the tougher of the two. Excellent pen signatures are seen on relatively firm surfaces of this **Very Fine** note.
From The Lincoln Collection **(600-900)**

14504 **Hindsboro, IL** - $10 1882 Date Back Fr. 545 **The First NB** Ch. # (M)5538
This ex-Lynn Shaw collection **Very Good** note is from a tougher issue for the bank, with this piece the only $10 Date Back reported from here.
From The Lincoln Collection **(850-1,250)**

14505 **Hindsboro, IL** - $20 1902 Plain Back Fr. 659 **The First NB** Ch. # 5538
This attractive issue is the finer of only two known Plain Back $20's from this bank. **Fine.**
From The Lincoln Collection **(600-800)**

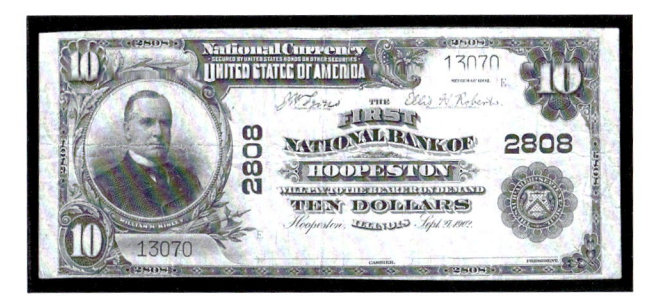

14506 **Hoopeston, IL** - $10 1902 Plain Back Fr. 624 **The First NB** Ch. # 2808
An attractive and wholly original note from this Vermilion County locale. It has been more than four years since another note from this bank has been offered at auction. **Fine-Very Fine.**
From The Lincoln Collection **(500-750)**

14507 **Hoopeston, IL** - $20 1929 Ty. 1 **Hoopeston NB** Ch. # 9425
A note from one of three issuers located here. A pencilled "9" is seen in red on the face. **Fine. (350-500)**

14508 **Humboldt, IL** - $10 1902 Plain Back Fr. 624 **The First NB** Ch. # 7168
A mere four notes make up the entire large size census from this one bank Coles County location, a figure which, with a meager $365 in large outstanding from here, is not likely to see much increase in the future. Pen signed **Fine-Very Fine.**
From The Lincoln Collection **(2,000-3,000)**

14509 **Hume, IL** - $10 1902 Plain Back Fr. 632 **The First NB** Ch. # 11108
The paper exhibited here is most pleasing and bright for the grade. This note likely spent only a very short time in circulation, sustaining a few folds and a little bit of handling. We were the last auction house to offer a note from this bank and that was back in September of 2005. **Very Fine.**
From The Lincoln Collection **(700-900)**

14510 **Irving, IL** - $10 1902 Plain Back Fr. 626 **The Irving NB** Ch. # 8647
A very rare Montgomery County bank, with the Kelly census showing just four large (and three small) notes extant from here. Pen signed **Very Good.**
From The Lincoln Collection **(1,000-1,500)**

14511 **Ivesdale, IL** - $10 1902 Plain Back Fr. 634 **First NB** Ch. # (M)6133
The paper quality here is consistent with a Fine grade, though the print quality is a bit faded. The signature of the Cashier has been reapplied. **Fine,** from well collected Champaign County.
From The Lincoln Collection **(500-700)**

14512 Jacksonville, IL - $10 1882 Brown Back Fr. 484 **The Jacksonville NB** Ch. # (M)1719
The Vice-President has signed this nice high denomination example which is perfect for type. Bright pen signatures. **Very Good.**
From The Lincoln Collection **(500-750)**

14513 Jacksonville, IL - $10 1902 Date Back Fr. 619 **The Jacksonville NB** Ch. # (M)1719
This is an attractive **Fine** that boasts two bold signatures. In place of the President, Chas B. Goff signed as Vice President. Some minor pinholes are noted but do not distract from the overall eye appeal.
From The Lincoln Collection **(600-800)**

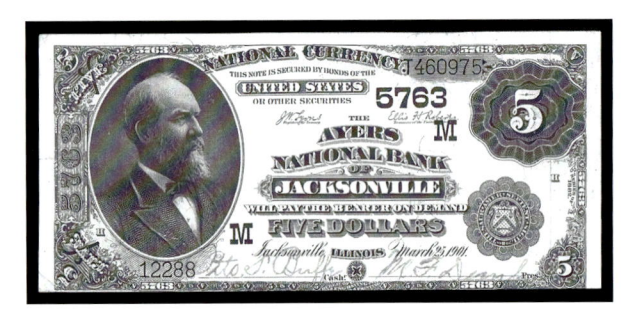

14514 Jacksonville, IL - $5 1882 Value Back Fr. 574 **The Ayers NB** Ch. # (M)5763
A pleasing example of this very scarce type, perfect for the collector who wants a decent yet affordable piece. **Very Fine,** with a tight bottom margin.
From The Lincoln Collection **(600-900)**

14515 Jacksonville, IL - $10 1882 Value Back Fr. 577 **The Ayers NB** Ch. # (M)5763
The stamped signatures are barely present on this tougher type which remains bright. **Very Fine.**
From The Lincoln Collection **(600-900)**

14516 Joliet, IL - $10 1882 Brown Back Fr. 484 **The Joliet NB** Ch. # (M)4520
A lovely Brown Back from this much collected Will County community, home to one of the oldest operating penitentiaries in the United States. This is the earliest note we know of from here, and by far the finest example known from this bank as well. **Choice Crisp Uncirculated.**
From The Lincoln Collection **(2,500-4,500)**

Unique for the Bank

14517 Joliet, IL - $10 1902 Red Seal Fr. 613 **The Citizens NB** Ch. # (M)6423
This Red Seal is the sole note extant from this short lived Joliet bank which was in business only until 1911. The bank issued Red Seals and Date Backs only until its demise, with our records showing that this is not only the only note known from here but that collectors are getting their first opportunity this evening to own any note from this prohibitively rare bank. **Fine,** a great note worthy of a very strong bid. **(8,000-12,000)**

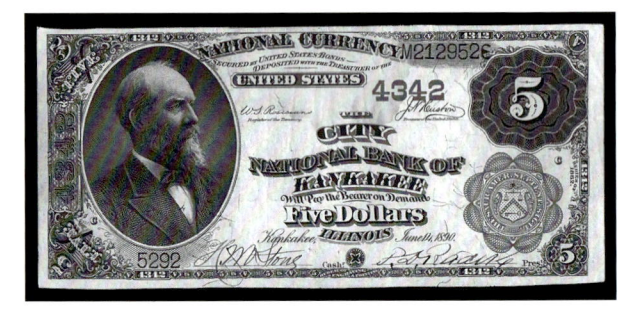

14518 Kankakee, IL - $5 1882 Brown Back Fr. 471 **The City NB** Ch. # 4342
Lovely pen signatures grace the surface of this pleasing example from this locale south of Chicago. Crisp, well inked surfaces give way to a slight stain at top center along with a few pinholes. Almost 30 years have passed since this denomination has been available at public auction. **Extremely Fine.** **(1,250-1,750)**

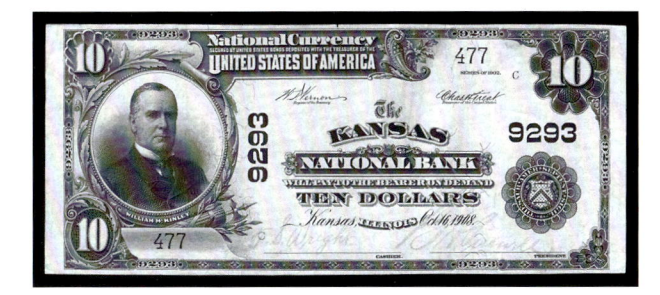

14519 **Kansas, IL** - $10 1902 Plain Back Fr. 626 **The Kansas NB** Ch. # 9293
From our 2006 Central States sale, "The signatures remain, though they are a touch faded. The paper surfaces are purely original and the paper waves created by the printed process are as fresh as ever. There is a touch of handling that prevents the note from going higher than **Crisp Uncirculated**." (1,000-1,300)

14520 **Kansas, IL** - $20 1902 Plain Back Fr. 652 **The Kansas NB** Ch. # 9293
Stamped signatures are still visible on this crisp **Extremely Fine** note which has a few foxing spots present.
From The Lincoln Collection (400-600)

14521 **Kewanee, IL** - $10 1902 Plain Back Fr. 627 **The First NB** Ch. # (M)1785
The paper is bright for the grade while the purple stamped signatures have nearly faded completely away. **Fine**.
From The Lincoln Collection (300-500)

14522 **Kewanee, IL** - $20 1882 Date Back Fr. 550 **The Kewanee NB** Ch. # (M)4854
This note has never been offered at public auction and is one of only three notes known from this Henry County issuer. The other two notes are Brown Backs and are in no better states of preservation than this **Fine**. We are pleased with the overall appearance of this note as the devices and overprint are bold.
From The Lincoln Collection (2,500-3,500)

14523 **Kinmundy, IL** - $20 1902 Plain Back Fr. 660 **The First NB** Ch. # 6143
Stamped signatures still show up on this **Very Good-Fine** 1922 dated Plain Back. A few pinholes are noticed on lightly aged surfaces.
From The Lincoln Collection (400-600)

14524 **Kirkwood, IL** - $10 1902 Plain Back Fr. 632 **The First NB** Ch. # (M)2313
Most of the large size survivors from this institution are heavily circulated. This piece shows moderate, even wear. **Very Good**.
From The Lincoln Collection (500-700)

14525 **Knoxville, IL** - $10 1902 Plain Back Fr. 624 **The Farmers NB** Ch. # 3287
The paper quality on this wholly original piece is most pleasing with remaining signatures and bright white paper for the condition. The margins are also solid. **Very Fine**.
From The Lincoln Collection (600-800)

14526 **La Harpe, IL** - $5 1902 Date Back Fr. 592 **The First NB** Ch. # (M)8468
An extremely rare note from one of the state's smallest banks. Only three examples are recorded from here in large size, and, with only $720 outstanding at the bank's close in 1933, it's unlikely very many more will appear. We've sold this note, the finest of the three examples known, three times over the past twenty seven years, once to Lynn Shaw, once when we sold Lynn's collection, and again this evening. It was one of the highlights of Lynn's collection, and will be one of the highlights of the collection it now enters as well. Bright **Very Fine+**.
From The Lincoln Collection (2,250-3,250)

14527 **Lacon, IL** - $50 1902 Date Back Fr. 667 **The First NB** Ch. # 347
A very scarce bank which issued high denomination examples only after Brown Backs. Eight large examples are recorded in the Kelly census. Nice **Very Fine**.
From The Lincoln Collection **(1,500-2,500)**

14528 **Lacon, IL** - $50 1902 Date Back Fr. 667 **The First NB** Ch. # (M)347
Another example from this very scarce bank which issued high denomination examples only after Brown Backs. Nine large examples are recorded in the Kelly census. Nice **Very Fine**.
From The Lincoln Collection **(1,500-2,500)**

14529 **LaSalle, IL** - $20 1882 Value Back Fr. 581 **The LaSalle NB** Ch. # (M)2503
This colorful **Very Good-Fine** example is a touch soft along the top margin.
From The Lincoln Collection **(750-1,000)**

14530 **Lawrenceville, IL** - $20 1902 Plain Back Fr. 659 **The First NB** Ch. # 5385
Frederick W. Keller served as President from 1906 until it closed its doors in 1932 while Edna E. Thorn served as Cashier from 1919 on. A slight paper skin affects the front of this **Very Good-Fine** piece.
From The Lincoln Collection **(500-750)**

14531 **Lewistown, IL** - $10 1902 Plain Back Fr. 631 **The Lewistown NB** Ch. # 4941
Only the President's signature appears on this Fulton County issue. Plenty of crispness remains on this **Very Fine-Extremely Fine** note which still exhibits some embossing.
From The Lincoln Collection **(400-600)**

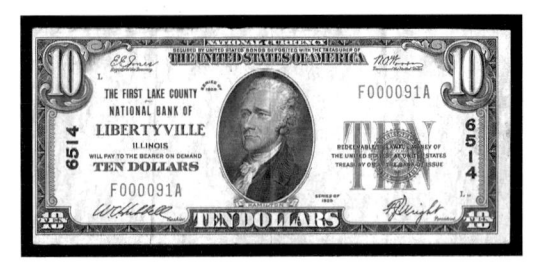

14532 **Libertyville, IL** - $10 1929 Ty. 1 **The First Lake County NB** Ch. # 6514
This note increases the second title census for this charter number up to a mere four serial numbers. This embossed **Very Fine-Extremely Fine** note is much closer to the high end of the split grade and it is also the nicest of the notes with a reported grade. In 2005 we sold a Type 1 $10 in Fine on this title and it brought $1380. This note could easily exceed that amount. **(1,250-1,750)**

14533 **Libertyville, IL** - $10 1902 Plain Back Fr. 624 **The Lake County NB** Ch. # 6670
This is an odd community. Despite its proximity to Chicago, and despite its importance as the Lake County seat, large notes from here are exceptionally scarce from both of the town's issuing banks. This piece traces its provenance back to the Shaw collection. **Fine**.
From The Lincoln Collection **(1,000-1,500)**

14534 **Lincoln, IL** - $5 1902 Date Back Fr. 591 **The Lincoln NB** Ch. # (M)3369
The purple stamped signatures remain bright as does the deep blue overprint. **Very Fine**.
From The Lincoln Collection **(600-700)**

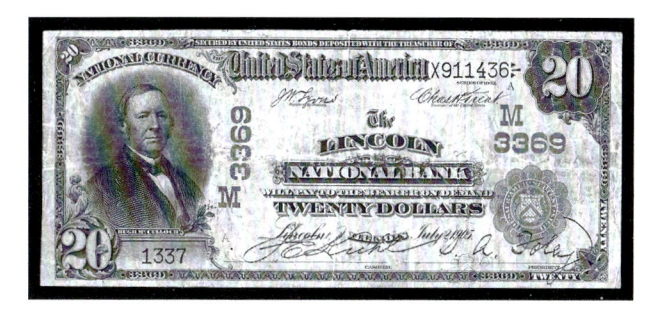

14535 Lincoln, IL - $20 1902 Red Seal Fr. 640 The Lincoln NB Ch. # (M)3369
Another very scarce Red Seal, with this the only Red Seal known from this bank, and from the city of Lincoln as well. **Fine**, ex-Lynn Shaw collection.
From The Lincoln Collection (1,500-2,500)

Rare & Lovely Lincoln $5 Brown Back

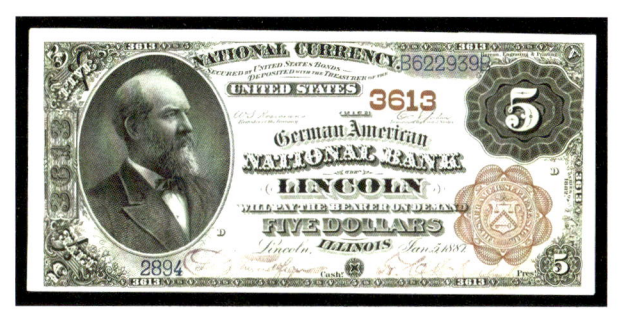

14536 Lincoln, IL - $5 1882 Brown Back Fr. 469 The German American NB Ch. # 3613
An absolutely gorgeous note which has everything a collector could desire in a National. It's the only Brown Back known from this institution, it bears an interesting ethnic title, it comes with a great "circus poster" layout, and it possesses more than enough grade to count, with broad margins, great color, and enormous eye appeal. When last offered at public sale, this piece realized $8800 at auction back in February of 2000. While the market for Illinois notes has clearly changed in seven years, the market for great Nationals remains quite solid, and our very realistic estimate here might well prove conservative for this truly outstanding note. **Extremely Fine+**.
From The Lincoln Collection (3,000-5,000)

14537 Lincoln, IL - $20 1902 Date Back Fr. 644 The German American NB Ch. # (M)3613
Only six large are recorded for this first title note from a town which lies just minutes north of the capital of Illinois. Dark stamped signatures are noticed along with a few pinholes. **Very Good**.
From The Lincoln Collection (500-750)

14538 Lincoln, IL - $5 1902 Plain Back Fr. 606 The American NB Ch. # 3613
Once named the German American National Bank, this institution adopted a new name during World War I. It issued $5 Plain Backs and Type 1 only under the new nomenclature prior to its failure in the Spring of 1934. The purple stamped signatures are fully intact, but the bottom margin is slightly cut in at lower left. **Very Fine**.
From The Lincoln Collection (400-600)

14539 Lincoln, IL - $20 1929 Ty. 2 First NB Ch # 14118
This exciting 14000 Charter Number bank has only 12 recorded notes. This bright **Fine-Very Fine** note is sure to please an Illinois or 14000 Charter Number collector. (500-750)

Uncirculated Brown Backs

14540 Litchfield, IL - $10 1882 Brown Back Fr. 483 The First NB Ch. # (M)3962
A lovely example which is one of a small run of uncirculated Brown Backs known from here. There is a crease in the right margin, and but for that one detraction this would easily merit the full Choice designation. **Crisp Uncirculated**.
From The Lincoln Collection (2,250-2,750)

14541 Litchfield, IL - $20 1882 Brown Back Fr. 497 The First NB Ch. # (M)3962
A lovely $20 Brown Back with plenty of original embossing and loads of eye appeal. Bright **Choice Crisp Uncirculated**.
From The Lincoln Collection (3,000-4,000)

14542 **Litchfield, IL** - $10 1902 Date Back Fr. 620 **The Litchfield NB** Ch. # (M)10079
Three vertical folds and a lone horizontal fold prohibits a full EF grade on this attractive note. The signatures remain bold as does the seal, serial numbers, and charter numbers. **Very Fine-Extremely Fine.**
From The Lincoln Collection (1,000-1,250)

14543 **Macomb, IL** - $1 1875 Fr. 383 **The First NB** Ch. # 967
Even circulation is seen on this pleasing Ace with a few tiny pinholes. The blue end security paper is easily detected and the signatures still remain legible. Original series notes appear at auction with regularity, but this 1875 marks the first to appear in eight years. **Very Good.** (1,000-1,500)

14544 **Macomb, IL** - $10 1902 Plain Back Fr. 628 **The Union NB** Ch. # (M)1872
Pleasing pen signatures still remain on this note that survived much time in commerce. **Very Good.**
From The Lincoln Collection (300-500)

14545 **Macomb, IL** - $20 1902 Plain Back Fr. 654 **The Union NB** Ch. # 1872
Pleasing stamped signatures remain on this still crisp **Fine** note.
From The Lincoln Collection (400-600)

14546 **Macomb, IL** - $20 1902 Plain Back Fr. 652 **The Macomb NB** Ch. # 9169
A couple of rust spots distract little from the charm of this **Very Fine** note. Bright surfaces with visible signatures are sure to please.
From The Lincoln Collection (400-600)

14547 **Madison, IL** - $5 1902 Plain Back Fr. 600 **The First NB** Ch. # 8457
This was the only note issuing national bank in town and it has left behind just 10 large to be counted for the census. This example has the stamped signatures of E.G. and A.W. Baltz. A lightly pencilled "1600" is found to the left of the bank title. **Fine.**
From The Lincoln Collection (600-900)

14548 **Maquon, IL** - $10 1902 Plain Back Fr. 626 **The First NB** Ch. # 8482
A **Very Good+** piece that still possesses traces of purple stamped signatures. Only nine large size examples are enumerated.
From The Lincoln Collection (500-750)

14549 **Marengo, IL** - $10 1902 Plain Back Fr. 628 **The First NB** Ch. # 1870
A most attractive piece from this very scarce McHenry County issuer. Although this bank, the only one in town, lasted until 1932, it was one of the smallest and most thinly capitalized in the state, as evidenced by its miniscule issue of both large and small notes. Pleasing **Fine-Very Fine,** with strong pen signatures.
From The Lincoln Collection (1,250-2,250)

14550 **Marion, IL** - $10 1902 Plain Back Fr. 627 **The First NB** Ch. # 4502
Stamped signatures are found on this nicely margined $10 that exhibits a little bit of edge wear. **Very Fine-Extremely Fine.**
From The Lincoln Collection (400-600)

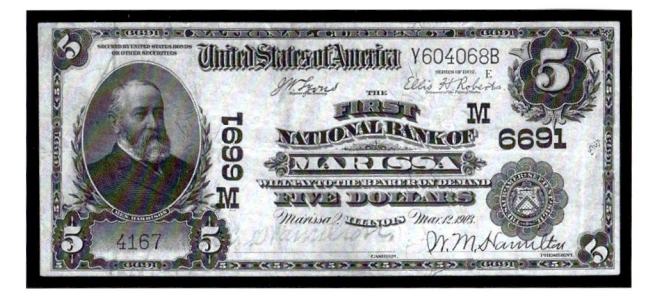

14551 Marissa, IL - $5 1902 Plain Back Fr. 598 **The First NB** Ch. # (M)6691
This bank was reorganized and rechartered in 1933 under the same name. A pleasing mix of stamped and pen signatures is noticed. Bright **Very Fine,** from an always in demand location.
From The Lincoln Collection **(1,000-1,500)**

14552 Marissa, IL - $20 1902 Plain Back Fr. 650 **The First NB** Ch. # 6691
From our 2002 Central States sale where it was described as, "An extremely scarce Illinois bank, particularly in large size, where virtually every note known from here is ensconced in a long term holding. This example is the first we've had to offer in over fifteen years. **Fine,** certain to be a most popular lot."
From The Lincoln Collection **(900-1,200)**

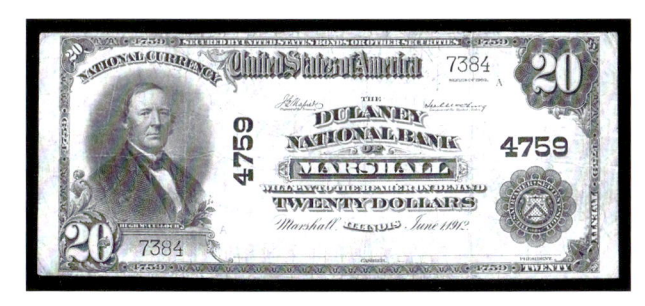

14553 Marshall, IL - $20 1902 Plain Back Fr. 654 **The Dulaney NB** Ch. # 4759
A few pinholes can be seen on this bright **Fine-Very Fine** example that has lost its signatures. Just five large notes are reported, with this the only $20.
From The Lincoln Collection **(600-900)**

14554 Martinsville, IL - $5 1902 Plain Back Fr. 598 **The First NB** Ch. # 6721
This **Fine** Clark County example has the distinction of being ex-Lynn Shaw collection.
From The Lincoln Collection **(500-750)**

14555 Martinsville, IL - $10 1902 Plain Back Fr. 624 **The First NB** Ch. # 6721
Two other consecutively numbered notes are known in CU, attributing to the originality of this piece. The paper is perfectly original with solid embossing. A hint of handling is noted, though the note is still fully **Crisp Uncirculated.**
From The Lincoln Collection **(1,000-1,200)**

14556 Mason City, IL - $10 1882 Brown Back Fr. 485 **The First NB** Ch. # 1850
This is a great note from an obscure one bank town in which the bank issued only First Charters and Brown Backs before liquidating in 1898. Only three notes are known from here, with only a literal handful of offerings in the past six decades. **Very Good+,** the face a bit better, the back well worn but quite intact.
From The Lincoln Collection **(2,500-3,500)**

14557 Mattoon, IL - $10 1902 Plain Back Fr. 628 **The State NB** Ch. # (M)10144
This attractive **Very Fine** saw some time in the Midwest channels of commerce. One signature remains and the overprint is deeply printed.
From The Lincoln Collection **(600-800)**

14558 Mattoon, IL - $20 1902 Plain Back Fr. 654 **The State NB** Ch. # (M)10144
Ten large size only for this Coles County issue are recorded. **Very Good** with stamped signatures still visible.
From The Lincoln Collection **(300-500)**

14559 Mazon, IL - $5 1902 Plain Back Fr. 602 **The First NB** Ch. # 10186
This one bank town in Grundy County was able to issue over $600,000 in Nationals and at its close in 1932, far less than 1% of that total was still outstanding in the form of large size notes. This piece is attractive and solid for the grade, though the signatures have faded. **Very Fine.**
From The Lincoln Collection **(600-800)**

14560 Mazon, IL - $10 1902 Plain Back Fr. 628 **The First NB** Ch. # (M)10186
This Grundy County institution was around for a touch over 20 years. **Very Good.**
From The Lincoln Collection **(300-500)**

14561 Metcalf, IL - $20 1902 Plain Back Fr. 651 **The First NB** Ch. # 7954
This is one of only four large size notes known from this institution and one-bank town, and the last offering of one at public auction was in 2005. The paper is pleasing though the signatures have been lightly retraced. **Fine.**
From The Lincoln Collection **(1,250-1,500)**

14562 Metropolis, IL - $10 1882 Value Back Fr. 577 **The National State Bank** Ch. # (M)5254
A few pinholes and aging are seen on this early note from here. Only five large size are known and this **Very Good** example has been off the market for some time.
From The Lincoln Collection **(1,000-1,500)**

14563 Metropolis, IL - $10 1902 Plain Back Fr. 633 **The National State Bank** Ch. # (M)5254
Five large size comprise the census from this Massac County issuer chartered at the turn of the 20th century. **Very Good** with stamped signatures still visible.
From The Lincoln Collection **(500-700)**

14564 Minooka, IL - $10 1902 Plain Back Fr. 626 **The Farmers' First NB** Ch. # (M)9208
While small notes are often available from this one bank location, large examples are truly scarce, with this one of just five pieces known. It's also perhaps the finest of the group, with sharp pen signatures and an overall pleasing appearance. **Very Fine,** with a tiny bit of tape residue on each end.
From The Lincoln Collection **(1,500-2,000)**

Excessively Rare Moline Note

14565 Moline, IL - $20 1882 Brown Back Fr. 499 **The Moline NB** Ch. # (M)1941

An excessively rare note which was formerly part of the Shaw collection. It comes from a bank with just two examples extant, one of which has never been offered for sale and the other this piece, which has been offered at public sale only once. Moline is by far the largest community in Illinois that remains just about unobtainable to collectors, a fact demonstrated by the realization for this note when we sold it back in September of 2000, when it realized $11,000 in spirited bidding. We don't believe that sum is attainable tonight, as another example is now known from here, but a realization in the area of two thirds that number for this pen signed **Fine** Brown Back is certainly a real possibility.
From The Lincoln Collection **(6,000-9,000)**

14566 Monmouth, IL - $1 Original Fr. 382 **The Monmouth NB** Ch. # 1706

This excessively rare bank has just two notes listed in the census, our offering tonight, which has been variously cataloged as Very Good and Fine in different auction appearances, as well as an Original $5. We've sold this note once before, at our Greater Cincinnati Numismatic Exposition Signature Sale in September of 2000, where it will appear after tonight to be a bargain at $715. **Very Good,** with reasonable claims to the next higher grade. The market for better Nationals is considerably stronger today than in when we last offered this elusive note, leading us to predict a realization in the range of... **(3,000-5,000)**

14567 Monmouth, IL - $50 1902 Date Back Fr. 670 **The Peoples NB** Ch. # 4313

This is the only Date Back on this denomination listed in the census. Off the market for over six years, this pleasing **Fine-Very Fine** should be welcomed back with open arms. A couple of margin nicks and a pencilled "32" are the only detractions on this example with pleasing pen signatures.
From The Lincoln Collection **(2,000-3,000)**

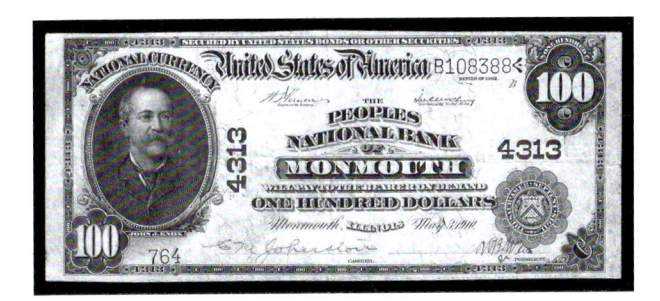

14568 Monmouth, IL - $100 1902 Date Back Fr. 692 **The Peoples NB** Ch. # 4313

This is now the third time this piece has appeared at public auction. The census shows only three large size are known from here. It is a lovely **Fine** with wonderful pen signatures and a few pinholes noticed.
From The Lincoln Collection **(2,000-3,000)**

14569 Monmouth, IL - $10 1882 Date Back Fr. 539 **The NB of Monmouth** Ch. # (M)4400

Signatures are still strong on this tough type note. **Fine** with the margin cut in a bit at lower left.
From The Lincoln Collection **(750-1,250)**

14570 **Monticello, IL** - $10 1882 Brown Back Fr. 485 **The First NB** Ch. # (M)4826
A moderate amount of circulation is noted on this piece. For the grade it is especially attractive and colorful. The signatures of the cashier and president remain bold. **Fine-Very Fine.**
From The Lincoln Collection **(750-1,000)**

14571 **Morris, IL** - $20 1882 Brown Back Fr. 494 **The Grundy County NB** Ch. # 531
This ex-Lynn Shaw collection note has evidence of pencil on the signatures. **Fine-Very Fine.**
From The Lincoln Collection **(750-1,000)**

14572 **Morris, IL** - $5 1902 Plain Back Fr. 601 **The First NB** Ch. # 1773
This piece is essentially uncirculated save for two folds. The stamped signatures are still bold and it is interesting to note that the stamped signature on the President line is followed by a penned V.P. **Extremely Fine-About Uncirculated.**
From The Lincoln Collection **(600-800)**

14573 **Morris, IL** - $5 1902 Plain Back Fr. 601 **The First NB** Ch. # 1773
Stamped signatures offer excellent contrast on the bright white surfaces of this **Extremely Fine-About Uncirculated** note.
From The Lincoln Collection **(600-1,000)**

14574 **Morris, IL** - $50 1902 Date Back Fr. 670 **The First NB** Ch. # (M)1773
No signatures are noticed on this **Fine+** note. This bank was originally chartered as the FNB of Seneca which lasted about one and a half years.
From The Lincoln Collection **(1,250-1,750)**

14575 **Morris, IL** - $10 1902 Plain Back Fr. 625 **The Farmers & Merchants NB** Ch. # 8163
Overall this is a bright note for the grade with just some soiling on a back quarter panel. The purple stamped signatures are light, yet legible. **Fine+.**
From The Lincoln Collection **(300-500)**

14576 **Morrisonville, IL** - $10 1902 Plain Back Fr. 624 **The First NB** Ch. # 6745
This **Fine** note comes from the only issuer in this Christian County community. Six large size are listed in the Kelly census. Stamped purple signatures still reside on somewhat snappy surfaces.
From The Lincoln Collection **(600-900)**

14577 **Mount Auburn, IL** - $10 1902 Plain Back Fr. 627 **The First NB** Ch. # (M)9922
This is a rare bank in large with ten recorded serial numbers and that includes this **Very Good** $10. However, marketplace activity on this charter number is even far sketchier as the only large note traded publicly in the last 30 years is a $20 1902 PB in Fine during our May 2002 auction that went for over $1600. Even the wonderful Lynn Shaw collection only had this town covered with a Series 1929 note. The signatures have faded from this example and the bottom edge slopes inside the frame line, but history informs us that the opportunity to own large notes on this bank is much rarer than the notes themselves.
From The Lincoln Collection **(1,000-2,000)**

14578 **Mount Carmel, IL** - $10 1902 Plain Back Fr. 627 **The First NB** Ch. # 4480
Superior edges for the grade are noticed on this $10. Printed signatures are of K.F. Putnam and Walter R. Kimzey. **Fine+.**
From The Lincoln Collection **(400-600)**

14579 **Mount Carmel, IL** - $20 1902 Plain Back Fr. 659 **The American NB** Ch. # 5782
Although small size notes from here do show up, large examples are quite difficult to obtain. Stamped signatures remain dark on this **Very Fine-Extremely Fine**.
From The Lincoln Collection **(400-600)**

14580 **Mount Carmel, IL** - $20 1902 Plain Back Fr. 659 **The American NB** Ch. # 5782
This pleasing **Very Fine-Extremely Fine** note is from the first title. The paper remains crisp and bright with fully stamped signatures. **(400-800)**

14581 **Mount Olive, IL** - $5 1902 Plain Back Fr. 598 **The First NB** Ch. # 7350
This piece is the lowest recorded serial number among the $5s known to collectors. The paper is solid except where the corners are a touch rounded. **Very Good.**
From The Lincoln Collection **(400-600)**

14582 **Mount Sterling, IL** - $20 1882 Date Back Fr. 555 **The First NB** Ch. # (M)2402
Neat pen signatures are still visible on this vivid example of a not so common issue. **Fine-Very Fine.**
From The Lincoln Collection **(750-1,250)**

14583 **Mount Sterling, IL** - $10 1902 Plain Back Fr. 632 **The First NB** Ch. # 2402
This discovery piece is from a one bank town. **Very Good-Fine.**
From The Lincoln Collection **(350-450)**

14584 **Mount Vernon, IL** - $10 1882 Date Back Fr. 545 **The Third NB** Ch. # (M)5689
Bright surfaces and stamped signatures are the hallmark of this crisp example from this Jefferson County issuer. **Very Fine-Extremely Fine.**
From The Lincoln Collection **(750-1,250)**

14585 **Moweaqua, IL** - $5 1902 Plain Back Fr. 598 **The First NB** Ch. # (M)7739
This is a scarce bank that was the only issuer in town and it issued large notes only. Eleven pieces are listed in the census, a figure which is quite deceptive, as one collector owns over one-fourth of the known notes. We have recorded a total of only six public offerings from here in almost seventy years. This figure is far more indicative of the real availability of notes from this Shelby County bank. **Very Good**, with traces of purple stamped signatures.
From The Lincoln Collection (700-1,000)

14586 **Moweaqua, IL** - $10 1902 Plain Back Fr. 624 **The First NB** Ch. # (M)7739
Large notes only from this Shelby County bank. **Fine**, with clear signatures.
From The Lincoln Collection (500-700)

14587 **Mulberry Grove, IL** - $10 1902 Plain Back Fr. 624 **The First NB** Ch. # 7379
The penned signatures add to the eye appeal of this moderately circulated issue. **Very Good**.
From The Lincoln Collection (650-850)

14588 **Murphysboro, IL** - $50 1902 Plain Back Fr. 677 **The First NB** Ch. # 4019
This **Very Fine-extremely Fine** ex-Lynn Shaw collection piece is the much scarcer of the two issuing Murphysboro banks, with a total of eight large from here recorded in the Kelly census. Lovely pen signatures are noticed.
From The Lincoln Collection (1,250-1,750)

14589 **Murphysboro, IL** - $100 1902 Date Back Fr. 691 **The First NB** Ch. # (M)4019
Pen signatures are still visible on this crisp **Very Good-Fine** note which has toned a touch. This is the only known example for its type.
From The Lincoln Collection (900-1,200)

14590 **Murphysboro, IL** - $10 1902 Date Back Fr. 620 **The City NB** Ch. # (M)4804
This bank opened its doors for business on November 2, 1892 after organizing a few months earlier. The dark pen signatures of Cashier Charles F. Chapman and President John G. Hardy grace the pleasing surfaces. **Very Fine**.
From The Lincoln Collection (500-700)

Rare Naperville Note

14591 Naperville, IL - $10 1902 Date Back Fr. 619 **The First NB** Ch. # (M)4551
A great note from the sole issuer in this Du Page County community. Although the census shows four notes known from here, most all have been closely held for years. Don't look for many new examples to show up either, as this bank chose to redeem its circulation in 1917, leaving a total of only $715 outstanding when the bank closed in 1934. This pen signed **Extremely Fine** example is the highest grade specimen known from here.
From The Lincoln Collection **(4,500-6,500)**

14592 Nashville, IL - $5 1902 Plain Back Fr. 598 **The First NB** Ch. # 6524
Purple stamped signatures remain visible on this bright representative from the larger of this community's two issuers. **Very Fine.**
From The Lincoln Collection **(400-600)**

14593 Nashville, IL - $10 1902 Plain Back Fr. 625 **The Farmers & Merchants NB** Ch. # 8221
This note was last sold by us in 2001 at our FUN sale. Five large size make up the current census from this institution which was not the only bank in town. Pleasing pen signatures still decorate the surface of this **Fine** example.
From The Lincoln Collection **(750-1,250)**

14594 National City, IL - $20 1902 Date Back Fr. 644 **The National Stock Yards NB** Ch. # (M)9118
This is not to be confused with the higher charter bank with a similar title, as this bank was actually chartered with the location of "National Stock Yards." Four years have passed since this **Very Good** last visited us.
(600-900)

14595 Nebo, IL - $20 1902 Plain Back Fr. 657 **The First NB** Ch. # 10492
This piece has been off the market for over six years last appearing with CAA in 2001. The signatures are mostly faded away, but the paper remains firm with a slight margin tear at right. **Fine-Very Fine.**
From The Lincoln Collection **(750-1,250)**

14596 Neoga, IL - $5 1902 Plain Back Fr. 607 **The Cumberland County NB** Ch. # 5426
This piece has been off the market since we last offered it over six years ago. The paper is solid for the grade though some edge nicks are reported. **Very Good.**
From The Lincoln Collection **(400-500)**

14597 **Neoga, IL** - $10 1902 Plain Back Fr. 625 **The Neoga NB** Ch. # (M)7841
Five large notes reside in the Kelly census. This bank succumbed in 1925 after almost 25 years in business. Beautiful pen signatures more than offset a minor rust stain near the title on this **Fine-Very Fine** specimen.
From The Lincoln Collection **(750-1,000)**

New Addition to the Census

14598 **Newman, IL** - $5 1902 Plain Back Fr. 598 **The Newman NB** Ch. # 7575
Bold pen signatures grace the surface of this scarce issue. With only three large size known, this is the first $5 Plain Back of record to make an appearance with us this evening. Hard folds account for the circulation sustained on this **Very Fine** note.
From The Lincoln Collection **(1,000-1,500)**

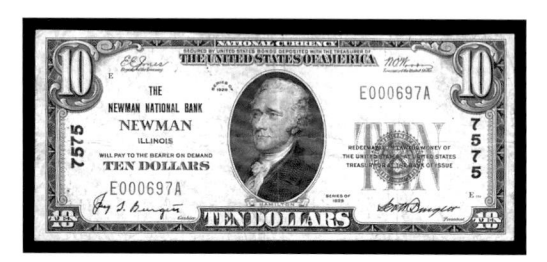

14599 **Newman, IL** - $10 1929 Ty. 1 **The Newman NB** Ch. # 7575
Here is a neat town name that would appeal to Cool Hand Luke fans everywhere. **Fine-Very Fine. (500-700)**

14600 **Newton, IL** - $10 1882 Brown Back Fr. 490 **The First NB** Ch. # (M)5869
One of just three Brown Backs listed in the census from this tougher Jasper County bank. **Very Good-Fine.**
From The Lincoln Collection **(600-800)**

14601 **Newton, IL** - $20 1882 Value Back Fr. 581 **The First NB** Ch. # (M)5869
A solid **Very Good** with a touch of softness and roughness.
From The Lincoln Collection **(500-700)**

14602 **Nokomis, IL** - $5 1882 Brown Back Fr. 472 **The Nokomis NB** Ch. # (M)1934
A scarce early note from this Montgomery County bank, with just two $5 Brown Backs known along with one $100 Brown Back. This is the nicest example in that trio, with good signatures, nice color, and little actual circulation. **Very Fine.**
From The Lincoln Collection **(1,800-2,200)**

14603 **Nokomis, IL** - $5 1902 Date Back Fr. 594 **The Nokomis NB** Ch. # (M)1934
This **Very Fine** ex-Lynn Shaw collection note remains as bright as it did in 2000. Deep pen signatures are noticed. Expect this note to be highly contested as only eight large size are recorded.
From The Lincoln Collection **(750-1,250)**

Gem Nokomis Red Seal

14604 Nokomis, IL - $10 1902 Red Seal Fr. 613 **The Farmers NB** Ch. # (M)7547
A beautiful Red Seal which is head and shoulders above any other note known from this scarce large only bank. We sold this back in May of 2000 and like it just as much today. **Gem Crisp Uncirculated,** with great color, margins, and signatures. (3,500-5,500)

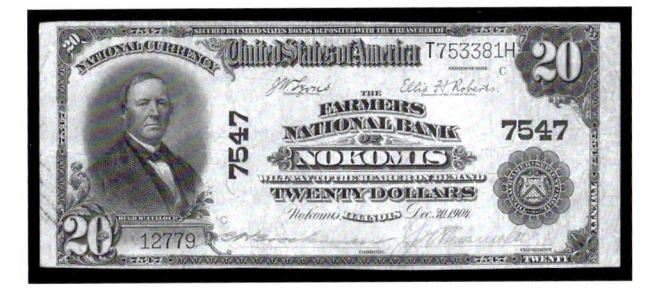

14605 Nokomis, IL - $20 1902 Plain Back Fr. 650 **The Farmers NB** Ch. # 7547
Eight large are all that are known on this Montgomery County institution which was assumed by the Nokomis NB in 1929. This **Fine** note with visible pen signatures has been off the market for seven years.
From The Lincoln Collection (600-800)

14606 Norris City, IL - $10 1902 Plain Back Fr. 625 **The First NB** Ch. # (M)7971
A very scarce bank in large size which is on the want lists of many Illinois collectors. We've sold the only three Norris City notes to reach the market since 1973, with this piece, from the Shaw collection, fetching $1870 back in May of 2001. **Fine-Very Fine,** with good signatures and no defects whatever.
From The Lincoln Collection (1,500-2,500)

14607 Oakford, IL - $20 1902 Plain Back Fr. 651 **The First NB** Ch. # (M)8256
Nice pen signatures grace this elusive issue that is a touch on the softer side. **Very Good-Fine.**
From The Lincoln Collection (400-600)

14608 Oakland, IL - $10 1882 Date Back Fr. 542 **The Oakland NB** Ch. # (M)2212
An attractive early note from this one bank Coles County location. Pen signed **Fine-Very Fine,** ex-Shaw and Lonnon collections.
From The Lincoln Collection (1,200-1,600)

14609 Oakland, IL - $10 1902 Plain Back Fr. 631 **The Oakland NB** Ch. # 2212
The paper quality for this **Very Good** is solid considering the grade. A lone pinhole is noted, but only when the note is candled. The signatures of the President and Cashier are still bold.
From The Lincoln Collection (100-600)

14610 Oblong, IL - $20 1902 Plain Back Fr. 652 **The First NB** Ch. # 8607
Ten large size are listed in Kelly from this town with a great name. Stamped signatures remain legible on this **Fine** note.
From The Lincoln Collection (1,000-1,500)

14611 Oblong, IL - $10 1902 Date Back Fr. 618 **The Oil Belt NB** Ch. # (M)8696
This piece bears one of the great titles from this state, and is the sole Date Back known from this bank as well. Pen signed **Very Fine**, with all four corner tips trimmed off.
From The Lincoln Collection (1,250-2,250)

14612 Oblong, IL - $20 1929 Ty. 1 **The Oil Belt NB** Ch. # 8696
A lovely example from this much sought after bank, which possesses one of the most interesting titles of any issuer. This is one of only two notes extant from here in this high a grade, and one of just eight Series 1929 examples reported in all grades combined. Perhaps the finest known, bright **PMG Uncirculated 62 EPQ.** (1,500-2,500)

14613 Odin, IL - $10 1902 Plain Back Fr. 626 **The First NB** Ch. # 9525
A rare note from a bank which had but $900 outstanding in large notes in 1935. While four examples are known in large, the last offering from here came back in 2001. Bright **Fine-Very Fine,** with vivid two color pen signatures.
From The Lincoln Collection (1,250-1,750)

14614 Ogden, IL - $10 1902 Plain Back Fr. 633 **The First NB** Ch. # 5304
A beautiful example from this scarce Champaign County bank, which had a meager $620 outstanding in large size notes in 1935. This piece appears new until closely examined, and bears the bold signatures of Lee Freese and J.A. Freese. **Extremely Fine-About Uncirculated.**
From The Lincoln Collection (1,750-2,250)

14615 Olney, IL - $10 1902 Date Back Fr. 617 **The First NB** Ch. # 1641
The life of this institution spanned almost 70 years. An even dozen survivors are recognized with this **Very Good** large size note still intact with visible signatures.
From The Lincoln Collection (300-500)

14616 Oneida, IL - $10 1902 Plain Back Fr. 632 **The First NB** Ch. # (M)10752
This **Good-Very Good** ex-Lynn Shaw collection piece last appeared in a May 2001 CAA auction. This well circulated note is from a scarce Knox County issuer.
From The Lincoln Collection (400-600)

14617 Ottawa, IL - $5 1902 Plain Back Fr. 598 **The National City Bank** Ch. # 1465
No problems to report on this **Very Good-Fine** note.
From The Lincoln Collection (300-500)

14618 Pana, IL - $20 1902 Plain Back Fr. 650 **The Pana NB** Ch. # (M)6734
This Christian County issuer almost lasted 27 years. Average circulation has affected this **Very Good** note. A few small holes have developed due to wear.
From The Lincoln Collection (300-500)

14619 Paris, IL - $20 1902 Plain Back Fr. 651 **The First NB** Ch. # 3376
Red stamped signatures stand out on this **Very Fine** note. A few edge nicks at right do not affect its overall pleasing eye appeal.
From The Lincoln Collection **(500-750)**

Unique Paxton Lazy Deuce

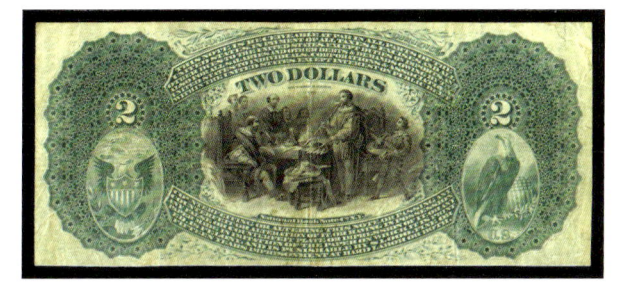

14620 Paxton, IL - $2 Original Fr. 389 **The First NB** Ch. # 1876
This Lazy Deuce is one of the highlights of tonight's Illinois offering, coming from a bank which was in business for less than five years before disappearing in January of 1876. By 1910, a miniscule $471 was listed as outstanding from here. The Kelly census confirms that this is the only Lazy Two known from the bank, and, fortunately for collectors, it is a most attractive example, with minimal wear, good signatures, decent margins, and a most pleasing overall appearance. Just four notes are known from this bank, with this the nicest by far. If rarity, desirability and grade are any criteria, expect this outstanding example, which grades a strong **Very Fine-Extremely Fine,** to see considerable action before the hammer falls tonight.
From The Lincoln Collection **(8,000-12,000)**

14621 Paxton, IL - $20 1902 Plain Back Fr. 650 **The First NB** Ch. # 2926
The Cashier's signature can still be seen beneath the circulation this note endured. The design elements remain legible on this **Good-Very Good** example that is lightly soiled.
From The Lincoln Collection **(250-400)**

14622 Pekin, IL - $5 1882 Date Back Fr. 534 **The Farmers NB** Ch. # (M)2287
Only one date back is known in the census. The signatures can still be seen despite the heavy use seen in commerce. **Very Good.**
From The Lincoln Collection **(500-750)**

14623 Pekin, IL - $20 1882 Date Back Fr. 552 **The Farmers NB** Ch. # (M)2287
The blue overprint and finely executed devices are still vivid. For the grade, the paper is most pleasing. **Fine-Very Fine.**
From The Lincoln Collection **(750-1,000)**

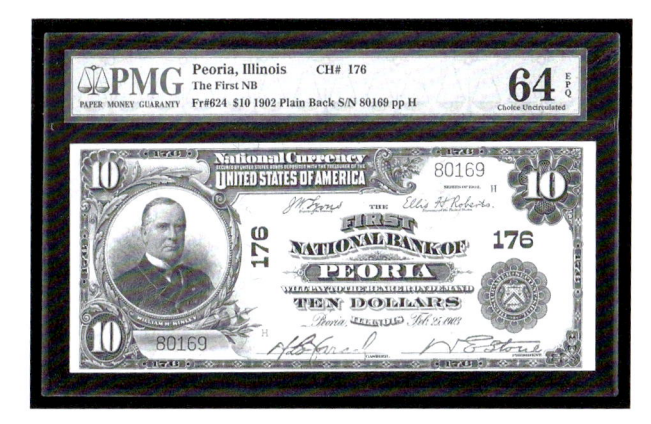

14624 Peoria, IL - $10 1902 Plain Back Fr. 624 **The First NB** Ch. # 176
This handsome $10 is unreported, but it drops neatly within a run of like-graded notes on this charter number. **PMG Choice Uncirculated 64 EPQ.** **(600-800)**

14625 Peoria, IL - $10 1902 Plain Back Fr. 624 **The First NB** Ch. # 176
Bright, fresh, and looking fully new, with just the lightest of handling and a close bottom margin keeping it from Gem. **PMG Choice About Unc 58 EPQ.** **(350-550)**

One of Three Known

14626 Peoria, IL - $10 Original Fr. 409 **The Second NB** Ch. # 207
First Charters only from this very rare bank, with this one of just three examples known from here. **Fine**, ex-Walter Herget collection sale.
From The Lincoln Collection (3,000-5,000)

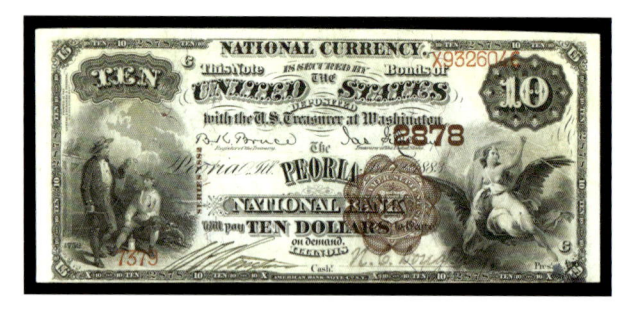

14627 Peoria, IL - $10 1882 Brown Back Fr. 479 **The Peoria NB** Ch. # 2878
An extremely rare Peoria bank which issued only Brown Backs and Red Seals during its twenty two years of operation, ending in 1905. Just three examples are known, a pair of Brown Backs and a single Red Seal, with this specimen by far the finest of the trio. **Very Fine-Extremely Fine**.
From The Lincoln Collection (2,750-4,250)

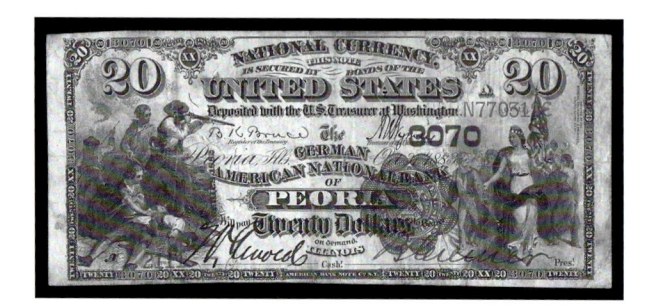

14628 Peoria, IL - $20 1882 Brown Back Fr. 494 **The German-American NB** Ch. # 3070
An extremely scarce bank which issued Brown Backs and Red Seals only before liquidating in January of 1904. Only a handful of notes are known from this ethnically titled institution, with this the only $20 Brown Back. **Fine**, ex-Shaw collection.
From The Lincoln Collection (1,750-2,250)

14629 Peoria, IL - $20 1902 Plain Back Fr. 650 **The Central NB & TC** Ch. # 3214
It appears that someone forgot to stamp the signature of the President onto this example. This is the second title for this institution. **PCGS Choice New 63**. (500-750)

14630 Peoria, IL - $10 1929 Ty. 1 **Merchants & Illinois NB** Ch. # 3254
A scarcer Peoria bank, especially in small size, where this institution issued Type ones only in relatively limited quantities before its doors closed forever in February of 1930. **Choice Crisp Uncirculated**, a high grade piece which will likely realize... (450-650)

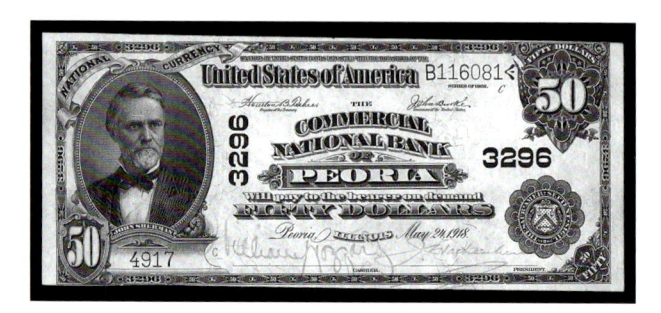

14631 Peoria, IL - $50 1902 Plain Back Fr. 682 **The Commercial NB** Ch. # 3296
This high denom boasts bright white paper but is precluded from an uncirculated grade by three light bends. **Extremely Fine**.
From The Lincoln Collection (900-1,100)

14632 Peoria, IL - $50 1929 Ty. 1 **Commercial Merchants NB &TC** Ch. # 3296
This $50 is blessed with original surfaces. A tiny ink mark is to the left of the right-hand charter number. **Very Fine**. (250-350)

14633 Peoria, IL - $5 1882 Brown Back Fr. 477 **The Illinois NB** Ch. # (M)5361
A very scarce Peoria bank which issued only Brown Backs and Second Charter Date Backs before liquidating in 1915. The Kelly census shows six examples known from here, three of which are in this sale. **Very Fine**, with a couple of minor splits.
From The Lincoln Collection (1,250-1,750)

Rare $50 Peoria Brown Back

14634 Peoria, IL - $50 1882 Brown Back Fr. 518 **The Illinois NB** Ch. # 5361
A very tough bank which issued only Brown Backs and Second Charter Date Backs before liquidating in June of 1915. This is the only high denomination Brown Back known from here. It is a most attractive example, displaying strong signatures and great color and body for the grade. Nice **Fine-Very Fine**, certainly rare enough to bring a very significant amount.
From The Lincoln Collection (4,250-6,250)

14635 Peoria, IL - $5 1882 Date Back Fr. 537 **The Illinois NB** Ch. # (M)5361
The paper exhibited here is relatively solid for the **Good-Very Good** grade. To date only a half dozen notes are known from this scarce bank.
From The Lincoln Collection (800-1,000)

14636 Peru, IL - $10 1902 Plain Back Fr. 624 **The Peru NB** Ch. # (M)2951
This LaSalle County bank failed during the depression in 1934, leaving the community without a National Bank. The ink signatures remain quite readable. **Very Good.**
From The Lincoln Collection (300-500)

14637 Peru, IL - $20 1902 Plain Back Fr. 650 **The Peru NB** Ch. # (M)2951
It has been a couple of years since a large size note from here has been available. Neat pen signatures with a few minor margin nicks. **Fine.**
From The Lincoln Collection (500-750)

14638 Petersburg, IL - $10 1902 Red Seal Fr. 613 **The First NB** Ch. # (M)3043
We know of no other Red Seals from this Menard County town save for this specimen, which traces its pedigree back to the Lonnon and Shaw collections. **Fine-Very Fine**, with a small area of light brown stain which barely detracts from the appeal of the note.
From The Lincoln Collection (1,200-1,800)

14639 **Petersburg, IL** - $20 1902 Plain Back Fr. 650 **The First NB** Ch. # (M)3043
Dark and complete pen signatures leap off the paper of this note with well embossed original surfaces. **Extremely Fine-About Uncirculated.**
From The Lincoln Collection **(500-700)**

14640 **Pinckneyville, IL** - $10 1882 Value Back Fr. 577 **The First NB** Ch. # (M)6025
Stamped signatures are still present on this note from the only bank in town. **Fine-Very Fine.**
From The Lincoln Collection **(750-1,250)**

14641 **Plymouth, IL** - $5 1902 Plain Back Fr. 609 **The First NB** Ch. # 12658
This **Fine-Very Fine** ex-Lynn Shaw collection note is one of nine reported from here. Purple stamped signatures still are visible
From The Lincoln Collection **(600-900)**

14642 **Pontiac, IL** - $10 1882 Brown Back Fr. 484 **The Livingston County NB** Ch. # 1837
A simply gorgeous example which is easily the finest note of any type known from here. It's a crackling fresh beauty with great color and eye appeal that somehow picked up a few folds from storage over the years. **Extremely Fine,** a note certain to please the most discriminating of collectors.
From The Lincoln Collection **(2,000-3,000)**

14643 **Potomac, IL** - $10 1902 Plain Back Fr. 624 **The Potomac NB** Ch. # 6824
This is a scarce **Good-Very Good** note from Vermilion County with only four specimens reported in Kelly to date.
From The Lincoln Collection **(750-1,000)**

14644 **Prophetstown, IL** - $10 1902 Plain Back Fr. 624 **The Farmers NB** Ch. # (M)6375
This **Fine** ex-Lynn Shaw collection piece is still a tougher Whiteside County note to locate.
From The Lincoln Collection **(750-1,000)**

14645 **Quincy, IL** - $5 1902 Plain Back Fr. 600 **The Quincy-Ricker NB & TC** Ch. # 3752
The Quincy National Bank absorbed the Ricker National Bank when the latter was placed in voluntary liquidation on June 12, 1923. The bottom edge is along the frame line. **Very Fine.**
From The Lincoln Collection **(250-450)**

14646 Rantoul, IL - $5 1902 Plain Back Fr. 606 **The First NB** Ch. # (M)5193
This is one of only nine large documented in the census for this Champaign County bank. Purple stamped officer signatures are of B. Rice and W.H. Wheat. **Fine,** ex-Lynn Shaw collection.
From The Lincoln Collection **(500-800)**

14647 Ridge Farm, IL - $10 1882 Value Back Fr. 577 **The First NB** Ch. # 5313
To date, this is the only Value Back reported from this Vermilion County bank. The details are consistent with a **Very Good,** though there is some softness of the margins to report.
From The Lincoln Collection **(1,000-1,250)**

14648 Ridge Farm, IL - $10 1902 Plain Back Fr. 633 **The First NB** Ch. # 5313
The First NB is the scarcer of Ridge Farm's two large size issuers. This note is one of only 8 large in the census. The signatures are present and it can be determined that this note was signed by the vice president. **Very Good,** with staining.
From The Lincoln Collection **(400-600)**

14649 Ridge Farm, IL - $5 1902 Plain Back Fr. 600 **The City NB** Ch. # (M)8630
The Foster family ran this bank for many years. This example has lightly handled edges and nice color for the grade. **Fine.**
From The Lincoln Collection **(500-800)**

14650 Rochelle, IL - $1 Original Fr. 382 **The Rochelle NB** Ch. # 1907
This is a more than presentable example that is one of four First Charter Aces to survive from here. Included in the census are all the sheet mates of this nicely margined note, including the Lazy $2, as well as one additional Ace. While two banks issued from this small community, this is the only one to have any documented survivors. Although there is an approximate quarter inch split at top center, a couple other margin separations, and a few filled pinholes, the note has the folds of a **Very Fine** example and still should merit serious attention from any Illinois collector who appreciates better First Charter material. **(1,500-2,500)**

14651 Rock Island, IL - $10 1882 Brown Back Fr. 487 **The Peoples NB** Ch. # (M)2155
This attractive Brown Back earns a grade of **Fine** due to its excellent color. Some toning of the paper is seen at the top of the note. Ex-Lynn Shaw collection.
From The Lincoln Collection **(1,500-2,500)**

14652 Rockford, IL - $5 1902 Date Back Fr. 593 **The Rockford NB** Ch. # (M)1816
The edges are nice for the grade, while the cashier's stamped signature is dark and the stamped signature of the president is weak. **Very Good+.**
From The Lincoln Collection **(300-500)**

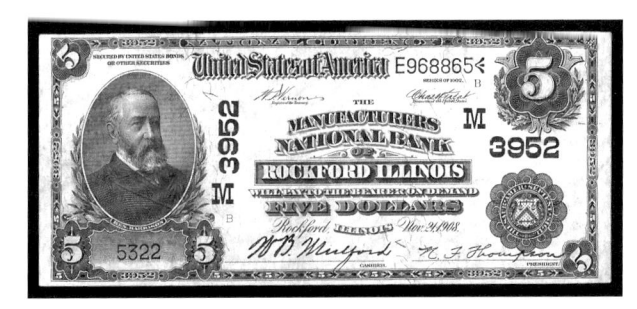

14653 Rockford, IL - $5 1902 Date Back Fr. 592 **The Manufacturers NB** Ch. # (M)3952
Bright signatures complement crisp surfaces on this **Extremely Fine-About Uncirculated** example.
From The Lincoln Collection **(500-800)**

14654 **Rockford, IL** - $10 1902 Plain Back Fr. 626 **The Manufacturers NB** Ch. # 3952
This has always been one of our favorite notes, with the unusual tombstone containing both the city and the state names. We've sold this incredibly margined beauty twice in the past, and mentioned both times that we had never seen a large example from here even close to this in grade. We still haven't. **Gem Crisp Uncirculated.**
From The Lincoln Collection **(1,500-2,500)**

14655 **Rockford, IL** - $10 1902 Plain Back Fr. 626 **The Manufacturers NB & TC** Ch. # 3952
This **Fine-Very Fine** note which last appeared in a CAA sale in September 2001 carries dual serial number 221. The second title is only known on four examples.
From The Lincoln Collection **(700-1,200)**

14656 **Rockford, IL** - $20 1902 Plain Back Fr. 653 **The Forest City NB** Ch. # 4325
This is one of the scarcer banks in this avidly collected city, with only ten large examples listed in the census, including this piece. This is one of the very nicest notes we have seen on this bank and the census data bears this out as it lists only one large note with a higher grade. **Very Fine,** with sharp pen signatures of both officers.
From The Lincoln Collection **(600-800)**

14657 **Rockford, IL** - $20 1902 Plain Back Fr. 653 **The Forest City NB** Ch. # 4325
One of the scarcer banks in this avidly collected city, with only ten large examples listed in the Kelly census. This is one of the nicer ones we've seen. **Fine-Very Fine,** with sharp pen signatures
From The Lincoln Collection **(500-800)**

14658 **Rockford, IL** - $5 1902 Plain Back Fr. 601 **The Swedish-American NB** Ch. # 9823
Another note for the ethnic bank title collector which has a pinhole visible along the horizontal fold line. **Very Good-Fine.**
From The Lincoln Collection **(350-550)**

14659 **Rockford, IL** - $10 1902 Plain Back Fr. 627 **The Swedish-American NB** Ch. # 9823
This pleasing ethnic title example lets us know who the first settlers to the area were. A nice **Very Good-Fine** last sold by CAA in September 2000.
From The Lincoln Collection **(400-600)**

14660 **Rockford, IL** - $10 1902 Plain Back Fr. 633 **The Commercial NB** Ch. # 11679
Bright and original paper are highlights of this $10. The Commercial issued only the $10 denomination in Plain Backs and the 1929 series during its 12 year run which ended in 1932. **Very Fine.**
From The Lincoln Collection **(350-550)**

14661 **Roodhouse, IL** - $10 1902 Date Back Fr. 618 **The First NB** Ch. # (M)8637
This Greene County example brings the number known from here to nine. A half-inch tear at upper center and a small piece missing at the bottom left are noted. **Very Good-Fine.**
From The Lincoln Collection **(400-600)**

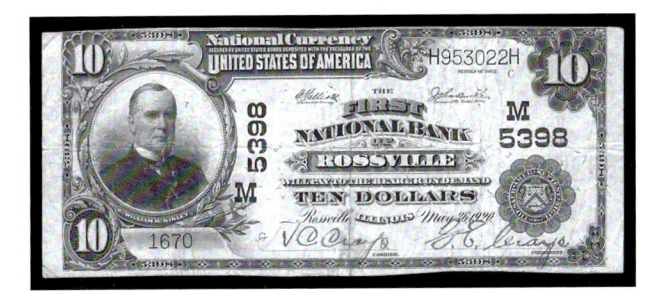

14662 Rossville, IL - $10 1902 Plain Back Fr. 633 **The First NB** Ch. # (M)5398
This note is one of a mere six large reported on charter number 5398 in the census. The penned signature of H.C. Crays and the purple stamped signature of G.E. Crays are dark. A repair is found through the cashier's signature. This note also has many pin holes. Still it is rare enough to be a worthwhile addition to any collection. **Fine.**
From The Lincoln Collection **(600-900)**

14663 Rushville, IL - $1 Original Fr. 380 **The First NB** Ch. # 1453
First Charters only from this bank, the only issuer in town. Well circulated but intact **Very Good,** with a few splits and small body holes.
From The Lincoln Collection **(1,000-1,500)**

14664 Saint Charles, IL - $10 1902 Plain Back Fr. 624 **The St. Charles NB** Ch. # (M)6219
The Cashier's signature is quite legible while the President's is completely gone. A couple of internal tears and a rough top margin have also left their mark on this 1902 dated example from this popular Kane County locale. **Very Good.**
From The Lincoln Collection **(400-600)**

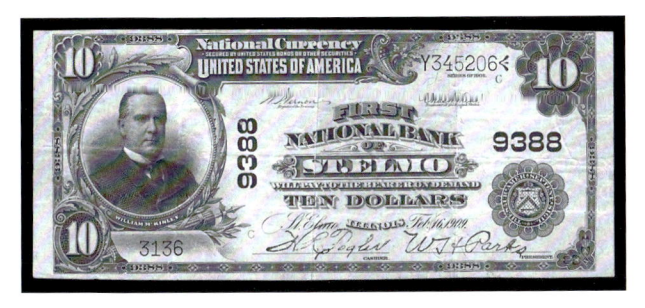

14665 Saint Elmo, IL - $10 1902 Plain Back Fr. 626 **The First NB** Ch. # 9388
A very tough large note from the only bank in town. **Very Fine,** with pleasing signatures.
From The Lincoln Collection **(1,000-1,500)**

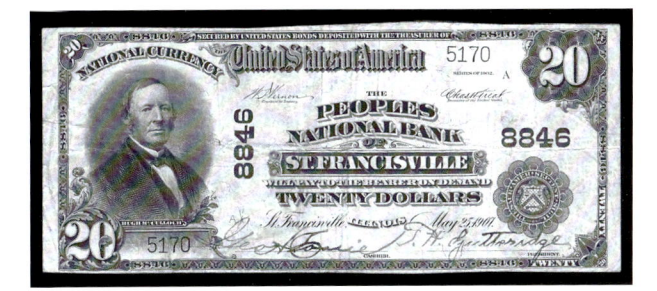

14666 Saint Francisville, IL - $20 1902 Plain Back Fr. 652 **The Peoples NB** Ch. # 8846
This **Very Fine** ex-Lynn Shaw collection note is usually not seen in this grade range.
From The Lincoln Collection **(600-900)**

14667 Saint Peter, IL - $20 1902 Plain Back Fr. 653 **The First NB** Ch. # (M)9896
This is one of only 8 large for this bank. There is also some staining. A small internal split affects the last digit in the bank serial number. The president's signature is darker than the cashier's. **Very Good.**
From The Lincoln Collection **(500-800)**

14668 Salem, IL - $20 1902 Plain Back Fr. 653 **The Salem NB** Ch. # 1715
CAA last sold this note in January 2001. Signatures are barely legible on this **About Fine** example.
From The Lincoln Collection **(400-600)**

14669 Savanna, IL - $10 1902 Plain Back Fr. 626 **The First NB** Ch. # 8540
A tougher example from the only bank here to issue large notes in this Mississippi River community. **Fine**, with stamped signatures.
From The Lincoln Collection **(400-600)**

14670 Secor, IL - $20 1902 Plain Back Fr. 660 **The First NB** Ch. # 6007
A very scarce note from the only bank to issue in this Woodford County hamlet. The census stands at just five large notes, with this one of only two Plain Backs. **Fine-Very Fine**, with two color pen signatures.
From The Lincoln Collection **(1,200-1,800)**

14671 **Shawneetown, IL** - $5 1902 Plain Back Fr. 598 **The NB of Shawneetown** Ch. # 7752
This is one of only 8 large in the census for this Gallatin County bank. Of those eight notes, only a couple have a higher grade than this example. This bank went into receivership on May 26, 1930 leaving a large size outstanding of only $1350. The penned signatures are in black ink for the cashier and blue for the president. Shawneetown served as an important United States government administrative center for the Northwest Territory after the American Revolution. The only towns chartered by the United States government are Shawneetown and Washington, D.C. **Fine.**
From The Lincoln Collection (1,000-1,500)

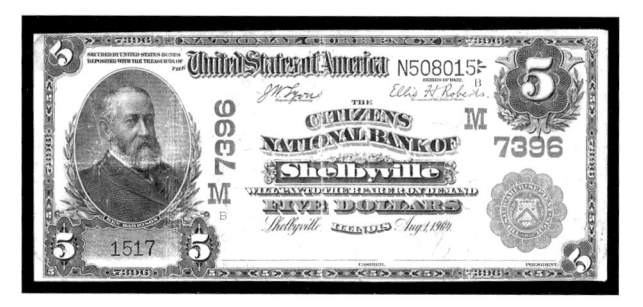

14672 **Shelbyville, IL** - $5 1902 Red Seal Fr. 587 **The Citizens NB** Ch. # (M)7396
Only two Red Seals are known from this Shelby County issuer. The center folds are a bit heavy. **Fine.**
From The Lincoln Collection (1,500-2,000)

14673 **Shelbyville, IL** - $5 1902 Plain Back Fr. 598 **The Citizens NB** Ch. # 7396
A little over a dozen notes are in the census for this Shelby County bank. The purple signatures which are a bit faded are still legible. **Fine.**
From The Lincoln Collection (500-700)

14674 **Sidell, IL** - $10 1902 Plain Back Fr. 626 **The First NB** Ch. # (M)8374
This is one of 6 large examples recorded from this Vermilion County bank that would pass from the banking scene in September 1933. Almost ten years have passed since CAA initially offered this **Very Good** piece that has a little scuff along the signature line at bottom right.
From The Lincoln Collection (600-1,000)

14675 **Springfield, IL** - $10 1882 Brown Back Fr. 479 **The First NB** Ch. # 205
Bold color for the grade makes this an attractive piece. The signatures are bold as are the details on the back. **Very Good.**
From The Lincoln Collection (600-800)

14676 **Springfield, IL** - $20 1882 Brown Back Fr. 493 **The First NB** Ch. # 205
We are most pleased with the originality and color of this Brown Back. All of the design elements are bold as is the all important back design. Some ink burn is noted in the signature of the cashier but it does not compromise the paper. **Fine-Very Fine.**
From The Lincoln Collection (800-1,000)

14677 **Springfield, IL** - $10 1882 Brown Back Fr. 482 **The Ridgely NB** Ch. # 1662
A nice early note from this state capital private name bank. **Fine-Very Fine,** signed by H. Ridgely as Cashier.
From The Lincoln Collection (900-1,200)

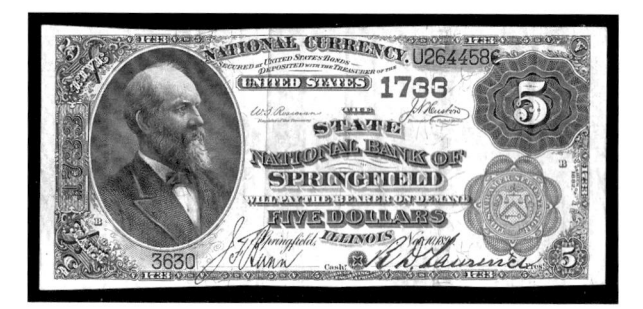

14678 **Springfield, IL** - $5 1882 Brown Back Fr. 471 **The State NB** Ch. # 1733
This is a glorious state capital note that would make a great example for type. The layout is wonderful and the pen signatures stand out. **Very Fine-Extremely Fine.**
From The Lincoln Collection (900-1,500)

14679 **Springfield, IL** - $10 1882 Brown Back Fr. 484 **The State NB** Ch. # 1733
The paper and signatures are particularly attractive for this moderately circulated issue. The overprint is bold and the margins solid. **Very Fine.**
From The Lincoln Collection **(900-1,100)**

14680 **Springfield, IL** - $10 1882 Date Back Fr. 539 **The State NB** Ch. # (M)1733
Large notes only from this tougher Springfield bank, with this piece formerly part of the Shaw collection. Pen signed **Very Fine+++,** a high end early state capital note.
From The Lincoln Collection **(800-1,000)**

14681 **Springfield, IL** - $10 1902 Date Back Fr. 619 **The State NB** Ch. # (M)1733
Strong stamped signatures remain on this bright **Very Fine** capital issue.
From The Lincoln Collection **(350-500)**

14682 **Springfield, IL** - $10 1882 Brown Back Fr. 482 **The Illinois NB** Ch. # (M)3548
One of the nicer Brown Backs we've seen from here. Pen signed **Very Fine,** a quality piece which is certain to please.
From The Lincoln Collection **(700-900)**

14683 **Springfield, IL** - $10 1902 Red Seal Fr. 615 **The Illinois NB** Ch. # (M)3548
This attractive example is by far the finest of the three Red Seals listed in the census from this state capital bank. Bright **Very Fine-Extremely Fine,** and further enhanced by the two color signatures of H.M. Merriam, Cashier, and Chas. G. Brown, V. President.
From The Lincoln Collection **(1,250-1,750)**

14684 **Springfield, IL** - $10 1902 Plain Back Fr. 618 **The Illinois NB** Ch. # (M)3548
Dark inks, stamped signatures, and original paper surfaces adorn this state capital $10. The top edge is inside the frame line and the bottom edge is inside the adjacent note. The census contains only one large graded note with a higher grade than this unreported $10. **Extremely Fine,** with original surfaces.
From The Lincoln Collection **(400-600)**

14685 **Springfield, IL** - $10 1902 Plain Back Fr. 626 **The Illinois NB** Ch. # (M)3548
Here is another pleasing state capital issue which has lost its signatures. **Very Fine+.**
From The Lincoln Collection **(350-500)**

14686 **Springfield, IL** - $20 1902 Red Seal Fr. 641 **The Illinois NB** Ch. # (M)3548
Numerous large size notes are known from this bank, though only three of those are Red Seals. This piece has wholly original paper and a gold overprint. **Fine,** ex-Lynn Shaw collection.
From The Lincoln Collection **(750-1,000)**

14687 **Staunton, IL** - $5 1902 Plain Back Fr. 602 **The First NB** Ch. # 10173
This **Fine-Very Fine** example is nicely margined, but the officers' signatures have faded away.
From The Lincoln Collection **(600-900)**

14688 **Streator, IL** - $50 1902 Plain Back Fr. 681 **The Union NB** Ch. # 2176
Few mid-grade high denomination Nationals have the eye appeal that this note boasts. The paper is wholly original and especially bright. Add two strong remaining signatures and a deep blue overprint, and this piece will sell itself. **Very Fine+++.**
From The Lincoln Collection **(1,400-1,700)**

14689 **Stronghurst, IL** - $10 1902 Plain Back Fr. 633 **The First NB** Ch. # 5813
This **Very Fine-Extremely Fine** note is the highest grade example from here to appear at auction in a long time. An interesting two color signature combination graces this well margined Henderson County piece with only eight enumerated in census data to date.
From The Lincoln Collection **(750-1,250)**

14690 **Sumner, IL** - $20 1902 Plain Back Fr. 650 **The First NB** Ch. # 6907
While small notes are occasionally available from this one bank location, large examples are another matter entirely, with this one of only three such examples known from here. It's as nice as any, not surprising considering its pedigree, which traces back to the Lonnon and Shaw collections, two of the three finest holdings of Illinois notes ever assembled. Pen signed **Very Fine.**
From The Lincoln Collection **(1,750-3,250)**

14691 **Sumner, IL** - $10 1929 Ty. 1 **The First NB** Ch. # 6907
This is a welcome addition to the census that previously had stood at four small and an uncut sheet for this Lawrence County bank. **Very Good.** (500-750)

14692 **Sycamore, IL** - $50 1902 Date Back Fr. 671 **The Sycamore NB** Ch. # (M)1896
An attractive high denomination example from this avidly collected location which is new to the census. Sharp **Very Fine,** with great pen signatures.
From The Lincoln Collection **(2,500-3,500)**

14693 **Sycamore, IL** - $10 1902 Plain Back Fr. 628 **The First NB** Ch. # 1896
The second title used by this much collected bank, which is none too common in large with either title. Pleasing **Fine.**
From The Lincoln Collection **(400-600)**

14694 **Sycamore, IL** - $10 1902 Plain Back Fr. 626 **The Citizens NB** Ch. # 9572
This pleasing **Fine** issue from this DeKalb County bank is represented by less than ten examples in the Kelly census.
From The Lincoln Collection **(600-1,000)**

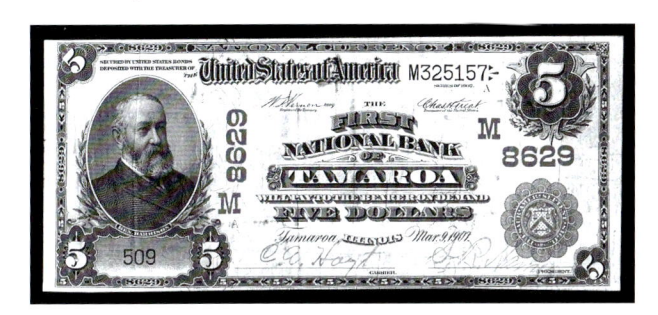

14695 **Tamaroa, IL** - $5 1902 Red Seal Fr. 589 **The First NB** Ch. # (M)8629
This colorful Red Seal is the only such example known from this small Perry County bank. It's one of just six large notes known from the bank, which was the sole issuer here. Bright **Fine+**, with some glue spots on the reverse which affect little.
From The Lincoln Collection **(3,500-5,500)**

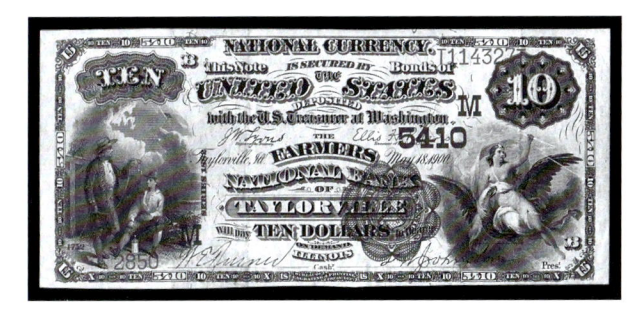

14696 **Taylorville, IL** - $10 1882 Brown Back Fr. 490 **Farmers NB** Ch. # (M)5410
A lovely Brown Back with great color and eye appeal which is perfect for type. **Extremely Fine+++**, with the bright blue pen signatures contrasting perfectly with the overall chocolate color of the remainder of the note. **(1,200-1,600)**

14697 **Taylorville, IL** - $10 1902 Plain Back Fr. 626 **The Taylorville NB** Ch. # (M)8940
Purple stamped signatures of F.C. Achenbach and Trey L. Long decorate this **Extremely Fine-About Uncirculated** $10.
From The Lincoln Collection **(450-650)**

14698 **Thomasboro, IL** - $10 1902 Plain Back Fr. 625 **The First NB** Ch. # 8155
Six large notes are reported from this Champaign County institution. This piece spent many months in a wallet and the corners are quite rounded. **Good.**
From The Lincoln Collection **(500-800)**

14699 **Toledo, IL** - $10 1902 Plain Back Fr. 633 **The First NB** Ch. # (M)5273
Great signatures are seen on this example which was signed by the Asst. Cashier and Vice President. **Very Fine-Extremely Fine.**
From The Lincoln Collection **(400-800)**

Finest of Three Known

14700 **Toluca, IL** - $20 1882 Brown Back Fr. 499 **The First NB** Ch. # (M)4871
A superlative item originally sold as part of the Shaw collection in January of 2000. This is one of three notes known from this bank, which issued Brown Backs only during its brief twelve year run. Just three notes are known, with this example the finest. **About Uncirculated,** a wonderful combination of rarity, grade, and desirability.
From The Lincoln Collection **(5,000-7,000)**

14701 Tremont, IL - $20 1902 Date Back Fr. 642 **The First NB** Ch. # (M)6421
Twelve large size notes are known from this Tazewell County issuer. **Fine.**
From The Lincoln Collection **(400-600)**

14702 Vermilion, IL - $5 1902 Plain Back Fr. 604 **The First NB** Ch. # 10365
Excellent pen signatures are seen on this Edgar County issue from which auction appearances are very slim. This note appeared with CAA at FUN 2001 and there is no telling when another opportunity will arise to acquire a note from here. **Fine.**
From The Lincoln Collection **(1,000-1,500)**

14703 Vienna, IL - $10 1902 Plain Back Fr. 627 **The First NB** Ch. # 4433
This **Fine** ex-Lynn Shaw collection piece has stamped signatures and a sprinkling of pinholes.
From The Lincoln Collection **(750-1,000)**

14704 Vienna, IL - $20 1902 Plain Back Fr. 653 **The First NB** Ch. # (M)4433
Eight large size notes are known for this Johnson County issuer. Lightly stamped signatures grace this issue which is a survivor of the $3130 in large size left outstanding. **Fine.**
From The Lincoln Collection **(750-1,000)**

14705 Virginia, IL - $20 1902 Date Back Fr. 642 **The Farmers NB** Ch. # (M)1471
A very scarce "two state" bank which was liquidated in 1918. Just seven examples make up the entire census from here, with this one of only two Date Backs. **Very Good-Fine.**
From The Lincoln Collection **(600-900)**

14706 Waddams Grove, IL - $5 1902 Plain Back Fr. 607 **The First NB** Ch. # (M)11675
This was the only bank in this tiny Stephenson County community, and this is the only type and denomination issued from here during this institution's short existence, which spanned less than four years before ending in 1923. Five notes are known from here, with this the finest by at least a full grade. Pen signed **Very Fine,** a great note from this outstanding Illinois collection.
From The Lincoln Collection **(4,000-7,000)**

14707 Waukegan, IL - $20 1902 Plain Back Fr. 650 **The First NB** Ch. # 945
A light pink stain is noticed along the bottom margin at center. The purple stamped signatures retain some brightness. Only eleven examples in large size are currently enumerated on this bank from a community along the shore of Lake Michigan between Chicago and Milwaukee. **Fine.**
From The Lincoln Collection **(600-800)**

14708 **Waverly, IL** - $20 1902 Plain Back Fr. 660 **The First NB** Ch. # 6116
This attractive and fully margined issue is one of only two pieces from this institution that is fully uncirculated. The paper quality is original and the embossing is bold. **Choice Crisp Uncirculated.**
From The Lincoln Collection **(800-1,200)**

14709 **White Hall, IL** - $10 1902 Date Back Fr. 616 **The White Hall NB** Ch. # (M)7077
Lovely pen signatures are exhibited on this piece which has a touch of soiling on the back. **Fine-Very Fine.**
From The Lincoln Collection **(400-600)**

14710 **White Hall, IL** - $10 1902 Plain Back Fr. 624 **Peoples-First NB** Ch. # (M)7121
This bank bears the second of two titles under which it circulated large size notes. Last appearing in May 1999, this **Very Fine** example is one of seven documented with this nomenclature in large and is scarce enough to be worth in the range of...
From The Lincoln Collection **(600-900)**

14711 **Wilmington, IL** - $50 1902 Plain Back Fr. 679 **The Commercial NB** Ch. # 1964
Only five large size notes are mentioned in Kelly from this Will County issuer southwest of Chicago. Bright signatures with a touch of roughness in the margin at right. **Fine.**
From The Lincoln Collection **(1,500-2,000)**

14712 **Witt, IL** - $10 1902 Plain Back Fr. 624 **First NB** Ch. # (M)7538
This was the second of two titles used by this prohibitively rare bank, which issued large notes only before bowing out in 1928. Just three notes are listed in the census, with this piece formerly residing in the Shaw collection. Nice **Fine.**
From The Lincoln Collection **(1,750-2,750)**

One of Two Known

14713 **Witt, IL** - $10 1902 Date Back Fr. 620 **The Witt NB** Ch. # (M)10264
This is considerably the rarest of Witt's four issuing banks, none of which are anything less than very scarce. This short lived bank issued only large notes, with this one of only two examples known. Pen signed **About Fine,** a truly rare item worthy of a strong bid.
From The Lincoln Collection **(3,000-4,000)**

14714 Wood River, IL - $5 1902 Plain Back Fr. 607 **The First NB** Ch. # 11876
Common in small size, but quite scarce in large. This pleasing **Fine** has been hidden away for a number of years.
From The Lincoln Collection **(500-700)**

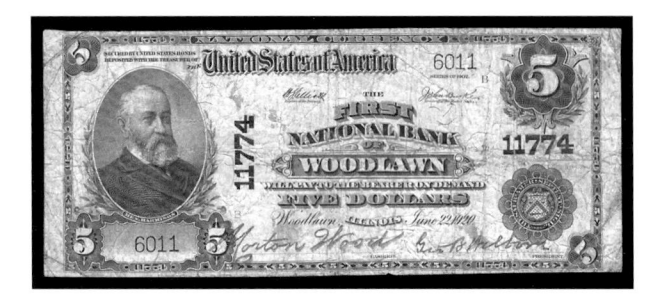

14715 Woodlawn, IL - $5 1902 Plain Back Fr. 607 **The First NB** Ch. # 11774
Two bold stamped signatures are noted on this moderately circulated issue. **Very Good.**
From The Lincoln Collection **(400-600)**

14716 Woodstock, IL - $10 1902 Plain Back Fr. 624 **The American NB** Ch. # (M)6811
A bright pen signed example from this very scarce northern Illinois bank. Sharp **Very Fine,** a note which will likely prove to be a most popular item.
From The Lincoln Collection **(700-1,000)**

14717 Wyanet, IL - $20 1902 Plain Back Fr. 652 **The First NB** Ch. # (M)9277
Ten large size are known from this Bureau County institution. Purple stamped signatures are still noticed on lightly soiled, crisp surfaces of this **Fine-Very Fine** note.
From The Lincoln Collection **(600-900)**

14718 Xenia, IL - $5 1902 Plain Back Fr. 608 **The First NB** Ch. # 12096
This is one of a scant 7 large in the census for this Clay County bank. The First NB of Xenia is essential in putting together an A-Z set for Illinois. Illinois and Ohio are the two states where this is possible. A mere $690 was outstanding from here in large size by 1935. A small internal hole is noticed along with an approximate quarter inch edge tear. A large moisture stain also covers most of this **Very Good** note.
From The Lincoln Collection **(500-800)**

INDIANA

14719 East Chicago, IN - $5 1929 Ty. 1 **The United States NB of Indiana Harbor** Ch. # 12058
This bank has one of the longer titles in Series 1929 notes. This $5 has original surfaces that camouflage its three light folds. Auction records are spotty for this charter number. In fact we can uncover only six appearances since 1973. We did sell a much lower grade $10 on this bank in 2004 for $575. **Extremely Fine. (750-1,000)**

14720 Franklin, IN - $10 1902 Plain Back Fr. 626 **The Citizens NB** Ch. # 3967
This is one of only two $10 Plain Backs found in the census. Purple stamped signatures of Jno. H. Tarleton and A.A. Alexander add to the value of this note. Red ink from the corner of a teller stamp is noticed. **Fine+.** (500-700)

14721 Franklin, IN - $20 1902 Plain Back Fr. 652 **The Citizens NB** Ch. # (M)3967
This bright $20 has purple stamped signatures of the cashier and vice president. This $20 carries a geographic sort letter, while the $10 listed above does not. A small skin mark is also found at the bottom center, along with a brown streak down the middle of the reverse. **Extremely Fine.** (700-900)

14722 Goshen, IN - $5 1929 Ty. 1 **The City NB** Ch. # 2067
This note would certainly qualify for Gem if the lower right margin were larger. **Very Choice Crisp Uncirculated.** (350-500)

14723 Goshen, IN - $5 1929 Ty. 1 **The City NB** Ch. # 2067
Here is a consecutive pair of original notes that were cut a bit tight along the top margin. **Choice Crisp Uncirculated.** (Total: 2 notes) (600-800)

14724 Goshen, IN - $20 1929 Ty. 1 **The City NB** Ch. # 2067
Plenty of punch through embossing is seen on this bright piece. (350-500)

14725 Green Castle, IN - $10 1902 Plain Back Fr. 624 **The Central NB** Ch. # (S)2896
A **Fine** note from a sought after community. (400-600)

14726 Greenwood, IN - $10 1902 Plain Back Fr. 626 **The First NB** Ch. # (M)8422
An extremely rare bank in this well collected location, with the census showing just four large examples. This piece is new to that listing, and is nicer than all but one example in that count. **Very Fine.** (2,000-3,000)

14727 Hammond, IN - $10 1902 Plain Back Fr. 632 **The Citizens NB** Ch. # 8199
Less than ten examples are known with the second title for this blue collar institution. The signatures have all but faded away, but the edges remain intact. **Very Good-Fine.** (500-700)

14728 Huntingburg, IN - $20 1902 Plain Back Fr. 652 **The First NB** Ch. # 8929
A very scarce bank in large size, with just six such examples in the census. Most all are very closely held, as we have seen no large examples offered at public sale since 1998. This piece is the only $20 reported to date, and grades a pleasing **Fine++,** with sharp pen signatures. (900-1,200)

14729 Indianapolis, IN - $20 1882 Brown Back Fr. 494 **The Merchants NB** Ch. # 869
While not a particularly attractive note, only two other Brown Backs are known on this bank, so the wait for another example may be lengthy. Some splits and pinholes are noted. **About Good** (400-600)

14730 **Indianapolis, IN** - $20 1902 Plain Back Fr. 650 **The Merchants NB** Ch. # 869
Printed signatures are seen on this note signed by members of the Frenzel family. It has been graded **CGA Gem Uncirculated 67** due to the prominent embossing and blazing color. (800-1,200)

14731 **Indianapolis, IN** - $10 1929 Ty. 1 & Ty. 2 **The Merchants NB** Ch. # 869
This is a pleasing pair of both types of small size $10 notes. Bright, well embossed surfaces are seen on both notes. **Choice Crisp Uncirculated.**
From The Bill and Kathy Stella Currency Collection (Total: 2 notes) (500-750)

14732 **Indianapolis, IN** - $10 1902 Plain Back Fr. 626 **The Continental NB** Ch. # 9537
Only thirteen large are reported on this tougher Indianapolis bank. **Fine.** (400-500)

14733 **Jeffersonville, IN** - $5 1902 Plain Back Fr. 598 **The First NB** Ch. # 956
A well circulated but intact **Very Good** example with a small paper clip stain. (300-500)

14734 **Lebanon, IN** - $1 Original Fr. 382 **The First NB** Ch. # 2057
This note last appeared on the scene 25 years ago as Choice New. PMG has graded it **Uncirculated 60** due to some margin roughness and some corner dings. The officers' signatures are every bit as strong as the day this note was originally signed. (2,000-3,000)

14735 **Logansport, IN** - $10 1902 Plain Back Fr. 632 **The City NB** Ch. # (M)5076
This is a problem-free **Fine** with excellent stamped signatures. (400-500)

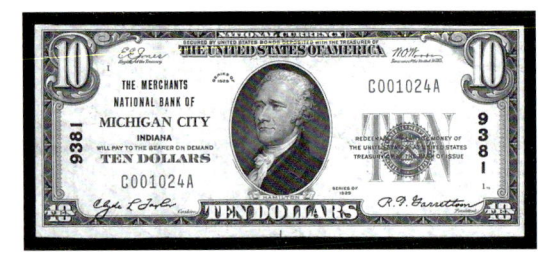

14736 **Michigan City, IN** - $10 1929 Ty. 1 **The Merchants NB** Ch. # 9381
Last appearing at our 2006 Central States sale, "This lightly circulated **Extremely Fine** $10 has the appearance of an even higher grade example. It still retains its white paper and rich brown ink, and is as nice as any note listed in the new Kelly census." (450-650)

14737 **Muncie, IN** - $10 1902 Plain Back Fr. 631 **The Merchants NB** Ch. # (M)2234
Here is a pleasing note from the third title for this issuer graded **CGA Extremely Fine 40.** (300-500)

14738 **New Albany, IN** - $10 1902 Date Back Fr. 616 **The New Albany NB** Ch. # (M)775
This fully original note has solid margins all around and nothing but even circulation to speak of. The stamped signatures have survived the test of time. Of the eleven large size notes listed in the census only three are Series 1902 Date Backs. **Fine.** (700-900)

First Offering Since 1977

14739 **New Albany, IN** - $1 Original Fr. 380 **The Merchants NB** Ch. # 965
An extremely rare New Albany bank which went out in 1909. Just four notes are listed in the census, with this the only First Charter Ace. More important for collectors is the fact that this marks the first public offering of any kind from here since the Donlon sale of September, 1977, a mere three decades ago. **Fine-Very Fine,** with a reverse repair of a long tear that is barely visible. If rarity is any guide, expect a realization in the vicinity of... (2,500-4,500)

Newly Discovered Serial Number 1 Note

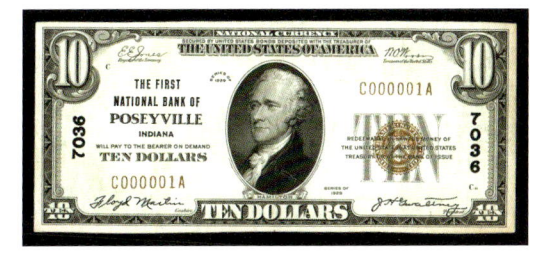

14740 Poseyville, IN - $10 1929 Ty. 1 **The First NB** Ch. # 7036

An extremely rare bank with the census showing just two large and three small notes. This piece is new to the census, and is the only serial number 1 Series 1929 example reported to date. There is a small amount of very light foxing in the right margin, but the note is an attractive **Very Fine-Extremely Fine** specimen with no other problems worthy of mention. Expect a realization in the range of... **(2,000-4,000)**

14741 South Bend, IN - $100 1929 Ty. 1 **The Citizens NB** Ch. # 4764

This is the first of two notes from the same sheet, both **Very Choice Crisp Uncirculated. (1,000-1,250)**

14742 South Bend, IN - $100 1929 Ty. 1 **The Citizens NB** Ch. # 4764

Plate position E is noted, which was next to last on the original sheet of six notes. **Very Choice Crisp Uncirculated. (1,000-1,250)**

14743 Tipton, IN - $5 1902 Plain Back Fr. 598 **The First NB** Ch. # (M)6251

Despite excessive wear, this note is graded **Very Good** with solid paper and no pinholes. Only thirteen large size notes have been reported on this bank that only issued Series 1902 notes. **(600-800)**

14744 Vincennes, IN - $10 1902 Plain Back Fr. 633 **The American NB** Ch. # 3864

This was formerly the German NB until the United States entered World War I. Officers are E.W. Drennan and Geo. R. Alsop. Charter number embossing remains on this $10. **Fine+. (300-500)**

14745 Vincennes, IN - $10 1882 Brown Back Fr. 485 **The Second NB** Ch. # (M)4901

This is one of only seven large size in the census with this being the only $10 Brown Back enumerated. The left edge has a thin skin mark that runs almost the entire length, while the right edge shows adhesive residue. We sold a $5 Brown Back one full grade higher on this bank in May 2000 for $1850. **Very Good. (500-800)**

14746 Wabash, IN - $5 1902 Plain Back Fr. 598 **The Farmers & Wabash NB** Ch. # 6309

This $5 is on the much scarcer second title on this bank that came into being on December 31, 1927. This gave the F&W roughly only 18 months to issue large size $5s under this title. This note can be added to the current census of a mere 4 large for this title. In January 2001 we sold a similar $5 for $880 on this bank. This example, with nicely stamped signatures, original surfaces, and even wear, should surpass that figure. **Very Fine. (750-1,000)**

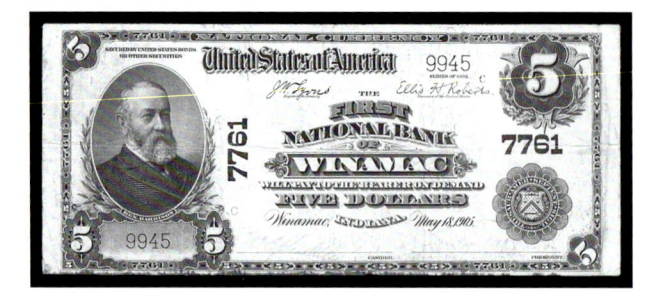

14747 Winamac, IN - $5 1902 Plain Back Fr. 598 **The First NB** Ch. # 7761
A little bleed through is seen along the bottom margin on this issue with twelve large size known. Signatures are still visible on brightly inked surfaces. **Fine.** (500-700)

IOWA

Scarce Iowa Lazy Deuce

14748 Clinton, IA - $2 Original Fr. 387 **The Clinton NB** Ch. # 994
Any Iowa Lazy Deuce is a tough note indeed, with this piece the first such example reported from Clinton. It's a very attractive example, with good color and signatures, with its sole defect a few small rust spots that affect nothing and are mentioned solely for the sake of full accuracy in cataloguing. **Very Fine.** (4,500-6,500)

14749 Davenport, IA - $10 1875 Fr. 418 **The Citizens NB** Ch. # 1671
A beautiful example which was saved for this generation of collectors when it was set aside as part of the Davenport bank hoard. The colors and overall appearance are those of an uncirculated specimen, with the only detraction a top margin which is a bit trimmed into the design at the center. **Extremely Fine,** a perfect type example. (3,250-5,250)

14750 De Witt, IA - $20 1902 Plain Back Fr. 650 **The First NB** Ch. # (M)3182
A lovely note which is one of the very nicest large examples known from here. Bright **Extremely Fine+,** with strong pen signatures. (500-700)

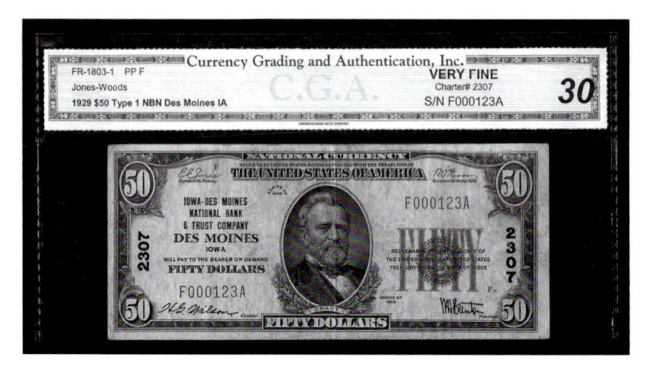

14751 Des Moines, IA - $50 1929 Ty. 1 **Iowa-Des Moines NB & TC** Ch. # 2307
Only 416 sheets of $50s were issued by this Midwest bank. This bright example is graded **Very Fine 30** by CGA. Just thirteen banks in Iowa issued this denomination. (400-600)

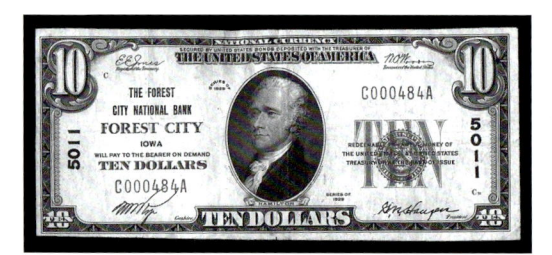

14752 Forest City, IA - $10 1929 Ty. 1 **The Forest City NB** Ch. # 5011
The example we offer tonight is a solid **Very Fine** that appears to have had a few paper clip rust stains nicely removed, leaving only faint traces. While two banks were located here, this was the sole issuer of the 1929 series. We anticipate that bids should reach no less than... (350-450)

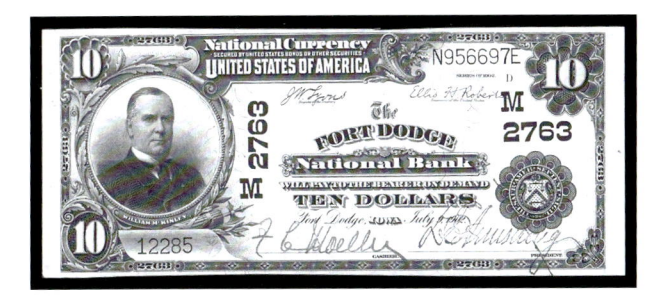

14753 Fort Dodge, IA - $10 1902 Plain Back Fr. 624 **The Fort Dodge NB** Ch. # (M)2763
A bright and vividly inked example from a small run of high grade large notes from here. **About Uncirculated** with clear signatures and great eye appeal. (450-650)

14754 Glenwood, IA - $50 1929 Ty. 1 **The Mills County NB** Ch. # 1862
Closed pinholes are noted on the left side of the note. **Fine-Very Fine.** (700-900)

14755 Greenfield, IA - $10 1902 Plain Back Fr. 634 **The First NB** Ch. # (M)5334
Large notes only from this bank, with the census standing at just over a dozen pieces. **Fine,** with two color signatures. (400-600)

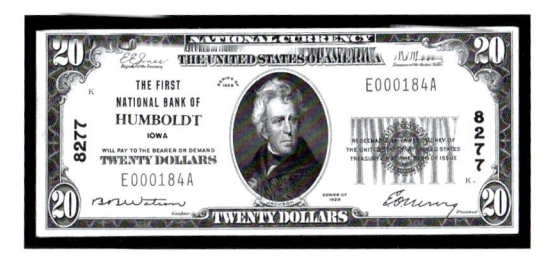

14756 Humboldt, IA - $20 1929 Ty. 1 **The First NB** Ch. # 8277
A high end example from the earlier of the two banks to issue here. Sharp **Extremely Fine.** (400-600)

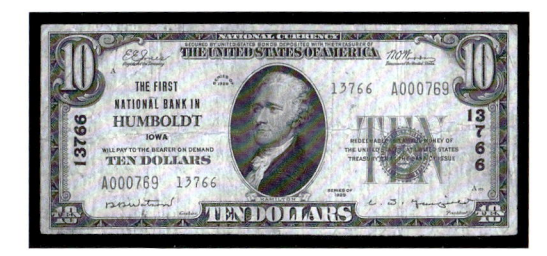

14757 Humboldt, IA - $10 1929 Ty. 2 **The First NB** Ch. # 13766
This late chartered institution only issued Type Two Fives and Tens. **Fine.** (500-700)

14758 Knoxville, IA - $5 1882 Brown Back Fr. 472 **The Knoxville NB** Ch. # (M)1871
Although well worn and low grade, this Brown Back is one of only three early notes known from here. **Very Good.** (400-600)

Lovely $50 Nevada Brown Back

14759 Nevada, IA - $50 1882 Brown Back Fr. 518 **The First NB** Ch. # (M)2555
The census reveals just twelve $50 Brown Backs known from all Iowa banks combined. It is, in fact, the only Brown Back known from this community. Fortunately for collectors, it is an absolute peach of a note, with broad even margins, great color, bold pen signatures, and loads of eye appeal. If you are a collector who can afford the best, this is an item you should absolutely try to bring home this evening. **Very Fine.** (8,000-12,000)

14760 Ottumwa, IA - $50 1902 Date Back Fr. 667 **The First NB** Ch. # (M)107
Pleasing pen signatures are noticed on this piece which is only the second of this type and denomination we have offered in five years. A few inconsequential spots near the top on the back do not distract. **Fine.**
From The Jacob and Heather Dedman Collection
(900-1,200)

Unique for the State- The Only Known Iowa Original Series $20

14761 Pella, IA - $20 Original Fr. 429 **The Pella NB** Ch. # 2063
This is an extraordinary new discovery from a state which, over the past two generations, has been as avidly collected as any in the country. Populated by dealers such as Art and Paul Kagin, Dean Oakes, John Hickman and Lyn Knight, and home to collectors such as Bill Higgins, who established a museum in his home town of Okoboji dedicated exclusively to National Bank Notes, Iowa notes have been more thoroughly researched, counted, and sought after than the issues of virtually any other state. Despite fifty years of searching however, no collector has ever had the opportunity of owning an Original Series $20 from Iowa before the discovery of this piece. While well circulated and displaying all of the defects associated with a note in this state of preservation, this example is fully intact, decently colored, and eminently collectible. Any estimate here is but a guess, but after the hammer falls this evening, only one collector or institution can hope to ever complete a type set of nationals from the state of Iowa. **Very Good. (10,000-15,000)**

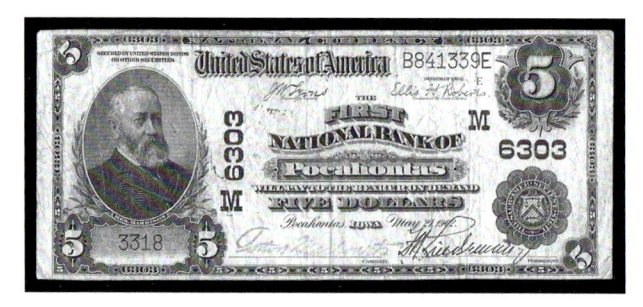

14762 Pocahontas, IA - $5 1902 Plain Back Fr. 598 **The First NB** Ch. # (M)6303
Large notes only from this bank, which features one of the most desirable of Iowa's many interesting town names. **Fine+,** a very scarce item from a bank which has had only three offerings at public sale in the past sixty years. **(1,250-1,750)**

14763 Shannon City, IA - $10 1902 Plain Back Fr. 627 **The First NB** Ch. # 9723
It has been over a decade since any large examples from this small Union County community has been available at public sale to collectors. Fortunately for those who waited, this piece, which is new to the census, is as nice or nicer than any previously listed example. Bright **Very Fine+. (1,100-1,400)**

14764 Terril, IA - $10 1902 Date Back Fr. 620 **The First NB** Ch. # (M)10238
Embossing is prevalent on this lightly circulated $10 that was pen signed flowingly by the assistant cashier while the president had his signature rubber stamped in purple ink. The purple ink shows some smudging, but this does not hinder the overall attractiveness of this delightful note. **Extremely Fine. (350-550)**

KANSAS

14765 Alma, KS - $10 1902 Plain Back Fr. 632 **The Alma NB** Ch. # (W)5104
The signatures of the Cashier and President are both present and add to the overall eye appeal of this note. While five different banks issued National Currency in Alma, surviving notes from all five banks total less than thirty! **Very Good-Fine. (500-700)**

14766 Ashland, KS - $10 1929 Ty. 1 **The Stockgrowers NB** Ch. # 5386
While this piece faces up quite nicely, there are several noticeable folds. Decent margins surround this **Very Fine-Extremely Fine** note. **(350-550)**

14767 Chanute, KS - $5 1902 Date Back Fr. 592 **The First NB** Ch. # (W)3819
The signatures are gone from this Neosho County example. **Very Good. (250-350)**

14768 Chanute, KS - $5 1929 Ty. 2 **The First NB** Ch. # 3819
Pleasing margins surround this bright example which has been graded **PMG Gem Uncirculated 65 EPQ.** (350-550)

14769 Colby, KS - $5 1929 Ty. 2 **The Thomas County NB** Ch. # 13076 Uncut Sheet
There is a soft corner fold in both the top and bottom notes of this uncut sheet, both of which are hard to see and essentially meaningless, but otherwise this sheet is absolutely pristine. There are no folds between the notes and each of them is a well margined Gem. **Gem Crisp Uncirculated. (4,000-6,000)**

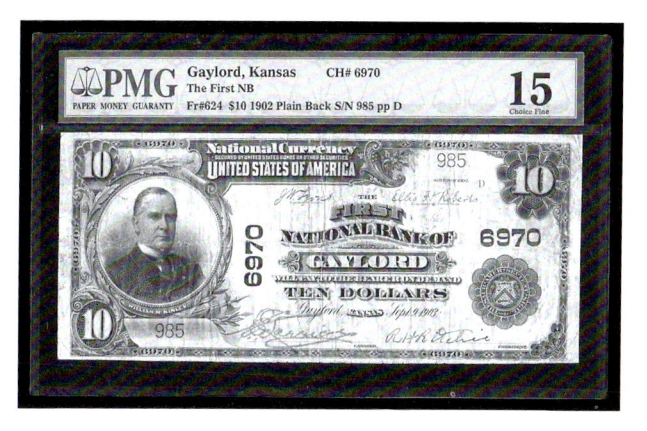

14770 Gaylord, KS - $10 1902 Plain Back Fr. 624 **The First NB** Ch. # 6970
Auction appearances of large size from here have been virtually non-existent, no surprise considering that only three large size specimens are known from here. Graded **PMG Choice Fine 15. (1,500-2,000)**

14771 Jewell City, KS - $10 1929 Ty. 1 **The First NB** Ch. # 3591
Ten small are reported for this bank from Jewell County. **Very Good-Fine. (350-500)**

First Ever Public Offering

14772 Kansas City, KS - $5 1902 Red Seal Fr. 589 **The Bankers NB** Ch. # (W)8602
A great Kansas note from a bank which was in business for less than two years before disappearing forever in January of 1909. Only one other note is known from here, with the whereabouts of that example unknown, as it has never been available at public sale to the collecting fraternity. Even the massive C. Dale Lyon collection was missing any note from this bank. **Very Good-Fine,** with great color for the grade, a truly rare item worthy of a very strong bid... **(7,500-12,500)**

One of Two Known

14773 Kingman, KS - $5 1882 Brown Back Fr. 469 **The Kingman NB** Ch. # 3559
A newly discovered note from this excessively rare bank which issued Brown Backs only. The Kelly census shows only one note extant from here (which has never been offered at public sale), no surprise as this bank was in existence for a mere four years and had but $370 outstanding in 1915. It is well circulated, but with nice pen signatures. Intact **Good-Very Good,** easily likely to see bidding reach or exceed... **(5,000-8,000)**

14774 Parsons, KS - $50 1929 Ty. 1 **The First NB** Ch. # 1951
In Series 1929 notes this bank only issued Type 1 $50s and $100s. Today there are 10 $50s known including this note, but not a single $100 has been reported. A pencilled "159" is next to the portrait. **Fine-Very Fine. (200-400)**

KENTUCKY

14775 Adairville, KY - $20 1902 Plain Back Fr. 652 **The First NB** Ch. # 8814
A very scarce bank in large size, with the Kelly census listing just five such examples, including this piece. It's the highest grade of any, and is a most attractive example. **Very Fine,** with a small area of light stain on the reverse that affects nothing. **(1,500-2,500)**

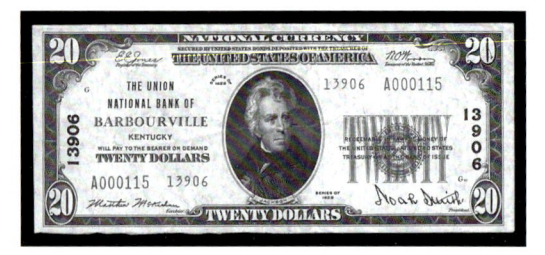

14776 Barbourville, KY - $20 1929 Ty. 2 **The Union NB** Ch. # 13906
A pleasing high grade example from this tougher Barbourville bank. **Very Fine+. (450-650)**

14777 Bowling Green, KY - $10 1882 Brown Back Fr. 490 **The Citizens NB** Ch. # (S)5900
A well margined Brown Back which is encapsulated in a **PMG Choice Uncirculated 64** holder. It certainly appears to be a conservative grade based on the note's appearance, which is that of a full Gem and more. **(3,000-4,000)**

14778 Burnside, KY - $5 1902 Date Back Fr. 592 **The First NB** Ch. # (S)8903
From our sale of the Bill Gale Collection where the description read, "This is a very rare bank in large size, with the Gale collection containing two of the three known large examples from here. This well circulated but intact **Very Good** example is no prize for grade, but it's significantly better than the only other reported Date Back, which was in the Martin collection and makes this specimen look like a gem by comparison." This note has found its way into a **CGA Very Good 08** holder since that sale. **(1,000-1,500)**

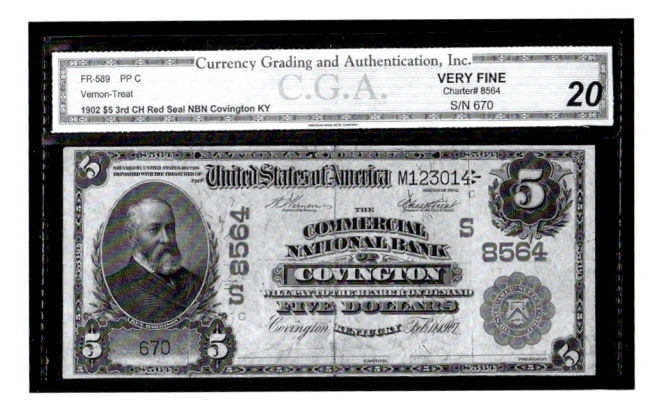

14779 **Covington, KY** - $5 1902 Red Seal Fr. 589 **The Commercial NB** Ch. # (S)8564

An excessively rare Covington bank which issued Red Seals and Date Backs only during its brief seven year stint. The red overprints remain bright on this **CGA Very Fine 20** that looks to have a center split repaired. (1,500-2,500)

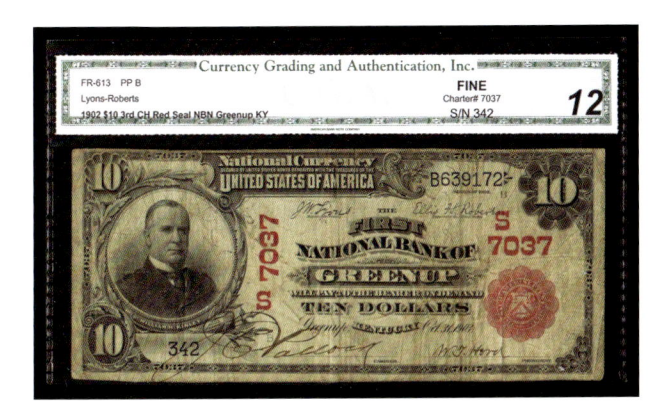

14780 **Greenup, KY** - $10 1902 Red Seal Fr. 613 **The First NB** Ch. # (S)7037

A scarce Kentucky Red Seal $10 certified as **CGA Fine 12**. The census from here includes only six large size notes of all varieties. A scant two are of the Red Seal persuasion, this $10 and a single $20. The particular note we bring to the collecting fraternity this evening was previously sold in St. Louis in 2002. It went for $4,888. The market for rare Nationals is considerably more robust now than when this prohibitively rare Red Seal was previously hammered down. We fully expect that the previous realization will be nothing more than a rather timid starting point for bids tonight. (4,500-6,500)

One of Two Known

14781 **Harlan, KY** - $20 1902 Date Back Fr. 645 **The First NB** Ch. # (S)9791

An extremely rare bank with just two examples reported from here to date. This marks only the second public appearance of any note from the earliest bank to issue in "Bloody Harlan," a location immortalized in many books and films. **Very Good-Fine.** (3,000-5,000)

14782 **Lancaster, KY** - $20 1902 Plain Back Fr. 650 **The NB** Ch. # (S)1493

This **Fine-Very Fine** $20 Plain Back comes from a community with only 12 large survivors documented from both issuers combined. The note we offer here is one of but three $20 Plain Backs listed from its parent institution. Given its scarcity as a type and denomination and the difficulty of acquiring any large note at all from this locale, we expect that bidding will end at least in the range of... (1,000-1,500)

14783 **Lancaster, KY** - $20 1929 Ty. 1 **The NB of Lancaster** Ch. # 1493

This piece is listed in the census as VF, and it is no wonder why, as it has great eye appeal for a moderately circulated National. **Fine.** (550-750)

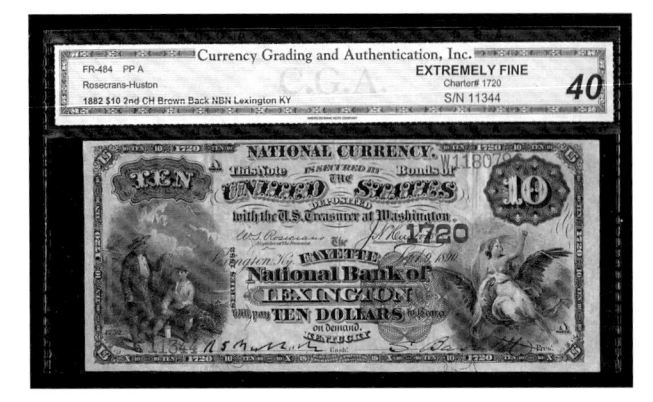

14784 **Lexington, KY** - $10 1882 Brown Back Fr. 484 **The Fayette NB** Ch. # 1720
Blazing white paper and bold signatures complement each other on this colorful Brown Back. **CGA Extremely Fine 40.** (1,000-1,200)

14785 **Louisville, KY** - $20 1882 Brown Back Fr. 501 **The Citizens NB** Ch. # (S)2164
A well margined and brightly colored $20 Brown Back which is a perfect note to represent this popular type. Sharp **Extremely Fine+,** with plenty of original embossing still evident. (1,400-1,800)

14786 **Louisville, KY** - $10 1902 Plain Back Fr. 632 **The Citizens Union NB** Ch. # 2164
From our 2006 FUN sale of the Bill Gale Collection, "This note bears the second of two large size titles utilized by this institution. It has nice margins as well as strongly stamped signatures. The paper surfaces display an unmistakable original crispness and it is an unquestionably **Extremely Fine** by even the most conservative standards, although it is listed in the census as VF. (400-600)

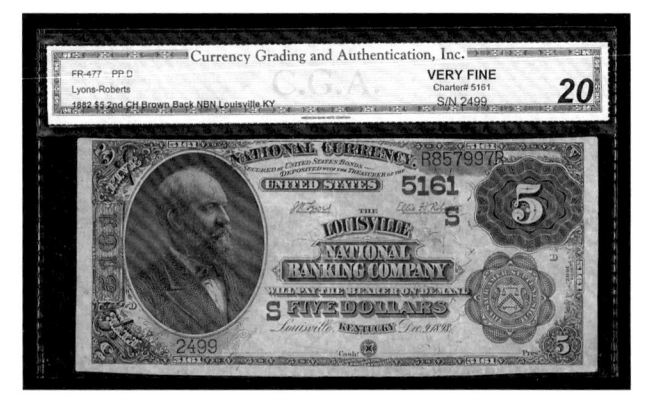

14787 **Louisville, KY** - $5 1882 Brown Back Fr. 477 **The Louisville National Banking Company** Ch. # (S)5161
The colorful design remains bold on this **CGA Very Fine 20.** (1,000-1,200)

14788 **Louisville, KY** - $100 1882 Brown Back Fr. 530 **The Louisville National Banking Company** Ch. # (S)5161
A very scarce type and denomination from any location. This $100 Brown Back grades **About Fine** or a bit better, but there are a few small stains at the top and bottom, and a small piece is missing from the top left corner. The note actually appears considerably nicer than the description would indicate, and, as a $100 Brown Back, will likely realize... (5,500-6,500)

14789 **Louisville, KY** - $10 1902 Date Back Fr. 618 **NB of Commerce** Ch. # (S)9241
From our sale of the Bill Gale Collection, "A tougher Louisville bank which went out in 1919. Just nine examples, including this piece, are listed in the census. **Fine-Very Fine,** with purple stamp signatures. (500-700)

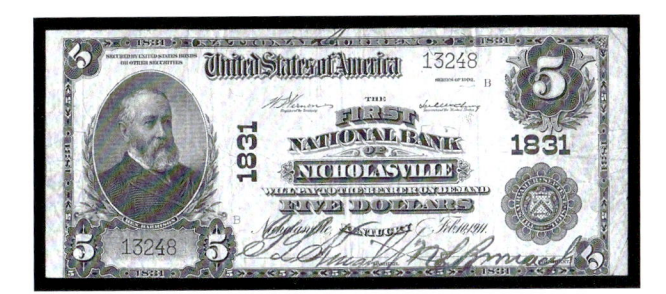

14790 **Nicholasville, KY** - $5 1902 Plain Back Fr. 601 **The First NB** Ch. # 1831
The First was the only issuing bank located in this Jessamine County locale. By 1935 only $3,675 in large size remained outstanding. Dark printed signatures are found on this evenly circulated **Fine-Very Fine** $5. **(600-800)**

14791 **Nicholasville, KY** - $10 1902 Plain Back Fr. 627 **The First NB** Ch. # (S)1831
This $10 has some staining at upper left and a partial paper clip rust outline at top center. Printed signatures are of G.L. Knight and N.L. Bronough. The layout of this note is different from the $5 above by having an added geographic sorting letter and a bank and Treasury serial number instead of two bank serial numbers. **Fine-Very Fine. (600-800)**

Unique for the Bank

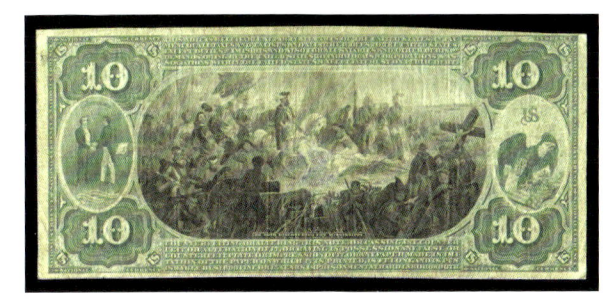

14792 **Owenton, KY** - $10 Original Fr. 414 **The NB of Owen** Ch. # 1963
A great Kentucky rarity, coming in a $10 Original Series note, a rarity from this state in itself. This bank issued First Charters only before liquidating in 1883. By 1910, just $505 remained unredeemed. This piece was part of the Martin and Gale holdings, and is the only example known on this short lived bank. It is an attractive piece which grades **Fine** overall, but there is a repair in the center, where a small hole previously existed. Nevertheless, there are no others, so even the most discriminating of collectors has no choice here. Buy this note, or go without, likely forever. **(7,500-12,500)**

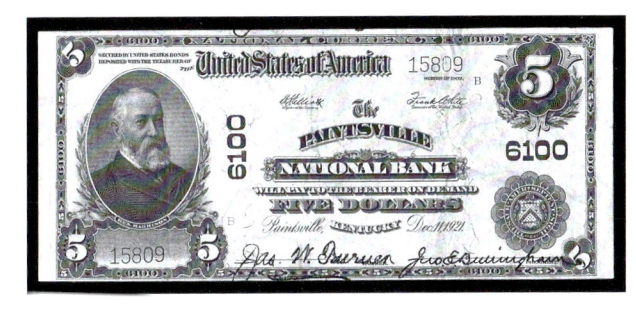

14793 **Paintsville, KY** - $5 1902 Plain Back Fr. 608 **The Paintsville NB** Ch. # 6100
This bank is the first of the so-called Fourth Charter banks with its extension date of December 11, 1921. Printed signatures are dark on this $5 with original paper surfaces. **Very Fine. (500-700)**

14794 **Pikeville, KY** - $10 1902 Plain Back Fr. 624 **The First NB** Ch. # 6622
The paper is perfectly original and the signatures of John M. Yost and George W. Green are bold. **Fine-Very Fine.** (600-800)

14795 **Pikeville, KY** - $20 1929 Ty. 2 **The First NB** Ch. # 6622
This bank title embossed $20 has the folds of an **Extremely Fine** note, but it has toned a shade from wallet confinement. Type 1s outnumber Type 2s on this bank by almost seven to one. (250-350)

14796 **Princeton, KY** - $20 1902 Plain Back Fr. 650 **The First NB** Ch. # 3064
An attractive large size example with oversize red signatures. **Very Fine.** (500-700)

14797 **Richmond, KY** - $10 1882 Brown Back Fr. 484 **The Madison NB** Ch. # (S)1790
The first of three titles used by this bank, which took its name from the county in which it operated. **Fine,** with good color and body for the grade. (1,250-1,750)

14798 **Richmond, KY** - $20 1882 Brown Back Fr. 498 **The Richmond NB** Ch. # 4430
This discovery piece raises the population of survivors from this bank to three. Only $10 and $20 Brown Backs were issued by this institution before it was liquidated in 1897. The paper exhibited here is solid for the grade thus the design is still bold. **CGA Very Good-Fine 10.** (3,500-5,500)

14799 **Somerset, KY** - $20 1882 Brown Back Fr. 504 **The Farmers NB** Ch. # (S)5881
This is one of only two Brown Backs known from this bank, with the other, a $10, not listed by serial number in the Kelly census. **Fine-Very Fine,** with a small paper clip stain. (1,500-2,000)

14800 **Somerset, KY** - $10 1902 Plain Back Fr. 633 **The Farmers NB** Ch. # 5881
Track and Price currently records 18 large size notes. Only four, including this **PCGS Very Fine 25** are of the $10 Plain Back persuasion. The stamped officers' signatures remain quite strong and enhance the overall appearance of this Pulaski County issue. (600-800)

LOUISIANA

14801 Stanford, KY - $10 1902 Plain Back Fr. 624 **The First NB** Ch. # 2788
Last appearing in our 2006 Central Sale sale, and described, "Despite a decent size issue that spanned several decades, large notes from this Stanford bank are in short supply, with nothing listed in the census before 1902 Plain Backs. Even there, the selection is limited, as only four pieces are listed, including this note. This attractive example is as nice as any. **Very Fine.** (1,100-1,400)

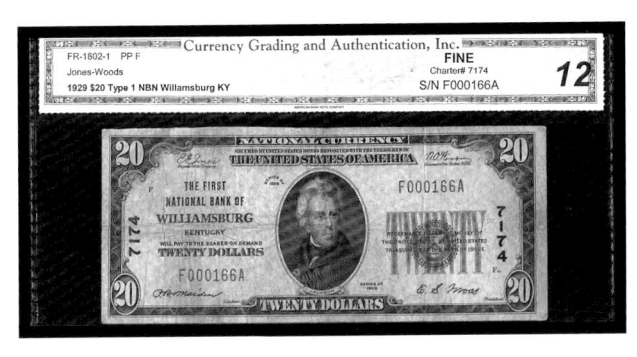

14802 Williamsburg, KY - $20 1929 Ty. 1 **The First NB** Ch. # 7174
Only five small notes are recorded for this Whitley County institution. **CGA Fine 12.** (600-800)

14803 Wilmore, KY - $5 1902 Plain Back Fr. 601 **The First NB** Ch. # 9880
This comes from a very rare bank which was the sole issuer in this tiny Jessamine County community. Just five notes make up the entire census in large size from here, with this the nicest of the group. **Very Fine+,** with vivid purple signatures. (2,000-3,000)

14804 Abbeville, LA - $10 1902 Plain Back Fr. 633 **The First NB** Ch. # 5807
This recently surfaced $10 can be added to the miniscule census of only 7 large known on this solo national bank in Vermilion Parish. There is some staining on the face and back particularly near and on the right charter number. The signatures are a bit hazy, yet J.G. La Blanc and J.N. Greene can be deciphered. **Very Good.** (1,500-2,500)

14805 Hammond, LA - $5 1902 Plain Back Fr. 608 **The Citizens NB** Ch. # 11977
A very tough bank in large size, with just eight such examples listed in the census. **About Fine.** (750-1,250)

14806 Jeanerette, LA - $10 1902 Plain Back Fr. 624 **The First NB** Ch. # 7768
This newly discovered $10 raises the census to eleven for this one national bank town in Iberia Parish. The signatures have faded and there is some scattered staining on the face and back. We have sold two notes on this bank in the past, the last one being in 2000. **Very Good.** (1,000-1,200)

14807 **Minden, LA** - $10 1902 Plain Back Fr. 631 **The First NB** Ch. # (S)10544
An excessively rare note from the only bank to issue in Webster Parish. The census shows four notes extant from here, with only two identified by serial number. The last offering from here came back in 1998, with few appearances before that date. Well circulated but intact **Very Good,** with no problems save honest circulation. (2,000-4,000)

14808 **New Orleans, LA** - $5 1882 Brown Back Fr. 469 **The Louisiana NB** Ch. # (S)1626
One of only thirty five $5 Brown Backs listed in the latest Kelly compilation from all issuing banks in Louisiana combined, and the nicest of the seven listed examples from this bank. We sold this piece back in May of 2004, when it realized $2070. Expect a similar if not a bit higher realization today. Nice **Very Fine,** with bold signatures. (1,800-2,200)

14809 **New Orleans, LA** - $5 1882 Date Back Fr. 537 **The Commercial NB** Ch. # (S)5649
This attractive Date Back has sufficient remaining color and solid margins. **Very Fine.** (1,250-1,500)

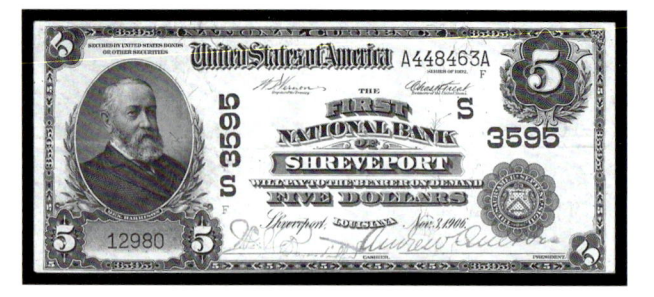

14810 **Shreveport, LA** - $5 1902 Date Back Fr. 592 **The First NB** Ch. # (S)3595
While this hardly ranks as a rare bank, this vividly colored Date Back is one of the very nicest large examples we've seen from here. Bright **Very Fine++,** with bold blue signatures. (500-700)

MAINE

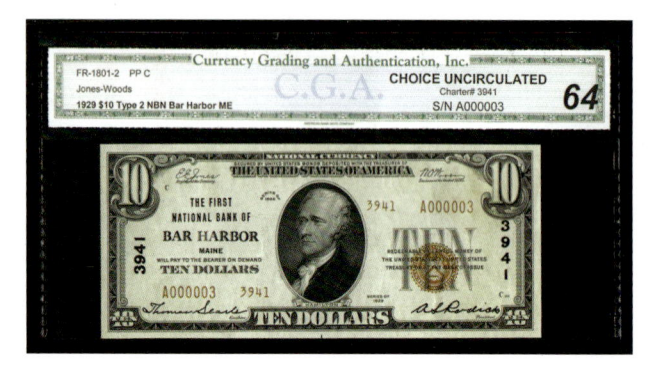

14811 **Bar Harbor, ME** - $10 1929 Ty. 2 **The First NB** Ch. # 3941
All but one of the small size notes known on this one bank town were once part of the first two sheets printed. This piece boasts serial number 3 and is complemented by wholly original paper quality and bold embossing. **CGA Choice Uncirculated 64.** (2,500-3,500)

14812 **Bath, ME** - $5 1902 Plain Back Fr. 598 **The Bath NB** Ch. # 494
Printed signatures of F.D. Hill and Wm. D. Sewall grace this $5. **Fine.** (300-400)

14813 **Lewiston, ME** - $5 1902 Plain Back Fr. 605 **The Manufacturers NB** Ch. # (N)2260
This $5 exhibits clean surfaces with darkly printed signatures. **Fine-Very Fine** (300-500)

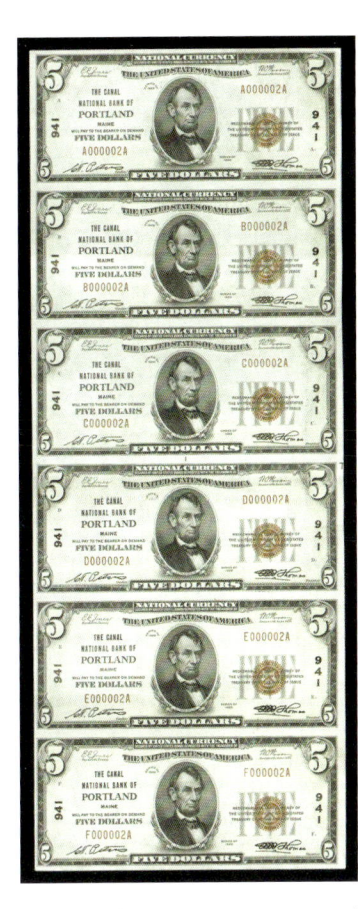

14814 **Portland, ME** - $5 1929 Ty. 1 **The Canal NB** Ch. # 941 Uncut Sheet
This is an all serial number 2 sheet that shows lateral bends in the second, fourth, and fifth notes. **Choice Crisp Uncirculated.** (4,000-6,000)

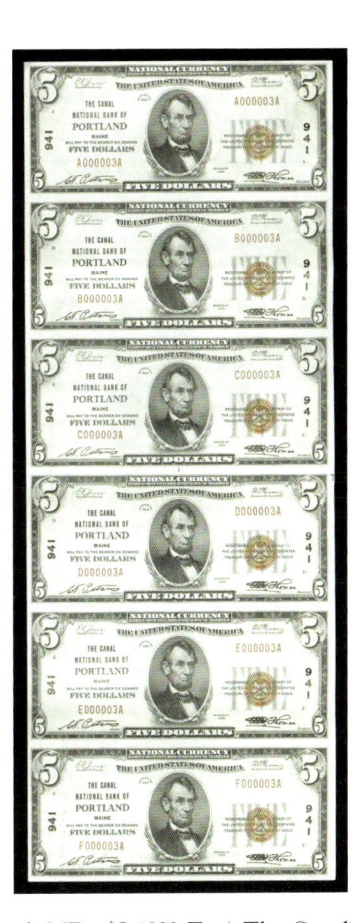

14815 **Portland, ME** - $5 1929 Ty. 1 **The Canal NB** Ch. # 941 Uncut Sheet
This lot is similar to the previous uncut sheet on this bank in every regard except serial number. In this case, this is an all serial number 3 sheet. **Choice Crisp Uncirculated.** (4,000-6,000)

14816 **Waterville, ME** - $1 1875 Fr. 383 **The Merchants NB** Ch. # 2306
An extremely rare Maine bank which issued Series 1875 and Brown Backs only before calling it quits in 1905. The entire census from here consists of five notes, with only two offerings of any kind from here since 1956. This Ace is new to the numismatic marketplace, and, even with a substantial restoration at the bottom left end, is a decent looking note with good color and body for the grade. **Very Good+++.** (2,000-4,000)

MARYLAND

14817 Baltimore, MD - $100 1929 Ty. 1 **The Western NB** Ch. # 1325
The paper is solid and a survey of the census reveals no uncirculated small size $100s are known. **Very Fine.** (400-500)

14818 Baltimore, MD - $100 1929 Ty. 1 **The First NB** Ch. # 1413
A total of four small size $100's are reported from this harbor city. The paper here still has a lot of life. **Very Fine.** (400-500)

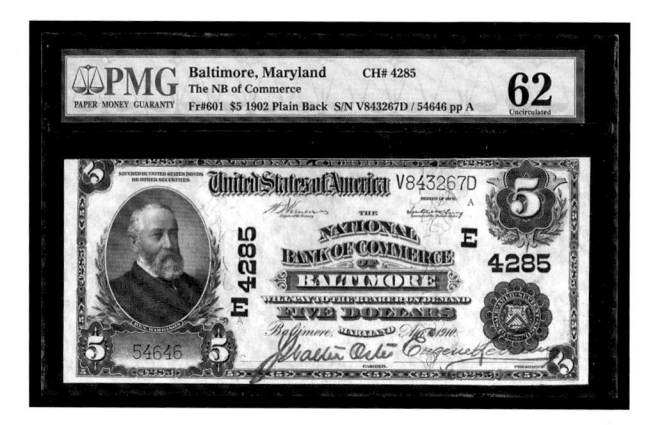

14819 Baltimore, MD - $5 1902 Plain Back Fr. 601 **The NB of Commerce** Ch. # (E)4285
As is so often the case from here a tightly trimmed top margin has limited the grade of this piece. Graded **PMG Uncirculated 62,** it has bright white surfaces and deeply stamped signatures. (600-800)

14820 Brunswick, MD - $10 1929 Ty. 1 **Peoples NB** Ch. # 8244
A beautiful small example. **Gem Crisp Uncirculated,** easily the finest non-number 1 Series 1929 example known from this bank. (900-1,200)

14821 Brunswick, MD - $20 1929 Ty. 1 **Peoples NB** Ch. # 8244
This issue faces up like a full EF and boasts low serial number A000080A. **Very Fine.** (500-600)

14822 Cumberland, MD - $10 1882 Date Back Fr. 545 **The Citizens NB** Ch. # (E)5332
A just plain rare bank which issued Second Charter notes only before liquidating at the expiration of its charter in 1920. The census shows just four specimens extant, one Brown Back and three Value Backs, with this the first Date Back of any denomination reported. **Very Good-Fine.** (1,500-2,500)

MASSACHUSETTS

Newly Discovered Hampstead Date Back

14823 Hampstead, MD - $20 1902 Date Back Fr. 645 **The First NB** Ch. # (E)9755
An excessively rare large size note from this Carroll County bank. Just two large notes are known from Hampstead, with one having been sold by us as part of the Armand Shank, Jr. collection back in May of 1998 (it graded Fine and realized $4620) and the second having been auctioned in February of 2000 (it graded Extremely Fine and realized $5225.) This is the only Date Back known from here, and, fortunately for collectors, it is a peach of a note, with even circulation, good color for the grade, and clear pen signatures. Nice **Fine+.** (4,000-6,000)

14824 Hancock, MD - $5 1902 Plain Back Fr. 599 **The First NB** Ch. # 7859
An extremely rare western Maryland note, with the census showing just four large examples, with this one of those four. All have been closely held for many years, with our records showing only Series 1929 offerings from here at public sale for at least the past decade. **Fine,** with the bottom margin trimmed very slightly into the design on the right end. (2,250-2,750)

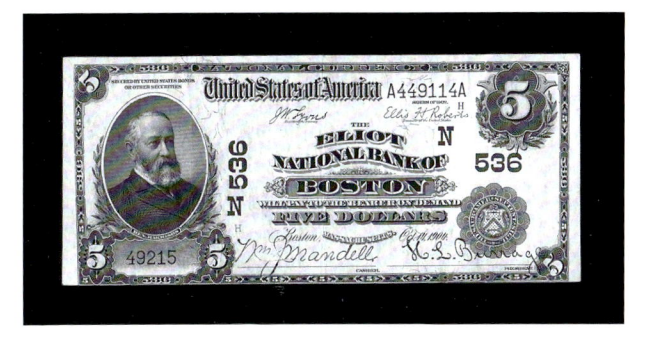

14825 Boston, MA - $5 1902 Date Back Fr. 590 **The Eliot NB** Ch. # (N)536
The last type issued by this scarcer Boston bank, which went out in 1912. Pleasing **Very Fine-Extremely Fine** with clear signatures, one of the higher grade pieces known from here. (500-700)

14826 Boston, MA - $5 1875 Fr. 401 **The National Webster Bank** Ch. # 1527
A very rare note with this title, the first used here. The census shows just four specimens extant with this nomenclature, with just one 1875 $5 listed, with a grade of "Good." This newly discovered piece is considerably nicer, with good color, body, and plenty of eye appeal for the grade. **About Fine.** (2,250-3,250)

14827 Boston, MA - $5 1902 Plain Back Fr. 609 **Engineers NB** Ch. # 12540
The second title used by this union organized bank, one of several chartered by railway labor organizations during the 1920s. Most failed before the end of the decade due to inexperienced management, and the onset of the Depression served to kill off those few banks that remained. This is one of the nicer large examples we've encountered. **Extremely Fine,** with a tiny bit of writing in the reverse margin. (700-900)

14828 Fall River, MA - $10 1902 Plain Back Fr. 624 **The Massasoit-Pocasset NB** Ch. # (N)6821
This bright **Very Good** example exhibits the usual circulation with a touch of soiling more prevalent on the back. **(600-900)**

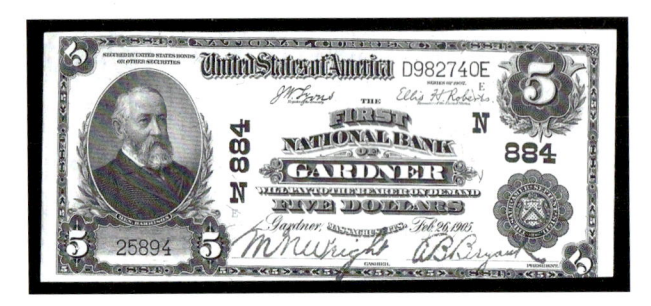

14829 Gardner, MA - $5 1902 Plain Back Fr. 598 **The First NB** Ch. # (N)884
A slight sloppy cut does not detract from this solid **Extremely Fine-About Uncirculated** with strong stamped signatures and plenty of eye appeal. We sold an XF from here at FUN 2006 for $586.50. We should expect more of the same this evening. **(500-700)**

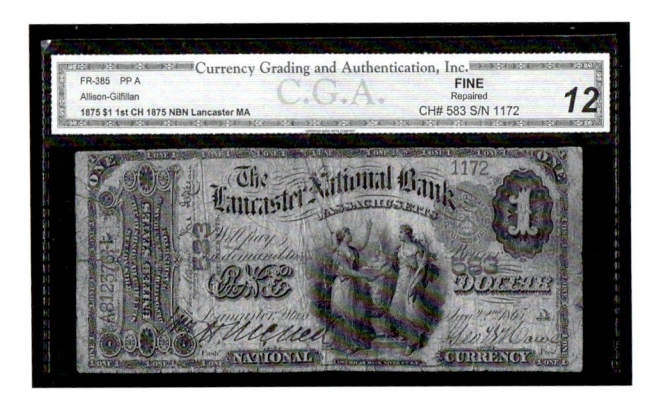

14830 Lancaster, MA - $1 1875 Fr. 385 **The Lancaster NB** Ch. # 583
A **CGA Fine 12** with the holder noting "Repaired." This very scarce bank issued First Charter notes only before closing in 1886 with only seven examples enumerated in the Kelly census. **(600-900)**

14831 Milford, MA - $10 1902 Plain Back Fr. 624 **The Milford NB** Ch. # (N)866
The paper retains much crispness and the stamped signatures are still dark on this newcomer to the census. Pleasing **Very Fine-Extremely Fine**. **(300-500)**

Serial Number 1 Nantucket Brown Back

14832 Nantucket, MA - $5 1882 Brown Back Fr. 467 **The Pacific NB** Ch. # 714
A gorgeous serial number 1 $5 Brown Back which has been encapsulated by PCGS and assigned the grade of **Choice About New 58PPQ**. It has the distinction of being the only serial number 1 example of any type which we have had the privilege of handling from this avidly collected location, and will serve as the centerpiece of any collection of notes from the Cape and Islands. **(10,000-14,000)**

14833 Nantucket, MA - $5 1882 Brown Back Fr. 467 **The Pacific NB** Ch. # 714
An attractive $5 Brown Back from this sought after bank which has been graded as **Extremely Fine 40PPQ** by PCGS. **(2,000-3,000)**

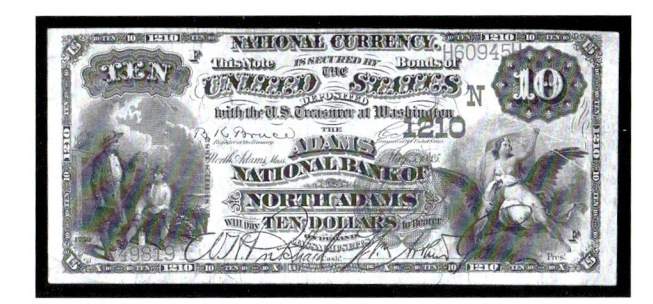

14834 **North Adams, MA** - $10 1882 Brown Back Fr. 481 **The Adams NB** Ch. # (N)1210
A nice example which is the earliest type known from this western Massachusetts institution. It bears the very scarce first title adopted by this bank, which was used only until 1905. Bright **Very Fine.**
From The Collection of Greg Southward (1,500-2,500)

14835 **Northampton, MA** - $5 Original Fr. 394 **The First NB** Ch. # 383
There is a small repair at the bottom of this First Charter five. **Very Good+.** (900-1,200)

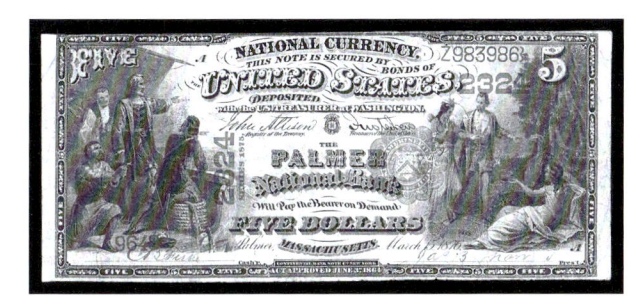

14836 **Palmer, MA** - $5 1875 Fr. 401 **The Palmer NB** Ch. # 2324
This $5 1875 is one of only a handful of First Charters of all denominations known from this institution, which was Palmer's only issuing bank. **Fine-Very Fine.** (1,750-2,250)

14837 **Springfield, MA** - $5 1882 Brown Back Fr. 466 **The First NB** Ch. # 14
A nice Brown Back from this scarcer low charter bank. **Fine**, with just a tiny bit of bleed through onto the back from the seal and charter number. (1,500-2,000)

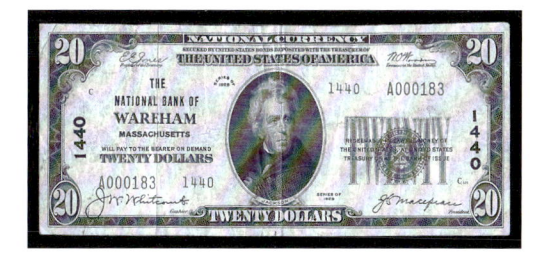

14838 **Wareham, MA** - $20 1929 Ty. 2 **The NB of Wareham** Ch. # 1440
No Type 2 notes were listed in the current Kelly census until this piece recently turned up. **Fine-Very Fine.** (400-600)

14839 **Webster, MA** - $5 1902 Plain Back Fr. 606 **The Webster NB** Ch. # 11236
Although the bottom margin is a bit tight on this **Very Fine** example, the officers' signatures are dark and legible. This institution was chartered in 1918 and failed in 1933, issuing only the $5 denomination in Plain Backs and 1929 Type 1 and 2. Just $2,470 of its large circulation remained available to the public when it closed. (350-450)

MICHIGAN

14840 Blissfield, MI - $5 1929 Ty. 1 **The First NB** Ch. # 11813
Fives were the sole denomination issued by this bank, which is quite common in large size and very scarce in small, not surprising as this institution closed its doors in July of 1931. Only five series 1929 examples are known, with this evenly circulated **Fine** specimen a new addition to that count. (1,000-1,500)

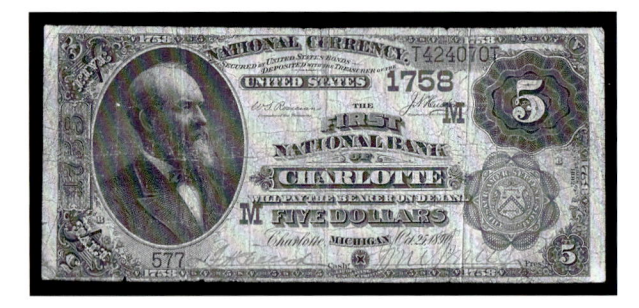

14841 Charlotte, MI - $5 1882 Brown Back Fr. 471 **The First NB** Ch. # (M)1758
This is the only $5 Brown Back reported to date from this scarce Eaton County bank. Pen signed **About Fine**. (1,250-1,500)

14842 Charlotte, MI - $50 1929 Ty. 1 **The First NB** Ch. # 1758
This Eaton County bank was the only issuer from Charlotte to issue this type and denomination. **Fine**. (650-850)

14843 Detroit, MI - $50 1929 Ty. 1 **Guardian NB of Commerce** Ch. # 8703
A beautifully margined example which is perfect for type. It's been slabbed by PMG, who have assigned this piece the grade of **Gem Uncirculated 66 EPQ**, which it certainly appears to have well deserved. (1,000-1,500)

14844 Detroit, MI - $100 1929 Ty. 1 **Guardian NB of Commerce** Ch. # 8703
All the 1929 emissions from here were printed bearing this, the second title under which the bank issued. It printed just 433 sheets of the Type 1 $100. A bit of charter number fading is seen with some ink at right. **Extremely Fine-About Uncirculated**. (400-600)

Serial Number 1 Large Size Gladstone

14845 Gladstone, MI - $5 1902 Plain Back Fr. 606 **The First NB** Ch. # (M)10886
A new discovery, with this example the only serial number 1 example, large or small, reported to date from this Upper Peninsula issuer. Pen signed **Very Fine** or a bit better, with a split at one of the folds. (3,000-5,000)

14846 Gladstone, MI - $5 1902 Plain Back Fr. 606 **The First NB** Ch. # 10886
An evenly circulated example with a higher serial number. **Fine-Very Fine**. (500-800)

Unique Serial Number 1 14000 Charter Michigan Uncut Sheet

14847 Gladstone, MI - $5 1929 Ty. 2 First NB Ch. # 14111
Uncut Sheet
A newly discovered serial number 1 uncut sheet from this hitherto extremely rare 14000 charter bank. Before this sheet turned up, the census from here totalled just three notes, with one of that number selling in a recent auction for $4025. There are folds either in or between each note here, and the bottom note has a few storage folds, but most of the other notes are uncirculated. We will be conservative here and label this exciting 14000 charter sheet as **About Uncirculated,** and assign a conservative estimate of... **(12,000-16,000)**

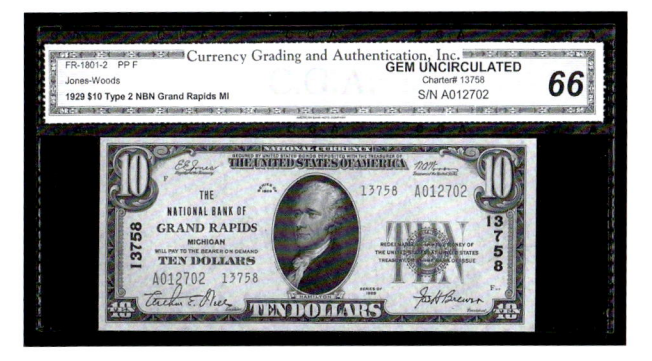

14848 Grand Rapids, MI - $10 1929 Ty. 2 The NB of Grand Rapids Ch. # 13758
A fully embossed and crackling fresh beauty graded **Gem Uncirculated 66** by CGA.. **(400-600)**

14849 Greenville, MI - $10 1902 Plain Back Fr. 633 The Greenville NB Ch. # 11843
A very scarce bank in large size, with the census standing at just six such examples, including this piece. CGA has graded this note as **Very Good-Fine 10. (800-1,200)**

Rare Lawton $10

14850 Lawton, MI - $10 1929 Ty. 1 The First NB Ch. # 12084
A center fold is found on this $10 that has "great embossing" according to PMG and this cataloguer. There is only six small in the census for this bank and that does not include this recent find. In fact, of the notes listed in the census with a grade, this is the nicest by a long shot. **PMG About Uncirculated 55. (900-1,200)**

MINNESOTA

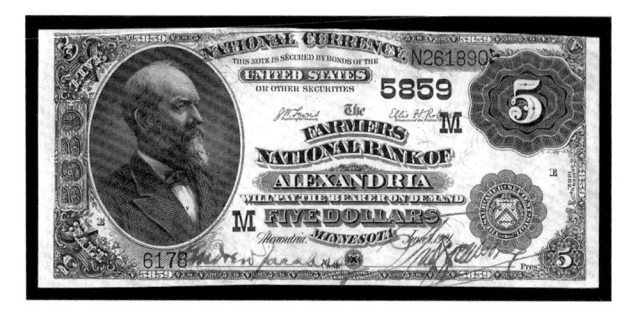

14851 Alexandria, MN - $5 1882 Date Back Fr. 537 **The Farmers NB** Ch. # (M)5859
A lovely example with the brightness and appeal of a note fresh from the press. **Choice Crisp Uncirculated,** kept from the gem class only because of the trimmed-in top right margin.
From The Rolling Plains Collection (1,750-2,250)

14852 Carlton, MN - $10 1929 Ty. 1 **The First NB** Ch. # 6973
Ten small are known on this Carlton County bank. The paper is bright and the folds not too distracting. A couple of pinholes are noticed at upper left. **Very Fine-Extremely Fine.** (750-1,000)

14853 Cloquet, MN - $10 1929 Ty. 2 **The First NB** Ch. # 5405
An attractive and bright white **About Uncirculated** specimen. The last issue in this grade that we handled was a few serial numbers away and realized $575 about a year ago. (400-500)

14854 Duluth, MN - $100 1929 Ty. 1 **The Northern NB** Ch. # 9327
This institution's issuance of small size only included $50s and $100s. This piece has no folds of significance. **PCGS Very Fine 30.** (400-500)

14855 Duluth, MN - $100 1929 Ty. 1 **The Northern NB** Ch. # 9327
An attractive piece with solid paper save for a couple of pinholes. **Very Fine.** (400-500)

14856 Hendricks, MN - $20 1929 Ty. 1 **The Farmers NB** Ch. # 9457
A very scarce note with no offerings of any kind from this bank in over five years. **About Fine,** with the top margin close at the right. (650-950)

14857 **Hibbing, MN** - $5 1902 Plain Back Fr. 609 **The Hibbing NB** Ch. # 12568
A very scarce bank which was in business for less than four years before bowing out in 1928. Just three notes are listed in the census from here, with the Gengerke data showing exactly the same number of public offerings during the past six decades. Pen signed **Fine. (2,750-3,750)**

14858 **Nashwauk, MN** - $20 1902 Plain Back Fr. 657 **The First NB** Ch. # 10736
There were only two issuers in this community and both are quite scarce. This was the first local financial institution to be awarded its Federal charter. As of 1935, only $1,300 of its large emissions were still unredeemed. The latest published Kelly census lists a population of only four large survivors, so plan on some competition from other Minnesota collectors tonight. **Very Fine,** with the signatures still legible and margins all around. **(1,750-2,500)**

14859 **Pine City, MN** - $10 1902 Plain Back Fr. 633 **The First NB** Ch. # (M)11581
One of the very nicest of the dozen large notes reported from this institution, the sole issuer in this rural Pine County hamlet. Pen signed **Very Fine. (900-1,200)**

14860 **Rochester, MN** - $20 1902 Plain Back Fr. 655 **The Union NB** Ch. # 2088
From our 2006 Central States sale, where we noted "Only two banks in the state of Minnesota issued notes with the scarce Napier-Thompson Treasury signature combination. This note also carries dark signatures of the cashier and vice president." **Fine. (400-600)**

14861 **Welcome, MN** - $10 1902 Plain Back Fr. 624 **The Welcome NB** Ch. # 6331
A nice grade example from this not terribly common bank. Pen signed **Very Fine,** an always sought after note bearing an interesting town name. **(800-1,000)**

MISSISSIPPI

14862 Aberdeen, MS - $10 1929 Ty. 1 **The First NB** Ch. # 3656
This **Fine+** note comes from a state with far fewer notes to go around than there are collectors seeking them. Outside of a few banks, almost all Mississippi notes, including those from this institution, are quite difficult to acquire. **(400-600)**

14863 Brookhaven, MS - $20 1902 Plain Back Fr. 657 **The First NB** Ch. # (S)10494
A pleasing large size note from the only bank to issue in Lincoln County. **Fine. (1,000-1,400)**

14864 Gulfport, MS - $10 1902 Plain Back Fr. 634 **The First NB** Ch. # 6188
This is a perfectly original **Very Fine** with bright, unadulterated paper. Two different plate dates were used for Gulfport Series 1902 Nationals. The bank was chartered in 1902 and the charter was renewed in 1922, explaining the two dates. **(400-500)**

14865 Laurel, MS - $10 1929 Ty. 2 **The First NB** Ch. # 6681
This note was 20 away from the end of the run. Pleasing colors and solid margins dominate the surfaces of this note. **Fine-Very Fine. (300-400)**

14866 Laurel, MS - $5 1902 Plain Back Fr. 607 **The Commercial NB & TC** Ch. # (S)11898
This was the only national bank in Mississippi to issue notes entirely under a trust designation. The president's signature has faded, while the cashier's partially remains. This is one of 14 Large in the census. **Very Good-Fine. (250-500)**

14867 Meridian, MS - $20 1902 Plain Back Fr. 650 **The Citizens NB** Ch. # (S)7266
We can't find a record of a $20 1902 Plain Back on this charter number being sold at auction. This example has dark stamped signatures of C.L. Hughes and Paney Brown. In fact the signatures are so dark that a large amount of black ink bleeds through on to the back. This community was originally named by settlers in the 1850s who mistakenly thought the word "meridian" meant "junction." **Fine. (400-600)**

MISSOURI

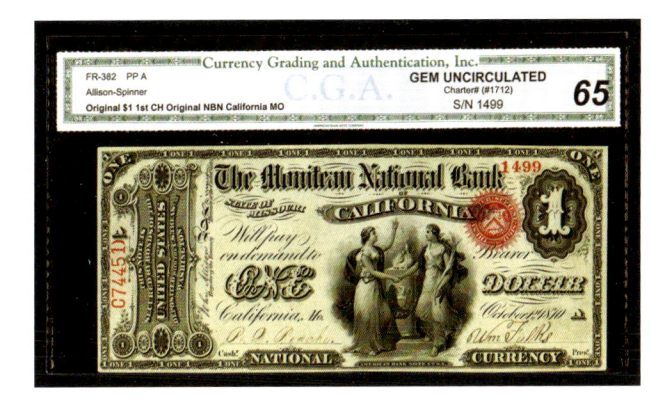

14868 California, MO - $1 Original Fr. 382 **The Moniteau NB** Ch. # 1712
A bright and well printed example of this classic hoard note. It has been encapsulated by CGA, which has assigned a grade of **Gem Uncirculated 65**. (3,500-4,500)

14869 Fairview, MO - $10 1902 Plain Back Fr. 626 **The First NB** Ch. # 8916
A truly rare note from the only bank to issue in this small Newton County location. This is one of only four large notes extant from here, and, luckily for collectors, it is a most attractive piece, with brightly colored inks contrasting nicely with its bold two color pen signatures. We've seen no large notes from here for sale for many years, and it would not surprise us at all if this **Very Fine** example easily bested our likely conservative estimate of... (5,000-7,000)

14870 Joplin, MO - $50 1929 Ty. 1 **The Joplin NB & TC** Ch. # 4425
An attractive $50 with a mere three folds. **Extremely Fine**. (625-725)

First Offering in Seventeen Years

14871 Kansas City, MO - $20 1902 Date Back Fr. 644 **The Southwest NB** Ch. # (M)9311
An excessively rare note from a bank which issued 1902 Date Backs only during its short three years in existence. Just three examples have been reported to date, with the last offering of any kind from here coming back in our first sale in November of 1990. This attractive pen signed specimen is new to the census, and offers collectors an opportunity they have not had for almost seventeen years. Sharp **Fine-Very Fine**. (1,750-2,750)

Serial Number 1 Kansas City Rarity

14872 Kansas City, MO - $5 1902 Plain Back Fr. 606 **The Midwest NB** Ch. # (M)10892
A lovely serial number 1 note from a rare bank which lasted only four years before bowing out in 1920. The Kelly census shows just five notes extant from this institution, with this example the only number 1 and the only note from here grading higher than Fine. Bright **Extremely Fine**. (5,000-7,000)

14873 Maryville, MO - $10 1902 Plain Back Fr. 624 **The First NB** Ch. # 3268
The last time we auctioned off a large note on this bank was during our first auction in November 1990. The signatures have faded on this **Fine** example. (400-600)

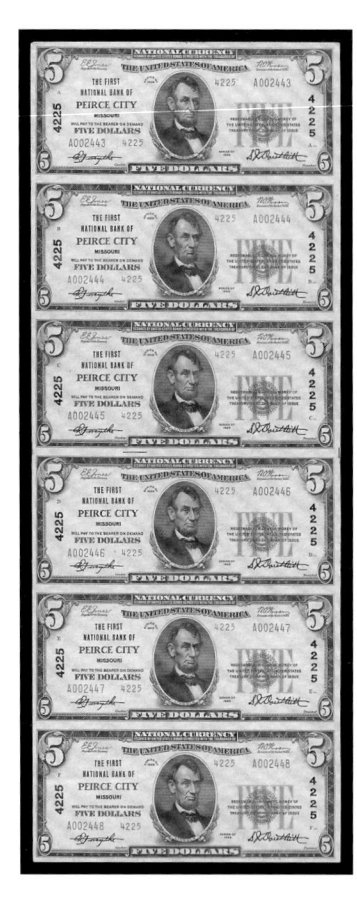

14874 **Peirce City, MO** - $5 1929 Ty. 2 **The Peirce City NB** Ch. # 4225 Uncut Sheet
Three small areas of tape are found on this **Choice Crisp Uncirculated** sheet. The bottom note has a light lateral bend. (4,000-6,000)

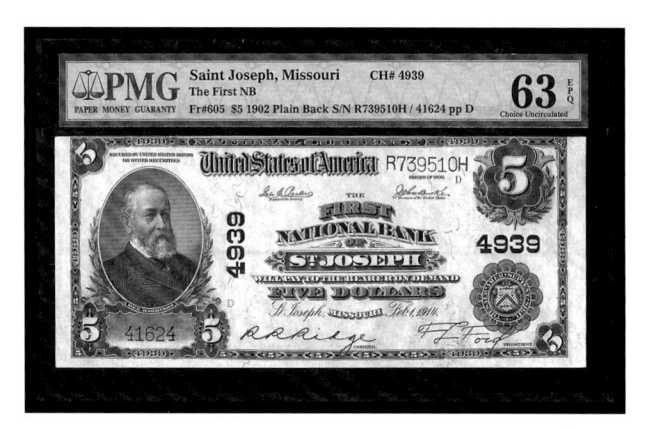

14875 **Saint Joseph, MO** - $5 1902 Plain Back Fr. 605 **The First NB** Ch. # 4939
BEP engraved signatures adorn this $5 that received its grade due to its top margin at the frame line. Nonetheless, a handsome note. **PMG Choice Uncirculated 63 EPQ.** (750-950)

D.N. Morgan Courtesy Autographed National

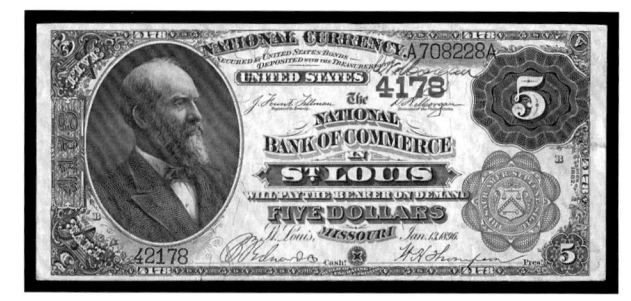

14876 **Saint Louis, MO** - $5 1882 Brown Back Fr. 474 **The NB of Commerce** Ch. # 4178
An intriguing note with a long and distinguished pedigree which can be traced back to the Grinnell sale. This note bears the courtesy autograph of D.N. Morgan over his printed signature as Treasurer of the United States. While Morgan was a prolific author of courtesy autographs, examples on Nationals are actually quite scarce, with this the first we've handled in many years. **Extremely Fine.** (1,200-1,800)

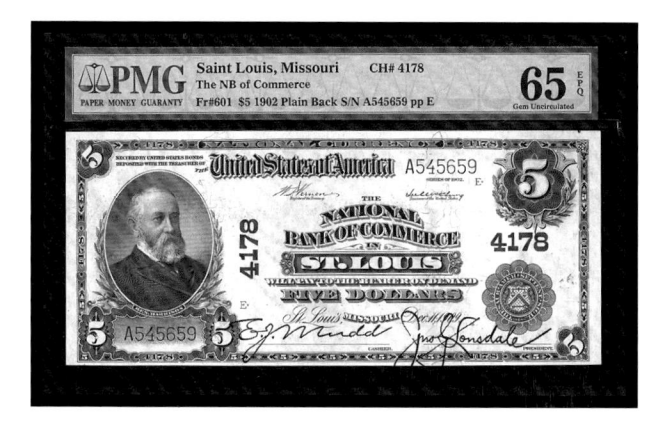

14877 **Saint Louis, MO** - $5 1902 Plain Back Fr. 601 **The NB of Commerce** Ch. # 4178
This bank issued many Third Charter Fives resulting in the needed use of a prefix letter A for its serial numbers near the end of the large note era. The plate letter is E5 on this A prefix note. **PMG Gem Uncirculated 65 EPQ** (800-1,200)

PCGS Superb Gem New 67PPQ $5 Brown Back

14878 Saint Louis, MO - $5 1882 Brown Back Fr. 477 **The State NB** Ch. # 5172
A simply spectacular $5 Brown Back with broad even margins all around and not a trace of a flaw. We saw this note before it was encapsulated by PCGS and fully concur with the grade it received, which is **Superb Gem New 67PPQ.** Notes of this quality will never be common, and prices for type Nationals are still inexpensive compared to just about all other large size type notes. **(5,500-7,500)**

14879 Saint Louis, MO - $5 1902 Plain Back Fr. 608 **The Security NB Savings & TC** Ch. # 12066
This is a considerably scarcer St. Louis bank in large size, with this fully margined example easily one of the nicest we know of from here. **Very Fine-Extremely Fine,** with the appearance and appeal of a note several grades higher. **(800-1,200)**

14880 Saint Louis, MO - $5 1929 Ty. 1 **The Security NB Savings & TC** Ch. # 12066
A perfectly printed and adequately margined issue. **PMG Gem Uncirculated 65 EPQ. (450-550)**

MONTANA

14881 Miles City, MT - $10 1902 Plain Back Fr. 632 **The Commercial NB** Ch. # (W)5015
A solid specimen that spent a bit of time in a wallet. Track & Price indicates there has been only one auction appearance of this issue since 2004. **(1,500-2,500)**

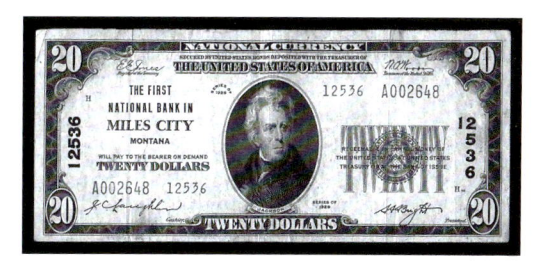

14882 Miles City, MT - $20 1929 Ty. 2 **The First NB** Ch. # 12536
A higher grade example from this bank which elected to issue Type 2 notes only in small size. Ten of this denomination are listed in Track & Price census data. **Fine-Very Fine. (650-850)**

NEBRASKA

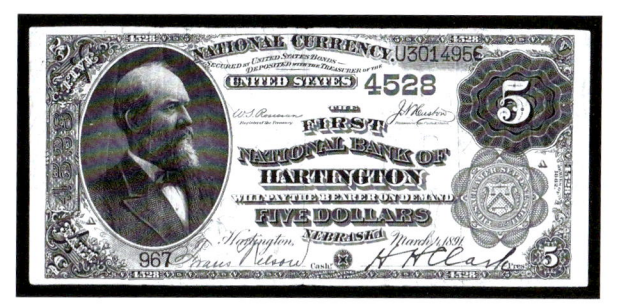

14883 Hartington, NE - $5 1882 Brown Back Fr. 471 **The First NB** Ch. # 4528
This is one of only two early notes known from this bank, both of which are $5 Brown Backs. One is a serial number 1 example which has been off the market since a 1992 auction appearance, and this is the other. Pen signed **Very Fine,** a premium piece worthy of a strong bid. **(1,750-2,250)**

14884 **Imperial, NE** - $20 1902 Plain Back Fr. 653 **The First NB** Ch. # 9762
A very scarce large size note from the only bank to issue in remote Chase County, hard by the Colorado border. This is a peach of a note with great signatures, color, and eye appeal. Sharp **Very Fine. (1,750-2,250)**

14885 **Lincoln, NE** - $10 1902 Plain Back Fr. 635 **City NB** Ch. # 13017
One of this capital city's scarcest and shortest lived banks, in operation for less than two years between December of 1926 and May of 1928. This is one of the nicest notes we've seen from here, although, with only nine notes listed in the Kelly census, there is relatively little to choose from. **PMG Uncirculated 62 EPQ,** a gem but for the cut into top margin, a feature more than offset by the most unusual signature of E.H. Mullvaney, who signs as "Vice-Pres. and Cashier." **(800-1,200)**

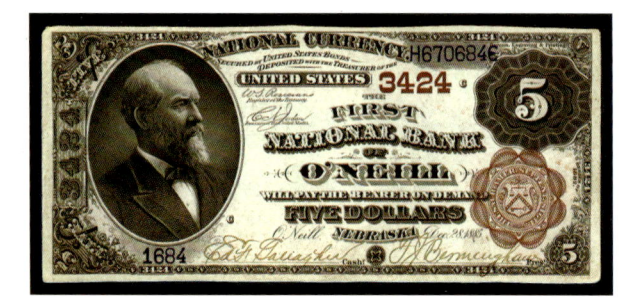

14886 **O'Neill, NE** - $5 1882 Brown Back Fr. 469 **The First NB** Ch. # 3424
A fresh and original $5 Brown Back with everything a collector could want, including vibrant colors, bold pen signatures, a neat layout, and great eye appeal. The corners are a bit rounded and there is a touch of handling, but this beautiful piece is certain to please its fortunate new owner. **Crisp Uncirculated. (3,000-4,000)**

14887 **Omaha, NE** - $100 1929 Ty. 1 **The Omaha NB** Ch. # 1633
A pleasingly original piece. **PCGS Very Fine 35. (250-350)**

14888 **Plainview, NE** - $10 1902 Plain Back Fr. 626 **The First NB** Ch. # (W)9504
Large notes only from this scarce bank, the sole issuer in this rural Pierce County community. This pen signed example is as nice as any listed in the census. **Very Fine. (800-1,200)**

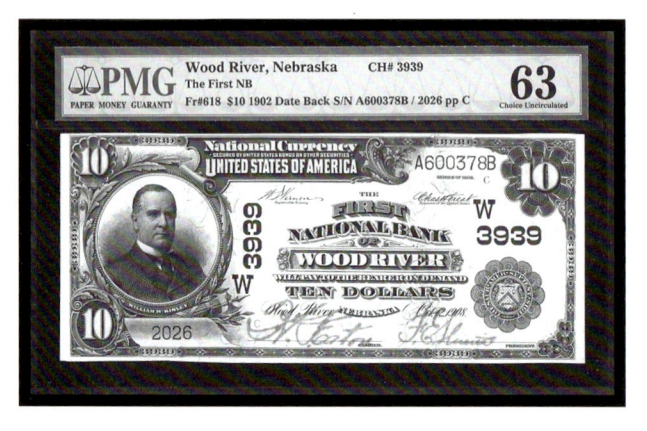

14889 **Wood River, NE** - $10 1902 Date Back Fr. 618 **The First NB** Ch. # (W)3939
This is a nicely margined **PMG Choice Uncirculated 63** that exhibits a few stains as mentioned on the holder. **(700-1,000)**

NEVADA

Nixon NB $10

14890 Reno, NV - $10 1902 Date Back Fr. 618 **The Nixon NB** Ch. # (P)8424

This note is on the much scarcer first title for this charter number. The signatures are darkly printed while the note exhibits even circulation, save for an approximate half inch split above the portrait. This private named bank was founded by George S. Nixon who was also president at the same time of the First National Bank of Winnemucca, Nevada. The Winnemucca bank was robbed of $33,000 by the outlaws Butch Cassidy and the Sundance Kid in September 1900. Newspaper accounts credit Nixon with shooting at the famous bank robbers. Nixon would also go on to become a United States Senator from Nevada. This lot is accompanied by photocopies of articles from *Bank Note Reporter* and *Coins Magazine* that mention George S. Nixon. **Fine.** (4,500-6,500)

NEW HAMPSHIRE

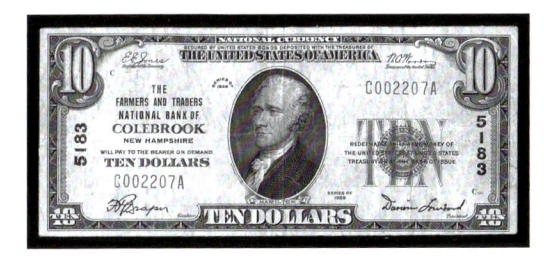

14891 Colebrook, NH - $10 1929 Ty. 1 **The Farmers & Traders NB** Ch. # 5183

This pleasing **Very Fine** example serves up solid margins with decent centering. (400-600)

14892 Nashua, NH - $1 Original Fr. 380 **The Indian Head NB** Ch. # 1310

This is one of just three Aces documented on this bank that carries one of the more intriguing bank titles in the state. The last time an Ace on this charter was offered was way back in 1997 and that was by us. The signatures have faded and there are a couple of small skin marks on the face. Still a nice note for the grade that sports a New England trim. **Very Good.** (1,500-2,000)

14893 Portsmouth, NH - $1 Original Fr. 380 **The First NB** Ch. # 19

The signatures of Kimball and Hackett stand out boldly on this perfectly original Ace. The paper is bright, the inks vivid and the margins are wide for the issue. Sharp **Very Fine+.** (4,500-5,500)

NEW JERSEY

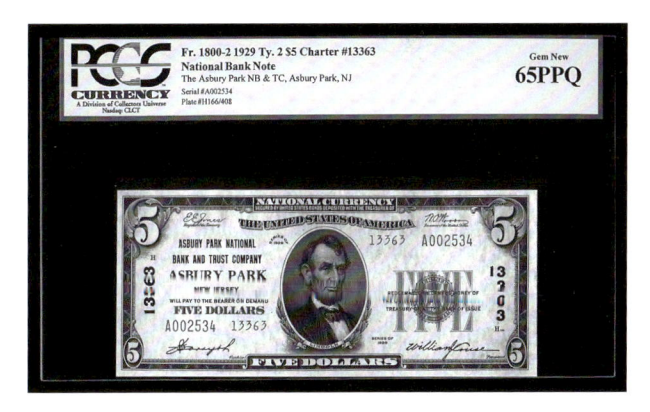

14894 Asbury Park, NJ - $5 1929 Ty. 2 **The Asbury Park NB & TC** Ch. # 13363

Simply as nice as examples from here are seen. Blast white surfaces exhibiting in your face embossing are framed by decent margins. **PCGS Gem New 65PPQ.** (800-1,200)

14895 Bogota, NJ - $5 1902 Plain Back Fr. 607 **The Bogota NB** Ch. # 11543
While small size notes from this Bergen County bank are plentiful, large examples from here are another story entirely, with the census listing just six such specimens. Pen signed **Fine,** with the bottom margin trimmed into the design at right. (1,000-1,400)

14896 Bordentown, NJ - $10 1929 Ty. 1 **The First NB** Ch. # 9268
A tougher note from the only bank to issue in this Burlington County community. **Fine.** (350-550)

14897 Bridgeton, NJ - $5 1902 Plain Back Fr. 600 **The Farmers & Merchants NB** Ch. # (E)9498
This piece last appeared in a CAA sale in 2001. With the popularity of notes from this state ever increasing expect this problem-free **Very Fine-Extremely Fine** piece to realize in the area of. . . (750-1,250)

14898 Burlington, NJ - $20 1929 Ty. 1 **The Mechanics NB** Ch. # 1222
A pleasing **Fine+++** example from this well collected southern New Jersey location. (250-350)

14899 Cape May, NJ - $20 1929 Ty. 1 **The Merchants NB** Ch. # 9285
A scarce and much in demand Series 1929 example from this avidly sought after resort community. Nice **Fine.** (1,750-2,750)

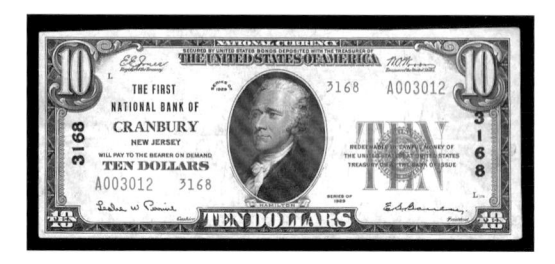

14900 Cranbury, NJ - $20 1929 Ty. 2 **The First NB** Ch. # 3168
Offerings of better grade notes like this bright, crisp example from here are few and far between. **Very Fine+.** (400-600)

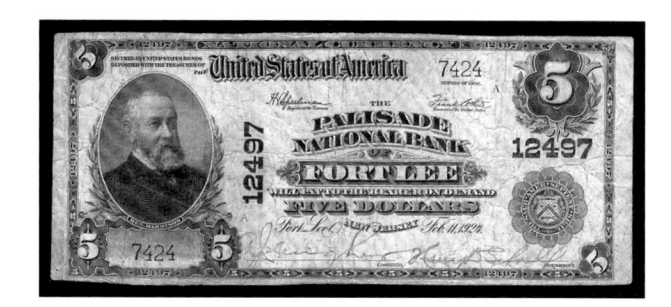

14901 Fort Lee, NJ - $5 1902 Plain Back Fr. 609 **The Palisade NB** Ch. # 12497
A very scarce Bergen County bank, with this the sole denomination issued from here. The census shows just five large notes extant from this bank, and a total of $780 in large notes outstanding from here in 1935. Evenly circulated **About Fine,** with a bit of light staining that barely detracts. (1,500-2,500)

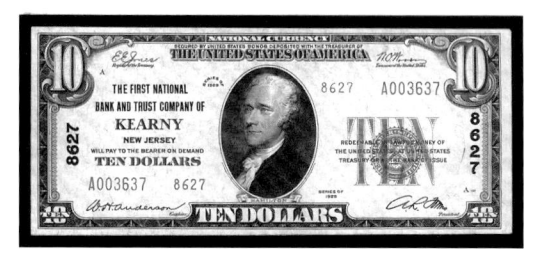

14902 Kearny, NJ - $20 1929 Ty. 2 **The First NB & TC** Ch. # 8627
This is a lightly circulated example from this second title institution. Well embossed surfaces give way to a center fold along with a light diagonal bend. **About Uncirculated.** (400-600)

14903 **Laurel Springs, NJ** - $5 1929 Ty. 2 **The Laurel Springs NB** Ch. # 12022
This thinly capitalized institution issued small size only and placed a meager $59,110 in circulation. The census documents only seven survivors from here. **Fine.** (1,250-1,750)

14904 **Little Ferry, NJ** - $5 1929 Ty. 2 **The Little Ferry NB** Ch. # 12378
A tiny notch missing in the top margin does little to detract from this otherwise **Fine** note. (1,250-1,750)

Excessively Rare Small Size Mays Landing Note

14905 **Mays Landing, NJ** - $20 1929 Ty. 1 **The First NB** Ch. # 8582
A great South Jersey note from one of the scarcest banks in the entire state. This was the sole issuer in this small Atlantic County community, with offerings from here of any kind few and far between. We note no appearance from this bank even in the landmark small size New Jersey collection sold at auction last November. Expect this attractive **Fine-Very Fine** example, which is on the want list of most every collector, to easily reach well into the range of... (6,000-9,000)

14906 **Merchantville, NJ** - $5 1929 Ty. 1 **Merchantville NB & TC** Ch. # 8323
Despite better than average census numbers, small size notes just do not turn up at auction as most are in tightly held collections. This piece spent much time in a wallet, but retains some crispness. **Fine.** (750-1,250)

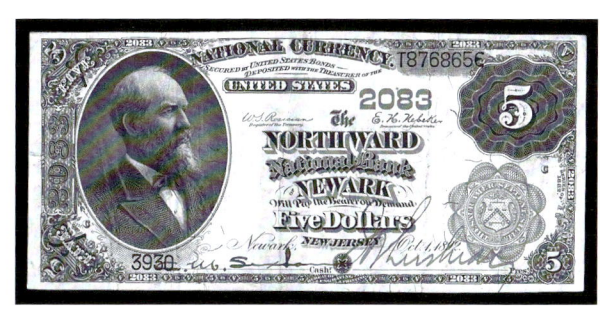

14907 **Newark, NJ** - $5 1882 Brown Back Fr. 472 **The North Ward NB** Ch. # 2083
An attractive $5 Brown Back from this seldom seen Newark issuer. Pen signed **Very Fine.** (1,200-1,400)

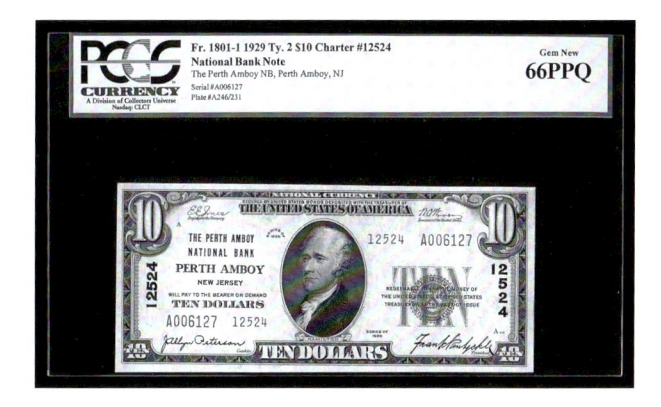

14908 **Perth Amboy, NJ** - $10 1929 Ty. 2 **The Perth Amboy NB** Ch. # 12524
Nice even margins are seen on this PCGS **Gem New 66PPQ** example that is very fresh. (500-700)

14909 **Prospect Park, NJ** - $10 1929 Ty. 1 **The Prospect Park NB** Ch. # 12861
This note would make a nice companion piece with the Type 2 listed below. **Fine.** (600-800)

14910 Prospect Park, NJ - $10 1929 Ty. 2 **The Prospect Park NB** Ch. # 12861
This is an average circulated example from this elusive Passaic County issuer. **Very Good-Fine.** (400-600)

14911 Town of Union, NJ - $10 1902 Plain Back Fr. 626 **The First NB** Ch. # (E)9544
A very scarce note bearing the first title used by this Hudson County bank, which began its large size issue located in the "Town of Union" before changing its issuing location to Union City in 1925. Just five notes are listed in the census bearing this nomenclature, with Track & Price showing only two appearances at public sale since 1996. Pleasing **Fine.** (800-1,200)

14912 Washington, NJ - $5 1902 Plain Back Fr. 598 **The First NB** Ch. # 860
A nicely circulated Third Charter $5 from this Warren County bank that operated from 1865 until the close of the National Banking period, some 70 years. **Fine.** (400-500)

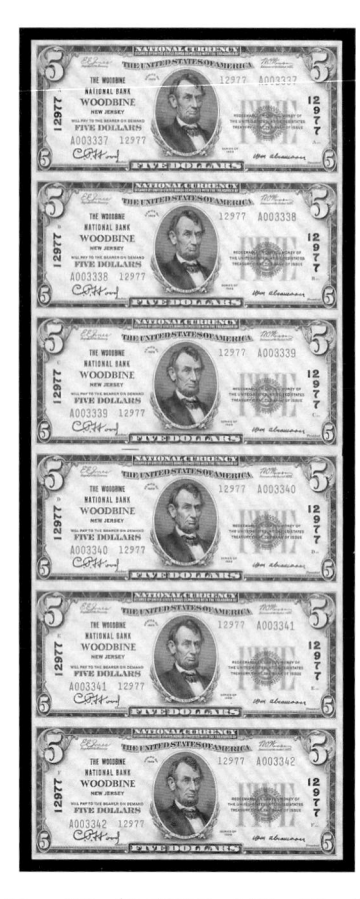

14913 Woodbine, NJ - $5 1929 Ty. 2 **The Woodbine NB** Ch. # 12977 Uncut Sheet
This is a nicely centered sheet that shows light handling on the second note. **Choice Crisp Uncirculated.** (4,000-6,000)

NEW MEXICO

14914 Raton, NM - $5 1902 Plain Back Fr. 602 **The First NB** Ch. # (W)4734
A solid circulated example from this Colfax County community in northern New Mexico. **PCGS Fine 15PPQ.** (1,000-1,500)

14915 Raton, NM - $10 1929 Ty. 1 **First NB** Ch. # 12924
This bank was chartered in April 1926 and elected to issue Series 1929 notes only. A couple of trivial edge tears are noticed. **Fine+.** (350-550)

14916 Raton, NM - $20 1929 Ty. 1 **First NB** Ch. # 12924
This is a nice Series 1929 example from one of the more common banks in this overall scarce western state. **Fine-Very Fine. (400-600)**

14917 Santa Fe, NM - $5 1929 Ty. 1 **The First NB** Ch. # 1750
This state capital note bears the autographed signature of Chas. J. Eckert over his printed signature as Cashier. **Very Fine,** ex-Jack Everson collection. **(600-900)**

NEW YORK

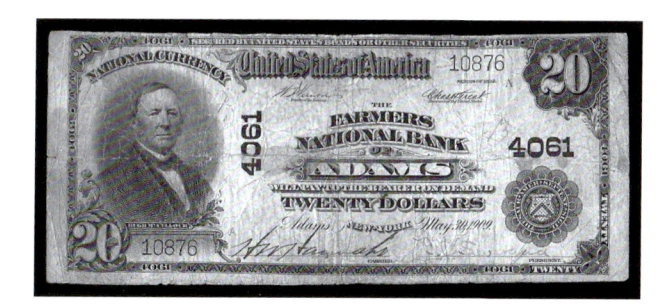

14918 Adams, NY - $20 1902 Plain Back Fr. 652 **The Farmers NB** Ch. # 4061
The edges are a little rough in a couple of places, though the paper is solid. **Very Good. (550-750)**

14919 Beacon, NY - $10 1902 Plain Back Fr. 631 **The Matteawan NB** # (E)4914
A pleasing example bearing the second title used by this bank, adopted when the towns of Matteawan and Fishkill Landing combined to form the city of Beacon in 1914. **Fine-Very Fine,** with clear signatures. **(600-900)**

14920 Bliss, NY - $10 1902 Plain Back Fr. 632 **The Bliss NB** Ch. # 10754
A very scarce large example from this one bank Wyoming County community. Our records show no offerings of any large notes from here for over five years, hardly a surprise considering the meager $690 outstanding from this issuer in 1935. This new to the census specimen is at least tied for finest known from here, and could easily be the best in a head to head competition. Bright **Extremely Fine.** **(1,750-2,750)**

14921 Boonville, NY - $10 1882 Brown Back Fr. 487 **The First NB** Ch. # (E)2320
While not an exceptionally rare bank, this note is the sole Brown Back of any denomination reported from here to date. There are a few pinholes and a small split at the right margin, but the note has good color for the grade and has retained clear pen signatures. **Fine. (1,000-1,500)**

14922 Brasher Falls, NY - $10 1902 Plain Back Fr. 632 **The Brasher Falls NB** Ch. # (E)10943
A very rare bank in large size, with the census standing at just two examples, both of which are ensconced in major New York collections and unlikely to return to the market any time soon. This specimen has been off the market for the better part of three decades, and offers collectors an unlikely to be repeated opportunity to obtain an example from a bank which had a miniscule $940 outstanding in large when the bank went into receivership in August of 1933. **Fine-Very Fine,** with one rather inconspicuous small body hole more than offset by the attractive purple signatures. **(3,000-5,000)**

14923 **Bridgehampton, NY** - $5 1929 Ty. 1 **The Bridgehampton NB** Ch. # 9669
A bright high grade example which is new to the census from this avidly sought after Suffolk County community. Sharp **Very Fine-Extremely Fine,** certain to be a popular item which will likely see bidding end in the range of... **(1,500-2,000)**

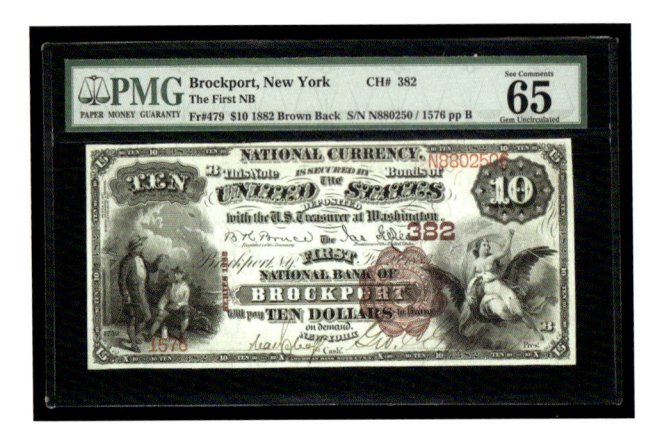

14924 **Brockport, NY** - $10 1882 Brown Back Fr. 479 **The First NB** Ch. # 382
A lovely pen signed Brown Back which has been graded by PMG as **Gem Uncirculated 65 EPQ,** with the EPQ designation noting the note's "Exceptional Paper Quality." **(4,500-6,500)**

14925 **Buffalo, NY** - $5 1902 Date Back Fr. 590 **The Marine NB** Ch. # (E)6184
Bright surfaces are still seen on this crisp **Very Fine** piece with deeply stamped officer's signatures. **(350-500)**

14926 **Chittenango, NY** - $5 1875 Fr. 401 **The First NB** Ch. # 179
An extremely rare note from the only bank to issue in this Madison County hamlet. This short lived institution issued First Charter examples only before liquidating in 1883, with a mere three pieces comprising the entire census. Our consignor has owned this note for nearly three decades, and its appearance here after all those years affords the opportunity for one other fortunate collector to add a note from this most elusive location to his holdings. Nice **Fine-Very Fine.** **(4,000-6,000)**

14927 **Clyde, NY** - $10 1902 Plain Back Fr. 633 **The Briggs NB** Ch. # (E)2468
A very scarce bank which redeemed its circulation early and issued nothing after emitting a small quantity of Third Charter Plain Backs, only one of which is listed in the census. Pen signed **Very Fine.** **(1,500-2,000)**

Only Known Small Size

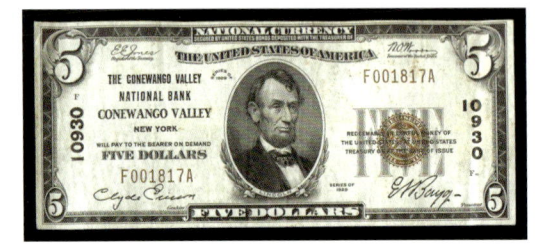

14928 **Conewango Valley, NY** - $5 1929 Ty. 1 **The Conewango Valley NB** Ch. # 10930
From our 2007 FUN Signature sale where it was described, "This Cattaraugus County issuer is extremely rare, with just four large examples previously reported. This is the discovery note from here for the 1929 series. Any estimate will be pure speculation, as an item of this rarity is worth whatever it takes to acquire. One thing, however, is quite certain, that when the hammer falls tonight, one New York collection will have its stature significantly increased by the addition by the addition of this rare note. Given small issue from here, it is doubtful that another example will surface during the lifetimes of the current generation of New York collectors. In addition to its rarity, this note is also quite attractive, grading an unchallenged **Very Fine,** with some justifiable claims to the next highest grade." **(6,000-9,000)**

14929 **Dundee, NY** - $10 1902 Plain Back Fr. 633 **The Dundee NB** Ch. # 2463
A very scarce note from the only issuer in this tiny Yates County community. Pen signed **Fine-Very Fine** with one small edge split, the paper a bit oil soaked, likely from storage in a PVC tainted holder. **(1,000-1,500)**

Gorgeous Uncut Sheet

14930 Forestville, NY - $10-$10-$10-$20 1902 Plain Back Fr. 630/656 **The First NB** Ch. # 10444 Uncut Sheet
An absolutely lovely uncut sheet which has retained its full top and bottom selvage. The colors and paper quality are those of a sheet printed this morning, and the eye appeal of this item is as good as it comes. **Gem Crisp Uncirculated.** (10,000-15,000)

14931 Fulton, NY - $1 Original Fr. 380 **The First NB** Ch. # 968
Gorgeous signatures remain on this Ace that has undergone some surgery to repair a couple of major tears. It has been over ten years since any original note has been seen at auction. Despite the appearance it remains scarce. *No returns will be permitted on this lot for any reason.* (750-1,250)

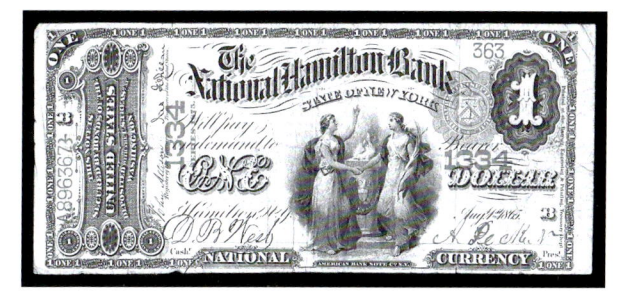

14932 Hamilton, NY - $1 1875 Fr. 385 **The National Hamilton Bank** Ch. # 1334
A brightly colored Series 1875 ace from this college community. This is by far the nicest of the three reported 1875 aces from here, grading **Fine+++,** with its sole defect a small split at the bottom that truly affects little. (1,200-1,600)

14933 Hammond, NY - $10 1902 Plain Back Fr. 628 **The Citizens NB** Ch. # (E)10216
Just five large notes are known from this one bank St. Lawrence County community, with this attractive specimen off the market since our consignor obtained it as part of the George Decker collection offering by NASCA in September of 1981. It's as nice or nicer than any other large note from here, grading **Very Fine** with clear pen signatures. Expect a realization in excess of the Sabis collection example from here, which we sold back in 2003 for $1955. (2,000-3,000)

14934 Hancock, NY - $20 1902 Plain Back Fr. 652 **The First NB** Ch. # (E)8613
Although a fair number of large notes are known from this small, one bank Delaware County locale, very few have traded publicly in recent years, with our records showing only two such offerings since 1996. This piece is one of only two Twenties in the census, and has been in our consignor's collection for so long it is listed in the Kelly census with no grade and no bank serial number. **Very Fine.** (1,000-1,500)

14935 Heuvelton, NY - $10 1902 Date Back Fr. 621 **The First NB** Ch. # (E)10446
An excessively rare bank in large size, with just $690 outstanding in 1935. Only three large examples are recorded from here, with this piece, in the hands of our consignor for three decades, the only Date Back extant and by far the nicest of any. Bright **Fine-Very Fine,** with bold inks and sharp two color signatures. (2,750-4,250)

14936 Homer, NY - $10 1902 Date Back Fr. 616 **The Homer NB** Ch. # (E)3186
While series 1929 examples from this bank are not terribly rare, large notes are another matter entirely, with the census standing at just four pieces, one of which has never been offered publicly and is listed without any grade or serial number. This is the only Date Back reported, and, although well circulated, is flawless for the grade. **Very Good.** (1,200-1,800)

14937 Jamestown, NY - $10 1902 Plain Back Fr. 624 **The First NB** Ch. # 548
A bright and attractive specimen which appears New until closely examined. **Extremely Fine.** (500-800)

14938 Jordan, NY - $10 1902 Plain Back Fr. 635 **The Jordan NB** Ch. # 12375
As nice as any large example from this just plain scarce bank, which had but $640 outstanding in 1935. **Extremely Fine,** a premium example from this Syracuse area community likely to easily reach and very possibly exceed... (3,000-5,000)

14939 Kingston, NY - $1 Original Fr. 380 **The National Ulster County Bank** Ch. # 1050
The census reveals this is one of only three known Aces from this bank. Only one of the other Aces has shown up at public auction, the consecutive note to this was part of a 1983 NASCA Sale. The technical wear on this note is consistent with a Very Fine grade, though the folds are a bit too heavy. The result is a fairly eye appealing piece with only a couple of splits in the paper at the folds. The paper remains bright as does the seal. **Very Good.** (800-1,000)

14940 Le Roy, NY - $10 1882 Date Back Fr. 545 **The Le Roy NB** Ch. # (E)6087
An evenly circulated Second Charter Date Back from this very much sought after location. **Fine,** with pen signatures. (2,000-3,000)

14941 **New York, NY** - $100 1902 Date Back Fr. 689 **The First NB** Ch. # (E)29
This high denomination note faces up well with bright paper. There are a few minor repairs that were professionally executed. **Very Fine. (1,000-1,400)**

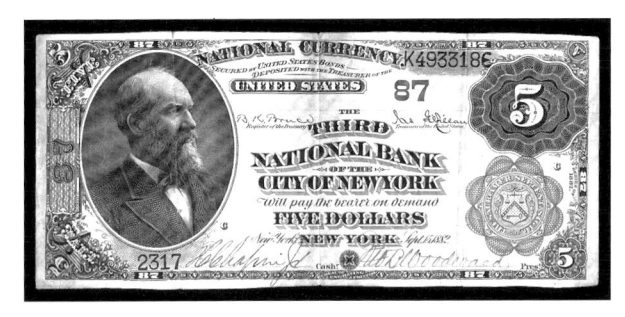

14942 **New York, NY** - $5 1882 Brown Back Fr. 466 **The Third NB** Ch. # 87
Only large size notes were issued by this bank which commenced business in 1863 and folded in 1897. Wonderful pen signatures still remain intact and dark as the day they were done. Margin splits are noticed along the hard center fold with some age staining visible, but the eye appeal of the piece is still great. **Fine. (850-1,250)**

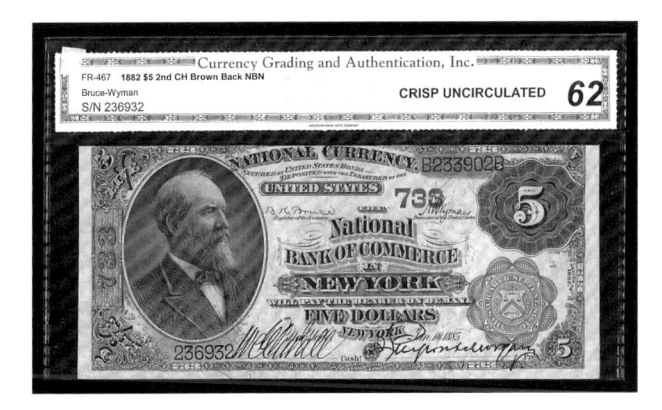

14943 **New York, NY** - $5 1882 Brown Back Fr. 467 **The NB of Commerce** Ch. # 733
These notes are always in demand due to the fact that they carry the penned signature of J. Pierpont Morgan as vice president. The top margin runs along the frame line on this **CGA Crisp Uncirculated 62** graded $5.
From The Collection of Greg Southward **(1,750-2,250)**

14944 **New York, NY** - $5 1882 Brown Back Fr. 467 **The NB of Commerce** Ch. # 733
The paper on this Brown Back is solid and the folds that account for the grade do not interfere with the design. **Fine. (600-800)**

14945 **New York, NY** - $10 1882 Brown Back Fr. 480 **The NB of Commerce** Ch. # (E)733
A nice average circulated Brown Back with good color and body for the grade. **Fine,** with clear signatures. **(600-800)**

14946 **New York, NY** - $20 1882 Brown Back Fr. 494 **The NB of Commerce** Ch. # 733
A well margined $20 Brown Back which is perfect for type. Evenly circulated **Fine-Very Fine,** with clear signatures and no problems whatsoever. **(900-1,200)**

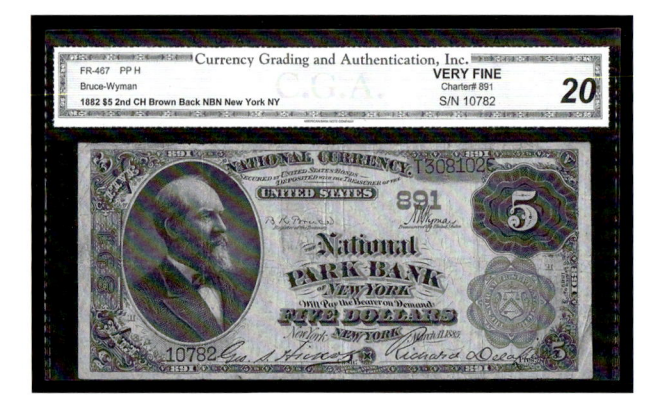

14947 New York, NY - $5 1882 Brown Back Fr. 467 The National Park Bank Ch. # 891
The officers' signatures are printed on this ideal representative for type. **CGA Very Fine 20.** (500-700)

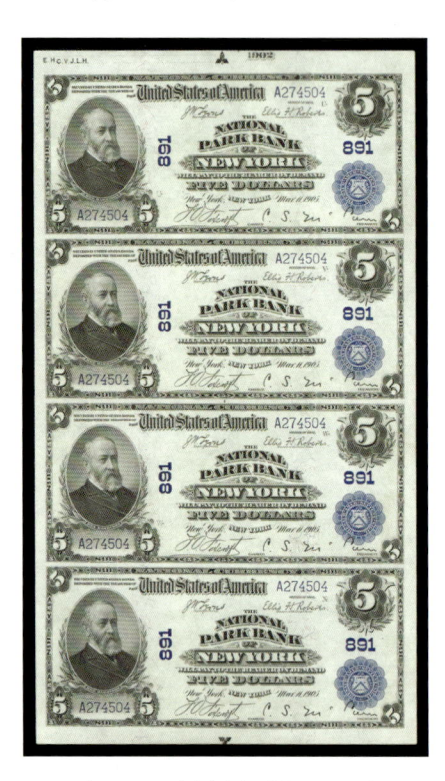

14948 New York, NY - $5-$5-$5-$5 1902 Plain Back Fr. 598 The National Park Bank Ch. # 891 Uncut Sheet
The National Park Bank issued over 999,999 sheets of 1902 $5s. Therefore it became one of the few banks in the country that had to go to having an "A" prefix tacked onto its later serial numbers for $5 notes. This "A" prefix serial number sheet presented here also carries U4-V4-W4-X4 plate letters. This shows how many plates were used to print this denomination for this bank as this is at the very end of the fourth time through the alphabet for $5 plates. This recent discovery makes it only the third sheet on this bank to survive with the A prefix serial numbers. Further, this **Gem Crisp Uncirculated** sheet is well preserved with bold embossing, wide margins, and nice color. (7,000-10,000)

14949 New York, NY - $10-$10-$10-$10 1902 Plain Back Fr. 624 The National Park Bank Ch. # 891 Uncut Sheet
This delightful uncut sheet is well preserved. Also, since it is of the rarely used $10-$10-$10-$10 format it has this added identifier to its printing plate. A portion of President C.S. McCain's engraved signature is incomplete. **Gem Crisp Uncirculated.** (7,000-10,000)

14950 New York, NY - $5 1902 Date Back Fr. 590 The Chatham NB Ch. # (E)1375
Bright paper, dark inks, ample margins, and the printed vanity signature of the bank president are traits of this **Very Fine** $5. (250-450)

14951 New York, NY - $5 1902 Red Seal Fr. 588 **The American Exchange NB** Ch. # (E)1394
This attractive note boasts pleasing margins that are sufficient all around as well as a bright red overprint. Unfortunately, a lone fold to the right of the bank title accounts for the grade of **Choice About Uncirculated.** (1,000-1,500)

Serial Number 1

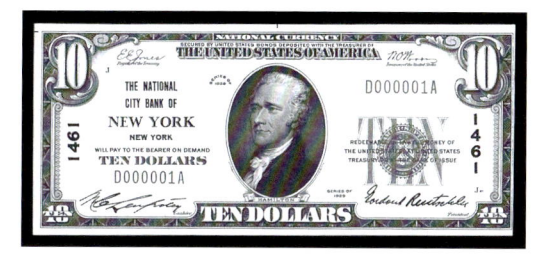

14952 New York, NY - $10 1929 Ty. 1 **The National City Bank** Ch. # 1461
While this bank was one of New York City's most prolific issuers, this example is the only Series 1929 serial number 1 specimen which appears to have survived. **Choice Crisp Uncirculated,** a significant New York City item worthy of the finest of collections. (2,000-2,500)

14953 New York, NY - $20 1882 Date Back Fr. 555 **The Lincoln NB** Ch. # (E)2608
The wear is more consistent with a Fine or better grade though the center fold is a bit too heavy and the edges a bit soft. **Very Good.** (500-750)

14954 New York, NY - $5 1902 Plain Back Fr. 601 **The Gotham NB** Ch. # (E)9717
This bank was chartered in 1910 and issued Date Backs and Plain Backs only during its 15 year run. While the top margin is cut in a bit, the stamped officers' signatures remain dark and legible. Enhanced by a great big city title. **Extremely Fine+.** (350-500)

14955 Ossining, NY - $5 1902 Plain Back Fr. 598 **The Ossining NB** Ch. # (E)6552
This tougher Ossining bank issued large notes only. In 2003 we saw a similar $5 on this bank just one grade higher cross the auction block at over $3000. **Very Good.** (1,000-1,500)

14956 Oxford, NY - $5 1902 Plain Back Fr. 598 **The First NB** Ch. # 273
This is a scarce Chenango County bank. We sold a slightly better note on this bank in January 2005 for almost $1100. **Very Good** with dark printed signatures. (400-600)

14957 **Palmyra, NY** - $1 Original Fr. 380 **The First NB** Ch. # 295
This ace is somewhat nicer than its assigned grade, but the margins are a bit ragged and there are a few splits and chips missing as well. **Very Good-Fine. (500-700)**

14958 **Ripley, NY** - $10 1902 Red Seal Fr. 613 **The First NB** Ch. # (E)6386
A gorgeous Red Seal which is being offered here for the first time to the numismatic community. While lightly circulated, the colors are exceptionally bright, with a vivid red overprint contrasting with crisp white paper. The bottom margin is a bit close, but that minor quibble is easily offset by the presence of two bold pen signatures. **Extremely Fine,** a significant new discovery certain to see some spirited bidding before the hammer falls tonight. **(5,000-7,000)**

14959 **Rochester, NY** - $10 1902 Plain Back Fr. 624 **The Traders NB** Ch. # (E)1104
This **Choice Crisp Uncirculated** example is a new addition to the census from this bank which ceased operating in 1924. The paper is very original with plenty of embossing. The serial number is raised into the design a bit. **(500-1,000)**

Serial Number 1 Sandy Hill $5 Brown Back

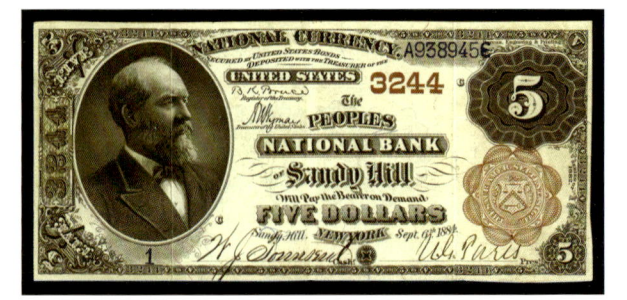

14960 **Sandy Hill, NY** - $5 1882 Brown Back Fr. 467 **The Peoples NB** Ch. # 3244
If ever a New York note had everything a collector looks for, this specimen is it. It combines real bank scarcity, a wonderful layout used only on $5 Brown Backs, enough grade to matter, and, in addition, is a serial number 1 example. This marks the first time this example has entered the numismatic marketplace, and it would not surprise us at all to see this lovely **Extremely Fine** specimen blow right by our estimate of... **(8,000-12,000)**

14961 **Scarsdale, NY** - $5 1902 Plain Back Fr. 607 **Scarsdale NB & TC** Ch. # 11708
The bottom margin is very slightly cut in on this Westchester County note. **Very Fine. (400-600)**

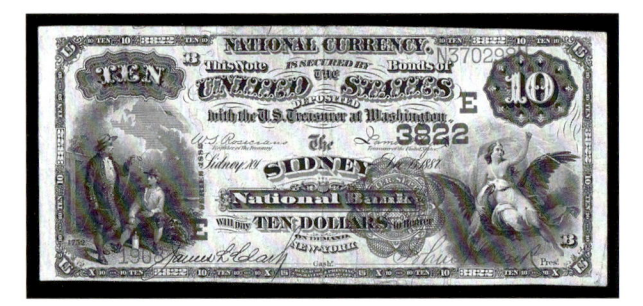

14962 **Sidney, NY** - $10 1882 Brown Back Fr. 483 **The Sidney NB** Ch. # (E)3822
A bright and attractive example which is the sole $10 Brown Back reported from here to date. **Very Fine,** with pen signatures of James L. Clark and John A. Clark. **(2,250-3,250)**

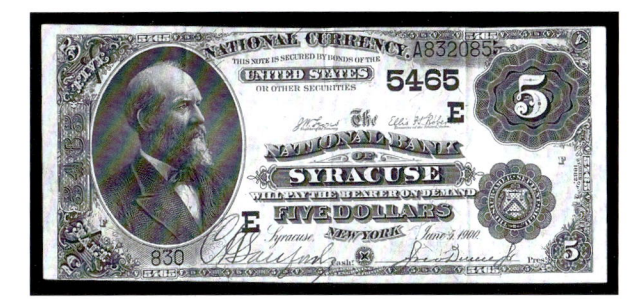

14963 **Syracuse, NY** - $5 1882 Date Back Fr. 537 **The NB of Syracuse** Ch. # (E)5465
This is one of just four $5 1882 Date Backs known from this bank, which issued Second Charter examples only. The note we offer tonight is a bright and crisply original **Extremely Fine**, with the officers' signatures every bit as fresh and vivid as the day the note was signed. A high grade example with all the eye appeal of an uncirculated note, and at considerably less money at that. (1,250-1,750)

Newly Discovered Serial Number 1 Troy Red Seal

14964 **Troy, NY** - $10 1902 Red Seal Fr. 613 **The Manufacturers NB** Ch. # (E)721
A beautiful serial number 1 example which is not only the only serial number 1 example of any type known from this bank but is also the only Red Seal of any denomination to be reported from here. Vividly colored **Extremely Fine,** a great new discovery which is certain to delight its fortunate new owner. (7,500-12,500)

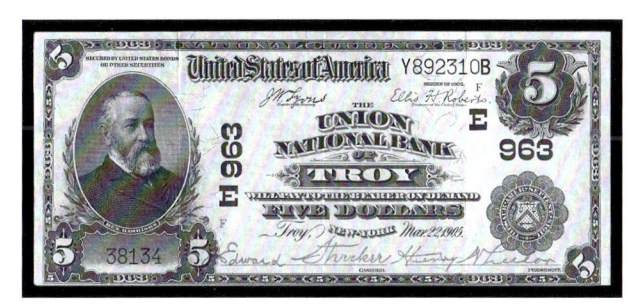

14965 **Troy, NY** - $5 1902 Plain Back Fr. 598 **The Union NB** Ch. # (E)963
A barely circulated three fold note which has retained its full original embossing. **Extremely Fine.** (400-600)

14966 **Unadilla, NY** - $10 1902 Plain Back Fr. 626 **The Unadilla NB** Ch. # 9516
Simply a gorgeous piece which has plenty of embossing with excellent eye appeal. A touch of handling holds this well margined note from the gem designation. **Very Choice Crisp Uncirculated.** (1,000-1,500)

14967 **Utica, NY** - $10 1902 Date Back Fr. 616 **The Oneida NB** Ch. # (E)1392
Bank officers G.A. Niles and Geo. L. Bradford are found on this note. Mr. Niles would go on to serve this bank as president. **PCGS Very Fine 25.** (250-350)

14968 **Westfield, NY** - $5 1902 Red Seal Fr. 587 **The NB of Westfield** Ch. # (E)3166
A gorgeous Red Seal which is the first example of its denomination and type reported from here. This is an absolute peach of a note, with great pen signatures, loads of original embossing, and a fiery red overprint that appears to have been applied this morning rather than one hundred years ago. There is a bit of handling evident, but it would be an utter travesty to grade this piece any less than **Choice Crisp Uncirculated.** (2,500-3,500)

Cut Sheet Four $5 Plain Backs

14969 Westfield, NY - $5 1902 Plain Back Fr. 598 **The NB of Westfield** Ch. # (E)3166
This glorious cut sheet is graced with wonderfully embossed surfaces. Kelly lists an uncut sheet in his census data. The likelihood that this sheet has been cut is very great. Most every note grades **Choice Crisp Uncirculated** with the only exception the "F" plate note which has suffered a corner fold into the design. The Cashier has signed in pen while the President's signature is stamped in purple. Expect a realization in the area of . . . (Total: 4 notes) **(3,000-4,000)**

14970 Yonkers, NY - $5 1902 Plain Back Fr. 601 **The Yonkers NB** Ch. # (E)9825
A decent evenly circulated example bearing the first title used by this Westchester County bank. **Very Good-Fine.** **(450-650)**

NORTH CAROLINA

Asheville Red Seal

14971 Asheville, NC - $10 1902 Red Seal Fr. 615 **The American NB** Ch. # (S)8772
A nice note which is one of just three Red Seals known from Asheville, none of which, to our knowledge, have ever been available at public sale to North Carolina collectors. Evenly circulated **Fine+,** and rare enough to reach or exceed... **(12,500-17,500)**

Excessively Rare North Carolina Lazy Deuce

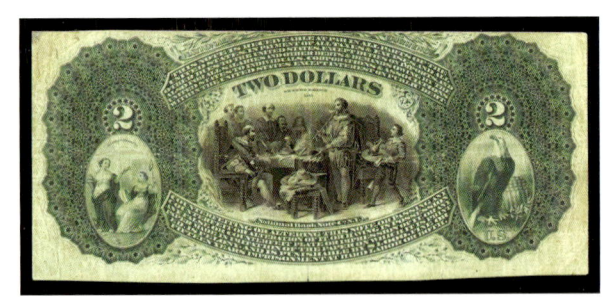

14972 Charlotte, NC - $2 Original Fr. 389 **The Merchants & Farmers NB** Ch. # 1781
This is one of the greatest North Carolina rarities we have ever had the privilege of offering. It is the only Lazy Two known from this bank, and one of just seven known from all banks in the state combined, one of which is held in the state museum collection and another of which is heavily repaired. Fortunately for collectors, this example is an evenly circulated piece displaying great color and body for the grade. It easily grades **Fine,** and perhaps a touch better, making it the second highest grade Lazy Two known from North Carolina by a considerable margin. A tiny corner tip repair must be mentioned for the sake of total accuracy in cataloguing, but it is miniscule and affects nothing. If rarity and desirability are any guide here, expect this true North Carolina trophy item to easily exceed our likely conservative estimate of... **(30,000-50,000)**

High Grade Original North Carolina $5

14973 Charlotte, NC - $5 Original Fr. 399 **The Merchants & Farmers NB** Ch. # 1781
A beautiful First Charter North Carolina note which is in extraordinary condition for its type. This is one of only eight Original fives from all banks in the state combined, and it certainly ranks as one of the very finest of any in the census. The colors are spectacular and the note displays only the barest traces of any real circulation. The only detraction at all worthy of mention is two tiny nicks in the right margin which affects nothing. **Very Fine-Extremely Fine,** a rarity worthy of a place of honor in any serious North Carolina collection. (15,000-20,000)

14974 Charlotte, NC - $10 1929 Ty. 1 **The Charlotte NB** Ch. # 5055
This **PMG Gem Uncirculated 65 EPQ** note would be ideal for a state collection in this condition. (500-750)

14975 Elkin, NC - $10 1902 Plain Back Fr. 633 **The Elkin NB** Ch. # 5673
A just plain rare note from the only bank to issue in this small Surry County community. Only five large (and one small, which is offered below) notes are known from here, with this at least as nice as any. **Fine.** (3,000-5,000)

Unique for the Bank

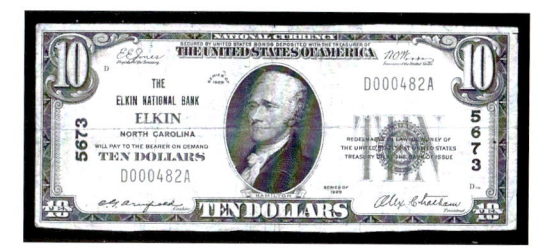

14976 Elkin, NC - $10 1929 Ty. 1 **The Elkin NB** Ch. # 5673
This is the only small size note known from this one bank town, and is one of the highlights of the North Carolina grouping offered here tonight. Our records show that it has only been offered once in the past six decades, with that auction appearance coming over ten years ago. **Fine,** a great item worthy of a substantial bid. (3,500-5,500)

14977 Goldsboro, NC - $20 1902 Plain Back Fr. 658 **The NB of Goldsboro** Ch. # 5048
An evenly circulated large example from the first of this community's two issuing banks. **Very Good-Fine.** (400-600)

One of Two Known

14978 High Point, NC - $10 1882 Brown Back Fr. 482 The NB of High Point Ch. # (S)3490
An extremely rare High Point bank which issued Brown Backs and Red Seals only before liquidating in 1907. Just two examples are known, both Brown Backs, with the only previous offering of any kind from this institution coming back in 1996. **Very Good-Fine**, with the top margin restored. **(10,000-14,000)**

14979 Leaksville, NC - $10 1902 Plain Back Fr. 635 The First NB Ch. # 12259
A scarce large example from this one bank community, which today no longer exists, having merged with the nearby communities of Spray and Draper to create the city of Eden. **Fine**, with a tear in the right margin. **(1,250-1,750)**

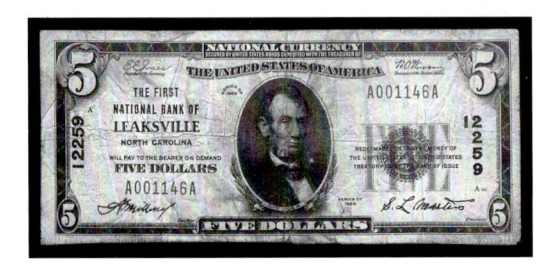

14980 Leaksville, NC - $5 1929 Ty. 1 The First NB Ch. # 12259
Small notes from this one bank location are considerably scarcer than are large, with the census standing at just three such examples, including this piece. **About Fine**, with a bit of soiling. **(1,500-2,000)**

14981 Lincolnton, NC - $10 1902 Plain Back Fr. 624 The First NB Ch. # 6744
While small notes from this bank are relatively common, large notes from here are another story entirely, with the census standing at just four pieces, including this example. All are in about the same grade, with this the sole Plain Back reported. **About Fine. (3,000-4,000)**

First Ever Public Appearance

14982 New Bern, NC - $5 1929 Ty. 1 The First NB Ch. # 13298
Talk about short lived...this bank came and went within seven months of receiving its charter in early 1929. The bank issued Series 1929 examples only, with a miniscule 184 sheets printed in the $5 denomination only. Although four notes are listed in the census, the whereabouts of the other three are unknown, with no record of grade or prior appearances during the past six decades. In fact, this evening's offering represents the first appearance of any note from this bank at public sale. Well circulated but intact **Very Good**, a truly rare item worthy of a strong bid despite its condition. **(2,000-3,000)**

14983 Raleigh, NC - $5 1875 Fr. 402 The Raleigh NB of North Carolina Ch. # 1557
Low grade, but the only $5 1875 known from this bank, which issued First Charters only before liquidating at the end of its charter in 1885. Well circulated but intact **Very Good. (5,000-7,000)**

Unique North Carolina Jeffries-Spinner $10

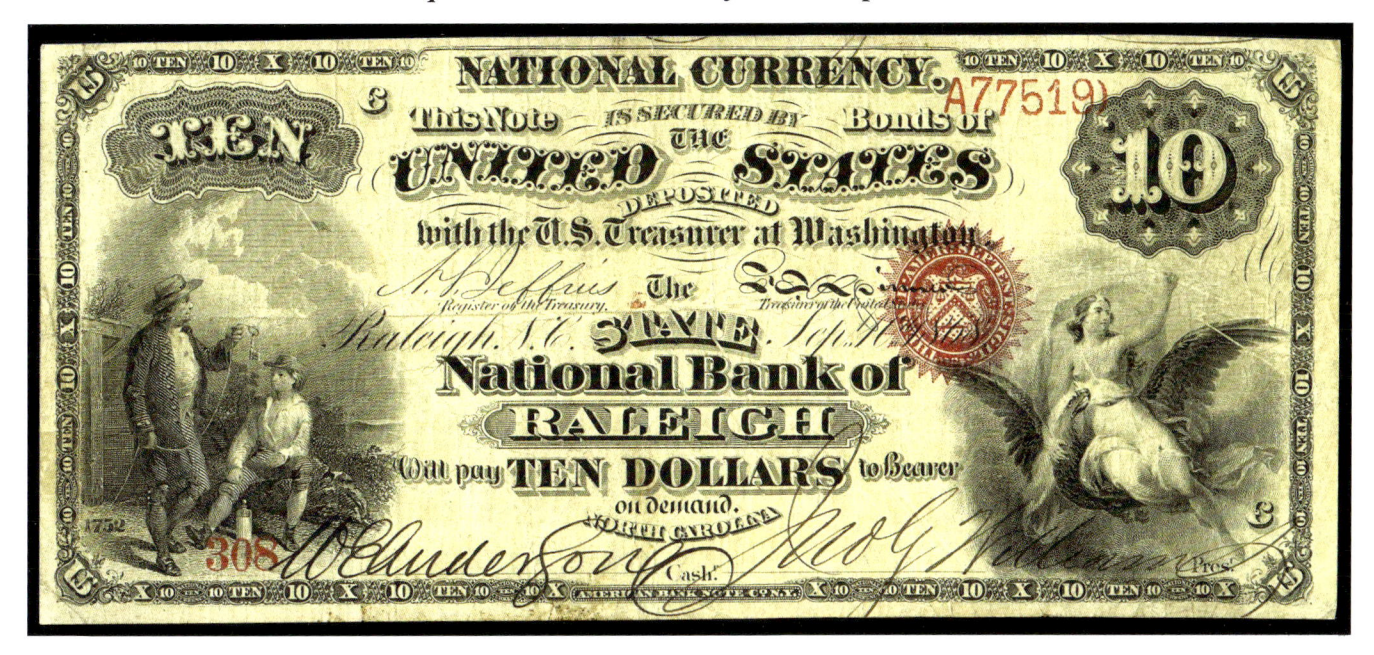

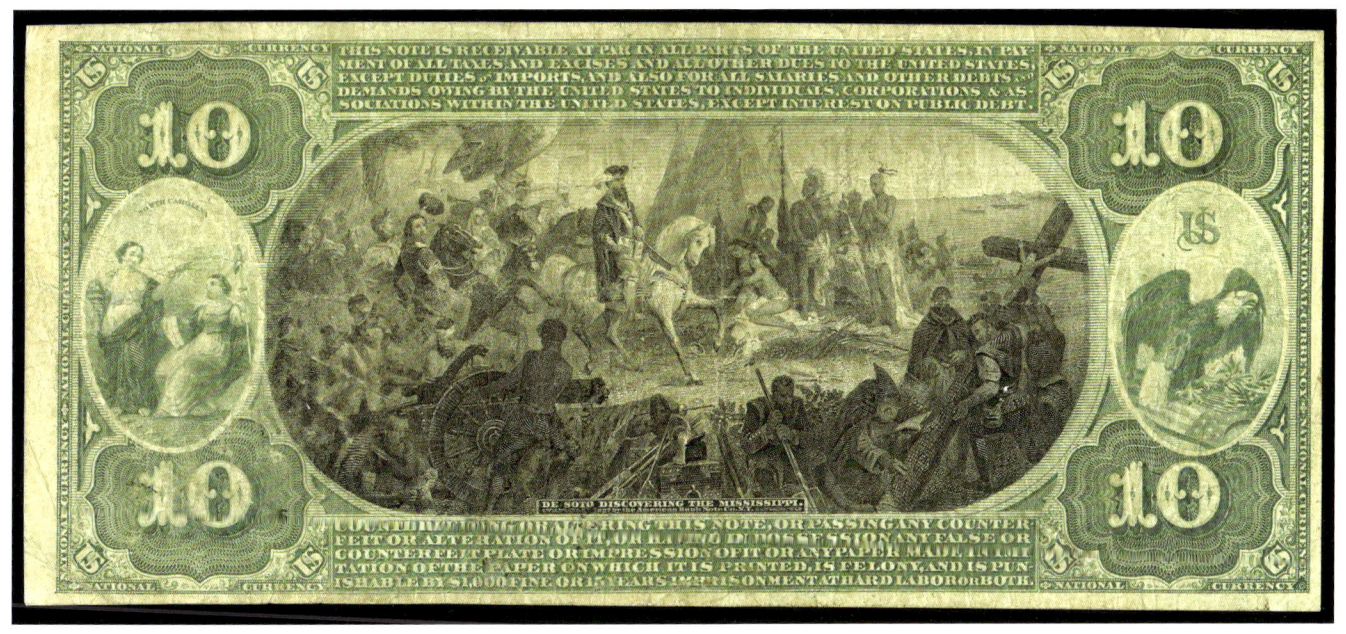

14984 Raleigh, NC - $10 Original Fr. 413 **The State NB** Ch. # 1682

If ever a First Charter had everything going for it, this one does. It is one of two notes known from this state capital institution that issued First Charter examples only before liquidating in 1888 at the expiration of its charter. It also bears the excessively rare Jeffries-Spinner Treasury signature combination, with this not only the only $10 example from North Carolina with these signatures but the sole reported $10 from any bank in the entire country. Fortunately for collectors, it is a most attractive specimen as well, being a nicely margined piece displaying great color and eye appeal for the grade. When we last offered this note six years ago, it sold to a major North Carolina collector at a then record price of $23,100 against a pre-sale estimate of $10,000-15,000. Expect this trophy item to bring more, and likely substantially more, before the hammer falls this evening. **Fine-Very Fine. (30,000-40,000)**

14985 **Raleigh, NC** - $10 1902 Plain Back Fr. 627 **The Citizens NB** Ch. # 1766
A nice large size example from the state capital. **Fine-Very Fine,** with black signatures. (500-700)

Unique With This Title

14986 **Rocky Mount, NC** - $10 1929 Ty. 1 **The Planters NB** Ch. # 10608
A truly rare note from this none too common bank, with this example the only Series 1929 specimen which bears the first title used from here. This nomenclature was used for only six months on small size notes, with a very minimal issue, making this an example well worth a very strong bid. **Fine.** (1,750-3,250)

NORTH DAKOTA

14987 **Anamoose, ND** - $5 1902 Plain Back Fr. 600 **The Anamoose NB** Ch. # (W)9390
Large notes only from this seldom seen bank, which is the only collectible issuer in this remote locale. While several notes do exist from here, most all have been very closely held, with the last offering of any kind at public sale coming over eight years ago. Bright **Fine-Very Fine,** with two color pen signatures of W.E. Schmidt as V. Cashier and J.J. Schmidt as President. (1,250-1,750)

14988 **Dickinson, ND** - $10 1929 Ty. 1 **The Liberty NB** Ch. # 12401
This thinly capitalized bank was chartered in 1923 and ordered only $60,910 worth of notes, all in the $10 and $20 Plain Back and the 1929 Type 1 designs. Seven small survivors are documented in the latest edition of the Kelly census. This **Fine** displays normal circulation soiling for the grade and light indications of a purple bank stamp on the face. (450-650)

14989 **Ellendale, ND** - $10 1902 Plain Back Fr. 624 **The First NB** Ch. # (W)6398
An attractive example from the first of three banks which issued in this small community. Pen signed **Fine-Very Fine,** as nice or nicer than any of the large notes reported to date from here. (800-1,200)

14990 **Grafton, ND** - $10 1929 Ty. 1 **The Grafton NB** Ch. # 3096
This is one of the few banks from North Dakota with any quantity of uncirculated notes available. Tonight's example is pack fresh and would unquestionably be a Gem but for a slight centering shift to the left. **PCGS Very Choice New 64.** (550-750)

OHIO

14991 Oakes, ND - $20 1929 Ty. 2 **The First NB** Ch. # 6457
Serial number six graces this pleasing Type 2 example that retains much crispness, though has a few spots on the front. **Fine. (500-800)**

14992 Page, ND - $20 1902 Plain Back Fr. 650 **The First NB** Ch. # 6463
A truly rare note in large size, with the census showing just four such examples, with this the equal of any in grade and the sole $20 as well. Bright **Very Fine**, with vibrant two color signatures and great eye appeal. **(2,000-3,000)**

14993 Taylor, ND - $20 1929 Ty. 1 **The Security NB** Ch. # 12502
Small notes only from this elusive North Dakota bank, with this the town's only issuer. **Fine+. (500-800)**

14994 Arcanum, OH - $5 1929 Ty. 1 **The First-Farmers NB** Ch. # 4839
In 1928 this institution changed its name to the First-Farmers National Bank after it assumed the Farmers National Bank and their circulation. In addition to its status as being from the first small size #1 sheet issued, it may well be the finest as this **Extremely Fine** was folded in three and never circulated. The embossing is still bold as are the printed details. **(1,000-1,500)**

14995 Arcanum, OH - $10 1902 Plain Back Fr. 626 **The Farmers NB** Ch. # (M)9255
This **Fine** addition to the census makes only three $10 Plain Backs now documented from here. This is quite a difficult bank to locate and should see bids top out in the range of... **(900-1,200)**

14996 Bethel, OH - $10 1882 Value Back Fr. 577 **The First NB** Ch. # (M)5627
The bright blue overprint adds to the eye appeal of this Value Back. **Very Fine. (800-1,200)**

First Appearance in Over Two Decades

14997 Bethesda, OH - $10 1929 Ty. 1 The First NB Ch. # 5602
A truly rare Belmont County bank where the entire census stands at just two large and four small examples, including this piece. All have been tightly held for many years, with the last offering we know of coming back in a 1984 Hickman-Oakes auction. **Fine.** (1,000-1,500)

14998 Bucyrus, OH - $20 1902 Date Back Fr. 642 The Second NB Ch. # (M)3274
The signatures remain bold on this deeply printed $20. There is a tiny corner tip fold that remains fully in the margin on this **Crisp Uncirculated** issue. (750-850)

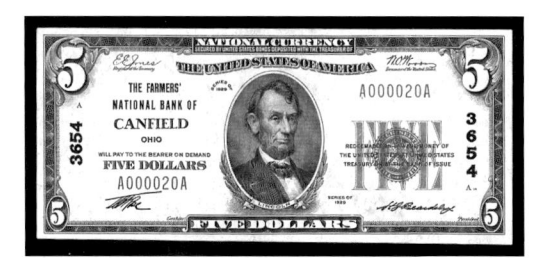

14999 Canfield, OH - $5 1929 Ty. 1 The Farmers NB Ch. # 3654
This is the first of two near-consecutive notes from this Mahoning County locale. The margins are near perfect as is the embossing and overall eye appeal. There is a bit of handling and a crease that account for a **Choice About Uncirculated** grade. (400-500)

15000 Canfield, OH - $5 1929 Ty. 1 The Farmers NB Ch. # 3654
This low serial numbered note is two away from the above lot. It is as nice, though a light centerfold separates it from a full CU grade. **Choice About Uncirculated.** (400-500)

15001 Centerburg, OH - $10 1902 Plain Back Fr. 625 The First NB Ch. # (M)8182
Large notes only from this very scarce Knox County issuer, the sole bank in this small community. Our records show just three offerings of any kind from here over the past sixty years, with the last coming back in 2002. **Very Good-Fine.** (1,500-2,500)

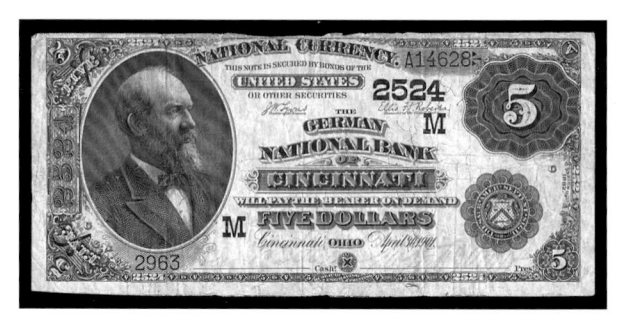

15002 Cincinnati, OH - $5 1882 Date Back Fr. 537 The German NB Ch. # (M)2524
The top margin is trimmed a bit close, with the back a bit off center as well. **Very Good-Fine.** (500-700)

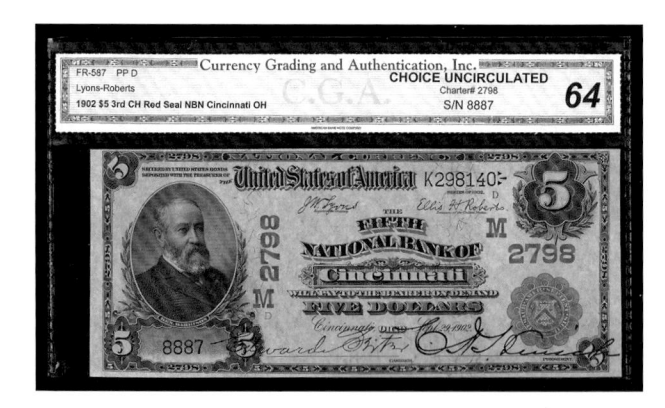

15003 Cincinnati, OH - $5 1902 Red Seal Fr. 587 The Fifth NB Ch. # (M)2798
The red overprint is bright and complements the white, original paper. Printed signatures of the Cashier and President are noted. **CGA Choice Uncirculated 64.** (1,500-2,000)

Serial Number 1 Red Seal

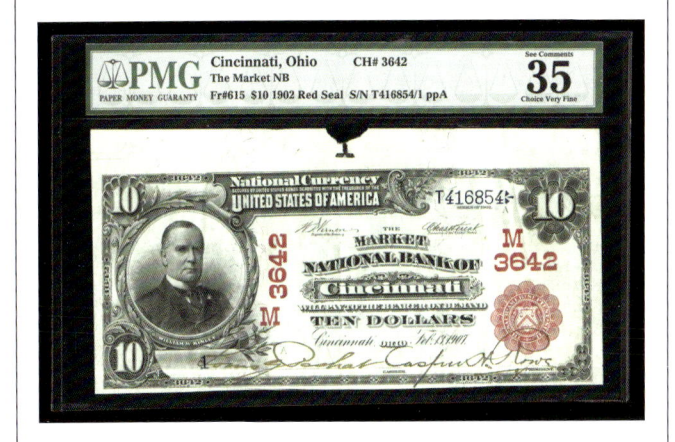

15004 Cincinnati, OH - $10 1902 Red Seal Fr. 615 The Market NB Ch. # (M)3642

A lovely serial number 1 example from this scarcer Cincinnati bank, which issued Brown Backs, Red Seals, and Date Backs only before it liquidated in 1919. This "A" position serial number 1 Red Seal has a small piece out of the expansive top selvage, and has been graded by PMG, which assigned a grade of **Choice Very Fine 35** with the additional comment "Great Color." With its bold pen signatures and attractive overall appearance, that grade certainly appears conservative to this cataloguer. (7,000-9,000)

15005 Cleveland, OH - $5 1882 Brown Back Fr. 471 The Central NB Ch. # (M)4318

The colors on this Brown Back remain bold. **PCGS Very Fine 20.** (600-800)

15006 Cleveland, OH - $5 1902 Plain Back Fr. 607 Brotherhood of Locomotive Engineers Co-Operative NB Ch. # (M)11862

A fresh and high grade example which bears a sought after title. Bright **Extremely Fine-About Uncirculated.** (600-900)

15007 Columbus, OH - $5 1882 Brown Back Fr. 474 The Ohio NB Ch. # 5065

This is a bright and colorful Brown Back with a neat title layout. The lightly penned date "Feb. 1898" in the left margin simply indicates how little actual circulation this specimen received and adds considerably to its charm and appeal. Boldly pen signed with original surfaces. **Very Fine.** (700-1,100)

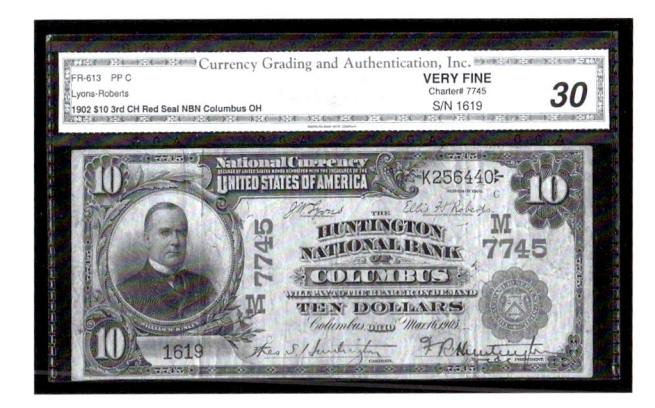

15008 Columbus, OH - $10 1902 Red Seal Fr. 613 The Huntington NB Ch. # (M)7745

This is the only $10 Red Seal reported to date on this charter number. This institution represents a classic American success story, starting as a small family owned bank in 1905 and eventually becoming one of the largest banks in the country with 594 branches in six states. Bright **CGA Fine-Very Fine 30,** with nice pen signatures of Theo S. and F.R. Huntington, Vice President. (800-1,200)

15009 **Crestline, OH** - $5 1929 Ty. 1 **First NB** Ch. # 13273
Small notes only from this bank, with rather few recent appearances despite a healthy census population. **Very Fine. (300-500)**

15010 **Delphos, OH** - $5 1882 Brown Back Fr. 466 **The Delphos NB** Ch. # 2885
An excessively rare bank which issued Five, Fifty and Hundred dollar Brown Backs only before liquidating in 1902. While two other examples are known to exist, our records disclose that neither has been offered to collectors at public sale since our data span began in 1944. There is some very minor damage along with a few stains, but where can another example from this bank be obtained at any price? **Very Good. (3,000-4,000)**

15011 **Dunkirk, OH** - $10 1929 Ty. 1 **The First NB** Ch. # 6628
This pleasing example from a tougher bank is graded **Fine 15** by CGA. **(400-600)**

15012 **East Liverpool, OH** - $20 1882 Brown Back Fr. 504 **The Potters NB** Ch. # (M)2544
Here is an unusual occupational title for this **PCGS Very Good 10** note. Darkly printed signatures are found on this $20 with Cashier R.W. Patterson holding down that position well into the Series 1929 era. There are only seven Brown Backs in the census for this charter number and this $20 is one of them. **(600-900)**

Attractive Serial Number 1 Red Seal

15013 **East Palestine, OH** - $10 1902 Red Seal Fr. 613 **The First NB** Ch. # (M)6593
A single $10 and lone $20 Red Seal make up the entire population of serial Number 1 examples from this very scarce Ohio bank. Both are virtually identical in grade, and neither has been available at public sale within the past fifteen years. While lightly circulated, this example has the appearance of a new note, with a vivid red overprint and bold pen signatures. With even mediocre Number 1 Red Seals flirting with the five figure area, expect this considerably above average **Very Fine+** specimen to surpass our likely conservative pre-sale estimate of... **(8,000-12,000)**

15014 **Greenwich, OH** - $20 1929 Ty. 1 **The First NB** Ch. # 7001
This fresh **Extremely Fine** example is from the only bank located here and retains a fresh and snappy originality. This institution printed only 166 sheets of the $20 Type 1. **(550-750)**

15015 **Hamilton, OH** - $5 Original Fr. 394 **The First NB** Ch. # 56
This nice mid-grade $5 is one of just two First Charters known on this bank. It is neatly margined and pen signed. **Fine-Very Fine. (2,000-3,000)**

15016 Hamilton, OH Trio.
$5 1902 Plain Back Fr. 598 **The First NB & TC** Ch. # 56 **VG**
$5 1902 Plain Back Fr. 598 **The First NB & TC** Ch. # 56 **VF**
$10 1902 Plain Back Fr. 624 **The First NB & TC** Ch. # 56 **Fine**.
The $5s are different in this lot as the VG note is of the Treasury and bank serial number variety and the VF note is of the two bank serial number variety. All notes have the printed signatures of E.M. and E.G. Ruder. (Total: 3 notes) (400-600)

15017 Hamilton, OH - $5 1882 Brown Back Fr. 467 **The Second NB** Ch. # 829
Pen signatures remain on this low grade $5 Brown Back. An approximate one inch tear extends from the right-hand side. **Good+.** (200-300)

15018 Hamilton, OH - $10 1882 Brown Back Fr. 483 **The Miami Valley NB** Ch. # 3840
The edges are healthy and the surfaces are soft on this $10 Brown Back. Some of the dark brown ink of the back is seen through the face. The purple stamped signatures are almost gone, but we do know it was the vice president's signature on this note at one time. **Fine-Very Fine** with a bottom edge just inside the frame line. (600-900)

15019 Kenton, OH - $20 1902 Plain Back Fr. 659 **The First NB** Ch. # 2500
A lovely example which is far above average from this location. **Very Fine-Extremely Fine,** with bright white paper and bold pen signatures, a premium piece in all respects. (600-800)

Rare $50 Uncut Sheet

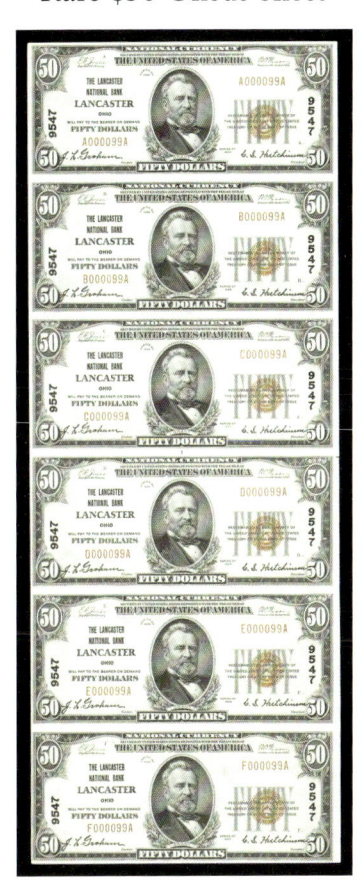

15020 Lancaster, OH - $50 1929 Ty. 1 **The Lancaster NB** Ch. # 9547 Uncut Sheet
This is the only $50 uncut sheet known from Ohio and it is one of only a literal handful of $50 uncut sheets known from all states combined. There are a couple of miniscule corner tip folds and one center fold was carefully done between the third and fourth notes, but the notes of this all serial number 99 sheet grade **Choice Crisp Uncirculated.** Expect this great item to reach or exceed... (15,000-20,000)

15021 Lockland, OH - $10 1929 Ty. 1 **The First NB** Ch. # 4133
A seldom seen example from this Cincinnati suburb, where this bank was the sole issuer. Nice **Fine-Very Fine.** (300-500)

15022 **Mount Vernon, OH** - $1 Original Fr. 380 **The First NB** Ch. # 908

This bank only had four large enumerated before the appearance of this note. Only one other of those counted notes is a First Charter note and it has never come up for auction. The upper right-hand corner is missing and there is a repair in the same vicinity on the back. Still the Ace faces up well for what it has gone through. **Good-Very Good.** (900-1,400)

Scarce Mt. Vernon $10 Red Seal

15023 **Mount Vernon, OH** - $10 1902 Red Seal Fr. 613 **The New Knox NB** Ch. # (M)7638

This is only the third Red Seal to be documented in the census for this Knox County bank. Not surprisingly, it is also the first Red Seal on the bank to go under the gavel. The note is a snappy **Fine** with a nice red overprint for the grade and the penned officer signatures are dark, too. There is a paper clip rust outline to the left of the portrait. A relatively modern First-Knox National Bank envelope comes with this lot. (2,500-4,500)

15024 **Mount Vernon, OH** - $10 1902 Plain Back Fr. 624 **Knox NB** Ch. # 7638

This new note for the census is nicer than any large note currently listed with a grade. It has original surfaces, embossing, and dark stamped signatures. **Very Fine-Extremely Fine.** (800-1,100)

15025 **Mount Vernon, OH** - $10 1902 Plain Back Fr. 624 **Knox NB** Ch. # 7638

This $10, that was handed down among the cashier's family, displays original paper surfaces that include embossing and boldly stamped signatures of the Cashier and Vice President. A paper tag accompanies this note and it says, "first one with rubber stamp signature permitted." **Very Fine+.** (700-1,000)

15026 **Mount Vernon, OH** - $20 1902 Plain Back Fr. 650 **Knox NB** Ch. #(M)7638

This is another quality, original note on this charter number in this auction. The other 1902 Blue Seals in this auction have rubber stamped signatures, while this $20 has well executed penned signatures of the Cashier and President, J. Gordon Bone and H.C. Devin. These notes come from the cashier's family. Included is a paper tag mentioning that this was the "first one J.G.B signed when he was cashier." A paper clip impression is noticed. **Extremely Fine.** (900-1,200)

15027 **Mount Vernon, OH** - $20 1902 Plain Back Fr. 650 **Knox NB** Ch. # (M)7638

The stamped signatures of the Cashier and Vice President are well executed on this $20. This note is also from the period when geographic sorting letters were added to notes. This $20 shows just a little more circulation than the other large notes in this auction on this bank. There is an approximate quarter inch split at top center and a small spot in the top margin. **Fine-Very Fine.** (600-900)

Serial Number 1 Mt. Vernon

15028 **Mount Vernon, OH** - $10 1929 Ty. 1 **Knox NB** Ch. # 7638

A paper tag comes with this serial number A000001A note saying, "first small sized with my signature JGB." Mr. Bone put another great note away for posterity. This note has embossing and original paper surfaces. The handling is mostly restricted to the far right hand quarter panel. The lower left corner is slightly shaved, yet it remains far from the frame line. There is not another number one note in the census on this bank. **Extremely Fine.** (2,000-4,000)

15029 **Mount Vernon, OH** - $20 1929 Ty. 1 **Knox NB** Ch. # 7638

There is only one graded Series 1929 note in the census that can rival the condition of this note on this bank. This $20 has natural paper ripple. **Choice Crisp Uncirculated.** (300-500)

15030 Mount Vernon, OH - $20 1929 Ty. 1 **Knox NB** Ch. # 7638
This is a crispy $20 with brown ink that bled through to the back. A couple of tiny edge nicks are noticed. **Very Fine.** (200-400)

15031 Mount Vernon, OH - $20 1929 Ty. 2 **Knox NB** Ch. # 7638
Type Ones outnumber Type Twos on this bank by over six to one. In fact we cannot find a record of any Type Two for #7638 ever being offered at auction. The lower left corner has a small moisture spot and there is a tiny spot of teller ink on the face. **Very Fine.** (400-600)

15032 Newark, OH - $1 Original Fr. 380 **The First NB** Ch. # 858
This well margined Ace comes from a run of uncirculated surviving examples. The overprint is excellent as is the overall eye appeal. **PMG Uncirculated 60 Net,** Top Left Margin Repaired. (2,250-2,750)

Gem Uncirculated 65PPQ $50 Brown Back

15033 Newark, OH - $50 1882 Brown Back Fr. 508 **The First NB** Ch. # 858
A $50 Brown Back whose original embossing is so pronounced that it can easily be seen through the front of the third party holder. PCGS has slabbed this note and assigned a grade of **Gem Uncirculated 65PPQ,** making this one of only a handful of $50 Brown Backs from either service to receive a grade this high. Expect to see bidding reach or exceed... (25,000-35,000)

15034 Piqua, OH - $1 Original Fr. 380 **The Piqua NB** Ch. # 1006
This is one of a scant three Aces known from this bank and appears at least **Fine** when looked at from the face and it also exhibits dark officer signatures. Unfortunately, there are numerous tape repairs on the back, which cover many different splits. A little bit of graffiti is also noticed. In May 2004 we sold an Ace in Fine on this bank for $3450. This is a great opportunity representing a lot of history for the money. (600-900)

15035 Saint Paris, OH - $20 1929 Ty. 1 **The Central NB** Ch. # 8127
Pleasing paper quality is noted on this Serial Number 21 issue. **Very Fine.** To date, none of the nine recorded surviving specimens grades higher than VF. (300-400)

15036 Steubenville, OH - $10 1882 Brown Back Fr. 487 **The Commercial NB** Ch. # 5039
A just plain rare note from a bank which liquidated in 1919. Just five notes of all kinds make up the entire census, with this the first example from this institution we've ever had the pleasure of handling. Pen signed **Very Fine.** (1,500-2,500)

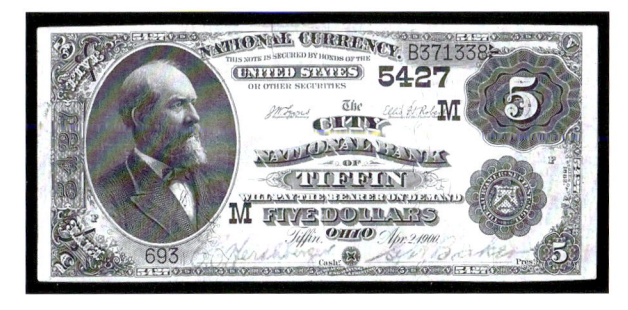

15037 Tiffin, OH - $5 1882 Date Back Fr. 537 **The City NB** Ch. # (M)5427
This is one of only three early notes known from this scarcer Tiffin bank, and the only one available to collectors in recent years. **Very Fine,** with a split at the top that affects little. (1,200-1,600)

West Milton, OH Unreported in Large Size

15038 West Milton, OH - $10 1902 Plain Back Fr. 626 The First NB Ch. # 9062
This **Very Good** example hails from a tough locale to acquire small size examples and has remained unreported in large size until this evening. Well circulated, but complete, it is a true miracle of survival as there was only $260 outstanding at close. Any estimate is but a guess, but this evening one lucky Ohio collector will be one step closer to a complete collection. Expect this currently unique piece to reach or exceed… **(6,000-9,000)**

OKLAHOMA

15039 Ada, OK - $10 1929 Ty. 2 The First NB Ch. # 12591
A scarce note which is considerably nicer than the example from here which we sold for $546.25 back in September of 2006. **Fine-Very Fine.**
From The Rolling Plains Collection **(500-700)**

15040 Alex, OK - $10 1929 Ty. 1 The First NB Ch. # 10193
A just plain scarce note from the only issuer in this tiny Grady County community. It is as nice or even a bit nicer than the example we sold from here in our September, 2006 sale, with that piece realizing a strong $1495. **About Fine.**
From The Rolling Plains Collection **(1,200-1,600)**

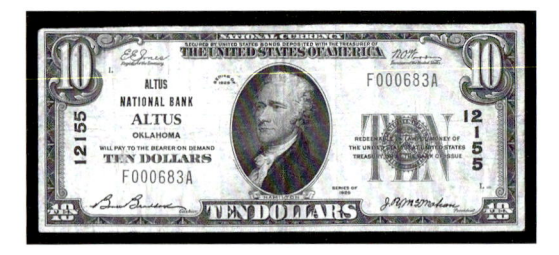

15041 Altus, OK - $10 1929 Ty. 1 Altus NB Ch. # 12155
Large notes are unknown from this Altus bank, which was one of five issuers here, leaving collectors no alternative than Series 1929 examples. This is a nice one. Sharp **Fine-Very Fine.**
From The Rolling Plains Collection **(500-700)**

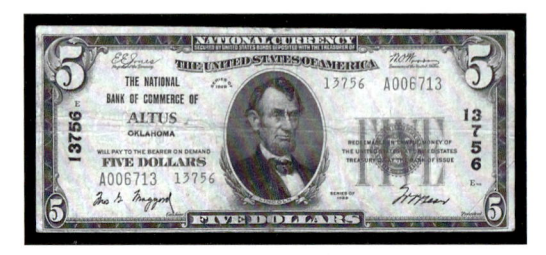

15042 Altus, OK - $5 1929 Ty. 2 The NB of Commerce Ch. # 13756
This late chartered bank only issued Type 2 notes, and currently has 12 in the latest Kelly census. Expect to see spirited bidding on this **Fine** example in the range of… **(600-800)**

15043 Anadarko, OK - $5 1929 Ty. 2 The First NB Ch. # 5905
This was the only bank chartered in this small Caddo County community which lasted long enough to issue Series 1929 examples. **Fine+.**
From The Rolling Plains Collection **(350-550)**

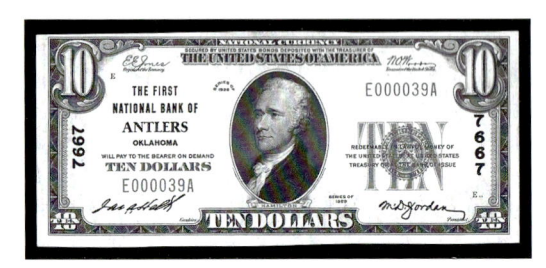

15044 Antlers, OK - $10 1929 Ty. 1 The First NB Ch. # 7667
This lovely example is one serial number removed from the note we sold from here back in our Long Beach sale in September, 2006. That piece realized over $5,000 against a pre-sale estimate of $2000-3000. Expect this most desirable specimen to approach or perhaps even exceed that figure before the hammer falls this evening. **Choice Crisp Uncirculated.**
From The Rolling Plains Collection **(4,000-6,000)**

15045 **Apache, OK** - $10 1929 Ty. 2 **The American NB** Ch. # 12120
An always in demand note from a town which bears a sought after Native American name. **Fine,** with just a touch of soil.
From The Rolling Plains Collection **(750-950)**

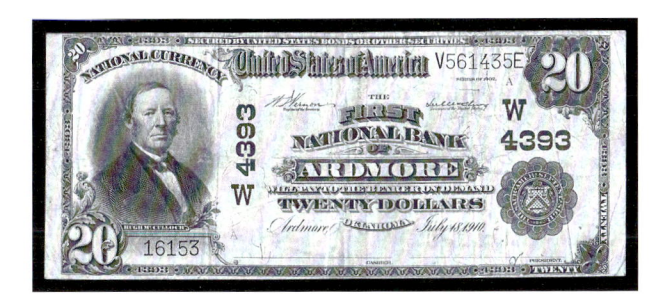

15046 **Ardmore, OK** - $20 1902 Plain Back Fr. 653 **The First NB** Ch. # (W)4393
A very scarce Ardmore bank which issued large notes only. Our records show only three offerings from here during the past fifteen years, including this piece, which we sold back in January of 1992. **Fine.** **(600-900)**

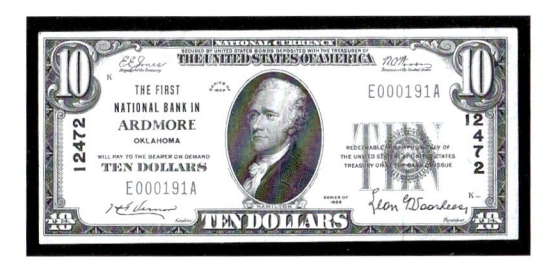

15047 **Ardmore, OK** - $10 1929 Ty. 1 **The First NB** Ch. # 12472
Although chartered in 1923, this institution elected to issue Series 1929 examples only before liquidating in 1933. Just eight notes make up the entire census, with this the finest of that small group. **Very Fine-Extremely Fine.**
From The Rolling Plains Collection **(600-900)**

15048 **Ardmore, OK** - $20 1929 Ty. 2 **First NB** Ch. # 13677
This is one of the highest grade examples known from this seldom offered bank, with this piece off the market since our consignor obtained it from us back in 1996. **About Uncirculated,** with a bit of foxing around the edges. **(300-500)**

15049 **Bartlesville, OK** - $5 1882 Date Back Fr. 538 **The First NB** Ch. # (W)5310
An extremely scarce Bartlesville bank with just eight examples reported to date. This is the sole $5 Date Back listed in the census. Well circulated but completely intact **Very Good+,** with clear signatures of Frank Bucher and Geo. B. Keeler, V. President. **(1,200-1,600)**

15050 **Blackwell, OK** - $10 1929 Ty. 1 **The First NB** Ch. # 5460
An exceptionally high grade piece which may be the finest Series 1929 example known from this Kay County community. **Very Fine-Extremely Fine.**
From The Rolling Plains Collection **(600-900)**

15051 **Blair, OK** - $10 1929 Ty. 1 **First NB** Ch. # 12130
An attractive note from this none too common bank which is listed in the census as CU. It's nice, but not nearly that nice. **Very Fine-Extremely Fine,** with a miniscule margin repair that affects little.
From The Rolling Plains Collection **(750-1,250)**

15052 **Blanchard, OK** - $20 1929 Ty. 1 **The First NB** Ch. # 8702
A very tough note which is as nice as any Series 1929 example listed in the census. **Fine-Very Fine.**
From The Rolling Plains Collection **(600-800)**

15053 Boynton, OK - $20 1929 Ty. 1 **The First NB** Ch. # 6511
An evenly circulated example from this small Muskogee County location. **About Fine,** with an edge split at the top. (400-600)

15054 Braggs, OK - $10 1902 Plain Back Fr. 630 **The First NB** Ch. # 10437
A pleasing high grade example with plenty of eye appeal. **Very Fine,** with vivid purple signatures. (450-650)

15055 Braman, OK - $20 1929 Ty. 1 **The First NB** Ch. # 10003
This was the sole bank chartered in this speck of a town, which is located in Kay County in the northernmost reaches of the state. With large notes unreported from this bank, collectors who want any example from this community are restricted to the six Series 1929 examples which make up the entire census from here. This pleasing **Fine+** specimen is as nice as any recorded to date.
From The Rolling Plains Collection (750-1,250)

15056 Calvin, OK - $10 1929 Ty. 1 **The First NB** Ch. # 6980
This is a tough bank to find in large size, but small notes from here are truly rare, with this example one of just three recorded in the census, one of which is listed without a grade. Pleasing **Fine+,** and desirable enough to easily reach or exceed...
From The Rolling Plains Collection (1,250-1,750)

15057 Carmen, OK - $20 1929 Ty. 2 **The First NB** Ch. # 12498
A decent example from the only one of the four banks chartered here to issue Series 1929 notes. **Very Fine-Extremely Fine.**
From The Rolling Plains Collection (600-800)

15058 Checotah, OK - $20 1882 Date Back Fr. 556 **The First NB** Ch. # (W)5128
An unusually high grade Oklahoma Date Back, although, as in the case with so many notes of this type, the top margin is tightly trimmed. Although not an exceptionally rare bank, this is the only Date Back of any denomination reported from here. **Very Fine-Extremely Fine.** (1,500-2,500)

Unique With This Title

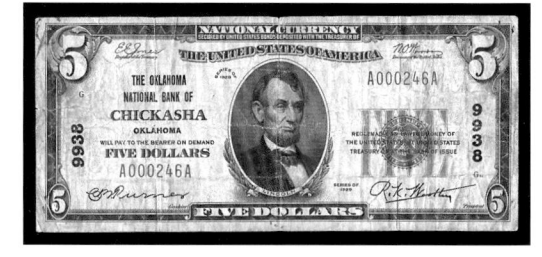

15059 Chickasha, OK - $5 1929 Ty. 1 **The Oklahoma NB** Ch. # 9938
This piece, which is new to the census, is the only Series 1929 example recorded to date bearing the first title used on notes from here. It may well remain unique for many years, as only a very limited number of small size examples bore this title, which was changed in May of 1930. Decent **About Fine,** a perfectly acceptable specimen likely destined for an important Oklahoma collection.
From The Rolling Plains Collection (1,250-2,250)

15060 Chickasha, OK - $10 1929 Ty. 1 **Oklahoma NB** Ch. # 9938
A high grade example bearing the second title used here. Bright **Extremely Fine-About Uncirculated,** considerably nicer than most notes known from here.
From The Rolling Plains Collection (300-500)

15061 Claremore, OK - $20 1902 Plain Back Fr. 654 **The NB of Claremore** Ch. # (W)10117
Seven large notes are reported in Kelly from here, which is also known as the home of Will Rogers. This **Fine** example last appeared in a CAA auction May of 2000. (500-750)

15062 Cleveland, OK - $5 1882 Value Back Fr. 575 **The First NB** Ch. # (W)5911
This is one of only twenty five $5 Value Backs reported from the entire state of Oklahoma, and the sole specimen known from Cleveland. **Very Good-Fine,** with a repaired top right corner.
From The Rolling Plains Collection (900-1,200)

15063 Clinton, OK - $10 1929 Ty. 1 **The First NB** Ch. # 6940
A high grade piece which is almost certainly the finest small size note reported from this Custer County locale. Bright **Very Fine+.**
From The Rolling Plains Collection (500-800)

15064 Comanche, OK - $10 1929 Ty. 1 **The First NB** Ch. # 6299
This is a just plain rare note from the only collectible bank in this Stephens County community, with this piece the finest Series 1929 example reported from here to date. **Very Fine,** with some light soiling on the back that affects nothing.
From The Rolling Plains Collection (1,200-1,600)

15065 Commerce, OK - $5 1929 Ty. 1 **The First NB** Ch. # 10689
This was the only issuer in this otherwise unremarkable small town whose only claim to fame was being the home town of Yankee's slugger Mickey Mantle. Well circulated but intact **Very Good.**
From The Rolling Plains Collection (350-550)

15066 Cordell, OK - $10 1929 Ty. 1 **The Farmers NB** Ch. # 9968
This was the only bank of the five chartered in this community of fewer than 3000 people that lasted long enough to issue Series 1929 examples. **Very Fine,** with the top margin trimmed just a bit close at the right end.
From The Rolling Plains Collection (400-600)

15067 Cushing, OK - $20 1929 Ty. 1 **The Farmers NB** Ch. # 10332
By far the scarcer of Cushing's two small size issuers, with the Series 1929 census from here standing at just seven pieces. **Fine-Very Fine,** with a few minor ink spots that affect nothing.
From The Rolling Plains Collection (600-900)

15068 **Custer City, OK** - $20 1929 Ty. 1 **The First NB** Ch. # 8727
A decent small example from this always in demand Custer County community. **Fine++.** (400-600)

15069 **Davis, OK** - $10 1929 Ty. 1 **The First NB** Ch. # 5298
A tougher bank from a community that was missing from the major Oklahoma offering in our last couple of sales. **Fine-Very Fine.**
From The Rolling Plains Collection (500-700)

15070 **Depew, OK** - $10 1929 Ty. 1 **The State NB** Ch. # 12104
This bank, which issued Series 1929 examples only, was the sole National Bank chartered in this Creek County location. The census from here stands at just seven notes, including this evenly circulated and problem free **Very Good-Fine** specimen.
From The Rolling Plains Collection (500-700)

15071 **Duncan, OK** - $20 1929 Ty. 1 **The Security NB** Ch. # 12065
This was the last of the five National Banks in Duncan to receive its charter, and one of only two which survived long enough to issue series 1929 examples. With this city's other small size issuer unreported to date, notes from this none too common bank afford collectors their only opportunity to obtain a Series 1929 note from here. This piece is sure to please its new owner. **Very Fine.**
From The Rolling Plains Collection (500-700)

15072 **Durant, OK** - $20 1882 Date Back Fr. 556 **The Durant NB** Ch. # (W)5590
Large notes only from this bank, with this attractive $20 Date Back one of the nicer examples we've seen from here. **Very Fine,** with purple signatures. (1,000-1,200)

15073 **Durant, OK** - $20 1929 Ty. 2 **The First NB** Ch. # 14005
This is a very scarce 14000 charter, with the census from here standing at just five pieces, including this one. There are a few small holes in the margins, but the body of the note is solid and the overall grade is at least **Fine**.
From The Rolling Plains Collection (600-900)

15074 **El Reno, OK** - $5 1902 Plain Back Fr. 602 **The First NB** Ch. # (W)4830
A rather common bank in small, but not so in large, where offerings are considerably fewer. Evenly circulated **Fine,** with bold violet signatures. (450-650)

15075 **El Reno, OK** - $20 1882 Date Back Fr. 556 **The Citizens NB** Ch. # (W)5985
A very scarce early El Reno note from a bank where small notes outnumber large by roughly a five to one ratio. **Very Good+,** with a small portion of bank stamp on the reverse. (800-1,200)

15076 El Reno, OK - $20 1929 Ty. 1 **The Citizens NB** Ch. # 5985
A nice example of this classic hoard note. **Choice About Uncirculated.**
From The Rolling Plains Collection (250-350)

15077 Elk City, OK - $20 1902 Plain Back Fr. 653 **The First NB** Ch. # 9952
A tough note from the only collectible bank in town, with this city's other two issuers both unreported. **Fine**, the signatures faded.
From The Rolling Plains Collection (1,200-1,600)

15078 Eufaula, OK - $10 1902 Plain Back Fr. 630 **The State NB** Ch. # 10388
While common in small size, large notes from here are another story entirely, with the census showing just six such examples. **Fine+**, rare enough to see bidding end in the vicinity of... (800-1,200)

First Offering in Twenty Years

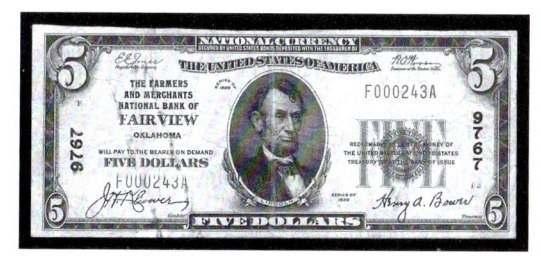

15079 Fairview, OK - $5 1929 Ty. 1 **The Farmers & Merchants NB** Ch. # 9767
This is a truly rare note from a bank which has not had an offering at public sale since 1988. With this small community's other bank unreported, and with the less than a handful of examples known from here all ensconced in major Oklahoma holdings, it may well be years before the opportunity of adding any note from Fairview arises again. **Fine**, with a few spots on the front visible because of a light stain on the back that barely detracts.
From The Rolling Plains Collection (2,000-4,000)

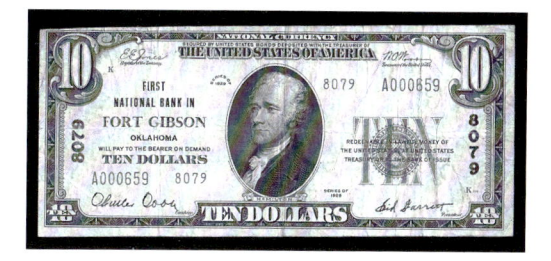

15080 Fort Gibson, OK - $10 1929 Ty. 2 **First NB** Ch. # 8079
A very presentable Type 2 example from this none too common Muskogee County bank. **Fine.** (300-500)

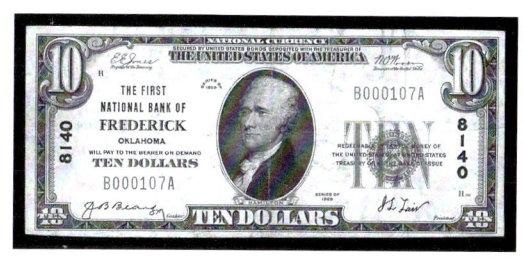

15081 Frederick, OK - $10 1929 Ty. 1 **The First NB** Ch. # 8140
This new to the census example is easily the finest of the four extant Series 1929 notes from this extremely scarce bank, and is considerably nicer than the specimen from here we sold in January for over $1000. Bright **Fine-Very Fine**, a certain to please item.
From The Rolling Plains Collection (1,000-1,500)

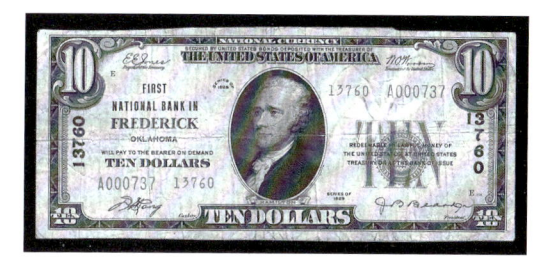

15082 Frederick, OK - $10 1929 Ty. 2 **First NB** Ch. # 13760
Only three notes are known from this scarce high charter Frederick issuer, with no offerings of any kind at public sale in the six decades before we sold one of the three extant examples last September for $1725. This piece is another of that trio, and is being offered to the collecting public at public sale for the first time in this outing. It is just about identical in grade to the other two reported pieces, and offers the underbidders in last September's sale a rare second opportunity to obtain a note from this rare charter. **Fine**, with a tiny pencil erasure.
From The Rolling Plains Collection (1,250-1,750)

15083 Guymon, OK - $20 1902 Plain Back Fr. 652 **The First NB** Ch. # (W)8138
A just plain rare example from this much sought after Oklahoma panhandle community. This is the only large $20 note reported from here to date, and it is the first large note of any kind from here to be offered since 2003, when a large note in just about the same grade as this piece realized $4600. Expect some stiff competition before the hammer falls on this pen signed **Very Fine** specimen. (3,500-5,500)

15084 Guymon, OK - $20 1929 Ty. 1 **The First NB** Ch. # 8138
Notes from this remote Oklahoma panhandle location have long been sought by this state's collectors, and are seldom available in either large or small size. In this case, however, large notes are considerably more common than are small, which have a population of just three pieces in the latest Kelly census. All but one have been off the market for many years, and our records disclose only one sales record for a Series 1929 example within the past decade. **Very Fine.**
From The Rolling Plains Collection (1,500-2,500)

First Offering Since 1989

15085 Harrah, OK - $20 1929 Ty. 1 **The First NB** Ch. # 9980
This is one of the highlights of the collection being offered here tonight, as this bank is unknown in large and extremely rare in small. In fact, this is the first offering of any kind from here since an example appeared on a fixed price list back in 1989. With this bank on several Oklahoma want lists, any estimate is but a guess, but the hammer likely will fall on this evenly circulated **Fine** example somewhere in the vicinity of...
From The Rolling Plains Collection (1,750-2,750)

15086 Haskell, OK - $10 1929 Ty. 1 **The First NB** Ch. # 7822
One of the nicer examples known from this bank. **Very Fine.**
From The Rolling Plains Collection (500-700)

15087 Helena, OK - $5 1929 Ty. 1 **The Helena NB** Ch. # 12081
This is one of just seven notes reported from this very scarce Alfalfa County community, and the first to be offered publicly in several years. **Fine.**
From The Rolling Plains Collection (750-1,250)

15088 **Hennessey, OK - $10 1902 Plain Back Fr. 633 The First NB** Ch. # 5473
This is just one of five large notes from this bank listed in the census. **About Fine,** with a few pinholes which barely detract. (700-1,200)

15089 **Hennessey, OK - $10 1902 Plain Back Fr. 628 The Farmers & Merchants NB** Ch. # (W)10209
While this bank is relatively abundant in the 1929 series, Large Size offerings are few and far between. This **Very Good** offering is one of only two 1902 Plain Backs known in the $10 denomination with a grand total of only 4 large in the census. In view of its scarcity, plan on going a few extra increments to acquire this challenging bank. (1,000-1,500)

15090 **Hennessey, OK - $10 1929 Ty. 1 The Farmers & Merchants NB** Ch. # 10209
This crisp, bright $10 from this popular collecting area sports the serial number 9. **Very Fine.** (500-700)

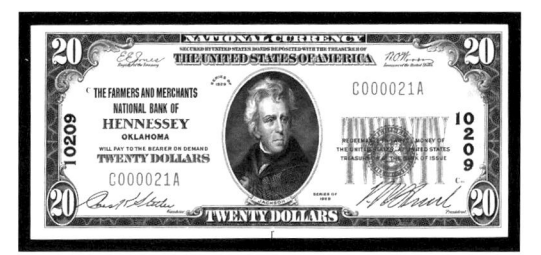

15091 **Hennessey, OK - $20 1929 Ty. 1 The Farmers & Merchants NB** Ch. # 10209
One of a small group of high grade examples known from here, most of which have been off the market for many years. **Choice Crisp Uncirculated,** with a small stain on the back that affects little.
From The Rolling Plains Collection (700-900)

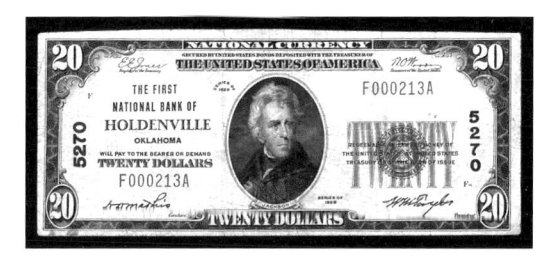

15092 **Holdenville, OK - $20 1929 Ty. 1 The First NB** Ch. # 5270
This bank was the first of five chartered here to issue, and the only one which lasted long enough to circulate Series 1929 examples. **Fine.**
From The Rolling Plains Collection (400-600)

15093 **Hollis, OK - $10 1902 Plain Back Fr. 628 The NB of Commerce** Ch. # 10240
Four large size notes are known from this bank, which had a meager $330 outstanding in large at the bank's closing in 1935. Through the vagaries of fate, and our good fortune in selling two major Oklahoma collections within the past year, we have now had the pleasure of offering three of the four reported examples. Once this piece is gone, don't expect many more opportunities to obtain a large note from here in the foreseeable future. Pen signed **Fine.**
From The Rolling Plains Collection (1,200-1,800)

15094 **Hollis, OK** - $10 1929 Ty. 1 **The NB of Commerce** Ch. # 10240
Series 1929 examples are even tougher than are large notes from here, with the census standing at just two pieces, one of which is offered here. Decent **Very Good-Fine,** rare enough to see bidding easily reach or exceed...
From The Rolling Plains Collection (1,500-2,500)

15095 **Hominy, OK** - $20 1929 Ty. 1 **The First NB** Ch. # 7927
An attractive note which is as high a grade Series 1929 example as we've ever seen for sale from here. **Very Fine-Extremely Fine.** (600-900)

15096 **Hydro, OK** - $10 1929 Ty. 1 **The First NB** Ch. # 9944
This note, bearing one of the more interesting Oklahoma place names, comes from the only bank here to issue Series 1929 examples. Offerings from here of any kind have been few and far between, with the last from this bank coming back when this note was sold to our consignor back in 1997. Nice **Fine-Very Fine.**
From The Rolling Plains Collection (1,000-1,500)

15097 **Idabel, OK** - $20 1929 Ty. 1 **The Idabel NB** Ch. # 11913
This hard to find SE Oklahoma bank issued Series 1929 examples only, with the last public offering coming some ten years ago when our consignor obtained this note. Pleasing **Very Fine.**
From The Rolling Plains Collection (600-900)

15098 **Kaw City, OK** - $20 1929 Ty. 1 **First NB** Ch. # 10075
An always popular note bearing an unusual and interesting town name. Sharp **Very Fine.**
From The Rolling Plains Collection (450-650)

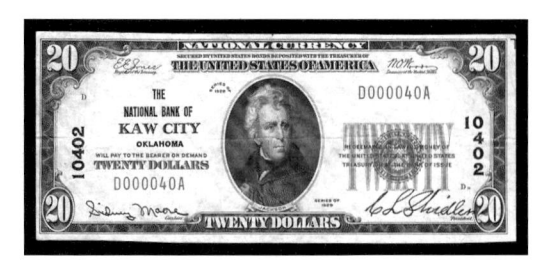

15099 **Kaw City, OK** - $20 1929 Ty. 1 **The NB of Kaw City** Ch. # 10402
This was by far the weaker of Kaw City's two banks which survived long enough to issue Series 1929 examples, with this institution succumbing to the ravages of the Depression early in 1932. Only a handful of small notes were issued from here, with the total population now standing at just three pieces. This example is likely the finest of that trio, and is worthy of a strong bid. Nice **Very Fine.**
From The Rolling Plains Collection (1,000-1,500)

15100 **Kingfisher, OK** - $20 1929 Ty. 1 **The First NB** Ch. # 5328
Although this Kingfisher bank was established during territorial days, it proved the smaller and weaker of this community's two banks which survived to issue series 1929 notes. This is one of just six small size notes reported from here to date. **Fine-Very Fine.**
From The Rolling Plains Collection (700-900)

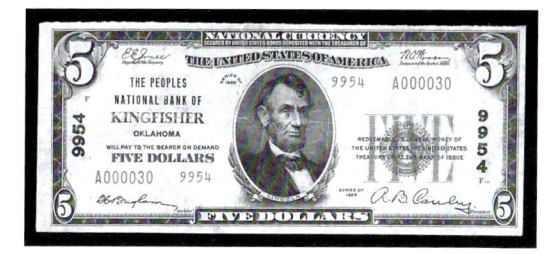

15101 **Kingfisher, OK** - $5 1929 Ty. 2 **The Peoples NB** Ch. # 9954
While hardly a rare bank, this piece is the only $5 example reported from this institution to date. **Fine.**
From The Rolling Plains Collection **(500-700)**

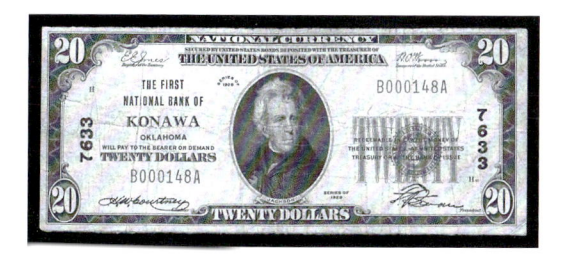

15102 **Konawa, OK** - $20 1929 Ty. 1 **The First NB** Ch. # 7633
This is a just plain rare town, with the community's other issuer unreported after liquidating in 1915. Just three large and five small notes are known, with the last offering coming back in 2004 when we sold a similarly graded Series 1929 example for over $1000. **Fine.**
From The Rolling Plains Collection **(800-1,200)**

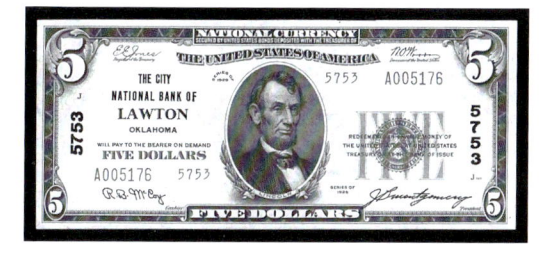

15103 **Lawton, OK** - $5 1929 Ty. 2 **The City NB** Ch. # 5753
A lovely example which is easily the highest grade small note known from here. **About Uncirculated.**
From The Rolling Plains Collection **(400-600)**

15104 **Lawton, OK** - $10 1882 Date Back Fr. 546 **The First NB** Ch. # (W)5914
Although this bank lasted just long enough to issue Third Charter examples, only Second Charter specimens are known from here. This Date Back is a very nice looking piece for the grade. **Fine.** **(1,000-1,500)**

15105 **Lindsay, OK** - $10 1902 Plain Back Fr. 634 **The First NB** Ch. # 6171
This is a just plain rare bank in large size, with the census showing just four such examples extant, all of which bear the second title used here. We sold this piece back in 2003, and it remains the only large note from here offered to the collecting fraternity in the past three decades. **Fine,** with the paper just a bit toned. **(1,500-2,500)**

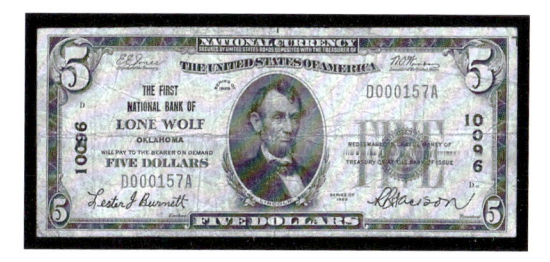

15106 **Lone Wolf, OK** - $5 1929 Ty. 1 **The First NB** Ch. # 10096
This is one of only a literal handful of circulated small notes we've seen from this always sought after location. **Very Good.**
From The Rolling Plains Collection **(600-900)**

15107 **Luther, OK** - $20 1902 Plain Back Fr. 652 **The First NB** Ch. # (W)8563
This newly discovered piece is far nicer than most from this tougher one bank community. Pleasing **Fine-Very Fine.** **(750-950)**

15108 **Luther, OK** - $20 1929 Ty. 1 **The First NB** Ch. # 8563
A perfect companion to the large example from here offered above, and one of the very nicest, if not the nicest, Series 1929 notes from this one bank location. **Very Fine-Extremely Fine.**
From The Rolling Plains Collection (500-700)

15109 **Madill, OK** - $10 1929 Ty. 1 **The First NB** Ch. # 13021
A more than acceptable note from this scarce bank which bears the second type style used in the title. **Fine+,** a virtual duplicate to the example from here which realized $632.50 in our last sale.
From The Rolling Plains Collection (500-700)

15110 **Mangum, OK** - $20 1902 Plain Back Fr. 659 **The First NB** Ch. # 5508
A most attractive large example which is very likely the highest grade example of any kind known from here. Sharp **Very Fine-Extremely Fine,** with bold pen signatures.
From The Rolling Plains Collection (1,000-1,500)

15111 **Marlow, OK** - $10 1929 Ty. 1 **The State NB** Ch. # 9946
A nice note from this better Marlow bank which has been off the market since our consignor obtained it from a 1997 auction. Pleasing **Very Fine.**
From The Rolling Plains Collection (450-650)

15112 **Marlow, OK** - $5 1929 Ty. 1 **The First NB** Ch. # 12129
A nicely centered and crackling fresh example of this hoard note. **Very Choice Crisp Uncirculated.**
From The Rolling Plains Collection (450-650)

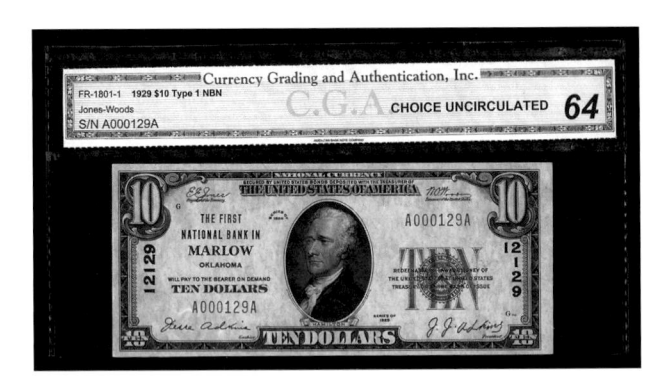

15113 **Marlow, OK** - $10 1929 Ty. 1 **The First NB** Ch. # 12129
An attractive example of this hoard note which is in a **CGA Choice Uncirculated 64** encasement. (450-650)

15114 **Marlow, OK** - $10 1929 Ty. 1 **The First NB** Ch. # 12129
A second $10 example from here, with this piece also grading **Choice Crisp Uncirculated.** (400-600)

15115 **Medford, OK** - $20 1929 Ty. 1 **The First NB** Ch. # 5796
An evenly circulated small example from the only National Bank chartered here. **Fine-Very Fine.**
From The Rolling Plains Collection (450-650)

15116 **Mill Creek, OK** - $10 1929 Ty. 1 **The First NB** Ch. # 7197
Although three banks were chartered here, this was the only one to last long enough to issue Series 1929 examples. **Fine** or a bit better.
From The Rolling Plains Collection (400-600)

15117 **Minco, OK** - $5 1929 Ty. 1 **The First NB** Ch. # 8644
This is one of just six small notes reported from this rare one bank locale. With the one large example known from here firmly ensconced in a major Oklahoma holding, Series 1929 notes are all that a collector can hope to find, with even those offerings few and far between. **Fine,** the top margin trimmed just a hair close to the design.
From The Rolling Plains Collection (1,250-1,750)

Excessively Rare Moore Note

15118 **Moore, OK** - $10 1929 Ty. 1 **The First NB** Ch. # 12035
This is the first note we have ever had to offer from this exceedingly rare Oklahoma City suburb. Just one large note exists from here, along with four small examples, with the note offered here perhaps the nicest of the four pieces extant. **Fine,** with a small blue teller stamp residue on the front that barely detracts.
From The Rolling Plains Collection (1,500-2,500)

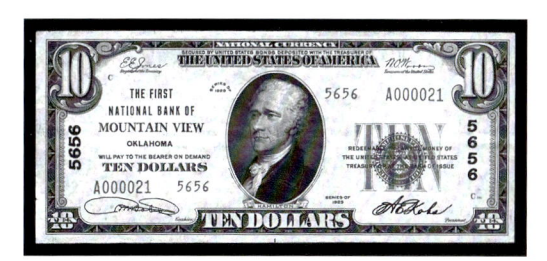

15119 **Mountain View, OK** - $10 1929 Ty. 2 **The First NB** Ch. # 5656
This is actually a tougher bank to obtain in small size than large, with this note coming from the only institution to issue in this rather unlikely named Oklahoma community. **Very Fine.**
From The Rolling Plains Collection (600-900)

15120 **Muskogee, OK** - $50 1902 Plain Back Fr. 678 **The First NB** Ch. # (W)4385
This **Very Good** $50 with faded signatures carries the second of two titles under which this bank issued large size and the only one to bear this nomenclature for the $50 Plain Backs. This is a sharply folded wallet keepsake with margin roughness at left and rounded corners. However, being a wallet keepsake is the only reason why this note survives today. (600-900)

15121 **Muskogee, OK** - $10 1902 Plain Back Fr. 635 **The Commercial NB** Ch. # 12890
Although almost seventy Series 1929 examples have been reported from here, only ten large examples are known from this bank in all grades and denominations combined. This bright example is as nice as any listed in the census. **Very Fine.** (600-900)

15122 **Nash, OK** - $5 1929 Ty. 2 **The First NB** Ch. # 11306
This was the only denomination issued by this bank in both large and small size. Pleasing **Fine-Very Fine.**
From The Rolling Plains Collection (300-400)

15123 Newkirk, OK - $10 1902 Plain Back Fr. 626 **The Eastman NB** Ch. # 9011
A well circulated but fully intact large example from this rather scarce bank. **Very Good. (600-900)**

15124 Newkirk, OK - $20 1929 Ty. 1 **The Eastman NB** Ch. # 9011
This pleasing example is the highest grade small note in the census from here. **Very Fine+.**
From The Rolling Plains Collection **(450-650)**

15125 Noble, OK - $10 1929 Ty. 1 **The First NB** Ch. # 9937
Although we have offered a pair of Series 1929 notes from here in recent sales, this is actually a very tough one bank community where large notes are easier to obtain than small. This **Fine** specimen bears the signatures of A.E. Ellinger and R.F. Ellinger.
From The Rolling Plains Collection **(700-900)**

15126 Norman, OK - $10 1882 Date Back Fr. 546 **The First NB** Ch. # (W)5248
This early Norman note is new to the census. **Very Good** or a bit better, with a small piece missing at the bottom left corner. **(500-900)**

15127 Norman, OK - $10 1929 Ty. 2 **The Security NB** Ch. # 12036
Small notes only from this considerably scarcer Norman bank. **Very Good.**
From The Rolling Plains Collection **(300-500)**

15128 Nowata, OK - $20 1929 Ty. 2 **The First NB** Ch. # 5401
This high grade example is the only Type 2 listed in the census from here. Sharp **Very Fine. (300-500)**

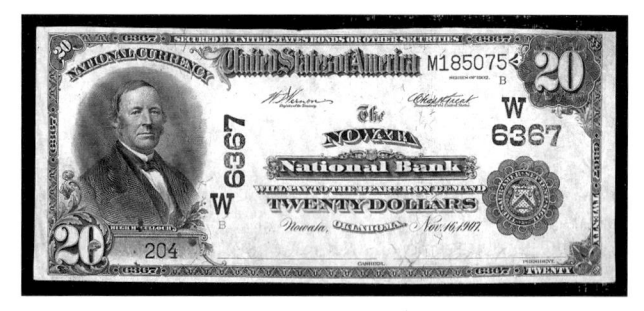

15129 Nowata, OK - $20 1902 Plain Back Fr. 652 **The Nowata NB** Ch. # (W)6367
Large notes only from this just plain rare Nowata bank, which disappeared forever early in 1924. Just three examples are known from here, with the last appearance at public sale coming back in 1992. **Very Fine,** but with some fading of the blue overprint and a few tiny rust spots at the lower left. **(1,500-2,500)**

15130 Oklahoma City, OK - $10 1902 Plain Back Fr. 626 **The Farmers NB** Ch. # (W)9564
A very scarce Oklahoma City bank which issued large notes only. Our records show no public offerings from here in almost ten years. **Fine. (600-900)**

15131 Okmulgee, OK - $20 1902 Plain Back Fr. 659 **The First NB** Ch. # (W)5418
This was the first of no fewer than seven banks chartered in this small county seat community. Like its siblings, it had a relatively short and undistinguished life, with this institution failing to survive beyond 1924. Just five notes are known from here, with this one of that limited number. Evenly circulated **About Fine. (900-1,200)**

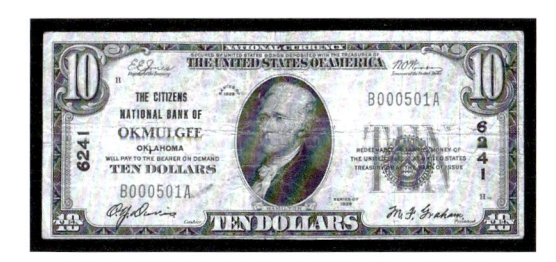

15132 Okmulgee, OK - $10 1929 Ty. 1 **The Citizens NB** Ch. # 6241
A tougher bank in small than large, no surprise considering this institution's limited Series 1929 emission. **About Fine.**
From The Rolling Plains Collection **(400-600)**

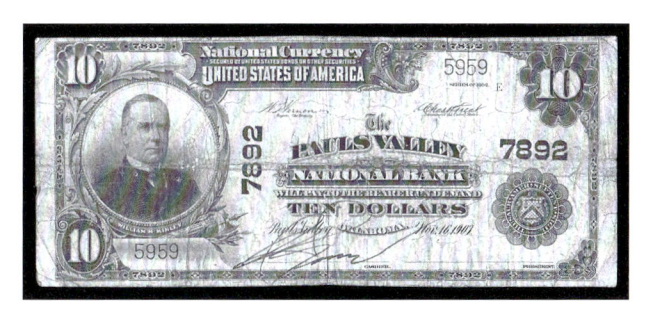

15133 Pauls Valley, OK - $10 1902 Plain Back Fr. 626 **The Pauls Valley NB** Ch. # 7892
While small notes are occasionally available from this institution, large examples are another matter entirely, with the current census standing at just three pieces. **Very Good**, with no problems save for even wear. **(1,500-2,500)**

15134 Pauls Valley, OK - $20 1929 Ty. 2 **The Pauls Valley NB** Ch. # 7892
This bank is considerably the scarcer of the two from here which survived long enough to issue Series 1929 notes. **Fine-Very Fine.**
From The Rolling Plains Collection **(500-800)**

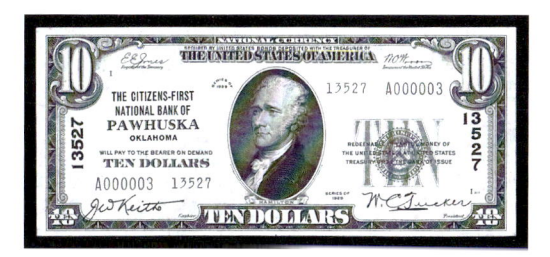

15135 Pawhuska, OK - $10 1929 Ty. 2 **The Citizens-First NB** Ch. # 13527
While the serial number 1 sheet of $5 Type 2 notes was preserved for collectors, the notes on the $10 Type 2 sheet obviously circulated, at least for a brief period, because the serial number 1 example grades only Very Fine and this example, bearing serial number A000003, grades **Extremely Fine. (300-500)**

15136 Pawhuska, OK - $20 1929 Ty. 2 **NB of Commerce** Ch. # 14304
This is one of the scarcer 14000 charter banks, with just four examples recorded in the census. All are Type 2 Twenties, the sole denomination this bank opted to issue. Pleasing **Fine-Very Fine**, likely to see bidding end in the range of...
From The Rolling Plains Collection **(1,000-1,400)**

15137 Pawnee, OK - $10 1902 Plain Back Fr. 632 **The First NB** Ch. # 5224
A nice native American name adorns this by no means common large example, which bears the pen signature of female Assistant Cashier Nellie Livesay. **Very Good-Fine.** (750-1,250)

15138 Pawnee, OK - $20 1929 Ty. 2 **The First NB** Ch. # 5224
A considerably above average small example from this bank. **Very Fine,** with a couple of tiny rust spots and a bit of old writing, neither of which is terribly significant.
From The Rolling Plains Collection (400-600)

15139 Pawnee, OK - $10 1929 Ty. 2 **The Pawnee NB** Ch. # 7611
This was Pawnee's only other issuer of Series 1929 notes. **Very Fine,** with a small amount of bleed through showing on the reverse.
From The Rolling Plains Collection (400-600)

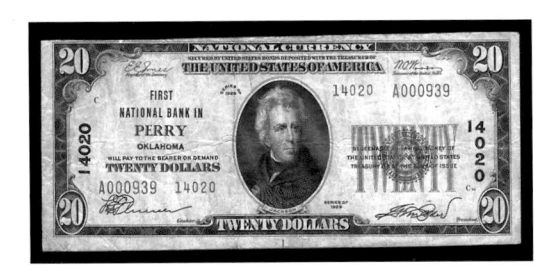

15140 Perry, OK - $20 1929 Ty. 2 **First NB** Ch. # 14020
A more than acceptable example from this hard to find 14000 charter issuer. **Fine.**
From The Rolling Plains Collection (600-900)

15141 Pocasset, OK - $10 1929 Ty. 2 **The First NB** Ch. # 10960
An extremely scarce note from the only bank to issue in this tiny Grady County location. Just four large and three small notes comprise the entire census from here, with no offerings of any kind since 1998 save for the considerably lower grade example we sold in our January sale. **Fine-Very Fine,** with a well disguised repaired split on the right side.
From The Rolling Plains Collection (1,400-1,900)

15142 Ponca City, OK - $20 1929 Ty. 2 **First NB** Ch. # 9801
An attractive piece which is the only Type 2 example of any denomination reported from here. **Fine-Very Fine.** (450-650)

15143 Porter, OK - $20 1929 Ty. 2 **The First NB** Ch. # 7615
A very scarce note from the sole Porter issuer that lasted long enough to emit Series 1929 notes. **Very Fine,** and the only Type 2 of any denomination known from here.
From The Rolling Plains Collection (600-900)

15144 Prague, OK - $10 1929 Ty. 2 **The First NB** Ch. # 7177
This new to the census piece is as high grade as any we've seen offered from here in small size. Bright **Very Fine,** with the bottom left margin a touch close. (400-600)

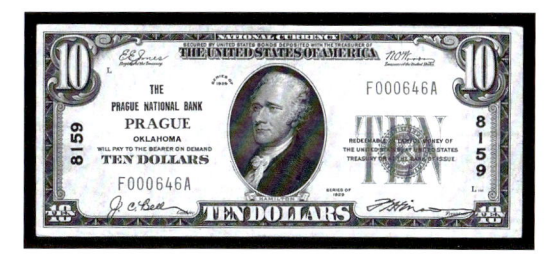

15145 **Prague, OK** - $10 1929 Ty. 1 **The Prague NB** Ch. # 8159
A really nice example which is considerably above the average of notes from here. Bright **Extremely Fine.**
From The Rolling Plains Collection (400-600)

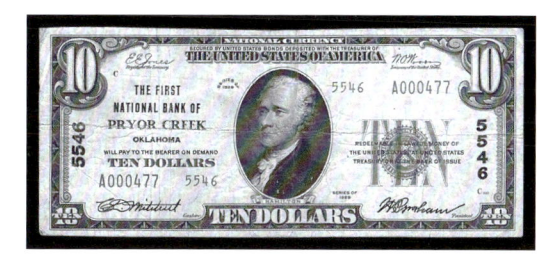

15146 **Pryor Creek, OK** - $10 1929 Ty. 2 **The First NB** Ch. # 5546
This is one of only two Type 2 examples listed in the census from here. **Fine.**
From The Rolling Plains Collection (400-600)

15147 **Purcell, OK** - $5 1929 Ty. 2 **The McClain County NB** Ch. # 12134
Small size only notes from this issuer, the last of Purcell's four banks to receive its charter. **Fine.**
From The Rolling Plains Collection (300-500)

Second Offering in Six Decades

15148 **Ralston, OK** - $10 1929 Ty. 1 **The First NB** Ch. # 6232
This truly rare note comes from the only bank chartered in this tiny Pawnee County community. The census here stands at just five pieces, three large and two small, all of which save one have been off the market in major collections for many years. In fact, our records show no offerings whatever of any Series 1929 example before this evening. With this bank issuing only a handful of small notes before disappearing in December of 1930, it would be unwise to expect many more such examples remain to be discovered. Sharp **Fine-Very Fine,** a great Oklahoma item worthy of a strong bid.
From The Rolling Plains Collection (2,000-4,000)

15149 **Rush Springs, OK** - $20 1929 Ty. 1 **The First NB** Ch. # 8336
It is only when important collections are dispersed that collectors have the opportunity to obtain truly scarce items such as this specimen. Until we sold the small note from here in our January sale, it had been fifteen years since any example from this one bank town had been available to the collecting fraternity. That piece, which was just about identical to this in grade, brought $2530 against a pre-sale estimate of $1250-1750. Expect this attractive **Very Fine** specimen to see the hammer fall within a few dollars of that figure, if not even a bit more.
From The Rolling Plains Collection (1,750-2,750)

15150 **Sand Springs, OK** - $10 1902 Plain Back Fr. 634 **The First NB** Ch. # 12079
A very scarce Tulsa County bank which issued large notes only during its brief seven year tenure. **Fine-Very Fine**, the signatures faded, a virtual twin to the note we sold in our last sale from here which realized $2300.
From The Rolling Plains Collection **(1,750-2,750)**

15151 **Sapulpa, OK** - $10 1929 Ty. 2 **The American NB** Ch. # 7788
An elusive bank which was this community's only small size issuer. **Fine.**
From The Rolling Plains Collection **(500-700)**

15152 **Sayre, OK** - $20 1902 Plain Back Fr. 653 **The First NB** Ch. # (W)9959
A seldom seen bank, with this piece off the market since our consignor obtained it back in 1998. **Very Good-Fine.**
From The Rolling Plains Collection **(600-800)**

Finer of Two Known

15153 **Sayre, OK** - $10 1929 Ty. 1 **The Beckham County NB** Ch. # 9976
Another great Oklahoma rarity from this outstanding collection. This institution was one of the most thinly capitalized in the state, and consequently issued just a literal handful of notes, both large and small. No large examples have ever been seen from here, and the small size population stands at just two pieces, with this the higher grade of the pair. This marks only the second opportunity in over sixty years for collectors to obtain any example from here, with the first appearance coming when our consignor purchased this piece for his holdings several years ago. **About Fine.**
From The Rolling Plains Collection **(2,250-4,250)**

15154 **Seiling, OK** - $10 1929 Ty. 2 **The First NB** Ch. # 8615
Large notes are just about uncollectible from this one bank town with just two examples reported, one of which is a serial Number 1 Territorial Red Seal. That leaves small size only for collectors, with even those seldom appearing for sale. This is a nice circulated specimen which is certain to please. **Fine-Very Fine.**
From The Rolling Plains Collection **(700-900)**

15155 **Seminole, OK** - $20 1929 Ty. 2 **The First NB** Ch. # 9514
A more than decent example bearing a nice Native American title. **Fine-Very Fine.**
From The Rolling Plains Collection **(500-700)**

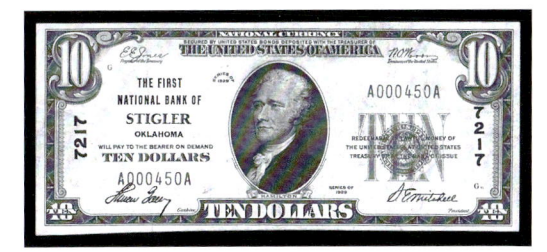

15156 **Stigler, OK** - $10 1929 Ty. 1 **The First NB** Ch. # 7217
A nice evenly circulated piece which is the finest example known from this very scarce Haskell County community. **Very Fine.**
From The Rolling Plains Collection (800-1,000)

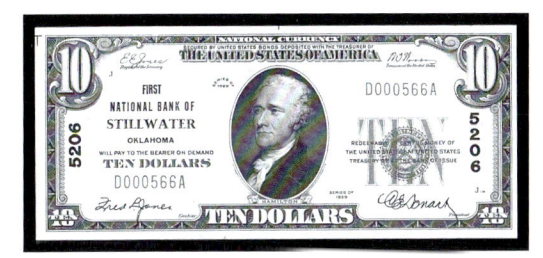

15157 **Stillwater, OK** - $10 1929 Ty. 1 **The First NB** Ch. # 5206
This lovely note is the only example from here, large or small, which is listed in the census in higher grade than Very Fine. Sharp **Choice About Uncirculated,** just the lightest of center bends away from the full Choice New designation.
From The Rolling Plains Collection (500-700)

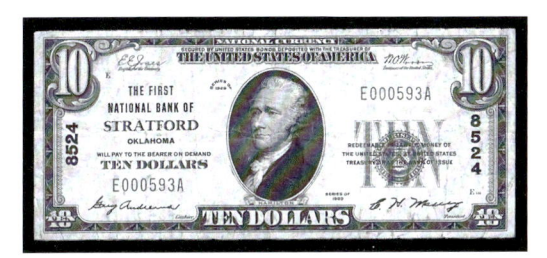

15158 **Stratford, OK** - $10 1929 Ty. 1 **The First NB** Ch. # 8524
A better note from a bank which is just about as difficult to find in small size as large. **Fine-Very Fine.**
From The Rolling Plains Collection (400-600)

15159 **Stroud, OK** - $10 1929 Ty. 1 **The First NB** Ch. # 6306
A most attractive example which is several grades higher than the note we sold from here last September which realized just under $500. Nice **Extremely Fine-About Uncirculated.**
From The Rolling Plains Collection (600-900)

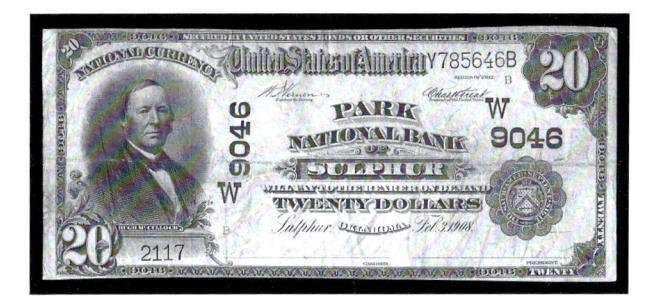

15160 **Sulphur, OK** - $20 1902 Plain Back Fr. 652 **Park NB** Ch. # (W)9046
This is one of only six large notes listed in the census from here. It's recorded there as "Very Fine," which, even on its best day, it most assuredly is not. **Very Good-Fine,** and accompanied by two early checks from the same bank. (1,250-1,750)

15161 **Sulphur, OK** - $10 1929 Ty. 1 **Park NB** Ch. # 9046
This bank is considerably scarcer in small than large, with this piece one of only four Series 1929 examples in the census. It has been off the market since our consignor purchased it from our May, 1999 Rosemont sale, and is as nice as the example from here we sold last year which fetched a strong $1380. **Fine+.**
From The Rolling Plains Collection (1,000-1,500)

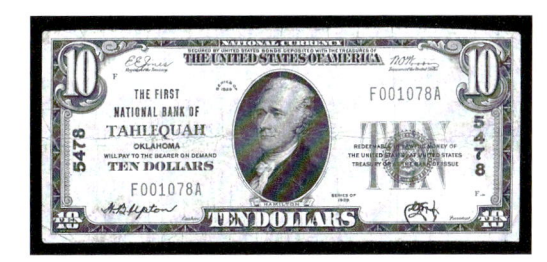

15162 **Tahlequah, OK** - $10 1929 Ty. 1 **The First NB** Ch. # 5478
This was the first of five banks chartered in this Cherokee County location, and the only one which survived long enough to issue Series 1929 examples. **Fine.**
From The Rolling Plains Collection (350-550)

15163 **Tecumseh, OK** - $10 1929 Ty. 1 **The Tecumseh NB** Ch. # 10304
This bank was the only issuer of Series 1929 examples in this small Pottawatomie County community. **Fine.**
From The Rolling Plains Collection **(500-800)**

First Ever Public Offering

15164 **Texhoma, OK** - $10 1929 Ty. 1 **The First NB** Ch. # 8852
This is a geat note from an excessively rare flyspeck of a community located in the far reaches of the Oklahoma panhandle smack on the Texas border. The total census population from this bank, the town's sole issuer, stands at just four notes, one a Red Seal Territorial, one a Blue Seal, and two small notes, with this the nicer of the pair. Our records show no offerings from here of any kind for a decade, and no offerings of any Series 1929 example at public sale at any time during the past sixty years. **Fine-Very Fine,** with a bit of inconsequential soil on the back, an item rare enough to see bidding easily reach or exceed...
From The Rolling Plains Collection **(4,000-7,000)**

15165 **Thomas, OK** - $10 1929 Ty. 1 **The First NB** Ch. # 7278
While the census shows more than a few Series 1929 examples extant from here, the number of actual offerings from this community suggests that either many of the notes are closely held by one institution or there are an inordinate number of collectors named Thomas who each own one of these items and are not selling. **Very Fine.**
From The Rolling Plains Collection **(600-900)**

15166 **Tulsa, OK** - $20 1929 Ty. 2 **The NB of Commerce** Ch. # 9942
While eight large notes are listed in the census from this very scarce Tulsa issuer, small notes are even tougher, with the count standing at just three such examples, including this attractive note. Sharp **Very Fine+++.**
From The Rolling Plains Collection **(900-1,200)**

15167 **Tyrone, OK** - $10 1929 Ty. 1 **The First NB** Ch. # 10032
A tougher note from a small town in the Oklahoma panhandle. **Very Good** or a bit better, trimmed in just a touch at the bottom left.
From The Rolling Plains Collection **(350-550)**

15168 **Vian, OK** - $10 1929 Ty. 1 **The First NB** Ch. # 10573
While large notes are fairly common, small notes from this one bank community are most certainly not, with the census standing at just four pieces, including this example. **Fine,** as nice or nicer than any of the three other reported series 1929 notes from here.
From The Rolling Plains Collection **(700-900)**

15169 **Vinita, OK** - $10 1902 Plain Back Fr. 628 **The First NB** Ch. # 4704
A nice example which is one of the higher grade Third Charters we've encountered from here. **Very Fine.**
(400-600)

15170 Walters, OK - $10 1929 Ty. 1 **The Walters NB** Ch. # 7811
A very scarce bank with just four large and four small notes comprising the entire census. **Fine. (700-900)**

15171 Waukomis, OK - $10 1929 Ty. 1 **The Waukomis NB** Ch. # 10227
This was the only denomination issued by this scarce bank, with this note signed by the same individual, John R. Camp, as both Cashier and President. Although not common, this cost saving expedient was used by several banks during the Depression. **Fine.**
From The Rolling Plains Collection **(500-800)**

15172 Waurika, OK - $10 1929 Ty. 1 **The Waurika NB** Ch. # 8861
For many years this was one of just a pair of notes known from this small bank, but the discovery of a number of uncirculated specimens almost twenty years ago changed the census from here significantly. **Uncirculated,** with a small partial teller stamp on the face.
From The Rolling Plains Collection **(500-800)**

15173 Wetumka, OK - $20 1929 Ty. 1 **The American NB** Ch. # 7724
A tough note from this small family owned bank. **Fine-Very Fine** with a few pinholes, signed by D.G. Hall and E.S. Hall.
From The Rolling Plains Collection **(500-700)**

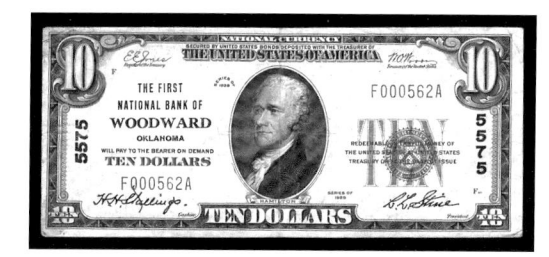

15174 Woodward, OK - $10 1929 Ty. 1 **The First NB** Ch. # 5575
Although a fair number of notes from here have been reported, offerings from this single bank community have been quite scant during the past decade. **Fine+++. (500-800)**

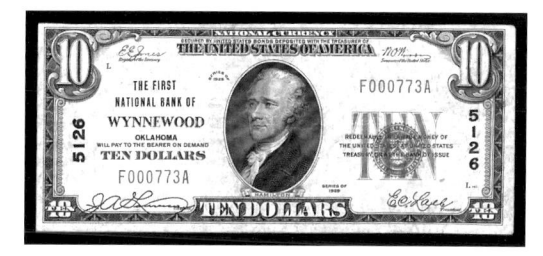

15175 Wynnewood, OK - $10 1929 Ty. 1 **The First NB** Ch. # 5126
A nice evenly circulated example from the slightly more common Wynnewood small size issuer. **Fine-Very Fine.**
From The Rolling Plains Collection **(500-700)**

15176 Wynnewood, OK - $20 1929 Ty. 1 **The Southern NB** Ch. # 5731
This was Wynnewood's second and last issuer, with notes from here rather hard to find. **Fine.**
From The Rolling Plains Collection **(600-800)**

15177 Yale, OK - $10 1929 Ty. 1 **The First NB** Ch. # 10014
A more than acceptable small example from the only bank here to issue. **Fine-Very Fine.**
From The Rolling Plains Collection **(500-700)**

15178 **Yukon, OK** - $20 1929 Ty. 1 **The First NB** Ch. # 6159
This is by far the scarcer of the two banks chartered in this small Canadian County locale, with a census consisting of just three large and six small notes. **Fine.**
From The Rolling Plains Collection **(700-900)**

15179 **Yukon, OK** - $10 1929 Ty. 1 **The Yukon NB** Ch. # 10196
This **Very Good** example is from a Canadian County institution that can be a considerable challenge to locate. A few scattered pinholes are noted. **(500-800)**

15180 **Yukon, OK** - $20 1929 Ty. 1 **The Yukon NB** Ch. # 10196
This is one of the very few high grade examples available from this institution. Bright **Very Fine.**
From The Rolling Plains Collection **(400-600)**

PENNSYLVANIA

15181 **Allentown, PA** - $10 1929 Ty. 2 **The Second NB** Ch. # 373 Uncut Sheet
This is a serial number 1-6 sheet that has slightly toned a shade. The notes grade **Choice Crisp Uncirculated** and there is a neatly done fold between the third and fourth notes. **(6,000-9,000)**

15182 **Allentown, PA** - $10 1929 Ty. 1 **The Merchants-Citizens NB & TC** Ch. # 6645
The edges are sound and the color is nice on this $10 from this bank's four year lived second title. **Very Fine.** **(200-300)**

15183 **Beaver, PA** - $5 1902 Plain Back Fr. 599 **The Fort McIntosh NB** Ch. # (E)8185
A popular town name graces this **Very Good** example which has a small notch at top center. **(250-400)**

15184 **Bethlehem, PA** - $20 1929 Ty. 1 **The First NB** Ch. # 138
This perfectly margined issue boasts a fairly low serial number for the issue. The margins are near perfect. **CGA Gem Uncirculated 66.** **(300-400)**

15185 **Bethlehem, PA** - $1 Original Fr. 382 **The Lehigh Valley NB** Ch. # 2050
This discovery note brings the population of Original Aces from this institution to only three pieces. It boasts pleasing paper quality though a minor edge split is noted at bottom. Overall, the eye appeal is excellent with the two boldly penned signatures. **Very Fine. (1,200-1,400)**

15186 **Blue Ball, PA** - $10 1929 Ty. 1 **The Blue Ball NB** Ch. # 8421
This is an immensely popular bank title with this Lancaster County town taking its name from the time when a blue ball was hung at the train station in order to signal the train that the station had a mail pickup. Officers during the late 1920s and 30s were H.S. Shirk and Jacob Hartz. July 1, 2005 saw this bank shed this title as it became part of Communitybanks. **Fine. (2,000-3,000)**

15187 **Bradford, PA** - $20 1902 Date Back Fr. 645 **The Commercial NB** Ch. # (E)4199
This is one of only seven large in the census, with this note also being the only 1902 Date Back reported. This $20 has printed signatures of R.L. Mann and W.H. Powers, wholesome edges, and crispy paper. **Fine+. (700-900)**

15188 **Brookville, PA** - $100 1929 Ty. 1 **The NB of Brookville** Ch. # 3051
Any $100 Series 1929 example bearing serial Number 1 is a very scarce item indeed, with the new Kelly census showing considerably under 100 such specimens in all grades combined from all banks in the country. This is one of the few we've handled in recent years, and one of the nicer pieces as well, which has been graded as **Choice Uncirculated 64 EPQ** by the folks at PMG. An added bonus is that L.V. and A.D. Deemer ran this bank. A.D. was brought into office after the presidency of the bank sat vacant for awhile during 1927. **(6,000-9,000)**

15189 **Confluence, PA** - $20 1929 Ty. 1 **The First NB** Ch. # 5307
Fewer than a half dozen small size notes are known from this institution, all of which are heavily circulated. This **Fine** example boasts the status of lowest serial number with D000006A. **(400-600)**

15190 **Connellsville, PA** - $20 1902 Plain Back Fr. 653 **The Second NB** Ch. # (E)4481
The stamped signatures are nicely executed on this $20. President Worth Kilpatrick had more than one cashier during his tenure. A spot is to the left of the portrait. **Fine. (250-450)**

15191 **Crafton, PA** - $5 1902 Plain Back Fr. 607 **The First NB** Ch. # 6010
This solid serial number 8 issue displays boldly printed signatures. The paper is pleasing though there are some breaks in the paper on the center fold in the margins. **CGA Fine 12. (350-450)**

15192 **Dawson, PA** - $10 1902 Plain Back Fr. 628 **The First NB** Ch. # 4673
The printed signatures are well executed on this $10 from Fayette County. Service as a wallet piece toned half of the back a shade. Small splits are noticed at top center and bottom, too. **Very Fine. (250-450)**

Rare Edinboro Note

15193 **Edinboro, PA** - $20 1902 Plain Back Fr. 650 **The First NB** Ch. # 7312
There were only 5 large examples in the census before this note crossed our desk. Of those five, four of the notes do not have a reported grade, telling us that those notes were reported a long time ago. We were also not able to find a single auction offering of this Erie County bank in large. The stamped signatures are almost completely gone, but E.P. Campbell and G.W. Minium can be discerned. **Very Good-Fine. (600-1,000)**

15194 **Emporium, PA** - $5 1902 Plain Back Fr. 598 **The First NB** Ch. # (E)3255
A single fold is noted at center, though we must use a split grade of **Extremely Fine-About Uncirculated** as there is a bit of handling noted. The paper is perfectly original and the signatures of B. Lloyd and Josiah Howard are still legible. **(300-400)**

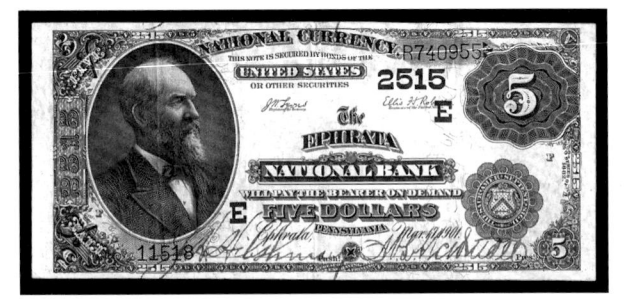

15195 **Ephrata, PA** - $5 1882 Value Back Fr. 574 **The Ephrata NB** Ch. # (E)2515
A handsome Lancaster County Value Back with unusually broad margins for this normally poorly margined issue. Bright **Very Fine**, a premium example. **(1,200-1,400)**

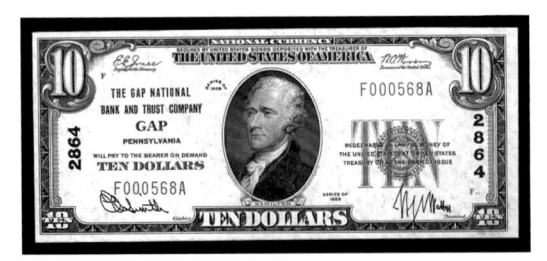

15196 **Gap, PA** - $10 1929 Ty. 1 **The Gap NB & TC** Ch. # 2864
A little bigger left margin and this crisp example would be a solid gem. **Very Choice Crisp Uncirculated. (400-600)**

15197 **Greenville, PA** - $20 1882 Brown Back Fr. 501 **The Greenville NB** Ch. # (E)2251
A scarce early note from this Mercer County bank. Nice **Fine**, a more than acceptable $20 Brown Back. **(700-900)**

15198 **Grove City, PA** - $20 1902 Plain Back Fr. 658 **The First NB** Ch. # 5044
A lone center fold is noted on this bright **About Uncirculated** issue. The overprint is bold as are the signatures of F.W. Daugherty and A.M. Allen. **(400-600)**

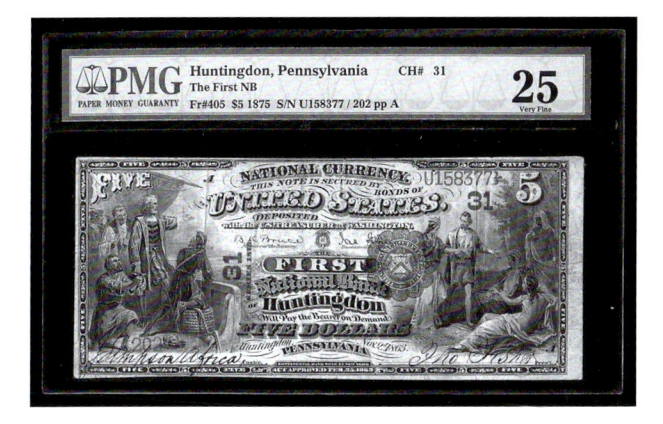

15199 Huntingdon, PA - $5 1875 Fr. 405 **The First NB** Ch. # 31
A nice early example from this low charter institution. It has been slabbed by PMG, which has assigned the grade of **Very Fine 25** to this problem free specimen. (1,200-1,600)

High Grade Large Intercourse

15200 Intercourse, PA - $5 1902 Plain Back Fr. 600 **The First NB** Ch. # (E)9216
A most attractive example of a large size note which everyone wants but few can own. We've sold only two large examples from Intercourse during the past five years, both grading Fine, with the first going for $4140 and the second realizing $4312.50. This piece is far superior in grade, and in fact is the nicest large size example from here to be offered at public sale in at least the past decade. Bright **Very Fine,** with great color and eye appeal, a winner of a note in all respects. (5,000-7,000)

15201 Jenkintown, PA - $5 1902 Plain Back Fr. 609 **Citizens NB** Ch. # 12530
A most attractive large example from this sought after Montgomery County bank. It has been encapsulated and graded by PMG, which has assigned a grade of **Very Fine 25.** (900-1,200)

15202 Jerome, PA - $5 1902 Plain Back Fr. 608 **The First NB** Ch. # 12029
A very rare Somerset County bank, with this by far the nicer of the two reported large size examples. A miniscule $520 was outstanding from here at the bank's close in early 1935, so few other large notes can be expected to surface. **Very Fine,** with sea green signatures. (1,500-2,500)

15203 Manheim, PA - $5 1902 Plain Back Fr. 600 **The Keystone NB** Ch. # (E)3635
While Series 1929 examples abound from here, large notes from this Lancaster County issuer are scarce indeed, with the census standing at under ten pieces of all kinds. This attractive note is as nice as any we recall seeing from here. **Very Fine,** with clear signatures. (600-800)

15204 McAlisterville, PA - $10 1902 Plain Back Fr. 626 **The Farmers NB** Ch. # (E)9526
A scarcer Juniata County note from a bank which had a meager $990 outstanding in large notes by 1935. **Fine.** (500-700)

15205 **McKeesport, PA** - $10 1902 Plain Back Fr. 631 **The First NB** Ch. # 2222
This bank is always popular due to its solid "2" charter number. The signatures are boldly stamped on this $10. **Fine. (300-500)**

15206 **Mifflin, PA** - $5 1902 Plain Back Fr. 601 **The Peoples NB** Ch. # 9678
This was the second title used here, after this bank changed its issuing location from Paterson to Mifflin in 1923. Only three large examples bearing this title are listed in the census, with this piece new to that compilation. Pleasing **Fine+,** scarce enough to see bidding reach or exceed... **(800-1,200)**

15207 **Mount Carmel, PA** - $5 1902 Plain Back Fr. 601 **The Union NB** Ch. # (E)8393
Strong stamped signatures are noted on this lightly circulated piece. The paper quality is exceptional with embossing of the seal and serial numbers still present. **Very Fine++. (300-400)**

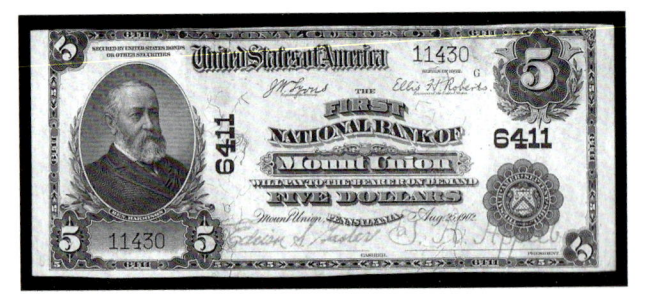

15208 **Mount Union, PA** - $5 1902 Plain Back Fr. 598 **The First NB** Ch. # 6411
Just five large examples are known from this Huntingdon County bank, with this the finest of the group by several grades. Bright **Extremely Fine-About Uncirculated,** with clear purple signatures. **(700-1,000)**

Serial # 1 Dateback - Only 30 Known Nationwide

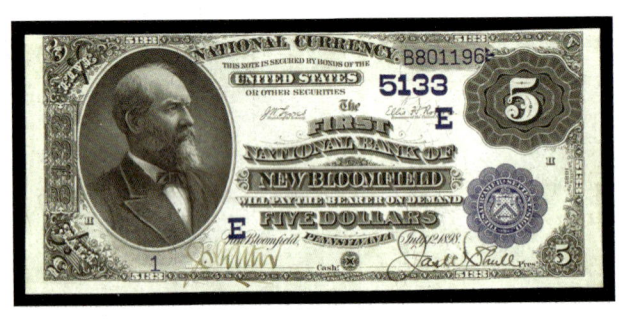

15209 **New Bloomfield, PA** - $5 1882 Date Back Fr. 537 **The First NB** Ch. # (E)5133
Last appearing in our 2006 Central States sale, and described, "A quick glance at the Kelly census reveals immediately how rare this Serial Number 1 Date Back is. Only 30 serial number 1 Date Backs have been reported in total from over 5,000 reported survivors from all banks in all states. Compare that with the rarity of Serial Number 1 Red Seals, which total 66 survivors from Pennsylvania alone! This particular issue has perfectly preserved signatures and received a light bend in storage which accounts for the grade. The bold blue overprint and the deeply printed black ink remain unmolested to this day. **Choice About Uncirculated. (5,000-7,000)**

15210 **New Milford, PA** - $5 1929 Ty. 1 **The Grange NB of Susquehanna County** Ch. # 8960
One of the rarest of the Grange banks, and one of the few that survived long enough to issue Series 1929 examples. The census here shows just four small notes, with this piece one of that quartet. Our records show no offerings of any Series 1929 example from here during the past two decades, a good indication of the desirability of this specimen. **Fine. (1,500-2,000)**

15211 **Olyphant, PA** - $10 1929 Ty. 2 **The NB** Ch. # 14079
Two banks issued notes in this Lackawanna County locale. The First National only issued large size notes and was liquidated in 1929. This institution was chartered in early 1934 and thus bears a popular 14000+ charter number and only issued small size notes. The total issue was fairly significant, $71,100 in total. To date a total of seven examples have been reported, though this is one of only three to appear in public auction. **Fine.** (500-700-up)

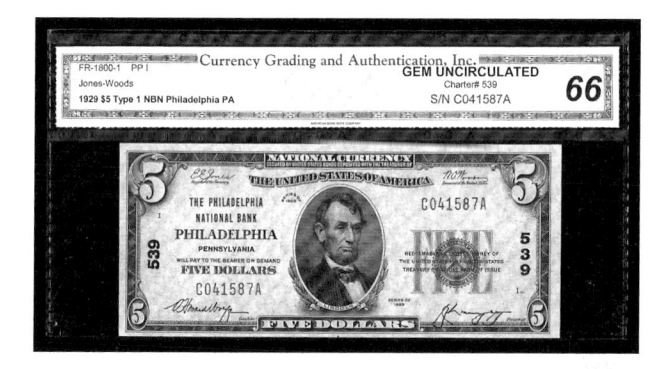

15212 **Philadelphia, PA** - $5 1929 Ty. 1 **The Philadelphia NB** Ch. # 539
The margins of this bright, well embossed piece are nicely spaced. CGA has awarded the grade of **Gem Uncirculated 66.** (350-500)

15213 **Philadelphia, PA** - $10 1929 Ty. 1 **The Philadelphia NB** Ch. # 539
Though this institution shows a plethora of reported surviving notes, it is likely this is the finest. Perfectly even margins and wholly original paper are noted on this **PCGS Superb Gem New 68PPQ.** (600-900)

15214 **Philadelphia, PA** - $5 Original Fr. 397 **The Bank of North America** Ch. # 602
An evenly circulated Original Series $5 from this historic institution, which was exempted by an Act of Congress from the requirement that all banks accepting a federal charter under the National Banking Act use the word "National" somewhere in their title. Legend has it that this legislation was passed in recognition of this bank's leading role in selling U.S. Treasury debt to the public during the darkest days of the Civil War. All notes from this bank are avidly collected, with this piece the first early example from here we've had to offer in fifteen years. **Fine.** (2,000-3,000)

15215 **Philadelphia, PA** - $10 1882 Brown Back Fr. 480 **The Bank of North America** Ch. # 602
A second note from this sought after bank, this a $10 Brown Back with the early seal and charter placement. **Fine.** (1,500-2,000)

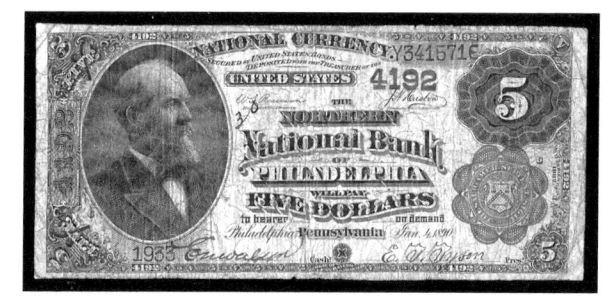

15216 **Philadelphia, PA** - $5 1882 Brown Back Fr. 471 **The Northern NB** Ch. # 4192
A very scarce early note from a very tough to find Philadelphia bank. Pen signed **Very Good-Fine,** with a small inked number on the face that barely detracts. (750-1,250)

15217 **Pittsburgh, PA** - $100 1929 Ty. 1 **The Farmers Deposit NB** Ch. # 685
This well margined $50 escaped circulation. **PCGS Choice New 63.** (450-650)

15218 **Pittsburgh, PA** - $100 1929 Ty. 1 **The Farmers Deposit NB** Ch. # 685
A number of pinholes at upper left and a bank teller stamp are seen near the portrait area on this **Fine** example. (350-500)

Marine National Bank Serial Number 1

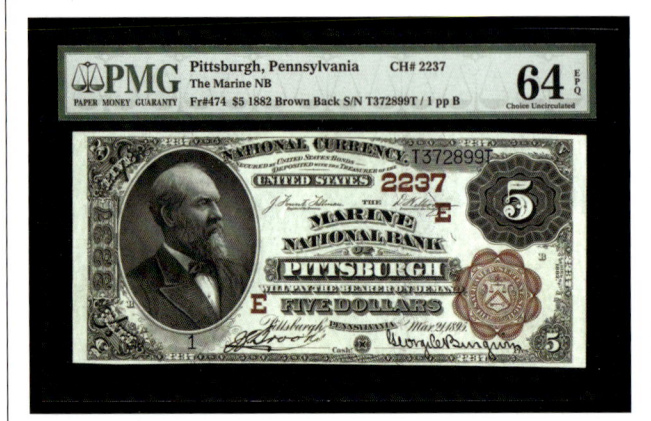

15219 Pittsburgh, PA - $5 1882 Brown Back Fr. 474 **The Marine NB** Ch. #(E)2237

We were ecstatic when the following three notes on this charter number were consigned for this auction, as they have been kept in the Burgwin family for the past 100+ years. This 1-B note is the only serial number 1 known on this bank and only the third known serial number 1 Brown Back for all of the Pittsburgh banks combined. George C. Burgwin was a prominent lawyer who appeared regularly before state and federal courts, including the US Supreme Court. In 1891 he also became a director of the Marine National Bank. This led to him becoming vice president in 1900 and president in 1903. He would stay at that post for over twenty years until his death on April 18, 1925. Along the way Mr. Burgwin was also involved in many civic, fraternal, and social organizations. This $5 is third-party graded **PMG Choice Uncirculated 64 EPQ** with the added comments of "exceptional paper quality, great embossing & color." We see that as certainly the case as this original note has been well preserved over the years. The inks are dark and the paper is white. The penned signatures of J.S. Brooks and George C. Burgwin look like they were laid down earlier today with ink from an ink well. The only thing that keeps this note from climbing higher on the grading scale is the thin bottom margin. This is still a true trophy note worthy of the finest collection. **(6,000-9,000)**

Marine National Bank Serial Number 2

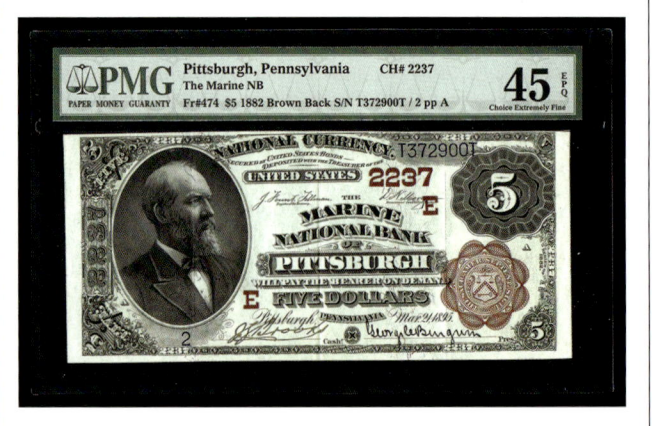

15220 Pittsburgh, PA - $5 1882 Brown Back Fr. 474 **The Marine NB** Ch. #(E)2237

This serial number 2-A Brown Back possesses bright white paper and dark inks. The penned signatures are dark on this note, too. The note did not circulate, but George Burgwin folded it into fourths and took it home. This left the note with three folds and in **PMG Choice Extremely Fine 45 EPQ** condition. Then the note was carefully stored leaving it with its "Exceptional Paper Quality" natural surfaces. **(3,000-5,000)**

Delightful $10 Brown Back

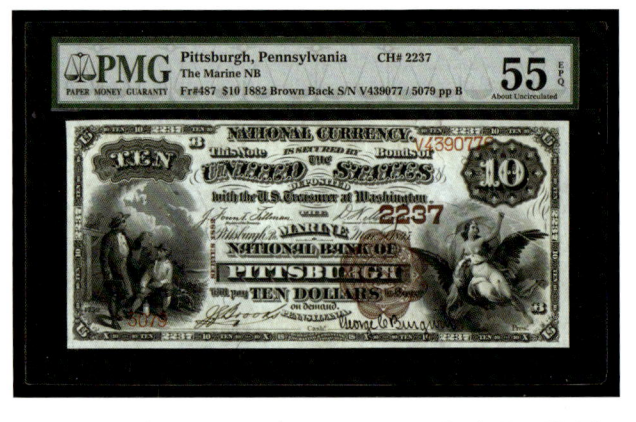

15221 Pittsburgh, PA - $10 1882 Brown Back Fr. 487 **The Marine NB** Ch. # 2237

This is the third note to come to us from the Burgwin family. This original note has dark inks, bold pen signatures, wide face margins, and bright paper. PMG adds to its label that this $10 has "Exceptional Paper Quality, Great Embossing & Color." We concur as we can see no impairments through the third-party holder. **PMG About Uncirculated 55 EPQ. (2,500-4,500)**

15222 **Pittsburgh, PA** - $10 1882 Date Back Fr. 542 **The Duquesne NB** Ch. # (E)2278
A great local flavor name adorns this $10 that has some wallet staining in two back corners. Still the edges and color are nice for the grade. **Very Fine.** (600-800)

15223 **Pittsburgh, PA** - $5 1902 Plain Back Fr. 598 **The Mellon NB** Ch. # 6301
Crackling fresh, fully embossed, and with great eye appeal. Graded **Superb Gem Unc 67 EPQ** by PMG, with the Treasury engraved signature of R.B. Mellon as President. (1,250-1,750)

15224 **Portland, PA** - $20 1929 Ty. 1 **Portland NB** Ch. # 6665
A scarcer Northampton County bank with just six Series 1929 examples reported to date. Pleasing **Very Fine.** (250-350)

15225 **Scranton, PA** - $5 1902 Plain Back Fr. 601 **The Union NB** Ch. # 8737
This picture perfect **Extremely Fine** exhibits some remaining embossing and bold color. (300-400)

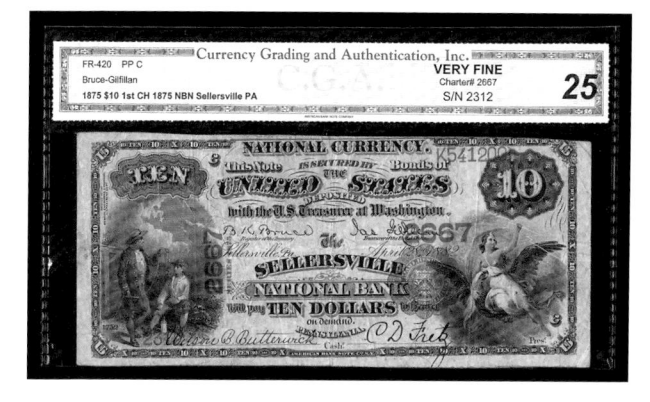

15226 **Sellersville, PA** - $10 1875 Fr. 420 **The Sellersville NB** Ch. # 2667
The paper quality exhibited here is pleasing allowing the detailed design to remain bold. The signatures of Wilson B. Butterwick and C.D. Fritz remain as bold as the day they were penned. **CGA Very Fine 25.** (1,500-2,500)

15227 **Shenandoah, PA** - $10 1929 Ty. 1 **The Miners NB** Ch. # 13619
Fully Uncirculated with deep embossing. **CGA Choice Uncirculated 64.** (200-300)

15228 **Shingle House, PA** - $5 1929 Ty. 2 **The First NB** Ch. # 6799
A very scarce piece possessing one of the greatest town names to be found on any National Bank Note. It's a virtual twin in grade to the example from here we sold back in 2004, when a $10 Type 1 realized $2185 in our May Central States sale. **Fine+**, likely to bring at least the same figure and quite likely more. (1,750-2,250)

15229 **South Fork, PA** - $5 1929 Ty. 2 **The First NB** Ch. # 6573 Uncut Sheet
This serial number 1 through 6 sheet is bright, original, and without folds. Problem-free **Gem Crisp Uncirculated.** (6,000-9,000)

15230 **Spring Grove, PA** - $10 1929 Ty. 1 **The Spring Grove NB** Ch. # 6536
A high grade small example from this well collected York County location. Bright **Very Fine+++.** (450-650)

15231 **Tyrone, PA** - $10 1902 Plain Back Fr. 627 **The First NB** Ch. # 4355
Extremely Fine, but with a separation beginning at the heavier central fold. Darkly stamped officers' signatures are noted, as is the bright and crackling-fresh paper. This is the later variety with the two bank serials rather than one bank and one treasury serial, and will likely sell for no less than... (350-500)

15232 **Warren, PA** - $10 1902 Plain Back Fr. 631 **The Citizens NB** Ch. # 2226
A high grade large example from this tougher Warren bank. **Very Fine,** with jet black signatures. (300-400)

15233 **Washington, PA** - $20 1929 Ty. 1 **The Citizens NB** Ch. # 3383
Interestingly only about four CU examples of this issue have been reported of more than one hundred surviving examples. **CGA Choice Uncirculated 63.** (300-400)

15234 **Wilkes-Barre, PA** - $5 1882 Brown Back Fr. 467 **The Wyoming NB** Ch. # (E)732
The signatures of the Cashier and President remain bold on this nice **Fine** Brown Back. (700-900)

15235 **Wyoming, PA** - $5 1929 Ty. 2 **The First NB** Ch. # 8517
This is a wonderful example of a misplaced state note which is new to the census. The surfaces are bright with several hard folds noticed. **Very Fine-Extremely Fine.** (400-600)

15236 **York, PA** - $5 1902 Plain Back Fr. 598 **The York NB & TC** Ch. # 604
The paper here is bright and the stamped signature remain strong. **Crisp Uncirculated. (450-550)**

RHODE ISLAND

15237 **Pawtucket, RI** - $1 Original Fr. 380 **The First NB** Ch. # 843
A scarcer Rhode Island bank which has had no offerings at public sale since 2002. **Fine** in appearance, but with a well executed repair after the note had been severed in two. **(1,000-1,500)**

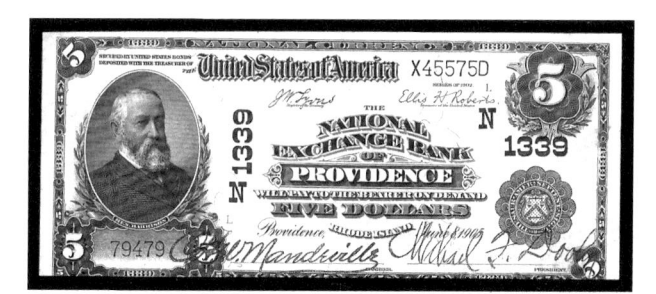

15238 **Providence, RI** - $5 1902 Plain Back Fr. 598 **The National Exchange Bank** Ch. # (N)1339
"United States of America" at top center and the charter numbers produced easily viewed embossing on this $5. The handling of this note consists of a little bit of counting soil, a center fold, and a tiny brown spot on the back. The bottom edge is also inside the frame line. **About Uncirculated. (300-500)**

SOUTH CAROLINA

15239 **Camden, SC** - $10 1902 Plain Back Fr. 626 **The First NB** Ch. # 9083
A very tough **Fine** note from the only bank in this historic community to issue. Thirteen examples make up the current census with this one having a few pinholes and minor margin foxing. **(1,000-1,500)**

15240 **Gaffney, SC** - $5 1902 Plain Back Fr. 605 **The Merchants & Planters NB** Ch. # 10655
A very tough bank in large size, with few such offerings in recent years. Evenly circulated **Very Good-Fine,** with no defects whatever for the grade. **(1,000-1,500)**

15241 **Greenville, SC** - $10 1902 Plain Back Fr. 628 **The First NB** Ch. # 1935
This is a delightful **Very Fine** note with original surfaces and turquoise-blue stamped signatures of H.J. Winn and F.F. Beattie. This bank also has charter number 1935, the year that the national bank note program came to a close. **(900-1,200)**

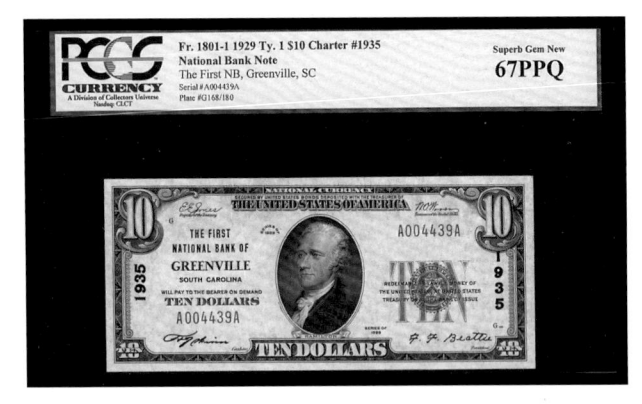

15242 Greenville, SC - $10 1929 Ty. 1 **The First NB** Ch. # 1935
Hulking margins are noticed on this nice looking example from a popular state. **PCGS Superb Gem New 67PPQ.** (800-1,200)

SOUTH DAKOTA

15243 Clear Lake, SD - $5 1902 Plain Back Fr. 609 **The Deuel County NB** Ch. # 12877
A just plain rare note in large size, with this bank reporting a miniscule $180 outstanding in large notes at its last compilation in 1935. We sold this piece back in April of 2001 for $1610, and it should certainly be worth that or more this evening as well. Pen signed **Very Good-Fine.** (1,400-1,800)

15244 Highmore, SD - $10 1929 Ty. 1 **The First NB** Ch. # 7794
This bank was the only institution to issue from Hyde County. The example we offer tonight retains considerable original paper body. **Very Fine.** (300-500)

15245 Hudson, SD - $10 1902 Plain Back Fr. 624 **The First NB** Ch. # 7335
A very nice example which is the highest grade large note reported to date from this scarce Lincoln County bank. **Very Fine,** enhanced by bold two color signatures. (900-1,200)

15246 Milbank, SD - $20 1902 Plain Back Fr. 650 **The First NB** Ch. # 6473
A lovely note from this none too common bank which issued large examples only. We note no offerings from here of any kind since a 2001 auction appearance. **Very Fine,** with a small split at the bottom more than offset by the brilliant green signatures adorning this note. (750-950)

15247 Mitchell, SD - $10 1882 Date Back Fr. 545 **The First NB** Ch. # (W)2645
The first time this note participated in an auction was a John Hickman affair that took place in October 1991. This is one of only seven 1882 Date Backs listed in the census. The cut is a bit off, so that a portion of the note below shows and the top margin is trimmed in. There are also two small rust holes near the left and right edges respectively. **Fine-Very Fine.** (500-700)

15248 Rapid City, SD - $10 1929 Ty. 2 **The Rapid City NB** Ch. # 14099
A bright example from this 14000 charter bank which PCGS has encapsulated and graded **Very Choice New 64PPQ.** (600-800)

TENNESSEE

15249 Chattanooga, TN - $100 1929 Ty. 1 The First NB Ch. # 1606
Healthy edges and paper are found on this C-note. This is a prime candidate for a type note. **Fine-Very Fine.** (600-900)

15250 Elizabethton, TN - $20 1902 Plain Back Fr. 658 The Holston NB Ch. # (S)10976
This private named bank was organized on March 6, 1917 and it lasted a little over 15 years before going into receivership. This $20 is cut a little tight at the bottom and at the top, but it is still above average in grade for this bank. The purple stamped signatures are of H.C. Hathaway and J.B. Nova. **Fine-Very Fine.** (600-900)

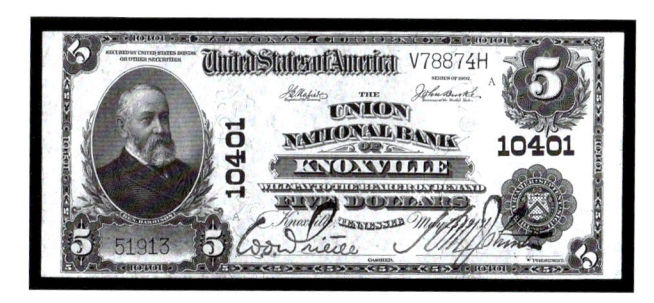

15251 Knoxville, TN - $5 1902 Plain Back Fr. 604 The Union NB Ch. # 10401
Officers W.O. Whittle and H.M. Johnston would close the Union's doors for the last time on March 31, 1928. This bright **Choice Crisp Uncirculated** specimen serves as a testimonial to their struggles. (500-750)

15252 Memphis, TN - $20 1929 Ty. 2 The First NB Ch. # 336
This is perhaps the finest known Type 2 example from here. Widely margined with plenty of originality, it grades PMG **Gem Uncirculated 66 EPQ.** (600-800)

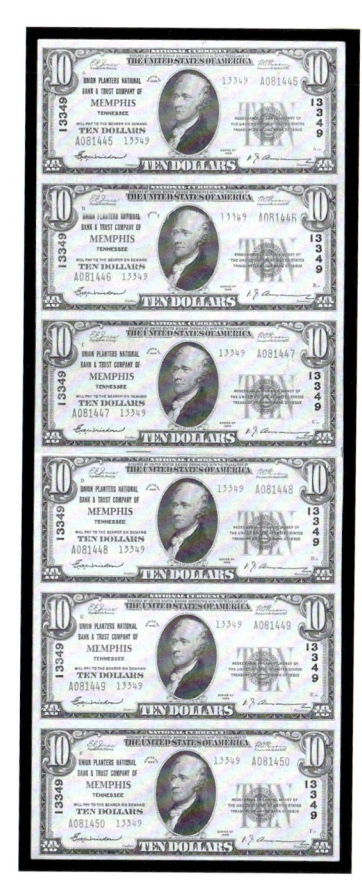

15253 Memphis, TN - $10 1929 Ty. 2 Union Planters NB & TC Ch. # 13349 Uncut Sheet
A fold is found between the third and fourth notes of this uncut sheet. This fold comes into contact with the top frame line of the fourth note. This sheet also has a couple of partial paper clip rust outlines at top center. It is not unusual to find these oversized paper money items folded in half. **Choice Crisp Uncirculated.** (4,000-6,000)

15254 Memphis, TN - $100 1929 Ty. 1 **Union Planters NB & TC** Ch. # 13349
This $100 has strong embossing. It also has a center fold and counting crinkles near the left and right edges. **Extremely Fine-About Uncirculated.** (400-600)

15255 Memphis, TN - $100 1929 Ty. 1 **Union Planters NB & TC** Ch. # 13349
This $100 is an evenly circulated **PCGS Very Fine 25**. Several different signature combinations are found on Series 1929 notes of the Union Planters. (300-500)

15256 Trenton, TN - $10 1902 Plain Back Fr. 635 **The Citizens NB** Ch. # 12438
A very scarce note from the second of two banks chartered in this small Gibson County locale. Just five notes make up the entire large size census from here, and, with a meager $640 large outstanding in 1935, few examples are likely awaiting discovery. **Very Fine,** with the signatures a bit faded. (1,750-2,750)

TEXAS

Type 2 Serial Number 1

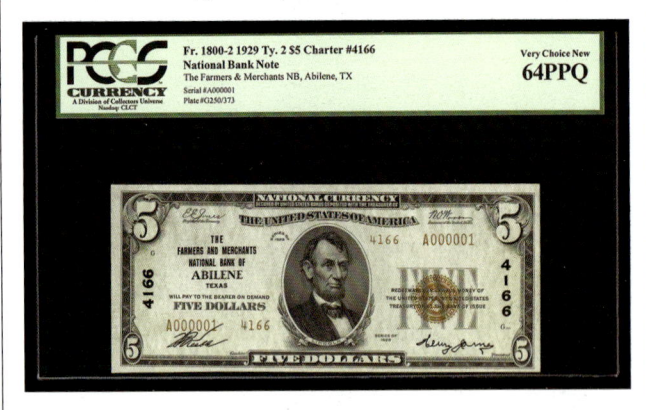

15257 Abilene, TX - $5 1929 Ty. 2 **The Farmers & Merchants NB** Ch. # 4166
A beautiful Type 2 serial number 1 example which has been given the grade of **Very Choice New 64 PPQ** by PCGS. Expect to see bidding for this prize easily reach or exceed... (2,500-3,500)

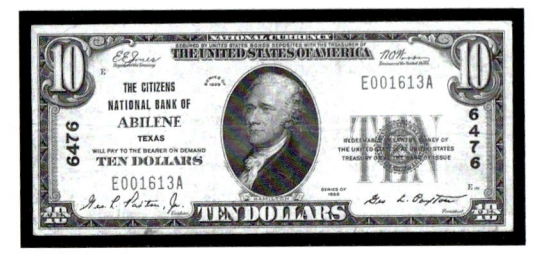

15258 Abilene, TX - $10 1929 Ty. 1 **The Citizens NB** Ch. # 6476
This family run institution was one of Abilene's smaller issuers. **Very Fine,** with signatures of Geo. L Paxton as President and Geo. L. Paxton, Jr. as Cashier.
From The Rolling Plains Collection (350-550)

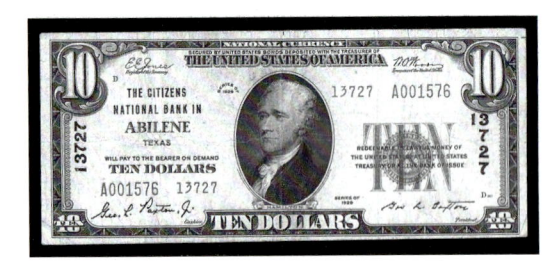

15259 Abilene, TX - $10 1929 Ty. 2 **The Citizens NB** Ch. # 13727
By far the scarcest of Abilene's three issuers of Series 1929 examples, with only seven pieces recorded in the census. This was a small family owned bank, with Geo. L Paxton signing as President and Geo. L. Paxton, Jr. signing as Cashier. **Fine-Very Fine.**
From The Rolling Plains Collection (450-650)

15260 **Albany, TX** - $10 1929 Ty. 1 **The First NB** Ch. # 3248
A decent **Fine** example which our consignor purchased from our 2001 Central States sale.
From The Rolling Plains Collection (400-600)

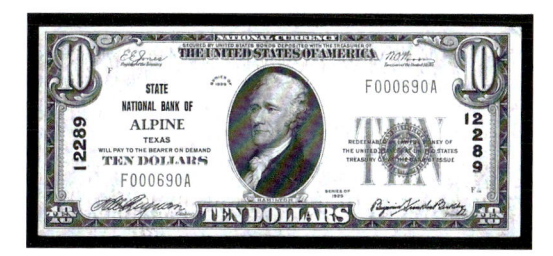

15261 **Alpine, TX** - $10 1929 Ty. 1 **State NB** Ch. # 12289
A very attractive example from this far west Texas community where the antelope roam; Pronghorn, that is. **Extremely Fine.** (800-1,000)

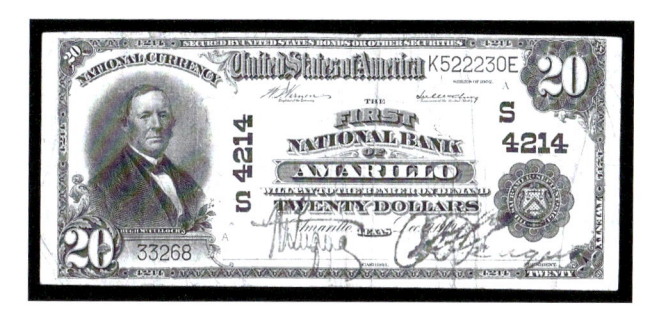

15262 **Amarillo, TX** - $20 1902 Plain Back Fr. 653 **The First NB** Ch. # (S)4214
An attractive large example with even circulation and no problems whatever. **Fine-Very Fine,** with oversize purple signatures.
From The Rolling Plains Collection (450-750)

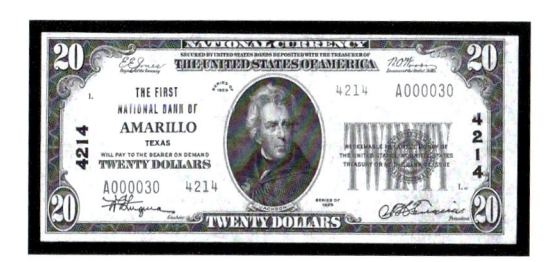

15263 **Amarillo, TX** - $20 1929 Ty. 2 **The First NB** Ch. # 4214
A fresh and attractive example with loads of eye appeal. We sold this piece to our consignor in our 1994 Memphis sale, where we noted that it was the finest Series 1929 example from here we had ever seen. Thirteen years later, it is still the finest small note from this bank listed in the census. Sharp **About Uncirculated.** (450-650)

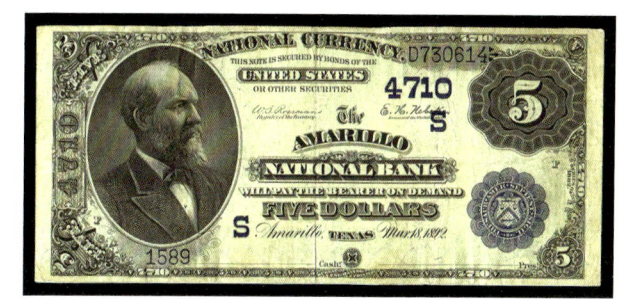

15264 **Amarillo, TX** - $5 1882 Date Back Fr. 533 **The Amarillo NB** Ch. # (S)4710
The census shows just eight large notes extant from this tougher Amarillo bank, with this piece, off the market for over a decade, the only Date Back of any denomination. **Fine,** with a small paper pull visible only on the reverse. (2,000-3,000)

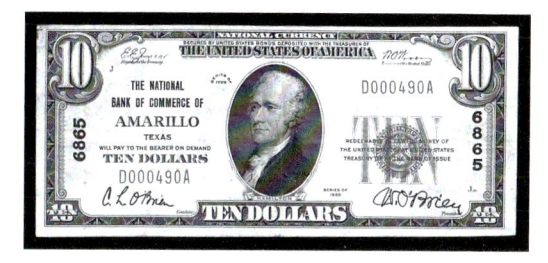

15265 **Amarillo, TX** - $10 1929 Ty. 1 **The NB of Commerce** Ch. # 6865
It has been a full ten years since any Series 1929 example from this bank has been available to collectors at public sale and, with just five such examples in the census, it may be at least that long until another shows up. This piece, signed by C.L. O'Brien and W. O'Brien, grades a nice Very Fine on the face, but we have reduced the grade to **Fine-Very Fine** due to some soiling on the back.
From The Rolling Plains Collection (700-900)

15266 **Anderson, TX** - $20 1929 Ty. 1 **The First NB** Ch. # 7337
A very tough note from the only bank to issue in this Grimes County location. Nice **Fine-Very Fine**.
From The Rolling Plains Collection (750-1,050)

15267 **Angleton, TX** - $20 1929 Ty. 2 **The First NB** Ch. # 14204
While we sold a pair of uncut sheets from here plus one high grade single note in our last sale, this is by no means a common bank. **Fine-Very Fine,** with a few tiny rust spots, the only bank to issue in this small Brazoria County location. (900-1,100)

Lovely Serial Number 1 Aransas Pass Note

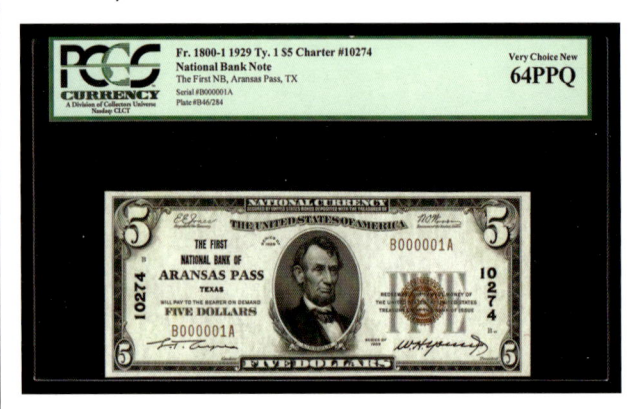

15268 **Aransas Pass, TX** - $5 1929 Ty. 1 **The First NB** Ch. # 10274
A very rare bank, as six of the eight Series 1929 examples reported from this small coastal community are serial number 1 specimens. Most have long been ensconced in major Texas holdings, with this piece and one other the only such notes offered within the past decade. Fortunately for collectors, this piece is a real beauty, having been graded as **Very Choice New 64 PPQ** by PCGS. (3,000-5,000)

15269 **Atlanta, TX** - $10 1929 Ty. 1 **The First NB** Ch. # 4922
A tougher east Texas bank which is seldom available. **About Fine.** (300-500)

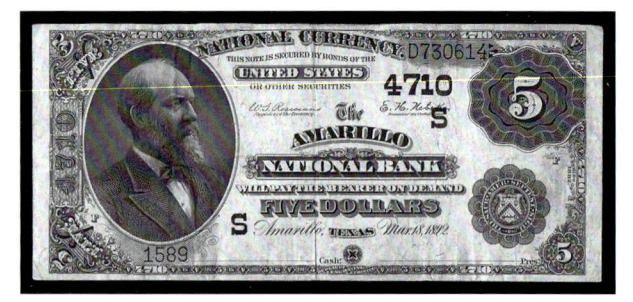

15270 **Austin, TX** - $20 1902 Plain Back Fr. 653 **The Austin NB** Ch. # 4308
A high grade example from this always in demand state capital. Bright **Very Fine-Extremely Fine,** ex-Jack Everson collection. (550-850)

15271 **Ballinger, TX** - $5 1929 Ty. 2 **The First NB** Ch. # 3533
A tougher note from the only really collectible bank in this small Runnels County community. **Fine.** (400-600)

15272 **Bellevue, TX** - $5 1929 Ty. 1 **The First NB** Ch. # 8672
A seldom seen note from the sole bank to issue in this Clay County community. Pleasing **Fine+++.**
From The Rolling Plains Collection (500-700)

15273 **Belton, TX** - $5 1929 Ty. 2 **The Farmers NB** Ch. # 13810
A very scarce high charter Belton note from a bank with just about a half dozen examples extant in all grades. **Very Fine.** (450-650)

15274 **Big Springs, TX** - $10 1929 Ty. 1 **The West Texas NB** Ch. # 6668
A great bank title which says it all about the desirability of this better note. **Fine-Very Fine.**
From The Rolling Plains Collection **(600-900)**

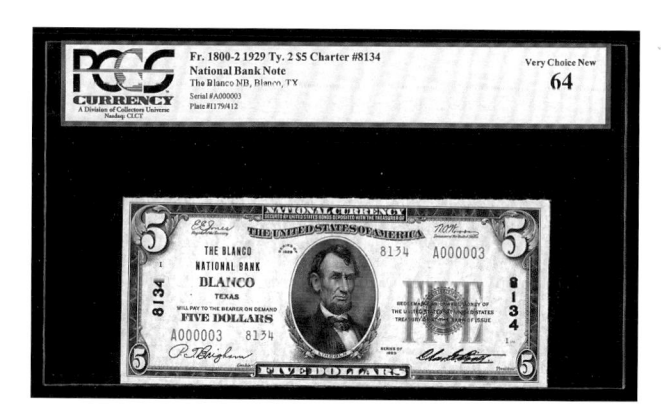

15275 **Blanco, TX** - $5 1929 Ty. 2 **The Blanco NB** Ch. # 8134
An attractive and well centered example bearing low serial number A000003. This Hill Country bank still exists, and is located just across the square from the historic Blanco County courthouse. This piece has been encapsulated by PCGS, which has assigned the grade of **Very Choice New 64. (600-900)**

15276 **Bowie, TX** - $20 1929 Ty. 2 **The First NB** Ch. # 4265
A great Texas town name combines with enough grade to count on this attractive Type 2 example, which is at least equal to if not finer than any other reported Series 1929 example from here. Sharp **Very Fine.**
From The Rolling Plains Collection **(750-1,250)**

15277 **Brady, TX** - $10 1929 Ty. 2 **The Brady NB** Ch. # 7827
Last appearing in our 2006 FUN, this McCulloch County bank now shows an even dozen survivors, according to the latest Track and Price census. **Very Fine. (650-850)**

One of Only Two Reported for City

15278 **Breckenridge, TX** - $10 1929 Ty. 1 **The First NB** Ch. # 7422
A truly rare small note from this virtually impossible to obtain west Texas community. The census shows just two Series 1929 examples reported from here, with the town's other issuer unreported. **Fine,** certainly rare enough to see bidding easily reach and likely exceed...
From The Rolling Plains Collection **(2,500-3,500)**

15279 **Brownsville, TX** - $10 1902 Plain Back Fr. 635 **The First NB** Ch. # 12792
Signatures are still visible on this note that retains much crispness and is quite clean. This Cameron County institution liquidated in 1932. **Very Fine-Extremely Fine. (1,000-1,300)**

15280 **Brownwood, TX** - $100 1929 Ty. 1 **First NB** Ch. # 4695
High denominations only in small size from this Brown County bank, with this piece right in the middle of the condition census from here. **Fine-Very Fine.**
From The Rolling Plains Collection **(500-800)**

15281 **Caldwell, TX** - $20 1929 Ty. 1 **The Caldwell NB** Ch. # 6607
This is the only collectible bank in this community, with the town's other issuing institution being represented by just one Red Seal. The census stands at just nine small notes from this none too common issuer. **Very Fine.** (350-550)

15282 **Canyon, TX** - $10 1929 Ty. 2 **The First NB** Ch. # 5238
This attractive panhandle note is one of only two Type two examples extant from this none too common bank. **Very Fine.**
From The Rolling Plains Collection (500-700)

15283 **Canyon, TX** - $5 1929 Ty. 2 **The First NB** Ch. # 14090
This institution, the successor to the failed First NB of Canyon, issued fewer notes than most any other bank in Texas, with a total emission of only 260 sheets of both five and ten dollar bills. By happenstance (or perhaps due to Colonel Blake's efforts), both serial number one sheets were saved, with both being cut within the past decade. This lovely note is the bottom note from the first sheet of fives, and gives both Texas collectors and those interested in 14000 charters the opportunity to add one of these notes to their holdings. **Choice Crisp Uncirculated.**
From The Rolling Plains Collection (1,250-2,250)

15284 **Childress, TX** - $20 1882 Value Back Fr. 581 **The City NB** Ch. # (S)5992
This just plain scarce west Texas bank issued large notes only, with this one of just two $20 Value Backs reported from here to date. Excluding the three notes in the Moody Foundation holdings, just four notes are listed in the census, with this piece among that number. The colors are a bit muted and the paper somewhat soft, and, as the photo here discloses, the trim is less than optimal, but if rarity is any guide, expect this **Very Good-Fine** specimen to see bidding reach the vicinity of...
From The Rolling Plains Collection (2,000-2,500)

15285 **Childress, TX** - $10 1929 Ty. 2 **The First NB** Ch. # 12666
Small notes only from this rather scarce bank, which comes from a west Texas town named for George C. Childress, author of the Texas Declaration of Independence. **Fine-Very Fine,** ex-Irish and Ivy collections.
From The Rolling Plains Collection (600-900)

15286 **Clarendon, TX** - $10 1902 Plain Back Fr. 633 **The First NB** Ch. # 5463
A scarce west Texas bank located in Donley County in the Texas panhandle. **Fine,** ex-Ivy collection sale, lot 4083.
From The Rolling Plains Collection (1,500-2,000)

15287 **Claude, TX** - $10 1929 Ty. 1 **The First NB** Ch. # 7123
With just one large note known from here, collectors are forced to settle for Series 1929 examples, which are not exactly common either. This piece grades **Fine-Very Fine**, but there is some staining on the back that shows through to the face as well.
From The Rolling Plains Collection **(500-700)**

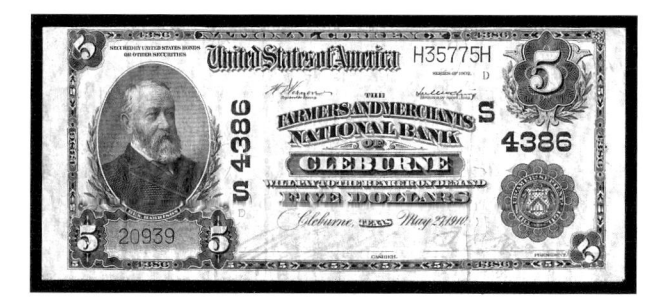

15288 **Cleburne, TX** - $5 1902 Plain Back Fr. 601 **The Farmers & Merchants NB** Ch. # (S)4386
Large notes only from this scarcer Cleburne bank. **Very Fine**, ex-Jack Everson collection. **(450-650)**

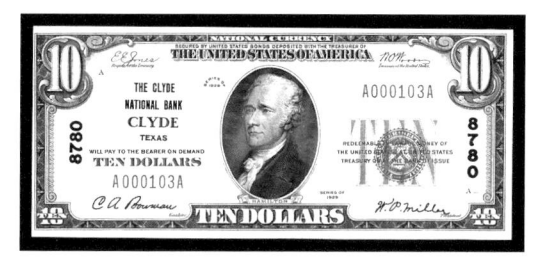

15289 **Clyde, TX** - $10 1929 Ty. 1 **The Clyde NB** Ch. # 8780
A nice example of one of the classic Texas hoard notes. **About Uncirculated.**
From The Rolling Plains Collection **(300-400)**

15290 **Coleman, TX** - $10 1929 Ty. 2 **First Coleman NB** Ch. # 13595
Do not let the census persuade you that this is not a very tough bank, as 36 of the 42 known examples from this institution are preserved in uncut sheets, leaving only six single notes for collectors to pursue. **Fine.**
From The Rolling Plains Collection **(350-550)**

15291 **Comanche, TX** - $20 1929 Ty. 1 **The Comanche NB** Ch. # 4246
A tougher small note from the Comanche County seat. **Fine**, ex-Ivy collection sale, lot 4096.
From The Rolling Plains Collection **(500-700)**

15292 **Corsicana, TX** - $20 1902 Plain Back Fr. 658 **The State NB** Ch. # 11022
A high end large example from this Navarro County bank. **Very Fine++,** with a tiny bit of purple bank stamp on the reverse that affects nothing. **(450-650)**

15293 **Cotulla, TX** - $20 1929 Ty. 1 **The Stockmens NB** Ch. # 7243
This none too common bank bears a most evocative Texas title. **Very Fine. (450-650)**

Serial Number 1 Crockett Note

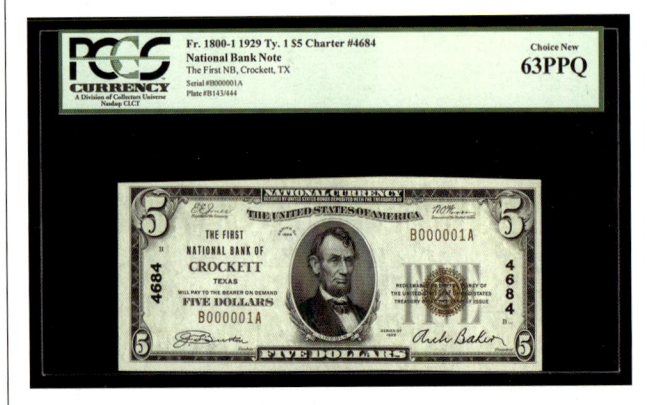

15294 Crockett, TX - $5 1929 Ty. 1 **The First NB** Ch. # 4684
An attractive serial number 1 example from a community bearing a name redolent of Texas history. PCGS has graded this note **Choice Crisp Uncirculated 63 PPQ**, a grade with which we have no disagreement whatever. (2,750-4,250)

15295 Daingerfield, TX - $20 1929 Ty. 1 **The NB of Daingerfield** Ch. # 4701
A very tough east Texas location with two issuing banks, one scarce and the other extremely rare. This example is as nice as any we've seen. Bright **Very Fine+**. (550-850)

15296 Dalhart, TX - $10 1902 Plain Back Fr. 624 **The First NB** Ch. # (S)6762
A better panhandle note which has been off the market in the collection of our consignor for almost a decade. Pleasing **Very Fine**.
From The Rolling Plains Collection (900-1,200)

Second Public Offering in Six Decades

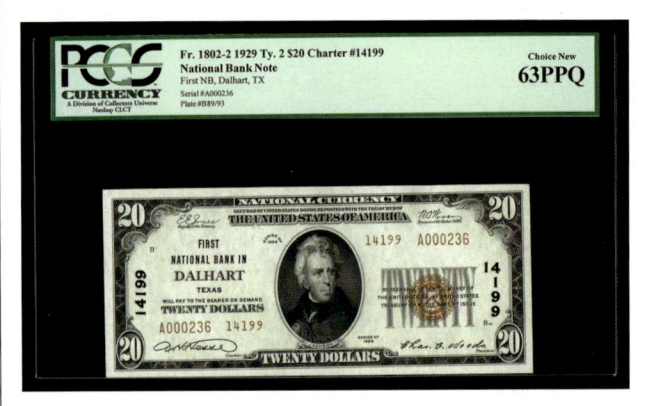

15297 Dalhart, TX - $20 1929 Ty. 2 **First NB** Ch. # 14199
While four notes are reported from this just plain rare panhandle bank, this specimen is the only one ever to be offered to collectors at public sale, having been part of the Irish holdings. Our consignor obtained it at that sale, where it brought $3025 against a pre-sale estimate of $500-1000. It is a truly lovely item, with its full original embossing easily observed inside the PCGS **Choice New 63 PPQ** holder it now resides in. Expect this beauty to surprise once again, with a realization likely in the area of... (2,500-4,500)

Newly Discovered Dallas First Charter

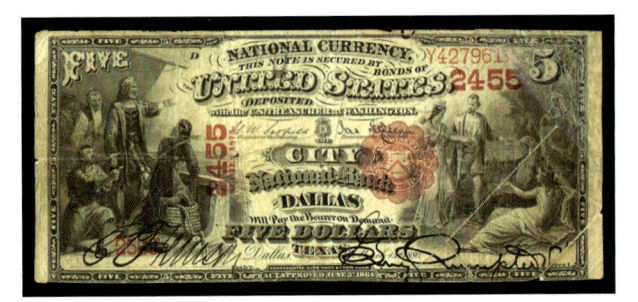

15298 Dallas, TX - $5 1875 Fr. 404 **The City NB** Ch. # 2455
This Dallas First Charter five is new to the census, and is one of only about twenty such examples known from all banks in the state combined. While grading **Fine**, with bright colors and good signatures, there is a substantial repair where a portion of the top right corner has been replaced. With any Texas First Charter likely to realize close to a five figure price if problem free, expect this piece, which still retains considerable eye appeal, to easily reach and perhaps well exceed... (5,000-7,000)

15299   Dallas, TX - $5 1882 Date Back Fr. 537 **The City NB** Ch. # (S)2455
An attractive high grade Second Charter example. The bottom margin is a bit tight, but the broad top margin helps considerably. This piece brought $1150 when we sold it back in January of 2003, and will likely fetch more this evening. Sharp **Very Fine-Extremely Fine.** (1,200-1,600)

15300   Dallas, TX - $100 1929 Ty. 2 **Republic NB & TC** Ch. # 12186
This **Fine-Very Fine** piece was recently discovered in a bank deposit. There are a few pinholes, but the paper still has plenty of snap. (750-1,000)

15301   Dallas, TX - $20 1902 Plain Back Fr. 661 **North Texas NB** Ch. # 12736
This bank was located on the first two floors of the Magnolia Oil Building. Signatures of D.W. Forbes and Everett S. Owens are engraved. The surfaces are pleasing on this **Fine+** $20 with a slight hole near the portrait area. (350-500)

15302   Dallas, TX - $50 1902 Plain Back Fr. 685 **North Texas NB** Ch. # 12736
A very scarce large size high denomination example from here, with this new to the census example one of only about half a dozen large fifties reported from this bank to date. Pleasing **Fine-Very Fine,** and sporting engraved bank signatures. (1,200-1,600)

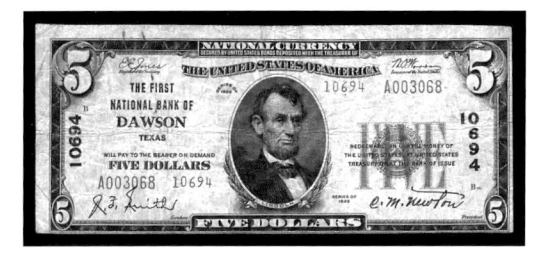

15303   Dawson, TX - $5 1929 Ty. 2 **The First NB** Ch. # 10694
This is the scarcer of Dawson's two banks, with the small size census somewhat skewed by the presence of two serial number 1 sheets, one of which has now been cut. **Fine,** with a bit of paper clip residue. (400-600)

15304   De Leon, TX - $20 1929 Ty. 1 **The Farmers & Merchants NB** Ch. # 7553
A high grade small example from this very scarce Comanche County issuer. Bright **Extremely Fine+.**
From The Rolling Plains Collection (550-750)

15305   Decatur, TX - $10 1929 Ty. 2 **The First NB** Ch. # 13623
A very scarce Wise County bank despite the existence of a cut sheet of serial number 1 twenties. **Very Fine,** ex-Irish and Ivy collections.
From The Rolling Plains Collection (400-600)

15306   Del Rio, TX - $5 1929 Ty. 1 **The First NB** Ch. # 5294
A considerably scarcer bank in small size than large, with this the sole type and denomination issued from here. **Fine-Very Fine.** (450-650)

15307 Dublin, TX - $20 1902 Plain Back Fr. 655 The Dublin NB Ch. # 4865
A very tough bank from this small Erath County community, reputedly the only remaining location in the state of Texas where one can obtain a Dr. Pepper with its original cane sugar recipe. Pen signed **About Fine,** with a couple of small problems at the lower left end.
From The Rolling Plains Collection **(900-1,200)**

15308 Dublin, TX - $10 1882 Value Back Fr. 577 The Citizens NB Ch. # (S)5836
This is a truly scarce bank with only seven examples listed in the census, two of which are permanently impounded in the Philpott/Moody Foundation collection. This Value Back is new to that listing, and, save for one of the Philpott notes, is likely the finest specimen known from here. Sharp **Very Fine,** with vivid purple signatures.
From The Rolling Plains Collection **(3,000-5,000)**

Newly Discovered Texas $20 First Charter-One of Eight Known

15309 El Paso, TX - $20 1875 Fr. 435 The First NB Ch. # 2532
A truly rare Texas note which is one of only eight known $20 First Charters from all banks in the state combined, and the only one from any El Paso bank. This piece has been encapsulated by PCGS, which has assigned a grade of **Very Good 10,** a conservative figure considering the good color and strong signatures the note displays. The Kelly premium here is $15,000, and we see no reason at all to disagree with that figure, which, if anything, might well be somewhat conservative. **(15,000-25,000)**

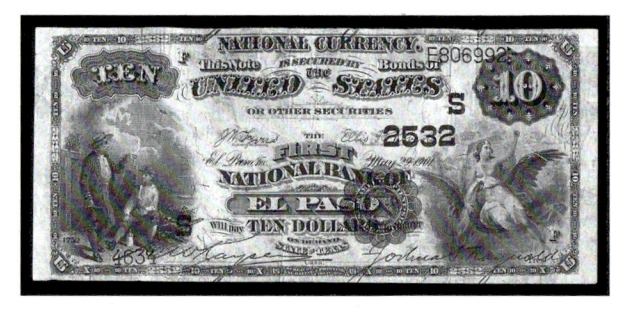

15310 El Paso, TX - $10 1882 Date Back Fr. 545 The First NB Ch. # (S)2532
This is a bright **Fine** $10 with officers E.W. Kayser and Joshua G. Reynolds. An approximate quarter inch top edge tear is noticed. **(600-900)**

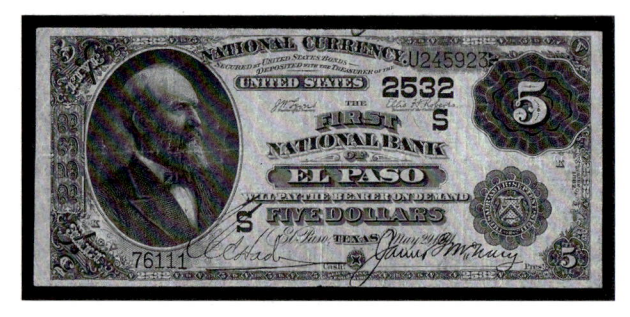

15311 El Paso, TX - $5 1882 Value Back Fr. 574 The First NB Ch. # (S)2532
A scarcer type and denomination from this well collected west Texas location. **Fine-Very Fine,** and more than adequately margined for a $5 Value Back. **(900-1,200)**

15312 **El Paso, TX** - $20 1882 Value Back Fr. 581 **The First NB** Ch. # (S)2532
This $20 has officers M.C. Hade and James G. McNary. As a type of note $20 Value Backs on Texas are scarce. **Fine. (700-1,000)**

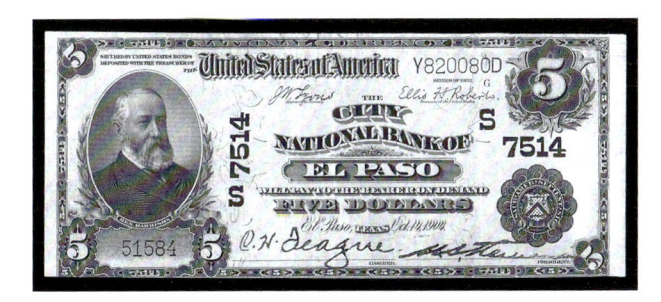

15313 **El Paso, TX** - $5 1902 Plain Back Fr. 598 **The City NB** Ch. # (S)7514
This is a bright, crisp example with bold printed signatures of C.H. Teague and M.S. Stewart. The folds are hard to see on this example from a bank that went into receivership in 1924. This note has the highest grade of all the graded notes in the census for the City National. **Extremely Fine. (500-800)**

Rare Short-Lived El Paso Bank

15314 **El Paso, TX** - $5 1902 Plain Back Fr. 602 **The Commercial NB** Ch. # (S)10140
This crisp, well centered note is bright and bold, and has only one light vertical fold to limit the grade. There are no signatures, but this is one of just four documented notes on this rare bank that was chartered in 1912 and liquidated a brief five years later in 1917. To throw fuel on to the fire, one of those four notes is locked away in the Philpott/Moody Collection leaving a true collectible population of only three notes. This charter number was even able to escape the Irish Collection. Simply a great Texas note. **Choice About Uncirculated. (2,500-4,500)**

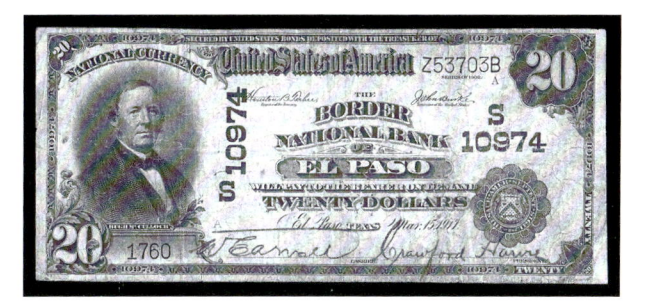

15315 **El Paso, TX** - $20 1902 Plain Back Fr. 658 **The Border NB** Ch. # (S)10974
This is a great bank title that was only on the El Paso banking scene for a little less than seven years. This new addition to the census becomes only the fourth $20 1902 Plain Back documented on this bank. The printed signatures are of W.E. Arnold and Crawford Harvie. **Fine. (500-800)**

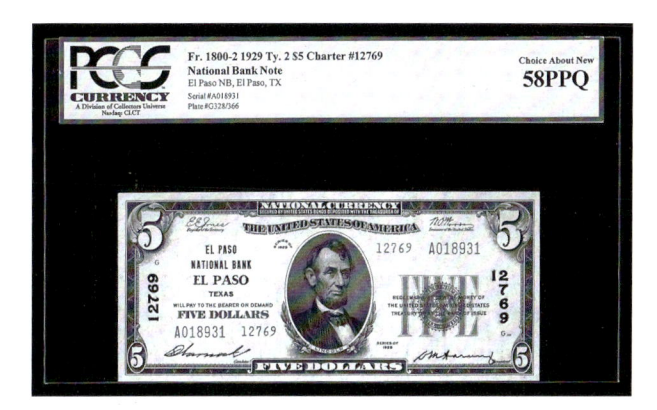

15316 **El Paso, TX** - $5 1929 Ty. 2 **El Paso NB** Ch. # 12769
An attractively centered example with great color and appearance. We must admit being somewhat perplexed at the PCGS assigned grade of **Choice About Uncirculated 58 PPQ**, as we can discern no folds through the third party holder and the note comes from a small run of consecutive notes, all of which are listed in the census as CU. (300-500)

15317 **El Paso, TX** - $10 1929 Ty. 2 **El Paso NB** Ch. # 12769
Ample margins and bold embossing are traits of this $10 that has a corner fold. This was the smallest of three national banks in El Paso during the Series of 1929 era. This note sports the second officer tandem found on small size notes of this charter number. **Choice About Uncirculated. (300-500)**

15318 **Ennis, TX** - $20 1929 Ty. 1 **The First NB** Ch. # 12110
Although an even dozen large notes are known from this Ellis County bank, just three Series 1929 examples have been reported from here to date, no surprise since this bank's small size issue was terminated by this institution's entry into receivership in February of 1930. **Fine.**
From The Rolling Plains Collection (900-1,200)

15319   **Floydada, TX** - $20 1929 Ty. 1 **The First NB** Ch. # 7045
An attractive small example from this agricultural community which serves as the county seat of Floyd County. This was the sole National Bank in town, and notes from here are decidedly scarce. Nice **Fine-Very Fine.**
From The Rolling Plains Collection **(750-950)**

15320   **Follett, TX** - $10 1929 Ty. 1 **The Follett NB** Ch. # 12101
Only one large note is known from this better bank, leaving just a veritable handful of small examples to satisfy collector demand to cover this tough one bank town. This piece, formerly in the Ivy holdings, is tied for finest known with one other. **Very Fine+.**
From The Rolling Plains Collection **(750-1,250)**

15321   **Forney, TX** - $5 1902 Plain Back Fr. 608 **The City NB** Ch. # 6078
Kelly lists seven known for large size examples from here. Purple signatures are still discernible on this **Fine-Very Fine** note which has been cut askew. **(1,000-1,500)**

15322   **Forney, TX** - $10 1929 Ty. 1 **The Farmers NB** Ch. # 9369
This is a tougher Kaufman County bank, with this note, although grading only a nice **Fine+,** one of the nicest Series 1929 examples reported to date. **(350-550)**

15323   **Fort Worth, TX** - $50 1929 Ty. 1 **The Fort Worth NB** Ch. # 3131
A high grade example which looks new at first glance, and, in fact, was sold as such in the August, 2002 Dallas auction. It's still as nice or nicer than any other small fifty listed in the census. **Extremely Fine-About Uncirculated.** **(600-900)**

15324   **Fort Worth, TX** - $5 1902 Plain Back Fr. 601 **The Farmers & Mechanics NB** Ch. # (S)4004
A very attractive piece which is one of the highest grade examples known from here. Vivid **Extremely Fine.** **(450-750)**

15325   **Franklin, TX** - $5 1929 Ty. 2 **The First NB** Ch. # 7838
A nice example from the only bank in this small Robertson County locale to issue. Pleasing **Fine-Very Fine. (450-650)**

15326   **Galveston, TX** - $5 1929 Ty. 1 **The First NB** Ch. # 1566
This $5 carries a pretty high grade for a national - **PMG Gem Uncirculated 66 EPQ.** The embossing is strong and the margins are ample. This note is not in the census, but there is not a graded Series 1929 note in the census for this bank that can compare with it. **(350-550)**

15327 Galveston, TX - $10 1929 Ty. 2 **The City NB** Ch. # 8899
A lovely example which was the bottom note on the first sheet of Type two tens sent to this bank. It's signed as President by W.L. Moody, Jr., the then-patriarch of one of Galveston's most prominent families. **Choice Crisp Uncirculated.** (500-800)

15328 **Charter Number 12475 Bonanza.**
Galveston, TX - $5; $10; $20 1902 Plain Back Fr. 609; 635; 661 **The United States NB** Ch. # 12475
The $5 grades **VG**, missing corner and graffiti, the $10 grades **Fine,** and the $20 grades **VG-Fine.** (Total: 3 notes) (300-400)

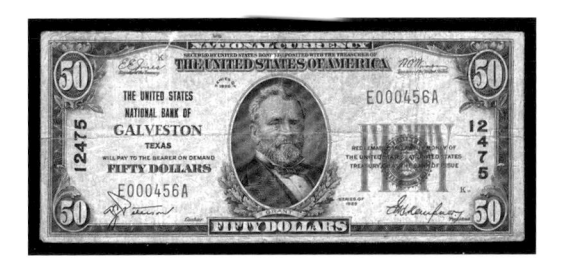

15329 Galveston, TX - $50 1929 Ty. 1 **The United States NB** Ch. # 12475
This is an uncommon denomination on this "forbidden title" bank, with this example representing one of only nine serial numbers in the census. This note served time as a wallet piece and this probably accounts for its survival. A small scuff spot is found at the top margin. **Very Good-Fine.** (450-650)

15330 Galveston, TX - $100 1929 Ty. 1 **The United States NB** Ch. # 12475
This is one of only seven Type 1 $100s in the census on this "forbidden title" bank. **Fine.** (900-1,200)

15331 Gilmer, TX - $10 1929 Ty. 1 **The Farmers & Merchants NB** Ch. # 5741
The more available of Gilmer's two banks which issued Series 1929 examples. **Fine.**
From The Rolling Plains Collection (300-500)

15332 Gonzales, TX - $10 1929 Ty. 1 **The Farmers NB** Ch. # 8392
While certainly not a rare note in small size, fewer than a handful of examples are listed in the Kelly census in this state of preservation. PCGS graded **Choice New 63 PPQ.** (500-800)

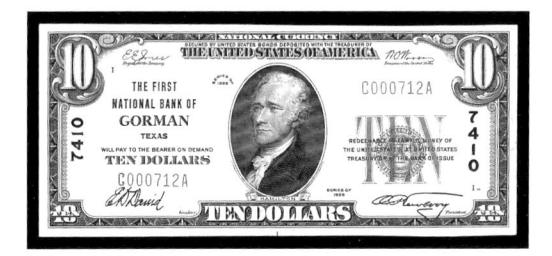

15333 Gorman, TX - $10 1929 Ty. 1 **The First NB** Ch. # 7410
A very scarce Eastland County issuer and the sole National Bank chartered here. This piece, which is new to the census, is easily the nicest example known from here, large or small. **Extremely Fine.**
From The Rolling Plains Collection (700-900)

15334 Graham, TX - $20 1929 Ty. 1 **First NB** Ch. # 4418
This bank was somewhat the scarcer of Graham's two Series 1929 issuers. **Fine.**
From The Rolling Plains Collection (400-600)

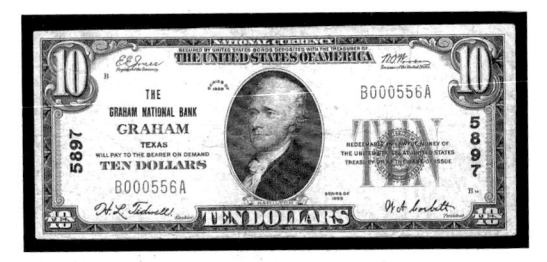

15335 Graham, TX - $10 1929 Ty. 1 **The Graham NB** Ch. # 5897
An attractive and utterly problem free example from this community's other small size issuer. **Fine-Very Fine.**
From The Rolling Plains Collection (350-550)

15336 Granbury, TX - $20 1929 Ty. 1 **The First NB** Ch. # 3727
A bright and attractive note which is the finest Series 1929 example recorded in the census from here. **Very Fine++.** (400-600)

15337 Grandview, TX - $5 1929 Ty. 1 **The First NB** Ch. # 4389
As nice a small size example from this Johnson County location as we've ever seen or heard of. **Very Fine-Extremely Fine.**
From The Rolling Plains Collection (500-700)

15338 Grandview, TX - $10 1929 Ty. 1 **The First NB** Ch. # 4389
A very scarce note from the only bank to issue Series 1929 examples in this small Johnson County community. Less than a dozen examples are now noted in the Kelly census. Nice **Fine-Very Fine.** (400-600)

15339 Groveton, TX - $10 1929 Ty. 1 **The First NB** Ch. # 6329
A tougher bank with only eight small notes making up the entire Series 1929 census from this bank. **Fine-Very Fine.** (400-600)

15340 Hebbronville, TX - $5 1929 Ty. 1 **The First NB** Ch. # 12995
Small notes only from this Jim Hogg County bank. **Fine-Very Fine.** (300-500)

15341 Hereford, TX - $20 1902 Plain Back Fr. 659 **The First NB** Ch. # 5604
An always popular note from the county seat of Deaf Smith County. This location took its distinctive name from the breed of cattle brought to the area by local ranchers. We can find only one offering of any large note from here since this example was sold as part of the Ivy collection holdings back in January of 2001. Pleasing **Fine+++,** with two color signatures.
From The Rolling Plains Collection (1,000-1,400)

15342 Hereford, TX - $20 1902 Plain Back Fr. 650 **The Western NB** Ch. # (S)6812
Somewhat the scarcer of Hereford's two issuers, with this piece bearing a distinguished pedigree, hailing first from the Everson holdings and then appearing in the Ivy sale, where it was lot 4234. **Fine.**
From The Rolling Plains Collection (1,000-1,500)

15343 **Hillsboro, TX** - $20 1902 Plain Back Fr. 655 **The Citizens NB** Ch. # (S)4900
This $20 has the scarce Napier-Thompson Treasury signatures. Only ten Texas banks issued notes with this signature combination. The bank officer signatures have faded away. **Fine.** (300-500)

15344 **Hondo, TX** - $10 1929 Ty. 1 **The First NB** Ch. # 5765
This Medina County bank is considerably scarcer in small size than large, with this example from this ranching community's only issuer matched in grade by just one other Series 1929 example in the census. **About Uncirculated.**
From The Rolling Plains Collection (750-950)

Serial Number 1 Honey Grove

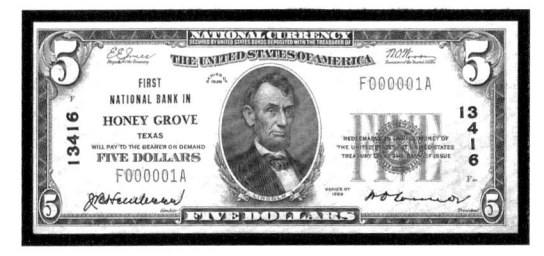

15345 **Honey Grove, TX** - $5 1929 Ty. 1 **First NB** Ch. # 13416
Serial number F000001A, the bottom note on the first sheet issued. There are a couple of folds picked up in storage, and a trace of mounting residue on the reverse bottom corner tips, but the note is still bright, crackling fresh, and quite appealing. **About Uncirculated.** (2,000-3,000)

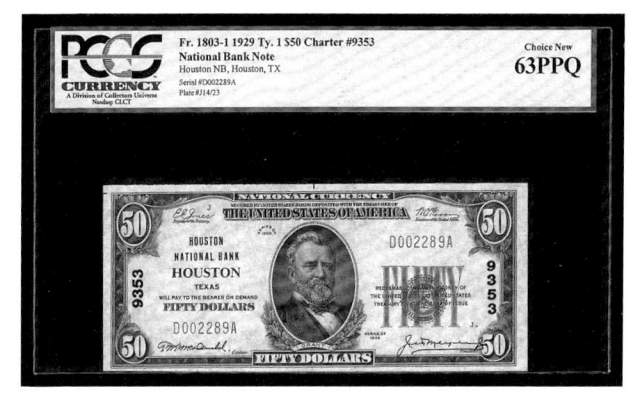

15346 **Houston, TX** - $50 1929 Ty. 1 **Houston NB** Ch. # 9353
One of the very nicest examples of this denomination known from here, with less than a handful of pieces listed in the Kelly census in CU or better condition. PCGS **Choice New 63 PPQ.** (600-900)

15347 **Houston, TX** - $10 1929 Ty. 1 **The Union NB** Ch. # 9712
Fresh, bright, and fully Gem save for its close top margin. **Choice Crisp Uncirculated.**
From The Rolling Plains Collection (250-450)

15348 **Houston, TX** - $100 1929 Ty. 1 **South Texas Commercial NB** Ch. # 10152
A less than common denomination from an otherwise extremely common bank. **Very Fine-Extremely Fine**, and bearing low serial number D000006A as a bonus. (350-550)

15349 **Houston, TX** - $100 1929 Ty. 1 **South Texas Commercial NB** Ch. # 10152
Three banks in Houston issued Series 1929 $100s. A light four-digit pencilled number is to the left of the portrait. **PCGS Fine 15.** (300-500)

15350 **Huntsville, TX** - $20 1929 Ty. 1 **The First NB** Ch. # 4208
A seldom available note from the only issuer in town. **Fine-Very Fine.**
From The Rolling Plains Collection (300-500)

15351 **Italy, TX** - $20 1929 Ty. 2 **The First NB** Ch. # 5663
An above average example from this Ellis County issuer, and the only Type 2 $20 reported from here to date as well. **Very Fine.**
From The Rolling Plains Collection **(300-400)**

15352 **Jacksboro, TX** - $10 1902 Plain Back Fr. 627 **The First NB** Ch. # 4483
A decent **Fine** example from the first of three banks chartered here. Purple signatures help as well.
From The Rolling Plains Collection **(600-900)**

15353 **Jacksboro, TX** - $20 1929 Ty. 1 **The Jacksboro NB** Ch. # 7814
This is a just plain rare Jacksboro bank, with just four large and four small notes comprising the entire census from here. Expect a realization for this evenly circulated **Fine** example in the range of...
From The Rolling Plains Collection **(700-1,100)**

15354 **Kaufman, TX** - $20 1929 Ty. 1 **The First NB** Ch. # 3836
A very scarce bank in small size, with a total census population of only seven such examples, including this specimen. Nice **Fine-Very Fine.**
From The Rolling Plains Collection **(400-600)**

15355 **Kingsville, TX** - $10 1929 Ty. 2 **The First NB** Ch. # 12968
A high grade note from Kleberg County, the home of the fabled King Ranch. **About Uncirculated,** actually a new note with a couple of rounded corners and one tiny corner tip fold.
From The Rolling Plains Collection **(300-400)**

15356 **Knox City, TX** - $20 1929 Ty. 1 **The First NB** Ch. # 7953
With large examples from this small one bank community unknown in public hands (the sole reported piece is ensconced in the Moody Foundation holdings), small notes from this none too common institution are even more desirable than otherwise. This piece, originally from the Ivy collection, grades **Fine** and has been off the market since our consignor purchased it back in 2001.
From The Rolling Plains Collection **(600-900)**

15357 **La Grange, TX** - $10 1929 Ty. 2 **The First NB** Ch. # 3906
A high grade Series 1929 example from a Fayette County bank which is actually scarcer in small size than large. **Very Fine-Extremely Fine.** **(350-550)**

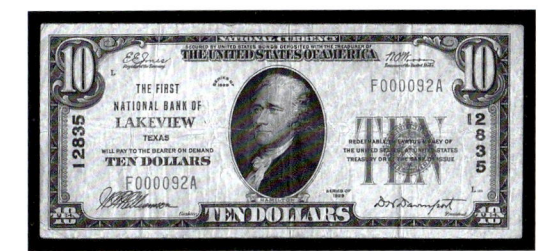

15358 Lakeview, TX - $10 1929 Ty. 1 The First NB Ch. # 12835
Although chartered in October of 1925, this bank opted not to issue any currency until the advent of small notes almost four years later. Even then the number of pieces printed were limited, at least in part certainly due to the fact that this remote panhandle location could barely support even one National Bank. Notes from here are just plain scarce, with this location missing from both the Everson and Ivy collections. Pleasing **Fine-Very Fine.**
From The Rolling Plains Collection **(1,000-1,500)**

15359 Laredo, TX - $50 1882 Date Back Fr. 563 The Milmo NB Ch. # (S)2486
Just 18 of this type and denomination are listed in the census for Texas, just under half of them from here, including this otherwise **Very Fine** example which has been closely trimmed all around, displays a bit of residue on the lower right corner and has a small worm hole near the right side sorting letter. It is, nonetheless, reasonably nice looking and is an exceptionally scarce type for the state, meriting bids of at least... **(5,000-7,500)**

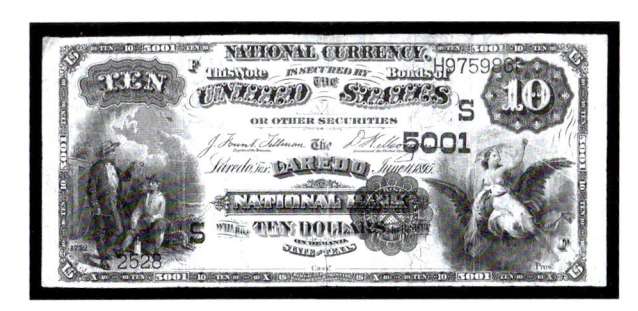

15360 Laredo, TX - $10 1882 Date Back Fr. 542 The Laredo NB Ch. # (S)5001
A much tougher early type from this bank, and one which is certain to be of interest to all collectors of south Texas material. **Fine-Very Fine.** **(1,750-2,750)**

15361 Laredo, TX - $20 1902 Plain Back Fr. 658 The Laredo NB Ch. # 5001
Just one quarter of the 33 large notes listed in the census from here are of the $20 Plain Back variety. This **Fine-Very Fine** example has especially generous margins and still displays the officers' stamped signatures. This always popular South Texas border town is seldom available in large size. We expect tonight's offering will sell for about... **(700-900)**

Unique in Small Size

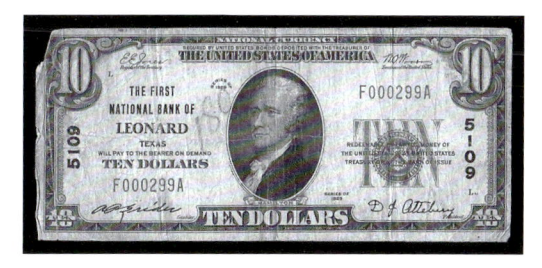

15362 Leonard, TX - $10 1929 Ty. 1 The First NB Ch. # 5109
While large examples from this north Texas institution are scarce but available, small notes are another matter entirely, with this bank on the unknown list before the appearance of this piece. Only a very small quantity of Series 1929 examples were issued from here before the liquidator arrived to close the bank in February of 1930, a mere seven months after the start of the small size issuing period. While hardly an example for the condition conscious, for those collectors who care about rarity this is about as good as it gets. **Very Good,** with a blue pencil number on the front and a corner tip missing. **(1,000-2,000)**

15363 Lipan, TX - $20 1929 Ty. 1 The First NB Ch. # 10598
Although a fair number of notes have been recorded from this one bank Hood County location, few are in this state of preservation. Bright **Extremely Fine-About Uncirculated.**
From The Rolling Plains Collection **(400-600)**

15364 Longview, TX - $5 1929 Ty. 1 The Rembert NB Ch. # 12411
The only denomination issued by this east Texas bank, with this piece considerably nicer than most known from here. **Very Fine. (300-400)**

One of Three Known

15365 Lufkin, TX - $20 1882 Brown Back Fr. 504 The Angelina County NB Ch. # (S)6009
This is by far the rarer of Lufkin's two national banks, having issued only Brown Backs and Second Charter Date Backs before exiting the scene in 1912. Just three notes are known, all Brown Back twenties and all in the same grade. This is an attractive piece with vivid inks and sharp two color pen signatures. The Kelly premium of $10,000 might be a bit high, but a realization of close to that figure for this **Very Fine-Extremely Fine** rarity is certainly not out of the question. **(6,000-9,000)**

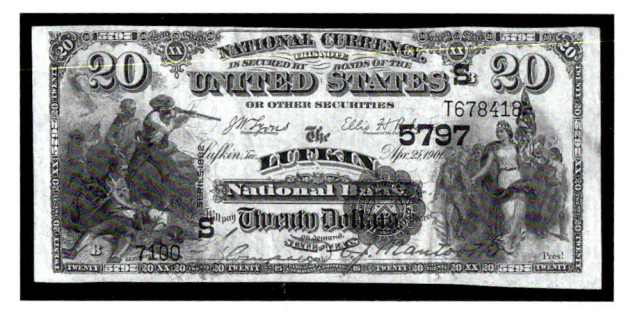

15366 Lufkin, TX - $20 1882 Value Back Fr. 581 The Lufkin NB Ch. # (S)5797
A very scarce type and denomination from any bank, with this one of only three such examples known from here, one of which is permanently impounded in the Philpott/Moody holdings. **Very Fine,** with bold blue signatures, a premium piece. **(2,000-3,000)**

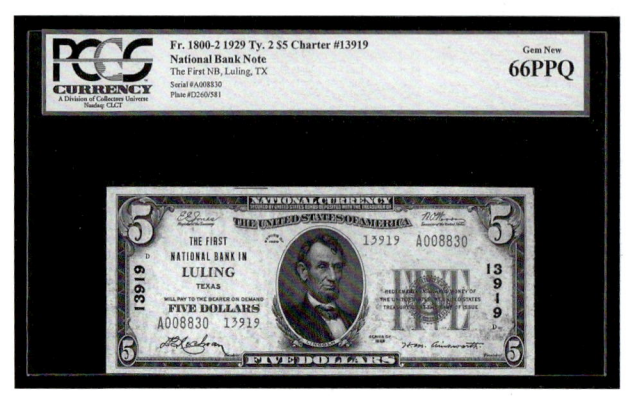

15367 Luling, TX - $5 1929 Ty. 2 The First NB Ch. # 13919
Uncirculated notes from this Caldwell County community are certainly not rare, but few will be the equal of this blazer. PCGS has given it a grade of **Gem New 66 PPQ,** an accolade it certainly appears to more than merit. **(600-900)**

15368 McGregor, TX - $20 1929 Ty. 1 The First NB Ch. # 4076
A just plain rare Waco area bank which is actually considerably scarcer in small size than large. This piece, which is new to the census, is the finest known Series 1929 example from here by a very wide margin. Bright **Extremely Fine-About Uncirculated. (750-1,250)**

15369 **Melissa, TX** - $5 1929 Ty. 2 **The Melissa NB** Ch. # 10008
A much in demand Collin County note from the only bank here to issue. This new to the census example is the only Type 2 $5 reported from here to date. Evenly circulated **Fine. (800-1,200)**

15370 **Memphis, TX** - $5 1902 Plain Back Fr. 608 **The First NB** Ch. # 6107
A decent **Fine** example from this scarce panhandle bank. This piece bears the so-called "Fourth Charter" plate date of January 11, 1922.
From The Rolling Plains Collection **(600-900)**

15371 **Memphis, TX** - $5 1929 Ty. 2 **The First NB** Ch. # 6107
A bright and fresh example bearing desirable low serial number A000006, the bottom note from the first sheet of Type twos sent to this bank. **Choice Crisp Uncirculated**, ex-Ivy collection sale.
From The Rolling Plains Collection **(500-800)**

15372 **Memphis, TX** - $10 1929 Ty. 1 **The Hall County NB** Ch. # 8005
This bank was by far the scarcer of this rural community's two issuers. **Fine-Very Fine.**
From The Rolling Plains Collection **(400-600)**

15373 **Mercedes, TX** - $5 1929 Ty. 1 **The First NB** Ch. # 11879
An evenly circulated example from Hidalgo County in far south Texas. **Fine. (400-600)**

15374 **Mineola, TX** - $10 1902 Plain Back Fr. 632 **The First NB** Ch. # (S)5127
This is a new note for the Kelly census which bumps it up to a mere eight large, but then you have to also consider that two of the notes are locked away in the Philpott/Moody Collection. This is also only the third different large note on this charter number to cross the auction block since 1997. **Fine** with light purple stamped signatures of Jas. D. Harris and R.J. Gaston. **(1,000-2,000)**

15375 **Mission, TX** - $10 1929 Ty. 1 **The First NB** Ch. # 10090
This small town is, somewhat surprisingly, one of the prime tourist meccas of Texas, serving as the home to 10,000 "winter Texans," mostly denizens of the snowy midwest who make the trek to far south Texas every fall to escape the harsh winters at home. Year round it is a major citrus producer, and home to the Texas ruby red grapefruit. This was the only bank chartered here. **Fine. (750-1,150)**

15376 **Munday, TX** - $20 1929 Ty. 1 **The First NB** Ch. # 7106
This is just a plain rare town, with one of the community's two issuers unreported and this bank represented in the census by only four large and three small notes, including this example. **Very Fine,** certain to be a popular item this evening.
From The Rolling Plains Collection **(1,250-1,750)**

15377 **Nacogdoches, TX** - $5 1929 Ty. 1 **The Stone Fort NB** Ch. # 6627
This historic east Texas community was home to three National Banks, two of which are unreported. Only one large note is known from here, leaving collectors who want any example from here the option of a Series 1929 specimen only. **Fine-Very Fine,** with a couple of red pencil marks on the right side. **(350-550)**

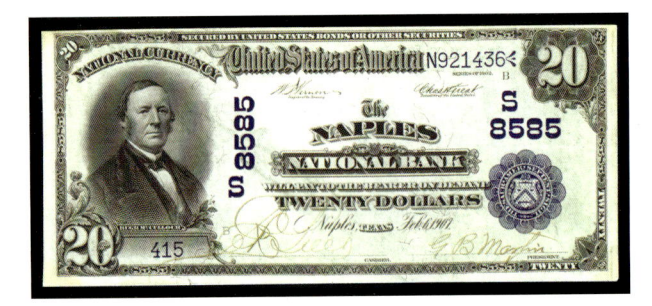

15378 **Naples, TX** - $20 1902 Date Back Fr. 644 **The Naples NB** Ch. # (S)8585
Just five notes are known from this short lived institution, which issued Red Seals and Date Backs only before liquidating in 1916. This piece is by far the finest of the group, grading a nice **Extremely Fine-About Uncirculated.** If rarity and desirability are any guide, expect this most attractive specimen to realize... **(3,500-4,500)**

15379 **Navasota, TX** - $10 1929 Ty. 1 **The First NB** Ch. # 4253
An attractive example from this Grimes County bank. Small notes from here are considerably scarcer than are their large size compatriots. **Very Fine.** **(350-550)**

15380 **Nevada, TX** - $10 1882 Value Back Fr. 577 **The First NB** Ch. # (S)5721
While three Value Backs from this small Collin County community are listed in the census, this is the only example that is available to collectors, as the other two are ensconced in the Philpott/Moody foundation holdings. The margins are a bit close, and there is a touch of light staining evident, but the purple signatures are visible and the rarity here unquestioned. **Fine.** **(2,500-3,500)**

15381 **Nocona, TX** - $20 1882 Date Back Fr. 555 **The Nocona NB** Ch. # (S)5338
The second title used by this very tough bank which went out in 1921. There is a small corner tip off, along with some light staining on the left side, but the note still retains plenty of eye appeal, not surprising for an example with a pedigree dating back to the Everson and Ivy collections. **Fine.**
From The Rolling Plains Collection **(1,500-2,500)**

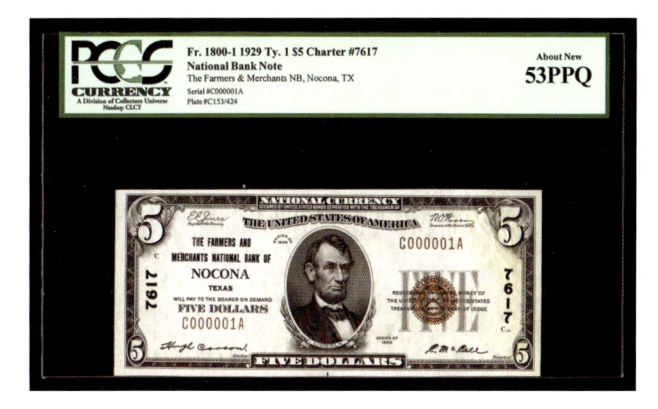

15382 Nocona, TX - $5 1929 Ty. 1 **The Farmers & Merchants NB** Ch. # 7617
An attractive and well centered serial number 1 example which is just one sharp fold from new. PCGS **About New 53 PPQ.** (2,250-3,250)

15383 Nocona, TX - $10 1929 Ty. 2 **The Peoples NB** Ch. # 11959
Despite receiving its charter in 1921, this bank elected to issue Series 1929 examples only. **Fine,** with a bit of soiling on the back.
From The Rolling Plains Collection (300-400)

15384 Odessa, TX - $20 1929 Ty. 1 **The Citizens NB** Ch. # 8169
A very rare small note from this much collected west Texas community, with this piece one of just three reported Series 1929 examples from here. **Fine.** (1,250-1,750)

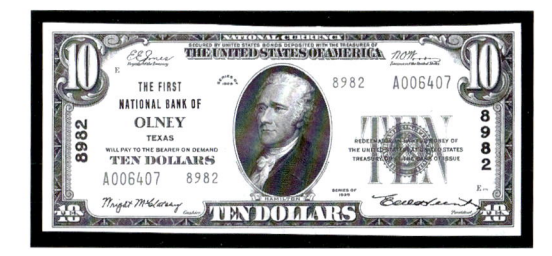

15385 Olney, TX - $10 1929 Ty. 2 **The First NB** Ch. # 8982
This is an interesting bank. We handled a small hoard of large notes from here over twenty years ago, and a handful of small size sheets are also known, but this example is the first uncirculated Series 1929 example we've ever seen for sale. **Choice Crisp Uncirculated.**
From The Rolling Plains Collection (400-600)

15386 Ozona, TX - $5 1929 Ty. 2 **The Ozona NB** Ch. # 7748
Fives, fifties and hundreds only in small size from this remote west Texas community. This is the only $5 note recorded. **Very Fine.** (1,500-2,500)

15387 Paducah, TX - $10 1902 Plain Back Fr. 628 **The First NB** Ch. # (S)10230
This piece, from the only bank chartered in this remote little town in rural Cottle County, is just plain rare, as it is one of only four large examples to have been reported from here to date. It traces its pedigree to the Ivy collection, and is, according to our records, the only large note from here which has been offered at public sale for at least the past ten years. **Very Good-Fine.**
From The Rolling Plains Collection (2,000-3,000)

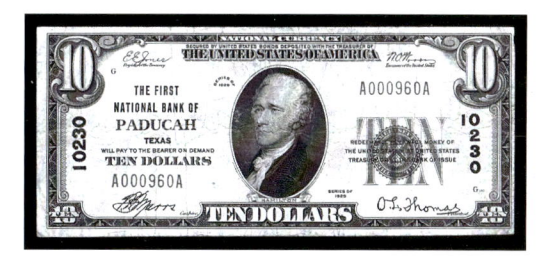

15388 Paducah, TX - $10 1929 Ty. 1 **The First NB** Ch. # 10230
An evenly circulated example from the only bank chartered in Cottle County, certainly one of the least celebrated of Texas' 254 counties. Pleasing **Fine.**
From The Rolling Plains Collection (500-700)

15389 Paris, TX - $50 1929 Ty. 1 **The First NB** Ch. # 3638
A nice high denomination example from this elusive east Texas bank. **Very Fine.** (900-1,200)

15390 **Pittsburg, TX** - $50 1929 Ty. 1 **The First NB** Ch. # 4863
This is a truly rare note which is one of just two Series 1929 examples extant from here. With this bank issuing only a tiny number of high denominations only (just 184 sheets of fifties and 35 sheets of hundreds) expect this to be rare forever as well. Bright **Very Fine+**. (3,000-5,000)

Flashy Plano Serial Number 1

15391 **Plano, TX** - $5 1929 Ty. 1 **The First NB** Ch. # 13511
A beautiful serial number 1 example from this fast growing Dallas bedroom community. **Gem Crisp Uncirculated.**
From The Rolling Plains Collection **(3,000-4,000)**

15392 **Port Arthur, TX** - $10 1902 Plain Back Fr. 633 **The First NB** Ch. # 5485
A decent circulated example from a bank which is quite common in small size but very scarce in large. **Fine-Very Fine.** (750-950)

15393 **Post City, TX** - $10 1929 Ty. 1 **The First NB** Ch. # 9485
A tougher note from this small family owned west Texas bank. **Very Good-Fine**, with signatures of J.T. Herd and H.B. Herd. (500-700)

15394 **Quanah, TX** - $10 1929 Ty. 1 **First NB** Ch. # 12307
This small NW Texas community was named in honor of legendary Comanche chief Quanah Parker, and was home to no fewer than six banks, four of which are as yet unreported and one which is represented by two large notes. This is the sole bank which lasted long enough to issue series 1929 examples, with this specimen one of just seven reported in the census. **Fine.**
From The Rolling Plains Collection **(700-900)**

Series 1929 Rising Star-One of Two Known

15395 **Rising Star, TX** - $20 1929 Ty. 1 **The First NB** Ch. # 7906
This piece bears one of the great Texas town names, and is a rare and desirable item indeed even forgetting about its title. This example is one of just two Series 1929 specimens known from Rising Star, a small Eastland County community with a current population of under 1000 people. When last sold this note realized a strong $2990 and we see no reason that it will not reach or exceed that level again tonight. **Fine.**
From The Rolling Plains Collection **(3,000-4,000)**

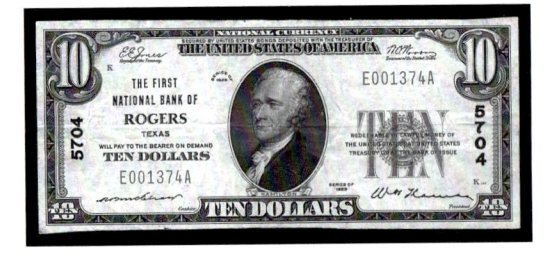

15396 **Rogers, TX** - $10 1929 Ty. 1 **The First NB** Ch. # 5704
As is the case with so many Texas banks, large notes outnumber small by a two to one ratio. This is the finest of the seven Series 1929 notes listed in the census. Bright **Very Fine.**
From The Rolling Plains Collection **(400-600)**

15397 Rotan, TX - $10 1929 Ty. 1 **The First NB** Ch. # 8693
This was the only bank to issue in this rural Fisher County location. As is often the case with agriculturally dependent communities, large notes are far more numerous than small because of the contraction of rural economies which began in the early 1920's and accelerated with the onset of the Depression. This bank is typical of many others, with eight large notes reported but only three small, a total which includes this example. **About Fine.** (1,000-1,500)

15398 Roxton, TX - $10 1902 Plain Back Fr. 633 **The First NB** Ch. # (S)5710
This **Fine+++** note from an extremely challenging East Texas bank came to the collecting fraternity by way of the Midwest Cash Hoard, which we sold in September of 2005. The census from this Lamar County issuer numbers just nine large notes, two of which are permanently impounded in the Moody Foundation holdings. Tonight's example is one of only two $10 Plain Backs known to survive and should see bids that will reach at least and possibly eclipse... (2,000-3,000)

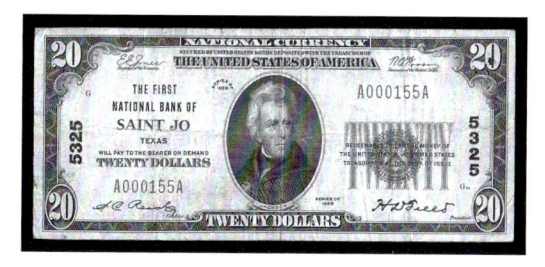

15399 Saint Jo, TX - $20 1929 Ty. 1 **The First NB** Ch. # 5325
A more than acceptable example from this tough Montague County bank. **Fine+,** with a small split in the top margin.
From The Rolling Plains Collection (500-800)

15400 San Antonio, TX - $100 1902 Plain Back Fr. 704 **The City NB** Ch. # (S)5217
A low grade but fully intact high denomination example. **Very Good.** (600-900)

15401 San Augustine, TX - $10 1929 Ty. 1 **The First NB** Ch. # 6214
This is a rare note from the only collectible bank in this historic east Texas community, the site of one of the first Anglo settlements in what was then part of Mexico. The census reveals just four large and six small notes extant from here, with two of the large examples impounded in the Moody Foundation holdings. This attractive small example is certain to please. Sharp **Very Fine.**
From The Rolling Plains Collection (800-1,000)

15402 Santo, TX - $20 1902 Plain Back Fr. 651 **The First NB** Ch. # (S)8176
This note last appeared at auction in 1998. This tough Palo Pinto issuer is represented in the Kelly census by five large size examples, and is the only Large $20 available, as the other example is tied up in the Philpott/Moody holdings. Bright signatures are an interesting color on this **Very Good+** example that was harshly trimmed. (1,250-1,750)

15403 **Schwertner, TX** - $20 1929 Ty. 1 **The First NB** Ch. # 10956
A very scarce central Texas note from the only bank chartered in this rural Williamson County location. **Fine++**, signed as president by Adolph Schwertner. (600-900)

15404 **Seguin, TX** - $50 1929 Ty. 1 **The First NB** Ch. # 5097
A very tough to find note from the only issuer in this small Guadalupe County community. The census lists just two high denomination examples from here, with this one of the pair. **Fine** or a bit better, with a couple of paper clip stains at the top. (900-1,300)

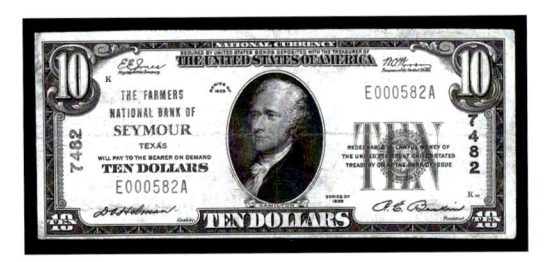

15405 **Seymour, TX** - $10 1929 Ty. 1 **The Farmers NB** Ch. # 7482
This was the last of three banks chartered in this small Baylor County community, and one of two that persevered long enough to issue Series 1929 examples. Just a half dozen such notes are recorded from here, making this a difficult to find bank until collections such as this are dispersed. **Fine.**
From The Rolling Plains Collection (600-900)

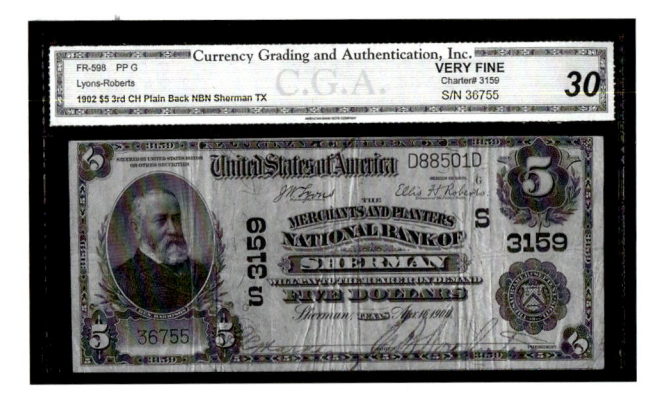

15406 **Sherman, TX** - $5 1902 Plain Back Fr. 598 **The Merchants & Planters NB** Ch. # (S)3159
This was the biggest bank between St. Louis and Galveston for many years due to railroad and Indian Territory accounts. This example is bright for the grade with natural surfaces. **CGA Very Fine 30.** (300-500)

15407 **Shiner, TX** - $5 1882 Brown Back Fr. 477 **The First NB** Ch. # (S)5628
A bright and well embossed example of the only easily obtained $5 Brown Back from the state of Texas. Were the margins on this pen signed specimen just a bit broader, it would easily have merited the full Choice grade, rather than is PCGS assigned designation of **New 62 PPQ**. (2,250-3,250)

15408 Silverton, TX - $10 1902 Plain Back Fr. 626 **The First NB** Ch. # (S)8816
This is about as rare as any Texas National is likely to be, as only three notes are known from this one bank community in Briscoe County. One is listed in the census without a serial number, the second is a serial number 1 Red Seal, and this is the third. It comes from the Irish and Ivy holdings, and has been off the market since its last offering in January of 2001. While hardly unappealing in its overall appearance, there is an old time tape repair on the back which affects the front of the note as well. As the Red Seal is now part of a prominent collection, and the other Blue Seal has never, to our best knowledge, been offered publicly, this may be the only chance for many years for serious collectors of this state's notes to obtain any example from this small panhandle community. **Good-Very Good.**
From The Rolling Plains Collection **(2,500-4,500)**

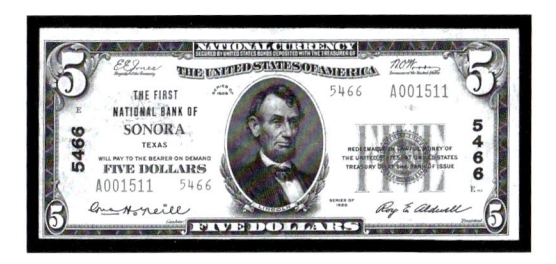

15409 Sonora, TX - $5 1929 Ty. 2 **The First NB** Ch. # 5466
A more than acceptable Type 2 example from this county's only issuing bank, which was located in this desert county's only town. **Very Fine. (350-550)**

15410 Spur, TX - $5 1929 Ty. 2 **The Spur NB** Ch. # 9611
A scarce west Texas note bearing one of the most evocative titles found on any National. **Very Good-Fine.**
From The Rolling Plains Collection **(600-900)**

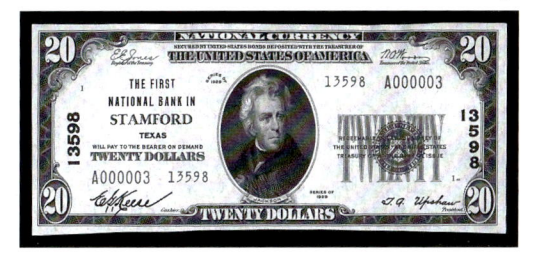

15411 Stamford, TX - $20 1929 Ty. 2 **The First NB** Ch. # 13598
A lovely example bearing low serial number A000003. **Choice Crisp Uncirculated.**
From The Rolling Plains Collection **(600-900)**

15412 Stanton, TX - $20 1929 Ty. 1 **The First NB** Ch. # 8094
A better Series 1929 note from a small west Texas community located about one hundred miles south of Lubbock. The town was settled in the early 1880's by German Catholic immigrants, who christened their new home Marienfeld. Although advised by earlier settlers that ranching was the only reliable economic mainstay, the success of a demonstration farm during the colony's first couple of years lulled the newcomers into believing that agriculture could become an economic mainstay in west Texas. The drought of 1886 and 1887 took the colony by surprise, and, combined with a series of vicious blizzards during the winter of 1886, were enough to nearly destroy the the settlement, with most of the Germans moving away. In 1890, the town was renamed Stanton, after Lincoln's Secretary of War, Edwin M. Stanton. **Very Good-Fine.**
From The Rolling Plains Collection **(450-650)**

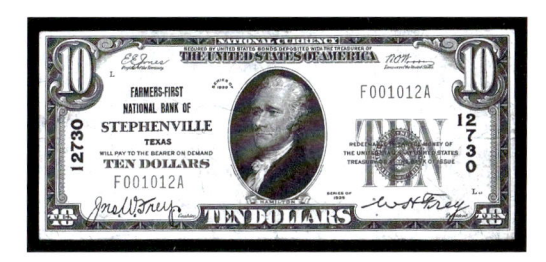

15413 Stephenville, TX - $10 1929 Ty. 1 **Farmers-First NB** Ch. # 12730
The fourth bank chartered in this Erath County community, and the sole issuer of Series 1929 notes from here. Pleasing **Very Fine.**
From The Rolling Plains Collection **(300-500)**

15414 **Strawn, TX - $10 1929 Ty. 1 The First NB Ch. # 10229**
Strawn is located in Palo Pinto County and named for Bethel Strawn, who helped settle the area in 1875. Oil and gas production are the economic mainstays here, although the town never developed into much more than a wide spot in the road, with a population peak of just 1000 back in 1940. Just two large and three small notes are known from this bank, with one of the large notes forever impounded in the Philpott/Moody holdings. **Fine,** with the bottom left margin a bit chewed into. (1,250-2,250)

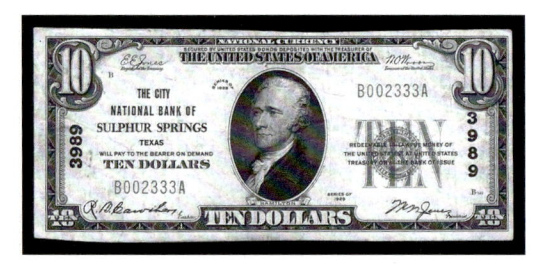

15415 **Sulphur Springs, TX - $10 1929 Ty. 1 The City NB Ch. # 3989**
A tougher example from this NE Texas community. **Fine-Very Fine.** (300-500)

15416 **Texarkana, TX - $5 1902 Plain Back Fr. 600 The Texarkana NB Ch. # (S)3785**
Original paper surfaces are found on this **Fine+** $5 that has the signatures printed a little higher than normal.
From The Jacob and Heather Dedman Collection **(400-600)**

15417 **Thornton, TX - $20 1929 Ty. 1 The First NB Ch. # 8538**
A lovely example which is easily the finest small note known from this one bank Limestone County location. Bright **Very Fine-Extremely Fine.** (700-900)

First Reported Large

15418 **Tom Bean, TX - $5 1902 Plain Back Fr. 606 The First NB Ch. # (S)11019**
What a happy day it was when this note strolled into our offices. This is the first large size Tom Bean note to be documented. None of the great Texas collections in the past had an example and that includes the high-powered Philpott Collection. This bank was chartered in 1917, but by 1935 there was only $880 large size outstanding. This town has always been on the top of collector want lists due to its interesting nomenclature. Tom Bean was a surveyor from Bonham and he donated a fifty-acre tract for a town site and railroad right-of-way in Grayson County. The penned signatures of the assistant cashier and president have held up well over the years adding to the romance of this unique item. A small skin mark is found on the back at bottom center, but it does nothing to detract from this historic note. **Very Good.** (10,000-20,000)

15419 **Trinity, TX** - $5 1929 Ty. 2 **First NB** Ch. # 13706
A well margined beauty bearing low serial number A000002. All but two of the notes known from this bank come from or are part of one of three serial number 1 Type 2 sheets, the $5 having been cut over a decade ago. PCGS **Gem New 65 PPQ.** (1,200-1,800)

15420 **Tulia, TX** - $10 1929 Ty. 2 **The First NB** Ch. # 6298
This Swisher County hamlet was marinating in its well deserved obscurity before a scandal combining a perjurious drug informant and an ambitiously unethical small town sheriff made this town's name a by-word for prosecutorial abuse throughout the southwest. **Fine.**
From The Rolling Plains Collection (500-700)

15421 **Vernon, TX** - $5 1929 Ty. 2 **The Herring NB** Ch. # 7010
The second of Vernon's two banks to issue Series 1929 examples. **Fine.**
From The Rolling Plains Collection (350-550)

Pleasing Victoria Brown Back

15422 **Victoria, TX** - $10 1882 Brown Back Fr. 484 **The First NB** Ch. # (S)4184
This is an attractive Texas Brown Back with great color, signatures, and margins. It's the first type issued by this none too common bank, which lasted only from 1889 through 1913, when it was liquidated and replaced by the Victoria National Bank. Sharp **Fine-Very Fine,** a premium example.
From The Rolling Plains Collection (3,000-4,000)

15423 **Waco, TX** - $10 1902 Plain Back Fr. 631 **The First NB** Ch. # 2189
An attractive note which is certainly one of the higher grade large examples we've handled from here. **Extremely Fine,** with engraved bank signatures. (300-400)

15424 **Waco, TX** - $50 1902 Date Back Fr. 674 **The First NB** Ch. # (S)2189
A tougher type and denomination from this otherwise easy to obtain bank. **Very Good-Fine,** with a bit of grafitti in the back margin. (900-1,200)

15425 Waco, TX - $100 1902 Plain Back Fr. 698 **The Citizens NB** Ch. # 3135
An attractive piece which is one of only three large size hundreds known from here. It's as nice as any, and an item which is certain to please. **Very Fine,** with purple signatures.
From The Rolling Plains Collection **(1,500-2,000)**

15426 Waco, TX - $20 1929 Ty. 2 **The National City Bank** Ch. # 6572 Uncut Sheet
The first note of this serial number 1-6 uncut sheet formerly of the Irish Collection has a trivial counting crinkle. A $5 and $10 sheet are also known on this bank, but this sheet is the nicest of the trio. **Gem Crisp Uncirculated. (7,000-9,000)**

15427 Waxahachie, TX - $5 1929 Ty. 1 **Citizens NB** Ch. # 13516
A neat note from this well collected community. **About Uncirculated,** ex-Irish collection and bearing serial number A000005A. **(400-600)**

15428 Weatherford, TX - $10 1882 Date Back Fr. 545 **The First NB** Ch. # (S)2477
A nice example which is one of only a literal handful of early notes known from here. **Very Fine.**
From The Rolling Plains Collection **(1,500-2,000)**

Serial Number 1 Wellington Note

15429 Wellington, TX - $10 1929 Ty. 1 **The First NB** Ch. # 13249
A gorgeous serial number 1 example, which, other than three uncut sheets (all serial number ones as well), is all that is available from here. **Gem Crisp Uncirculated,** a premium piece certain to delight its fortunate new owner.
From The Rolling Plains Collection **(2,500-3,500)**

15430 **West, TX** - $10 1929 Ty. 2 **The West NB** Ch. # 13935
A beautiful note which is likely as nice as any note you will ever see from this elusive high charter institution. **Gem Crisp Uncirculated,** and bearing desirable low serial number A000003.
From The Rolling Plains Collection (1,000-1,500)

Unique in Small Size

15431 **Whitesboro, TX** - $10 1929 Ty. 1 **The First NB** Ch. # 5847
This tiny Grayson County bank limped along for thirty years before the Depression put it out of its misery in January of 1930. This is the only survivor of a miniscule small size issue which lasted for only six months before the bank shut down. While well circulated, it is fully intact and, as the question goes, where can another be found at any price? **Very Good-Fine,** a remarkable opportunity for the serious collector of this state's 1929 issue.
From The Rolling Plains Collection (2,000-4,000)

15432 **Whitesboro, TX** - $20 1929 Ty. 1 **The City NB** Ch. # 10634
This is one of a mere 8 small in the census for this Grayson County bank. **Fine.** (400-600)

15433 **Whitewright, TX** - $10 1929 Ty. 1 **The Planters NB** Ch. # 6915
By far the scarcer of this Grayson County's two issuers, with just eight small examples recorded from here. This one is a pleasing problem-free **Fine.** (400-600)

15434 **Wichita Falls, TX** - $10 1902 Plain Back Fr. 624 **The First NB** Ch. # 3200
When we sold this beauty four years ago, we called it "As nice a large note as we've ever seen from this community. Brightly colored and very fresh Choice Crisp Uncirculated, just the lightest of handling from the full gem grade." PCGS clearly agrees, having slabbed and and graded this example as **Very Choice New 64 PPQ.** (900-1,200)

15435 **Wichita Falls, TX** - $10 1929 Ty. 1 **The First NB** Ch. # 3200
A bright and fresh example removed from the Choice designation by one hard to spot corner fold. **Crisp Uncirculated.**
From The Rolling Plains Collection (300-400)

15436 **Wichita Falls, TX** - $5 1929 Ty. 2 **Wichita NB** Ch. # 13676
As nice a note as one could ever hope to find from this high charter Wichita Falls bank. **Gem Crisp Uncirculated.**
From The Rolling Plains Collection (450-650)

15437 **Wichita Falls, TX** - $5 1929 Ty. 2 **Wichita NB** Ch. # 13676
This bank was a late entry on the national currency scene, not receiving its charter until 1933, and therefore its issue is confined to the 1929 series. This **PCGS New 62PPQ** would likely have earned a few more grade points, but for a centering shift on the face. Most of the $5 type 2 survivors from here are in the "CU" range, making this a popular type note. (300-500)

15438 **Winnsboro, TX** - $20 1929 Ty. 1 **The First NB** Ch. # 5674
This is one of only seven small in the census for this scarce bank. The note looks **Fine** with an approximate one inch tear that runs upwards through the left-hand serial number. There was also an attempt to remove a blue hand-written "37" from the face. Officers are Tobe A. Wright and Alf Morris. Alf followed in the footsteps of C.H. Morris as president of this Wood County bank. (400-600)

Lovely Serial Number 1 Wolfe City Note

15439 **Wolfe City, TX** - $5 1929 Ty. 2 **The Wolfe NB** Ch. # 13199
A lovely serial number 1 example which boasts a neat town name as a bonus. **Choice Crisp Uncirculated.** (2,500-3,500)

15440 **Yoakum, TX** - $10 1902 Plain Back Fr. 626 **The Yoakum NB** Ch. # 8694
In 2004 we saw a 1902 $10 PB in a similar grade on this bank go for almost $1800. Yoakum is the only National Bank Note issuing town in Texas with a name that begins with the letter "Y." **Fine,** the signatures faded. (400-600)

15441 **Yoakum, TX** - $20 1929 Ty. 1 **The Yoakum NB** Ch. # 8694
A pretty note from the only collectible bank in this south Texas community. Nice **Very Fine.** (300-500)

UTAH

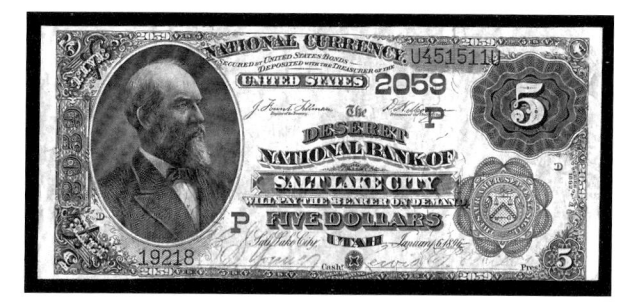

15442 Salt Lake City, UT - $5 1882 Brown Back Fr. 474 **The Deseret NB** Ch. # (P)2059
This perfectly original Brown Back boasts its original color, embossing and overall eye appeal. It is likely this note saw very little circulation as the paper is still bright white and unadulterated. Folds, and some handling ultimately account for the **Very Fine** grade. (3,500-4,500)

15443 Salt Lake City, UT - $20 1929 Ty. 1 **The Deseret NB** Ch. # 2059
This title is always in demand. **Very Fine.** (200-300)

VERMONT

15444 Fairhaven, VT - $10 1902 Plain Back Fr. 624 **The First NB** Ch. # 344
This is a scarce Rutland County bank. A left edge tear reaches the frame line. The purple stamped signature of Cashier R.R. Ellis is somewhat faded, while the pen signature of President G.E. Adams is bold. Notes of this bank have a BEP engraving error as the town name is "Fair Haven" not "Fairhaven" as it is laid out in the tombstone and postal location. **Fine.** (400-600)

15445 North Bennington, VT - $20 1902 Plain Back Fr. 650 **The First NB** Ch. # 194
This is another Vermont bank which is exceedingly common in small size but seldom appears in large. It's an attractive piece with bold signatures that well deserves the grade of **Fine 15** awarded it by PCGS. (350-500)

15446 Orwell, VT - $5 1902 Plain Back Fr. 598 **The First NB** Ch. # 228
This **Fine** is an attractive example of a note from this institution. (600-800)

15447 Wells River, VT - $5 1902 Plain Back Fr. 598 **The NB of Newbury** Ch. # (N)1406
An especially appealing note from an elusive bank to acquire in large. **PCGS Very Fine 35PPQ** and quite attractive in its overall presentation. (500-700)

VIRGINIA

15448 **Bassett, VA** - $10 1929 Ty. 1 **The First NB** Ch. # 11976
This one bank town in Henry County issued more than $1 million in National Currency. Today less than $200 in total face value is known to collectors. This piece, is likely the finest of all the large and small survivors according to the Kelly census. **Very Fine. (600-800)**

15449 **Leesburg, VA** - $10 1902 Plain Back Fr. 626 **The Peoples NB** Ch. # 3917
The signatures are missing on this **Very Good-Fine** $20.
From The George P. Hammerly Collection **(400-600)**

15450 **Leesburg, VA** - $20 1929 Ty. 1 **The Peoples NB** Ch. # 3917
We last had a Series 1929 note on this bank almost six hears ago where it went for over $350. Today's offering should surpass that. **Very Fine.**
From The George P. Hammerly Collection **(300-500)**

15451 **Leesburg, VA** - $10; $20 1929 Ty. 1 **The Peoples NB** Ch. # 3917
The $10 grades a bright **Fine+**. Also, a few pinholes are noticed with some black ink on the back of the **Fine** $20.
From The George P. Hammerly Collection (Total: 2 notes) **(400-600)**

15452 **Lynchburg, VA** - $20 1902 Plain Back Fr. 650 **The Peoples NB** Ch. # 2760
The legible stamped signatures are of W.W. Dickerson and Jno. Victor. **Fine-Very Fine.**
From The George P. Hammerly Collection **(300-500)**

15453 **Norfolk, VA** - $10 1882 Date Back Fr. 545 **The NB of Commerce** Ch. # (S)6032
Signatures are present on this note that has two rounded corners and a few rust spots at or near the top and bottom edges. **Very Good-Fine.**
From The George P. Hammerly Collection **(350-550)**

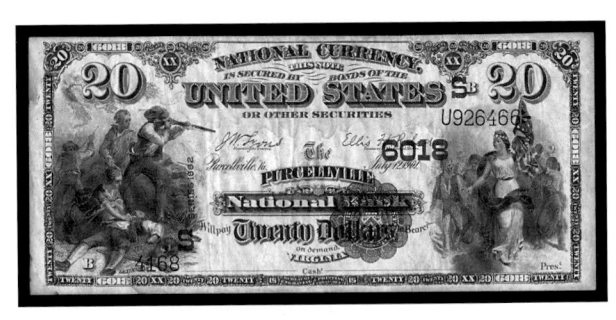

15454 **Purcellville, VA** - $20 1882 Value Back Fr. 581 **The Purcellville NB** Ch. # (S)6018
In January 2003 we sold a $5 Value Back in a similar grade on this bank for over $3600. We don't expect this moisture stained **Fine** $20 to go for that much, but we could see prices settling in the range of ...
From The George P. Hammerly Collection **(800-1,200)**

Previously Unreported Second Title

15455 **Radford, VA** - $10 1929 Ty. 2 **The First & Merchants NB** Ch. # 6782
This discovery piece is the only known note to feature this bank's second title. Its paper quality is exceptional, showing very little evidence of actual circulation. **Very Fine. (2,250-3,250)**

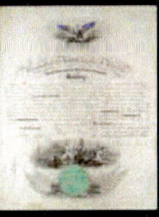

Specialists Sought

Heritage Auction Galleries, located in Dallas, Texas, is looking for top experts in a variety of fields to join our world-class team of auction professionals. If you have experience buying, selling and appraising fine collectibles, from fine art, movie posters and comic books, political memorabilia and autographs, sports, coins....this is the opportunity you've been looking for! The successful candidate will be responsible for reviewing incoming inquiries, appraising property, communicating with clients, writing and proofing catalogue essays, as well as developing and generating business.

Must be willing to relocate to Dallas. Excellent communication and interpersonal skills are important. Full compensation package with benefits commensurate with experience.

EXPERTS WANTED IN ALL COLLECTIBLE FIELDS, INCLUDING:

Fine Arts • Decorative Arts • Rare Books & Manuscripts • Comic Books and Original Comic Art • Vintage Movie Posters • Sports Collectibles • Jewelry & Gemstones • Political Memorabilia & Americana • Hollywood, Celebrity & Music Memorabilia • U.S. Coins & Currency • Ancient Coins • World Coins

Please send resume by email to **Jobs@HA.com**.

HERITAGE HA.com
Auction Galleries
The World's Largest Collectibles Auctioneer
3500 Maple Avenue • 17th Floor
Dallas, Texas 75219
214-528-3500 • 800-872-6467

WASHINGTON

15456 Seattle, WA - $10 1929 Ty. 2 **First NB** Ch. # 11280
Embossing, natural paper wave, and original sheen are noticed on this nicely margined $10 graded **PMG Choice Uncirculated 64 EPQ.** (350-500)

WEST VIRGINIA

15457 Fairview, WV - $10 1929 Ty. 1 **The First NB** Ch. # 10219
This **Extremely Fine** piece is one of the nicest known to become available from here in quite some time. A bright example with decent margins and good centering. (1,500-2,000)

15458 Fairview, WV - $20 1929 Ty. 1 **The First NB** Ch. # 10219
This is by far the nicest example from a very rare bank in any format. This Marion County institution printed a mere 578 small size sheets total. Three vertical folds are the only circulation sustained. **Extremely Fine.** (1,500-2,500)

15459 Kenova, WV - $20 1929 Ty. 1 **The First NB** Ch. # 9913
This moderately circulated issue is eye appealing and original. Of the dozen or so reported notes from this locale, none is graded higher than VF. **Fine.** (350-450)

15460 Weston, WV - $20 1929 Ty. 2 **The Weston NB** Ch. # 13634
An attractive example which is new to the census, and only the second $20 Type 2 specimen reported to date. **Very Fine+.** (400-600)

15461 Wheeling, WV - $20 1882 Date Back Fr. 555 **The National Exchange Bank** Ch. # (S)5164
The edges are nice for the grade on this $20. The signatures were darkly printed including the "V" for "Vice President." **Very Good.** (500-700)

WISCONSIN

15462 **Darlington, WI** - $5 1929 Ty. 2 **The First NB** Ch. # 3161
Although not a terribly rare bank, notes from this community are avidly collected, and bring substantial prices whenever they are offered. This example, however, is a rare item, as it is the only Type 2 note of any denomination reported from here. Bright **Fine-Very Fine**, considerably closer to the higher grade than the lower. (750-1,250)

15463 **Grand Rapids, WI** - $10 1929 Ty. 1 **The First NB** Ch. # 1998
One of two near sequential examples of this Grand Rapids bank. The paper quality is exceptional. **Choice Crisp Uncirculated.** (300-400)

15464 **Grand Rapids, WI** - $10 1929 Ty. 1 **The First NB** Ch. # 1998
A pleasingly original piece with solid, even margins. **Choice Crisp Uncirculated.** (300-400)

15465 **Kenosha, WI** - $10 1929 Ty. 1 **The First NB** Ch. # 212
You will find at least two different presidents on the Series 1929 notes of this bank. This **Very Fine** is adorned with natural paper surfaces. (250-350)

15466 **Lake Geneva, WI** - $10 1929 Ty. 1 **The Farmers NB** Ch. # 5592
This note comes from the second of two banks chartered in this resort community. **Very Good+.** (400-600)

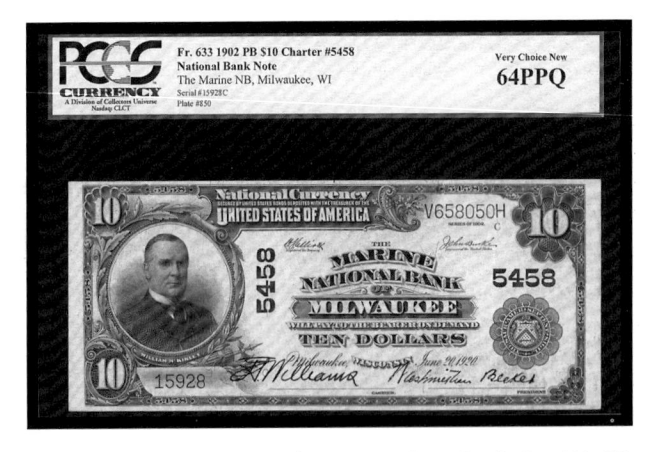

15467 **Milwaukee, WI** - $10 1902 Plain Back Fr. 633 **The Marine NB** Ch. # 5458
While not from an especially challenging bank to locate, with the latest Kelly census standing at 172 pieces in large, this PCGS **Very Choice 64PPQ** example is one nice example, with darkly stamped signatures and broad margins all around. (500-700)

15468 **Milwaukee, WI** - $5 1929 Ty. 1 **Sixth Wisconsin NB** Ch. # 12628
A hint of handling is noted. **Crisp Uncirculated.** (400-500)

15469 **Viroqua, WI** - $10 1929 Ty. 1 **The First NB** Ch. # 8529
A tougher note from the only bank in town to issue. Evenly circulated **Fine.** (350-550)